LEGAL PHILOSOPHY FROM PLATO
TO HEGEL

LEGAL PHILOSOPHY FROM PLATO TO HEGEL

BY

HUNTINGTON CAIRNS

THE JOHNS HOPKINS PRESS · BALTIMORE

Originally published, 1949

Second printing, 1949

Third printing, 1956

Fourth printing, 1966

Johns Hopkins
Paperbacks edition, 1967

TO

JOSEPH HERGESHEIMER

We have to think of them as forever bailing,
Setting and hauling, while the North East lowers
Over shallow banks unchanging and erosionless
Or drawing their money, drying sails at dockage;
Not as making a trip that will be unpayable
For a haul that will not bear examination.

T. S. ELIOT

PREFACE

*" Tell me," said Faraday to Tyndall,
who was about to show him an
experiment, " tell me what I am to
look for."*

THIS BOOK is a study of the legal systems put forward by
philosophers from Plato to Hegel. It seeks to ascertain
the views which those philosophers took of law, what problems
they considered significant, and the nature of the solutions
they proposed. The book is a continuation of a task initiated
almost twenty years ago. I thought it important to look at
law from three points of view, that of the social sciences, that
of logic and the empirical sciences, and that of philosophy.
The present volume is thus associated with my *Law and the
Social Sciences* (1935) and my *Theory of Legal Science* (1941).
The object of all three volumes is the same: To construct the
foundation of a theory of law which is the necessary antecedent
of a possible jurisprudence. I trust that a fourth volume, *The
Elements of Legal Theory*, in which the conclusions of the three
preceding ones are applied and expanded, can be completed
with reasonable expedition.

I have not, therefore, in the present book attempted to write
either a history of legal philosophy or to present a systematic
view of the field. I have long held the belief that modern
jurisprudence in its essentials is a prolongation of the great
philosophical systems, and so far as this book may be said
to have a thesis it is that proposition which I hope to demonstrate. But that task is a subsidiary one. In its basic character
jurisprudence is philosophical. Its problems have been the
subject of intensive investigation by almost every major
philosopher from Plato to Hegel. The primary task of this book
has been, therefore, to set forth as precisely as may be the
results of these investigations. I have concerned myself only
with the conclusions reached by professional philosophers and

not with what other perhaps equally gifted men in jurisprudence, such as Grotius, have done with their conclusions.
This volume is therefore concerned with a group of thinkers
whose main efforts at speculative construction have lain in
fields other than the juristic. It is unnecessary to add that
Cicero, whose legal philosophy is treated in the book, is not a
professional philosopher. My excuse for including him is that
he summed up the views of a school of philosophers whose
theories are of legal importance but whose works unfortunately
are lost.

So far as possible, I have let the subjects of this study speak
in their own words. I have endeavored to omit no significant
idea, but in the interests of space I have been obliged for the
most part to forego discussion of biographical details and
analysis of the cultural influences which may have shaped the
philosopher's attitude towards particular problems. It would
be hopeless, except under the broadest categories, to attempt
to reconcile the diverse philosophical attitudes expressed in the
volume. In the exposition of them I have taken a neutral
position and have treated them as impartially as possible.
I have not attempted to answer questions which these thinkers
have left unanswered. At the same time, I have not treated
their ideas as historical facts, but as propositions to be judged
on their own merits.

The life of *a priori* philosophies of law, Holdsworth has
observed, is short. In the sense that jurisprudence does not
build upon *a priori* systems in the way that mathematicians
add to algebraical theorems, Holdsworth's statement is a true
one. But jurisprudence at all times employs propositions which
have been developed in earlier philosophical systems. Unless,
indeed, there is to be a great amount of wasted effort it is
necessary that it should do so; however disguised the fact may
be, jurisprudence is still a branch of philosophy, and the insight
that philosophers have brought to its tasks is its most valuable
capital. What produces confusion is the failure to recognize
frankly that jurisprudence, as a part of philosophy, has under-

standing as its first aim and the reformation of practice as only a secondary hope. Jurisprudence's primary objective, in its philosophical aspect, is to understand the function of law in human society. Philosophers such as Hegel insist that that is its sole concern. They argue that philosophy must not mix with the world, and that its work is to protect the possessions of Truth. How the actual present-day world is to escape from its predicament must be left to the world to settle. Other philosophers, such as Bacon and Spinoza, take a different view. They hold that jurisprudential speculation can be a guide to practice; but they make this suggestion with grave reservations. Bacon observed that the powers of our ancestors were the equal of our own, and that we have no more chance of success than they unless we develop a new method. Spinoza held that the past disclosed all possible commonwealths which permit men to live in unity; he therefore conceived his problem to be the determination of what is in best agreement with practice. Today there is a growing scepticism that social problems are soluble. If there is a single thread in the speculations of the philosophers discussed in the present volume, it is the recognition of the necessity of keeping the inquiry directed upon the main issues, which sustain the possibility of novelty, and which preclude a lapse into an abandonment of effort. Stated concretely, it is an understanding of the precariousness of the social structure and the significance of law as a sustaining factor. It is not impossible that in this thread lies the contribution, even for a sceptical age, that justifies the labors expended upon the development of *a priori* legal systems.

The book as a whole served as the basis for lectures delivered under the James Schouler Lectureship at the Johns Hopkins University in 1947 under the auspices of the Department of Political Science. I wish to express my gratitude to the members of that faculty for their many kindnesses. I wish to thank also James K. Feibleman, Graduate Professor of Philosophy, Tulane University, New Orleans, Louisiana, who generously read the manuscript in its entirety, and Mr. L. O. Teach of Baltimore, Maryland, for assistance on research problems.

Portions of this book have appeared in the *Columbia Law Review*, the *Harvard Law Review*, *Seminar*, and *Interpretations of Modern Legal Philosophy*, edited by Paul Sayre, Oxford University Press, New York. Translations of portions have also appeared in the *Revista de la Escuela Nacional de Jurisprudencia*, Mexico, the *Revista de la Universidad Nacional de Cordoba*, Argentina, and *El Actual Pensamiento Jurídico de los Estados Unidos*, a volume published under the auspices of Biblioteca del Instituto Argentino de Filosofía Jurídica y Social, Buenos Aires, Argentina. I am indebted to the editors and proprietors of those publications for their kind permission to reprint. I am also indebted to Mr. T. S. Eliot and Messrs. Harcourt, Brace and Company, Inc., New York, for permission to use the lines from Mr. Eliot's *The Dry Salvages* which appear as the epigraph.

Huntington Cairns

National Gallery of Art
Washington, D. C.

CONTENTS

CHAPTER I

PHILOSOPHY AS JURISPRUDENCE

The final problem is to conceive a complete fact.

A. N. Whitehead

L AW AS A FIELD of speculative inquiry is a subject in which philosophers nowadays evince little interest. This is a relatively new attitude on the part of philosophers, and an unfortunate one in its consequences for both disciplines. Law until the time of Hegel had been historically one of the main concerns of philosophy. It was a subject of prime importance for the philosophers of ancient Greece, and every philosopher of the first rank from Plato to Hegel occupied himself with its elucidation. Through this activity the problems of law were first established—the problems on the solution of which every task of modern legal thought turns. As a matter of written history, a philosopher and not a lawyer first asked the still basic question, " What is law? " But as philosophy during the nineteenth century became increasingly concerned with the theory of knowledge, and as law itself in its practical aspects during the same period became increasingly technical, philosophers gave it less and less attention. The separation of law and philosophy was also promoted by the attitude of the lawyers themselves. They reflected a general mental outlook which came to full fruition in the nineteenth century. This was a period marked by the establishment of separate subjects of study. Economics, anthropology, sociology, and human geography, notwithstanding their extensive historical antecedents, came to be clearly differentiated branches of inquiry only during the late eighteenth and nineteenth centuries. Although these fields of knowledge were held to possess subject matters capable of independent investigation, it was also recognized that they were parts of the study of man, and

1

therefore had interconnections with one another. But the tendency of jurisprudence, which had broken with theology in the sixteenth century but had maintained an association with political science and international law in the seventeenth and eighteenth centuries, was towards complete independence. Jurisprudence, the analytical jurist insisted, was a wholly self-sufficient science. This view culminated in the opinion, at least in the Anglo-American world, that jurisprudence was a formal science of relations, and the divorce of jurisprudence from philosophy appeared complete.

At the same time, the relations between philosophy and science have never been closer. Since the renascence of scientific ideas in the seventeenth century, scientific conceptions have continually attracted the interest of philosophers. Mathematical physics under the influence of Newton, biology under that of Darwin, and the new theories that in the twentieth century have developed in physics and mathematics, have all been potent forces in shaping the course of philosophical inquiry. These influences have been productive of large benefits to philosophy. They have provided a fresh impetus to speculation in the form of a novel subject matter, they have worked a radical transformation in the traditional methods of philosophy, and they have created a doubt in the basic metaphysical assumption that philosophy yields knowledge of a reality which transcends the world of science and common sense and thus have prompted philosophy to reexamine its own premises. Science has also contributed to philosophy's detour from the main highway which it has followed since the days of ancient Greece. Philosophy's attempt to emulate the methods of science has resulted in its assuming as its mode of inquiry the chief characteristic of science. That is to say, like the temper of the present age, philosophy's dominant trend is analytic and not synthetic. The emphasis of this trend is upon knowledge of the part and not the whole. It has abandoned the elaboration of total systems and the point of view which attempts to comprehend the world as a whole. In its constructive phases it proceeds like science in a piecemeal fashion and provisionally. However, the interest of Anglo-American philosophy in science has been largely in the activities of the natural sciences. On the Continent the philosopher has continued to participate critically in the development of the less exact disciplines such as history and jurisprudence. In the main, science for the Anglo-American philosopher means the natural sciences. Philosophy is held to be ultimately indistinguishable from science, and to differ from it merely in the fact that its problems are more general and that its initial hypotheses lack immediately substantiating empirical evidence.

Science's relations with jurisprudence since the seventeenth century have been as intimate as with philosophy. The immediate impact of mathematical thought upon the legal thought of Hobbes, Leibniz, Pufendorf and Grotius is plain. By the time of Burke and Blackstone, jurisprudence had become firmly established as a " science," expressly recognized as such by both of them, with mechanics as its obvious model. With the differentiation and development of the social sciences during the eighteenth and nineteenth centuries, and with jurisprudence in the latter stages claiming to be one of them, the relationship between science and jurisprudence became even closer. For their aims and methods the social sciences have looked much more to science than to philosophy, and this practice has been shared to a marked extent by jurisprudence. It has never lost contact with philosophy to the same degree as the other social sciences, but its methodology today, both in its application and in the justifications which are advanced on its behalf, are almost exclusively taken over from science.

Thus we are confronted with the situation that an extensive and reciprocal cross-fertilization exists between philosophy and science, and a one-way fertilization obtains between science and the social sciences, including jurisprudence. But in the case of jurisprudence its chief well-spring for sixty generations of European thought, outside of its own special domain, has dried up; even the incidental contributions made by philosophers today to jurisprudence are of a critical and didactic character, aimed at revealing the concealed dilemmas inherent in juristic speculation that ignores metaphysical presuppositions. This stands in sharp contrast with the earlier philosophical practice directed at the working out of a general theory of law founded upon expressly articulated philosophical premises.

Today there is a growing interest on the part of lawyers in what is termed the philosophy of law, a subject much deprecated by the dominant jurisprudence of the latter part of the last century, in spite of its earlier record as a vitalizing power in the hands of such judges as Marshall and Story. But the philosophy of law is one thing in the hands of lawyers and quite a different thing in the hands of philosophers. For the lawyer the starting point is the juridical institution, practice or ideal, and the end sought is its establishment on a rational basis. For the philosopher, the premise lies beyond the domain of law in the realm of natural existence or human nature from which the function of law in society is deduced and harmonized with man's other activities. A philosophy of law constructed by the lawyer still stands in need of correlation with other phases of human existence and nature; a philosophy of law outlined by the philosopher is merely another brick laid into place in an edifice which purports to encompass the totality of existence in its outline.

Philosophy's effort, like that of jurisprudence, is thus directed at knowledge. But the knowledge it seeks, even of the legal process, is different from that sought by jurisprudence in the sense that the questions it asks will not be the same or, if they should coincide, the answers proposed may be different. Thus the philosopher may answer in response to the question, " What is law? " that it is the discovery of that which is; and the jurist may respond that it is a command emanating from a sovereign authority. Philosophy possesses no exclusive preserve as the source of knowledge which is not accessible to jurisprudence, but its point of view differs so materially from that of jurisprudence that the results of its speculations may be distinct. It aims at the construction of a system of general ideas that will explain all the events of human experience. Jurisprudence has a similar aim, but more circumscribed. It seeks to frame a system of general ideas that will account for the events of the legal process. The answers which philosophy finds to the questions it raises in the legal domain must not contradict the solutions which it determines in other spheres of human behavior, such as economics, history, and psychology. But the jurist, at least until very recent times, has not felt himself to be under any such compulsion. Whether his solutions were in accord with data established in other fields of endeavor was an irrelevance. Even today we find courts deciding cases on premises the data of which have been established as a matter of empirical evidence to be erroneous, *e. g.*, the tests employed to ascertain the mental competency of witnesses. Jurisprudence may achieve the construction of a coherent system of propositions about legal behavior, but unless those propositions are correlated with the propositions of other domains, they may rest upon inconsistent assumptions. Since jurisprudence studies only one aspect of human behavior, just as the other social sciences study other aspects, its conclusions will be operative in just that limited area. But inasmuch as the characteristics of that confined area are subject to the influences of the whole domain of human activity, the determinations of jurisprudence are necessarily incomplete to the extent those influences are ignored. Those determinations are also erroneous to the extent that the influences which are not allowed for in juristic speculation affect the characteristics of the jurisprudential system in a way that would cause them to be explained differently if they had been perceived. Jurisprudence as it stands today is therefore necessarily incomplete, and the propositions which it has proposed may be erroneous. If jurisprudence achieves a system of propositions that possesses internal consistency it must still be adjusted to the like systems of the other sciences, and all of them together made into a coherent and unified whole. That has been the special point of view from which philosophy in the past has approached the problems of law.

Philosophy's concern with law in the past has affected legal speculation in three directions, apart from its efforts to incorporate law in some total explanatory system. It has influenced the development of its methodology, it has contributed ideals which jurists have proposed as the end of legal activity, and it has added a profound practical intelligence to the abstractions in which jurisprudence is likely to become enmeshed.

METHODOLOGY

Both philosophy and jurisprudence share the characteristic that they have perfected no techniques either for the discovery of knowledge or for its successful application once that goal has been reached. Mathematics may be taken as an example where the perfecting of method has attained a high level of success, and mechanical engineering is equally fortunate in the possession of techniques which permit the manipulation of conditions in the light of verified propositions. However, philosophy and jurisprudence follow in the main the same general techniques employed in the fields of thought that have not attained the rigor of the exact sciences. Their primary instrument is reason, which in view of the attacks upon it, even by philosophers themselves, cannot be taken for granted as a self-evidently valid tool. For Hume,[1] " reason is, and ought only to be the slave of the passions, and can never pretend to any other office than to serve and obey them." Reason means only the statement of arguments in a logical order, and in view of its imperfections Hume was ready " to reject all belief and reasoning " and could " look upon no opinion even as more probable or likely than another." In answer to Hume's position Reid and other members of the Scottish school advanced the doctrine of intuition and common sense. If it be argued that reason must be rejected because

---

[1] *Treatise of Human Nature* (1739) Bk. II, sec. III; Bk. I, sec. VII.

of inherent infirmities which are always present in the effort to move from the object to the knower, then, according to the Scottish school, this impediment can be overcome by reliance upon our immediate apprehension of reality. Belief founded upon sense or memory is an act of consciousness, and as such is intuitive, and is therefore self-evident and needs no further justification. Thus the doctrines of both Hume and Reid amount to an abandonment of philosophy as it has been traditionally understood. Reason has always been its main weapon, and if we are denied its use because it is untrustworthy, or if we are to substitute intuition for it, which is explicitly intended to obviate the necessity of proof, we have lost the redoubt which philosophy must hold or perish. But the principle of intuition itself is unsatisfactory since, even assuming that through it we reach the object, that is merely the beginning of our quest. What we want is knowledge of the object, and that is what intuition does not purport to supply. In legal speculation the intuitionalist fallacy is still prevalent, as in the attempt to ground the enforcement of promises on the proposition that they are self-evidently sacred.

Nevertheless, reason, as philosophy's instrument of inquiry, still awaits its final vindication. Whitehead,[2] as one of philosophy's chief contemporary spokesmen, has suggested an analysis of the function of reason that is intended, in part at least, to reveal some of the dangers of Hume's position. He shows that reason, when it seeks a solution of practical problems, degenerates in the end into a static methodology and becomes a mere habit remote from the affairs of the world. Jhering was making this point when he imagined a Heaven of Jurisprudential Conceptions, with its dialectic-hydraulic-interpretation press that could extract an infinitude of meanings from any text or statute, and with its hair-splitting machine which could divide a single hair into 999,999 equal parts; that operated by really expert jurists it could split each of these parts again into 999,999 equal parts. In Whitehead's view this

[2] *The Function of Reason* (1929).

aspect of reason is corrected by speculative reason which seeks with disinterested curiosity an understanding of the world. In its essence it is untrammelled by method. " Its function," he writes, " is to pierce into the general reasons beyond limited reasons, to understand all methods as coördinated in a nature of things only to be grasped by transcending all method." But its special function is to bring novelty into the appetitions of mental experience. " In this function," he adds, " there is a sheer element of anarchy." But the anarchical element is canalized by reason, and a higher appetition discriminates among the mind's own anarchic productions. This process has been a continually evident one in legal history. We need think only of the statement of Hippodamus in the fifth century B. C. that there were but three subjects of law suits—insult, injury and homicide—to formulate some estimate of the range of novelty which speculative reason has introduced into the legal order and, at the same time, brought under control. In the law, as elsewhere, novelty through the instrument of reason has been assimilated and it has been rejected, as in the failure of the common law at the end of the eighteenth century to accept Lord Mansfield's doctrine that want of consideration was no objection to the validity of a mercantile contract. Although Whitehead has not answered Hume's criticism, he has added to Hume's conception of reason as logical habit the idea of novelty as an anarchical element which is a part of the rational process and, because of that, is also subject to orderly control.

Although reason is the main instrument of philosophy, it has not developed a method for the discovery of truth that commands general assent. In Socrates' hands, philosophic methodology was the putting of questions of the kind " What is law? " with a view to ascertaining the essence of the matter inquired about. That question must be answered, he held, before other questions can be raised. If we do not know what virtue is, he says, we cannot advise someone how to acquire it.[3] The history of legal speculation reveals one of the principal

[3] *Laches* 190 B.

objections to which this method is open. What warrant have we for assuming that the term " law " is univocal and that it has an essence? Although the question " What is law? " is still asked by jurists, the history of the efforts to respond to it show that there is little likelihood that it can ever be answered in the sense intended by Socrates. For Plato dialectic was the great instrument of discovery, and its essential form was the question-and-answer method, the cross-examination technique of the lawyer. To this Aristotle answered that in fact we more readily fall into error in conversation than when we inquire into a problem by ourselves. Nevertheless, there is an element of truth in Plato's position. The question-and-answer method does not possess the supreme virtue which was assigned to it by Plato, but it occasionally does lead to the discovery of truth, as courtroom practice shows. Also, for those who work in the domain of the so-called non-exact sciences, where techniques for rigorous proof have not been established, it is still the most satisfactory method for testing conclusions. A rôle of great importance is claimed for the method in the history of Roman jurisprudence. It was through dialectic alone, as it is believed, that Roman jurisprudence " became fully logical, achieved unity and cognoscibility, reached its full stature and developed its refinement. . . . It proved to be verily the fire of Prometheus." [4] With Aristotle formal logic, induction, and his own kind of dialectic, among other procedures, were added to the methodology of philosophy. By the latter, Aristotle meant the type of reasoning that justifies first principles through a refutation of all the objections which can be raised against their validity, a methodology which became highly formalized in the hands of such mediaeval schoolmen as St. Thomas. From a study of logic, geometrical analysis and algebra, Descartes arrived at the idea that all the objects of knowledge are mutually connected and may be known through one another, and that no object is so remote or hidden that it cannot be discovered, provided only that we do not accept the

[4] Schulz, *History of Roman Legal Science* (1946) 48.

false for the true and always follow the order necessary for the deduction of one truth from another. To this end he proposed four rules: accept no proposition as true, unless it is known to be so; divide each of the difficulties under examination into as many parts as possible, or as might be necessary for an adequate solution; begin the analysis with the simplest and easiest known objects and proceed step by step to knowledge of the more complex; make the enumerations so complete and the review so general that nothing is omitted.

No one can deny the logical excellence of Descartes' rules or their extreme helpfulness in all kinds of inquiry, mathematical and non-mathematical. As a summation of technique, they describe as well as may be the method of most well-constructed judicial opinions. But in non-mathematical thought, as exemplified by social and legal speculation, they do not reveal the power of discovery that they disclose in mathematical analysis. A chain of mathematical reasoning not infrequently culminates in a single symbol, the permissible operations of which are thoroughly known. This symbol itself can then be utilized as a tool for further discovery, without additional investigation of the complexities that preceded its construction. Hertz's employment for his radio experiments of the wave equations of mathematical physics formulated by Clerk Maxwell is an example. But legal analysis reveals no such power. In the first place its rigor of analysis is so elementary compared with that of mathematics that it is more than doubtful that it could arrive at any summary idea which could be employed as summary mathematical symbols are employed. It is true that the history of mathematics is in part the history of an increase in the rigorousness of proof, and that what satisfied Euclid would not pass in any well-conducted freshman course in geometry today. It is also true that inasmuch as perfection in this respect is apparently unattainable it has been wittily remarked that " sufficient unto the day is the rigor thereof." But in the construction of its summary ideas legal speculation is remotely pre-Euclidean. In the second place, in legal speculation the opposite rule seems to prevail than obtains in mathematics. Russell's suggestion with respect to science may be extended to mathematics: its internal development may be summed up as the passage from contemplation to manipulation. In legal thought the passage, so far as the construction of summary ideas is concerned, seems to be from manipulation to contemplation. Thus the Austinian concept of sovereignty ended in the hands of his followers in the confession that it was a purely juristic idea, *i. e.*, that no actual state exhibited its characteristics.

Since Descartes, the search for a method peculiar to philosophy itself has continued with unabated vigor. Kant proposed the transcendental method which, in its synthetical aspect, began with experience, proceeded to the discovery of its necessary presuppositions, and then passed to the validation of *a priori* truths. He concluded that definitions in philosophy should come rather at the end than at the beginning of the inquiry, a position the opposite of that maintained by Socrates; philosophy possesses no axioms, no self-evident truths, and two concepts must be connected discursively by means of a third; philosophy's proofs are not demonstrative but acroamatic, that is to say, in mathematics it is possible to proceed from premises through a strict chain of arguments to a conclusion, but in philosophy we must always be on guard to discover defects which have been overlooked in the premises and which make it necessary to revise them or even change them entirely. He adds that reason can never refuse to submit to criticism, and that nothing is exempt from reason's searching examination; but the procedures of reason end, he holds, in antinomies for which there is no solution. Since no one will ever prove the opposite of a philosophical proposition we must accept those propositions that are consistent with the speculative interest of our reason, such as that there is a God, and that there is a future life. Hegel took up the problem and added his method of dialectic, or the attempt to reconcile opposites (which are not illusions) in a unity (which is also not an illusion).

In modern times, under the stimulus of the great successes of science, philosophy has once again turned to it, as philosophy did with Socrates and Descartes, for a model methodology. The analysis has progressed beyond the formulation of specific techniques to the isolation of the elements necessarily present in any adequate technique. These elements are abstractions, generality, concepts and possibility. When reason is confronted with a specific object or situation it attempts to abstract the essential features and to eliminate the non-essential. The abstraction that results permits the grouping of a great many objects or situations under one rubric, *e. g.* " chair " or " tort." But the abstraction is increased in usefulness and importance in proportion to its generality. The more cases subsumed under an abstraction, whether physical or legal, provided there is no loss of definiteness, the more successful the abstraction. If a legislature were compelled to consider the case of every individual and to frame rules of conduct for everyone in turn its task would be impossible. It therefore resorts to abstract generality and may provide, *e. g.*, that no one shall operate an automobile unless it possesses a windshield wiper. But at this point " the ballet of bloodless categories," that William James and Bergson feared, begins. In one American state, at least, the magistrate applied the legislative rule as it was written and fined a motorist for operating an automobile without a windshield wiper although his automobile had no windshield. In such cases, Aristotle pointed out, we need a rectification of law where it is defective because of its generality. The process of abstraction and generalization leads to the formation of the concept, which is the term applied to the way of conceiving the significant elements which have been abstracted. It is one of the functions of philosophy to reveal to us the order of compatible concepts which, since their conceivable relations are more numerous than the relations of the actual world, takes us beyond the actual into the wider realm of the possible. Here it is that philosophy and legal speculation join hands with art, religion and science in the exploration of the indefinite world of contingency.

In the discussion so far, no place has been assigned to logic as an instrument of philosophic methodology. That it had such a function seemed clear to Aristotle. Its principles were to be acquired by the student before embarking upon the study of any particular science, and it would teach him the kinds of propositions for which proof could be demanded and the kind of proof he could expect.[5] Logic would supply the tools for all the sciences, including philosophy, and would establish the formal conditions of proof that guaranteed certainty. This way of viewing logic was emphasized by the Scholastics, who attempted to formulate the rules to be followed in the solution of problems, *e. g.*, the rules of definition and of classification and division. It is this aspect of logic which Mill also emphasized. " Logic does not pretend to teach the surgeon what are the symptoms which indicate a violent death," he wrote. " This he must learn from his own experience and observation, or from that of others, his predecessors in his peculiar science. But logic sits in judgment on the sufficiency of that observation and experience to justify his rules, and on the sufficiency of his rules to justify his conduct. It does not give him proofs, but teaches him what makes them proofs, and how he is to judge of them." [6] He concluded that Bacon had correctly isolated logic's main characteristic when he called it *ars artium*— the science of science itself.

In spite of the impressive authority which can be adduced in support of an applied logic, the main effort of logicians has been directed at the study of logic itself, and not at its utilization. That is to say, logic as a methodology has as its object the attainment of true propositions; but logic as a department of knowledge aims at a statement of the necessary conditions for the formulation of true propositions. Logic's concern is with the attainment of truth in its own sphere of inquiry, and not with the application of those truths to problems in other fields. Moreover, there is little evidence that a knowledge of

[5] *De Sophisticis* 169ᵃ37; *Meta.*, 1005ᵇ3, 1006ᵃ6; *E. N.* 1094ᵇ23.
[6] *Logic* (1864) 6.

logical rules is of much assistance in the analysis of philosophical questions. As Locke pointed out, " Nobody is made anything by hearing of rules, or laying them up in his memory; practice must settle the habit of doing, without reflecting on the rule: and you may as well hope to make a good painter or musician, extempore, by a lecture and instruction in the arts of music and painting, as a coherent thinker, or strict reasoner, by a set of rules, showing him wherein right reasoning consists." [7] And Bradley, author of one of the subtlest and most influential of all *Logics,* admitted that " in my actual reasonings, I myself certainly have never troubled myself about any logic." [8] All this is not to deny that logic may be put to certain uses after its validating forms have been established. It is merely to insist that logic is not a philosophic methodology, a handmaiden of metaphysics in the sense that mathematics is the handmaiden of the exact sciences; further, logic is becoming identified with the wider study of scientific method, which may eventually crystallize into a technique of scientific discovery. But in that event, since the discipline known as scientific method is almost exclusively concerned with the problems of science, its technique will scarcely be applicable to what is traditionally recognized as philosophy. Finally, there is no intention to deny a usefulness to logic in legal speculation. In jurisprudence, no more than in philosophy, is it a methodology for the purposes of reasoning; for that kind of assistance jurisprudence must keep pace with scientific method itself. But for progress in the development of law as a deductive system, for the estimation of the validity of proof, for the detection of fallacies in reasoning, logic has a fair share to contribute. However, it is well to remember that even in this capacity its effectiveness is limited. No philosophy has ever been refuted, it has been remarked; it has only been abandoned. It is a rare instance when a legal controversy between jurists turns for its solution on a purely logical argu-

---

[7] *Conduct of the Understanding* (1706) § 4.
[8] *Principles of Logic* (2nd. ed. 1922) 621. *cf.* 534.

ment. " The law," as Thayer remarked conversely, " has no mandamus to the logical faculty." [9] Against a position passionately maintained, logic is as powerless in the law as elsewhere. At the Versailles Peace Conference, President Wilson determined to support the inclusion of pensions in the Reparation Bill. It was explained to him that not a single lawyer on the American Delegation would give an opinion in favor of including pensions. " All the logic was against it. ' Logic! logic! ' exclaimed the President, ' I don't care a damn for logic. I am going to include pensions! ' " [10]

Although philosophy has never succeeded in developing a distinctive method of its own, it is plain that the methods which it has followed have been closely imitated in juristic inquiries. Legal speculation, throughout most of its history, in spite of the fact that its subject matter in large part is existential, has drawn more on philosophy than on science. Perhaps it is to this factor that jurisprudence owes its advanced position among the social sciences. It learned early and has only rarely forgotten (as in Savigny's historicism), that rigorous reasoning is the indispensable element in all analysis. It has seldom yielded to the blandishments of a pure empiricism. At the same time, not infrequently it has fallen into the opposite error of dependence upon an exclusive attention to the logical analysis of concepts. Only in modern times has it come fully to appreciate the lesson of physical science that advances arise through joint manipulation of data and ideas. In its attachment to philosophical methodology, juristic methodology has experimented with both the form and the substance. For the most successful utilization of the form we need look only at St. Germain's two *Dialogues of the Doctor and the Student.* That his philosophical reading was extensive is apparent; and that some of his leading ideas, such as his insistence on the fact that general rules cannot cover all particular cases, are Aristotelian or even Platonic in origin, is also clear. Not the least of the

[9] *A Preliminary Treatise on Evidence* (1898) 314n.
[10] House, ed., *What Really Happened at Paris* (1921) 272.

reasons that account for the great influence which the treatise has exercised upon the development of modern equity, an influence comparable to that exercised by Bracton's treatise upon the development of the common law, is the dialogue form in which it was cast. That form, derived from Cicero or Plato, made possible the popular exposition of foreign principles in such a manner that there was a reception of them in English law.[11] For the substance the examples are endless, and it is sufficient to examine only the most notable work on jurisprudence in the English language—Austin's *Lectures on Jurisprudence*. His object in his first six lectures is clearly to mark out the boundaries of his subject, and his declared method to achieve that end is stated as follows:

> I determine the essence common to all laws properly so called: in other words, I determine the essence of a law imperative and proper.
>
> I determine the respective characters of the several classes into which laws (proper and otherwise) may be divided, assigning to each class the appropriate marks by which laws of that class are distinguished from laws of the others.

That this is the Socratic-Platonic method of inquiry scarcely needs to be pointed out. It is not surprising that the jurist should be guided in his methodology more by philosophy than by science, for the philosopher has concerned himself with juristic problems and the scientist scarcely at all. The jurist, if his writings are to possess any significance, must acquaint himself with the philosopher's work in jurisprudence, and thus observe at first hand the methods of philosophy. But he is under no such compulsion to study the product of the pure scientist. If, for the purposes of his own work, he studies it at all, it is solely from the methodological point of view, and instances of that kind are rare in the history of juristic thought.

---

[11] 5 Holdsworth, *History of English Law* (1924) 268-9.

IDEALISM

Most major juristic disputes of the present day have been under continuous analysis in philosophic thought since their crystallization by the ancient Greeks, and that dispute which centers around the rôle of the ideal in the judicial process is no exception. At the close of Book IX of the *Republic,* Plato, in one of his most famous passages, remarks that the wise man will regulate his life not in accordance with the rules of the city of his birth, but with the standards of " the city whose home is in the ideal." [12] That such an ideal could be known was a tradition of Greek political thought, considered even by practical statesmen, although Plato was the first to realize that the discovery of the constitution of the ideal state did not mean that a remedy had been found for the difficulties of actual political life.[13] Plato's ideal city was the basis of the City of God and the Communion of Saints of the Stoics and Christians, that vision, in Pater's words, " of a reasonable, a divine order, not in nature, but in the condition of human affairs, that unseen Celestial City, Uranopolis, Callipolis." Pater's phrase contains what, for our purposes, is the central idea behind Plato's difficult conception. The wise man, in attaching himself to the standards of the Celestial City, has not passed from the realm of the social to the private. His judgments are not those of a radical individualism, but are grounded in what he conceives to be social necessity. He is appealing, in other words, to standards that are applicable to existing societies. Now the question at once arises, Are there any such standards? Elsewhere, Plato, as was his custom, states the point of view of his opponents. In the *Theaetetus* the idea is associated with the name of Protagoras: in politics Protagoras' followers affirm " that just and unjust, honorable and disgraceful, holy and unholy, are in reality to each state such as the state thinks and makes lawful, and that in determining these matters no

---

[12] 592A. (Shorey's trans., Loeb), τῇ ἐν λόγοις κειμένῃ, literally, " the city which is founded in words."

[13] Aristotle, *Politics* 1267ᵇ29; 1 Newman, *The Politics of Aristotle* (1887) 85-86.

individual or state is wiser than another. . . . When they
speak of justice and injustice, piety and impiety, they are
confident that in nature these have no existence or essence of
their own. . . . The ordinances which the state commanded
and thought just, were just to the state which imposed them,
while they were in force." [14] It is scarcely necessary to add
that the problem is still unresolved, and today occupies a fair
share of the attention of philosophers, moralists, social scientists
and jurists. But because the problem has proved to be a
baffling one, that does not mean that juristic inquiry should
ignore it. There is a strong tendency in philosophy today, the
influence of which is already felt in jurisprudence, to abandon
the persistent problems as permanently insoluble. Whatever
may be the outcome of that movement in philosophy, the case
of jurisprudence is different. Problems of the kind with which
we are here concerned cannot be ignored so long as assumptions
based on one solution or another are almost an everyday factor
in the legislative, judicial and administrative processes.

In its ordinary meaning an ideal is that which, if we were
able to attain it, would be completely satisfying. It is thus
a standard of value against which actual behavior is to be
measured. As a standard it is expressible in propositional form,
and is therefore true or false. Thus, Plato's ideal of justice
could be stated: Justice is doing one's own business and not
being a busybody. If we can agree that that proposition correctly sets forth a course of conduct which will lead to the
realization of justice, then we have the statement of an ideal.
But the ideal may not be identifiable with the end. The end
may be happiness which might be attained through the realization of Plato's conception of justice; but it may be insisted
that the idea of justice as minding one's own business is
erroneous, that justice consists of something else or of many
other things, *e.g.*, equality of income, rendering to each his
due, etc. In that case we have a number of ideals all pointing
to the same end.

[14] 172A, 177D (Jowett's trans.)

A rule of law or a statutory enactment differs from a proposition expressing an ideal in at least two respects. First, the rule of law or statute as a norm is a concrete particularization of a consciously or unconsciously held ideal. Such ideals are not infrequently stated in the preamble to statutes, and are sometimes embodied in the text itself in the so-called "policy section." [15] Thus, the District of Columbia Rent Control Act, enacted October 22, 1919, laid it down as an ideal that the Federal Government ought not to be embarrassed in the transaction of the public business.[16] The Act therefore attempted to prevent such embarrassment by controlling rent conditions that were declared to be dangerous to the public health and burdensome to public officers and employees. Second, the rule of law or statute as a norm usually embodies an enforceable ideal. Apart from the difficulty of enforcement, there is no limitation in legal theory on the degree of generality of a statute, and Congress, if it so desired, could enact that all persons are prohibited from embarrassing the Federal Government in the transaction of the public business. However, both of these distinctions are merely distinctions of degree. In the popular sense, as Hegel observed, ideals are chimeras, or they are something far too excellent to possess reality, or far too feeble to procure it for themselves. Nevertheless, that does not seem to prevent ideals from influencing the course of public affairs. In January, 1914, the French Ministry succeeded in passing a bill appropriating 20,000 francs for a national funeral for General Picquart. A member in the Senate rose to inquire just what services the General had rendered the country. The premier, M. Doumergue, replied: "You ask me what services General Picquart has rendered the country! He believed in immanent justice and truth!" [17]

Modern sociological opinion, like ancient Greek thought, is divided on the value of ideals in society. For Sumner,[18] " an

---

[15] *E. g.*, National Industrial Recovery Act, Act of June 16, 1933, Ch. 90, 48 Stat. 195.

[16] 41 Stat. 297 § 122.

[17] 3 Pareto, *The Mind and Society* (1935) 1311.   [18] *Folkways* (1906) 32, 201.

ideal is entirely unscientific." They cause men to waste and
dissipate their energy, to turn their backs on welfare and
reality, in order to pursue beauty, glory, poetry, and dithyr-
ambic rhetoric, pleasure, fame, adventure, and phantasms which
have little or no connection with fact. He denied flatly that
there was any process by which to reach an ideal or any tests
by which to verify it. It is therefore impossible to frame a
proposition about an ideal which can be proved or disproved,
and the attempt to use ideals in social inquiry does not deserve
serious consideration. Pareto,[19] however, believes that society
will never be able to subsist without them. They set a goal,
however irrational and illogical, for which mankind should aim,
although in the nature of things it is unattainable and man's
achievement will always fall short of it. Nevertheless, the
general result is to raise achievement to a level which would
not have been reached in the absence of the ideal. That a
system of the highest ideals is not incompatible with the basest
behavior is, of course, well attested. Writing of the Chinese
Government in the latter part of the nineteenth century, Col-
quhoun [20] observed that it " exhibits the widest discrepancy of
any known system between theory and practice, the purest
ideal cloaking the grossest aims; a terrible example, in fact, of
corruptio optimi pessima. And the preternatural exaltation of
the ideal, places it so far beyond the reach of the highest attainment in real life that the standard of public duty, lost in the
clouds of inflated verbiage, is wholly disconnected from practical affairs. . . . Whereas in other countries there is still some
relation between the profession and the procedure—as, for
instance, when the minor is alleged as the major reason—this
relation has practically disappeared in China, and the substitution of the false for the true has become an organized system,
already consecrated by unwritten law." Midway between the
views expressed by Sumner and Pareto are those of Cicero, who
raised the question whether the ideal, in any matter so com-

[19] *Op. cit.* supra note 17 at 1306 *et seq.*
[20] *China in Transformation* (1898) 188.

plicated as that represented by human affairs, could be known by one individual. To Cato the Censor he attributes the opinion that a satisfactory conception of an ideal State could never be rationally constructed. Cicero held that no man has ever lived possessed of so great genius that nothing could escape him, nor can the combined powers of all the men living at one time possibly make all necessary provisions for the future without the aid of actual experience and test of time. A State therefore advances by what may be called Nature's road, through many generations, and finally reaches its ideal condition (*optimus status*).[21] Cicero does not make it clear by what tests men will know the State has finally reached its perfect form.

In spite of the vague and unsatisfactory condition in which the theory of ideals at present stands, we are confronted with the inescapable fact that ideals play a rôle of major importance in the judicial, legislative and juristic processes. In legal analysis the jurist has had his eyes predominantly upon the rule of law, although the rule of law is nearly always the concrete formulation of a consciously or unconsciously held ideal. We need a combing of the books,—analogous to the scrutiny of case and treatise for the rule of law,—for the discovery of the ideals behind the case and treatise. We need a statement of them in propositional form, so that they may be clearly understood and their implications developed. At that point Sumner's argument that all ideals are nonsensical because no known method of testability exists becomes pertinent. There is no need to deny that the difficulties in the way of verification of normative propositions are immense. But they are not necessarily insuperable, or at least have not been proved so. Until a critical theory of ideals is developed, they are subject to verification through the two prime means of scientific method, the dialectical and the empirical. For the dialectical, Plato's *Republic* can be taken as an example, where hypotheses are proposed, necessary exceptions admitted, and

[21] *De re publica* 2. 1. 3; 2. 16. 30.

the hypotheses are then abandoned or reformulated. The argument, it is true, usually turns on human preferences; but those preferences themselves are also subject to verification through dialectical and empirical means. For the empirical method, Hobbes' theory of law can serve as an illustration. It is grounded in a theory of human nature that purports to be purely empirical. Having set forth certain observations with respect to the nature of man, such as his powers of understanding, his motives, the needs of his body, etc., all of which are of a nature to admit of empirical verification, he proceeds to develop a series of hypotheses and their alternatives based upon those observations, which after many chapters of analysis leads to a theory of positive law. In neither the case of Plato nor that of Hobbes am I suggesting that the methods there followed are to be taken as representing perfection. On the contrary, it has been a large part of the business of their commentators to point out their numerous weaknesses. But that both the dialectical and the empirical methods can be used, at least provisionally, to test ideal norms, seems clear from these examples. In the end, in spite of the increasing rigor of our methods of verification, we will, with these methods, get no more than contingency. But at least we will know that our propositions are contingent, and to some extent the limits of that contingency. That seems a better ideal at which to aim than our present method of acquiescence in a state of ignorance as to the ideals we are presumed to be supporting, or in the acceptance of idealistic absolutisms from the courts, untested by anything save blind preference or prejudice.

Into the current of the law from its very inception philosophy has provided a never-ending stream of influential ideals. From Plato's ideal of a society in which everyone is to do that for which he is fitted, from the point of view of its social consequences, to the varying ideals of the absolutisms of today, all have left their mark at one stage or another on the legal process.[22] In the long-standing debate between the idealists

[22] Pound, *The End of Law as Developed in Juristic Thought* (1914) **27 Harv.**

and the realists the argument has turned on the illusory character of ideals as social forces. To the phenomenalists, the psychological realists, and the economic determinists, the illusory nature of ideals is plain. There is a strong tendency to answer this position by showing that ideals are not only forces of as influential a nature as, say, economic factors, but to show also that they are forces for good. There is no denying that some ideals have resulted in certain particular benefits to the legal process, such ideals as those of good faith, universality, authority and the idea of law behind and above law.[23] For such ideals, the law undoubtedly owes a great debt to philosophic speculation. But philosophic inquiry is not infallible. It can hold up to us the ideals of present satisfactions as in Epicurus, future satisfactions as in nineteenth-century evolutionary thought, primitive simplicity as in Rousseau, indifference as in Stoicism, progress as in philosophic thought from the eighteenth century to the present, and contemplation as in Plato. No doubt there is an element of effectiveness in all these ideals; but carried to the point to which their exponents insist it seems plain that they can yield nothing but harm. Descartes once played with the idea that the world might be ruled by a malicious demon, who arranged things so that the more we strove for truth the more we were deceived, and the more we strove to do right the greater our wrongdoing. There are many examples, in addition to two World Wars as the culmination of the moral optimism of the nineteenth century, to give point to his remark. Legal speculation must acknowledge its indebtedness to philosophy for the ideal goals that philosophy has formulated. But philosophy has not provided jurisprudence with a critical theory of ideals, nor has jurisprudence developed one of its own. The absence of such a

L. Rev. 605, (1917) 30 Harv. L. Rev. 201; *id. Twentieth Century Ideas as to the End of Law, Harvard Legal Essays* (1934) 357; Yntema, *The Rational Basis of Legal Science* (1931) 31 Col. L. Rev. 925, 934; Cohen, *Law and the Social Order* (1933); 2 Vinogradoff, *Collected Papers* (1928) 341; Cahn, *Justice, Power and Law* (1946), 55 Yale L. Jr., 336; *id., Freedom, Order and Law* (1948), 23 N. Y. Univ. L. Q. Rev. 20.

[23] Pound, *The Church in Legal History, Jubilee Law Lectures* (1939) 3 *et seq.*

theory which would show us in part the way to handle many of our own difficulties is the major weakness of idealistic inquiry today. The debate over the existence or non-existence of ideals as forces in the legal process can be safely treated as irrelevant pending the construction of such a theory.

PHILOSOPHY AND THE LEGAL PROCESS

Philosophy in its jurisprudential form is a special mode of inquiry concerned with particular problems, and from this point of view it has the same logical status as the other special sciences. It brings to a focus through the process of analytic differentiation a problematic situation that it endeavors to resolve by its own methods for its own end. Its approach is theoretic, that is, it seeks to construct a logical system which is complete and the parts of which are interconnected. We need not linger over the debate in modern logic whether the institution of such a system exhausts the work of science or, in other words, whether the use of scientific generalizations to determine singular cases is extra-scientific and merely practical.[24] The history of science seems to show that it has more chance of attaining its end of a system of true propositions if the scientist keeps that goal before him and is not distracted by considerations of the use to which his conclusions can be put. At the same time it is impossible to deny that logically applications of hypotheses are confirmatory or not, and to that extent are an essential element of the verificatory aspect of scientific method. The elimination of swamps where anopheles mosquitoes breed helps in the control of malaria, but as it has been observed it also, from the point of view of scientific method, is an experiment that confirms an hypothesis. But whatever the solution of this controversy may be, it is a fact that philosophical speculation has, in numerous instances, become exemplified in legal practice. One reason is that philosophers, at least in their juristic endeavors, have not been

[24] 2 Bradley, *The Principles of Logic* (2nd. ed. 1922) 713; Dewey, *Logic* (1938) 437, 493; Cohen, *Reason and Nature* (1931) 83 *et seq.*

as remote from practical affairs as opinion generally credits them. It is plain from their works that Plato and Aristotle had an extensive knowledge of law and legal history. Moreover, Aristonymus, Phormion, Menedemus, Eudoxus and Aristotle went as experts from the Academy under Plato's direction to assist a number of Greek states in matters of legal revision, a circumstance which leads Calhoun [25] to conclude that the Academy itself may have exercised a real influence upon the Hellenistic law, that was to contribute in its turn to the Roman. Among later philosophers—Cicero, St. Thomas, Kant, Fichte and Hegel, and for English law, Bacon, Hobbes, Locke and Hume—we find a knowledge of law and legal practice precise and extensive in a number of cases, but in every instance sufficiently adequate to channel the speculative inquiry in the direction of the concrete. Sometimes the results have been fantastic, as in Kant's reduction of marriage to a mutual lease of the sexual organs; sometimes they have been brilliant formulations of legal doctrines which are now, because of their necessity, commonplaces, but which at the time of their proposal were novelties or debatable. An instance is Plato's denial that a code of law can possess finality, at least when first enacted, and his insistence that allowance must be made for amendment. This concern of philosophers with the practical has added a concrete element to their inquiries, which in turn has given their propositions a usefulness when the legal system has stood in need of revision.

Perhaps the most famous conception taken into the legal process from philosophical inquiry is the distinction developed by the Greek thinkers of the fifth century B. C., who inquired whether the right or the just was right and just by nature or only by convention and enactment. The problem had first arisen in physics, in the effort to find a constant element in the apparent world of flux, and thus we find Democritus, the originator of the atomic theory, taking the position that color and taste exist by convention and that reality is to be found in

---

[25] *Greek Legal Science* (1944) 70.

the atom and the void. It was inevitable that the same problem should arise with respect to law. It received its classic exposition in chapter seven of Book Five of the *Nicomachean Ethics,* where Aristotle drew a distinction between the rules of natural justice which have the same validity everywhere and do not depend on our accepting them or not, and rules of conventional justice which in the first instance may be settled in one way or the other indifferently. As examples of the latter type Aristotle instances the rule that the ransom for a prisoner shall be a mina and that a sacrifice shall consist of a goat and not of two sheep. The subsequent history of this idea is well known. From later Greek thought to Cicero, from Cicero to the classical jurists, to mediaeval and renaissance thought, to English law, Hobbes and Blackstone, and finally to the court decisions of the nineteenth and twentieth centuries, the idea has never ceased to be a leavening one. Another principle, almost as influential as the one that distinguishes between nature and convention, is that law, because it is the expression of justice, is supreme, an unjust law being no law at all. The roots of this principle, that dominated mediaeval thinking and is not without its force today, are clearly discernible in Plato's question in the *Politicus,* whether it is more advantageous to be subject to the best man or the best laws. It is scarcely necessary to add that the adoption into the legal process of principles of the type here being discussed is not due to the compulsion of their transcendent merit. They become important, and impinge upon legal activity, for compelling social and economic reasons. On all occasions of social upheaval difficulties tend to be interpreted in moral terms, and the moral principles enunciated by the philosophers thus possess a peculiar relevance. In the struggle in fifth-century Greece between the aristocracy and the people, the distinction between right by nature and right by convention served to place law on a foundation to which both sides could appeal with more security than to such an old-fashioned idea as that law was the gift of a god.[26]

[26] Pound, *Law and Morals* (2nd. ed. 1926) 5.

Similarly, the principle of the supremacy of law as the expression of justice was bound to be a powerful weapon from the ninth century A. D. onwards, in the struggle over the authority of the kingship. On the same basis we may expect in our own day, if indeed it is not already present, to find reflected in legal practice doctrines which have their origin in the recent speculations with respect to philosophical relativism and its offspring, absolutism.

Philosophers have also not infrequently evinced an interest in practical reforms and distinctions, but whether their suggestions have been the actual sources of later changes in legal administration, it is impossible to say. Thus we find Plato advocating the desirability of statutory preambles, and proposing an approximation to the modern classification of first and second degree murder and manslaughter, and Hobbes insisting on the necessity of bringing statutes and rules of law to public notice. Nevertheless, however interesting or influential such contributions may be on their own account, as contributions from philosophers they are incidental.

Law generally in its substance is a reflection of the social environment in which it functions, and inasmuch as society is in an incessant state of flux, law itself is in a continuous state of readjustment, and, not infrequently, even transilience. In the past, philosophy has been the chief extra-legal source to which the jurist has turned for help in the solution of the never-ending series of novel problems with which he is confronted. That he will continue this practice is likely, and, in fact is already apparent in the solutions proposed by jurists to meet certain of the problems of our own age. Whether we approve of the new philosophies to which contemporary jurists are turning for sustenance is a matter of opinion. They may contain germs of ideas that will help to see law through its current crisis, or they may share in the second-rateness and thus in the social ineptitude which is the general mark of our age. In any event, the contemporary jurist suffers from a disadvantage that did not burden his predecessors. Philosophy offered his

predecessors not only the aid of a system of general ideas, but
a concrete working out of those ideas by philosophers in the
realm of law. Today the jurist is offered the first, but not the
second. Whether this state of affairs will make any significant
difference in the progress of law will depend upon how skillful
the jurist will be as a philosopher. Would the jurist of classical
times have seen the relevance of the controversy with respect
to nature and convention to the idea of justice to the extent
developed by Aristotle? We do not know; but we can at least
take warning from the abortive efforts of the contemporary
popularizing physicist to interpret modern philosophy that the
task is not an easy one.

CHAPTER II

PLATO

> *Still, quotations from time to time
> met with, have lead me to think that
> there are in Plato detached thoughts
> from which I might benefit had I the
> patience to seek them out.*
>
> Herbert Spencer

PLATO TOOK the widest possible view of law. He held that it was a product of reason and he identified it with Nature itself. Law was a subject which he kept constantly before him, and there is scarcely a dialogue in which some aspect of it is not treated explicitly. His theory of law is a fundamental part of his general philosophy and it illumines and is illumined by the entire Platonic corpus. Like the law of the Greeks, his legal thought was never systematized as we have become accustomed to regard system in law since the last century of the Roman Republic; yet it was remarkably coherent in relation to his major philosophical ideas. He was a layman in the field, as were all the Greeks, in the sense that there were no professional lawyers as we conceive their function today. But, in his juristic thinking, he isolated a range of legal ideas among the most important in the history of law and which have been the basis of much subsequent speculation. His influence on the law has been large in both its theoretic and its practical aspects. The Roman jurists " have taken many ideas from Plato," said the learned Cujas; [1] and his influence upon Hellen-

---

I have in general, for the quotations appearing in the text, followed the translations of Bury, Shorey (for the *Republic*), Jowett and Taylor, though sometimes in combination or with modifications. My debt to the felicitous translations which England occasionally ventures to append to his edition of the *Laws* and to his notes will be readily apparent. My obligations to the commentaries of Grote, Shorey, Taylor, Nettleship and Ritter will also be obvious.

[1] 5 Cujas, *Opera Omnia* (1722) 666, where instances in the *Digest* of specific borrowings from Plato are cited. *Cf.* 3 *Ibid.* 702-3. Milton's *Tractate on a Free Commonwealth* borrowed many of its ideas from the *Republic* and the *Laws*. Shorey points out that through that medium many of Plato's thoughts were

istic law, and through its practices upon Roman law, and thus directly and indirectly upon much of the law of modern times, has even yet not been fully appreciated.

How much Plato owed to his predecessors in legal speculation is not clear, since their works survive only in fragments and are sometimes unintelligible. Many attempts have been made to determine the meaning of the fragments and for some of them it is still anyone's guess. We owe their preservation to the fact that they were quoted by later writers who apparently regarded them as stating doctrines of importance. If we cannot in some cases make much of their meaning we are nonetheless affected by their note of passion.

From Solon, Plato undoubtedly inherited a tradition that the happiness of the state depended upon the faithful observance of sound laws, and that it was the duty of the good citizen to see that such laws were made. In his poetry, Solon took the view that law should be impartial, assigning proper spheres to the rich and the poor, " protecting both with a strong shield, and suffering neither to prevail unjustly." [2] Herodotus and Pindar had a similar opinion of the importance of law. To Herodotus it was the " Master." Demaratus, the exiled King of Sparta who was marching with Xerxes against Hellas, told him that the Lacedaemonians were the best warriors on earth. " Free they are," he said, " yet not wholly free; for law is their master, whom they fear much more than your men fear you. This is my proof—what their law bids them do, that they do; and its bidding is ever the same, that they must never flee from

transmitted to America and some of them to the Constitution of the United States: Patrick Henry's return to a state of nature when the ruler breaks the covenant; the necessity of a ruler's neglecting his own affairs; the requirement that the general council be always in session, because the ship of state is always under sail; partial rotation in the senate, a third part going out according to the precedence of their election; the need of maintaining a balance against the dangers of " a licentious and unlimited democracy "; ingenious devices to qualify and refine election; the idea that wisely chosen legislators will not be distrusted but will be " the true keepers of our liberty "; local self-government and locally controlled schools. Shorey, *Platonism Ancient and Modern* (1938) 186.

[2] Aristotle, *Constitution of Athens*, xii, 1. *Cf. Politics*, 1273^{b}35. For the history of legal ideas prior to Plato, see Hamburger, *The Awakening of Western Legal Thought* (1942).

the battle before whatsoever odds, but abide at their posts and there conquer or die." [3] To Pindar it was " Lord of all." " Law, lord of all, mortals and immortals, carrieth everything with a high hand, justifying the extreme of violence." [4] Anaximander [5] declared that " the beginning of that which is, is the boundless; but whence that which is arises, thither must it return again of necessity; for the things give satisfaction and reparation to one another for their injustice, as is appointed according to the ordering of time." Among many interpretations of this sentence it has been suggested that it depicts a lawsuit before the judgment seat of Time where things present their rival claims of a right to exist. Pythagoras,[6] in a statement which belongs to that realm of arbitrary speculation which has for its subject matter the ethical import of numbers, asserted in a much vexed sentence that justice was a square number. Aristotle [7] seemingly knew what the assertion meant since he denied that it was true. Modern commentators differ with Aristotle and profess to find great wisdom in the remark. The poignant sayings of Heraclitus do not always speak for themselves: " Men would not have known the name of Justice were it not for these things [*i. e.*, justice is known only through injustice]"; [8] " The people must fight for its law as for its wall "; [9] " It is law, too, to obey the counsel of one." [10] Some of his utterances might be interpreted as demanding an accurate description of what happens in fact in society as a necessary basis for speculative political thought. In this aspect he may be the forerunner of modern juristic realism.

Whatever meaning may attach to those fragments, by the

---

[3] *History* VII, 104.

[4] *Frag.* 169 (151).

[5] 1 Diels, *Die Fragmente der Vorsokratiker* (5th ed. 1934) 89.

[6] Aristotle, *Magna Moralia*, 1182ª13.

[7] *Magna Moralia*, 1182ª13. The judgment passed by Photius, the ninth-century patriarch of Constantinople, is, however, a sufficient summary of the matter. " It is necessary, so it seems, to have spent a whole lifetime in diligent study in order to understand these prodigious theological fictions concerning numbers; such application will permit one to rave in a profound fashion." 103 Migne, *Patrologiae Cursus Completus, Series Graeca* (1860) 594.

[8] *Frag.* 60.　　　　[9] *Frag.* 100.　　　　[10] *Frag.* 110.

time Plato had begun to write the doctrine of subjectivism and relativism had taken distinct forms. They were put forward by numerous groups—among them the sophists, the dramatists, and the historians—and were expressed in many tendencies. The issue was sharply raised by the question: Does what is just depend upon nature or convention? In one direction the answer leads to Antigone's [11] assertion of a " higher law " which commanded her to bury her brother, an act forbidden by the law of the state; and in the other to the position that state laws were merely arbitrary enactments promulgated and made effective by those who had the power to do so and for their own advantage. The form which Plato undertook to refute maintained that laws were an invention of man and that in devising them he was restricted by no compulsion of nature.

From his predecessors, particularly the sophists, Plato learned the value of empiricism, although if experience did not yield a theory he regarded it as having failed in its purpose. In the main, however, his method was to trace the logical consequences of a theory and to refute or uphold it, not through empiricism, but by exhibiting its logical contradictions or harmonies; but the empirical was rarely absent from his mind. From the sophists who were intent not upon acquiring knowledge but on an advantageous manipulation of social phenomena, Plato learned the value of the practical. He saw law as a form of social control and his theories were, therefore, adjusted to meet both theoretical and practical objections. He kept steadily before him both the λόγος and the πρᾶγμα, the formula and the fact.

This account of Plato's legal ideas is meant to include a description of his principal theories of law and his application of them to the practical affairs of society. It endeavors to bring together in one place the numerous suggestive ideas on the law scattered throughout the dialogues. His principles are open to much criticism; but as that has been the main business

[11] Sophocles, *Antigone,* 450.

of Platonists and others from Aristotle to the present day, it has here been kept to a minimum. To state as precisely as may be exactly what he thought about a subject to which he gave so much reflection has appeared to be a task of sufficient value in itself. There are numerous points on which it would be profitable to have further information; but, as a general rule, conjectural attempts to repair omissions on the part of Plato have been left to the reader.

The Nature of Law

In a dialogue remarkable for its anticipation of subsequent analysis, Plato states that law seeks to be the discovery of reality.[12] He arrives at this position by the following argument. Socrates asks abruptly: " What is law? " " What kind of laws do you mean? " his companion asks. Socrates makes short work of this question by inquiring if there is any difference between law and law in the very point of being law, or if gold differs from gold in being gold. His companion then defines law as that which is accepted as legal. To this the objection is made that speech is not the thing that is spoken, nor is vision merely the visible things nor hearing the audible things. Law must therefore be distinct from that which is accepted as legal. Suppose it is assumed that it is by " law " that " the laws " are accepted, how would the " law " whereby they are thus accepted be defined? Socrates is here raising what we are accustomed to think of in modern terms as the problem of " authority." His companion answers that, in this sense, law is the decrees and pronouncements of the community, or, to state it generally, law is the opinion of the state. That is to say, as Plato expresses it elsewhere, when a judgment of society

---

[12] *Minos* 315 B. I leave to the philologists the dispute over the genuineness of this dialogue. It was accepted in ancient times as by Plato, and in recent times this view was shared by Bentley, Ruhnken and Grote. It is rejected by most modern scholars although opinion is now beginning to veer in its favor. It is generally agreed that its thought is thoroughly Platonic. For a recent discussion see Chroust, *An Anonymous Treatise on Law: The Pseudo-Platonic Dialogue Minos* (1947), 23 Notre Dame Lawyer 47.

takes the form of a public decision of the state, it has the name
of law.[13] Socrates observes that perhaps this is right, but he
does not believe that the conversation has reached the essence
of the matter. Law is a good thing, and public opinions which
are evil would not be law. Granting that law is some sort of
opinion, which Socrates believes it is, it must be good opinion.
Now good opinion is true opinion, and true opinion is discovery
of reality. Socrates therefore concludes that law seeks to be
the discovery of reality, or more precisely, it is the true reality
with respect to the administration of a state.[14]

Nevertheless, it is common knowledge that the laws of
the different communities differ on the same subject matter.
Perhaps, Socrates suggests, law may not always achieve its
ideal of discovering true reality. Still, he adds, no society, not
even the Persians, believes that the just can really be unjust.
It is thus a universal rule that realities, and not unrealities,
are accepted as real; whoever fails then to reach reality, fails
to find law. However, answers the companion, we are continually changing our laws in all sorts of ways. Perhaps it is
because you do not reflect that when we change our pieces
at draughts they are the same pieces, replies Socrates. Those
who know always accept the same views, whether Greeks or

---

[13] *Laws* 644 D.

[14] *Minos* 315 B, 321 A. That this is sound Platonic doctrine is evidenced by the
Politicus, where it is maintained that law is an imitation of truth, which for Plato
equals reality. 300 C, 301 B. It is to the *Minos*, however, that we must turn for the
explicit justification. Other Greek definitions of law are: Xenophon (*Memorabilia*
I, ii, 43), "Whatsoever the ruling power in the state, after deliberation, enacts and
directs to be done is known as a law"; Demosthenes (*Against Aristogeiton*, 774),
"The law is that which all men ought to obey for many reasons, but above all,
because every law is an invention and gift of the gods, a tenet of wise men, a
corrective of errors voluntary and involuntary, and a general covenant of the whole
state in accordance with which all men in that state ought to regulate their lives"
(This definition was repeated by Hermogenes, see Spengel, *Rhetores Graeci* II, 289
1853); Anaximenes of Lampsacus (Aristotle, *Rhetoric to Alexander*, 1420ᵃ),
"Law is reason defined in accordance with a common agreement of the state setting
forth how men are to act in each matter"; Chrysippus (Diog. Laert., VII, 88),
"The end [the goal of living] may be defined as life in accordance with nature, or,
in other words, in accordance with our own human nature as well as that of the
universe, a life in which we refrain from every action forbidden by the law common
to all things, that is to say, the right reason which pervades all things, and is
identical with Zeus, Lord and ruler of all that is."

foreigners; they will not write differently at different times on the same matters, nor will they ever change one set of accepted rules for another in respect of the same matters. If we see some persons anywhere doing this, we can say that they have no knowledge; and if they are mistaken in what they describe as law, then that law is mere appearance and ought not to be accepted as "law." In answering the case of the relativists, Socrates appears to be asserting a distinction between principles and rules, *e. g.*, the difference between the principles of mechanics which are everywhere the same and the specific instructions followed by the bridge builder which vary with every work of construction.

In holding that law seeks to be the discovery of true reality, Plato was defining its proper sphere in his philosophical view of the world. It represents part of his effort towards a constructive metaphysics and through it, as with any other thread we pick up in Plato, we reach the core of the entire Platonic system—the general theory of Forms or Ideas. Elsewhere, in an aside, Plato offers another definition of law as the apportionment of reason; [15] but inasmuch as reason is apprehension of reality [16] we are brought to the same point as in the first definition. What did Plato mean by reality? He once tentatively defined it as power, by which he meant that anything has real existence if it has inherent in it the power of being affected or of affecting others, no matter how small the thing. [17] Plato remarks, however, that "the easy use of words and phrases and the avoidance of strict precision is in general a sign of good breeding; indeed, the opposite is hardly worthy of a gentleman." [18] Although Plato nowhere sums up his doc-

---

[15] *Laws* 714 A. In the Golden Age the Deity ruled through its ministers the "daemons," but they have been supplanted by the divine in man, which is to say, the intellect, which rules through its ministers, those "arrangements of the intellect" we term "law."

[16] *Phaedr.* 249 B.

[17] *Soph.* 247 E, 248 C. *Cf.* Cornford, *Plato's Theory of Knowledge* (1946) vii.

[18] *Theaet.* 184 C. Plato adds that "sometimes precision is necessary." As a logician of great powers he could be extremely precise in his use of words. Philosophers like Whitehead however have found it necessary to devise their own

trine in final form, if the pieces are put together they make an intelligible picture. When he asserted that law was the discovery of true reality he appeared to mean that the moral value of law increases as it approximates the ideal law which exists in the world of reality. The philosopher in the Platonic system is one who knows true reality and who therefore knows what the ideal thing to do is. If the philosopher is a king he will prescribe laws for the state based upon the ideal laws which he has perceived in the world of reality. They will therefore be the best possible laws, and by following them, the members of the community will be directed to the way of the good life.[19] Thus the laws of a city, if they are to be of moral worth, must be modeled upon the laws of reality so that they are the objective expression in the state structure of the system of ideas which alone represents the real.

There are obscurities in Plato's views on the nature of law and gaps in his reasoning. In a handful of pages, however, he raised many of the problems which have been the staple of juristic thought from his day down to the present time. His first question, literally the first sentence of the dialogue, still remains the first question asked of itself by every school of legal thought: What is law? He did not distinguish between society and the state nor between ethics and politics. There was only one place for the realization of the good life and that was in the community. After twenty-four hundred years during which the notion of the good life was kept distinct from that of the political life, the state philosophies of the twentieth century are reasserting the Platonic thesis in one form or another. By insisting upon a rigid distinction between the

vocabulary in order to avoid the obscurities of ordinary language. Plato did not employ a technical vocabulary and expressed his ideas in constantly changing words.

[19] *Rep.* 473 C-D; *Epistle* VII, 324 B, 328 A-B. Rulers identified at various times in the popular imagination with Plato's philosopher-king are Marcus Aurelius, Constantine, Julian the Apostate, Arcadius, Saint Louis, James I, Frederick the Great, and Napoleon. It seems scarcely necessary to caution the reader that Plato's doctrine of ideas has received numerous interpretations; it is even urged, although inconclusively, that he abandoned the theory in later life. Burnet, *Platonism* (1928) 35 *et seq.*

idea of law and the positive enactments of the state, Plato prepared the way for natural law speculation and the perception of an ideal element in law-making. He answers the commonplace distinction, of fifth and fourth-century discussion, between nature and convention by setting in opposition the theory of Ideas which leads him to the conclusion that law is discovered and not invented. He puts forward the theory that law is an instrument of social control and thus suggests the problem of the end of law. By assenting in part to the notion that laws are the public resolutions of the community, he raises for later speculation the question of the relation between the state and law. The connection between law and morals is never absent from his thought. By suggesting (though rejecting the idea) that law might be defined as the aggregate of laws, he anticipated the position which was taken by the majority of jurists from the Middle Ages to the analytical jurists and beyond. He made clear the function of principle in the construction of a legal system. So far as the extant evidence shows, he was in all this, particularly when coupled with the tremendous power of his philosophical method, the first to exhibit the possibility of a general science of law.

The Function of Law

Three hypotheses are assumed as the basis of Plato's thinking about law. They have been championed by influential schools of thought since his day; they have also been the source of much anguish in admirers whose political beliefs are of a different complexion than Plato's. He held that the end of law was to produce men who were " completely good "; this could be done because, as the institutional idealists of the nineteenth century also asserted, human nature was capable of almost unlimited modification; the method to be used was a benevolent dictatorship: philosophers must become kings or kings, philosophers. Those hypotheses have received as much attention as anything else in Plato, and it is necessary only that they be properly understood.

As a philosopher, Plato could not accept anything less than complete goodness in men; he therefore rejected all laws that did not incline to that end.[20] " Keep watch on my present law-making," says the Athenian, " in case I should enact any law either not tending to goodness at all, or tending only to a part of it." [21] This is not the place to examine the role of ideals in legal thought, except to observe that the conception men have of a better condition of affairs has frequently been a potent element in lawmaking; nor is it necessary to examine Plato's views on the relation of law and morals; his legal and moral views are so intertwined as to be inseparable, and lead him upon occasion, as we have already seen from the *Minos*, even to assert that a bad law is no law.[22] He was as aware as Hobbes and Austin of the distinction between law and morals, of the idea of law as a command,[23] but he would have none of it.[24] Although, if men would listen to him, his goals were possible of achievement, he understood fully that his proposal was visionary,[25] an old man's game of jurisprudence,[26] and he had no expectation that his ideal would be realized in practice. He was merely insisting upon the necessity of abstractions or hypotheses as controls in societal inquiry.[27]

He was wedded to his belief in the malleability of human nature, and he had no doubt that the children would accept the new laws even if the parents would not.[28] That is a common presupposition of reform movements; it was given one of its most rigid tests, and with complete success, during two centuries of the Ottoman Empire (*circa* A. D. 1365-1564) which witnessed in practice the closest approximation to his proposals that the world has perhaps ever known.

---

[20] *Laws* 630 C.

[21] *Laws* 705 E.

[22] *Hipp. Maj.* 284 B-E; *Minos* 314 E; *Laws* 715 B. *Cf.* Xenophon, *Memor.* I, ii 40-46.

[23] *Laws* 723 A.   [25] *Laws* 632 E, 712 B; *Rep.* 376 D.

[24] *Laws* 857 C-D.   [26] *Laws* 685 A; *cf. Phaedr.* 276 D, *Parm.* 137 B.

[27] *Rep.* 472 C; *Laws* 739 E. Strictly, Platonic Ideas are not abstractions from sense-data inasmuch as sense-data are only approximations of the Ideas.

[28] *Laws* 752 C; *Rep.* 541 A.

What is possibly the best defense devised by Platonists for the doctrine of the philosopher-king argues that it represents the principle that government is an art or science as opposed to the politicians' idea of government by oratory under law; [29] that this doctrine is merely a further expression of his theory of ideal postulates [30] and the combination of intellectual and moral perfection it envisages has never been known on this earth and is *a priori* fictional; that it is a recognition of the demand that the state be ruled by the highest available intelligence,[31] and represents only the autocratic discretion of the true shepherd, pilot, or physician; [32] and finally that (though Plato always insisted upon the proposition that it is better for the unwise, whether they consent or not, to be ruled by the wise) [33] in practice he everywhere yields to the reign of law and the consent of the governed. A marked feature of Plato's writings is the extraordinary care he takes to limit his proposals by explicit qualification or an ironical turn of phrase. The defense offered for him, therefore, is not an impossible one.

Was Plato hostile to law? That is a necessary question in any account of Plato's jurisprudence. There is no doubt that as a seeker after an ideal the Plato of the *Republic* preferred the adaptable intelligence of the all-wise autocrat to the impersonality of the rule of law. As it appeared on this earth, it was the despot of mankind and often forced men to do many things which were opposed to nature. It was the lord of the state. In the nature of things, moreover, law aimed at the impossible. Through the medium of the fixed, inflexible general rule laws sought to direct men and actions which were constantly

---

[29] *Gorgias.* The doctrine plainly needs a defense, since it led even Mill to assert that it postulated infallibility, or something near it, in the rulers of the state, "or else ascribes such a depth of comparative imbecility to the rest of mankind, as to unfit them for any voice whatever in their own government, or any power of calling their scientific ruler to account." 4 Mill, *Dissertations and Discussions* (1868) 325. Earlier, in his *Prospect for a Perpetual Peace* (1795), Kant had remarked, "That kings should philosophize or philosophers become kings is not to be expected. But neither is it to be desired; for the possession of power is inevitably fatal to the free exercise of reason."

[30] *Laws* 711 A.
[31] *Laws* 711 A.
[32] *Laws* 684 C; *Polit.* 296 B, 290 D.
[33] *Rep.* 590 D; *Polit.* 296 B; *Laws* 684 C.

changing and always different. In such a system it was impossible to avoid the " hard case." [34] He knew well the simple truth, as the trial of Socrates had shown him, that the debating method of the courtroom, as distinguished from cross-examination, was perhaps the least likely to lead to the discovery of truth.[35] Against this the Plato of the *Laws* and *Statesman* had come to realize that on this earth benevolent dictatorship was a counsel of perfection and that he would better propose a solution which had a possibility of realization. In the arts we trust the experts absolutely; but in the realm of government the expert is rarer than in any other art. In the human hive no king-bee [36] was produced so pre-eminently fitted in body and mind to rule as an expert that he might ignore the instructions of law. Plato therefore believed that society should fall back upon law as a second-best,[37] perhaps even as something in the nature of a *pis aller,* the supremacy of the rigid rule adapted to the " average " man and the general situation [38] and incapable of dispensing equity in the particular case.[39] He had no doubt whatever that fixed laws are to be preferred to the personal administration of the unscientific ruler which is the type society usually receives.[40]

Plato thus came to his final view on the necessity of law. He insisted that it was indispensable; without it we were indistinguishable from animals. It was the instructor of youth. Its noblest work was to make men hate injustice and love justice. The laws are intended to make those who use them

---

[34] *Protag.* 337 D, *Symp.* 196 C, *Polit.* 294 B; *Rep.* 405 A-C.

[35] *Rep.* 492 B-C; *Laches* 196 B; *Theaet.* 172 C-E; *Phaed.* 272 D-E; *Apol.* 17 D. *Cf.* Frank, *Say It With Music* (1948), 61 Harv. L. Rev. 921, 946, where it is argued that in the work of the trial judge the conditions indispensable to all really scientific knowledge are completely lacking, and that at best such work can be described only as a " subjective art." See also *Ibid.* 923 n. 9 where *Theaet.* 201-2 is cited for the proposition that the conclusions of trial judges are matters of opinion and not knowledge.

[36] *Polit.* 301 D-E; *Rep.* 520 B. Xenophon employed the same metaphor. *Cyrop.* V, 1, 24; *Oecon.* VII, 32.

[37] *Polit.* 300 C; *Laws* 875 D.

[38] *Polit.* 295 A.

[39] *Polit.* 295 A-B. Plato again brings in the idea of equity in *Laws* 875 D.

[40] *Polit.* 300 A *et seq.*

happy; and they confer every sort of good. It was hard, Plato pointed out, for men to perceive that the preoccupation of social science was with the community and not with the individual; loyalty to the community's interest bound a state together; the pursuit of the individual's interest tore it asunder. Plato stated that it was hard for men to see also that the interests of both alike were better served by the community's prosperity than by that of the individual. There was not a man among us whose natural equipment enabled him both to see what was good for men as members of a community, and, on seeing it, always to be both able and willing to act for the best. Irresponsible power for mortal men always led to grasping and self-interested action, or, as Acton was to rephrase it later, " all power corrupts and absolute power corrupts absolutely." If ever a man were providentially endowed with a native capacity to apprehend the true power and position of the irresponsible autocrat he would need no laws to govern him; for no law had the right to dictate to true knowledge. But, as things were, such insight nowhere existed, except in small amounts; that was why we had to take the second best—law the generality of which could not always do justice to particular cases.[41]

Anticipating subsequent analysis, Plato considered the suggestions that law is of divine origin and that man's function is to discover its true rules;[42] that it is a product of impersonal social and natural forces—economic, geographical and sociological or, as he expressed it, the result of chance and occasion;[43] and that it is an invention of man to meet social needs, Art cooperating with Occasion.[44] He accepted all these views as being in some sense partly true; but his ultimate idea was in the nature of a compromise. In his final position he regarded law as the art of adjusting human conduct to the

---

[41] *Apol.* 24; *Protag.* 326 D; *Laws* 862 E, 874 E *et seq.*

[42] *Laws* 624 A, 835 C; *Minos* 333 *et seq.* Plato believed that law was unknown in primitive society. *Laws* 680 A.

[43] *Laws* 709 A. *Rep.* 471.

[44] *Gorg.* 482 E; *Rep.* 551 B; *Laws* 889 D *et seq.* In the *Minos* 314 B the idea also is stressed that it is through art ($\tau\acute{\epsilon}\chi\nu\eta$) that reality is discovered.

circumstances of the external world. Sometimes, as Montesquieu was later to insist, the conditions of society shape the laws and sometimes, as Condorcet urged, the laws shape the conditions. Plato thus regarded law as both a genetic and teleologic process whose primary function as an art is to correct the inequalities in the relationship between society and its environment.[45] Stated concretely, the precise end of law is the achievement of group unity,[46] which cannot be obtained if minority groups are disregarded or by legislating for single classes.[47] This, in Plato's theory, is the philosophic or highest view, and it leads to the position that if the function of law as the interest of the entire community is observed faithfully, in the end it will yield an understanding of the ideal laws in the world of Forms which may then be utilized as models. In the world of opinion, however, as distinguished from that of philosophy, group unity may perhaps be achieved only by means of laws devised in the interest of the governing or stronger group.[48]

Plato's conception of the end of law as the achievement of group unity has not, at the level of his discussion, been improved upon by later analysis. He is asserting no more than that the function of law is to assist in the maintenance of societary order. If we divorce the proposition from its Platonic associations we can view it naturalistically and interpret it to mean that law is a constituent of societary order in the sense that hydrogen is a constituent of water; that it is one of the elements from which societary order is constructed. Every society has its own structure, and the order that prevails in any society is nothing more than a relationship among its members of a kind that demands behavior in accord with that structure.

But society is as inconstant and uncertain as the sea. Its structure is always in a state of modification. Jurisprudence

---

[45] *Laws* 709.
[46] *Rep.* 462 C-D, 423 B; *Laws* 664 A, 739 C-E.
[47] *Rep.* 419 *et seq.*; 466 A.
[48] *Rep.* 343 B *et seq.*

has therefore never rested content with the theory that the end of law is the maintenance of order. It has demanded that the order which is to be achieved shall rest upon some principle in terms of which the order itself can be evaluated. The history of legal thought, we are told by Pound, reveals that four such principles have been proposed: It has been held that law exists to keep the peace in a given society; that its end is the preservation of the social *status quo*; that its purpose is to make possible the maximum of individual free self-assertion; finally, that its function is the adjustment of conflicting interests. All these principles contain some elements of truth. But they also rest upon assumptions which are far from established, and which, from the point of view of a sound jurisprudence, it may be unwise to adopt.

They assume the possibility of a purposive social control in a matter so fundamental as the determination of the nature of the society's structure and function. It may be necessary to believe this in order to sustain the labors of jurists; but that the proposition is not self-evident ought to be clear from the elaborate arguments of Spencer and Sumner to the contrary. The principles assume further that the elements which they isolate are the significant elements in the social structure. The modifications which constantly occur in the social structure are the product of some factor or set of factors; it is assumed that if those factors are properly controlled the modifications which take place can be directed to socially desirable ends. Modern juristic theory, as well as contemporary sociological theory, assumes that the key factor is " interest," defined as the claims, wants, and desires involved in social life in civilized society. At bottom this is an effort to explain social phenomena in terms of psychic impulses to action. That this method of approach has been fruitful no one would deny; we will see its special value when we come to the consideration of Aristotle's theory of teleological explanation in social science. But it is also clear that the principle fails to account for the great changes that have occurred in the structure of Western society and which in turn have modified the legal order itself. The French and Russian Revolutions set in motion forms of energy which will continue to modify the structure of the world's societies for generations to come. Those modifications are beyond the explanatory range of the doctrine of psychic impulses. The psychic impulses which the theory of interests brings to the foreground have their place in the explanation of social change; but they are out of perspective as an effort to account for the important modifications of the social structure.

If jurisprudence insists upon devising a principle in terms of which the order of the society is to be evaluated, that principle must be formulated at the same level of generality as the theory of order itself. In its concrete working out by its Anglo-American adherents the doctrine of interests is a rationalization of Anglo-American law. The application of the same method to other systems of law would yield an Anglo-American jurisprudence, a Russian jurisprudence, a German jurisprudence, and so on. As a matter of fact, it is in that direction we are tending. But a national quality is not characteristic of any of the advanced sciences. Nationalism in jurisprudence is a symptom of immaturity, and a warning of the extensive labors still demanded before it can meet the requirements of scientific method. The ideal of jurisprudence, like that of the other sciences, must be one of complete generality.

THEORY OF LEGISLATION

At the root of Plato's theory of legislation is the idea, developed later by the proponents of natural law, that the legislator through reason alone is able to formulate a set of rules which will be adequate for the needs of the community. That is an aspect of the doctrine of the philosopher-king and takes its origin in Plato's general theory of society. For all societies Plato recognized the necessity of the performance of three functions: supply, administration, and direction. In concrete terms, human needs such as food, shelter, and clothing

have to be satisfied; there must be order and security in some
measure for the individuals making up the group; and the
activities of the society must be intelligently guided. Want is
the general factor which results in the appearance of a society; [49]
its requirements may be met through reason represented by
the class of philosopher-kings; through force in the warrior
class; and through labor in the masses. The first class embodies
the virtue of wisdom, the second that of courage, and the third
temperance; altogether, when fused into a unity, there is justice.

For Plato the legislator is the philosopher in action. He is
the man who has seen the reality of the just, the beautiful,
and the good. Although the better life of reality is within his
power, he must be compelled to live an inferior life and rule
the state; this is so since the law is not concerned with the
special happiness of any class, but with the happiness of the
whole society. Furthermore, he has been engendered as a
king-bee and leader of the hive; he has received a better education than the others and is therefore more capable of sharing
both ways of life. Down from the clouds he therefore must
come. He will obey the command since it is a just one and he
is a just man. He will take office as an unavoidable necessity.[50]
The spectacle of a Henry Adams assuming the role of excluded
aristocrat and remaining aloof from public office is the antithesis of this view. Those who receive the laws from the legislator must have a full grasp of the principles underlying them,
otherwise the laws will not survive the legislator's death,
nor will they be prepared to modify them to meet changed
conditions.[51]

In thinking of legislation, Plato followed the traditional
Greek distinction between written and unwritten law. Antigone's rebuff to Creon was based upon " the immutable unwritten law "; [52] in *Oedipus Tyrannus* the chorus refers to
the " laws ordained from above "; [53] in Xenophon [54] unwritten

---

[49] *Rep.* 369 B *et seq.*
[50] *Rep.* 519 C, 521 B.
[51] *Rep.* 497 C-D; *Laws* 692; *Polit.* 295 D.

[52] *Antigone* 454.
[53] *Oedipus Tyrannus* 865.
[54] *Memor.* IV, iv, 19.

laws are defined as those uniformly observed in every country, and he remarks that they must have been made by the gods inasmuch as men could not all meet together and do not speak the same language. Thucydides [55] regarded the unwritten law as one of the forces which compel obedience to authority. Plato [56] thought the unwritten law was not law strictly so-called but that it was nevertheless important. The Anglo-American conception of the unwritten common law and the Continental doctrine of unwritten law, which attaches to the monarchical tradition and is administered by the executive department as distinguished from the courts, approximate but do not equal Plato's idea. Sometimes the idea of unwritten law has been treated as a natural law doctrine referring to society's basic theory of morality, its conception of right and wrong, which it regards as fundamental and which has authority over positive law and is of universal extent. Plato's theory of justice as an aspect of the doctrine of Forms may also be regarded as an expression of the natural law idea. In the *Republic,* he defined justice as a harmony of the state, in which each individual attended to his own business in the sense that he performed the necessary work which fell to his lot in the state organization. Justice is thus an idea applicable to all societies, and in the Platonic philosophy is an eternal Idea. Unwritten law represents specifically the rules or regulations founded upon immemorial tradition and social usage. Law is like a stubborn and ignorant man who allows no one to do anything contrary to his command, or even to ask a question, not even if something new occurs to someone which is better than the rule he has himself ordained. Human life is not simple, but the law, which is persistently simple, aims, nevertheless, to control that which is never simple. Unwritten law helps to make up this deficiency. Plato indulged in a riot of metaphors to describe it. It is the mortise of legislation, the connecting link between the statute laws already enacted and those yet

[55] II. 37. For Aristotle's discussion see *Politics,* 1287ᵇ; *Rhetoric,* 1373ᵇ.

[56] *Laws* 793 A-C, 841 B, 838 B, 680 A, 890 E; *Politicus* 294 C, 299 A, 300 A, 301 A, 302 A; *Rep.* 563 D.

to come, a true *corpus* of tradition, which, rightly instituted
and duly followed in practice, will serve as a screen for the
statutes already enacted. Unwritten laws are the braces or
clamps of metal which keep building stones in position; they
are also the main supports on which a superstructure rests.

Plato saw an advantage in reducing these basic laws to
writing; for, once put on record in writing, they stay written.
It does not matter if a man misunderstands them at first sight,
he can study them till he does understand them. The new
city which Plato is establishing in the *Laws* will not have an
inheritance of immemorial tradition; therefore its legislation
must go into petty detail so that the enacted laws will not fail
of their purpose.

Thus the legislation of a whole community can be framed by
an effort of reason. In later times this doctrine was to appear
in modified forms in the theories of Hume, Helvétius and
Bentham. Plato had no doubt that reason could arrive at
absolute knowledge and that our errors are the product of
our senses and are not due to any infirmity in our reason.
Reason is the lord of all things and has produced everything,
including law.[57] Plato liked to believe that the word for
" human reason " was etymologically connected with the word
for " law." [58] In the sense of the trained philosophic intellect
reason is the supreme authority in law. In a metaphor he
suggests that men are puppets activated by the strings of desire.
The leading-string is the golden and holy cord of reason entitled
the public law of the state. Man must always cooperate with
the golden cord of reason. By this he meant that a careful
calculation by the state of the end in view through an estimate
of the probable pleasures and pains would result in a law.
That is to say, the legislative process, including debate and
ultimate agreement, concludes in statutory enactment. Law
will thus guide man when he is attracted by the delights of
pleasure or repelled by the fear of pain. Law is therefore in a

---

[57] *Laws* 875 D, 890 D.
[58] *Laws* 957 C 4-7; 714 A. νόμος = νοῦ διανομή. *Cf. Rep.* 532 E.

sense the conscience of the state and possesses a direct educational influence. But behind it, as behind education, is the force of reason. It has been conjectured that Homer's picture of Zeus at one end of the golden rope, successfully resisting the pull of all the other gods and goddesses at the other, was perhaps here present to Plato's mind.[59]

Plato took the traditional moralist's view of legislation: it was to regulate the whole of life. At the same time he recognized that mischief is done by making trifles penal, thus bringing fundamental laws into contempt.[60] Nevertheless, there was little that was not subject to legal regulation in Plato's opinion: marriage, procreation, development of the citizen from infancy to old age, distribution of wealth, price-fixing, all relations between the citizens, shipping, merchandising, peddling, the control of emotions, innkeeping, the regulation of playgrounds, mines, loans and usury, the supervision of farmers, shepherds and beekeepers, including the preservation and supervision of their instruments, the appointment of magistrates, every activity in fact that entered Plato's mind, and concluding with the burial of the citizen and the celebration of the appropriate funeral rites and the assignment of proper marks of respect.[61] Plato found it unnecessary to enumerate all the laws which the legislator must promulgate. The enactments he proposed were in part intended to illustrate a theory of legislation. "I want to show," the Athenian says, "that there is a philosophy of law, a system, in the ordered code, to be discerned by the philosopher, and even by those who have lived under a perfect code: how it enables a man to judge of the relative importance and proper function of various enactments." [62]

At this point in his thinking Plato made a great leap into the future. He clasped hands firmly with Bentham. Under the influence of Newton, Bentham attempted to discover principles which would direct him in the construction of a complete and systematic code. In that field he believed that the equivalent

---

[59] *Laws* 644-645.
[60] *Laws* 788 B; *Rep.* 425 B.

[61] *Laws* 780 A; 631-632; 842 C-D.
[62] *Laws* 632 D.

of the Newtonian physical laws were the principle of utility and the principle of the association of ideas. Plato had precisely the same objective in view and the results of his efforts are an extraordinary anticipation of Bentham. He pointed out that existing codes were arranged by topics and that consequently the legislator, when he wished to provide for a situation which the code did not cover, was compelled to confine himself merely to tacking new provisions on to the appropriate chapter. In the matter of fraud, for example, the legislator in utilizing this method was in very truth trying to cut off a Hydra's head.[63] "Whatever kind of law any lawmaker finds to be needed," the Athenian remarks, "nowadays he devises, and adds it to its class: one adds a section on estates and their heiresses, another on unlawful beatings."[64] Plato thought, as Bentham was to do later, that an orderly and exhaustive code could be framed on the basis of a principle rather than by the hit-and-miss method of existing procedures. As that principle he proposed nothing less than a form of the felicific calculus itself. "Two considerations," he wrote, "go to the foundation of the philosophy of law: (1) What pleasures ought not to be sought? (2) What pains ought not to be avoided?"[65] The measure of the legislator's ability was a direct function of his capacity to answer those two questions. Furthermore, the legislator was to keep his feet on the ground. His legislation must be definite. "He must often ask himself these two questions: first, 'What am I aiming at?' and secondly, 'Am I hitting the mark or missing it?' In this way, and this only, he may possibly so discharge his task as to leave nothing for others to do after him."[66] Pleasure and pain were the stuff with which the legislator had to work; it was to be controlled through habits created by his legislation. It is scarcely necessary to state that the idea of principle in code-making, to the extent envisaged by Plato, still remains in the realm of the philosopher's stone.

---

[63] *Rep.* 427 A.
[64] *Laws* 630 E.
[65] *Laws* 636 D-E.
[66] *Laws* 744 A, 719, 769 D, 885 B, 916 E.

As an end the legislator was to have three objectives in view: freedom, unity of the state, and intelligence or temperance among the citizens.[67] Plato thought that liberty and despotism in the extreme were both bad. As a preliminary to the formulation of his own code, Plato had examined samples of various types of government, among them the Persian and the Athenian, and had found their laws wanting. He wished to know if their laws could be defended in theory; if they could, he then felt entitled to ask: Have they worked well in practice?[68] In the Persian monarchy he found an extreme of despotism and in the Athenian democracy there was an excess of liberty; both were fatal to good government and private happiness. He concluded that a mixed government was the only salvation. He observed that there were two forms in which statutes could be enacted: a peremptory mandate accompanied with provisions for pains and penalties in the event of noncompliance, or a statute prefaced by a preamble, preparing the citizen's mind for the directions contained in the statute and making him understand its reasonableness so that he will be encouraged to obey it. It is the same with physicians. Let us take a lesson from the children who beg the doctor to treat them by the mildest method. Some physicians run around the city, from patient to patient, giving their orders without explanation like autocrats and as if they had exact knowledge; other physicians, who are educated men, explain the whole matter to their patients, make them understand the treatment which is prescribed, and secure their help in the task of restoring them to health.[69] That analogy leads Plato to his doctrine of the preamble and of law as literature. He compares the preamble to the prelude to a musical composition or song.[70] Statutes will thus have two parts: the " despotic prescription," corresponding to the prescription of the autocratic doctor, which is pure law; there is also the prelude, which is not the text of the law, but its preamble. The same idea is given explicit

---

[67] *Laws* 701 B.
[68] *Laws* 683 B.
[69] *Laws* 719 C, 721.
[70] *Laws* 722 E.

application in some of the decree laws of present-day Spain. The legislator should take constant care to see that all laws have their preambles appropriate to the subject. It would be a mistake, however, to insist on a preamble for minor laws, just as one does not treat every song in that fashion. Whether a particular law needs a preamble must be left to the discretion of the legislator.[71]

In the theory of Anglo-American law the desirability of the preamble is far from agreed upon. Coke favored the preamble as an aid to the interpretation of the statute. It is " a good means," he said, " to find out the meaning of the statute, and is a true key to open the understanding thereof." Bentham also thought that the preamble was a help in the process of statutory construction, but that it should be brief. In English law the preamble commences with the word " Whereas," and in French law with the word " *Considérant.*" Bentham observes that the latter term is clearer and more expressive. The draftsman asks his reader *to consider.* " By myself," the draftsman says, " this whole mass of introductory matter was considered, all this whole mass of matter borne in mind at the same time, for the purpose of framing the enacting part; on you I impose the task of taking and bearing in mind all this elucidatory matter, as you would wish or hope to understand the enacting part." Macaulay has perhaps stated more effectively than anyone the case against the preamble. He denied that it is possible to prefix to acts preambles which really set forth the reasons which induce the legislators to pass the acts. Should a marriage between uncle and niece be authorized by law? The legislators might all agree in prohibiting such a marriage, but their reasons for doing so might extend from the belief that such unions were forbidden by nature to the consideration that public feeling ought not to be outraged. It is undoubtedly true that legislators can more often agree on what to do than on their reasons for doing it. But there are clear limitations upon that proposition. Compromise is essential to

[71] *Laws* 723.

the legislative process, and a legislator more frequently than not accepts a bill which does not accomplish all that in his opinion the situation requires. It should be noted also that whatever force Macaulay's argument may have is applicable equally to the committee report, a document which is undeniably an aid to the courts in construing statutes. There are at least two apparently unsurmountable objections to Macaulay's position: (a) No ground suggests itself why legislators may not agree upon the formal reasons for the enactment of a statute, whatever their real reasons may be, and why they may not state in the form of the preamble that they will be bound by those reasons; (b) the preamble may serve a function other than that of setting forth the reasons for the enactment of the statute.

The most striking preamble in American law is the preamble to the Federal Constitution. It purports to set forth the reasons for the establishment of the Constitution. Undoubtedly the reasons thus expressed were the ones which moved many who voted for its adoption; undoubtedly also, many who so voted were moved by other and different reasons. But the framers of the Constitution agreed upon the formal reasons, and agreed also that they would be bound by them. The fact that some of them may have thought that the reasons for adopting the Constitution were of a different nature seems irrelevant to the desirability of the preamble as formulated and its salutary effect in the long process of American constitutional interpretation. Further, the preamble may not only state the reasons for the adoption of the statute, it may also, as Plato suggested, act as a persuasive device to incite approval of the legislation; it may be an interpretative device to direct administrative and judicial application of the statute; and it may be a device to express legislative policy. As a device of legislative policy the preamble has plainly been of help to the courts, and has won the approbation of such a skilled constructionist as Holmes.[72]

---

[72] Co. Litt. 79a; Plowd. 369. 3 Bentham, *Works* (1843) 249. Dharker, *Lord*

Plato's theory was confusing to fourth century B. C. Austinians and realists who regarded law as a command and who wanted to know what the law was in fact. The Athenian makes their point fairly. He suggests that if one of the autocratic physicians should overhear the educated physician explaining the method of his treatment to a patient his merriment would be instantaneous and loud. " How silly of you! You are *teaching* your patient instead of curing him; he doesn't want to be made into a doctor, he wants to be made whole." Plato recognizes that there is merit in that view; but he is not merely legislating; as a matter of fact, he is also teaching. Law for Plato is a form of literature, and the legislator's responsibility is greater than the poet's.[73] The legislator is himself the author of the finest and best tragedy he knows how to make. In fact, all his polity has been constructed as a dramatization of the fairest and best life, which is in truth the most real of tragedies.[74] Plato apparently intended his code to be studied as a text-book.[75] Bentham also suggested that the father of a family might teach Bentham's code to his children and give to the precepts of private morality the force and dignity of public morals.

Plato based the duty of obedience to law on the idea of good faith and, to some extent, on the notion of honor, i. e., the moral worth a man possesses in his own eyes and in the opinion of society. He valued obedience to legislation highly for he

---

Macaulay's Legislative Minutes (1946) 146 *et seq.* For the various devices for which the preamble is employed, see Horack, *Cases and Materials on Legislation* (1940) 552, 647. *Block* v. *Hirsh*, 256 U. S. 135 (1921) (Opinion by Holmes). For a modern example of a legislative preamble, see the Preamble to the Employment Act of 1946, 15 U. S. C. § 1021.

[73] *Laws* 857 D, 858-859; in *Phaedr.* 257-258, he observes that our statesmen, who are sometimes contemptuous of authors, are most fond of writing. When a statesman produces a composition he insists upon signing it at the beginning, thus: " Be it enacted by the senate, the people, or both, on the motion of a certain person " who is the statesman. *Cf. Ibid.* 278 D. *Cf. Epist.* VII 344 C: " If anyone sees a written composition of anyone, whether by a legislator on laws, or anything else on any other subject, he must know that these are not that man's most serious interests, if he is a serious man."

[74] *Laws* 817 B.

[75] *Laws* 810 B, 811 B.

held that the man whose victory over his fellow-citizens took that form had the best claim to rule.[76] This view differs radically from a modern one, which, however, is still a paper expression in the attitude of governments generally, that legislation must secure allegiance through its inherent qualities. For Plato the issue was raised in a concrete case by the trial and condemnation of Socrates.[77] Crito suggests to his friend Socrates, who is in prison awaiting execution, that his escape can be arranged. Socrates refuses to disobey the law and thus wrong his country, even though the law has wronged him. He states simply that a man ought to do what he has agreed to do, provided it is right; he ought not to violate his agreements. The state cannot exist if its laws are flouted and the decisions of its courts made invalid and annulled by private persons. That is true even if the state has wronged the citizen and has not judged the case rightly. By his life-long residence in Athens, Socrates has impliedly promised obedience to the laws. There is no equality of right between legislation and the citizen, any more than between the father and child, the master and servant. The child if he is punished does not hit the father in return; nor does the good citizen undertake to destroy the laws if his country undertakes to destroy him. Socrates has always had the opportunity to move to another country if the Athenian laws displeased him; failing to do that he has confirmed his promise to obey. If he disobeyed the laws of his country and escaped to Thebes or Megara, he would properly be regarded as the enemy of law everywhere. This argument, it has been observed, leaves open the question whether it is wrong to disregard the sentence of an incompetent court. In Socrates' case the court was without jurisdiction; but the court thought itself competent, and Athenian law had no provision for the quashing

[76] *Laws* 715 C, 762 E. Whether or not a law was obeyed was partly determinative of its moral worth. Diog. Laert. III. 103.

[77] *Crito* 49 E, *et seq.* On the question whether orders made by a court having no jurisdiction to make them may be disregarded without liability, see *U. S.* v. *Shipp,* 203 U. S. 563, 573 (1906), *U. S.* v. *United Mine Workers,* 330 U. S. 258, 307 (1947) (Concurring opinion by Frankfurter, J.)

of findings as *ultra vires*; apparently Socrates thought that private judgment should not pass on the question of jurisdiction. It has also been suggested that Plato is not laying down a categorical imperative for the wrongfully condemned generally, but is merely exhibiting the actions of an individually great man. What Plato himself would have done in similar circumstances in his seventieth year is not clear.

Elsewhere [78] Plato gives full expression to the idea that law is a convention devised by the weak to suppress the strong and regulate their conduct. Law in that view is nothing but arbitrary power, and whether it should be obeyed is dependent solely upon one's capacity to flout it. Again,[79] Plato suggests that when the citizens consent to the authority of a code of laws as a substitute for the personal rule of the minority, there is apt to be greater unity in the state. That unity implies that the majority realize that it is in their own interest to obey the laws. Society does not act against its own will when it obeys its laws; when it does obey unwillingly they will be soon abolished.[80] He believed that once general respect was secured for a particular law, it would be implicitly obeyed. The difficulty was that public opinion is apt to stop half way, when the progress of the law in question is thwarted by some passionate feeling on the part of large numbers of the population. For instance, the difficulties attending the establishment of common meals were overcome in Sparta for men; but the obstinate hostility of the women made its extension to them seem an impossibility.[81]

The character and extent of a state's legislation was for Plato a yardstick to measure its worth. Altogether, he distinguished seven forms which he grades by the standard of respect for law. There is first the perfect and non-existent state of the philosopher-king which is above and beyond the rule of law. In the sphere of the practical, however, there are six possible

[78] *Gorg.* 483 D, 488 E; *Rep.* 359 A; *Laws* 714, 890 A.
[79] *Laws* 627 D-E.
[80] *Cf. Rep.* 359 *et seq.*
[81] *Laws* 839 C-D.

states: the rule of one, or monarchy under law, and its counter-part tyranny, where law is disregarded; the rule of the few, or aristocracy under law, and its counterpart oligarchy, which has no respect for law; the rule of the many, or a constitutional democracy, and its counterpart unrestrained democracy, which is characterized by contempt for law.[82] Thus, monarchy becomes the best of all governments and tyranny the worst, the government of the few intermediate, and democracy the worst of all lawful governments and the best of all lawless ones. At the core of this scheme, however, is a belief in the necessity of an ideal. In the state of the tyrant there are laws; and Plato recognizes in the great Wellsian romance on the origin of law in Book III of the *Laws* that law may be the product of what Maine termed "quasi-legislation," social and economic conditions, accretions of administrative customs, and other chance influences.

In the myth of the ring of Gyges, which made its wearer invisible, Plato attempted to answer the current argument that everyone would break the law if he dared, that law observance rests entirely upon force. If two men were each given such a ring the honorable man could readily be distinguished from the dishonorable one.[83] It is the ideal which makes all the difference for Plato. Without it law becomes merely a matter of force; with it the noblest and best life is possible for all members of the community and law itself becomes, in the Platonic scheme, in itself a good. As a practical philosopher, however, he knew how much depended upon the cooperation of the citizen. "Unless private affairs in a state are rightly managed," he wrote, "it is vain to suppose that any stable code of laws can exist for public affairs."

THE JUDICIAL AND ADMINISTRATIVE SYSTEM

Athenian justice was held in great contempt by Plato, and there are many indications throughout his writings that he gave

---

[82] *Politicus.*   [83] *Rep.* 359 D *et seq. Laws* 790 B.

much thought to its reform. He had grown to manhood in the atmosphere produced by the disastrous Sicilian expedition, when the Athenian Empire was falling apart. The large jury courts of Athens were judges of both law and fact, were unrestrained by precedent, and were swayed by the gusts of sentiment which moved the populace; in the end they became instruments of political blackmail and judicial murder, evidence of the disintegration of the state. Plato was present at the condemnation of Socrates, and the failure of the court to observe even the ordinary decencies of a fair trial, such as patience and the preservation of order in the courtroom, did not pass unnoticed in his description of the proceedings. When the multitude, that great beast, as Plato calls it, are seated together in the courtroom, and with loud uproar censure some of the things that are said and done and approve others, both in excess, with full-throated clamor and clapping of hands, in such a case, asks Plato, what is the plight of the young man? What private teaching will hold out and not rather be swept away by the torrent of censure and applause, and borne off on its current, so that he will affirm the same things that they do to be honorable and base, and will do as they do, and be even such as they? A chief count against courts was that they were exclusively places of punishment and not of instruction.[84] Plato, after long experience with the Athenian courts, became convinced that only drastic remedies could eliminate the evils which he observed.

As a matter of general principle, Plato held that judges must be men of superior intellect, and that the judicial system must be so constructed that there will be a clear presentation of issues and time for due deliberation.[85] A true judge, in deciding a matter, ought not to content himself with a safe legal yes or no, but ought to state the principles of his decision. He had no use for courts which were mean-spirited and inarticulate, where the judges never told each other what they thought, and hid their opinions from the public.[86] He observed that it

[84] *Apol.* 26 A; *Rep.* 492 B-D.   [85] *Laws* 766 D-E.   [86] *Laws* 876 B.

was sometimes difficult to distinguish between administrative and judicial functions. Every administrator was bound to exercise judicial functions in some matters, and every judge was an administrator of no little importance on the day when he concluded a suit by pronouncing judgment.[87] He followed the distinction of Attic law and divided causes into private suits, where the dispute was between individuals, and public suits, where the wrong was to the state.[88]

For private disputes [89] he proposed a system of three courts: a court of first instance, an intermediate appellate court, and a court of final appeal. The court of first instance was to be arranged by the parties themselves. They selected the judges from among their neighbors and common friends, the people who know most about the matter in dispute. This proposal was no doubt suggested to Plato by the excellent system of public arbitration which prevailed in Athens. The bulk of private suits were assigned to public arbitrators who were selected by lot. They were men in their sixtieth year, experienced and impartial, and their first duty was to effect a compromise. If they failed in this task, they heard the arguments and received the evidence. An appeal lay from their decisions, but was confined to the record made before the arbitrators, which was placed in a sealed casket until the day of the appellate hearing. Altogether it was an easy and inexpensive method of settling disputes, and the only innovation which Plato introduced was to permit the plaintiff and defendant to select their own arbitrator rather than to depend upon choice by lot. Undoubtedly the capacities of the Athenian public arbitrators varied, and Plato's modification of the system perhaps represented an effort to equalize the inequalities of chance. Plato remarked that if litigants were compelled first to resort to arbitration the issue between them would be sharpened, thus facilitating the work of the courts. He thought

[87] *Laws* 767 A.
[88] *Laws* 767 B. For the full distinction in Attic law, see Hermann, *A Manual of the Political Antiquities of Greece* (1836) 268 and notes.
[89] *Laws* 767 C *et seq.* 956.

that litigants ought to be debarred from taking oaths. If an action were instituted, the declaration ought to be in writing and the charges specified, but it ought not to be under oath. Similarly, the defendant's answer should be in writing and not under oath. It is a horrible thing to know, he writes, that well-nigh half the citizens are perjurers, inasmuch as lawsuits are frequent in a state.[90] Furthermore, the judiciary should put a stop to litigants in their speeches " calling gods to witness " or making whining appeals to pity. Let them behave like gentlemen, stating their case fairly and sticking closely to the subject.

From the arbitrators an appeal, as in Athenian practice, could be taken to an intermediate court composed of villagers and tribesmen. Apparently in these tribal courts Plato had in mind, as a model, the Athenian Dikastery. He insists that all citizens have a share in the settlement of even private disputes; for the man who has no share in helping to judge imagines that he has no part or lot in the state at all. The courts will, therefore, be popular ones, but at the same time they should be neither too large nor too small; " it is not easy for a large body of men to judge well, nor yet for a small one, if of poor ability."

No appeal could be had from the Athenian Dikastery. Plato, however, provided for an appeal from his popular court to a tribunal which was " to be organized in the most incorruptible way that is humanly possible, specially for the benefit of those who have failed to obtain a settlement of their case either before the neighbors or in the tribal courts." The judges were to be selected by the public officials, who were to assemble in a temple and choose from among their own ranks those who had most competently discharged their duties and who appeared the most likely to decide the suits for their fellow citizens during the ensuing year in the best way. When the selection had been made, there should be a reexamination by the electing body itself, and if any name be rejected, another

[90] *Laws* 948 D-E.

should be chosen in like manner. The hearings of the court should be held publicly, in the presence of the officials who elected it, and any others who wished to attend, and the judge's vote should be a matter of record. This latter provision was a departure from Attic practice, the vote of each dicast being secret. Elsewhere [91] Plato names thirty-five as the number of judges which should constitute the court, but the scheme of the *Laws* apparently contemplated a much smaller court.

Plato's proposals are, with the principal exception of the appellate procedure, an adaptation of Athenian theory and practice. He was convinced of the soundness of the conception that the law could be stated simply enough to be understood by the average man; he believed also that a popular court, one composed, that is, of a fairly large number of citizens, was perhaps the best insurance of justice and, as Machiavelli was to remark later, a court consisting of numerous judges was a guaranty against bribery. A court as large as the one which tried Socrates, possessing a membership of probably 501, was perhaps too unwieldy for Plato. He compromised by reducing the membership and by adding the element of publicity. To permit an appeal to a court of select judges from the large popular courts, which in Athenian democratic theory were supreme, since they were a committee of the sovereign people, was a decided innovation and Plato endeavored to provide what he thought were necessary safeguards. The judges were subject to fines or impeachment for improper decisions and could be compelled to correct their wrongs. Their one-year tenure of office, while inapplicable to our own professionalized system of law which demands an expertness acquired only after a long period of application, was no detriment to the non-professionalized system envisaged by Plato, and which obtained in the Attic world, inasmuch as the emphasis there was on the ascertainment of fact and upon decision according to common-sense ideas of justice.

[91] *Epist.* VIII 356 D-E; *cf. Epist.* VII, 337 B.

In matters involving wrongs against the state,[92] Plato thought it was necessary, first of all to admit the public to a share in the trial; for when a wrong was done the state, it was the whole of the people who were wronged. But before the case came before the popular court for decision, Plato desired to make certain that it was properly presented and prepared, a situation which did not always exist in the Attic legal system. So, while it was right that both the beginning and the ending of such a suit should be assigned to the people, the examination should take place before three of the highest officials, mutually agreed upon by both defendant and plaintiff, or by the Public Council if they were unable to agree. The three commissioners would conduct the inquiry and develop the issues by searching questions.[93]

Plato did not overlook procedure.[94] The judges should be seated, facing the plaintiff and defendant, in a closely-packed row in order of seniority, and all the citizens who had leisure to do so should attend and listen attentively to the trials. The prosecutor should state his case and the defendant reply to it, each in a single speech. When the speeches had been delivered the senior judge should first state his view of the case, in which he should review in detail the statements made. When he had finished, the rest of the judges, each in his order, should review any omissions or errors they found to complain of in the pleadings of either party, a judge who had no complaint to make leaving the right of speech to his neighbor; the written record of all statements pronounced to be relevant should be confirmed by the seals of all the judges and deposited on the sacred hearth of the courtroom. They should meet again the next day at the same place to continue the review of the case, and once more affix their seals to the documents. When this had been done for a third time, due weight being allowed to the evidence and witnesses, each judge should give a solemn vote, swearing by the altar to pronounce just and true judgment to the best of his power, and that should be the end of

---

[92] *Laws* 768 A. [93] *Laws* 766 D. [94] *Laws* 855 D-866 A.

the trial. Plato evolved a rule of thumb for testing the veracity of witnesses.[95] A single lapse from truth might be due to an unavoidable mistake; two such lapses indicated carelessness— such a man was no good as a witness; three lapses made him a knave. If anyone were unwilling to act as witness, he might be summoned and had to obey under penalty of damages. If he knew the facts and were willing to give evidence, he should give it; if he lacked knowledge, he should take an oath that he had no knowledge and he might then be dismissed. A judge summoned as a witness should not vote at the trial. A woman might act as a witness if over forty; and if unmarried might bring an action. If she had a husband alive she should only be allowed to give evidence. In murder trials, slaves and children might be witnesses provided they furnished bond that they would stand trial for perjury. Evidence might be denounced as perjured provided it was done before the trial was concluded. A new trial should be awarded if false evidence was found to have influenced the verdict.

Plato thought that life abounded in good things and that a fair judicial proceeding was one of mankind's boons. It was cursed, however, by the art of professional advocacy, which begins by asserting that there is a device for managing one's legal business and that this device would ensure victory equally whether the conduct at issue in the case had been rightful or not. The advocate who defended anyone for pay must be silenced and banished. If any attempted to pervert the influence of justice upon the mind of a judge, or wrongfully multiplied suits at law, or wrongfully aided others to such suits, they should be duly tried and punished. If the culprit acted for the sake of fame, he should be excluded from taking part in any trial, or maintaining a suit of his own, unless twice convicted, in which case he should be put to death; if he acted for money, he should be put to death if a citizen, or banished if a foreigner.

From Attic practice Plato borrowed the idea of a Board of

[95] *Laws* 937 C.

Examiners to watch over the conduct and audit the proceedings of administrative officials and judges.[96] Modern parallels to some extent are the American practice of the office of the Comptroller General and the theory behind some Congressional investigating committees, but the Platonic suggestion was on a much more elaborate scale. Some officials in Plato's state were chosen by lot, some by election, some for a year, some for a longer period. There were hazards in that method of selection and the state must have competent examiners in the event any of them acts at all crookedly through being burdened by the weight of his office and his own inability to support it worthily. Plato provides for the election of examiners by a carefully circumscribed method. The examiners, by means of honorable tests, were to judge the official acts and life of public servants. An appeal from their rulings might be taken to the court of select judges which heard final appeals, but if the appeal failed the penalty, if short of death, was doubled. The examiners themselves were not, however, above suspicion and Plato provides for an examiner of examiners. That was a special tribunal before which any citizen could bring impeachment proceedings. Conviction involved loss of all rank while alive and of the state funeral when dead. If the impeachment proceedings failed to gain one-fifth of the tribunal's votes, the prosecutor was subject to fine. It may be well to emphasize that the judiciary were subject to scrutiny by the examiners and were liable also to actions for damages by suitors for abuse of judicial power, an idea which was to appear later in Roman law and other systems.

Justice is the word that will be associated with Plato's name as long as he is read. But his theory of justice was a formulation of a general principle of human conduct and was not a rule for the law courts. He was familiar with the legal idea of justice—the rendering to each man his due. But he was able to show that as a guide for human behavior generally it was inadequate. His arguments against the rule do not meet the

[96] *Laws* 945 B-948.

real issue, as he was no doubt aware; but they were sufficient to eliminate it for the purposes of his dialogue and to permit his own argument to proceed. When he arrived at his ultimate conclusion, that justice was doing one's own proper business or one's duty, he admitted the legitimacy of the legal rule as a special case of his general rule.[97]

CONTRACT AND PROPERTY

Plato allowed recovery for failure to carry out the terms of an agreement unless the agreement were contrary to law, or made under duress, or frustrated by unforeseen circumstances beyond the control of the parties, the latter ground being perhaps an anticipation of the modern doctrine of " frustration of adventure " which came into being as a result of the circumstances created by World War I. He subscribed to the intuitionalist theory that promises should be enforced because good faith was the first of all the virtues. The man who failed to keep his promises would develop an ugly soul and come to a miserable end.[98] An action for nonfulfilment of agreement would lie in the tribal courts unless previously settled by the arbitrators. Agreements made with aliens were to be regarded as specially sacred.[99] If a craftsman culpably failed to complete work he had undertaken, he had to produce double value. If work was received which had been contracted for, and the price was not paid within the stipulated time, the price was recoverable twofold with interest for each month that payment was deferred.[100]

Plato was never able to develop a law of property adapted to a going society. He knew that the proper distribution of property was vital to the welfare of the state,[101] but his solutions of the problem were limited to the artificial conditions of ideal communities. In the strength of middle age he pro-

[97] *Rep.* 331 E *et seq.*, 433 E. *Cf.* I. 1. 1. pr. " Iustitia est constans et perpetua voluntas suum cuique tribuens."
[98] *Laws* 920 D, 730 C, *Gorg.* 525 A.   [100] *Laws* 921. *Cf. Laws* 847 B.
[99] *Laws* 729 E.   [101] *Laws* 736 E.

posed to abolish private property altogether,[102] which has been interpreted as a device to insure disinterestedness on the part of the ruling class. For the second best state of his old age, he felt that the rule of community property was beyond the capacity of the people who inhabit it and he therefore arranged for the portioning out of the land and houses.[103] He was well aware of the passions which would be aroused in any attempt at redistribution of property; if the legislator endeavored to disturb such things, everyone would confront him with the cry " Hands off " and with curses, with the result that he would be rendered powerless.[104] To regard other people's property as sacred was, he believed, the basis of mutual trust, and he therefore proposed the following as a comprehensive rule: So far as possible no one shall touch my goods nor move them in the slightest degree, if he has not my consent; and I must act in like manner regarding the goods of all other men, keeping a prudent mind. He laid down the doctrine that the citizen held his land of the state,[105] a rule which though latent still obtains in American law; he recognized that the state could impose restrictions on the transfer of property,[106] and he provided for a record office and the registration of title so that legal rights pertaining to all matters of property might be easy to decide and perfectly clear; [107] his system included also the valuation of the property.[108] Plato's fumbling effort at a classification of property was probably caused by the absence of a tradition of theoretical analysis, one of the rewards of professionalization. He was unable to perceive any place for the application of his favorite principle of bifurcation, something which was readily apparent to the Roman and common law lawyer though that perception was not grounded on a necessary scientific basis. Since he could not bisect, he divided property " like an animal that is sacrificed, by joints." [109] By this method

[102] *Rep.* 416 D, 420 A, 422 D, 464 C, 543 B-C.
[103] *Laws* 740 A.
[104] *Laws* 684 E, 736 D.
[105] *Laws* 740 A, 923 A.
[106] *Laws* 923 A.
[107] *Laws* 745 A, 754 E, 850 A, 855 B, 914 C.
[108] *Laws* 955 D.
[109] *Politicus* 287-289.

he obtained a sevenfold classification: implements, materials from which things are manufactured, receptacles, vehicles, articles for defense, playthings, and articles which provide nourishment. Plato observes that " the classification is somewhat forced " but that it took care of all property except tame animals including slaves.[110] He objected to the oligarchic system because it inevitably tended to make property a test of office.[111]

He attempted no systematic survey of the law of property, but he had made a thorough study of the traditional rules and practices, particularly in the Athenian state. He ventures numerous suggestions. On the troublesome question of boundaries,[112] he provides simply that no man shall move boundary marks of land; if he does so, anyone may report him, and if convicted, the court shall estimate the damages. Petty acts of annoyance on the part of a neighbor, Plato thought, particularly when they are frequently repeated, engender an immense amount of enmity. Invasions of real property, in Plato's view, were such a source of irritation that he provided that a man must, above all things, take special care not to encroach in the least degree on his neighbor's land. Whoever encroached on his neighbor's ground, overstepping the boundaries, should pay for the damage and, by way of penalty, should also pay twice the cost of the damage. Similarly, a man should be fined for the theft of bee swarms by the rattling of pans, and for injuries caused by fire or by the planting of trees too close to a neighbor's boundary. He also laid down elaborate rules, borrowed from the old laws, on irrigation, well-digging, and damage by flood. If the ownership of lost property was in controversy, it should be produced in court, and the magistrates should try the dispute with the help of the state register of property in case of registry; if it was not registered, the magis-

---

[110] As to property in slaves, see *Laws* 776 C.

[111] *Rep.* 551 B, *Laws* 698 B, 774 A.

[112] *Laws* 842 E-844 D. Cujas refers to Plato's proposed law on injury to a neighbor's land by the obstruction of the outflow of floodwaters or by permitting it to flow out too violently as the source of the rule in D. 1. 13. 1. See *supra* note 1.

trate had to decide the case within three days.[113] Plato proposed to abolish the power of testation on the ground that too much indulgence had been paid the dying man's desire to keep his possessions.[114] Let the preamble of the law state: "Poor creature of a day, in your present state you do not know what you have or what you are: you and yours belong not to yourself so much as to your family past and present, and both you and they belong to the state. So I will not suffer you to be cajoled by flattery, or reduced by sickness, into making a bad will: the state's interest must count before that of any individual. Depart from life in peace and charity: leave the rest to us lawgivers." He thereafter makes elaborate provision for the distribution of the deceased's property.

SALE OF GOODS

Plato's proposals for regulating sales of goods lack the concrete richness of the case law of sales. Human conduct, when confronted with the complex situation known as the transfer of property in goods, is so charged with the unexpected and the necessary that legislative devices to control it, unless grounded upon an intimate familiarity with actual practice, are apt to miss the mark. Plato again saved himself by legislating for a small city state of quasi-utopian construction, and by confining all transactions to an area of narrow dimensions.

He prohibits altogether certain transactions and methods of acquiring property. No finder of treasure trove shall disturb it, and penalties are laid down for the violation of the rule.[115] Similarly, anyone who finds property which has been left behind by another, whether voluntarily or not, shall leave it undisturbed, under penalty; such goods are under the protection of the Goddess of the Wayside.[116] Plato's [117] rule of treasure trove and lost property is regarded by him as an application of the purportedly Solonic maxim: "What thou hast not laid

---

[113] *Laws* 914 C-D.
[114] *Laws* 923 A *et seq.*
[115] *Laws* 913-914 B.
[116] *Laws* 914 B-D.
[117] *Laws* 914 E, 916 A-C.

down, take not up." A contributor to a mutual benefit association may not maintain an action with respect to any dispute arising out of his contribution.[118] Credit sales are frowned upon, and a man must not hand over to the other party his part of the transaction (whether it be goods or money) without getting the equivalent. Thus a vendor making a sale on credit had to rely upon the good faith of the purchaser for payment. It has been suggested that that is the best way to prevent the creation of debt in a state.[119] Runaway slaves may be seized by the owner or by friends or kinsmen of the owner. If a slave is sold and is found within six months to be diseased, or within twelve months to be epileptic, he may be returned unless the purchaser is a physician, a trainer, or was informed of the disease at the time of the sale. The purchaser of a murderer had the right to return the slave upon discovery of the fact. If the vendor of a diseased slave was an expert, who could be presumed to have knowledge, he must pay as damages twice the purchase price; if a layman, only the actual price received. His desire to treat contributions to benefit associations as an imperfect obligation is perhaps influenced by Attic law, which allowed recovery against citizens in good circumstance, but not otherwise.

Although Plato believes that the practice of selling goods gives rise to lying and cheating, and that retailers, businessmen, and innkeepers are never content with a reasonable profit, but always prefer to make an exorbitant one, he nevertheless recognized the necessity of such business, but limited the practice to non-citizens.[120] Market stewards are to have full charge of all matters concerning the markets, including keeping an eye on outrageous behavior.[121] There must be one fixed price for

---

[118] *Laws* 915 E.

[119] *Laws* 742 C, 849 E, 915 E; *Rep.* 556 A. This rule appears to be an adaptation to the special life of the Platonic state of the principle that promises will not be enforced if they are economically undesirable from the point of view of the community, a principle exemplified today in the refusal to enforce wagering contracts. See *Amory* v. *Gilman*, 2 Mass. 1, 11 (1806).

[120] *Rep.* 371 B-C; *Laws* 917 B, 918 D.

[121] *Laws* 849 A.

every article, and that price must be neither increased nor decreased during the day on which it is announced.[122] The law-wardens are instructed to meet in consultation with experts in every branch of retail trade and fix a standard of profits and expenses which is to be prescribed in writing.[123] Retailers must not engage in puffing or taking of oaths about anything offered for sale, under severe penalty.[124] Anyone who exchanges for money either money or anything else, living or not living, shall give every such article unadulterated. If anyone gives a security, it must be given in express terms, setting forth the whole transaction in a written record before at least three witnesses, if the amount be under 1,000 drachmae, and before not less than five, if over 1,000. The broker in a sale may be held as surety for a seller who does not have good title to the goods sold, or who cannot guarantee delivery, and an action may lie against the broker equally with the seller.[125] Plato's views on those matters represent an attempt to find a compromise between what he felt were the evils of Athenian trade and the necessity, in any state, of permitting the sale of goods. His solution was rigorous supervision, careful limitations, and increased penalties.

Notes on a Penal Code

By the time Plato had come to formulate the penal principles of the *Laws,* he had given much thought to the circumstances under which punishment was justified. His general view was that punishment was warranted only on the assumption that virtue can and must be taught. No one reproves another for an affliction which has come to him by nature or by accident; we have only pity for the ugly, the small, or the weak. But we are wrathful and reproving in the case of those who do not possess the qualities that people are supposed to acquire by application, practice, and teaching. That is the idea of punishment. No rational man, he maintained, undertakes to punish

[122] *Laws* 916-917.
[123] *Laws* 920 C.
[124] *Laws* 917 C.
[125] *Laws* 954 A.

in order to avenge himself for a past offense, since he cannot make what was done as though it had not come to pass. He looks rather to the future, and aims at preventing that particular person and others who see him punished from doing wrong again. His object in punishing must therefore be both reformation and deterrence; and by necessary implication we must draw the conclusion that virtue can be produced by training.[126] At this point Plato did not attempt to meet the argument on which the reformation and deterrent theories break down; both theories justify the punishment of innocent men; the deterrent theory if he is believed to be guilty by those likely to commit the crime in the future; and the reformation theory if he is a bad man, but not guilty of the offense charged. Plato also insists, from the sociological standpoint, that the wrongdoer is not alone in his guilt; that the entire community, because of its tolerance of bad government and faulty educational practices, is also guilty, a notion which sometimes is put into practice in the execution of Chinese criminal justice.[127]   In

---

[126] *Protag.* 323-324 C. *Cf. Gorg.* 480 B; *Laws* 934 A-B; *Rep.* 380 B.

[127] *Timaeus* 87 B. "A man named Chaong An-ching, aided by his wife Chaong Wongshee, flogged his mother. Upon the circumstances being made known to Tung-chee, in whose reign the crime was perpetrated, an imperial order was issued, to the effect that the offenders should be flayed alive, that their bodies should then be cast into a furnace, and their bones, gathered from the ashes and reduced to a powder, should be scattered to the winds. The order further directed that the head of the clan to which the two offenders belonged, should be put to death by strangulation; that the neighbours living on the right and left of the offenders should, for their silence and non-interference, each receive a flogging of eighty blows, and be sent into exile; that the head or representative of the graduates of the first degree (or B. A.), among whom the male offender ranked, should receive a flogging of eighty blows and be exiled to a place one thousand li distant from his home; that the granduncle of the male offender should be beheaded; that his uncle and his two elder brothers should be put to death by strangulation; that the prefect and the ruler of the district in which the offenders resided, should for a time be deprived of their rank; that on the face of the mother of the female offender four Chinese characters expressive of neglect of duty towards her daughter should be tattooed, and that she should be exiled to a province, the seventh in point of distance from that in which she was born; that the father of the female offender, a bachelor of arts, should not be allowed to take any higher literary degrees, that he should receive a flogging of eighty blows, and be exiled to a place three thousand li from that in which he was born; that the mother of the male offender should be made to witness the flaying of her son, but be allowed to receive daily for her sustenance a measure of rice from the provincial treasurer; that the son of the offenders (a child) should be placed

devising his penal principles, Plato had also to face the difficulty of the proposition which he had maintained a score or
more times: that all wrongdoing is involuntary and arises from
ignorance since right conduct is happiness, and wrong conduct
is unhappiness, and no one therefore would willingly choose
wrong conduct which would lead to unhappiness.[128]

Plato felt that it was a shameful thing to have to make
criminal laws since it assumed that the citizens of his state
would grow up to share in the worst forms of depravity practiced in other states.[129] The Golden Age was past, however,
and he was legislating for mortal men; besides there would be
foreigners and slaves in his state who would not have the
benefit of a sound education.

Plato's main argument appears to turn on what a present-day
lawyer would regard as a distinction between tort and crime;
but it is complicated because the idea was a new one.[130] He
was driven to make the distinction because of his assertion
that all bad men were unwillingly bad. He found himself
differing from popular opinion on that point and on another:
it is just and therefore beautiful to punish the temple-robber
by putting him to death; but punishment is shameful. Plato
asserts, however, that, if it is proper that the punishment should
be imposed, it cannot be improper for it to be suffered. At all
times and everywhere legal systems have made the necessary
distinction between voluntary and involuntary wrongdoing.
Plato could not accept this distinction because it ran counter
to his philosophical position that wrongdoing could not be
voluntary. What he must do, therefore, is to make clear what
jurists really have in mind when they distinguish between

---

under the care of the district ruler, and receive another name; and, lastly, that the
lands of the offender should for a time remain fallow." 1 Gray, *China* (1878) 237-8.

[128] *Protag.* 345 D; *Timaeus* 86 E; *Rep.* 589 C; *Laws* 731 C; *Apol.* 26 A; *Meno* 77-8;
Gorg. 466 E; *Hipp. Min.* 376 B.

[129] Plato's penal principles are most fully set out in *Laws* Bk. IX.

[130] Similarly, in the *Euthyphro*, before the invention of a grammatical vocabulary,
Plato seems to be attempting a philosophical distinction between the active and the
passive voice of a verb. From that point of view to us today the argument appears
unnecessarily complex.

voluntary and involuntary acts. His views and those of the jurists would then be reconciled. Plato's resolution of the difficulty was to make a distinction between acts which were remediable in damages and acts which require punishment, between injury and wrongdoing. If an injury had been inflicted, the court must make it good so far as possible; it must conserve what was lost, restore what was broken down, make whole what was wounded or dead; and when the injury had been atoned for by compensation the court must endeavor always, by means of the laws, to convert the parties who had inflicted it and those who had suffered it from a state of discord to a state of unity. If there had been wrongdoing, the guilty person must not only pay for the injury, but must also be punished so that he would not repeat the deed in the future; in other words, the court must teach him virtue, which for Plato is the basis of punishment.

In using the terms " voluntary " and " involuntary," Plato said that he meant something different from their popular usage. He would never call an unintended injury wrongdoing, as the public did. A man may even be committing a wrong when he confers a benefit on another. Thus, the so-called Socratic fallacy, that no man commits injustice voluntarily, was one with which the legislator need not concern himself. When someone had involuntarily caused a loss to another, it was a misnomer to describe his action as an " involuntary wrong "; he had merely damaged another. Once this distinction was grasped, it was, of course, important to consider the state of mind of the actor. The degree of his culpable intention must be taken into account. To make the matter clearer, Plato turned to psychology and classified offenses as follows: (1) those due to passion and fear; (2) those produced by pleasure and desire; (3) those prompted by a mistaken belief in what was for the best—which may come from simple ignorance, or from the false knowledge of the powerful or the insignificant. It is plain to perceive in all this, in spite of the obscurities, that Plato was endeavoring to extend his ideas of code-making from the civil to the criminal field, and to devise a penal code based upon rational principles.

He met the weakness of the reformation and deterrent theories—that they justify the punishment of innocent men— by maintaining that before a man can be punished he must by his conduct have done or failed to do some act which in itself called for the application of penal measures.[131] A man should not be punished merely because it might deter those who are likely to be criminals in the future, or merely because it might transform a bad man into a good man. Before a punishment could be imposed there must have been an offense. This view itself ends in difficulties which are still unresolved in penology. The measure of punishment is basically the offense and not the personality of the criminal. If the measurement of punishment is shifted to the criminal's personality, then there is a return to the position that the bad, though innocent, man ought to be punished for his own good; but that is a proposal which few have had the temerity to advocate.

At the head of his list of crimes came sacrilege and treason. The punishment was to be death or a lesser penalty in the discretion of the court, but the punishment should not descend upon the children, unless the father, grandfather and great-grandfather had been condemned on a capital charge, in which case the children should be deported. For theft, the culprit should pay twice the value of the stolen article; if he was unable to comply with this rule, he must stay in prison until he did so or was released by the prosecutor. In dealing with homicide, he distinguished between voluntary, involuntary, and justifiable homicide, the latter class embracing the killing of burglars, robbers, and rapists. He also provided penalties for wounding and beating. He devoted extensive treatment to the crime of outrage, which was generally committed by young men and fell into five groups: outrages against sacred things or places, private shrines and tombs, parents, magistrates, and civil rights of private citizens.[132] It was here, for the first time

---

[131] *Laws* 855 B-C, 862 D-E; *Polit.* 297-300.   [132] *Laws* 884-885 A.

in the Western World, that the idea of the Inquisition was proposed, an institution which would seek out, examine and punish heretics.

THE LAWYER

The case against the lawyer has not been stated more bitterly than by Plato.[133] Lawyers abounded, he observed, when wealth increased. It was a dishonor to go to court at all. What surer proof 'could there be of an evil and shameful state of education than the necessity of first-rate judges, not only for the uneducated, but also for those who profess to have had a liberal training? Is it not disgraceful for a man to have to go to others for his justice from lack of such qualities in himself, and thus put himself into the hands of men who become his masters and judges?

A philosopher has his talk out in peace, and wanders at will from one subject to another, not caring whether his words are many or few, if only he attains the truth. But the lawyer is always in a hurry; there is the water flowing through the water-clock to drive him on and not allow him to develop his points at will; there is his adversary standing over him, enforcing his rights; there is the pleading to be read, from which he must not deviate. He is a servant continually disputing before his master, who is seated, and has the cause in his hands. As a consequence, he has become tense and shrewd; he has learned how to wheedle his master with words and indulge him in deed; and his character becomes small and warped. His thoughts are never disinterested, because of the issue at stake, which is sometimes life itself. From his youth upwards he has been a slave and that has deprived him of growth, straightforwardness, and independence; dangers and fears, which were too much for his truth and honesty, came upon him in early years, when the tenderness of youth was unequal to them, and he has been

---

[133] *Theaet.* 175-177; *Rep.* 405. The scholiast advised that the passage from the *Theaetetus*, which in its entirety contrasted the man of affairs and the lawyer with the philosopher, be memorized in full. Cf. Pound, *Causes of Popular Dissatisfaction with the Administration of Justice* (1906), 40 Am. L. Rev. 729.

driven into crooked ways; from the first he has practiced deception and retaliation, and has become bent and stunted. Consequently, he has passed from youth to manhood with no soundness of mind in him; but he thinks he has become clever and wise. His narrow, keen, pettifogging mind reveals its helplessness when, divorced from its pleas and rejoinders, it is brought to the contemplation of the nature of right and wrong or of human happiness and misery. He can make a fawning speech smartly and neatly, but he cannot discourse intelligently on the meaning of the good life.

Conclusion

Kant's [134] comparison of Plato with the light dove piercing the air in her easy flight and imagining, upon perceiving its resistance, that flight would be easier still in empty space has little relevance to Plato's legal ideas. He knew in the long run that practice, at least in the legal world, outweighed theory. His study of actual laws and procedures was comprehensive and profound; its penetration is particularly evident in his continued insistence upon the limits of effective legal action. In the history of jurisprudence, however, no one has been more fully aware of the necessity of the reign of law for any state which desires to realize the ultimate values of happiness and well-being for its citizens. He had a complete understanding of the function of law as an agency of social control. His concrete proposals must always be understood in terms of the problems created by his age, and particularly against the background of the waste stretch in Crete where his Model City was to be placed. His philosophical statements about law are another matter. They are theories of law in its generality and, if they have validity in whole or in part, the measure of truth

[134] Kant, *Critique of Pure Reason* (Smith's trans. 1933) 47. Whitehead observes that in two fields at least the familiar charge that Plato was not sufficiently empirical is without substance. "So far as concerns political theory, and in particular jurisprudence," he writes, "this accusation is certainly untrue, and arises from the habit of concentrating interest on his Dialogues in proportion to their literary brilliance." Whitehead, *Adventures of Ideas* (1933) 193.

they contain is independent of their local setting. Some of his thoughts were never completely expressed, some were mere asides. Aristotle brought a number of his ideas into sharper focus; but others were to wait more than two thousand years for their validity to be urged again, occasionally by men who believed they were stating new doctrines. Whatever may be the attitude towards the " mystical " or " spiritual " aspects of Platonism, the questions raised by Plato have been among the most useful ever formulated for jurisprudence. Perhaps the best evidence of their suggestiveness is the fact that we must go beyond Platonism for the answers. His grasp of legal problems was so acute that it is enough to venture the paraphrase that Western jurisprudence has consisted of a series of footnotes to Plato. The extent of his practical effect on the legal institutions of the thousand or more city-states founded during Hellenic times, and which reflected in their constitutions the imaginary commonwealth of the *Laws,* is still locked in the mysteries of Hellenic jurisprudence. But it is reasonable to suppose that it was considerable. Until Rome conquered, it was a period of great dreams; but, under Roman rule, as has been observed, there was no place for dreams.

CHAPTER III

ARISTOTLE

*Aristotle spurns me, as colts kick
out at the mother who bore them.*

Plato

GREEK THOUGHT had formulated, by the time Aristotle began
to write, the frame of general legal conceptions which
from that day to the present has been the staple of Western
jurisprudence. Aristotle developed those conceptions in two
directions. He subjected them to the tests of a highly formalized methodology, and he incorporated them as thus refined
in a body of thought that was never closed, and that was
more complete than any previously known.

Methodology in Socrates' hands was the cross-examining
elenchus of the lawyer. He assumed, in opposition to the
Sophists, that although a word might be used in many senses,
nevertheless it properly stood for some one general meaning
which it was the goal of inquiry to discover. Thus in the *Minos*
his first question was " What is law," and he proceeded to elicit
by questions the various meanings of the term, arriving finally
at a general definition. In Aristotle's opinion this was a form
of induction, in the sense that the arguments were arguments
from analogy; he believed that Socrates was the first to recognize the importance of induction and the first systematically
to use the method to reach general definitions.[1] Plato's dialectic cannot be caught in a formula; in the wonderful efflor-
escence of methodological activity to be observed in the

Note on the Translations. The Loeb and Oxford translations have in general
been followed, though there have been some departures in favor of Welldon's more
literal versions of the *Politics, Ethics,* and *Rhetoric.* Barker's translation of the
Politics (1946) I have also found particularly illuminating. My debt to the great
commentaries of Cope (*Rhetoric*), Grant and Stewart (*Ethics*), Newman (*Politics*)
and Ross (*Physics* and *Metaphysics*) will be manifest to Aristotelians. I have
availed myself freely of their interpretations wherever they appeared helpful.

[1] *Meta.* 1078^b 28.

dialogues the elements of many of our modern procedures can be detected. Some of his principal methods had a strong influence upon lawyers. A characteristic legal expression of his method of the Idea as the hypothetical premise is the utilization by the courts of natural or " higher " law propositions as points of departure for the reasoning that leads to decision; his method of division has always been an approved technique in legal analysis, and appears for example in the separation of public and private law.

Aristotle took the methodology of his predecessors and cast it into a formal system of valid inference, which has never lost its dominance in logical thinking. Its importance for the law has been twofold. In the judicial process the Aristotelian logic has been the basis of effective legal analysis from Roman times to the present. For jurisprudence, Aristotle's works represent the first example of the use of a precise scientific method in the exploration of legal propositions. Platonists have made out a strong case that most of the roots of Aristotle's methodology, even the syllogism, are present in the writings of his great teacher. Nevertheless, putting aside the question of originality, the systematization of formal logic as a distinct domain of knowledge, if not as an independent science, is undeniably an achievement of Aristotle. In modern times the Aristotelian logic has been rectified and further generalized by later systems. Lukasiewicz and others have devised alternative systems of logic by basing their systems on new definitions and different primitive ideas. The major premise of the Aristotelian logic has been reduced by modern logic to the status of an hypothesis. Nevertheless, the basic principles of the Aristotelian logic operate in the domains of all the alternative systems. Notwithstanding many dogmatic statements to the contrary, no non-Aristotelian logic has yet been formulated in the sense in which we have non-Euclidean systems of geometry. That is to say, no logic has been devised which assumes the contraries of the laws of identity, contradiction and excluded middle to be true even when taken as necessary formal conditions of inquiry, and not in their Aristotelian ontological interpretation, and which permits the making of valid inferences. To his logical methodology Aristotle added an empirical procedure that included a constant reference to the facts of observation and the views of other investigators. Whatever may have been its limitations in Aristotle's hands when judged by its results or ontological bias, his methodology possessed all the requirements of modern scientific method. At bottom it was the method of hypothesis and verification. He had an extraordinary genius for the perception of problems, which he attempted to solve by methods that in their formal aspects are still the mainstay of valid inquiry. In all this he never lost sight of the necessity of system, the requirement that verified propositions should be systematically inter-connected.

Thus with Aristotle we are for the first time brought face to face with an effort to deal with legal materials systematically, by justified methods and as part of a larger whole. He took the legal ideas that Plato with a lavish hand had scattered throughout his dialogues, and arranged them in a scheme which as a whole attempted to explain human conduct in its most essential aspects. He assigned to jurisprudence what must always be its main task, the establishment of a rational legal order for a given society.

The Contingency of Legal Method

Aristotle held that the end of theoretical knowledge was *truth*, that of practical knowledge *action*.[2] He divided the sciences into the *theoretical*, which had as their object knowledge for its own sake, the *practical*, which sought knowledge as a guide to conduct, and the *productive*, which employed knowledge for the creation of beautiful or useful objects.[3] Politics, or what in view of the modern classificatory outlook we would term the social sciences, was the pre-eminent prac-

[2] *Meta.* 993^{b} 19.
[3] *Meta.* 1025^{b} 25; *Top.* 145^{a} 15; *E. N.* 1139^{a} 27. The origin of the classification is Platonic. *Phil.* 55C-59A; *Polit.* 258E-260D. Diog. Laert. iii, 84.

tical science.[4] It should be emphasized that Aristotle attempted
no separation of ethics and politics. Both were aspects of the
" philosophy of human affairs," [5] and he did not attempt, as
is done today, to draw any distinction between them on the
ground that the good of the state and the good of the individual
were different, or that there was a class of " political duties "
differing essentially from others. Inasmuch as Aristotle admitted only metaphysics, natural science and mathematics into
the group of theoretical sciences that study knowledge for its
own sake,[6] it follows that the modern practice of studying the
legal process for precisely that purpose runs counter to Aristotelian dogma. However, the unsoundness of the practice is
not apparent, and Aristotle's own contributions to the analysis
of jurisprudence could be taken as evidence that he ignored
his own rules. Aristotle's views may have been influenced by
what practical men, *e. g.*, statesmen, actually do; for, as he
observed, even if they investigate how things are, practical
men do not study the eternal, but what is relative and in the
present.[7]

Scientific reasoning in the Aristotelian system is distinguished
sharply from dialectical or popular reasoning. Metaphysics,
natural science and mathematics are alone regarded as sciences.
The ideal of science is knowledge, and it takes expression as
an ordered system of demonstrative syllogisms. Scientific
knowledge is knowledge that necessarily cannot be otherwise.[8]
The dialectical syllogism reaches conclusions that are true
upon the whole; its premises are probable, that is, they are
accepted by all, or by the majority, or by the wise.[9] Since
demonstration alone gives us knowledge, a syllogism which
reaches that result must have certain characteristics: (a) the
premises must be true; (b) they must be undemonstrable,
otherwise they will require demonstration in order to be known,
for knowledge of things which are demonstrable means pre-

---

[4] *E. N.* 1094ª 18 *et seq.*, 1141ᵇ 23 *et seq.*
[5] *E. N.* 1181ᵇ 15.
[6] *Meta.* 1026ª 18.

[7] *Meta.* 993ᵇ 23.
[8] *An. Post.* I. 33.
[9] *Top.* 100ᵇ 23.

cisely to have a demonstration of them; (c) they must be the causes of the conclusion, since we possess scientific knowledge of a thing only when we know its cause; (d) they must be better known and prior to the conclusion, prior in order to be causes, and prior and better known in the sense that the truth of particular causes is more readily perceived, being closer to sense than universal causes.[10] Aristotle's concept of nature had a pronounced influence on his view of the constituents of science. He held that every demonstrative science has three elements: the genus which is posited, the axioms which are the primary premises of the demonstration, and the essential properties of the genus revealed by the demonstration.[11] Aristotle is here plainly influenced by the fact that biology and geometry were the most advanced sciences of his time. Nevertheless, it is important to note that he generalized those elements beyond the model sciences of biology and geometry, and expressly recognized that some sciences might pass beyond them. His ultimate conclusion was that in the case of a demonstration the essential elements of demonstration were a subject matter, the basic premises, and that which is proved.[12]

As generalized, the three elements are present in the demonstrations of scientific methodology today. But the heart of the Aristotelian theory—that demonstrative knowledge is syllogistic—is no longer regarded as valid. To take Aristotle's own case of mathematics, it is plain that nothing would be gained by casting a modern mathematical argument into syllogistic form. Further, the material truth or falsity of the axioms is of no interest to the mathematician; he accepts them as given, and is concerned only with whether his theorems are implied by them. If he has a set of postulates he wants to know also if they are self-consistent and will never lead to a contradiction; but such knowledge has apparently never been vouchsafed to anyone. However, if we turn from mathematics to the empirical sciences the theory is still unacceptable. The

---

[10] *An. Post.* 71ᵇ 9 *et seq.*
[11] *An. Post.* 75ᵃ 42; 76ᵇ 14.
[12] *An. Post.* 76ᵇ 16 *et seq.*

axioms of contemporary scientific practice are hypotheses. That is to say, they are propositions asserted for the purposes of study, without any suggestion as to their truth or falsity. There is no necessary requirement that they should be known to be true, or be " better known " before we have knowledge of the warranted conclusions. Generally when the material truth of the conclusions has been established, it confirms the probability of the truth of the axioms.

Methodology was always a troublesome matter to Aristotle; he had difficulty in making people understand that its characteristics necessarily varied with the subject matter. It is the customary, he insisted, that is intelligible. We find the strength of the familiar in the ancient laws, in which the mythical element prevails by force of habit over our knowledge of its childishness. Thus, some people will not listen to a speaker unless he gives a mathematical proof; others demand examples; still others want a poet cited as authority. Some want exactness, while others are annoyed by it, either because they cannot follow the reasoning or because they think it is pettifoggery. There is something about exactness, in philosophy as well as in business, that repels people. We must be trained in the proper method before we begin the study of a subject, so that we will know when to expect mathematical accuracy and when it would be out of place. It is absurd to seek simultaneously for knowledge and for the method of obtaining it; as a matter of fact, it is not easy to get even one of the two.[13]

In the view of Aristotle, precision should not be looked for in jurisprudence, which is a part of the philosophy of human affairs; its conclusions are outside the realm of demonstration. They lie in the field of the contingent, the idea of which Aristotle asserted he was the first to investigate.[14] He begins by noting that some things always come to pass in the same way,

[13] *Meta.* 995ᵃ 3.

[14] *Phys.* 196ᵃ 17. In the *Protrepticus* written at the beginning of his philosophical career, Aristotle maintained the opposite position, that " the knowledge of unjust and just actions and of immoral and moral actions is similar to that of geometry and such like sciences." Rose, *Aristotelis Fragmenta* (1886) 58-59 (Frag. 52).

and others for the most part. There is a third class, consisting of the irregular and exceptional. He also looks at this class from another point of view. Things happen *per accidens* (κατὰ συμβεβηκός); that is to say, a carpenter may happen to be a cultivated person, so that this accidental quality becomes part and parcel of the direct cause of the building. Such qualities are not necessary in a carpenter, and thus the erection of buildings by cultivated carpenters will happen neither always nor for the most part.

So far, he has been talking about the incidental production of some significant result by a cause that took its place in the causal chain incidentally, and without the result in question being contemplated. In order to arrive at the idea of " chance," he adds " purpose-serving actions " that accomplish " ends " when the result is such that would have been recognized as a purpose and would have determined the action, had it been anticipated. Thus, a man goes to the market-place to buy bread; he discovers his debtor receiving money from a third person and collects the money from him. The collection of the money was an accident of his journey to the market to buy bread; but if he had anticipated the recovery of the money it might have determined his action in going. Altogether, we are in the presence of chance, which can be defined as an incidental cause in the sphere of action for the sake of something, and which involves purpose.[15]

In this treatment Aristotle does not allow for a true contingency. What happened may have been unforeseen but it was nevertheless determined; the actions of the bread-buyer and the debtor followed separate lines of strict causality that intersected. He once implies that determinism operates throughout the whole of existence, and that accidents are only unintelligible exceptions which are as much subject to laws as the intelligible.[16] Elsewhere, in denying the applicability of the law of excluded middle to statements about particular future events, he asserts the reality of an objective contingency, one

[15] *Phys.* II, 5.   [16] *Meta.* 1027ᵃ 25.

not a function of ignorance. If you state, tomorrow there will
either be a sea-fight, or there will not be a sea-fight, this assertion
will be necessarily true; but it is not the case either that
tomorrow there will be a sea-fight or tomorrow there will not
be a sea-fight.[17] Hobbes [18] attempted to meet this argument
by pointing out that it says " no more but that it is not yet
known whether it be true or not." Other statements by Aristotle imply a belief in a true contingency,[19] and nowhere in his
writings is there evidence of a belief in a general law of causality
of the kind conceived, for example, by Mill.

These views are important when considered in connection
with Aristotle's reflections on the methodology applicable to
the study of human conduct. He remarks, first, that his
analysis of conduct will be adequate if it achieves that amount
of precision [20] which belongs to its subject matter. We must
not expect the same precision in all departments of philosophy
alike, any more than in all the products of the arts and crafts,
e. g., we make more exact tools from metal than from wood.
The subject-matter of the science of human conduct, such as
justice and virtue, exhibits so great a diversity and uncertainty
that it is sometimes thought to have only a conventional, and
not a natural, existence. Hence, reasoning with such conceptions, we cannot expect demonstrative and exact conclusions; we must be content with rough and general theories.
Again, he inquires whether in appraising conduct we should
proceed *from* first principles or *to* first principles; and he concludes that we should begin inductively with what we know,
e. g., relative and not absolute truths.[21] Finally, after stating
the meaning of the idea of good, he observes that having drawn
the outlines he must now fill in the details; the idea of the good

[17] *De Int.* 19ᵃ 30.

[18] 1 *Works* (1839) 131.

[19] *Meta.* 1027ᵇ 10; *De Gen. et Corr.* 337ᵇ *et seq.; De Int.* 18ᵃ 33 *et seq.; E. N.*
1113ᵇ 14.

[20] *E. N.* 1094ᵇ 13. ἀκρίβεια here appears to mean " that *mathematical exactness*
is not suited to ethics, that too much *subtlety* is not to be expected, that too much
detail is to be avoided." 1 Grant, *Ethics of Aristotle* (3d ed. 1874) 450 n. 18.

[21] *E. N.* 1095ᵇ 5.

is also a leading principle and, having been found, it amounts to more than half the whole science. He repeats his warning against expecting too much exactness and points out that while a carpenter and a geometrician both want to find a right angle, they do not want to find it in the same sense.[22] Above all,[23] he insists upon the practical nature of the study of human conduct. In such an enterprise it is by the practical experience of life and conduct that the truth is really tested, since it is there the final decision lies. We must, therefore, examine all conclusions by bringing them to the test of the facts of life. If they are in harmony with the facts, we may accept them; if they are in disagreement, we must deem them mere theories. In a practical science the end is not to attain a theoretic knowledge of the subject, but rather to carry out theories in action.

All this amounts to the method Mill considered alone applicable to the social sciences. As a strict determinist, Mill believed that it was incorrect to say that any phenomenon is produced by chance. Nevertheless he observed that " if all the resources of science are not sufficient to enable us to calculate *a priori,* with complete precision, the mutual action of three bodies gravitating towards one another; it may be judged with what prospects of success we should endeavor, from the laws of human nature only, to calculate the result of the conflicting tendencies which are acting in a thousand different directions and promoting a thousand different changes at a given instant in a given society." [24] However, he did not despair of approximating some of the aims of science in that field. Aristotle and Mill both began with a " general conception," or in modern terms an hypothesis, which is subjected to verificatory tests. This procedure is often inverted, as we have seen, so that instead of deducing conclusions from principles, and verifying them by observation, we begin by obtaining them conjecturally

[22] *E. N.* 1098ª 17 *et seq.*
[23] *E. N.* 1179ª 16, 1179ᵇ 2.
[24] *Logic* (1864) 561. 1 Stewart, *Notes on the Nicomachean Ethics* (1892) 104.

from specific experience and afterwards connect them with general principles by a method of reasoning which provides a verification.

Inasmuch as the study of human conduct analyzes in Aristotle's opinion " things which are for the most part so," " things which are capable of being otherwise," his theory at bottom was that human affairs were ultimately contingent. Apart from human conduct the contingency of occurrences might be an appearance that was the product of partial knowledge; and if the logical connections of existence in that sense could be wholly understood, chance might be altogether eliminated. However, in human affairs he apparently accepted a radical contingency; thus the propositions formulated for that field of study would be approximate merely.

That is the generally accepted conclusion in all empirical sciences today. Locke [25] endeavored to maintain the opposite view, on the ground that " the precise real essence of the things moral words stand for may be perfectly known; and so the congruity or incongruity of the things themselves be certainly discovered, in which consists perfect knowledge." Thus he held that we could attain a demonstrative knowledge of justice. This argument overlooks the fact that in an empirical inquiry any general statement about justice is always an embodiment of contingent data. All data of that kind are obtained by observation, and observation is never otherwise than approximate. Thus the laws of all the empirical sciences cannot escape contingency. We are no better off if we establish a purely formal principle of justice, for it is impossible to apply it to particular instances. Pure universals, nineteenth century logic made clear, do not imply particular existential propositions. Non-Euclidean geometry and non-Newtonian mechanics showed that formal first principles are hypotheses, and unless an empirical element is added to the argument all deductions from them will remain hypotheses. As an example of a demonstrative moral proposition Locke suggested: " Man is subject to law " and defined

[25] Locke, *Essay on the Human Understanding* (1853) 376.

" man " as " a corporeal, rational creature." He intended to include children under the proposition, and even animals, if any were found that understood " general signs " and were able " to deduce consequences about general ideas." As a normative proposition, it is clear that children ought not to be held criminally responsible unless they possess a certain measure of understanding; but Locke's proposal does not tell us how much understanding we ought to demand. Modern experiments have shown that even pre-school children are capable of analyzing and reorganizing their impressions. Should we, in the interests of justice, revise downwards the common law standard of responsibility for felony and include them? Formally, on the basis of Locke's argument, the rule should be revised; but would a present-day community accept as adequate a standard that might result in the hanging of three-year old children? Like all juristic propositions it breaks down in specific application. That is so because the initial hypothesis is radically defective in the material statement of those facts which it will be called upon to meet.

In this characteristic the propositions of a legal science are not different from those of other empirical sciences. They are approximate merely. If we attempt to determine the position of the sun over Paris at any moment, to paraphrase Duhem, we begin by discarding the real sun, which has an irregular surface, for a perfect geometric sphere; it is the position of the center of this ideal sphere that we shall try to determine; or rather, we shall endeavor to determine the position that will be occupied by this point if astronomical refraction does not deviate the rays of the sun and if the annual aberration does not modify the apparent position of the stars. We shall use extremely complicated instruments, but all of them are imperfect, and we shall perform long and complex calculations. From this example, it is apparent that it is possible to devise any number of formulae to direct the experiment, and no differences will be detected in the observations, since the actual differences are too imperceptible to be detected by our crude instruments.

A comparable situation exists in the judicial process. Inasmuch as numerous principles can be suggested as the basis of any particular decision, it is foolish to assert that any particular case decides a principle as its *ratio decidendi*. From the example, the conclusion can also be drawn that every law of physics is an approximate law, and as a matter of strict logic, cannot be either true or false; all other laws which represent the same phenomena with the same approximation are able to claim, as justly as the first, the title of a true law, or to speak more rigorously, an acceptable law. Because of their approximate quality all laws of physics are thus of merely provisory validity.[26]

TELEOLOGY IN SOCIAL SCIENCE

In Aristotelian theory the grounds of contingency are not established as in modern thought on the basis of the approximate character of the elements of scientific procedure, the data, the propositions and the instruments, but rest on his view of nature. His ultimate explanation of nature, which is teleological in character, also involves a necessary way of viewing social phenomena and is an essential addition to his formal methodology.

Matter and form are the fundamental categories which for Aristotle explain the universe. We know a thing through its form and thus form is the basic reality; but Nature consists of forms which are materialized or embodied. Matter in the Aristotelian sense has a meaning beyond corporeality. A man's character is matter which has impressed upon it a certain form just as much as the copper in the copper vase. The principle of matter and form takes on a different meaning when the idea of change is added. Form then becomes the end or object of change, matter the potentiality that will receive the impress of

[26] Duhem, *La Théorie Physique* (1906) 274 *et seq.*, Poincaré, *La Valeur de la Science* (1925) 251; 1 Cournot, *Essai sur les Fondements de nos Connaissances* (1851) 96 *et seq.; id., Matérialisme, Vitalisme, Rationalisme* (1923) 250; Cohen, *Reason and Nature* (1931) 223.

form. When matter has received its form it has realized the aim of becoming. Hence, in the doctrines of matter and form, and of potentiality and actuality, we have a theory of a continuous development from the potential to the actual, from that which is capable of being to that which is. Now the realization of matter in actuality is the end or final cause. Development is always towards an end, and thus the end is itself the cause of becoming. For example, the form of the oak is potentially present in the acorn and determines its full development. In the sense therefore of its true being, the oak is really prior to the acorn. But in Nature conceived as the conquest of form over matter allowance must be made for the refractory character of matter. Too often the material with which form struggles displays itself as recalcitrant.[27] Thus we have imperfect conduct and the abnormalities of nature. Matter is therefore the passive recipient of impressions, the wax conforming to the die, the source of necessity in Nature to the extent of its capacity to achieve form; it is also the resister of impressions, the wax which refuses to receive the die, the source of contingency in Nature to the extent that it rejects form.[28]

From this metaphysical position Aristotle arrived at his teleological method of handling social phenomena. In the *Ethics* he sets the stage for that approach in the first sentence: "Every art and every inquiry, and similarly every action and pursuit, is thought to aim at some good; and for this reason the good has rightly been declared to be that at which all things aim." All that follows is a development and deduction from that principle. Similarly the opening sentence of the *Politics* is again teleological: "Every state is a community of some kind, and every community is established with a view to some good; for mankind always act in order to obtain that

[27] *De Part. An.* 640ᵃ 18.
[28] Aristotle's doctrine of form and matter appears in his writings on logic, natural science, metaphysics, social science and aesthetics, in brief, in nearly all the works. For a general discussion see Joachim, *Aristotle on Coming-to-be and Passing-away* (1922).

which they think good." And the rest of the discussion is an
effort to determine the end of the state, and the nature of the
matter or means which is necessary to a realization of that end.
This view led him to see the function of education and law as
instruments for the achievement of the good life; it permitted
him also to find a justification for slavery in the doctrine that
the end was thereby promoted.

It is not difficult to reduce a thoroughgoing teleology such
as Aristotle's to absurdity. The nose, Voltaire said, is made
to carry glasses. However, in a limited sense the theory contains some elements of truth. One of the aims of science is to
explain the events of experience. In the social sciences particularly, explanation in qualitative, as against quantitative, terms
is a customary practice. The object of explanation of that
kind is to determine the extent to which a given activity
achieves a purpose or conforms to a value. Does the infliction
of capital punishment affect the homicide rate? is clearly a
legitimate question in social science. Teleological explanation
assumes intelligent direction and evaluation; it looks to the
effect to make the earlier activity intelligible, to the future as
determining the present. In general, teleological explanation
seeks to answer the question *Why?* Why did the Constitution
provide for the Supreme Court? Why did the framers of the
Constitution seek that objective? Why did they not attempt
to realize it through the administrative power? There seems
to be no good reason why this is not a sound and enlightening
method of explanation. However, it possesses another aspect
which involves greater difficulty. Bosanquet's [29] argument that
nothing is properly due to mind which was never a plan before
a mind, meets the issue of the individual will as a factor in
social causation, but it does not dispose of the theory of social
purpose. The activities of the leader of a Greek colony to
Ionia in the eighth or ninth century B. C. paved the way to
Christianity, but it certainly was never part of his design any

---

[29] "The Meaning of Teleology" (1906) in *Proceedings of the British Academy*
235, 244.

more than the coral reef is the design of the coral insect.
Individual purpose is a factor in the immediate and apparent;
it is an inadequate element in the explanation of the radical
changes which are a feature of human history. " The human
will is *a* juridical cause," writes Tourtoulon,[30] " but it is nothing
more than a cause. It urges the law to the right or left, it
knows not whither. Must we compare it to Luther's tipsy
peasant, who cannot stay on his donkey, but falls sometimes
to one side, sometimes to the other? This would, perhaps, be
giving it too much honor, for the peasant knows that he has a
road and wishes to follow it, although he cannot. The juridical
will has no road to follow. It goes, as a poet says, ' *Où va
toute chose, où va la feuille de rose et la feuille de laurier.*' "
It is true that we frequently fail in the immediate social purpose
at which we aim. As Spinoza saw long ago, those who try to
determine everything by law foment crime rather than lessen
it. Nevertheless, social purpose, or the immediate ends at
which human action aims, is a standard which a sound methodology cannot ignore. To eliminate it would be to deprive
social behavior of much that makes it intelligible.

It is true of Aristotle's general theory as of history that any
one who endeavors to tell a piece of it must feel, in Maitland's
phrase, that his first sentence tears a seamless web. His theory
of jurisprudence cannot be wholly understood apart from his
political science and that in turn rests upon his ethics; ethics
presupposes certain psychological doctrines which are developed
in his metaphysics and his philosophy of nature. His great
strength lies in the coherent and comprehensive character of
his system which permits him to see things in their totality.
It was a system also not without its practical effect on the
course of the law. In 1829, when the question of ownership
of a finished article made by one man out of material belonging
to another was first fully considered in the United States we
find the court settling the problem in terms of " identity of
the material," " conversion into original species," " retention by

[30] *Philosophy in the Development of Law* (1922) 41.

the material of its specific character, or kind, or qualities,"
" change of mere form," " change of species," " specific but
not essential change," and " essence of material." It is not
improper to assert that the meaning of those words and phrases
stems, through Bracton and Justinian, from the significance
they acquired in the works of Aristotle.[31]

The Nature of Law

In the Platonic *Minos* we fortunately possess an inquiry into
the nature of law undertaken in the full panoply of the dialectic.
No comparable writing of Aristotle has come down to us. We
are without any analysis of his conducted for the express purpose of stating a general and ultimate theory of law. His
definitions of law are partial and are thus an anticipation of
the practices of modern science. They are always relative to
the problem before him, and the aspect of law which they
emphasize constantly shifts in order to permit different consequences to be drawn.

In the *Rhetoric to Alexander* it is pointed out that in a
democracy the final appeal on all matters is to the law, but
in a monarchy the appeal is to reason. A self-governing community is directed along the best path by its public law, and
so a king, as the embodiment of reason, guides along the path
of their advantage those who are subject to his rule. In a
clumsy attempt to bring the two ideas together, law is then
stated to be reason defined by the common consent of the
community, regulating action of every kind. Later, in the same
treatise, which is a handbook on how to persuade audiences,
another aspect emerges. Advice is offered on how to speak
in favor of a law (show that it affects all equally, that it is
beneficial to the city, etc.) or against a law (show that it does

---

[31] *Lampton v. Preston,* 1 J. J. Marsh. 454 (1829); 2 Woodbine, *Bracton* 43-47;
Gai. II, 79; D. XLI, 1.17 § 7. 1 Sokolowski, *Die Philosophie im Privatrecht* (1902)
69 *et seq.* Cf. Kunkel, *Book Review* (1928) 48 *Zeitschrift der Savigny-Stiftung für
Rechtsgeschichte* (Rom. Abt.) 709, 721; Guibal, *De l'Influence de la Philosophie sur
le Droit Romain et la Jurisprudence* (1937) 196 *et seq.*

not apply equally to all the citizens, etc.). For this purpose
law is defined as the common agreement of the state enjoining
in writing how men are to act in various matters.[32] Aristotle
argued that the nurture and occupations of the young should
be fixed by law so that they would become customary. He
agreed with Plato that legislation should teach virtue. Goodness, in men, he thought, could be secured if their lives were
regulated by a certain intelligence, and by a right system,
invested with adequate sanctions. Paternal authority does not
have the required force to accomplish this end. But law has
this compulsive power and it is at the same time a rule emanating from a certain practical wisdom and reason. Thus,
while people hate men who oppose their impulses, even if they
are right in so doing, they do not regard the law as invidious
if it enjoins virtuous conduct.[33] Similarly, in an action involving
a contract, if the contract's existence is admitted and if that is
a fact favoring the side of the speaker, that circumstance ought
to be "magnified" or strengthened. That can be done by
calling it a "law" because a contract may really be considered
as a private or special and partial law; and it is not of course
the contracts which make the law binding, but it is the laws
which give force to legal contracts. Aristotle therefore suggests
that, in a general sense, the law itself is a kind of contract, so
that whoever disregards or repudiates a contract is repudiating
the law itself. However, Aristotle believed that law was much
more than a contract. He pointed out that if the state did not
pay attention to virtue, the community became merely an
alliance; "the law would be a contract, and, as Lycophron the
Sophist says, a pledge of lawful dealing between man and
man."[34] Again, in arguing that it is difficult and perhaps
impossible for a state with too large a population to have good
legal government, he observes that law is a form of order, and

---

[32] 1420ª 25, 1422ª 2, 1424ª 9. For the authenticity of the dialogue, see Cope, *An
Introduction to Aristotle's Rhetoric* (1867) 401 *et seq*. The first definition may be
by Anaximenes of Lampsacus, purportedly a tutor of Alexander.
[33] *E. N.* 1180ª 21. Plato, *Laws* 722 D.
[34] *Rhet.* 1376ᵇ 10. *Polit.* 1280ᵇ 10.

good law must necessarily mean good order; but an excessively large number cannot be orderly.[35] Again, in considering whether the best men or the law should be supreme he observes that he who bids the law rule may be deemed to bid God and reason alone to rule, but he who bids man rule adds an element of the beast; for desire is a wild beast, and passion perverts the minds of rulers, even when they are the best of men. Hence, law is reason without appetite.[36] As he observed elsewhere, intellect is always right, but appetency may be right or wrong. Appetency aims at the practical good which may not be good under all circumstances.[37] Finally, Plato [38] had divided state organization into two parts, one the appointment of individuals to office, the other the assignment of laws to the offices. Both divisions came under the general topic of the " constitution " (πολιτεία). Aristotle [39] developed a distinction between " constitution " (πολιτεία) and " laws " (νόμοι). As a general principle he insisted that the laws should be laid down to suit the constitutions—the constitutions must not be made to suit the laws. A constitution is the organization of offices in a state, and determines what is to be the governing body, and what is the end of each community. But laws are not to be confounded with the principles of the constitution. They are the rules according to which the magistrates should administer the state, and proceed against offenders. Cicero [40] observed the distinction and differentiated the " optimus rei publicae status " from " leges " and thereafter it became firmly fixed in Western political thought.

---

[35] *Polit.* 1326ᵃ 30. *Cf.* 1287ᵃ 19.

[36] *Polit.* 1287ᵃ 32.

[37] *De An.* 433ᵃ 26. In the *E. N.* 1139ᵃ 23 he points out that pursuit and avoidance in the sphere of desire correspond to affirmation and denial in the sphere of the intellect. Hence, inasmuch as moral virtue is a disposition of the mind in regard to choice, and choice is deliberate desire, it follows that, if the choice is to be good, both the principle must be true and the desire right, and that desire must pursue the same things as principle affirms. He is here speaking of practical thinking, and of the attainment of truth in regard to action.

[38] *Laws* 735A; *cf.* 678A. *Cf.* 4 Newman, *The Politics of Aristotle* (1902) 142.

[39] *Polit.* 1289ᵃ 15; 1298ᵃ 17; 1292ᵇ 15; 1278ᵇ 8; *E. N.* 1181ᵇ 12.

[40] *De Leg.* I. 5. 15.

To the extent his works have survived, it is clear that Aristotle did not reach any final definition of law comparable, say, to his idea of substance or of justice; he reveals no general and leading conception of it from the point of view of its nature. This failure to state explicitly the meaning of a vital idea is not an anomaly. At the heart of Aristotle's theory of the State is the idea of κοινωνία; but nowhere are we told plainly what the conception stands for, and it is only by analyzing his incidental remarks when the term is emphasized that we are able to ascertain the idea behind it. If what has come down to us represents his true view of the nature of law then he attained a position which was not reached in jurisprudence again until the twentieth century. That is to say, he saw the inherent complexity of legal phenomena, and he found that no single description of it could embrace its manifold aspects. The identification of any aspect may have significance for the task in hand; and he therefore, so far as we can judge, allowed room for them all and did not insist upon the exclusive validity of any single one. In this approach he was on much sounder ground than Plato who saw law as a simple unitary phenomenon. All the elements which Aristotle emphasized have been taken separately as the single bases of subsequent systems, and most of them are factors in current legal analysis. He thought of law as a rule of conduct for the individual, perhaps the most discussed conception in jurisprudence; he stressed the ideal of reason, the doctrine that legal precepts should have some basis in intelligibility and not be the mere expression of arbitrariness, force or custom; the idea of law as a contract was adopted by Epicurus and Lucretius,[41] and appears in present day opinion in the theory that its naked function is to prevent attacks by individuals on each other; when he distinguished law from the constitution and defined it as the rules which regulate how the magistrates are to govern, he formulated a theory of law—that laws are the rules in accordance with which courts determine cases—which reappeared again in the

[41] Diog. Laert. 10. 150; Lucr. 5, 1143.

later development of analytical jurisprudence; when he pointed out that law was a form of order he put his finger on an aspect that since Kant has been dominant in continental legal thought.

Law itself, like everything in the Aristotelian system, had its end and to Aristotle it was clear that its task was to make men good.[42] This was deduced from his premise that the state does not exist for the sake of life only, but for the sake of the good life.[43] But what is goodness? Everyone agrees, Aristotle says, that the highest good is happiness or well-being; but that is merely a label and the main inquiry is to find out what the word means. Aristotle's [44] general definition is that happiness (ἐνδαιμονία) is an exercise of the powers of life in accordance with virtue throughout a whole life-time. He endeavors to show that this definition sums up and improves upon all that has been said on the subject. If it is asserted that happiness is virtue he claims to make an advance on this by insisting that happiness is an exercise and not a mere possession of virtue; if happiness is pleasure he says that happiness is necessarily accompanied by an inherent pleasure; if it is good fortune or external prosperity he says that the functions of happiness cannot be performed without it. Thus happiness takes its origin in virtue, it issues in pleasure, and material good-fortune is its ordinary equipment.

That this position is largely Platonic scarcely needs to be stated. Plato had held that a task of law was to produce happiness in the state as a whole and that through its instrumentality men could be taught virtue.[45] However, while Aristotle's definition satisfies the Platonic conditions for a happy life—that the goal is important on its own account and not as a means to other things, that its satisfactions appeal to us, and that it would be the final choice of the wise—as a juristic formula it has several defects. In his attitude towards the nature of law, Aristotle admitted a plurality of viewpoints.

---

[42] *E. N.* 1199[b] 33, 1102[a] 10, 1103[b] 3; *Polit.* 1280[b] 12.
[43] *Polit.* 1280[a] 30.
[44] *E. N.* 1098[a] 16.
[45] *Rep.* 519E; *Laws* 693, 701D, 705E.

Here, only one position has significance; no doubt this view is a product of his teleological method which has as its object the discovery of the final end. Now it is plain that the tasks of law can no more be caught within the net of a single formula than its numerous and contradictory aspects can be confined within the limits of one definition. If we look at the police functions of the legal order, the task of law is to keep the peace; if we look at law as one of the instruments of control in a complex society its task is also the harmonization of disparate claims. The task is a function of the problem; and since the problems are numerous, the tasks are alike multitudinous and are equally valid. Law may also be a means in the inculcation of established ethical ideals and the promotion of new ones. The maxim of the Institutes [46] that the precepts of law are to live honorably, not to hurt another, to give each man his due, gives expression to ideals which if insisted upon in applicable situations, such as those involving the issue of good faith in undertakings, may raise the entire moral tone of a people. Another defect in Aristotle's idea of the end of law is that it breaks down as soon as it is put into practice. However, as we have seen above, it shares this weakness with all other ideals that have been proposed. They do not contain enough elements to meet all concrete situations. Thus, Aristotle [47] excludes the man of pre-eminent virtue from the operation of the law. His principle is that the law is necessarily concerned only with those who are equal in birth and power. He maintained that anyone is ridiculous who attempts to make laws for exceptional men, for probably they would say what the lions said when the hares made speeches in the assembly and demanded that all should have equality: " where are your claws and teeth? " This position when stated conversely will also provide a justification of slavery. Some idea of the concrete model Aristotle probably had before him in depicting the actual

---

[46] *Inst.* I, 1, § 3. This is clearly the crystallization of a Greek conception. *Cf.* *E. N.* V, i, 14; Plato, *Rep.* 331E *et seq.,* 433E.

[47] *Polit.* 1284ª 12, 1287ª 17.

realization of the end of the law may be derived from the following summary: " Aristotle's political ideal is that of a small but leisured and highly cultivated aristocracy, without large fortunes or any remarkable differences in material wealth, free from the spirit of adventure and enterprise, pursuing the arts and sciences quietly while its material needs are supplied by the labor of a class excluded from citizenship, kindly treated but without prospects. Weimar, in the days when Thackeray knew it as a lad, would apparently reproduce the ideal better than any other modern State one can think of." [48] Goethe found Weimar the most satisfactory place in the world in which to live; nevertheless it seems possible to devise other ideals which would have a wider appeal.

Aristotle held that the law has no power to command obedience except that of habit, which can only be given by time. [49] This assertion, like many others, reveals the clear unity of his thought. If obedience to law is based on habit, then, as he says, a readiness to change from old to new laws enfeebles the power of the law. [50] Inasmuch as law has a psychological basis, education also has a major role in Aristotle's theory. It assists in making obedience to law second nature to the citizens. He believed that the best means to secure the stability of constitutions is a system of education suited to the constitutions; for there is no merit in the most valuable laws, ratified by the unanimous judgment of the whole body of citizens, if the citizens are not trained and educated in the constitution. The state must begin the education early, for if a man is to lead the good life he must practice it a long time. [51] Aristotle's aphorism " It is hard to be good " is often quoted. But he also said: " A life of virtue ceases to be painful when you get used to it." [52]

There is an apparent paradox here which should be noted

---

[48] Taylor, *Aristotle* (1919) 117.
[49] *Polit.* 1269^a 20, 1310^a 12; *E. N.* 1163^b 37; *Meta.* 995^a 2.
[50] *Polit.* 1269^a 23.
[51] *Polit.* 1310^a 12, 1337^a 14.
[52] *E. N.* 1180^a 1.

in passing. If the citizen is to be educated in the spirit of the constitution, what happens if the constitution is a bad one? Will the citizen be able to live the good life? Aristotle's answer, and it is not clear whether it is given normatively or descriptively, is that the citizen should be educated in the aims of the constitution, whether good or bad. Thus the citizen may be taught to be an evil man. During the Reformation the question took on practical importance and became sharply focussed in the test issue: Is it lawful to kill tyrants? Melanchthon [53] thought that Caesar was unjustly killed; but Luther [54] apparently took a different stand. In view of the rise of authoritarian government it may once again cease to be an abstract matter.

In the doctrine of the categories, conduct comes under the heading of Quality.[55] Virtue is a Quality and Aristotle assumes that that category has four divisions: habits, or tendencies to do a thing; capacities for doing a thing; feelings, passions and emotions prompting us to do a thing; and external form or shape.[56] In which classification does conduct fall? Aristotle does not trouble to mention form or shape, which is used in describing a man's appearance, since character is here alone in question. Conduct is not to be classified under feeling—*e. g.*, desire, anger, fear, confidence, envy, joy, love, hate, longing, emulation, pity—because no one is praised or blamed for having feelings, but only for having them in a certain way; similarly, good and bad conduct is not a capacity, for we are not said to be good or bad because we are capable of experiencing certain feelings, but for the manner in which we actually do so. If their conduct is neither a feeling nor a capacity, it must be a habit or settled tendency to act in a certain way. Good conduct is not acquired from nature; if it were it could not be changed and moral training would be impossible; however, we owe nature something, for she gives us the capacity

[53] 16 *Opera* (1850) 105.
[54] 2 Bossuet, *Histoire des Variations* (1770) 91.
[55] *Categ.* VIII. *E. N.* 1096ª 24.
[56] *E. N.* II, v.

for good conduct. Nor does it come from teaching. Character depends on what you do and not on what you are told to do. Most people, instead of acting, take refuge in theorizing; they imagine that they are philosophers and that philosophy will make them virtuous; in fact, they behave like people who listen attentively to their doctors but never do anything their doctors tell them. People who doctor themselves that way will never get well.[57] Habituation therefore is the only method of acquiring that settled tendency to do acts of a certain kind. It is by doing acts of a given kind and as a consequence of these acts that we become good or bad, as the case may be, just as in the arts; by playing well you come to be a good player, and by playing badly, a bad one. This truth is attested by the experience of states: lawgivers make the citizens good by training them in habits of right action—this is the aim of all legislation, and if it fails to do this, it is a failure; that is what distinguishes a good form of constitution from a bad one.[58]

Although his theory of legal sanction is essentially a psychological one, Aristotle is careful to point out that the lawgiver need not be a specialist in psychology any more than it is necessary for the medical practitioner to be a specialist in physiology. Nevertheless, since the aim of law is to make men good, and goodness is happiness which in turn is an activity, it behooves the lawyer to have some acquaintance with psychology just as physicians of the better class devote attention to the study of the human body.[59] Aristotle also recognized the element of compulsory force in the law; there must be some force to maintain it.[60] In the *Republic* [61] Glaucon had argued that the laws are obeyed, not from a sentiment of natural law-abidingness, but through a fear of the penalties which will be imposed if we break them. Those penalties are imposed by force, and thus the police and prisons are necessary elements

---

[57] *E. N.* 1105[b] 16.
[58] *E. N.* 1103[b] 5.
[59] *E. N.* 1102[a] 18.
[60] *Polit.* 1286[b] 32, 1255[b] 15; *E. N.* 1180[a] 22.
[61] 360C.

of a society. In analytical jurisprudence this doctrine has reappeared in the distinction taken between social orders which rest on voluntary obedience and the legal order which is based on coercion. It is true that in some communities conformity to a social order is a matter of choice, e. g. in large cities in the United States church attendance is voluntary; it is also equally true that sanctions for the violation of other orders may be more severe than the penalty for the violation of a law. In some Southern communities of the United States, the non-churchgoing member may find the sanction for the violation of a rule of the society so effective that he will be unable to obtain work of any kind and thus be compelled to move elsewhere. To argue otherwise than in a formal juristic sense that the sanctions of custom are imperfect because no man is under an absolute compulsion to visit the barber, or to wear garments of usual design is to shut the eyes to the true effectiveness of the sanctions behind custom. Which sanction would a railroad conductor choose for imposition on himself in the event he lost his temper and struck a passenger: ten dollars and costs in the police court for disorderly conduct or loss of his job and blacklisting throughout the business? Coercion is undoubtedly an element in the legal order, but it is also an element in many other orders. Aristotle's insistence upon habit as one of the bases of legal obedience is also sound and is a valuable corrective to the formal excesses of analytical jurisprudence.

THEORY OF LEGISLATION

Aristotle's normative view of law is clearly apparent in his theory of legislation. The law prescribes certain conduct; the conduct of a brave man (*e. g.* not to desert or run away or to throw away his weapons), that of a temperate man (*e. g.* not to commit adultery or outrage), that of a gentle man (*e. g.* not to assault or abuse), and so with all the other virtues and vices, prescribing some actions and prohibiting others—rightly if the law has been rightly enacted, not so well if it has been

made at random.[62] The science of legislation must be learned
like any other science. No doubt it is possible for a particular
individual to be successfully treated by some one who is not
a trained physician, but who has an empirical knowledge based
on careful observation of the effects of various forms of treatment upon the person in question; just as some people appear
to be their own best doctors, though they could not do any
good to someone else. Nevertheless, it would doubtless be
agreed that anyone who wishes to make himself a professional
and a man of science must advance to general principles, and
acquaint himself with them by the proper method: for science
deals with the universal. So presumably a man who wishes to
make other people better by discipline, must endeavor to
acquire the science of legislation—assuming that it is possible
to make us good by laws. For to mold aright the character
of any and every person that presents himself is not a task
that can be done by anybody, but only (if at all) by the man
with scientific knowledge, just as is the case in medicine and
the other professions involving a system of treatment and the
exercise of prudence.[63] This is an enlargement of the Socratic
theory that virtue is knowledge; since our passions and emotions
are not good or bad but are ethically neutral, they must be
trained to make us desire what is right; mere knowledge is
not sufficient to make us do right.

Plato [64] had held that legislation should be so framed that
it could be incorporated in a manual of instruction for the
young. Aristotle does not take exception to this view but he
indulges in a severe criticism of the Sophists for attempting
to teach legislation from existing codes of law.[65]

From whom then or how, Aristotle asks, can the science of
legislation be learned? He answers: Perhaps like other subjects,

---

[62] *E. N.* 1129[b] 20.

[63] *E. N.* 1180[b] 16.

[64] *Laws* 810B, 811B.

[65] *E. N.* 1180[b] 28. On whether Aristotle is here referring to the Sophists of the
fifth century, such as Gorgias and Protagoras, or to contemporary teachers of
rhetoric such as Isocrates, see Barker, *The Politics of Aristotle* (1946) 357-8.

from the experts, namely, the politicians; for legislation is apparently a branch of political science. But there is this difference between political science and all other sciences. In these, the persons who teach the science are the same as those who practice it, for instance, physicians and painters; but in politics the Sophists, who profess to teach the science, never practice it. It is practiced by the politicians, who apparently rely more upon a kind of empirical skill than on the exercise of abstract intelligence; for we do not see them writing or lecturing about political principles (though this might be a more honorable employment than composing forensic and parliamentary speeches), nor have they ever made their sons or friends into statesmen. Yet we should expect them to have done so if it were in their power; they could not have bequeathed any better legacy to their country. Still it must be admitted that experience does much good; for we see that those who live in a political environment become politicians.

It follows that those who aspire to a scientific knowledge of politics require practical experience as well as theory.

However, those Sophists who profess to teach politics are found to be very far from doing so successfully. In fact, they do not know what it is, or what it is concerned with; otherwise, they would not class it as identical with, or even inferior to, the art of rhetoric. They would not have thought it easy to legislate by merely collecting such laws as are held in high repute, and selecting the best of them—as if the selection did not demand intelligence—as if all did not depend on deciding rightly! Who, we would ask, is the intelligent judge of the product of any art—of the musical composition or painting? The experienced musician or painter. Now laws are the product, so to speak, of the art of politics. How then can a mere collection of laws teach a man the science of legislation, or make him able to judge which of them is the best. We do not see men becoming expert physicians from a study of medical handbooks. Yet medical writers attempt to describe not only general courses of treatment, but also methods of cure and modes of treatment for particular sorts of patients classified according to their various habits of body; and their treatises appear to be of value for men who have had practical experience though they are useless to the novice. Very possibly, therefore, collections of laws and constitutions may be serviceable to students capable of studying them critically and judging what measures are valuable or the reverse, and what kind of institutions are suited to what national characteristics. But those who examine such compilations without possessing a trained faculty cannot be capable of judging them correctly, unless, indeed, by accident, though they may very likely sharpen their political intelligence.

Aristotle concludes that as his predecessors had left the subject of legislation unexamined he will proceed to state its general postulates, a statement exceedingly unfair to Plato who had worked out an elaborate legislative theory.

Accordingly, Aristotle laid down a series of principles to control and guide the legislative process. The best legislators, he believed, were from the middle class, giving as instances Solon and Lycurgus and remarking that in fact almost the greatest number of the other lawgivers had that status.[66] In the *Laws* Plato had said that the legislator ought to have his eyes directed to two points—the people and the country.[67] As an example Plato cited the Cretan lawgiver who chose for the Cretans bows and arrows which were the most suitable arms for swift runners in a hilly country like Crete. Aristotle accepts this principle but adds to it the corollary that neighboring states must not be forgotten by the legislator if the state for which he legislates is to have a true political life, that is to say, a life of intercourse with other states. A nation's arms should be such as to enable it to meet its foes in its own territory and in theirs, something bows and arrows would not enable it to do. For this reason there must be a fleet, the government must be organized with a view to military strength, and the legislator

---

[66] *Polit.* 1296ᵃ 16.
[67] An uncertain reference. Perhaps *Laws* 704-709, 747D, 625C, 842C-E.

must pay attention to the foreign relations of the state.[68] Still, the legislator should not make conquest the aim of his state; it is the province of the legislative art, if the state has neighbors to consider what the practices should be in relation to each sort of neighbor. It was a mistake for the Lacedaemonian legislators to lay down one indiscriminating rule; the rule ought to vary in accordance with the character of the neighboring state. Isocrates had maintained that laws affect only the internal organization of states, and not their mutual relations. The legislator must know all possible forms of the state, and he should be able to find remedies for the defects of existing constitutions. He must know what sort of democratic institutions save and what destroy a democracy, and what sort of oligarchical institutions save and destroy an oligarchy; he must not think that a law is democratic or oligarchic which will cause the state to be democratically or oligarchically governed in the greatest degree, but which will cause it to be so governed for the longest time. In amending the constitutions of democracies and oligarchies it is necessary to distinguish between the different kinds and to handle each kind in a different way, so that those who recognize only one kind of democracy and one of oligarchy cannot properly amend their constitutions. The same political insight will enable a legislator to know which laws are the best, and which are suited to different constitutions; for the laws are, and ought to be, relative to the constitution, and not the constitution to the laws.[69] The legislator must know under what conditions each form of constitution will prosper and by what internal developments or external attacks each of them tends to be destroyed. By destruction through internal developments Aristotle means that all constitutions, except the best one of all, are destroyed both by not being pushed far enough and by being pushed too far. Thus, democracy loses its vigor, and finally passes into oligarchy, not only when it is not pushed

[68] *Polit.* 1265ᵃ 18, 1267ᵃ 20, 1327ᵃ 23, 1325ᵃ 11. Isocrates, *De Antid.* § 79.
[69] *Polit.* 1289ᵃ 7; 1309ᵇ 35; 1320ᵃ 2.

far enough, but also when it is pushed a great deal too far;
just as the aquiline and the snub nose not only turn into
normal noses by not being aquiline or snub enough, but also,
by being too violently aquiline or snub, arrive at a condition
in which they no longer look like noses at all, *e. g.*, it is altogether effaced or becomes a beak.[70] This is an application of
the doctrine that it is in the " mean " state alone that the
constitution can be said to keep its true character. For example,
if the principle of democracy is equality, and if this principle
is exaggerated so that everybody actually becomes equal, then
the government degenerates into mob-rule or anarchy and
thus loses its true democratic character; if it is relaxed and the
equality diminished, the democratic institutions become so
enfeebled that the inequalities increase until at last we are
in the presence of an oligarchy. Constitutions differ because
the deliberative, magisterial, and judicial elements are organized in different ways, and the legislator must have regard
to what is expedient in each state.[71] The legislator must not
trust to fortune to make certain of the virtue of the state;
to secure this is not the function of fortune but of science and
policy.[72] In his aims the legislator must always be modest
and never attempt the impossible.[73]

Shall legislation have in view the good of all or that of a
privileged class when several classes coexist in a state? Aristotle's reply is that the laws must be equal, and this means
that legislation must aim at the good of the whole state.[74]
Moreover, all should share alike in ruling and being ruled in
turn, for when the sharers are alike, equality demands that each
shall have an identity of political privilege.[75] The legislator

[70] *Rhet.* 1360ᵃ 22.
[71] *Polit.* 1297ᵇ 37. The legislative, executive and judicial elements of modern
theory do not correspond to Aristotle's three " elements of all constitutions." Aristotle's deliberative element had legislative functions but it also had executive and
judicial ones as well. 2 Zeller, *Aristotle and the Earlier Peripatetics* (1897) 283.
[72] *Polit.* 1273ᵇ 22, 1332ᵃ 32.
[73] *Polit.* 1265ᵃ 17, 1325ᵇ 38. This was a Platonic principle. *Laws* 709D, 742E,
Rep. 456C.
[74] *Polit.* 1283ᵇ 40.
[75] *Polit.* 1332ᵇ 25.

must always favor the middle class in order to give stability to the government; the laws must prevent oppression of the rich and tend permanently to increase the material prosperity of the poor. Nevertheless, in anticipation of the Marxists, he recognizes that the law in fact may be the expression of the will of a particular class.[76] In a well-ordered state the citizens should have leisure and not have to provide for their daily wants.[77]

In all this Aristotle was viewing law, and particularly legislation, as a concrete expression of a moral ideal. He saw legislation as an instrument through which the standard of human conduct could be lifted above the practices which prevailed in the societies he had studied. He is not so much intent upon telling legislators what laws to enact as upon instructing them in the general theory of legislation itself.

EQUITY

Equity ($\dot{\epsilon}\pi\iota\epsilon\iota\kappa\epsilon\dot{\iota}\alpha$) in Aristotle's [78] hands can be viewed narrowly in modern terms, as a rule of construction. It is also the Cerberus of the legal system; it is the attempt to work out philosophically the meaning of the idea of fairness in its application to concrete legal systems. Plato [79] had recognized that the appearance of a philosopher king, an expert who could be trusted to rule in disregard of the written law, was unlikely; we must therefore accept the second best, the

[76] *Polit.* 1296[b] 35; 1320[a] 4-1320[b] 16; 1281[a] 37, 1282[b] 10.

[77] *Polit.* 1269[a] 34, 1273[a] 32, 1331[b] 12.

[78] *Rhet.* 1373[b] 25-1374[b] 23; *E. N.* V, 10. It is not unusual to find Aristotle's treatment of this topic criticized as mere metaphysical web-spinning, and as evidence of the academic character of his thought, which is held to be "remote from legal practice and real problems." See, *e. g.*, Schulz, *History of Roman Legal Science* (1946) 75. For the opposite view see Allen, *Law in the Making* (1927) 201 *et seq.*; 2 Vinogradoff, *Outlines of Historical Jurisprudence* (1922) 64 *et seq.* As Vinogradoff observes, the idea has had such an influence on modern developments of the theory of law that the framers of the Code Napoléon in 1804 thought it necessary to restate Aristotle's doctrine in their introductory chapter. Contemporary opinion now accords Aristotle a wide knowledge of law and legal science. See Calhoun, *Introduction to Greek Legal Science* (1944) 72.

[79] *Polit.* 295AB.

government of fixed, inflexible law which cannot always do
justice to the individual case. Aristotle analyzed the idea with
care and gave it a wider scope.

To bring out his meaning he puts a concrete case. The law
provides a penalty for an offender who inflicts a wound by an
iron weapon, or by iron in general. If a man wearing an iron
ring strikes another, by the letter of the law he is liable to the
penalty and has committed a crime; but in truth and in fact
he is not guilty of the crime and in this fair interpretation
lies equity.[80] Equity therefore is a kind of justice, *e. g.*, fairness,
but beyond the written law. It is a rectification of the written
law, to supply deficiencies consequent upon its universality.
The failure of the legislature to provide for the particular case
is partly intentional, partly unintentional; involuntary, when
it may have escaped their notice, voluntary when it is necessary
to lay down a general rule, and this rule has exceptions which
cannot be foreseen and determined; and also by reason of the
infinite variety of possible cases that may arise, no two of
which are exactly alike. Legal rules, which are general, require
constant modification and adaptation to circumstances, and
this is equity, the mitigation of the austerity or the relaxation
of the exact rigor of the written law, and a leaning to the side
of mercy, indulgence, liberality.

Since law is general, equity must always be on the watch to
see that justice is done in the individual case. It is equity

[80] Quintilian gives the same case. *Inst. Orat.* VII. 6. 8. The present-day movement for individualization of justice favors greater discretion. See Pound, *Law in
Books and Law in Action* (1910), 44 Am. L. Rev. 12; Wigmore, *A Program for
the Trial of a Jury Trial* (1929), 12 J. Am. Jud. Soc'y 166; Frank, *Law and the
Modern Mind* (1930). Wigmore has shown that a satisfactory legal system has
functioned in which courts were expressly authorized to treat all cases as unique.
See Wigmore, *The Legal System of Old Japan* (1892), 4 Green Bag 403. These
writers have also shown that when the rules lead to results that offend the " sense
of justice," discretion enters by the back door through general verdicts by juries,
decisions by trial courts unaccompanied by findings of fact, or the twisting of such
findings so that they misreport the facts. All this has led Judge Frank to suggest
that we ought carefully to study the Japanese system " and to consider substantial
modifications of our own, instead of adhering to our present misleading and somewhat hypocritical practice of sanctioning furtive, unavowed, exercises of discretion."
See Frank, *Say It With Music* (1948), 61 Harv. L. Rev. 921, 953.

therefore to pardon human failings, and to look to the law-giver and not to the law; to the spirit and not to the letter; to the intention and not to the action; to the whole and not to the part; to the character of the actor in the long run and not in the present moment; to remember good rather than evil, and good that one has received, rather than good that one has done; to bear being injured; to wish to settle a matter by words rather than by deeds; lastly, to prefer arbitration to judgment, for the arbitrator sees what is equitable, but the judge sees only the law, and for this an arbitrator was first appointed, in order that equity might flourish. Indefinite circumstances require a flexible rule like the leaden one used by Lesbian builders, adapted to the shape of the stone used.

This view has theoretical merits, but it runs at once into a practical difficulty. Equitable principles in their application are governed by rules or they are not; if not, justice ceases to be uniform, one of its most valuable characteristics; if it is, equity itself soon becomes as rigid as the written law; in the first case, the leaden rule becomes so soft that it can hardly be used, in the second, so rigid that it is indistinguishable from an iron one.

Equity is a part of the unwritten law. Aristotle divided law into two classes, particular and general; the former is either written or unwritten, the latter is unwritten, is based upon nature and embraces the great fundamental conceptions of morality and is superior to all the conventional enactments of human society. Equity is that kind of unwritten law which belongs to particular law and is what is omitted by (*i. e.*, intended to supply the deficiencies of) the written law. It is, therefore, a law of mercy or clemency, the particular decision adapted to the special occasion where the written general law fails to meet the case.

Aristotle's treatment of unwritten law when coupled with his teleological doctrine suggests his answer to the question raised by the Sophists, whether law was right by nature or by convention. He regarded it as a commonplace argument for leading men into paradoxical statements. The man whose statement agrees with the standard of nature is met by the standard of the law, but the man who agrees with the law is met by the facts of nature. Aristotle refuses to accept the antithesis. In so far as the end of law is realized it is natural, for the realization of the nature of anything is its end. In discussing civil justice, Aristotle admits a natural element and a conventional element; that is natural which has the same force everywhere, and does not depend on being adopted or not being adopted; while that is conventional which at the outset does not matter whether it be so or differently, but when men have instituted it, then matters.[81] This assertion is difficult to reconcile with other statements of Aristotle; but it has been taken to be similar to the distinction drawn in modern treatises between moral and positive laws; natural justice is law because it is right, conventional justice is right because it is law. His meaning is further brought out by his criticism of the phrase " law is said to be the ' measure ' or ' image ' of the things which are by nature just." [82] This, he says, is a bad definition; such phrases are worse than metaphors; for the latter do make their meaning to some extent clear because of the likeness involved. Whereas this kind of phrase makes nothing clear; an image arises through imitation, and this is not the case with law.

ADMINISTRATION

Another commonplace antithesis of Greek thought which Aristotle attempted to reconcile was whether the rule of man or law is best, whether, in the historic phrase, it shall be a government of laws, and not of men. Pittacus [83] had early decided in favor of law, but Solon apparently thought otherwise, as did his people.[84] In fourth century Athens only two

---

[81] *Soph. El.* 173ᵃ 7, *E. N.* 1134ᵇ 18.
[82] *Top.* 140ᵃ 6.
[83] Diod. 9. 27. 4, Diog. Laert. I, 77.
[84] Plut. *Solon*, c. 18. 3, c. 14. 3. *Cf.* Plut. *Ad. Princ. Inernd.* c. 3.

principal forms of constitution were recognized: democracy and oligarchy. Democracy was the constitution under which law ruled, or should rule, and in oligarchy men ruled without regard to law. Theseus thus urges the case of democracy in the *Suppliants*:

> *No worse foe than the despot hath a state,*
> *Under whom, first, can be no common laws,*
> *But one rules, keeping in his private hands*
> *The law: so is equality no more.*
> *But when the laws are written, then the weak*
> *And wealthy have alike but equal right.*
> *Yea, even the weaker may fling back the scoff*
> *Against the prosperous, if he be reviled.*[85]

Socrates, by asserting that he who knows should rule, gave fresh vitality to the problem. Plato [86] urged the supremacy of the wise man to the rule of law on the principle that simplicity can never encompass complexity. If law determined what is noblest and most just for all, nevertheless it could not determine what is best for them; for the differences of men and actions are so numerous, and since change is always occurring, it is impossible for any science to promulgate a simple rule for everything and for all time. In attempting this very thing law is like an ignorant and stubborn man who permits no one to question his commands even though a sounder alternative has been proposed. Why make laws at all, if this analysis is sound? Plato answers the question on the analogy of the physical training instructor who issues general orders for his class as a whole and who cannot go into details in individual cases and order what is best for each man's physique; he makes a rough general rule which will be good for the physique of the majority, such as the assignment of equal exercise to whole classes. Similarly, the legislator who watches over the human herds will never be

---

[85] 429 *et seq.* (Way's trans.)
[86] *Polit.* 294A *et seq., Laws* 874E *et seq.*

able by making laws for all collectively, to provide exactly that which is proper for each individual; he will legislate for the majority and in a general way only roughly for individuals. In the nature of things this must be the case, for no one can sit beside each person all his life and tell him exactly what is proper for him to do. Thus, if laws are promulgated the king should be at liberty to change or depart from them as circumstances indicate.

In his old age when he wrote the *Laws* Plato still held to the view that law was only a second-best; but he was more aware of its indispensability. It is really necessary, he says, for men to make themselves laws and to live according to laws, or else they will not differ from savage beasts, a metaphor which Aristotle also employed. He urged this for several reasons: Human nature is such that it is impossible for man both to perceive what is of benefit to the civic life of men and, perceiving it, to be alike able and willing to practice what is best. Even if a man should fully grasp the principle that the public interest ought to prevail over private interest, should he afterwards get control of the State and become an irresponsible autocrat his mortal nature will always urge him on to grasping and self-interested action. It is not right for reason to be subject to anything, for no law is mightier than knowledge; but genuine reason does not exist anywhere and hence it is that we have to call on law to rule.

At this point Aristotle [87] took up the discussion and subjected the problem to an analysis from several points of view. It is important to notice when his analysis is aporetic and when he is speaking for himself. It is worthwhile to examine his position in full inasmuch as it bears directly upon the vital present-day question of the degree of power to be accorded administrative agencies.

In examining the subject of kingship as a type of normal constitution, Aristotle observes that those who are for a king will say that laws enunciate only general principles but do not

[87] *Polit.* 1286ᵃ 9 *et seq.*

give directions for dealing with the circumstances of the particular case. In an art of any kind it is foolish to govern procedure by written rules: even in Egypt, where the physicians are expected to treat their patients by stereotyped written rules, they are allowed to change the treatment after four days, if desirable. However, if the objection to law is that it embodies a general principle, we must not overlook the fact that the king also must possess the general principle, so that he is open to the same objection; moreover, in the case of the ruler it will be coupled with the unsettling influence of emotion and passion which every human soul necessarily has; it will consequently be inferior. It may be answered, however, as an offset that the ruler will be better able than the law to handle the particular case.

This analysis suggests that the ruler should make laws which will be binding in all cases except where they fail to give justice in some particular case. But this raises the question, ought the one best man govern or all the citizens in matters which it is impossible for the law either to decide at all or to decide well? Aristotle's answer seems to favor the citizens, on the ground that the many judge better than one, are less corruptible, and are as inherently virtuous as a single ruler.

So far Aristotle has been discussing the case of the king who rules subject to law except where justice requires that he set the law aside. What of the absolute monarch who rules according to his own will? Some people think that it is entirely contrary to nature for one person to rule over all the citizens when the state consists of men who are alike; everybody must govern and be governed alike in turn; but this constitutes law, for regulation is law. But it may be objected that any case which the law appears to be unable to determine, a human being also would be unable to decide. The law, however, does all that can be done to meet this difficulty, for it purposely trains the rulers to deal fairly and justly with these matters. The law has this merit, that it not only regulates but educates men to supply its own inevitable defects.

Furthermore, it permits the introduction of any amendment that experience has shown is better than the established code. The rule of law is the rule of God and reason: the rule of a man involves a part rule of the brute which is present in every man in the form of desire and anger. There is really no analogy with the art of medicine. A physician is seldom drawn by spite or favoritism in a direction contrary to that which reason dictates, whereas the ruler may have a personal interest in the matter which he has to decide. Moreover, physicians themselves call in other physicians to treat them when they are ill, believing that they are unable to judge truly because they are judging about their own cases and may be influenced by feeling. Hence it is clear that when men seek for what is just they seek for what is impartial; for the law is that which is impartial. The argument against curing men by written rule and governing by written rule also applies only to one sort of law— written law; unwritten, or customary law, which is the more authoritative sort, is not affected by it. Then, again, it is certainly not easy for the single ruler to oversee a multitude of things; he will have to delegate much of his authority; and if he does so why should not supreme authority be given to the whole number at once. He repeats that " two heads are better than one," especially after they have legal training, and he states again the argument from equality.

To this point Aristotle's discussion has been kept rigorously on an aporetic basis. He has stated fully the arguments for the rule of the best man under law, and he has taken account of Plato's position in the *Politicus* notwithstanding Plato's apparent abandonment of it in the *Laws*. In their precise problematic setting the arguments for Absolute Monarchy are in the realm of the abstract in relation to the modern state which could not be administered without the aid of law even by the wisest of men. At this stage of the argument Aristotle abandons the aporetic analysis and ends the discussion by giving his own position. He remarks that what has been said is a true account of the matter in some cases, but it does not apply in others;

specifically, the arguments against the rule of the superior man unrestrained by law do not apply in the case of the individual whose virtue exceeds that of all the others. It is clear, he says, that among people who are alike and equal it is neither expedient nor just for one to be sovereign over all—neither when there are no laws, but he himself is in the place of law, nor when there are laws, neither when both sovereign and subjects are good nor when both are bad, nor yet when the sovereign is superior in virtue, except in one particular instance, *i. e.*, when he surpasses all the others in virtue.

Aristotle began with the assumption that wherever supreme authority in the State was lodged, some hardships will result,[88] and that supreme authority should be given to laws which conform to normal constitutions.[89] His analysis drove him to make an exception to this rule: it holds only when the State is composed of individuals who are equal, and does not hold where it would work injustice. If the philosopher king of Plato should ever appear on this earth his will should be paramount in the State, even over law. He was driven to make this exception in order to make his study theoretically complete; he could not logically maintain the supremacy of law in the face of the hypothetical supposition that a Heracles might appear on earth. Moreover, to the fourth-century B. C. mind, the idea of the possibility of a philosopher-king was a familiar one. Xenophon and Isocrates had drawn convincing pictures of the ideal ruler. But the conception had a deeper root. It was supported by the conviction that the rule of the superior man or superior race was a natural one. " We do not," said Plato,[90] " set oxen to rule over oxen, or goats over goats "; and so in the golden age of the reign of Cronus, demigods were set by him to rule over man " and they with great ease and pleasure to themselves, and no less to us, taking care of us and giving us peace and reverence and order and justice

---

[88] *Polit.* 1281ᵃ 14.
[89] *Polit.* 1282ᵇ 1.
[90] *Laws* 713D. For a full discussion see 1 Newman, *op. cit.* 279.

never failing," secured a life of concord and happiness to the tribes of men. " This tradition," he adds, " tells us, and tells us truly, that for cities of which some mortal and not God is the ruler, there is no escape from evils and toils." " There is in nature a principle of slave mastery," said Aristotle.[91] He believed that the appearance of a philosopher-king was most improbable but he would not hold that it was impossible; if such a ruler appeared the " truest and most divine " form of the State would be realized.[92]

Aristotle [93] elsewhere again considered the problem of the necessary insufficiency of general rules of law when applied to particular cases. The question arose in a consideration of the kind of appeal to address to a judge or jury. Aristotle held that rhetoric was an art which could be treated systematically if not scientifically; previous discussions of the subject had contributed very little to an understanding of proof, the legitimate and most effective method of persuasion, which is the reputed end of the art. If trials were everywhere conducted, as they are in some well-governed cities, the rhetorician would have nothing to say. For in those trials all appeals to a judge's passions and feelings, all attempts to excite him to anger, jealousy, compassion are rightly excluded. It is clear that the parties to an action strictly speaking have nothing to do but prove their point; whether the fact is so or not, whether the thing alleged has or has not been done. Whether it is important or unimportant, just or unjust, in all cases in which the legislature has not laid down a rule, is a matter for the judge himself to decide; it is not the business of the litigants to instruct him.

Aristotle here indulges in a digression to discuss how much should be left to the discretion of the judge. Laws properly enacted should as far as may be determine everything themselves and leave as little as possible to the discretion of the

[91] *Polit.* 1288[b] 37.
[92] *Cf. Polit.* 1289[a] 40, 1261[a] 29 *et seq.*
[93] *Rhet.* 1354[a] 15 *et seq.*

judge: first, because it is easier to find one or a few men of good sense, capable of framing laws and pronouncing judgments, than a large number; and second, because legislation is the result of long consideration, whereas the decisions of a judge are given on the spur of the moment, without much time for reflection, so that it is difficult for the judges properly to decide questions of justice or expediency. But the most important consideration of all in favor of this view is that the judgment of the legislator does not apply to a particular case, but is universal and applies to the future: he lays down general rules with refernce to future acts and events, in which he himself has no immediate interest; but when we come to the judge, he has to decide present and definite issues in which he is, or may be, directly concerned, and in which his interests and affections may be engaged; and so from this conjunction of his personal feelings and private interests with the case before him, his judgment or power of decision is clouded and he is unable to discern the truth. Questions of fact, however, past, present and future, are a necessary exception to the application of this principle: these cannot be foreseen by the legislator, and it is impossible for him to provide for them by any general regulations; they must necessarily be left to be decided as occasion arises by the ordinary judges.

Some of Aristotle's analysis must be read against the background of Greek legal procedure, for example, that the judge is not allowed sufficient time in which to deliberate. His general conclusion that the law is better than the individual but should be coupled with a power to relieve in hard cases has been the usual historical practice since his time. It represents the over-all picture today. The wide latitude accorded jury and judge in criminal cases, executive clemency, bills for special relief, the power to grant new trials in civil cases, above all, the rise of administrative agencies, are instances of attempts, haphazard though they may be, to meet Aristotle's principle. There are many gaps to be closed, as in the so-called doctrine of the law of the case; but in the absence of a systematic approach to the problem the defects will always be numerous. Aristotle's great achievement, in spite of the unique character of Greek law, lay in reaching a position which has accorded with the ideal and practices of all subsequent legal systems.

JUSTICE

With the theory of justice worked out by Aristotle we pass to a theory rich in legal content. That is to say, we are concerned in large part with justice as an application of law as opposed to justice as the whole of virtue. In the latter sense it had been the subject of Plato's greatest dialogue; its legal significance was, of course, known to him, but he had scant interest in that aspect. Aristotle's approach is different. He is interested in justice as a particular virtue; specifically, as a virtue which must be analyzed in order to make his philosophical theory of the virtues complete. Moreover, in the *Ethics* and *Politics* he was setting forth a practical philosophy, guides which would make men good, and which would instruct legislators in the management of the State. Plato's theory of justice gave no help in legal practice inasmuch as he declared the " conduct within " to be justice in the only true sense of the word,[94] while the judge's primary concern is with external action. Justice is accorded a fuller treatment than any other virtue since it is the virtue most directly connected with the welfare of the State.

Justice is divided into Universal Justice and Particular Justice, and the latter is further subdivided into Distributive Justice and Corrective Justice; the latter is again subdivided into that concerned with voluntary transactions, and that concerned with involuntary transactions, which again are either furtive (theft, adultery, etc.) or violent (assault, murder, etc.) .[95] The conceptions underlying this classification have been notably influential in subsequent thought; but their precise meaning in Aristotle's mind is not clear and the mathematical analogies to which he resorts while helpful are not conclusive.

[94] *Rep.* 443CD   [95] *E. N.* V.

It has been thought that if his ideas are read in a legal context all difficulties will be resolved. This method has been more fruitful than any other but it is in danger of being carried to an excess.

Universal Justice means, Aristotle says, complete virtue. He arrives at this definition by an appeal to popular usage. A man is unjust if he breaks the law of the land or if he takes more than his share of anything. By " just " we mean therefore what is lawful, what is fair and equal. Universal Justice is the former and Particular Justice the latter. It is clear that in one sense all that is lawful is just; for the law aims either at the common interest of all, or at the interest of a ruling class determined either by excellence or in some other similar way; so that in one of its senses the term " just " is applied to anything that produces and preserves the happiness of the political community. The law speaks on all subjects and more or less rightly commands the practice of all the virtues. Justice, then, in this sense, may be said to be the practice of entire virtue towards one's neighbors. In an abstract sense therefore the just can be identified with all law and therefore with all morality. Hence Justice is often regarded as the best of the virtues—neither the evening star nor the morning star is so admirable. This kind of Justice is not a part of virtue but the whole of virtue. However, Aristotle remarks that he is not interested in Justice in this sense: " what we are investigating is the Justice which is a part of virtue."

Juristically, Universal Justice has been interpreted to mean that in Aristotle's intention it is the source of the conception of public law, the law of things and a large part of the law of persons. Particularly it is the source of the criminal law that the state enforces as distinguished from the appeal to the courts for the redress of private wrong to individuals.[96] This interpretation has been criticized on the ground that the jurist

---

[96] Vinogradoff, *Aristotle on Legal Redress* (1908) 8 Col. L. Rev. 548; *idem.*, 2 *Outlines of Historical Jurisprudence* (1922) 57; Barker, *Greek Political Theory, Plato and His Predecessors* (1918) 47.

is attributing his own point of view to Aristotle and making him reason as a lawyer when he is really thinking more of Platonic and traditional Greek ethics than of the systematic philosophy of law.[97] Aristotle's Universal Justice appears to be an ethical, rather than a legal, conception and the legal references are brought in only in subordination to, and in illustration of, the ethical idea. Aristotle wishes to get rid of, to dismiss aş he says, the broader Platonic conception of justice as the whole of virtue before entering upon the discussion specifically of justice as a distinctive virtue. Did Aristotle have in mind the legal classification the jurists have ascribed to him? The division of justice into the two classes " obedience to laws and equitàble treatment of neighbors " is not taken over from Athenian law, but is reached by Aristotle's topical method of examining the current use of terms ($\pi o\lambda\lambda\alpha\chi\hat{\omega}\varsigma$ $\lambda\epsilon\gamma\acute{o}\mu\epsilon\nu\alpha$). These appear to be, Aristotle says, the two chief current conceptions of the word. There is no conscious discrimination between public and private law when it is stated that the law enjoins all virtue. It is an illustration and confirmation of the Platonic notion Aristotle wishes to discuss. It is only the exigencies of the theory and not any explicit statement of Aristotle that classifies criminal justice under General Justice instead of under Corrective Justice. Lastly, there appears to be no shred of evidence for the further deduction of the technical process of $\delta\iota\alpha\delta\iota\kappa\alpha\acute{\iota}\alpha$ from this same conception of General Justice. The jurists' legal mind may connect the two ideas, but Aristotle did not.

This is a strong case and has not apparently been satisfactorily answered. It has been argued in reply that such an interpretation would leave certain parts of the juridical process unexplained. If we restrict the notion of juridical justice to Distributive and Corrective Justice we would fail to account for important parts of the law. The juristic view of Aristotle's

---

[97] Shorey, *Universal Justice in Aristotle's Ethics* (1924) 19 Jr. Class. Philol. 279. Ross, *Aristotle* (3rd ed. 1937) 215. Vinogradoff's answer to the criticism is printed at the end of Shorey's article.

scheme is based on the assumption that the great encyclopedist could not have disregarded such juridical categories as crime and punishment, property and possession, relations between the city and the citizen; men have to estimate them in all systems under some standard of justice and so did the Greeks. Neither Distributive nor Corrective Justice supplies such standards, but Justice in general does supply them from the point of view of compulsory morality. This interpretation is primarily juridical but it can hardly be maintained that the confronting of a passage on justice with fundamental categories in the administration of justice must be considered as a methodological defect.

However, is it not precisely such a defect unless there is some evidence that Aristotle intended in his theory of justice to account for all the primary legal categories? The object of the whole discussion is plainly not that. It is to show that the principle of the mean is applicable to Justice as well as to other forms of goodness. More exactly, he wants to show that Justice is the establishment of a sort of proportion (ἀναλογία) [98] and that the three kinds of justice involve three different kinds of proportion. In accomplishing this end he displaces Plato's theory, which maintained that justice was always proportion, and also that of the Pythagoreans who had asserted that it was reciprocity. That he did not, contrary to his usual practice, directly allude to Plato's theory has been best accounted for by Mme. de Staël's remark that it is more than commonly true that the names we forget are those which we remember only too well. It must not be forgotten also that when Aristotle says that " the various pronouncements of the law (νόμοι) aim at the common interests of all " [99] νόμος means *law* and *custom* as sanctioned by public opinion. If Aristotle was thinking of the fundamental categories of law he must also have been thinking of the fundamental categories of custom. But where is the evidence? Even if Aristotle desired, as he apparently did, the extension of law in its strict sense to the

[98] *E. N.* 1131ᵃ 30.   [99] *E. N.* 1129ᵇ 14.

whole of life, he could not have affirmed truthfully that " the laws, *in fact*, have something to say about all that we do," although it would be true to make that remark about custom whether sanctioned by law or by public opinion. If custom is neutral it does not forbid, and fashion decides.

Distributive Justice " is exercised in the distribution of honor, wealth, and the other divisible assets of the community, which may be allotted among its members in equal or unequal shares." [100] The principle of this distribution is one of geometrical proportion and is the one which should guide the legislator. If A and B be persons, C and D lots to be divided, then as A is to B, so must C be to D. A just distribution will produce the result that A + C will be to B + D in the same ratio as A was to B originally. Distributive justice, therefore, consists of the distribution of property, honors, offices, etc., in the State according to the merits of each citizen. Concretely, if you are twice as good a citizen as I am you should be twice as honored and twice as wealthy.

Aristotle seemed to think that the rule could be applied in concrete cases and that ideally it was capable of a wider application as a regulative principle for the distribution of property and all the distinctions of society. That it was impossible to measure the immeasurable apparently did not occur to him. Historically, it represents the Platonic ideas of a harmony and proportion ruling the world, and in addition the idea of two kinds of equality, one a mere equality of number and measure, the other, the " award of Zeus," which was the equality of proportion.[101]

Corrective Justice is the rule of arithmetical proportion and is a matter for the judiciary.[102] It operates in the realm of private transactions between citizens, and therefore in the field of private and not public law. The principle takes no account of persons, but treats the cases as cases of unjust loss and gain, which have to be reduced to the middle point of equality between the parties. Justice is a mean, and the judge

[100] *E. N.* 1130ᵇ 32.   [101] *Gorg.* 507E, *Laws* 757B.   [102] *E. N.* 1131ª 1.

a sort of impersonation of justice, a mediator or equal divider. The division of Corrective Justice into voluntary and involuntary corresponds to the modern classification of. contract and tort and in Roman law to *obligationes ex contractu* and *ex delicto*. It seems clear that Aristotle had before him the distinctions of Greek law and that he was speaking in terms of Greek legal practice and probably using Greek legal terminology in so far as there was one.[103]

To the conception of justice as a mean or proportion Aristotle adds the requirement of a state of mind. There must be a deliberate purpose. An action done in ignorance and which could not be reasonably expected is called an accident; an action done in ignorance and without malice but which might reasonably be expected is a mistake (it would be negligence for us); an action done with knowledge but without deliberation (*e. g.*, in anger) is unjust but it does not imply that the doer is unjust; an action done deliberately means that both the act and the doer are unjust.[104]

In all this Aristotle no doubt had an eye on Greek legal practice, and was perhaps rationalizing aspects of it. However, he was groping for an ethical and not a legal principle. That is to say, he was searching for general principles to the effect that inequality in the treatment of individuals must be justified by the requirements of the good life seen in all its aspects. If such a principle were found, legal justice, as Plato held, could be accounted for as a special case. Aristotle's movement towards a separation of the various kinds of justice is a step away from Plato, who wished to unite all activities under one supreme rule of goodness, towards the present-day practice of perceiving a multitude of problems. Because Aristotle's theory was more specific than Plato's its influence upon legal thinking has been more marked.

---

[103] For a full discussion see Lee, *The Legal Background of Two Passages in the Nichomachean Ethics* (1937) 31 Classical Quarterly 129.

[104] *E. N.* 1135ᵃ 15.

Conclusion

At Paris in 1536 Ramus defended the radical thesis that all
the doctrines of Aristotle were false. His opponents were plainly
hard-pressed since Ramus was silenced only by an edict of
Francis I which forbade him, under pain of corporal punishment, from " uttering any more slanderous invectives against
Aristotle." Ramus' revolt was really against scholasticism and
the equating of truth with authoritative dogma. The extent to
which he himself was entangled in the coils of Aristotelianism
is clear from his own logic which, in spite of his claims to the
contrary, amounted to no more than a formal improvement
upon that of his predecessor. However, his lesson for us is that
we need not assume that a philosophical position necessarily
states doctrines of truth or falsity. Our first question may be:
Is the doctrine a serviceable one? Does it help us in the verification of hypotheses and in the prosecution of our inquiry?

By this test there is no room for debate with respect to
Aristotle's contribution to legal thought. In the first systematic legal treatise ever put forward, the work of Q. Mucius
Scaevola, the definition and classification of legal concepts
proceeded on the basis of the Aristotelian logic. He was the
first, Pomponius remarked, to " arrange the *ius civile* in *genera* "
and a clue to the meaning of this statement may be found in
Gaius' observation that he distinguished five kinds of guardianship.[105] Aristotle's doctrine of law as passionless reason, as a
form of order, as a kind of a contract, his theory that its end
was to make men good, that it must be grounded on habit, his
instrumental view of legislation, his insistence upon the necessity of the rule of fairness or equity in any legal system, his
establishment of the fundamental principle of the administrative process, his conception of justice, all have had so
obvious an influence that it is impossible to examine the work
of any subsequent legal thinker of importance without finding
some of his ideas present in an explicit form. Whether true or

[105] Gai. I. 188. Jolowicz, *Historical Introduction to Roman Law* (1932) 90.

untrue their usefulness is apparent from the fact that they have never ceased to be employed. Between Aristotle and modern legal thought there are profound differences; but those differences are due in part to a working out of his own ideas by means of the consideration of the possible alternatives.

" The Athenians have invented two things," Aristotle [106] once remarked, " wheat culture and excellent laws. The only difference is that they eat the wheat, but make no use of the laws." No one knew better than Aristotle how false this witticism was. It is true that Greek law never had the benefit of the technical analysis of professional jurists. Moreover, it never achieved the complexity which marked the Roman system; but complexity in a legal system is a direct function of the complexity of the activities it regulates. A system controlling the behavior of a city-state will need fewer elements than one which seeks to maintain the order of an area which includes most of the known world. But it was the characteristic of the Athenians that they made use of their laws. Solon was once asked which was the best policed city. " The city," he replied, " where all citizens, whether they have suffered injury or not, equally pursue and punish injustice." This idea, which was carried out in practice through the institution of large jury courts, instilled in the Athenians a passion for litigation. The law became one of the chief agencies through which public opinion expressed itself. At the same time the solutions which were reached for the large problems of substantive law have, because of their soundness, never lost their appeal to subsequent generations.

To the historian of Greek law Aristotle has a special importance. His painstaking accounts of Greek law and procedure are the chief source of our knowledge of the system. That aspect of the Aristotelian encyclopedia is beyond the limits of the present study, but it must be mentioned for completeness. An example is the detailed account of the procedure of the dikastic courts which appears in the final chapters of the

[106] Diog. Laert. V, 1, 17.

Athenian Constitution. Until the year 1937 it was believed that Aristotle's description of the allotment process with respect to jurors was so ambiguous and contained so many omissions that the process could not be understood. However, in that year a Greek allotment machine (κληρωτήριον) was discovered, and when Aristotle's meticulous text was restudied the result was a complete vindication.[107] For the legislative process, the law of property, contract, inheritance, possession, crime and punishment, tort and the other divisions of the law his writings are equally important. He was an incomparable encyclopedist, and his interest in the law was a powerful one; for the legal historian as well as the legal theorist his works, in which he systematized much of the knowledge of his time, are a matchless source of information and stimulation.

---

[107] Dow, *Aristotle, the Kleroteria, and the Courts* (1939) 50 Harv. Stud. in Class. Philology 1.

CHAPTER IV

CICERO

Cicero was a very wise man; hee wrote more than all the Philosophers and read all the Grecian books through. . . . I hope God will be merciful to him.

Luther

CHRYSIPPUS opened his book *On Law* with the definition: "Law is the ruler of all things divine and human, the settled arbiter of good and evil, the guide to justice and injustice, the sovereign and lord of all who are by nature social animals. It directs what must be done and forbids the opposite." [1] When those words were written perhaps not more than a hundred years had passed since the death of Aristotle. However, they may be taken as establishing the bridgehead on this side the gulf between ancient and modern legal thought, as summing up a social philosophy which henceforth was to be dominant in Western thinking.

Alexander, at a dramatic moment in his career in the early summer of 325 B. C., revealed a policy which subsequently became the basis of the Hellenistic philosophies. At Opis in that fateful summer he announced, after the mutiny of his troops had subsided, that the Macedonians and the Persians were both his kinsmen and he prayed especially for harmony (ὁμόνοια) and fellowship in the empire between the two peoples. [2] Napoleon has noted the conspicuous skill with which Alexander appealed to the imagination of men. Aristotle had maintained the basic inequality of human beings; the idea of the State as a whole of which man is a part; the distinction between Greek and barbarian with its corollary that the Greek race, through the mechanism of an Hellenic city-state, was the one best fitted to rule. The Hellenic philosophies, or some of

---

[1] 3 von Arnim, *Stoicorum Veterum Fragmenta* (1903) 77, no. 314.
[2] Arr. *Anab.* VII, 11, 9.

them, stimulated by the Macedonian Persian policy asserted the equality of human beings; a theory of individualism; and the doctrine of a world state, a cosmopolis,[3] in which Greek and barbarian, Jew and Gentile should all be equal. For the ideal city-state of Plato and Aristotle, the device through which the good life could be realized, there was substituted the perfect wise man of Zeno and Epicurus, the sage who alone knew the way to right living.

Those doctrines had their antecedents in earlier Greek philosophy, and in that sense the belief that the systems of Plato and Aristotle were splendid digressions from the main line of ancient speculation rather than stages in its regular development has some justification. Zeno appears to have returned to Heraclitus for his doctrine that men should live according to a single, harmonious principle in accordance with universal law; and slavery was held by some sophists to be an unnatural institution. Plato himself recognized forms of individualism in the theory that laws are made by men to protect their own selfish interests,[4] thus doing violence to the natural badness of human nature; and in the idea that law, the despot of mankind, often constrains us against nature.[5] In the latter aspect individualism, as an expression of goodness, is led by law to unnatural deeds. Whatever may be the philosophical antecedents of the Hellenistic philosophies their humanistic tendencies were fully worked out when Cicero came to study them. Iambulus had sketched his great Utopia of the Islands and Children of the Sun in which humanitarian principles are developed to their ultimate political significance.[6] Christianity extended further the notion of equality as in the emphasis on the cardinal virtue of unlimited openhandedness; and the French Revolution, which enthusiastic French critics[7] trace to third century stoicism, gave new impetus to the Hellenistic ideas for the modern world; but the significant break in the

[3] Diog. Laert. VI, 2, 63. [5] 337C-D.
[4] *Rep.* 359A. [6] Diod. II, 55-60.
[7] 2 Denis, *Histoire des théories et des idées morales dans l'antiquité* (1856) 191; 1 Janet, *Histoire de la science politique* (n. d.) 249-250.

metaphysical foundations of ancient and modern legal thought lies in the Hellenistic period with its development on the ethical side to fuller dimensions of the idea of the " inhabited world " or οἰκουμένη.[8]

Cicero was the inheritor of this complex tradition. In philosophy he followed the teaching of Carneades and denied the certainty of knowledge; he held that the differences between opinions were differences merely of probability.[9] However, in the theory of law Cicero renounced agnosticism and followed the views of Antiochus who declared knowledge to be possible. Cicero was the statesman who was also the intellectual, one of the first since the classical days of Greece and the most influential of his type in the history of the West. No doubt he is open to the accusation, which has been brought against his great successor Burke, of approaching his philosophical problems with something of a sinister interest in solving them in one way rather than another. That weakness of the man of affairs turned philosopher is evidently a customary one. At the same time Cicero's speculations have all the strength of being brought to a focus upon the concrete. He was a Utopian, but he was also the statesman who had learned the value of testing ideas by reference to the actual affairs of men. How soundly his political and legal philosophies were conceived is made apparent by the fact that they served as the basis of the Augustan policy of restoration fifteen years after his death. The triumph of his humanism was even greater. It was perpetuated by the Fathers of the Church, and at the Renaissance his works became the touchstone of enlightened inquiry, thus extending the humanity of Stoicism to the present day.

---

[8] The first professed study of the Alexandrian revolution is Tarn, *Alexander the Great and the Unity of Mankind,* Proceedings of the British Academy (1933) 123. For a later view see Ehrenberg, *Aspects of the Ancient World* (1946) 175, where it is maintained that Alexander's idea was to build an empire which would unite the peoples of the earth without forcing any of them into slavery. Professor Ehrenberg believes it may be doubted that Alexander subscribed to the doctrine of the unity of mankind.

[9] *ad Att.* XII, 52.

Methodus Jurisprudentiae

Cicero in writing to Atticus took a modest view of his accomplishments: " You will say, ' What is your method in compositions of this kind? ' They are merely copies, and cost me comparatively little labor. I supply only the words, of which I have a copious flow." Elsewhere, however, he placed a different value on his compositions: " As is my custom, I shall at my own option and discretion draw from the Stoics in such measure and in such manner as shall suit my purpose." [10] " For our part we do not play the rôle of a mere translator, but, while preserving the doctrines of our chosen authorities, add thereto our own criticism and our own arrangement." [11] In the setting down of his legal philosophy he clearly had Plato's *Laws* open before him as he wrote and occasionally the writings of some of the Stoics. Nevertheless, his fusion of Greek and Hellenistic legal speculation is of a notable order and warrants study on its own account. Moreover, as we shall see, there is an original element in his legal philosophy. That originality is small in extent and is clearly suggested by his experiences as an advocate. It sounds a new note, however, in juristic thought and cannot be matched by anything in the writings that preceded him.

Cicero was the first to raise the question: Why is jurisprudence worth studying? Though he was the leading practicing lawyer of his day he had no use for the contemporary Diceys who held their noses when the subject was mentioned. It is not likely that the question would ever have occurred to a Greek of the Fourth Century B. C. since there was no body of positive law, maintained by a highly skilled class of advocates, from which jurisprudence could be rigidly separated. Cicero recognized the field of positive law as a domain for separate study; but he refused to write treatises on the law of eaves and house-walls, on contract and court procedure. Those subjects had been carefully treated by many writers

[10] *de off.* I, 6.   [11] *de fin.* 1, 6.

and were of a humbler character, he believed, than what was
expected of him. There were many eminent men in Rome whose
business it was to interpret the civil law to the people and
answer questions in regard to it. Those men, though they have
made great claims, have spent their time on unimportant
details. What subject indeed is so vast as the law of the state,
but what is so trivial as the task of those who give legal
advice? However, it is a necessary social function. The professional lawyers are not altogether ignorant of the principles
of jurisprudence; but they have carried their studies of the
civil law, from this point of view, only far enough to accomplish
their purpose of being useful to their clients. From the standpoint of knowledge all this amounts to little, though for practical purposes it is indispensable.[12] In maintaining this position
Cicero is perhaps insisting upon the Platonic thesis that knowledge is an ultimate value, important on its own account and
not as a means to other things.[13] He saw that it was a mistake
to defend jurisprudence on the ground of its usefulness to
positive law, a lesson which modern jurists have even yet not
learned. If the sole justification of jurisprudence is its usefulness to positive law then it will never achieve the status of an
independent science inasmuch as a science of means is always
controlled by the ends. It was clear to Cicero that jurisprudence was something more than a dependent science.

In fact, he expressly took an opposite position. His theory
of law was to possess complete generality, in particular to be
so general that the *ius civile* would be merely a special case
easily subsumed under a wider principle.[14] Like Plato he had
already written a treatise on the constitution of the ideal state,
and he now proposed to write one on its laws. He stated
with care the method which would lead him to those laws.
Cicero neither believed, as our present day realists and the
majority of his fellow workers believed, that the science of law

[12] *de leg.* 1, 14. Unfortunately Cicero's treatise *De Iure Civili in Artem Redi-
gendo*, mentioned by Aulus Gellius, I. xxii. 7, is lost.

[13] *Rep.* 475 *et seq.*

[14] *de leg.* 1, 17.

could be derived from the praetor's edict, nor did he believe, as the Austinians and his own immediate predecessors believed, that the science of law could be drawn from the Twelve Tables. A science of law must be based on the fundamental principles of philosophy. It must be borne in mind in such an inquiry, Cicero points out, that we are not learning how to protect ourselves legally, or how to advise clients. Those in truth are important tasks. But the present discussion is along wider lines than that called for by the practice of the courts. Cicero's declared subject is the whole range of universal law and enactments. In order to do this the nature of law must be explained, and it must be sought for in the nature of man; then the laws by which all states ought to be governed must be considered; and finally the *iura civilia* already formulated for particular countries, including Rome, will be studied. No other kind of discussion can reveal so clearly how much has been bestowed upon man by nature, what a wealth of endowments have been implanted in the human mind, why we have been born and placed in the world, what it is that united men, and what natural fellowship there is among them. For it is only after all these things have been made clear that the origin of law and justice can be discovered.

THE NATURE OF LAW

Cicero knew many kinds of law but his legal theory, under the influence of a commonplace Stoic idea, was dominated by the conception of a " true law " (*vera lex*). He knew *lex* as the written law, and *ius* not only as denoting what is right and fair, but as law in the most general sense of the word and also as referring to a particular system of law. In its plural form *iura* were the ordinances, rules, rules of law, decisions on points of law; *iura* were also the separate provisions, *lex* the whole enactment containing them. He knew also the divine law (*fas*). One of Cicero's contributions to philosophy was the invention of a Latin philosophical vocabulary which reappeared in modern European languages. Thus we find him using as importations from Aristotle *ius* or *lex naturae* (δίκαιον κατὰ φύσιν) in the sense of an ideal law which may or may not have an existence in universal practice, but which ought to have. Similarly, the *ius civile*, the law governing citizens, has its Aristotelian counterpart in the δίκαιον νόμιμον. As a corollary to the *ius naturae* Cicero employed the phrase *ius gentium*, which he stated had been used by his predecessors; by the phrase he apparently meant, when he wanted to distinguish it from the *ius naturae*, legal usage actually existing everywhere as distinguished from the ideal law (*ius naturae*) which might not exist. *Ius gentium* was a world common law, the principles applicable to cases in which the parties were not both Roman citizens and in which, therefore, no appeal could be made to the *ius civile*. He used the phrase *ius communis* to mean the law which he and the person whom he is addressing acknowledge. He thought of customary law (*consuetudo*) as that which has been approved by common consent of long standing and which may not have been ratified by statute. He drew a sharp distinction between public law and private law. He had many more phrases and combinations of phrases to denote further kinds of law.[15] Plainly, we are in the presence of a man to whom legal distinctions were important and who was fortunate enough to have before him a body of material which would permit the making of distinctions.

As a professed philosopher it was Cicero's business to systematize this miscellaneous collection of the kinds of law. He states expressly that he is following the method of the philosophers—not those of former times, but the modern ones who have built workshops, so to speak, for the production of wisdom.[16] Formerly, problems were argued loosely and at

[15] Nettleship, *Contributions to Latin Lexicography* (1889) 497 *et seq.* 1 Costa, *Cicerone Giureconsulto* (1927) 13 *et seq.*

[16] *de leg.* 1, 36. Cicero is here following Plato who insisted upon the trained philosophic intellect as the supreme authority in law. *Laws* 714A. *Cf. de leg.* 1, 17-18. Dialectics, in Cicero's opinion, was the instrument that would transform jurisprudence into an art and would make possible the systematic study of law. *Brut.* XLI. 152-3.

great length; Cicero thought they were now examined systematically and point by point. For that reason Cicero wanted to be especially careful not to lay down first principles that had not been wisely considered and thoroughly investigated. He does not expect to demonstrate his doctrine to the satisfaction of everyone for that is impossible; but he does look for the approval of all who believe that everything which is right and honorable is to be desired for its own sake, and that nothing whatever is to be accounted a good unless it is intrinsically praiseworthy, or at least that nothing should be considered a great good unless it can rightly be praised for its own sake. Of all such, therefore, Cicero expected the approval, whether they have remained in the Old Academy with Speusippus, Xenocrates, and Polemon; or have followed Aristotle and Theophrastus who differ slightly from the Old Academy in mode of presentation; or, in agreement with Zeno, have changed the terminology without altering the ideas; or even if they have followed the strict and severe sect of Aristo, now broken up and refuted, and believe everything except virtue and vice to be on an absolute equality. So far, however, as those philosophers (the Epicureans) are concerned who practice self-indulgence, are slaves to their own bodies, and test the desirability or undesirability of everything on the basis of pleasure and pain, Cicero bids them, even if they are right (for he feels no need to quarrel with them here) to carry on their discussions in their own gardens, and even requests them to abstain for a while from taking any part in matters affecting the state, which they neither understand nor have ever wished to understand. He implores the New Academy formed by Arcesilaus and Carneades to be silent, since it contributes nothing but confusion to all these problems; for if it should attack what Cicero thinks he has constructed and arranged so beautifully, it would do great mischief. At the same time he would like to pacify this school, and so does not dare to banish it from the discussion.

Two points stand out in this discourse. There is a clear

conception of system,[17] but it is rudimentary. As stated it means a strict and distinct enumeration of points. In practice, however, as will appear, it also includes the idea of classification and its corollary, subsumption. Nowhere do the notions of fact, hypothesis, verification, systematic doubt, axiomatization, simplicity, theory, abstraction, explanation, appear explicitly though the elements of some of them are evident in the subsequent analysis. Cicero's attempt to systematize the kinds of law, therefore, is self-conscious, and slightly more explicitly sophisticated than that of Plato and Aristotle. His practice does not go beyond theirs but what they take for granted he particularizes and states as a principle of all scientific systematization. Aristotle's method of aporetic analysis is an instance of Cicero's principle but the converse would not be true. From the discourse it is also clear that there will be an identification of the legal and the moral. Until modern times there has been no effort in natural law thinking to separate the law that is from the law that ought to be; although Cicero, as we shall see, was aware of the distinction in the field of positive law, he assumed, as have most jurists who have employed the natural law approach, that it was a necessary implication of the natural law doctrine that law and morals were to be identified.

Cicero perceived three kinds of law operating in the world and this classification apparently embraced all the forms with which he was familiar. There is first the heavenly law (*lex caelestis*).[18] He observes it has been the opinion of the wisest men that law is not a product of human thought, nor is it any enactment of peoples, but something eternal which rules the whole universe by its wisdom in command and prohibition.

[17] Cicero also proposed a plan for the systematization of positive law (*de or.* 1, 190) which was influential in the sixteenth century revival of juristic studies. See Hotman, *Dialecticae Institutionis Libri* IIII (1573) 117. Holland thought that Cicero's plan was "the clearest possible description of an analytical science of law." *Elements of Jurisprudence* (10th ed. 1906). 6n.1. However, it is now argued that the professional jurists had a better grasp of the nature of jurisprudence than Cicero. Schulz, *History of Roman Legal Science* (1946) 69.

[18] *de leg.* 2, 8.

Thus they have been accustomed to say that law is the primal and ultimate mind of God, whose reason directs all things either by compulsion or restraint. Therefore, that law which the gods have given to the human race has been justly praised; for it is the reason and mind of a wise lawgiver applied to command and prohibition.

Plato's [19] playful account of the origin of law may have been in the back of Cicero's mind as he set forth this idea, although as he develops its main foundations, it is obviously Stoic. In the old days Plato pointed out Cronos ruled us through his daemons (δαίμονες). Today there is in man a divine part— his *mind*—and this divine element must do as Cronos did and appoint subordinate ministers for our government. These ministers we may call not δαίμονας but νοῦ διανομάς, " the arrangements " or " appointments made by the intellect " and to which we give the name of "laws." Elsewhere Cicero refers to the contention that nothing is more divine than reason and quotes Chrysippus as identifying Jupiter with the mighty law, everlasting and eternal, which is our guide of life and instructress in duty, and which he entitles Necessity or Fate, and the Everlasting Truth of future events.[20] That he has in mind a kind of law distinct from natural law is clear from his discussion of wrongful gains as being contrary to the law of nature (in this case *ius gentium*), the statutes of particular communities, and the " Reason which is in Nature, which is the law of gods and men " (*ipsa naturae ratio, quae est lex divina et humana*).[21]

At the point in the dialogue of *De Legibus* at which Cicero first develops the idea of law as the ultimate mind of God his brother Quintus interrupts him and demands a fuller explanation. He remarks that Cicero has, on more than one

[19] *Laws* 714A. *Cf.* 715C, 762E. 1 England, *Laws of Plato* (1921) 441. England suggests that when Cicero connects νόμος with νέμειν, as being so called " a suum cuique tribuendo," he is very possibly thinking of Plato's association here of διανομή with νόμος, but he leaves Plato's τοῦ νοῦ out of sight. See also *Laws* 624A, 835C; *Minos* 333.
[20] *de n. d.* 1. 37; 1. 40.   [21] *de off.* 3. 23.

occasion, already touched on this topic. But before Cicero comes to treat of the laws of peoples, Quintus would be grateful if he would make the character of this heavenly law clear to him, so that the waves of habit may not carry him away and sweep him into the common mode of speech on such subjects.

Cicero agrees that there should be a true understanding of the matter. He quotes a rule from the Twelve Tables and observes that it, together with other rules of the same kind, is called " law." These commands and prohibitions of nations have the power to summon to rectitude and away from wrongdoing. However, this power is not merely older than the existence of nations and states, it is coeval with that God who guards and rules heaven and earth. For the divine mind cannot exist in a state devoid of reason; and divine reason must necessarily have this power to establish right and wrong. Prior to written law reason existed, derived from the nature of the universe, urging men to right conduct and diverting them from wrongdoing; and this reason did not first become law when it was written down, but when it first came into existence; and it came into existence simultaneously with the divine mind. Therefore, the true and supreme law, whose commands and prohibitions are equally authoritative, is the right reason of the Sovereign Jupiter.

Lactantius [22] has preserved for us an eloquent passage by Cicero describing the *lex caelestis* at greater length: There is in fact a true law, right reason, agreeing with nature, diffused among all men, unchanging and eternal; it summons to duty by its commands, and deters from wrong by its prohibitions. Its commands and prohibitions are not laid upon good men in vain, but are without effect on the bad. It is a sin to try to alter this law, nor is it allowable to attempt to repeal any part of it, and to annul it wholly is impossible. We cannot be

---

[22] *Inst. Div.* VI, 8. 6-9. Cicero, *de rep.* 3. 33. This passage is customarily quoted as an illustration of natural law. From the context in Lactantius it is clear, however, that the *lex caelestis* is meant.

freed from its obligations by senate or people, and we need not look outside ourselves for an expounder or interpreter of it. It will not lay down one rule at Rome and another at Athens, or different laws now and in the future; but there will be one law, eternal and unchangeable, binding at all times upon all peoples. There will be, as it were, one common master and ruler of men, namely God, who is the author of this law, its interpreter, and its sponsor. The man who will not obey it will abandon his better self, and in denying the true nature of a man, will thereby suffer the severest of penalties, although he has escaped all the other consequences which men call punishment.

That is a clear statement of the Stoic doctrine of the Logos carried over explicitly into jurisprudence. Heraclitus had laid it down that "all things happen in accordance with the Word"[23] and that men must "hold fast to that which is common to all, as a city holds fast to its law, and much more strongly still; for all human laws are nourished by the one divine law."[24] Assertions such as these were transformed by the Stoics into the doctrine of a κοινὸς λόγος which ruled the universe. An early work by Zeno, the *Republic*, was an attempt to answer the argument of Plato's *Republic* and to show that the perfect state must include the entire world. A man would not say "I am an Athenian," but would follow Socrates and regard himself as a native and citizen of the world. At the basis of this speculation was the belief, taken over from physics, that the universe is governed by law, which essentially is the law of reason. Morality as an expression of reason represents the commands and prohibitions of the divine law. "Act according to nature" summed up the general ethical teaching. In its legal sense the Logos becomes the Platonic rule of Right Reason (ὀρθός λόγος, *vera ratio*) which pervades all things and which commands what ought to be done and forbids the opposite.[25] Cicero could never understand how Zeno convinced

[23] *Fr. 2.*   [24] *Fr. 91.*   [25] Diog. Laert. VII, 88; Cicero, *de leg.* I, 18.

himself that this law was alive.[26] Eventually the conception took its place in the Digest in Chrysippus' definition of law as the Queen of all things, human and divine, a paraphrase of Pindar.[27]

Although the Roman jurists were able to work the Logos out in practice by means of the doctrine of the law of nature, the imagination of the Stoics was too idealistic to foresee the possibility of its use in positive law. Zeno wanted to abolish law courts altogether.[28] He also argued that the practice of permitting both sides to be heard in an action at law ended in a dilemma. If the plaintiff has plainly proved his case, there is no need to hear the defendant, for the question is at an end; if he has not proved it, it is the same case as if the plaintiff had not appeared to prosecute his cause when the case was called, or had appeared and offered no evidence; so that, whether the plaintiff has proved or not proved his case, the defendant should not be heard. To this Plutarch [29] replied that Plato had either proved or not proved those things which he set forth in the *Republic*; but in neither case was it necessary for Zeno to write against him.

Cicero as a practical lawyer attempted to give concrete meaning to the idea of a *lex caelestis*. As an instance he cited the case of Cocles who took his stand on a bridge alone, against the full force of the enemy, and ordered the bridge broken down behind him. He was obeying the "law of bravery," an illustration of the positive or command aspect of the *lex caelestis*. For its negative or prohibitory side Cicero cites the case of Sextus Tarquinius who broke the "eternal law" against rape by violating Lucretia.[30] It is a weakness of Cicero that in his efforts at concreteness he is not able to rise above the level of the wall motto in his moral precepts. Cocles' conduct was a noble act of bravery. But should the law command

[26] *de n. d.* I, 36.
[27] D. 1. 3. 2. Plato, *Gorg.* 484B.
[28] Diog. Laert. VII, 33.
[29] *Sto. rep.* 8, 1.
[30] *de leg.* 2, 10. See also *Phill.* Xi, Xii, 28; *pro Milo*, 10.

such conduct in all similar circumstances with penalties for disobedience? As a legal ideal the bare proscription of rape is too indeterminate to be a standard of much use. In English law a man may be guilty of rape upon a prostitute, but he cannot be guilty of rape upon his wife; a husband has no need to ask his wife's consent to sexual intercourse, whatever new circumstances may have arisen since the marriage, not even if he is knowingly suffering at the time from a venereal disease.[31]

For his second kind of law, Cicero turns to the idea of natural law. He observes that the divine mind is the supreme law, and that when reason is perfected in man that also is law; and this perfected reason exists in the mind of the wise man.[32] However, there exist rules which, in varying forms and for the need of the moment, have been formulated for the guidance of nations. They bear the name of law not so much by right as by favor of the people. For every law which really deserves that name is truly praiseworthy. When rules were drawn up and put in force which would make it possible for the people to live an honorable and happy life, it is clear that men called them "laws." When wicked and unjust statutes were formulated it is clear that something was put into effect that was not "law." Such statutes no more deserve to be called laws than the rules a band of robbers might pass in their assembly. For if ignorant and unskillful men have prescribed deadly poisons instead of healing drugs, these cannot possibly be called physicians, prescriptions; neither in a nation can a statute of

[31] Stephen, in the first edition of his *Digest of Criminal Law* (1877) 172 thought that under some circumstances a man might be indicted for rape upon his wife; however, in the fourth edition (1887) 194, he withdrew that opinion.

[32] *de leg.* 2. 11. Pollock points out that *lex naturalis* or naturae, *ius naturale*, came in as deliberate translations of the Greek term (φυσικόν δίκαιον) in the last period of the Republic. He thinks they must have been neologisms in Cicero's time, for in his earliest work, the *De Inventione*, the idea is found, but is expressed by periphrasis. The law derived from Nature, as there set forth, is identical, as might be expected with the morality of a high minded Roman gentleman. *The History of the Law of Nature* (1901) 1 Col. L. Rev. 11. "Natural law is that which has not had its origin in the opinions of men, but has been implanted by some innate force, like religion, affection, gratitude, retaliation, respect, truth." *de inv.* 2. 53. Cf. *Tusc.* 1, 30. The inclusion of "retaliation" in this group may seem strange, but is merely a further illustration of the variability of moral judgments.

any sort be called a law, even though the nation, in spite of its being a ruinous regulation, has accepted it. Therefore, Cicero says, law is the distinction between things just and unjust, made in agreement with that primal and most ancient of all things, nature; and in conformity to nature's standard are framed those human laws which inflict punishment upon the wicked but protect the good. This is his formal definition of natural law (*lex naturae*).

Plato had argued that law is a good and that what is not beneficial to the state is not a good, and hence a bad law is no law.[33] Cicero's analysis reproduces this argument, but adds the idea of nature as the standard by which to test the goodness or badness of a law. However, it is far from clear what Cicero meant by " nature." Chrysippus had defined the highest good " as life in accordance with nature, or, in other words, in accordance with our own human nature as well as that of the universe." [34] Apparently there was an order of nature which was rational throughout and man was to conform to it. Animals were able to preserve their lives because nature had given them impulse. In their case nature's rule was to follow the direction of impulse. To man nature had added reason, and for him life according to reason rightly becomes the natural life.[35] By " reason " Cicero understood that which teaches and explains what should be done and what should be left undone.[36] Cicero regarded a life in accordance with nature as the highest good. That meant the enjoyment of a life of due measure based upon virtue, or, in other words, following nature and living according to her law; that is to say, to spare no effort, so far as in us lies, to accomplish what nature demands, among those demands being her wish that we live by virtue as our law.[37]

For his third kind of law, Cicero turns to the naked idea of law as that which decrees in written form whatever it

---

[33] *Hipp. Maj.* 284B-E; *Minos* 314E; *Laws* 715B.
[34] Diog. Laert. VII, 88.   [36] *de off.* 1, 101.
[35] Diog. Laert. VII, 86.   [37] *de leg.* 1, 56.

wishes, either by command or prohibition.[38] Such, he observes
with contempt, is the crowd's definition of law. With those
words he dismisses the subject. Nevertheless, the idea was a
necessary one in order to make his system philosophically
complete. For one thing, it would serve as a catch-all for the
specimens of law which could not be fitted into the categories
of the *lex caelestis* or the *ius naturae*. It could contain even
those bad laws which were no laws at all.

What is extraordinary in this analysis of the nature of law
is that Cicero, although the most learned lawyer of his time,
does not reason from legal materials. His *lex caelestis* is pure
Stoicism; his *ius naturae* appears to be a Greek importation.
Only the *lex vulgus* refers directly to positive law. In this
respect Cicero is much closer to Plato than to Aristotle,
although his idea of law is completely different from either of
theirs. Plato, in working out his theory that law seeks to be
the discovery of reality, paid no more attention to legal
materials than did Cicero. Aristotle, however, in putting forward his numerous ideas on the nature of law plainly kept
positive law and legal procedure before him. Cicero's conceptions, nevertheless, were to be as influential as those of his
illustrious predecessor and are even today the basis of a revival
in juristic thought.

There was no inclination on Cicero's part to underestimate
law even in its opprobrious sense. In his hands the theory of
the state assumes a legalistic form unknown to the Greeks.
He maintains that nothing can be nobler than the law of a
state.[39] It was originally made for the security of the people,
for the preservation of the state, for the peace and happiness
of human life.[40] Law is the bond of civil society, and the state
may be defined as an association or partnership in law.[41] If a
state has no law, it cannot be considered a state at all.[42] Law
is even superior to philosophy. An art, even if unused, can

---

[38] *de leg.* 1, 19; *cf.* 3, 44.
[39] *de leg.* 1, 14.
[40] *de leg.* 2, 11.
[41] *de rep.* 1, 32; 1, 25.
[42] *de leg.* 2, 12.

still be retained in the form of theoretical knowledge, but virtue depends entirely upon its use; and its noblest use is the government of the state, and the realization in fact, not in words, of those deeds which philosophers rehearse in their secluded retreats. For, even when philosophers express just and sincere sentiments about these matters, they merely state in words what has been actually realized and put into effect by those statesmen who have given states their laws. From whom comes our sense of moral obligation and our reverence towards the gods? From whom do we derive that law which is common to all peoples (*ius gentium*), or that to which we apply the term civil (*ius civile*)? Whence justice, honor, fair-dealing? Whence decency, self-restraint, fear of disgrace, eagerness for praise and honor? Whence comes endurance, toils and dangers? Assuredly, from those statesmen who have developed these qualities by education and have embedded some of them in customs and have enforced others by statutes. Xenocrates, one of the most distinguished of philosophers, was once asked, so the story goes, what his pupils gained from his instructions. He replied that of their own free will they would perform the duties they would be enforced to do by the laws. A statesman, therefore, who by his authority and by the punishments which his laws impose obliges all men to adopt that course which only a mere handful can be persuaded to adopt by the arguments of philosophers, should be held in even greater esteem than the teachers who make these virtues the subject of their discussions. For what speech of theirs is excellent enough to be preferred to a state well provided with law and custom? [43]

JUSTICE

We know Cicero believed that justice was the supreme virtue and perhaps included all the others.[44] Why he thought so we do not know, since he stated the arguments of his opponents so fairly that he was unable to refute them. That, at any rate,

---

[43] *de rep.* 1, 2.   [44] *de fin.* 5, 65.

is the assertion of Lactantius, who was not a prejudiced witness, and to whom we owe much of the statement of the argument.

Justice is defined by Cicero as that sentiment which assigns to each his own and maintains with generosity and equity human solidarity and alliance.[45] It has its source in nature [46] and as a matter of fact, " we are born for justice." [47] The most foolish notion of all is the belief that everything is just which is found in the laws of nations. A law to the effect that a dictator might put to death with impunity any citizen he wished, even without a trial, is obviously not a just law. Justice is one; it binds all human society, and is based on one law, which is right reason applied to command and prohibition. Whoever does not know this law, whether it has been recorded in writing anywhere or not, is without justice.[48]

These are lofty sentiments, but Cicero knew well enough that they were not self-evident principles. Unless justified philosophically, they were no more than pious platitudes which awakened an echo in the minds of the morally inclined but which the cynical could pass by with a smile. In the *Republic* he assigns to Philus, who was regarded as an almost incomparable example of old-fashioned probity and honor, the task of stating Carneades' arguments in support of the conventional nature of justice and the equivalence of true justice and folly. Philus believed that to state the case against a position was the easiest means of reaching the truth.[49]

He first set forth the general propositions to be established. Men enacted laws for themselves with a view to their own advantage. These laws differed according to their characters and in the case of the same persons often changed according to the times. There was no natural law; both men and animals were directed by the guidance of nature to their own advan-

[45] *de fin.* 5, 65. See also *de inv.* 2, 160; *de n.* 3, 38. *de off.* 1, 42.
[46] *de fin.* 2, 59.
[47] *de leg.* 1, 28.
[48] *de leg.* 1, 42.
[49] *de rep.* 3, 8 *et seq.* For Cicero's views on self-evident principles see *de off.* 3. 33; *de inv.* 1, 65.

tage; therefore, there was no justice, or if any did exist, it was the greatest folly, because it injured itself by promoting the interests of others.

In support of these propositions, Philus turns to the argument from relativity. If the justice he is investigating is a product of nature, then, like heat and cold, or bitter and sweet, justice and injustice would be the same thing to all men. In actual fact, it is not. In Egypt animals are worshipped as divine; in Greece and Rome the sacred statues have a human form, a custom which the Persians considered wicked; many peoples believe in human sacrifice; the Cretans and the Aetolians considered piracy and brigandage honorable; the Gauls think it disgraceful to grow grain by manual labor, and consequently they go forth armed and reap other men's fields. Indeed, the Romans themselves, the most just of men, forbid the races beyond the Alps to plant the olive or the vine, so that their own olive groves and vineyards may be the more valuable. This is regarded as prudent, but not just, conduct. Not only are there differences among nations, but there have been a thousand changes in a single city, even in Rome, in regard to these things. Before the passage of the Voconian law the rights of women with respect to inheritance were different. That law itself is full of injustice to women. Why should a woman not have money of her own? Why may a Vestal Virgin have an heir, while her mother may not?

In short, if the supreme God had provided laws for us, then all men would obey the same laws, and the same men would not have different laws at different times. If it is the duty of a just and good man to obey the laws, what laws is he to obey? All the different laws that exist? But virtue does not allow inconsistency, nor does nature permit variation. Laws are imposed upon us by fear of punishment, not by our sense of justice. Therefore, there is no such thing as natural justice, and from this it follows that neither are men just by nature. Or will they tell us that, though laws vary, good men naturally follow what is truly just, not what is thought to be so? For, they say, it is the duty of a good and just man to give everyone that which is his due. Well then, first of all, what is it, if anything, that we are to grant to dumb animals as their due? For it is not men of mediocre talents, but those who are eminent and learned, such as Pythagoras and Empedocles, who declare that inevitable penalties threaten those who injure an animal.

At this point leaves of the manuscript are missing, but from other sources,[50] it appears that the argument continued as follows. The difference between codes of law can be accounted for by utility, which varies from place to place. But there is a wide divergence between justice and utility. Prudence demands that we have a care to self-interest, justice to the interests of others. But to follow justice is the height of folly, inasmuch as it leads us to injure ourselves to the advantage of others. Roman history itself is the best proof of this. Rome has won her empire by injustice both to gods and men; a policy of justice would make her again what she was originally, a miserable poverty-stricken village, inasmuch as it would require her to restore all that was not her own. What is commonly called justice in states is nothing but an agreement for mutual self-restraint, which is a result of weakness, and is based on nothing whatever but utility.

Wisdom urges us to increase our resources, to multiply our wealth, to extend our boundaries; for what is the meaning of those words of praise inscribed on the monuments of our greatest generals " He extended the boundaries of the empire " except that an addition was made out of the territory of others?[51] Wisdom urges us also to rule over as many subjects as possible, to enjoy pleasures, to become rich, to be rulers and masters; justice on the other hand, instructs us to spare all men, to consider the interests of the whole human race, to give everyone his due, and not to touch sacred or public

---

[50] Lactantius, *Inst. Div.* V, 16, 2-4; VI, 9, 2-4; VI, 6, 19 and 23; Tertullian, *Apolog.* 25 (p. 164 Oehl, p. 90 Mayor).

[51] *de rep.* 3, 24.

property, or that which belongs to others. What then is the result if you obey wisdom? Wealth, power, riches, public office, military commands, and royal authority, whether we are speaking of individuals or nations.

To such arguments as these it is replied by the Epicureans who are open and frank and do not themselves use crafty and rascally tricks of arguments, that a wise man is not good because goodness and justice in themselves give him pleasure, but because the life of a good man is free from fear, anxiety, worry, and danger, while on the other hand the minds of the wicked are always troubled by one thing or another, and trial and punishment always stand before their eyes. No advantage or reward won by injustice is great enough to offset constant fear, or the everpresent thought that some punishment is near or is threatening.[52]

However, I put the question to you: Let us suppose there are two men, one a pattern of virtue, fairness, justice and honor, and the other an example of extreme wickedness and audacity; and suppose a nation is so mistaken as to believe the good man a wicked, treacherous criminal, and the wicked man on the other hand a model of probity and honor. Then let us imagine that, in accordance with this opinion, held by all his fellow-citizens, the good man is harassed, attacked, and arrested; blinded, sentenced, bound, branded, and reduced to beggary, and finally is also most justly deemed by all men to be most miserable. Then let the wicked man, on the contrary, be praised, courted, and universally loved; let him receive all sorts of public offices, military commands, wealth and riches from every source; and finally, let him have the universal reputation of being the best man in the world and most worthy of all the favors of fortune. Now I ask you, who could be so insane as to doubt which of the two he would prefer to be? The same thing is true of states as of persons. No people would be so foolish as not to prefer to be unjust masters rather than just slaves.

---

[52] At this point a page of the manuscript is lost. With the following paragraph *cf.* Plato, *Rep.* 361-362.

Philus' defense of injustice from here on is lost, but from Lactantius we learn that he returned to the antagonism between prudence and justice. Let us suppose, he said, that a good man possesses a runaway slave or an infected house, and that he alone is aware of these defects. If on this account, he offers the slave or the house for sale, will he declare that he is putting on the market a runaway slave or an unhealthful house, or will he conceal these defects from a purchaser? If he admits them, he will be considered honest, but he will also be regarded as a fool, for he will either sell at a low price or he will not sell at all. If he conceals the defects, he will be prudent in that he considers his own interest, but he will be dishonest in that he deceives. Again let us suppose that a man finds a dealer who thinks he is selling copper, though it is really gold, or who thinks he is selling lead when it is really silver. Will an honorable man keep silence in order to buy at a low price, or will he disclose the truth and pay a higher price? Only a fool, it appears, would choose the latter course. Consider also the cases in which a man cannot be just without endangering his life. Certainly justice requires us not to kill human beings and not in any way to touch another's property. What then, will the just man do if he is in a shipwreck and someone weaker than himself has found a plank on which to keep afloat? Will he not push the weaker man off the plank, that he may get on it himself and thus make his escape, especially when there is no one in the middle of the sea to bear witness against him? If he is prudent he will do this, for he will inevitably lose his own life if he does not. If however, he would rather die than raise his hand against another man, he is indeed just but he is a fool, because in sparing another's life he fails to spare his own. Similarly, when the army in which he is fighting has been routed, and the enemy begin pursuit, if a man finds a wounded soldier mounted on a horse, will he spare the wounded man and be killed himself, or will he throw the other from the horse in order that he may himself escape the enemy? If he follows the latter course, he is prudent, but also wicked; if he takes the former course, it necessarily follows that, though just, he is a fool.

Accordingly, Lactantius goes on, after political and natural justice had been distinguished, Philus overthrew both, for political justice is in fact prudence and not justice, while natural justice, though it is really justice, is not prudence. " Clearly," he adds, " these arguments are subtle and ensnaring; indeed, Cicero could not refute them. For though he makes Laelius answer Philus and present the case for justice, Cicero left all these objections unrefuted, as if they were mere traps. The result is that Laelius appears as the defender not of natural justice, which had been subjected to the charge of being mere stupidity, but rather of political justice, which Philus had admitted to be prudent, though it was not just." Lactantius himself attempts to answer the argument by showing that a truly just man would not take a sea voyage. For why should he take a voyage when his own land is sufficient for him? However, he admits it is possible that a man may be compelled even against his will to make a voyage. In that case it is impossible that the just man should be unprotected by the guardianship of Heaven. Finally, he grants that the case Cicero puts is possible. In those circumstances, the just man will die because of his innocence; he abstains from all fault, because he cannot do otherwise, although he has the knowledge of right and wrong. He is the wisest man who prefers to perish rather than to commit an injury, that he may preserve that sense of duty by which he is distinguished from the dumb animals.

It may well be that Cicero's answer was the doctrine of the *lex caelestis*. That doctrine expressly denies that there will be different laws at Rome and at Athens, or different laws now and in the future, but asserts one eternal and unchangeable law valid for all nations and all times. He may have shown the identity of the *lex caelestis* and *iustitia*. Elsewhere,[53] Cicero states the same and similar cases as representative of the dis-

---

[53] *de off.* 3, 50 et seq.

pute between Diogenes of Babylonia who took one side, and his pupil, Antipater who took the other. The cases are given as evidence of the contradiction that seems often to arise between the expedient and the morally right. Cicero remarks that he must give his decision, for he does not propound the cases merely to raise questions, but to offer a solution. He does this by showing that the expedient is really the inexpedient. The man who sells the infected house without disclosing that fact opens himself to the charge of fraud, underhandedness, and slyness. Is it not inexpedient to subject oneself to all these terms of reproach and many more besides? Surely the philosopher Cicero is not speaking here, but rather the successful Roman careerist.

Such is the state of the manuscript Cicero left us, that the argument, although he did not believe it himself, clearly favors the great political tradition of Thucydides, Mandeville, Machiavelli, Hobbes, La Rochefoucauld, and Nietzsche. He himself belonged in the equally great tradition of Plato and Christianity which asserts that the just man, if he possess the ring of Gyges, would nevertheless abstain from injustice. The pure abbess locked in the cell with her lover on the eve of the summons to the guillotine will remain pure. Cicero shares with modern ethics the inability to improve upon Plato's statement of the dilemma. However, in Cicero's hands the problem of justice is beginning to assume a definite legal character. Plato is fully aware of the formula *suum cuique tribuere,* but he states it only to repudiate it. It is basic in Cicero's theory and becomes in time, of course, the classic legal definition. His essential problem, which he never succeeded in solving, was to give the phrase a meaning beyond the legal, in order to avoid an identification of the just and the legal, which would have invalidated his theory of an unjust law.

THE MAGISTRATE

Cicero's theory of the magistrate represents a combination of Aristotelianism and natural law doctrine. He set a high value on the administration of justice which he regarded as including the interpretation of the law.[54] It is the function of the magistrate to rule and to command what is just and beneficial and in conformity with the law. For as the laws govern the magistrate, so the magistrate governs the people, " and it can truly be said that the magistrate is a speaking law, and the law a silent magistrate." Aristotle[55] also took the view that the ruler was a " living law." Nothing, Cicero thought, was so completely in accordance with the principles of justice and the demands of nature (by which he says he means law) than authority (*imperium*); for without it neither household, city, nation, the human race, physical nature nor the universe itself could exist. For the universe obeys God; seas and lands obey the universe; and human life is subject to the decrees of supreme law.

INTERPRETATION

In legal theory, interpretation is the name of the methodology employed in the analysis of propositions, generally from the realm of legal discourse, to determine the mode of action to be induced. Law as a means of social control is a technology. Propositions from technological discourse, in the theory of modern logic, have the function of inducing modes of action, as contrasted with propositions from scientific discourse which report a situation or with propositions from aesthetic discourse which present a value. Technological discourse, which embraces medicine, engineering, agriculture, in short, all the technologies, is concerned with imperatives which prevail upon behavior. The propositions of legal discourse are distinguished by such words as " shall," " may," " authorized," " directed," and " shall not." There is today a vigorous effort on the part of logicians to work out a general theory of interpretation which would be comprehensive enough to embrace the results already obtained in logic, theology, law, biology, anthropology, aesthetics, and

---

[54] *de rep.* 5, 3.
[55] *Pol.* 1284ª 13. For the idea in Hellenistic thought see Goodenough, *The Political Philosophy of Hellenistic Kingship* (1928) 1 Yale Classical Studies 55.

the numerous other fields in which interpretation has been studied. It is thought that a theoretical structure simple in outline might unite the now disparate methods into a unified whole. However, that goal is still far to seek.

In the field of legal interpretation the judge, public official, and lawyer have at their disposal a technique formidable in dimension and flexible in content. In spite of a fair amount of analysis. the field remains confused, with its basic theory unsettled, and its rules for the most part, at least from the point of view of rigorous analysis, meaningless and contradictory. In the typical case the judge is free to take down from the shelf the rule which will produce the result he wishes, to reach. Thus, to cite a case, the results of which Blackstone [56] did not question, the statute 1 Edw. VI c. 12 enacted that those who are convicted of stealing *horses* should not have the benefit of clergy. Inasmuch as there is a rule that penal statutes must be construed strictly, the judges conceived that the statute should not extend to the man who stole but one horse. A different result could, of course, have been reached if the judges had applied the rule that the plural number includes the singular. Humanitarian considerations, not even today crystallized into a formal rule, may have moved the judges to their odd conclusion. This factor was plainly present in the second case cited by Blackstone. The statute 14 Geo. II c. 6 made the stealing of sheep, *or other cattle*, a felony without benefit of clergy. The general words " or other cattle " were looked upon as much too loose to create a capital offense, so the act was held to extend to nothing but mere sheep, a decision which Parliament cured at the next session by amending the statute to include bulls, cows, oxen, steers, bullocks, heifers, calves, and lambs by name.

In Cicero's hands the theory of interpretation reached a level of development which compares not unfavorably with that which obtains today. Traditionally, interpretation was a branch

---

[56] 1 Bl. Comm. 88. Lord Hale attempted to rationalize the case. 2 *Pleas of the Crown* 365.

of rhetoric and as such it had been intensively studied by some of the best minds of ancient times. In the *Phaedrus* Plato had conceived of rhetoric as an art based on philosophy. It was concerned with the influence of speech or words upon men's minds. Aristotle,[57] following Plato, regarded it as a branch or counterpart of dialectic and defined it as the power of discovering the possible means of persuasion in reference to any subject whatever. Like dialectic, rhetoric has no special subject matter but can discuss any subject whatever; exact demonstration and necessary conclusions are excluded from it, and no proof, or conclusion, or principle that it employs is more than probable, since belief and not scientific demonstration is the object aimed at; it has no special, appropriate first principles, such as those from which the special sciences are deduced, though it appeals to the ultimate principles common to all reasoning; it argues indifferently the opposite sides of the same question, and concludes the positive or negative of any proposition or problem, unlike science and demonstration, which can only arrive at one conclusion. Where the materials and the method are alike only probable, every question has, or may be made to appear to have, two sides, either of which may be maintained on probable principles. In rhetoric no certainty is attained or attainable.

All his life Cicero was a careful student of rhetorical theory, and he wrote extensively upon it. In a letter he describes one of his rhetorical works as being written " in the Aristotelian manner " and states that it " embraces all the theories of rhetoric held by the ancients, including those of Aristotle and Isocrates." [58] It was Cicero's avowed aim to provide the Romans with a discussion of every phase of philosophy treated by the Greek philosophers. Inasmuch as Aristotle and Theophrastus had joined rhetoric with philosophy it also appeared proper to Cicero to put his rhetorical works in the same category.[59] However, the important consideration is that from

---

[57] *Rhet.* 1354ª 1, 1356ᵇ 26. 1 Cope, *Rhetoric of Aristotle* (1877) 3.
[58] *ad. fam.* 1, 9, 23.   [59] *de div.* II, 4.

Cicero's works it is apparent that the Latin rhetors, following the Greeks, had worked out a complete rhetorical theory of interpretation.

Rhetorical theory was divided into a number of main divisions and it was under the heading *inventio* that interpretation was treated. Invention was defined by Cicero as the devising of reasons either true or credible, which make one's cause appear probable.[60] It is instructive to examine the history of this idea. In the *Politicus* Plato had concluded that the appearance of the expert who could be trusted in government was so unlikely that we must put up with law which is inflexible and cannot adapt itself equitably to the individual case. In an attempt to correct this theory Aristotle drew a distinction in his *Ethics* and *Rhetoric* between τὸ δίκαιον or justice and τὸ ἐπιεικές or equity and fairness. From this distinction certain rules followed, such as looking to the lawgiver rather than the law in interpreting the latter. That is to say, when the law lays down a general rule, and thereafter a case arises which is not covered by the general rule, then it is right, where the lawgiver's pronouncement because of its absoluteness is defective and erroneous, to say what the legislator himself would have said had he been present and would have enacted if he had been cognizant of the case in question.[61] Thus, what began as an ethical and political idea with Plato, and was treated both ethically and rhetorically by Aristotle, becomes in Cicero's theory a purely rhetorical notion altogether divorced from ethics. Interpretation is one branch of the theory of speaking and is exclusively concerned with persuasion. Plato himself had admitted that rhetoric included even the false dialectic which could make the same things seem like and unlike, one and many. But the effort to correct on ethical grounds an admitted deficiency in the rule of law has become transformed into the false dialectic itself.

In English law the Aristotelian doctrine of looking to the legislator rather than the law for help in statutory interpre-

---

[60] *de inv.* I, 7.   [61] *E. N.* 1137ᵇ 20.

tation became the so-called principle of the "equity of the statute" (*per l'cquite de le statut*) which was defined by Coke [62] as follows: "Equity is a construction made by the Judges that cases out of the letter of a statute yet being within the same mischief or cause of the making of the same, shall be within the same remedy that the statute provideth; and the reason thereof is, for that the law-makers could not possibly set down all cases in express terms." Plowden [63] cites Aristotle as authority for the principle, quoting him in the words of the Latin maxim *Equitas est correctio legis generatim latae qua parte deficit.*[64] Plowden observed "that is not the Words of the Law but the internal Sense of it that makes the Law, and our Law (like all others) consists of two Parts, *viz.* of Body and Soul, the Letter of the Law is the Body of the Law, and the Sense and Reason of the Law is the Soul of the Law, *quia ratio legis est anima legis.*" The principle has been now generally abandoned, at least by name. However, it was applied in a comparatively recent case where a murderer was not permitted to take under the will of his victim, although the statutes regulating the making, proof and effect of wills and the devolution of property, if literally construed, gave the property to the murderer. After citing Aristotle the Court asked: "If the lawmakers could, as to this case, be consulted, would they say that they intended by their general language that the property of a testator or of an ancestor should pass to one who had taken his life for the express purpose of getting his property?" [65] Although the principle of the equity of the statute is no longer looked upon with favor, a new principle is developing which occupies a portion of the field formerly covered by Aristotle's rule. The principle is an exception to the *casus omissus* rule which provides that omissions in a statute cannot, as a general rule, be supplied by construction.

---

[62] 1 Co. Inst. 24ᵇ.

[63] Plowd. 465. Blackstone cites Cicero. 1 Bl. 61.

[64] Equity is the correction of the law in those particulars wherein, by reason of its generality, it is deficient. Aristotle's words are καὶ ἔστιν αὕτη ἡ φύσις ἡ τοῦ ἐπιεικοῦς, ἐπανόρθωμα νόμον ᾗ ἐλλείπει διὰ τὸ καθόλου. E. N. 1137ᵇ 27.

[65] *Riggs* v. *Palmer*, 115 N. Y. 506, 22 N. E. 188 (1889).

The new rule holds that, where a statute deals with a genus, and a thing which afterwards comes into existence is a species thereof, the language of the statute should generally be extended to the new species, though it was not known or could not have been known to the legislature when the act was passed, *e. g.* the genus " railroad " when used in an 1860 statute included the species " steam railroad " and " city street or horse railroad " but in 1907 was extended to the new species " interurban and suburban railroad." [66] Although Aristotle is shoved out the front door, he reappears again by the back entrance.

Cicero classified disputes about the interpretation of written texts into five types. [67] For all cases, following standard rhetorical practice, Cicero obligingly supplies the kinds of arguments which should be used on both sides. *Scriptum* and *voluntas*: When the words of the document and the intention of the writer appear to be at variance. If the orator is speaking for the written law he should ask: Why did the draughtsman write like that if that was not his meaning? It is intolerable that the meaning of the legislator should be explained by anybody rather than by the law. What prevented the writer from inserting the exception which his opponent professes to have followed as though it were actually there? On the other hand one who bases his defense on the meaning and intention of the law will maintain that the force of the law resides in the purpose and intention of the person who drafted it and not in its words and letters. Then he must introduce examples of cases where all equity will be thrown into confusion if the words of the law are followed and not the meaning. Then he must arouse the hatred of the judge against cunning and chicanery of such a kind, with a note of resentful complaint in his voice. [68] *Leges contrariae* or ἀντινομία: When two or more laws contradict each other. For this type Cicero supplies an

---

[66] *McCleary* v. *Babcock*, 169 Ind. 228, 82 N. E. 453 (1907).

[67] *de inv.* 1, 13. 17. 4 Voigt, *Das jus naturale, aequum et bonum und jus gentium* (1875) 350 *et seq.* collects the instances.

[68] *part. or.* 38, 134, 135. *de inv.* II. 35. 130, II. 44. 128, II. 46. 135.

elaborate set of rules. Nothing like them has heretofore appeared in the history of jurisprudence as it is known to us. " It is necessary first," Cicero says,[69] " to compare the laws to determine which is concerned with the more important, that is to say, the more useful, honorable, and necessary matters. It follows that if it is not possible to preserve two or more laws which are contradictory, that one should be preserved which appears to include within its scope the most important matters. Next is the question, which is the most recent law: usually the latest law is the most important. Then, which is the law that commands and that permits; for that which is commanded must necessarily be done, but that which is permissive is optional. Then it is necessary to consider which of the two laws penalizes violations or which has the heavier penalty attached to it; for that law must be preserved which is protected by a more carefully contrived set of penalties. Again, inquire which law commands and which prohibits; for the law which prohibits may turn out to contain amendments to the law which commands. Then it is necessary to discover which is the general and which the particular law; which is applicable to a variety of matters, and which is applicable to a single matter only. The particular law and the special law may be more relevant to the case under consideration and be more helpful in reaching a conclusion. It should also be determined which law prescribes immediate action and which permits some delay and postponement; above all, that law must be first obeyed which brooks no delay. Next, there should be an endeavor to make it appear that the letter of the law is being followed with fidelity; that the opposite position requires a choice of two meanings or of a resort to syllogistic reasoning or definition: a law has more weight and authority if its meaning is clear. Argue also that there is full agreement between the letter and the spirit of the law; if the case allows it, attempt also to give to the opposing law a meaning different from its apparent one, so that the two laws will not seem

[69] *de inv.* II. 49.

contradictory. Thus, if your interpretation is adopted, both
laws are preserved, but if your opponent's interpretation is
adopted, one of the laws must be discarded. Also, take into
consideration the stock arguments suggested by the theory
of rhetoric and those which the case itself furnishes, as well
as those which may be drawn from the ample domains of honor
and profit. By developing those topics you will be able to
show which of the two laws ought to be followed." *Ambiguitas*
or ἀμφιβολία: When that which has been written signifies two
or more things.[70] *Ratiocinatio* or συλλογισμός: From that which
is written, something appears to be discovered which is not
written. This is the *casus omissus* of our law. " It is forbidden
to export wool from *Tarentum*: he exported sheep." Or, " The
man who kills his father shall be sewed up in a sack. He killed
his mother." [71] *Definitio legalis* or ὅρος: When the inquiry is
as to the exact meaning of a word which appears in a written
document.[72]

It may be well to look at an actual application of some of
these rules. In what Cicero describes as the famous case of
Curius v Coponius [73] a testator had left his estate to his
expected posthumous son, with a gift over to Curius in the
event of such child dying under the age of fourteen, the period
at which he emerged from guardianship. In fact no posthumous
son was born, and after ten months Curius claimed the estate
but was opposed by M. Coponius the next of kin. It was a
clear case of *scriptum vs voluntas*. Q. Mucius Scaevola argued
on the literal terms of the will and contended that Curius
could never inherit unless a posthumous son had in fact been
born and died before reaching puberty. How full and precise
he was, Cicero says, on testamentary law, on ancient formulas,
on the manner in which the will should have been drawn if
Curius were to be recognized as heir even if no son were born;

---

[70] For the stock arguments see *de inv*. II. 40, II. 41.
[71] The examples are from Quint. VII. 8. 3. For Cicero's arguments see *de inv*.
II. 50.
[72] For the stock arguments see *de inv*. II. 51.
[73] *de or*. I. 180; II. 140, 221. *Brut*. 52. 194 *et seq*.

what a snare was set for plain people if the exact wording of
the will were ignored, and if intentions were to be determined
by guesswork, and if the written words of simple-minded people
were to be perverted by the interpretation of clever lawyers.
How much he had to say about the authority of his father,
also a great jurist, who had always upheld the doctrine of
strict interpretation, and in general how much concerning
observance of the civil law as handed down: In saying all this
with mastery and knowledge, and again with his characteristic
brevity and compactness, not without ornament and with
perfect finish, what man of the people would have expected or
thought that anything better could be said?

L. Licinius Crassus, who represented Curius, began his re-
buttal with the story of a boy's caprice, who while walking
along the shore found a thole-pin, and from that chance
became infatuated with the idea of building himself a boat to
it. He urged that Scaevola in like manner, seizing upon a thole-
pin of fact and captious reason, had upon it made out a case
of inheritance imposing enough to come before the centumviral
court. He urged that the will, the real intention of the testator,
was this: that in the event of no son of his surviving to the age
of legal comptence—no matter whether such a son was never
born, or should die before that time—Curius was to be his
heir; that most people wrote their wills in this way and that
it was valid procedure and always had been valid. He then
passed over to general right and equity; defended observance
of the manifest will and intention of the testator; pointed out
what snares lay in words, not only in wills but elsewhere, if
obvious intentions were ignored; what tyrannical power Scaevola was arrogating to himself if no one hereafter should
venture to make a will unless in accordance with his idea. The
decision went to Curius.

There is a core of truth at the center of Cicero's theory of
interpretation which sets it over against our own attempts at
a " scientific theory of interpretation." His theory was frankly
opportunistic. It was wedded neither to *scriptum* nor *voluntas*,

to the intent of the legislature, to the " true meaning " of the words, or to the application of technical rules. At the center of the rhetorical theory of interpretation was the concrete case. In principle it could be solved with the aid of all the techniques which the rhetors had elaborated—or in the face of all of them. This would make for a thoroughly explored system of case law, tough and at the same time sufficiently flexible to meet the surprises of the future. However, the weakness of the rhetorical theory is the fact that its sole object is success, while a legal theory of interpretation demands that it be pointed towards desirable or just results. Cicero's assertion that in judicial argumentation the proper end is equity or some kind of honesty seems a pious afterthought not required by the theory.[74]

Whether the rhetorical theory of interpretation influenced Roman law is perhaps the most strongly contested point in the history of Roman law today. The jurists were certainly aware of the theories of the rhetors and were no doubt helped on some points by them; but that the theory had a more positive influence is still uncertain.[75]

CONCLUSION

Cicero thought of jurisprudence as the Roman counterpart to Greek philosophy.[76] He was wonderfully equipped to advance Rome's claim to distinction in that field of knowledge. With the exception of Varro he was probably the most learned Roman of his age. That a man should be well trained in the *artes liberales* which included literature, rhetoric, dialectics, arithmetic, geometry, astronomy, and music, he accepted as a matter of course. But his ideally educated man, his *doctus orator* or philosophic statesman (πολιτικὸς φιλόσοφος) must be specially at home in literature, rhetoric, history, law, and

---

[74] *de inv.* II. 51.
[75] The basic study is Stroux, *Summum ius summa iniuria* (1926); Italian translation by Funaioli with preface by Riccobono 12 *Annali Universita di Palermo* (1929) 639. The most complete discussion in English is Schiller, 27 *Vir. L. Rev.* (1941) 733.
[76] *de or.* 1. 195.

philosophy. "We are called men," he writes, "but only those of us are men who have been perfected by the studies proper to culture." [77] His own legal knowledge is a matter of dispute. That he was a brilliant orator is a commonplace. He prepared his cases with the utmost diligence; and a minute study of four of his orations has led to the assertion that he was a consummate jurisconsult, who combined with the practical a grasp of general principles which culminated in recommendations for legal reforms which were adopted. Still, Cicero himself hedged in the great debate between Crassus and Antonius on the question whether an orator could also be a jurist. Crassus argued that the orator should devote himself to a study of Roman law, but Antonius insisted that the subjects were separate sciences, each demanding a lifetime of study. [78] Cicero sympathized with the idealism of Crassus but he recognized an inevitable distinction between a good advocate and a good lawyer. Like Austin's, Cicero's knowledge of the law may have been deficient, but again like Austin, this did not prevent him from devising an influential jurisprudence. His training in the Greek scholastic rhetoric, with its logical subtleties but its emphasis on the practical, here stood him in good stead. For one thing it gave him a sense of system. One of his criticisms of Roman law was that it lacked systematic form.

With Cicero jurisprudence embraced an humanitarian ideal which was to persist in a vital form for many centuries, and which is still influential. At the center of his thinking was the belief that civil law, if it were true law, was not merely the external expression of the desires of a dominant class, but a realization of the rules of justice and reason. The effect of this principle is plainly apparent in his theory of rights. He held that men of high moral character were made kings in order that the people might enjoy justice. When the masses were oppressed by the strong, they appealed for protection to some one man who managed by establishing equitable con-

[77] *de rep.* 1. 28.
[78] *de or.* 1. 166-203, 234-55. For the whole subject see Gwynn, *Roman Education* (1926) 79 *et seq.*

ditions to hold the higher and the lower classes in an equality of right. This was also the reason for making constitutional laws. For what people have always sought is equality of rights before the law. For rights that were not open to all alike would be no rights. If the people secured their ends at the hands of one just and good man, they were satisfied with that; but when such was not their good fortune, laws were invented, to speak to all men at all times in one and the same voice.[79] Thus, the way was paved for the identification by the Roman jurists of law and morality. At the opening of the Digest was set Celsus' definition of *ius* as *ars boni et aequi*. Not until Hobbes propounded his theory of positive lawmaking was ethics to be dethroned from its position of dominance over law and jurisprudence.

[79] *de off.* 2. 41–42.

CHAPTER V

ST. THOMAS AQUINAS

> *In astonishment I ask myself how
> was it possible that such truths,
> once expressed, could have been
> forgotten by our Protestant schol-
> ars. What errors they might have
> spared themselves had they heed-
> ed these truths! I might not have
> written my book had I recogniz-
> ed them, for the basic thought
> that was important to me I find
> already in this mighty thinker in
> perfect clarity and in the most
> precise formulation.*
>
> Rudolf von Jhering

S<small>T</small>. T<small>HOMAS</small> sat down to compose his treatise on law at a significant moment in the history of jurisprudence. Most probably the treatise was written in 1269 or 1270. For the preceding one hundred and fifty years the mind of the West had given itself over to jurisprudence to an extent which is historically unique. " Of all the centuries," Maitland [1] wrote, " the twelfth is the most legal. In no other age, since the classical days of Roman law, has so large a part of the sum total of intellectual endeavor been devoted to jurisprudence." It was the period of the Glossators, of Irnerius, of the famous " Four Doctors "—Bulgarus, Martinus, Jacobus, and Hugo,

---

The Latin text is that of the Leonine Edition, edited by the Pontifical College of Editors. The standard English translation of the *Summa Theologica* was made by the Fathers of the English Dominican Province (1920) 21 vols. A two volume selection based upon this translation has been prepared by Professor Anton C. Pegis. It includes the material of interest to the legal student, and the translation has been revised, corrected and annotated. *Basic Writings of Saint Thomas Aquinas,* ed. Pegis (2 vols. 1944). The quotation at the head of the chapter is from Maritain, *St. Thomas Aquinas* (1933) 19.

[1] Pollock and Maitland, *Hist. Eng. Law* (2nd ed. 1899) 111. " Before the end of the century," Maitland adds, "complaints were loud that theology was neglected, that the liberal arts were despised, that Seius and Titius had driven Aristotle and Plato from the schools, that men would learn law and nothing but law."

of their followers Azo, Hugolinus, Accursius, and many others. Law provided a subject matter upon which the great resources of the medieval intellect could test itself. It yielded particularly to the mighty weapon of the medieval mind—the so-called scholastic method. Through the process of dialectical analysis the medieval lawyers were able to systematize legal thinking, to state the basic ideas with clarity, to develop the logical consequences of legal principles, to reconcile apparent contradictions, to define, classify, distinguish, to make interconnections manifest and to eliminate irrelevancies—in short, to subject legal thinking to perhaps the most intensive logical analysis it has ever known.

Parallel with the revival of jurisprudence, there came the influx of knowledge to the Latin West from Greece, Byzantium and Islam. As early as the second quarter of the twelfth century the translators began the work of putting Greek and Mohammedan philosophy and science, and Byzantine theology into Latin. For the most part the scholars of the early middle ages, knowing no Greek, had been confined to Latin sources. By the time St. Thomas came to write he had available for study the philosophy and logic of the Greeks in Latin translations. Those translations were as literal as they could be made; their word by word reproduction of the originals would not suit modern tastes, and they would be rated scarcely more than barely adequate by modern tests, but for St. Thomas, who knew no Greek, they were precisely the tools he needed. Their literalness was a guarantee that whatever interpretative impulses may have inspired the translators were kept to a minimum. St. Thomas' insight into Aristotle is due in no small part to the word for word method of the translators.

Of greater significance for juristic thinking, however, than the legal activity of the twelfth century and the transmission of Greek knowledge to Western Europe was the shift in the point of view in legal philosophy induced by the rise of Christianity and other factors. Cicero [2] had based his legal

---

[2] *de leg.* 1. 22 *et seq.*

philosophy on the nature of man. He held that reason and a
sense of justice had been implanted in man by Nature and
were derived ultimately from God. Although all men possess
the sense of justice and know right reason they are nevertheless
corrupted by the practice of separating the useful, or what is
expedient, from justice. This theory culminated in the idea
of the world immanence of natural law and rests on the two
basic Stoic ideas of God as the " First Cause " and the Logos
as the principle of order. Because of the adoption of the
theory by the Roman jurists of Imperial times it became woven
into the doctrines of positive law. But a major difficulty at
once presented itself for solution. Natural law was identified
by the Fathers of the Church with the law of God as expressed
in the " law and the Gospel." Natural law was therefore
immutable and was the source of positive law. But positive
law was frequently contrary to natural law; it was also frequently opposed to the social ideals of the Church. A solution
of the difficulty was attempted by adopting the idea of a
Primitive State in which a pure law of nature operated un-
impaired; unjust laws and institutions could therefore be
explained as due to Original Sin. However, this attempted
solution also contained a difficulty. Were positive law and
government to be looked upon as generally evil things inasmuch
as they did not belong to the primitive state of man? A final
solution was reached on the theory that the appearance of sin
in the world completely changed the conditions proper to
human life, and that while positive law and government were
a result of sin they were also a remedy for sin. Thus it was
possible to maintain that while government was not a natural
institution it was at the same time a divine one. This argument, which has its roots in the doctrines of St. Paul, culminated in the important idea of a relative natural law.[3] Man's
natural powers were impaired but not wholly destroyed by

---

[3] The tradition was carried on by St. Irenaeus, Justin Martyr, St. Ambrose, St.
Augustine, St. Gregory the Great, and St. Isidore. For the full history see 1 Carlyle,
History of Medieval Political Theory in the West (1903) c. XI. 1 Troeltsch, *The
Social Teaching of the Christian Churches* (1931) 151.

the Fall; his sense of justice led him to create a body of law which everywhere nearly all men obey—the *ius gentium*. This law of custom comes after the law of nature; there was also a third form, the *ius civile*, representing the law of a particular state. Thus, the Christian theory of natural law had several parts: a pure natural law of the primitive state, a relative natural law of the fallen state, and the positive law, with all its intolerable provisions; to these elements was added the theocratic idea of a true goodness expressed through the Church by the love of God which gave a divine strength to the elements of natural law within the state. This theory of the Church is complex, obscure and difficult to cast into a form that is not contradictory. It represents on the one hand an effort to reconcile the conflicting doctrines of Cicero, Seneca, the Stoics, the Christian teachings, the juristic theories of the Roman lawyers and, on the other, an attempt to adjust the resulting theory to the actual conditions of the world so that the Church could exert her full powers in the social and political realm. However unsatisfactory the theory may be in the final result, its decisive significance must be emphasized. " It is the real ecclesiastical doctrine of civilization," Troeltsch [4] writes, " and as such it is at least as important as the doctrine of the Trinity, or other fundamental doctrines."

It was against this background that St. Thomas developed his theory of law. In its completed form his theory stands as one of the great achievements of thirteenth-century thought, critical, original, fully adjusted to the complex nature of the world it is intended to encompass. Of the philosophies of law founded explicitly on a theological basis none surpasses it and only that of Suárez approaches it.

The Definition of Law

In the Thomistic scheme the theory of law is part of an elaborate metaphysical, psychological and ethical system. It

---

[4] *Op. cit.* note 3 at 160.

takes its immediate departure from a consideration of the human act. Moral behavior is first explained in terms of the will which is directed by reason and habit. However, this explanation is intrinsic; there are also extrinsic principles which affect the human will. One extrinsic principle inclines to evil and is the devil; the other moves to good and is God. This second principle falls into two parts: Law and Grace. Through the instruction of God's Law and the Assistance of His Grace we are helped to do right.

Two important results have been at once achieved by this analysis. Law has been given a firm theological foundation and it has been marked off as a separate domain of study. When we contrast St. Thomas' treatment of law with that of Plato the significance of the latter's achievement is immediately apparent. Plato's extraordinary insight into the problems of law are sparks generated in the midst of a discussion of any subject matter—dialectics, politics, love, art. Since there is no order in his analysis there are gaps in his theory. But the scholars of the thirteenth century had a passion for classification and their theory of classification was a sophisticated one. It was of such fundamental importance that St. Thomas treated it at the very beginning of the Summa Theologica. It was fundamental because the distinction taken between the sciences will influence the choice of facts and the perception of problems. Sciences are differentiated, St. Thomas [5] held, according to the point of view from which they regard their subject matter. That is to say, all sciences are occupied with objects which constitute their material; but every science sees that material from a different position, and that position is the point of view from which the mind is brought to a focus on the material. Thus, the mind is able to abstract from the material an aspect which is susceptible of separate study. Many sciences are concerned with the same object: for example, physiology, psychology, ethics, economics, sociology, law,

---

[5] *Summa Theol.* I, q. 1, art. 1. All references hereafter will be to the *Summa Theologica* unless otherwise indicated.

politics, anthropology, etc., all deal with human behavior. Their differentiation lies in the fact that the points of view from which they consider the object common to them are different. An important consequence of this approach is that the propositions established in one field are not necessarily valid in another. It is for this reason that the law is unable to accept without modification many of the results of ethical inquiry.

Law is defined by St. Thomas as an ordinance of reason for the common good, made by him who has care of the community, and promulgated.[6] In this definition there is plainly an attempt to reach a comprehensive position that will embrace all law, the eternal and the natural as well as the human; there is also an effort to include what is regarded as ethically necessary. In his definition St. Thomas is thinking primarily of legal precepts. He is not thinking of the lawyer's law of the present-day realists—the idea that law, as Llewellyn puts it, is whatever is done officially.

It is advisable to consider separately the elements that make up St. Thomas' definition. It is first an " ordinance of reason." Inasmuch as it is an ordinance it is a command and is therefore distinguished from hortatory precepts. In this view statutes which direct certain conduct but which are not provided with sanctions for their violation are not to be regarded as establishing rules of law. This idea, which was shared by Austin and Gray, is defective in so far as it fails to specify the place of such statutes, which are not uncommon, in the legal order. However, it is directed at the solution of a real difficulty: What is the distinction between law, which apparently carries an obligation of obedience, and counsel, which merely advises on conduct? " Reason " raises more important considerations.

St. Thomas points out that law is a rule or measure of acts whereby one is induced to act or restrained from acting. He argues that that is apparent from the etymology of the word *lex*, which he derives from *ligare*, to bind, because law binds

---

[6] I-II, q. 90, art. 4.

one to act. In modern terminology law creates a duty. We thus have human behavior submitting to the authority of a rule or a principle, respecting it as its measure, and recognizing a duty to obey it. Now the first principle of human acts is the reason; indeed, no other principle by which to measure human behavior was admissible. The modern substitutes for reason—authority, experience, *Volksgeist*, utility—have since crowded reason very much from the scene, but in the thirteenth century the supremacy of its position in matters of this sort was incontestable. Since reason is the universal rule and measure of action law then becomes an obligation prescribed by reason.

A principle which the common law has made its own is asserted here. That principle holds that the choice between alternative rules of law shall rest upon a deliberate balancing of possible ends and means and shall take account of all the facts. It stands in direct opposition to the equally well-established principle that the will of the sovereign is law. This latter idea is an inheritance from the Byzantine period of Roman law; St. Thomas saw that it could not be reconciled logically with the doctrine he was propounding and he therefore drew the necessary conclusion that the unreasonable directions of a sovereign may bear the nominal title of laws but are not real laws.[7] In the common law the principle of reasonableness has performed very much the same function that the law of nature has performed in continental law. So long ago as the sixteenth century the two ideas were regarded as identical [8] and that fact has been given explicit recognition in modern case law.[9]

That law must be for the common good is an ideal difficult to apply but is one nevertheless which has left its mark on the legal order. It rests on the ethical idea that the final end of life is happiness and that an individual guided in his conduct by reason always seeks happiness. Laws therefore are rules

[7] I-II, q. 90, art. 1.
[8] Saint Germain, *The Doctor and Student* (1874) 12.
[9] *Johnson* v. *Clark*, 1 Ch. 303, 311 (1908).

of conduct which have as their final end the realization of happiness. However, since there are no limits to the good at which law aims, it is not restricted to the good of particular persons; therefore, it is always directed to the common good. Here, again, St. Thomas makes the deduction that a precept limited to individual circumstances is devoid of the nature of a law, save in so far as it affects the common good. That last saving clause points directly to the difficulty which stands in the way of any precise application of the ideal. Before 1789 the legal privileges of the nobles under the *Ancien Régime* were defended as being necessary for the common good. We still recognize that there is an element of truth in the view that special privileges sometimes lead to the common good, as in the franchises, tax exemptions, subsidies, and special powers granted utilities, corporations and other bodies by modern law. In American law the influence of the ideal is directly apparent in the numerous constitutional provisions forbidding special legislation and requiring general laws wherever applicable. But exceptions have had to be made to this rule. Thus, private acts are allowed which compensate individuals for claims founded on contracts with the state, private acts which remove a cloud on the title of land acquired from the state, private statutes providing compensation for the negligence of the state, and, at one time, legislative divorces were also permitted.

A law, properly speaking, therefore, regards first and foremost the order to the common good. Now the responsibility to order anything to the common good belongs either to the whole people, or to someone who is the vicegerent of the whole people. Therefore, the making of a law belongs either to the whole people or to a public personage who has care of the whole people: for in all other matters the directing of any thing to the end concerns him to whom the end belongs. To this argument St. Thomas adds the argument from the idea of sanction. A private person cannot lead another to virtue efficaciously: for he can only advise, and if his advice is not taken, it has no coercive power, such as the law should have, in order to have an efficacious inducement to virtue. But this coercive power is vested in the whole people or in some public personage to whom it belongs to inflict penalties. Therefore, the framing of laws belongs alone to the holder of this power.

This idea, particularly when joined to the theory of sovereignty, has commended itself to many thinkers. It is under a cloud today in the main because it does not direct us with sufficient determinateness to the law with which the courts are concerned. Court law can be assigned a place in the Thomistic system, but it cannot be deduced from St. Thomas' theory without the aid of the theory of sovereignty. But the idea of sovereignty is itself under strong attack today, and the whole conception will have to be restudied.

"Laws are said to be promulgated," said Festus,[10] "when they are made known to the people for the first time, when, as it were, they are exhibited to the multitude." Promulgation, as a necessary element in the lawfulness of law, has had varying fortunes. That a man should be informed of the laws he was expected to obey seems a desirable ideal. Caligula's practice of writing his severe tax statutes in minute letters on a tablet which he then hung up in a high place with a view to subjecting the unwary to penalties, has usually been a ground of complaint against him.[11] In Japan, before 1870, the laws were given only to the officials who were charged with their administration. This practice was in accordance with the Chinese maxim "let the people abide by, but not be apprised of, the law." In the common law system it was decided as long ago as 1365 that "everyone is bound to know what is done in Parliament, although it has not been proclaimed in the country; as soon as Parliament has concluded any matter, the law presumes that every person has cognizance of it, for Parliament represents

---

[10] *De Verborum Significatione* (1839) 14. 123. 10. There is a pun here (*promulgari, provulgari*) which cannot be translated. For Roman law, see Bonfante, *Storia del diritto Romano* (1909) 252.

[11] Dio's *Roman History* 59. 28. 11.

the body of the realm." [12] In the United States promulgation
is apparently not always necessary, inasmuch as some secret
Federal statutes have been enacted.[13] Assuming that promulgation is desirable the question at once arises to what lengths shall
it be carried. Our present-day American system assumes that
the mere printing and distribution of the statutes in book form
is sufficient. Hobbes [14] strongly objected to this practice which
also prevailed in England. " I know that most of the statutes
are printed," he said; " but it does not appear that every man
is bound to buy the book of statutes, nor to search for them at
Westminster or at the Tower, nor to understand the language
wherein they are for the most part written." His solution was
to have the statute books circulated as widely as the Bible
and to make certain that every man that could read had a copy.
The Code Napoleon and subsequent enactments provided that
the promulgation of laws shall result from their insertion in the
Bulletin des Lois (later the *Journal Officiel*) and were binding
from the moment their promulgation could be known; and
that the promulgation should be considered as known in the
department of the Imperial residence one day after that promulgation, and in each of the other departments of the French
empire after the expiration of the same space of time, augmented by as many days as there were distances of twenty
leagues between the seat of government and the place. The
provision has been widely copied in Latin America.

" The provision shows a striking difference between the
French and the English mind," Gray remarks.[15] "A Frenchman says a man cannot know the law until he has heard or
seen it; it is unjust to hold a man bound by a statute which
he could not know; the further a man lives from the seat of
Government the longer will it be before the news of the making
of a statute reaches him; and not to have a provision like that

---

[12] Thorpe, C. J., *R.* v. *Bishop of Chichester,* Y. B. 39 Ed. III, 7. For promulgation
in English law see Allen, *Law in the Making* (1927) 265.

[13] 3 Stat. 471-472 (1846).

[14] 6 *Works* (1840) 28.

[15] *Nature and Sources of the Law* (2nd ed. 1924) 165.

of the Code Napoleon would be the greatest injustice. An Englishman would be likely to say: Who reads the *Bulletin des Lois?* If it contains a statute which is of great importance, the whole country will know that such a statute has been passed by the Legislature long before it is promulgated. If the statute is not one that has excited public interest, the arrival of the *Bulletin des Lois* at the *chef-lieu* of a department is one of the most insignificant factors in the general knowledge. Is it immediately known by one in a thousand or one in twenty thousand of the inhabitants? It is foolish to worry about one or more grains of sand in such a heap of ignorance. Does any man know all the Law governing his actions? It is a serious evil to complicate the Law, and offer tempting opportunities for litigation by making a statute applicable to some citizens on one day and to other citizens on another."

In *Panama Refining Co.* v. *Ryan,* decided in 1935, the case reached the United States Supreme Court before it was discovered that a provision of the Petroleum Code on which the controversy in part hinged had been eliminated by an unpublished Executive Order. The Court commented on " the failure to give appropriate public notice of the change in the section, with the result that the persons affected, the prosecuting authorities, and the courts, were alike ignorant of the alteration." [16] In order to prevent the occurrence of similar cases and to bring administrative documents to public notice the *Federal Register* was established. It seems clear that promulgation is a firmly established ideal of the legal order but its meaning in practice is still vague and inconclusive.

There are no elements in St. Thomas' definition of law which were not insisted upon by Plato. Like St. Thomas, Plato bases law ultimately on a theological foundation,[17] insists that it is a form of reason,[18] holds that it must be made for the common good,[19] by the guardians of the community,[20] and, inasmuch as its function is to teach men to lead the good life, assumes

---

[16] 293 U. S. 388, 412.
[17] *Laws* 624A, 835C.
[18] *Laws* 714A, 875D, 890D, 957C; *Rep.* 532E.
[19] *Rep.* 466A, 519E.
[20] *Rep.* 520D *et seq.*

that it will be notified to them.[21] Nevertheless, the fact that St. Thomas put forward a comprehensive definition represents an advance over Platonic thinking, at least with respect to the philosophy of law. His definition shows an improvement in methodology which has important consequences. Through the instrumentality of the definition he is striving to realize the ideal of system. That procedure possesses both negative and positive aspects. Negatively it means that many characteristics which Plato and others have assigned to law are rejected by St. Thomas as not essential to an understanding of the nature of law or as deducible from more fundamental elements. Positively it means that the elements which St. Thomas holds to be vital are brought into relation with each other and with the even more basic components of a wider system; by that process we are more likely to discover if the propositions of the definition have a special import than if they are considered by themselves and without reference to other facts. Plato asserted that law seeks to be the discovery of reality. That proposition would have little or no meaning if we were unable to relate it to other Platonic propositions which make it intelligible. St. Thomas' procedure also means that he is aiming at completeness—that he believes he has set forth all that is necessary to be taken into account to enable us to grasp the nature of law. Such a position has large advantages. It brings to an issue the crucial contents of the theory and permits it to be tested immediately from the point of view of omissions, surplusage, and alternative propositions.

For the philosophical system for which it was framed St. Thomas' definition of law is apparently satisfactory. It is, of course, accepted by modern Thomists; it is also the one still generally followed in canon law circles. It is rejected by

---

[21] *Laws* 630C, 705E. Plato did not develop the idea of promulgation *qua* promulgation; rather, he took it so much for granted, even to the extent of arranging that the laws should be written in a persuasive and readable form, that the idea that there might be secret laws did not occur to him. He thought of law very much as did the Hebrew lawgiver: "This law is no vain thing for you, it is your life, and through this ye shall prolong your days upon the land whither ye go over Jordan to possess it." *Deut.* 32. 47.

students of positive law because their philosophical assumptions are different. Their opposed assumptions lead them to definitions of law which would be as inadequate for St. Thomas' purposes as his is for theirs. Their relative definitions of law represent a return to Aristotelian practice and a repudiation of the effort to catch all legal phenomena within the net of a single formula. At the level of utility there is no question of ultimate truth or falsity. In the centuries since it was devised St. Thomas' definition has exhibited immense vitality; it has routed numerous competitors and still exhibits in its field undiminished power. By that test it has been more successful than any other definition of law ever proposed.

Natural Law

St. Thomas' legal writings are more than the working out of a jurisprudence adjusted to thirteenth-century thinking. They are also an epitome of the major juristic principles which had come down to him tested by all the resources of Scholasticism. His summing up is so complex and, at the same time, so unified that it is difficult to disentangle his primary assumptions. Certain principles should however be stated. He believed that the universe was an orderly system and that law operated throughout its whole extent. God was the Supreme Ruler, and inasmuch as law was derived ultimately from God, it was supreme in the State. In the famous words found in Bracton [22] the King rules under God and the law, or in Pindar's phrase "Law is Lord of all." Furthermore, man is a rational being: that is the differentia which in Scholasticism divides the genus "animal." All creatures are governed by rules and move toward ends, but man alone is conscious of them. We must look, therefore, to the nature of man for an understanding of law. Through his nature he participates in the Divine Reason which he is under a duty to discover and obey. Thus the human legal order takes its origin in the efforts of man as a rational creature to follow the dictates of the Divine Reason.

[22] *De Legibus,* Folio 107.

In order to achieve his ideal of completeness St. Thomas found it necessary to recognize four kinds of law—the eternal law, the natural law, the human law, and the divine law. Since the whole community of the universe is governed by Divine Reason, the very Idea of the government of things in God the Ruler of the universe has the nature of a law; and since the Divine Reason's conception of things is not subject to time but is eternal, this kind of law must be called eternal.[23] Natural law is man's participation in the eternal law. All things subject to Divine providence are ruled and measured by the eternal law; but man as a rational creature is subject to Divine providence in a more excellent way, in so far as he partakes of a share of providence by being provident both for himself and others: and this participation of the eternal law in man is called the natural law. The light of natural reason, whereby we discern what is good and what is evil, which is the function of the natural law, is nothing else than an imprint on us of the Divine light. It is therefore evident that the natural law is nothing else than man's participation in the eternal law.[24] Thus, man knows the precepts of the natural law, not as a matter of faith, but through a rational examination of his own nature. To the extent the natural law is thus ascertained man is participating in the eternal law; but it is important to note that natural law is not discovered through an inspection of the eternal law. Human laws [25] are the particular determinations drawn by human reason from the precepts of natural

---

[23] I-II, 91, art. 1.

[24] I-II, 91, art. 2. The ontological distinction between the eternal and the natural law has been well expressed by Gilson. " The eternal law is one with the Wisdom of God which moves and directs to their end all things it has created. And so we may say with St. Augustine that God ' concreated ' the natural law along with all things that he called into existence; just as, in virtue of their existence, they participate analogically in the Divine Being, so, in virtue of the fact that the law of their activity is inscribed in their essence, in the intimate structure of their being, they participate analogically in God's eternal law. How could they receive one without the other? The natural law is to the eternal law what being is to Being." *The Spirit of Medieval Philosophy* (1936) 334.

[25] I-II, 91, art. 3.

law to fit distinct conditions. Divine law [26] is the body of precepts promulgated for mankind by God Himself and revealed in the Scriptures. All kinds of law therefore lead back to God.

It is advisable to glance briefly at St. Thomas' theory of the eternal and divine law in view of their connections with his natural law doctrine. Eternal law is nothing but Divine Wisdom directing all actions; it is also the divine law, the twofold law of God revealed in the Old and New Testaments. But natural law is a participation in us of the eternal law. Why, therefore, do we need the divine law? St. Thomas suggests four reasons: (a) Man's final end is beyond his natural ability and it is necessary that he be directed to it by a law given by God. (b) Human judgment is uncertain, especially on contingent and particular matters; hence there are different and contrary laws. The divine law informs man without any doubt what he ought to do and what he ought to avoid. (c) Human law can deal effectively only with exterior acts which are observable; but for the perfection of virtue it is necessary for man to conduct himself rightly in both his exterior and interior acts. Divine law will direct interior acts. (d) If human law attempted to prohibit all evil actions it would do more harm than good; but the supervention of divine law forbids all sins. It should not be supposed that this argument is St. Thomas' answer to ethical relativism. Since he held that the right is not right because God wills it, but that God wills it because it is right, then right has a meaning apart from God's will.

To his natural law theory St. Thomas did not hesitate to ascribe a positive content. Modern defenders of natural law are able to make out a strong case for its necessity in the light of some juristic methods; but since all efforts to concretize natural law have failed to stand the test of rigorous criticism they are chary in suggesting new ideals. St. Thomas' ideals are put universally; in that respect his proposals differ from those of modern jurists who seek to meet the usual criticisms

---

[26] I-II, 91, art. 4.

levelled against Scholastic natural law by positing their ideals for a civilization of the time and place. But St. Thomas' justification, altogether apart from matters of faith, is that his precepts follow from a theory of the nature of man. St. Thomas' claim to put his precepts universally is based on the assumption that man everywhere exhibits the same basic psychology and physiology. That does not mean, however, that St. Thomas was able to clothe his ideals with a sufficient determinateness to make them useful in the solution of actual cases where the law, because of its generality, or for other reasons, stood in need of such assistance. It is hardly necessary to add that modern ideals exhibit the same defect.

Acting on the proposition that "good is that which all things seek after," St. Thomas concludes that the basic precept of the natural law is that "good is to be done and sought after, and evil is to be avoided." It should be noted that St. Thomas has cast an observed characteristic of human conduct into the form of a precept. He regards it as the fundamental precept of natural law and holds that all other natural law precepts are deductions from it. By basing his precept on a rule of human behavior he has avoided the charge of being arbitrary. He has identified "good" with the object sought and "evil" with the object avoided. Whatever is sought therefore as a good, or avoided as an evil, belongs to the precepts of the natural law as something to be done or avoided. Furthermore, since good has the character of an end of action, and evil the contrary character, it follows that all those things to which man has a natural inclination, are naturally apprehended by reason as being good, and their contraries as evil and objects of avoidance. If St. Thomas intends the argument to be taken strictly it is so far tautological. If it is a fact that all men always seek good, then nothing substantial has been added if we say all men ought always to seek good. From what he has said, however, he deduces that the order of the precepts of natural law corresponds exactly to the order of man's natural inclinations.

Man is first of all a substance, a being. At this ontological level his inclination to good is one common to all beings: self-preservation. Therefore whatever is a means of preserving human life, and of warding off whatever tends to destroy it, belongs to the natural law. This is the first precept of the law of nature. Man is secondly a living being. At the biological level his inclination to good is one which he has in common with other animals and is exemplified by sexual intercourse, the education of offspring and so forth. Man is thirdly a rational being. His inclination to good at the sociological level requires him to know the truth about God, to live in communities, to shun ignorance, to avoid offending those among whom one has to live, and to fulfill similar duties. Altogether, these are the primary natural laws.

Through his doctrine of the existence of an order among the precepts of natural law St. Thomas was able to rank the precepts in importance. This in part prepared the way for his allowance of the mutability of some of the applications of natural law precepts. The doctrine was an adaptation of the Aristotelian principle of the primacy of individual substance, the foundation presupposed by all the other categories. St. Thomas held that just as *being* is the first thing that falls under the apprehension absolutely, so *good* is the first thing that falls under the apprehension of the practical reason. Hence the first principle of the practical reason, and hence of natural law, is based on the nature of good. St. Thomas laid great stress upon the self-evident character of the idea of good as the substratum of the first principle of the practical reason. The view that certain principles were self-evident and their truth apprehended through a special faculty (Noûs) was a dogma of Aristotelian logic; the idea was apparently derived from Euclidean geometry which was regarded as a model of precise thinking. With the recognition that Euclidean axioms are not unquestionable first principles, but postulates that possess significance only from the point of view of the use to which they can be put, the idea of " self-evidence " has disappeared as a legitimate mode of argument. What is really valuable, however, in St. Thomas' analysis, is his conception of levels of order. It is a remarkable anticipation of the current tendency in sociological thought, which reduces all material phenomena to the inorganic, the organic, and the interorganic or societary. St. Thomas' classification and the modern one both recognize the inseparability of material phenomena and the reciprocity and interdependence of the different levels. " All observable phenomena," Comte wrote, " may be included within a very few material categories, so arranged that the study of each category may be grounded on the principal laws of the preceding, and serve as a basis for the next ensuing." St. Thomas' grasp of the importance of this methodological principle was as firm as that exhibited by present-day social thought.

As jural ideals, putting aside whatever value they may possess as moral precepts, St. Thomas' natural laws are plainly defective. It is impossible to imagine their being able to determine any crucial case. However, even as jural ideals they are not altogether devoid of positive value. Ideals are an ineliminable aspect of the legal order. Their precise formulation has been a never ending task of the philosophy of law; in large part it has been a process of trial and error. St. Thomas' efforts at a careful statement of them are valuable as a pioneer attempt; his principles are materials for subsequent generations to modify and reshape into more perspicuous guides.

Not all virtuous acts are claimed by St. Thomas to be prescribed by the natural law. He allows for the discovery of the virtue of certain acts through independent rational inquiry. In order to reach this result he is forced to distinguish two meanings of the word virtuous. If we speak of acts of virtue, considered as virtuous, then all virtuous acts belong to the natural law. For to the natural law belongs everything to which a man is inclined according to his nature, and since man is a rational animal there is in every man a natural inclination to act according to reason; and this is to act according to virtue. Consequently, all acts of virtue are prescribed by the natural law, since man's reason naturally dictates to him to act virtuously. However, if we speak of virtuous acts, considered in themselves, then not all virtuous acts are prescribed by the natural law. For many things are done virtuously, to which nature does not incline at first; but which, through rational inquiry, have been found by men to be conducive to well-living.[27] This argument opens the way for St. Thomas to insist later on the Platonic principle that human law is necessary as a discipline to train men to virtuous acts.

It is St. Thomas' position that the natural law is immutable, but here, again, he is forced to make a distinction, inasmuch as, an experienced moralist, he knew it to be the part of wisdom to allow for the possibility of an exception to any concrete moral rule. His distinction follows from the difference which he asserts between the speculative and the practical reason. The first is concerned with necessary things, which cannot be otherwise than they are, and its proper conclusions therefore contain the truth without fail. The second is occupied with contingent matters which are the domain of human actions; consequently, although there is necessity in the general principles, the more we descend to the particular, the more frequently we encounter defects. Accordingly, then, St. Thomas holds that in speculative matters truth is the same in all men, both as to principles and as to conclusions; although the truth is not known to all as regards the conclusions, but only as regards the principles. But in matters of action, truth or practical rectitude is not the same for all as to what is particular, but only as to the general principle. And where there is the same rectitude with respect to matters of detail, it is not equally known to all.

It is therefore evident that, as regards the general principles whether of speculative or of practical reason, truth or rectitude is the same for all, and is equally known by all. As to the

[27] I-II, 94, art. 3.

proper conclusions of the speculative reason, the truth is the same for all, but is not equally known to all. Thus, it is true for all that the three angles of a triangle are together equal to two right angles, although it is not known to all. But as to the proper conclusions of the practical reason, neither is the truth or rectitude the same for all, nor, where it is the same, is it equally known by all. Thus, it is right and true for all to act according to reason; and from this principle it follows that goods entrusted to another should be restored to their owner. Now this is true for the majority of cases; but it may happen in a particular case that it would be injurious, and therefore unreasonable to restore goods held in trust, *e. g.*, if they are claimed for use in a war against one's own country. This principle has less applicability the more we descend into detail. It will be of little assistance in determining whether goods held in trust on numerous conditions should or should not be restored to their owner. The same point had been insisted upon by Plato in the *Republic,* where Socrates pointed out that it was impossible to affirm without qualification that it was always just for a bailee to return to the owner objects which had been entrusted to him. Plato put the case of weapons acquired from a friend who was in his right mind, but who subsequently went mad and demanded them back.

Consequently, St. Thomas concludes, we must say that the natural law, as to general principles, is the same for all, both as to rectitude and as to knowledge. But as to certain matters of detail, which are attempted deductions from the general principles, it is the same for all in the majority of cases, both as to rectitude and as to knowledge; and yet in some few cases it may fail as to both. Thus Caesar reported that theft, although it is expressly contrary to the natural law, was not considered wrong among the Germans. It is interesting to note here that St. Thomas seems to be expressly providing for the relativity of moral behavior, a conception which has been often advanced as being inherently opposed to the idea of natural law.

In spite of its immutability the natural law can be changed

in two ways, provided the word " change " is understood in St. Thomas' meaning. It can be changed by way of addition, since many things for the benefit of human life have been added over and above the natural law, both by the divine law and by human laws. It may also be changed by subtraction, so that what previously was according to the natural law, ceases to be so. In this sense, the natural law is altogether unchangeable in its first principles; but in its secondary principles, which are the detailed proximate conclusions drawn from the first principles, the natural law is not changed, it remains right in most cases; but it may be changed in some particular cases of rare occurrence, through some special causes hindering the observance of such precepts, as in the case of goods deposited on trust.[28]

As a logical system St. Thomas' theory of natural law has much to recommend it. When we compare it with the Platonic and Aristotelian doctrines of the unwritten law, and with Cicero's theory of the natural law, it is apparent how much in the way of definiteness and extension has been added to the idea. However, in order to encompass the facts of both the legal and moral orders, St. Thomas has been forced to sacrifice concreteness for generality. But the generality he has achieved is so extensive that opposite principles can be subsumed, as he recognized, under his primary postulates. In a developed legal system the judges do not need guidance of the order of generality St. Thomas offers them. To be told to do good and to avoid evil is a meaningless injunction in the judicial process so far as concerns any help it renders in the decision of concrete cases. A theory of natural law, to fulfill a useful function in any system of developed law, must be sufficiently specific, or permit the drawing of specific deductions, to guide the judge in the decision of cases which the law fails to cover. Should the police in their pursuit of criminals be allowed to tap the wires of suspects? By no process of sound logic can the answer to that question, which is typical of those which courts must

[28] I-II, 94, arts. 4-5.

decide, be deduced from St. Thomas' premises. It is for that principal reason, putting aside the shift in the philosophical point of view since his time, that St. Thomas' theory has ceased to be a direct influence in contemporary legal thought. The ends he sought to achieve through a system of natural law are, after a period of eclipse, now the subject of revived speculation. His great contribution was in insisting upon a rational approach to the problem.

Human Law

Natural law, St. Thomas held, was written in the hearts of men, and its general precepts could not be blotted out. Now the natural law is a participation of the eternal law, and through the eternal law all things are ordered. It would seem therefore that the natural law suffices for the ordering of all human affairs and that consequently there is no need for human laws.

To avoid this difficulty St. Thomas appeals first to the logical procedures of thought generally. He had already established the proposition that a law is a dictate of the practical reason, and that in both the practical and the speculative reason the same reasoning process takes place, for each proceeds from principles to conclusions. He argues that in the speculative reason from naturally known indemonstrable principles we draw the conclusions of the various sciences; the knowledge of these sciences is not imparted to us by nature but is acquired by the efforts of reason. Similarly from the precepts of the natural law, as from general and indemonstrable principles, the human reason needs to proceed to the more particular determination of certain matters. These particular determinations, devised by human reason, are called human laws, provided the other essential conditions of law are observed. Thus man has a natural participation in the eternal law, according to certain general principles, but not as regards the particular determinations of individual cases, which are, however, contained in the eternal law. Hence the need for human reason to proceed further to sanction them by law. However, human laws have a particular infirmity. St. Thomas takes the Aristotelian position that the practical reason is concerned with practical matters, which are singular and contingent; but not with necessary things, with which the speculative reason is concerned. Therefore human laws cannot have that inerrancy that belongs to the demonstrated conclusions of sciences of the type of geometry.[29]

This argument establishes the necessity of human law insofar as the natural law is concerned. Putting to one side the theory of natural law, are human or statutory laws necessary? In the ideal tradition of Western thought they are apparently held to be undesirable, since there is usually an effort to exclude them in the construction of Utopias. Are not men more to be induced to be good willingly by means of admonitions, than against their will, by means of laws? Animate justice is better than inanimate justice, which is contained in laws. Is it not better for the execution of justice to be entrusted to the decision of judges, than to frame laws in addition? Every law is framed for the direction of human actions; but human actions are about particular things, which are infinite in number. But matters pertaining to the direction of human actions cannot be taken into sufficient consideration except by a wise man, who looks into each one of them. Is it not better for human acts to be directed by the judgment of wise men, than by the framing of laws?

To these questions St. Thomas gives the general Platonic answer. Man has a natural aptitude for virtue, but in its perfection virtue can be acquired only by training. It can scarcely be argued that man can give this training to himself, inasmuch as the essence of it requires man to abstain from immoderate pleasures to which he is inclined; this is especially true of the young, who are more capable of being trained. Man must therefore receive this training from some one else. Paternal training, *i.e.*, admonition, suffices for those among

[29] I-II, 91, art. 3.

the young who are inclined to acts of virtue by their good natural dispositions, or by custom, or by the gift of God. But the dissolute, who will not heed admonitions, must be restrained by force and fear. In time they will be inculcated with the habits of virtue and will do willingly what formerly they did from fear. Training of this kind, which compels obedience through fear of punishment, is the discipline of laws. Therefore, if man is to have peace and virtue, it is necessary for laws to be established. As Aristotle observed, man is the best of animals when perfected, but he is the worst of all when severed from law and justice. Through his reason man can find ways to satisfy his lusts and evil passions, an accomplishment not open to other animals.

St. Thomas reinforced this general argument with some additional observations. He conceded that men who are well disposed are led to virtue more willingly by admonitions than by coercion; but evilly disposed men must be forced to be virtuous. Again, not all men are fit to be judges, and even the justice which the judge is supposed to administer can be perverted; thus it is necessary for the law to determine, whenever possible, how to judge, and to leave few matters to the decision of men. Certain matters, of course, must necessarily be committed to judges. Legislation cannot determine, for example, in advance whether an event has or has not happened.

St. Thomas' argument for law as a necessity of human society is entirely an ethical one. In its insistence upon the good life as a primary aim of human association it is characteristically Greek in its point of view. The approach today is different. Now there is an attempt to show that law in some sense is an essential constituent of society generally, altogether apart from its function as an instrument in the promotion of ethical conduct. Suárez's conception of the human animal as the "legal man," so vital is law to him, and Bagehot's theory of man as "a custom-making animal," were steps in the direction of the present-day position. Nineteenth-century anthropology and, to a considerable extent, current sociology, advance the view that legal systems are unnecessary in primitive life, inasmuch as man at that level is restrained by other forces, such as religion, and is inherently law-abiding. This view is disputed by some modern anthropologists who insist, in Malinowski's words, that "there must be in all societies a class of rules too practical to be backed up by religious sanctions, too burdensome to be left to mere good-will, too personally vital to individuals to be enforced by any abstract agency. This is the domain of legal rules." This position has wide, but far from unanimous, support. It is an effort to account for the social structure at the level of descriptive empiricism. St. Thomas' theory envisages a different objective, namely, the task of ordering society on a rational basis.[30]

Is every human law derived from the natural law? St. Thomas accepts the ancient tradition that an unjust law is no law. Consequently, human laws have exactly the nature of law to the extent they are derived from the natural law. If a human law does not follow the natural law, it is not a law but a perversion of law. But there are two modes of derivation from the natural law. Some enactments are deduced from natural law premises. Thus " killing is unlawful " may be derived from the principle " one should do harm to no man." Other enactments are applications of principles, as when a builder adapts the general form of a house to some particular shape. Thus it is a principle of the law of nature that a wrongdoer shall be punished, but the manner in which he shall be punished is an application of the principle. Human law discloses both modes of derivation; but inasmuch as the former are not mere legal enactments they partake of some of the force of natural law; the latter have the force of human law only.

Many different conclusions, however, can be derived from the same premise, and the same premise can be applied in many different ways. It was therefore necessary for St. Thomas

[30] I-II, 95, art. 1. Suárez, *Tractatus de legibus deo legislatore* (1612) Bk. I; Bagehot, *Physics and Politics* (1873) 141; Malinowski, *Crime and Custom in Savage Society* (1926) 67-68.

to introduce an additional standard by which to measure human laws. If he adopted derivation from natural law as the sole test of the legitimacy of human law, he could be confronted with legal systems that conformed fully to that measure but which had no relevancy to society as a functioning association. He found this further test in the Aristotelian doctrine of teleology. He held that the form of anything that has an end must be determined proportionately to that end, *e. g.*, the form of a saw must be suitable for cutting. Furthermore, the form of anything that is ruled and measured must be proportionate to the rule and measure. Human law satisfies both these conditions. Its measure is the divine law and natural law. It is ordained to an end, which is to be useful to man. Thus human law conforms to the measure of the divine law when it is virtuous; it conforms to the measure of the natural law when it is just, possible to nature, in accordance with the custom of the country, and adapted to the time and place; it conforms to the criterion of usefulness when it is necessary, when it is clearly expressed (so that harm will not follow from the law itself), and when it is not framed for private benefit, but for the common good. These tests mean, among other things that human law will vary with the time and place, and properly so.

At this point in his argument St. Thomas raised the question of the power or authority of human law. Its end was the common good. Was its power to achieve that end unlimited? We have been taught today, in Pound's happy phrase, that there are limits to effective legal action. The admonition of Shelley's schoolmaster, " Boys, be pure in heart or I'll flog you " well illustrates one of the inherent limitations of the legal order. " Whenever the offense inspires less horror than the punishment," Gibbon wrote from another point of view, " the rigour of penal law is obliged to give way to the common feelings of mankind." St. Thomas' general conclusion does not differ materially from that of modern legal analysis; but he thought of the problem in much wider terms than does the present day jurist. Contemporary analysis has narrowed the question to a consideration of the failure of law in specific cases. Thus the requirement that money be paid as redress for injury to the character or reputation of an individual is often insufficient compensation. The modern jurist asks himself if it is not possible that some other remedy can be devised to meet this inadequacy of the law of defamation. That approach is perhaps the most remunerative one to increase the effectiveness of a legal order. St. Thomas' analysis, however, was confined to a treatment of the general problem.

He had first to decide whether laws should be framed for the community or for the individual. Specifically, since decrees are framed with individual actions in mind it would seem that law is framed not only for the community, but also for the individual. Again, human acts are about individual matters, and therefore law should be framed, not for the community, but rather for the individual. Further, law is a rule and measure of human acts. But a measure should be certain. Since, therefore, in human acts no general proposition can be so certain as not to fail in some individual cases it seems that laws should be framed not in general but for individual cases.

However St. Thomas' position was that whatever is for an end should be proportionate to that end. Inasmuch as the end of law is the common good, human laws should be proportionate to the common good. But the common good consists of many things which the law, in order to function properly, must notice. It must take account of persons, matters and times in all their multitudinous aspects. Since the community is comprised of many persons, its good is procured by many actions, and it is established to endure for a long time.

To the specific objections he replied that law is composed of more than decrees. Again, if there were as many rules or measures as there are things measured or ruled, they would cease to be of use, since their use consists in being applicable to many things. Further, we must not seek the same degree of certainty in all things. Consequently in contingent matters, such as natural and human things, it is enough for a thing to be certain, as being true in the greater number of instances, though at times, and less frequently, it fail.[31]

Our experience with the National Prohibition Law taught us some of the evils involved in the endeavor to repress some conduct by law. Although the end of law is the common good, the law is not the sole agency to accomplish that result. As St. Thomas remarks, " Man is not ordained to the political commonwealth to the full extent of all that he is and has." [32] He is firmly of the opinion that it is not a function of human law to control all undesirable behavior. If a law is a measure of human acts, then it ought to be homogeneous with that which it measures. Hence laws must take account of the differences among men. In St. Thomas' theory the springs of action take their origin in habit or disposition, and thus a man possessed of virtuous habits will be able to accomplish tasks beyond the range of one who has not formed such habits. For this reason St. Thomas insists that a child is not held to the same legal accountability as an adult. In Anglo-American law the legal irresponsibility of children under seven rests upon a different ground, namely their mental incapacity or, as Blackstone phrases it, their " defect of understanding." This ground would also permit the adoption of the rule of Chinese law which exempts from punishment persons of advanced age. St. Thomas points out that society allows by custom conduct which in a perfectly virtuous man would be intolerable. Human law itself is framed, not for the perfectly virtuous, but for human beings generally. Therefore human law does not prohibit all the vices from which the virtuous abstain, but only the graver excesses from which it is possible for the majority to abstain. It prohibits chiefly those excesses that are injurious to others, without the prohibition of which society could not be maintained, such as murder and theft. At this point St. Thomas' ethical approach exhibits a deficiency of analysis

---

[31] I-II, 96, art. 1.   [32] I-II, 21, art. 4.

which the present-day empirical reduction of the problem appears to have overcome. In the modern theory it is insisted that legal power is inherently limited whatever may be the wishes of the community. As Morris Cohen has pointed out, any proposal to repeal the New York State statute making adultery a crime would arouse widespread resentment. Many thousands of divorces have been granted for the offense, yet there are hardly any convictions for the crime. The statute is simply too difficult to enforce.

Human law, St. Thomas observes, aims at educating men in virtue by gradual steps, and not suddenly. Hence it makes no attempt to impose upon the multitude of imperfect men the burdens which are borne by the virtuous, *viz.*, that they shall abstain from all evil. Otherwise, as Spinoza was to argue later, these imperfect persons, unable to carry the burden of such precepts, will be instigated to greater evils. This is ancient wisdom. "He that violently bloweth his nose, bringeth out blood."[33] Again, if "new wine," *i. e.*, precepts of a perfect life, is "put into old bottles," *i. e.*, into imperfect men, "the bottles break and the wine runneth out,"[34] *i. e.*, the precepts are rejected and the men out of contempt rush into worse evils.[35]

However, in St. Thomas' theory, since the law is ordained to the common good, there is no virtue whose acts cannot be prescribed by the law. Nevertheless human law does not prescribe all virtuous acts, but those ordainable to the common good. However, human law prohibits some acts of each vice and also prescribes some acts of each virtue.[36]

St. Thomas was of the opinion that human laws, if just, have the power of binding in conscience.[37] He also considered at some length whether all are subject to law. This question at times takes on a practical importance. It appeared at one stage of the proceedings that the trial of Louis XVI could not be continued constitutionally. However, the report of the

[33] Prov. XXX, 33.
[34] Matt. IX, 17.
[35] I-II, 96, art. 2.
[36] I-II, 96, art. 3.
[37] I-II, 96, art. 4.

Committee of Legislation maintained that the nation was sovereign and was above its own constitution. St. Thomas addressed himself to the specific question whether the just, the spiritual, and the sovereign were subject to law. He pointed out that there were two essential elements in law: it is a rule of human conduct and it has coercive powers. Hence man is subject to law in two ways. When law is viewed as a rule of human conduct, whoever is subject to the power that frames the rule is subject to the rule framed by the power. Thus the citizen of one country is not bound by the laws of another country since he is not subject to the authority of that country. Again, the subject of a proconsul should obey his laws, but not in cases in which the subject receives his orders from the emperor. In those instances he is not bound by the mandate of the lower authority, since he is directed by that of a higher. This is, of course, a basic principle of American constitutional law, which traces most authority to the Constitution. Thus in *Kilbourn* v. *Thompson*, 103 U. S. 168 (1880), it was held that the sergeant-at-arms of the House of Representatives should have disregarded orders of the House which were contrary to the Constitution.

When law is viewed in the light of its coercive power St. Thomas held that the wicked, but not the virtuous, were subject to its commands. Coercion acts contrary to the will; but the will of the good is in harmony with the law and there is thus no occasion to call the power into operation. The spiritual are not subject to laws inconsistent with the guidance of the Holy Ghost, but an effect of that guidance is to subject men to human authority. The sovereign is exempt from the coercive power of law inasmuch as he cannot coerce himself, and law has no coercive power save from the authority of the sovereign. In that sense, if the sovereign disobeys the law, he is exempt from its penalties, because there is no one to pass sentence upon him. In its directive force, however, the sovereign is subject to the law by his own will, and he should obey it voluntarily. This is St. Thomas' effort to rationalize the Roman law doctrine of *legibus solutus,* that the Emperor was above the law.[38]

Aristotle had maintained that the law had no power to compel obedience except the force of habit, and habit only grows up in a long lapse of time, so that lightly to change from the existing laws to other new laws is to weaken the power of the law. "Law must be stable and yet it cannot stand still," Pound [39] has written in a now classic sentence. "Hence all thinking about law has struggled to reconcile the conflicting demands of the need of stability and of the need of change." St. Thomas inquired whether human law is changeable, whether it should be always changed whenever anything better occurs; whether it is abolished by custom, and whether custom obtains the force of law.[40]

If human law is derived from the natural law, which is immutable, human law is also immutable. It is also the essence of law to be just and right; but that which is right once is right always. Therefore that which is law once should be always law. To these arguments St. Thomas answered that law is a dictate of reason for the direction of human acts. Just changes of human law may spring therefore either from reason or from the condition of men whose acts are regulated by law. With respect to the former, it seems in accordance with nature for human reason to advance gradually from the imperfect to the perfect. We know that the teachings of the early philosophers were imperfect, and that they have been corrected by later thinkers. In practical matters the same rule obtains. Those who devise the structure of society are not able to take everything into consideration, and their institutions reveal many deficiencies which subsequent lawgivers must correct. With respect to the condition of man, it is right to

[38] I-II, 96, art. 5.

[39] *Interpretations of Legal History* (1923) 1.

[40] I-II, 97. "If I had the choice," writes Shorey, "of putting into the hands of a student of Aristotle the commentary of Thomas or the book of some recent interpreter of Aristotle, I would choose the medieval schoolman as more educative in sensible methods and less likely to mislead and confuse the student." *Platonism Ancient and Modern* (1938) 90.

change the law when man's condition changes. Law must be adapted to the time and place. St. Thomas cites an example from St. Augustine:[41] If the people have a sense of moderation and responsibility, and are careful guardians of the common welfare, a law allowing such a people to choose their own magistrates is a proper one. With the passage of time, if the people become corrupt, barter their votes, and entrust the government to scoundrels and criminals, then the people rightly forfeit their power to appoint their public officials, and the choice devolves upon a few good men.

Human law is rightly changed, in so far as such change is conducive to the common weal. To a certain extent, however, the mere change of law is of itself prejudicial to the common good, because custom itself is a main instrument in law observance. We know that statutes contrary to common custom, though right in themselves, seem burdensome. Hence, when law is changed, the binding power of the law is diminished, inasmuch as a custom is set aside. Hence human law ought not to be changed, unless the gain to the public advantage on one side is enough to balance the loss on the other.

It is clear to St. Thomas that custom could obtain the force of law. It is clear also that law may be altered by men's words, *e. g.*, by legislation which directs a change. Hence, also, by repeatedly multiplied acts, which make a custom, law may be altered, and even established. Custom could also operate to repeal a law.[42]

With respect to human law it should be noted finally that St. Thomas distinguished the *ius gentium* from the *ius naturale*. The former falls short of the latter, because the latter is common to all animals, while the former is common to men only.[43] Elsewhere, he says that positive law is divided into

---

[41] *De Lib. Arb.* i. 6.

[42] St. Thomas' argument here follows closely that of D. I, 3, 32. For an interpretation of the provision in the Digest and the abrogation of statutes by disuse, see Gray, *Nature and Sources of the Law* (1924) 190 *et seq.*

[43] II-II, 57, art. 3.

the *ius gentium* and the *ius civile*.[44] The *ius gentium* is a part of positive human law to the extent that it is law, but a part of the natural law to the extent that it is just. It thus occupies an intermediate position between natural and positive law, but it derives its binding force from both.

INTERPRETATION

By the thirteenth century the Fathers of the Church could be cited both for and against the proposition that the letter of the law should prevail. Thus on the basis of a sentence from St. Augustine [45] it was claimed that the letter of the law should prevail over the intention of the lawgiver. St. Hilarius,[46] on the contrary, could be brought forward in support of the principle that we should take account of the motive of the lawgiver, rather than his very words.

St. Thomas' solution follows strictly from his general conception of the nature of law and is in the nature of a compromise. Every law is ordained to the common welfare of men, and has so far the essence and force of law. Hence, the rule of the *Digest*:[47] By no reason of law, or favor of equity, is it allowable for us to interpret harshly, and render burdensome, those useful measures which have been enacted for the welfare of man. But we often see that the observance of a law is in accord with the common good in many instances, but, in some cases, is clearly harmful. The lawgiver cannot have every single case in view, and he must frame laws for the majority of cases, keeping the common good in mind. Hence, if a case arises in which the observance of a law would be harmful to the general welfare, it should not be observed. This rule is not applicable to everyone. If observance of the letter of the law does not involve a sudden risk needing instant remedy, it is not competent for everyone to expound what is useful and what is not useful to the state. That right is confined to those in authority, who have the power to make

[44] I-II, 95, art. 4.   [46] *De Trin.* iv.
[45] *De Vera Relig.* XXXI.   [47] D. 1. 3. *De Leg. et Senat.*

exceptions to the laws. However, if there is a sudden peril so that delay is impossible, the necessity brings with it a dispensation, because necessity knows no law.[48] In stating this last rule it appears from the context that St. Thomas is thinking of cases of military necessity. In American constitutional law, the doctrine in cases of military necessity is that " the emergency gives the right ";[49] in other cases it is stated that " while emergency does not create power, emergency may furnish the occasion for the exercise of power." [50]

Substantially the same argument is used by St. Thomas in discussing the end of equity [51] and the judicial process.[52] When the observance of the letter of the law is against the equality of justice and the public good it is equitable to disregard it; similarly, if the observance of the law's letter would be contrary to the natural law, it may be disregarded. Again, he who is placed over a community has the power of making exceptions to the human law that rests upon his authority, so that, when the law fails in its application to persons or circumstances, he may waive the precept of the law.[53]

JUSTICE AND THE JUDICIAL PROCESS

Ulpian's definition of justice as the constant and perpetual wish to give each man his due is accepted by St. Thomas provided it is understood correctly. In order to make it conform with his psychology he recast it to read: Justice is a habit whereby a man renders to each one his due by a constant and perpetual will.[54] Its fundamental idea is some kind of equality, and therefore it is proper to justice to direct man in his relations with others.[55] Aristotle's thinking is a potent factor in much of St. Thomas' discussion, and he follows him in

---

[48] I-II, 96, art. 6.
[49] *Mitchell* v. *Harmony*, 13 How. 115, 134 (1851); *U. S.* v. *Russell*, 80 U. S. 623, 628 (1871).
[50] *Home Building and Loan Assoc.* v. *Blaisdell*, 290 U. S. 398, 426 (1934).
[51] II-II, 120, art. 1.
[52] II-II, 60, art. 5.   [54] II-II, 58, art. 1.
[53] I-II, 94, art. 4.   [55] II-II, 57, art. 1.

the distinction between " distributive " and " commutative " justice.[56] His analysis, however, is elaborate, and he endeavors to bring into a consistent system Aristotle's thoughts on the subject and what appears to him meritorious from the thought of the intervening centuries. We may pass over the main discussion which is devoted to a consideration of justice as a moral virtue, and examine his idea of legal justice, which is given a concrete content in the description of the *judicium* or the judicial process.

Human acts, about which laws are framed, are so many singular occurrences of infinite possible variety. Hence it is impossible for any rule of law to be established that should in no case fall short of what is desirable.[57] Now a judge's conclusion is like a particular law regarding some particular fact.[58] Men have recourse to a judge, as Aristotle observed, as to animate justice.[59] Three conditions must be fulfilled for a judgment to be an act of justice: first, it must proceed from the inclination of justice; secondly, it must come from one who is in authority; thirdly, it must be pronounced according to the right ruling of prudence, or in accordance with that intellectual discernment which perceives the golden mean of moral virtue and the way to rescue that mean.[60] Judgment must not be formed from suspicions, that is, from slight indications;[61] doubts should be interpreted in favor of the accused;[62] judgment should be pronounced according to the written law;[63] in order for the sentence of the judge to have coercive power it is necessary that the judge have jurisdiction; a judge's judgment should be based on information acquired by him, not from his knowledge as a private individual, but from what he knows as a public person; finally, in criminal cases, the judge cannot condemn a man unless the latter has an accuser.[64]

In accusation the punishment of another's crime is intended.

---

[56] II-II, 61, art. 1.
[57] II-II, 120, art. 1.
[58] II-II, 67, art. 1. *Cf.* I-II, 96, art. 1. ad 1.
[59] I-II, 65, art. 1.
[60] II-II, 60, art. 2.

[61] II-II, 60, art. 3.
[62] II-II, 60, art. 4.
[63] II-II, 60, art. 5.
[64] II-II, 67.

In the case of a crime that conduces to the injury of the commonwealth St. Thomas held that a man is bound to accusation. In criminal cases the accusation should be put in writing. The accuser must be on guard against utterance of false accusations out of malice, collusion, and of withdrawing from the accusation. However, the accusation may be quashed by the sovereign who has the care of the common good. An accuser who fails to prove his indictment must suffer the punishment of retaliation. In support of this rule, St. Thomas argues that where the procedure is by way of accusation, the accuser is in the position of intending the punishment of the accused. It is the duty of the judge to establish equality of justice between them; and equality of justice requires that a man should himself suffer whatever harm he has intended to be inflicted on another, according to the *lex talionis.* Consequently it is just that he who by accusing a man has put him in danger of being punished severely, should himself suffer a like punishment.[65] This rule, which in one form or another had prevailed since the days of ancient Greece, continued throughout the Middle Ages and is given modern expression in the provision now common to many countries that innocent victims of unjust convictions shall be compensated by the State. In English law in the Middle Ages when a court occasionally permitted a witness to testify, the court's action protected the witness against proceedings for maintenance.

A defendant is duty bound to tell the judge the truth, which the latter exacts from him according to the form of law. He is not bound to divulge all the truth, but only such as the judge can and must require of him according to the order of justice. By not answering questions which he is not bound to answer he is merely acting prudently. However, he must never defend himself with calumny, guile or fraud. A man may appeal if he believes he is unjustly oppressed by the judge, but an appeal ought not to be allowed merely for the sake of delay. Also it ought not to be permitted from a

[65] II-II, 68.

judgment of arbitrators who were chosen by the litigants, since the litigants themselves by their choice approved of the judgment beforehand. These considerations do not in St. Thomas' opinion, apply in the case of an ordinary judge since his authority does not depend on the consent of those who are subject to his judgment. A man justly condemned to death must submit to the punishment, but if the sentence is unjust he may resist it to the point where a public scandal might ensue. St. Thomas believed that he might also endeavor to escape from prison, thus reversing Socrates' opinion.[66] However, the commentators of St. Thomas are far from agreeing on the validity of this conclusion.

St. Thomas went into the question of evidence with great care. His discussion is important because it shows him grappling with a problem which English law was not to settle for several centuries. At the time St. Thomas wrote it was " a general rule that no one could be compelled, or even suffered, to testify to a fact, unless when that fact happened he was solemnly ' taken to witness.' "[67] In 1291-92 the king attempted to force certain magnates to take an oath with respect to the existence of specific facts. They maintained that there was no precedent for such a proceeding, and they refused to take the oath until they had consulted with their peers.[68] Not until Parliament intervened with legislation in 1562 was it settled that witnesses could be compelled to testify to the court. Holdsworth points out that canonist theories of evidence were in the air in the thirteenth century in England, and that Bracton knew something of them. If this influence had continued it is quite possible that the English law of witnesses and evidence would have been worked out at a much earlier date than it actually was. But the result would have been, Holdsworth believes, a procedure modelled on that of the canon law, which would have eliminated the jury. " The jury would have been treated as witnesses; and, at a later date,

[66] II-II, 69.
[67] 2 Pollock and Maitland, *History of English Law* (2nd ed. 1899) 601.
[68] 9 Holdsworth, *History of English Law* (1926) 179.

the wish to reconcile the rules as to the strict proof required by the law, with the need to suppress crime, would have introduced into England, as into other states, the use of torture as a regular part of the judicial procedure." [69] This danger was averted, but it meant several centuries delay in the development of the use of witnesses.

At the outset St. Thomas raised the fundamental question whether there is a duty to give evidence. The rules he laid down in answer to the question were framed in accordance with the nature of the case in which the witness was to testify. The first class involves a witness subject to a superior whom he is bound to obey in matters of justice. In that case he is bound to give evidence on those points which are required of him in accordance with the order of justice, *e. g.*, on manifest things. He is not bound to give evidence, however, on secret matters. In the second class the witnesses' evidence is not called for by a superior authority. Under those circumstances, if his evidence is required to deliver a man from an unjust punishment, he is bound to give it; but he is not bound to give evidence tending to the condemnation of a man unless compelled by superior authority. St. Thomas attempts to support this rule with the argument that if the truth of such a matter is concealed, no particular injury is inflicted on anyone. How he reconciles this doctrine with his theory of the common good is not clear. In the same vein is his conclusion that a danger which threatens the accuser is of no moment since he risked the danger of his own accord. It is otherwise with the accused who is in danger against his will.

If the testimony of the witnesses is in conflict with respect to matters of substance (*i. e.*, matters of time, place or person), then the evidence, in St. Thomas' opinion, is of no weight. He rejects the evidence on the ground that the witnesses are manifestly speaking of different matters. He puts the case of a witness who says that a certain thing happened at such and such a time or place, while another says it happened at a

---

[69] *Op. cit.* 180.

different time or place. St. Thomas believes they are not speaking of the same event. If there is complete disagreement on such matters between the witnesses for the prosecution and defence, and if, on either side, they are of equal number and standing, the accused should have the benefit of the doubt. St. Thomas laid it down as a general rule that the judge ought to be more inclined to acquit than to condemn. It is possible, however, for the witnesses for the same side to disagree. In those circumstances the judge must use his discretion in determining which side to favor; he should take into consideration the number of witnesses, their standing, the favorableness of the suit, the nature of the matter involved and the evidence. The testimony of a witness who contradicts himself when questioned about matters he has seen and heard should be rejected; this rule is not to be applied, however, if he contradicts himself on matters of opinion and report.

The evidence is not to be regarded as weakened if there is a discrepancy in the testimony on minor matters of fact, as for instance, whether the weather was cloudy or fine, whether the house was painted or not. For the most part men are not apt to notice such things and easily forget them. It was clear to St. Thomas that discrepancies of this kind render the evidence more credible. If the witnesses agree in every particular, even in the minutest details, it gives rise to the legitimate inference that they have conspired together to say the same thing. This is a question, however, in St. Thomas' opinion, that must be left to the prudent discernment of the judge.

The authority of evidence is not infallible but probable; consequently the evidence for one side is weakened by whatever strengthens the probability of the other. St. Thomas approached this matter through a consideration of the rules with respect to the competency of witnesses. Sometimes a witness's testimony is weakened through some fault of his own, as in the cases of unbelievers, persons of evil repute, and those guilty of a public crime. Sometimes there is no fault on the part of the witness. Thus we have the cases of insufficient reason, as in children, imbeciles and women; cases of personal feeling, as in enemies or persons united by family or household ties; cases of external condition, as in the poor, slaves, and those under authority. In the latter instance it may be presumed that they might easily be induced to give evidence against the truth.[70] Rules of this character were listed by Bracton, Fleta and Britton as stating grounds on which jurors could be challenged. Salmond points out that the lists were influenced by the rules of the canon law. Thus, he writes, "the canon law rejected the testimony of all males under fourteen and females under twelve, of the blind and the deaf and dumb, of slaves, infamous persons, and those convicted of crime, of excommunicated persons, of poor persons and women in criminal cases, of persons connected with either party by consanguinity and affinity or belonging to the household of either party, and of Jews, heretics and pagans."[71] Although these rules were devised for jurors, some of them were adapted to the new class of witnesses in the fifteenth and sixteenth centuries.

An advocate is not always bound to defend suits of the poor but only when conditions of time, place, and circumstances require it. If a contrary rule prevailed he would have no time left for other business. An advocate who is defective in skill should be debarred from practice. A lawyer provides both assistance and counsel for the party for whom he pleads. Hence, if knowingly he defends an unjust cause, he sins grievously and is bound to make restitution of the loss unjustly incurred by the other party by reason of the assistance he has provided. If, however, he defends an unjust cause unknowingly, thinking it just, he is to be excused according to the measure in which ignorance is excusable. An advocate, however, may believe at the outset that the cause is just, and discover afterwards, while the case is proceeding, that it is

[70] II-II, 70.
[71] *Essays in Jurisprudence* (1891) 29, quoted 9 Holdsworth, *History of English Law,* 186.

unjust. In those circumstances he ought not to retire from the case in such a way as to help the other side or so as to reveal the secrets of his clients to the other party, but he can, and must, give up the case or induce his client to abandon it or to make some compromise without prejudice to the opposing party. A cause is not unjust in criminal matters merely because the client is guilty. It was once thought to be simony to sell the fruit of the mind since it was the sale of a spiritual thing. However, St. Thomas held that a lawyer might sell his advice, provided he takes a moderate fee with due consideration for persons, for the matter in hand, for the labor entailed, and for the custom of the country.[72]

CONCLUSION

There can be only admiration for the skill with which St. Thomas has knitted together the threads of legal speculation. He has done no less than to present the first systematically complete philosophy of law in the history of jurisprudence. His great synthesis combines the juristic tradition based on the data of Roman law and the Decretals of Gratian, the theological tradition of St. Augustine, the philosophical traditions of Plato, Aristotle, and Stoicism, the positive law of the Old and New Testaments, some principles from Germanic law, and other elements. Altogether he put forward a system which is a model in the inclusiveness of its approach and the rigor of its development. But he did more. He related that philosophy of law to a system of philosophy which itself was equally comprehensive; but his legal philosophy was not a mere adjunct of his philosophical system. His theory of the legal order is tied as closely to his theory of morals as it in turn is related to his view of the nature of man, which itself is directly affected by his metaphysics.

It is true, as the opponents of scholasticism urge, that the Thomistic system culminates in a theology, and is, therefore,

[72] II-II, 71.

throughout its whole extent not a philosophy but a theology. In practice, so far as the legal aspects of the system are concerned, this charge is immaterial. Truth for the thirteenth century could be known either by means of revelation or reason, and it was plainly St. Thomas' intention to construct a legal system the justification of which rested on rational grounds. His philosophy as a whole was directed ultimately towards the problems of revelation and faith; but it could in its legal aspects, at any rate, be tested at all points by the processes of reason.

St. Thomas' contribution to the philosophy of law may perhaps be summed up as an insistence that law, to achieve its ends, must be regarded, not as a mere external, arbitrary set of rules, but as dependent, in greater part, upon intrinsic factors which extend from habit to expressed ideals. That idea stands in direct opposition to the police conception of the state, to the theory that law is solely a guardian of rights or interests, and to the notion that all social ends can be realized through the mere promulgation of rules of conduct. Neither the Ancient World nor the Middle Ages ever accepted the validity of that latter position; but it is implicitly the view of much modern speculation.

Chapter VI

FRANCIS BACON

Incomparabilis Verulamius
Leibniz

Bacon's leading ideas are few in number, but they dominate his legal speculation as well as his philosophy. He was able to dismiss all earlier jurisprudence with two criticisms. "All those which have written of laws," he states,[1] "have written either as philosophers or as lawyers, and none as statesmen. As for the philosophers, they make imaginary laws for imaginary commonwealths: and their discourses are as the stars, which give little light because they are so high. For the lawyers, they write according to the states where they live, what is received law, and not what ought to be law." Knowledge, in Bacon's conception, must have a practical aim; it is his basic idea, and he dismisses all other objects of knowledge as "inferior and degenerate."[2] He insists also upon the unity of science. "The distributions and partitions of knowledge are not like several lines that meet in one angle, and so touch but in a point; but are like branches of a tree that meet in a stem, which hath a dimension and quantity of entireness and continuance, before it comes to discontinue and break itself into

Citations to the *Works* refer to *The Works of Francis Bacon*, edited by Spedding, Ellis and Heath, Boston, no date, 15 vols. Citations to *Spedding* refer to *The Letters and the Life of Francis Bacon*, by James Spedding, London (1861-1874) 7 vols.

[1] 6 *Works* 389. Bacon made the same point elsewhere in much the same words. "All who have written concerning laws have written either as philosophers or lawyers. The philosophers lay down many precepts fair in argument, but not applicable to use: the lawyers, being subject and addicted to the positive rules either of the laws of their own country or else of the Roman or Pontifical, have no freedom of opinion, but as it were talk in bonds. But surely the consideration of this properly belongs to statesmen, who best understand the condition of civil society, welfare of the people, natural equity, customs of nations, and different forms of government; and who may therefore determine laws by the rules and principles both of natural equity and policy." 9 *Works* 311.

[2] 8 *Works* 113; 6 *Works* 34.

arms and boughs." [3] Law itself has its appropriate place in
the divisions of knowledge, and although it exhibits many
aspects it too is a unity within it own sphere. " For there are
in nature certain fountains of justice, whence all civil laws
vary according to the regions and governments where they
are planted, though they proceed from the same fountain." [4]
Finally, since the mental capacities of our predecessors were
the equal of our own, we cannot hope to attain a greater
insight into nature than they did, unless we devise a new
method of inquiry. The rationalists, who depend upon reason
and neglect observation are like the spiders who spin webs
out of their own bodies; the empiricists, who construct their
theories from a few experiments, are like the ants which merely
collect their store of materials and feed upon them. True
science is like the bee which gathers its materials from the
flowers and then, through its own activities, elaborates and
transforms them into honey.[5] Bacon's purpose was to combine
the methods of rationalism and empiricism, and this in the end,
he believed, would lead to certainty,[6] an ideal which he never
tired of insisting upon. Certainty was the great objective which
he hoped to realize through his legal speculation.

It must not be supposed that Bacon's repudiation of the legal
theories propounded by the philosophers involves a complete
lapse on his part into a philosophy of the practical. Undeniably
it was his position that scientific speculation and research
should issue in an increase of man's power over nature; but
he singled out for special criticism those who were unduly hasty
in seeking for practical results. He knew that a full understanding of nature belonged to the distant future and that he
himself would scarcely reach the threshold. If there were men
who desired to apply the fragments of his work to practical
ends they were welcome to do so; those fragments might serve
as interest until the principal was forthcoming. For himself
he condemned as unseasonable and premature all attempts

---

[3] 6 *Works* 207. Cf. 9 *Works* 14.   [5] 7 *Works* 137.
[4] 6 *Works* 389.   [6] 8 *Works* 60.

at such applications. Those who stop for the production of works are like the runners diverted from the race by Atalanta's golden balls. Bacon refuses to run off like a child after golden apples, but will stake everything on the victory of art over nature in the race; nor does he make haste to mow down the moss or the corn in blade, but will wait for the harvest in its due season.[7] His objection to the juridical theories of the philosophers is the protest of the practicing lawyer and judge. Their legal precepts may be unassailable ethically but try as it may the legal profession can never squeeze any guidance from them for the decision of actual cases.

If the legal speculation of the philosophers errs by proceeding too far in one direction, that of the lawyers errs by moving too far in the other. They fail to see law as a whole, and perceive only that particular part of it which is under their noses. They are like the alchemists who work in the narrowness and darkness of a limited field.[8] It is true that the alchemists have made a good many discoveries, and have presented men with useful inventions;[9] but in the entirety their record is one of failure. Nature must be studied as a whole if it is ever to be understood. General scientific research must be carried on and applied to the particular sciences, and particular sciences be carried back again to general scientific theory. For want of this the particular sciences altogether lack profoundness, and merely glide along the surface and variety of things. That is so because after the particular sciences have been once distributed and established they are no more nourished by general scientific ideas, which might have drawn out of the true contemplation of their subject matters the means of imparting to them fresh strength and growth. Therefore, it is not strange if the sciences do not grow, seeing they are parted from their roots.[10]

With this set of ideas Bacon began the construction of a legal philosophy. He possessed a special competence in the

[7] 8 *Works* 149.   [9] 8 *Works* 119.
[8] 8 *Works* 93.   [10] 8 *Works* 112.

field because of his training as a lawyer. Of all the great, or
near great, philosophers who have ventured into the domain
of legal speculation Bacon and Leibniz stand alone in the fact
that they were experienced lawyers. Financial circumstances
compelled Bacon to take up the study of law, but he did so
with reluctance.[11] It was never his only, and was far from
being his favorite, study. He had the great stimulus of rivalry
with Coke to spur him to hard efforts, and he worked faithfully
at the law though always with distaste; from the beginning
he had resolved, however, that English laws should be the
better by his industry, than that he should be the better
by the knowledge of them.[12] At the end he could say he
was in good hope that when Coke's *Reports* and his own
Rules and *Decisions* should come to posterity there would be,
whatever the opinion of his contemporaries, some question as
to who was the greater lawyer.[13] There can be now no im-
pugning of his capacities as a lawyer. His little tract on *The
Maxims of the Law*, his *Reading on the Statute of Uses*, his
Ordinances in Chancery, his *Arguments of Law* leave no doubt
as to his technical competence. His great advantage over most
of his competitors at the bar lay in the organizing power which
his philosophy enabled him to exercise over his legal knowledge.
His philosophy gave him a point of view from which to arrange
the materials of English law in a systematic and critical form.
His knowledge of Roman law permitted him to escape from the
insularity of the precepts of his native legal system. Altogether,
his practical experience as a common law lawyer and chancellor
imparted to his legal philosophy the concreteness and applicability for use which is its chief characteristic.

His own estimate of himself is as near the mark as any
estimate is likely to be. At the age of thirty-one he had told
his uncle Lord Burghley that he had taken all knowledge to be
his province [14] and so far as the demands of an exceedingly full
life permitted he never lost sight of that ideal. He believed

---

[11] 1 Spedding 231; 2 *ibid.* 1.
[12] 14 *Works* 179.
[13] 6 Spedding 70.
[14] 1 Spedding 109.

himself fitted for nothing so well as the pursuit of knowledge. He found his mind nimble and versatile enough to catch the resemblances of things (which he thought was the chief point), and at the same time steady enough to fix and distinguish their subtler differences; a mind gifted by nature with desire to seek, patience to doubt, fondness to meditate, slowness to assent, readiness to reconsider, carefulness to dispose and set in order; that neither affects what is new nor admires what is old, and that hates every kind of imposture; a mind therefore especially framed for the study and pursuit of truth.[15]

GENERAL THEORY

On Bacon's agenda of unfinished works at the time of his death was a treatise on a system of jurisprudence, or, as he termed it, an exposition of that branch of knowledge which was concerned with the " laws of laws." [16] His object was to go to the fountains of justice and public expediency, and endeavor with reference to the several provinces of law to exhibit the character and idea of justice in general by comparison with which the laws of particular states might be tested and amended.[17] This project was not carried out, but he provided a specimen of what he had in mind in the form of ninety-seven aphorisms. Those aphorisms touch on nearly all the points which he enumerated as being the proper subject matter of jurisprudence. Thus we appear to have in a crystallized form the main positions which he had reached in a lifetime of reflection on legal theory.

Jurisprudence in Bacon's view must not be content with the construction of a platform of justice; it must also occupy itself with its application. In that latter task jurisprudence must consider by what means laws may be made certain, and what are the causes and remedies of the doubtfulness and uncertainty of law; by what means laws may be made apt and easy to be

[15] 3 Spedding 85; 6 *Works* 435.
[16] 9 *Works* 313; 6 *Works* 390.
[17] 9 *Works* 311.

executed, and what are the impediments and remedies in the execution of laws; what influence laws have which touch private right of *meum* and *tuum*, and how they may be made apt and agreeable; how laws are to be penned and delivered, whether in texts or in acts, brief or large, with preambles or without; how they are to be pruned and reformed from time to time; and what is the best means to keep them from being too vast in volumes or too full of multiplicity and entanglement; how they are to be expounded, when upon causes emergent and judicially discussed, and when upon responses and conferences touching general points or questions; how they are to be pressed, vigorously or tenderly; how they are to be mitigated by equity and good conscience; whether discretion and strict law are to be mingled in the same courts or kept apart in several courts; and how the practice, profession, and erudition of law is to be censored and governed. He also proposed to consider many other points touching the administration and what he termed animation of laws.[18]

In the outline of these objectives for jurisprudence, we are plainly in the presence of a man who has broken sharply with the traditional approach of philosophy to law. It might even be asserted that Bacon here was thinking more as a lawyer than as a philosopher. It is true that some of the great seventeenth century legal problems, such as the delimitation of the fields of law and equity, and the control and education of barristers and attorneys, were present to his mind. But that is a small part of the matter. At the outset he is careful to dismiss none of the problems which have occupied the thoughts of past philosophers; he admits expressly their legitimacy; but he insists their solution is only half the task of a science of law. It is not enough to frame the general theory of a legal science; equally important is the development of the principles of its application. In the twentieth century there has been overemphasis on the second half of that program. It is thought that legal systems can be reformed on the basis of an objective

[18] 6 *Works* 390.

analysis of the systems conducted with such a purpose in view. Bacon made no such mistake. He was aware that all technologies are dependent for their success upon the previously formulated principles of a general science. He determined therefore that his theory of law would be an entire one; it would be general in its ultimate principles, but applicable to use, taking into consideration the practical problems which many legal systems must meet.

He thought that the perfection of law was attained when it was certain in meaning, just in precept, convenient in execution, agreeable to the form of government, and productive of virtue in those that live under it. There was only one end of law and that was the happiness of the citizens. However, that end will be effected only if the people be rightly trained in religion, sound in morality, protected by arms against foreign enemies, guarded by the shield of the laws against civil discords and private injuries, obedient to the government and the magistrates, and rich and flourishing in forces and wealth. For all those objects, laws are the sinews and instruments.[19] He thought that education—duties taught and understood—was a surer obligation of obedience than blind habit. To assert otherwise was to affirm that a blind man may tread more certainly with a guide than a seeing man can with a light.[20]

Bacon's theory of the origin of law and justice rests on the principle that they are produced through the reaction of the group to behavior held to affect the well-being of the whole community. That principle had been clearly formulated by Polybius[21] and has been further developed in modern times by Bagehot and Sumner.[22] Bacon's views are colored by the great struggle of the seventeenth century over the problems of public law. He held that in civil society, either law or force prevails.[23] But there is a kind of force which pretends law,

[19] 9 *Works* 313.
[20] 6 *Works* 104.
[21] *The Histories*, VI, 6.
[22] Bagehot, *Physics and Politics* (1873); Sumner, *Folkways* (1906).
[23] 9 *Works* 311.

and a kind of law which savors of force rather than equity. Thus there are three fountains of injustice: mere force, a malicious ensnarement under color of law, and harshness of the law itself.

Private right rests on the following ground. A man who commits an injury, receives either pleasure or profit from the act, but incurs danger from the precedent. For others do not share in the particular pleasure or profit, but look upon the precedent as applicable to themselves. Hence they readily agree to protect themselves by laws in order to prevent the injury from occurring to them. But it may happen that those whom a law protects are not as numerous or as powerful as those whom it endangers. Under those circumstances the law is often overthrown. Furthermore, private right depends upon the protection of public right. For the law protects the people, and magistrates protect the laws; but the authority of the magistrates depends on the sovereign power of the government, the structure of the constitution, and the fundamental laws. Therefore, if this part of the constitution is sound and healthy, the laws will be of good effect, but if not, there will be little security in them. It is not, however, the only object of public law, to be attached as the guardian of private right, to protect it from violation and prevent injuries; but its purposes extend also to religion, arms, discipline, ornaments, wealth, and, in a word, to everything that regards the well-being of a state.

It is difficult to determine the extent to which Bacon's political opinions are here finding indirect expression. Indeed, it is no easy task to ascertain his theory of the English constitution. His views on the subject were never formally reduced to writing; they must be pieced together from his actions and from occasional expressions found in his works. At the same time, allowances must be made for the arguments he advanced in his capacity as an attorney, and for the opinions he suggested for the purpose of securing royal favor. Altogether, however, he appeared to believe in some form of benevolent despotism, in which an enlightened monarch moved unrestrainedly within

the imprecise limits of his royal prerogative, but advised by able
ministers and informed by a Commons upon the condition of
the country.[24]   In Elizabeth's reign he had argued that a
king's grant repugnant to law was void; [25] but by 1612 he was
apparently of a different view. A lawyer who had been retained
by clients to find objections to a commission in point of law,
which he did, was formally charged with slandering the King's
Commission and with censuring his prerogative. Bacon held
the offence to be a great one; first, that he presumed to censure
the King's prerogative at all; secondly, that he generalized his
opinion more than was pertinent to the question; and lastly,
that he had erroneously, falsely, and dangerously given opinion
in derogation of it. " I make a great difference," Bacon [26] said,
" between the King's grants and ordinary commissions of
justice, and the King's high commissions of regiment, or mixed
with causes of state."   The proceedings are not complete, but
the attorney admitted unreservedly that he had done wrong,
and this in the presence of Coke and Tanfield who were present as assessors; he would scarcely have done so, it would
seem, if the common law had given him any support.

It appears likely that Bacon's political views led him to
assert that private rights were dependent ultimately for their
security upon the preservation of public law, and that the
authority of public law extended to everything that affected
the well-being of the state. What did Bacon mean by public
law? In the Roman system it was that part which was concerned with the government of the Roman state; private law
was that part which looked to the interests of individuals.[27]
Ulpian added that public law was the law relating to religion,
to priests and to officials.[28]   When Bacon came to consider
the union of the whole of Great Britain under one law he seized
upon the distinction as a useful one. It enabled him to put to

[24] 2 Gardiner, *History of England* (1885) 192.
[25] 15 *Works* 12. The date is sometime before October 11, 1587.
[26] 4 Spedding 355.
[27] Institutes of Justinian I. 1. 4.
[28] D. I. 1. 1. 2.

one side, as inexpedient to be handled at that time, all law
affecting property. " I consider," he [29] said, " that it is a true
and received division of law into *jus publicum* and *privatum*,
the one being the sinews of property, and the other of government. For that which concerneth private interest of *meum* and
tuum, in my simple opinion, it is not at this time to be
meddled with." Thus putting private law aside, he thought
that the lawyers of Scotland and England should set down the
laws of their respective nations in brief articles, to be printed
in parallel columns for appropriate action by the King.[30] The
public law thus set forth would consist of four parts: First, the
criminal law; secondly, the law concerning the causes of the
church; thirdly, that having to do with magistrates, officers, and
courts, including the consideration of the regal prerogative, of
which the rest were but streams; finally, those concerning
certain special politic laws, usages, and constitutions, connected
with the public peace, strength and wealth of the state. As
a specimen Bacon appended a statement of the law of capital
crimes.

But a more important issue was at stake than a convenient
division for the purposes of legal exposition. It was an indirect
attack on Coke and the mediaeval tradition of the rule of law.
It was a wedge that would remove officials from the jurisdiction
of the law to which other persons were subject. That such
was his intention seems clear enough. The courts are not to
attempt to control the crown in the exercise of its prerogative.
The judges are lions supporting the throne on both sides: " let
them be lions, but yet lions under the throne; being circumspect
that they do not check or oppose any points of sovereignty." [31]
The issue took a concrete form in Bacon's efforts to prohibit
the common law judges by means of the writ *De non proceden-
do Rege inconsulto* from proceeding with a case in which the

[29] 15 *Works* 317.
[30] Montesquieu asserted that to determine which of two different systems of laws
is more agreeable to reason, we must take them each as a whole and compare them
in their entirety. *The Spirit of Laws* XXIX, 11.
[31] 12 *Works* 270.

interests of the crown were concerned. As a statesman and trained administrator Bacon was convinced that certain administrative actions of the state ought to be beyond the control of the common law, that the principles of the common law were not adapted for the handling of such matters. In his view, at least under James I, the chancellor's functions were political as well as judicial. " The writ," he [32] wrote the King, " is a mean provided by the ancient law of England, to bring any case that may concern your Majesty in profit or power from the ordinary Benches, to be tried and judged before the Chancellor of England, by the ordinary and legal part of this power. And your Majesty knoweth your Chancellor is ever a principal counsellor and instrument of monarchy, of immediate dependence on the king; and therefore like to be a safe and tender guardian of the regal rights." [33] " The working of this writ," Gardiner writes, " if Bacon had obtained his object, would have been, to some extent, analogous to that provision which has been found in so many French constitutions, according to which no agent of the Government can be summoned before a tribunal, for acts done in the exercise of his office, without a preliminary authorization by the Council of State." [34] Although the practice can be traced to the Middle Ages, we find the Council and the Star Chamber of Tudor and Stuart times especially solicitous in the protection of officials from the ordinary processes of law; thus, the Council directed a jailer to disobey a writ of habeas corpus, and to make a return that the commitment was by the queen's special command. " It is clear," Holdsworth [35] remarks, " that the ideas which underlie these activities lead directly to the growth of a system of administrative law, and that in all questions of doubtful jurisdiction the Council was claiming to exercise the powers of a *tribunal des conflits.*" However, as he [36] remarks elsewhere,

---

[32] 5 Spedding 234.

[33] 3 *History of England* 7 n. 2.

[34] For the American doctrine see *Marbury* v. *Madison*, 1 *Cranch* 137, 143 (1803); *Boske* v. *Comingore*, 177 U. S. 459 (1900).

[35] 4 *Hist. Eng. Law* (1924) 87.

[36] 1 *Hist. Eng. Law* (3rd ed. 1922) 515-16.

when the jurisdiction of the Council fell with the victory of the Parliament in 1641, English law was saved from a system of administrative law and developed instead a theory of ministerial responsibility. In Hale's *Analysis of the Law,* first published in 1713, officials are regarded as persons, and the general law of persons controls their conduct equally with that of private individuals.[37] Bacon's theory of a division of law into public law and private law had disappeared. Blackstone, who expressly [38] adopted Hale's scheme as the basis of the arrangement of the *Commentaries,* also treated officials as subject to the law of persons.[39] The significance of treating public law as part of the private law of persons was fully perceived by Austin who regarded Hale's adoption of this arrangement, which was held on the continent to be a great absurdity, as a striking indication of Hale's originality and depth of thought.[40] For himself, he had no doubt that public law should not be opposed to the rest of the law but should be treated under the law of persons. Bacon's idea of public law, however, has reappeared today in the struggle now going on with respect to the place of administrative agencies in the modern state. " Public law," Jennings [41] has written recently, " is gradually eating up private law. Industrial law is being controlled by administrative organs and is at the same time eating in the law of obligations. Quotas and marketing schemes under administrative control reduce the operation of commercial law. Housing and planning legislation takes the law of property under public control. This is only to say that *laisser-faire* has been abandoned, the public lawyer is ousting the private lawyer, and the rights and duties of institutions are superseding the ordinary rights and duties of private citizens." This analysis admittedly stems from continental views, particularly those of Hauriou; at the same time they represent a return, so far as English law is concerned, to Bacon's

[37] *The Analysis of the Law* (2nd ed. 1716) 4 *et seq.*

[38] *An Analysis of the Laws of England* (3rd ed. 1758) vii.

[39] 1 Blackstone, *Commentaries,* c. 3 *et seq.*

[40] 2 Austin, *Lectures in Jurisprudence* (Campbell's ed.) § 1024.

[41] *Modern Theories of Law* (1933) 72. *Cf.* Pound, *Public Law and Private Law* (1939) 24 Cornell Law Quarterly 469.

position. It may well be that Bacon finally will have his triumph over Coke.

Bacon believed that the common law exceeded the civil law in fitness for the English system of government; for the civil law was not made for the countries in which it rules.[42] As the common law is more worthy than the statute law, so the law of nature is more worthy than both of them.[43] The English law is grounded upon the law of nature, and from the latter law flow three things: preservation of life, liberty, and marriage. All national laws are to be taken strictly in any point in which they abridge and derogate from the law of nature.[44]

CERTAINTY

All Bacon's thinking, as we have seen, was directed towards the single end of the achievement of certainty in the various departments of knowledge. It was no less the ultimate ideal of his logical method than it was the constant objective of his proposals for reform in the affairs of men. In jurisprudence, it was the point of departure of his entire theory. Certainty was the primary necessity of law. It was so essential to law, he believed, that law cannot even be just without it. " For if the trumpet give an uncertain sound, who shall prepare himself to the battle? " [45] So if the law give an uncertain sound, who shall prepare to obey it? It ought therefore to warn before it strikes. He remarks also that Aristotle [46] had well said " that that is the best law which leaves least to the discretion of the judge "; and this can come about only if the laws are certain.[47]

This idea lay also at the basis of his proposals for the improvement of the laws of England. His project for the codification of English law, entitled *A Proposition touching the Compiling and Amendment of the Laws of England* [48] was advanced upon the express ground " that our laws, as they now

[42] 6 *Works* 391.
[43] 15 *Works* 202
[44] 15 *Works* 225-6.
[45] I Corinth. XIV. 8.
[46] *Rhet.* 1354a.
[47] 9 *Works* 314.
[48] 6 Spedding 61.

stand, are subject to great incertainties, and variety of opinion, delays, and evasions: whereof ensueth, 1. That the multiplicity and length of suits is great. 2. That the contentious person is armed, and the honest subject wearied and oppressed. 3. That the judge is more absolute; who, in doubtful cases, hath a greater stroke and liberty. 4. That the chancery courts are more filled, the remedy of law being often obscure and doubtful. 5. That the ignorant lawyer shroudeth his ignorance of law in that doubts are so frequent and many. 6. That men's assurances of their lands and estates by patents, deeds, wills, are often subject to question, and hollow; and many the like inconveniences." The project was not adopted, and English law followed the path of Coke and not Bacon. Nevertheless, his arguments for certainty in this specific field were later to be the subject of a remarkable testimony. In 1826, Sir Robert Peel as Home Secretary moved for leave to bring in his bill for the consolidation of the laws relating to theft and asked permission to use Bacon's paper for the preface of his speech, as comprising in a short compass every argument that could be cited in favor of the measure he proposed to introduce, and satisfactorily confuting every objection that could be brought against it. " The lapse of two hundred and fifty years has increased," he said, " the necessity of the measure which Lord Bacon then proposed, but it has produced no argument in favor of the principle, no objection adverse to it, which he did not anticipate." [49]

With the insight to be expected of him, Bacon has thus isolated the central problem of all juristic thinking. In the the jurisprudence of Plato and Aristotle it was expressed in the words: Shall the law or the just man rule? In the language of the present day we seek for the means of reconciling rule with discretion, the general security with individual needs, stability with change. Must we choose between justice according to law and justice without law? Maine [50] observed that " the more

[49] *Ibid.*
[50] *Ancient Law* (1931) 61. For the most extensive analysis of the question in contemporary literature, see Frank, *Law and the Modern Mind* (1930).

progressive Greek communities . . . disembarrassed themselves with astonishing facility from cumbrous forms of procedure and needless terms of art, and soon ceased to attach any superstitious value to rigid rules and prescriptions. It was not for the ultimate advantage of mankind that they did so, though the immediate benefit conferred on their citizens may have been considerable. . . . No durable system of jurisprudence could be produced in this way. A community which never hesitated to relax rules of written law whenever they stood in the way of an ideally perfect decision on the facts of particular cases, would only, if bequeathed any body of judicial principles to posterity, bequeath one consisting of the ideas of right and wrong which happened to be prevalent at the time. Such a jurisprudence would contain no framework to which the more advanced conceptions of subsequent ages could be fitted. It would amount at best to a philosophy, marked with the imperfections of the civilization under which it grew up." Unless there are rules, there will be no certainty in the judicial process; they are an assurance that human affairs will follow a general pattern and will not be at the mercy of ignorant or improperly influenced officials. They sometimes limit an able judge and prevent a full consideration of an individual's claim.[51] Nevertheless, it is important for people to know as precisely as may be the consequences of their actions before they act. If there are no rules to guide human conduct and to govern the

[51] Hans Schmidt, a religious fanatic, hacked his mistress to death and was found guilty of murder in the first degree. His defense was insanity; he claimed to have heard the voice of God calling upon him to kill the woman as a sacrifice and atonement. Among the grounds for a new trial, urged on appeal, was that his story at the trial was a fabrication, and that he was not mentally unsound. He insisted that the woman had died as the result of an abortion, the penalty for which was less than death since such a crime was manslaughter and not murder. He therefore asked that he be given another opportunity to put before a jury the true narrative of the crime. However, the rule is that the evidence must not have been discovered since the trial. Cardozo rejected Schmidt's contention on the ground that the evidence to support the new plea was not newly discovered, since it was known to Schmidt at the time of the trial. Carodozo suggested in his opinion that the matter be referred to the Executive, inasmuch as the Court was powerless to give relief. *People* v. *Schmidt*, 216 N. Y. 324, 110 N. E. 945 (1915). Schmidt was eventually executed. For the case from the psychiatrical point of view, which insists he was insane, see White, *Insanity and the Criminal Law* (1923) 61.

decision of controversies, human affairs would become so uncertain as to be intolerable.

But that is only one side of the question. Rules are made
for the general case, and in particular cases they may operate
too harshly. They may crystallize obsolete practices and
theories, as our law of insanity has crystallized discarded medical concepts; they may become too rigid and formalistic; they
may become too detailed and invade provinces they would do
well to omit.

If law is to be a sound agency of social control it must therefore find a place within its system for both the legal rule and
judicial discretion. Legal thought must solve the problem of
the limits to be allowed each sphere of activity, and the methods
by which they may be adjusted to each other. Bacon reduced
the task of solving this dilemma to two general cases. He
believed that uncertainty of law is of two kinds; the one, where
no law is prescribed; the other where the law is ambiguous and
obscure. His object was to find some rule of certainty for these
two situations. The narrow compass of human wisdom cannot
take in all the cases that time may discover; hence new and
omitted cases often present themselves. Thus, in the nature of
things, legal rules cannot be made for all cases. Judicial discretion, therefore, has an inescapable function; but it was
Bacon's position that that discretion was not to be anarchic in
its exercise, but itself be subject to certain general rules and
standards.

Omitted Cases

When an omitted case appeared Bacon thought the remedy
was threefold. There should be a reference either to similar
cases, or an employment of examples which have not yet grown
into law, or a decision by a court empowered to decide according to the arbitration of a good man and sound discretion.
Bacon considered each of the remedies in detail.[52]

In omitted cases, the rule of law is to be drawn from cases

[52] 9 *Works* 314-325.

similar to them, but with caution and judgment. A number
of rules are to be observed in the process. " Let reason be
esteemed prolific, and custom barren. Custom must not make
cases. Whatever therefore is received contrary to the reason
of a law, or even where its reason is obscure, must not be
drawn into consequence." [53] These are obscure assertions and
their meaning is far from clear. The last sentence is an adaptation of the troublesome view of Paulus that that which has
been received against the reason of the law is not to be drawn
into a precedent.[54] Paulus' statement appears to mean that a
custom not supported in reason is not necessarily invalid; but
it must not be used as a precedent either, for similar cases or
as a basis for logical deduction.[55] Bacon, however, appears to
go further than this. He seems to say that if a rule of law fails
to cover a case the omission must not be supplied by reference
to practices established by custom; the gap must be filled by
some process of reason. Yet the doctrine, however curious it
may now seem to us, was not a novel one to the lawyers of
the seventeenth century. The sixteenth century had witnessed
the settlement of the property rights of the villeins. Since
those rights were held to be customary the courts had been
compelled to analyze with great care the relationship of custom
to the common law. In order to work out a compromise
between the interests of the villeins and those of the lords it
had become necessary to confine sharply the force of custom.
Littleton [56] maintained that a custom had to be reasonable
before its validity was admitted, and Coke [57] devised the
standards of reasonableness by which customs were to be
tested. Custom came to be regarded as a perilous idea, the
sting of which must be pulled. In the *Case of Tanistry*,[58]

[53] 9 *Works* 315.
[54] Quod contra rationem juris receptum est, non est producendum ad conse-
quentias. D. 1. 3. 14.
[55] Brie, *Die Lehre vom Gewohnheitsrecht* (1899) 21.
[56] *Tenures*, § 80.
[57] *Copyholder*, § 33.
[58] (1608), Dav. 29. For a criticism of the case, see Maine, *Early History of
Institutions* (1888) 185 *et seq.*

decided in 1608, the common law tests of custom were applied to the Irish Brehon law of succession. Although the existence of the custom could not be denied, the judges with the aid of the tests were able to pronounce illegal the native Irish tenures of land.

Bacon gave no example of what he had in mind in his condemnation of custom, but there is no doubt that he shared in the general hostility of his time towards the notion. He seemed to favor entirely, to the disregard of custom, an extension of the law through the process of analogical reasoning. That is a legitimate device of the judicial process. For some years, for example, the United States Supreme Court had been troubled by the degree of control to be allowed state regulatory bodies over gas transported into the state in interstate commerce. It solved the problem finally on the analogy of the " original package "; when the gas passed from the distribution lines into the supply mains it was " like the breaking of an original package, after shipment in interstate commerce " and was therefore subject to local regulation.[59] However, custom itself is equally as potent a force in the legal process as analogical reasoning. Bacon himself stood at the very threshold of the classical instance of the development of the law through the transformation of customary rules into legal ones. It was from the customs of merchants that Lord Mansfield was to construct our modern mercantile law.

Nevertheless, Bacon pointed to a real difficulty. It is no longer fashionable to refer to the spirit of the law, but we still are permitted to remark upon its policy. Now a practice may be widely customary but be contrary to a law's policy. Thus Bacon himself was opposed to slavery but he could not deny that it was a widespread custom.[60] It was Mansfield himself who refused to follow mercantile custom and settled the English law that there was no right of property in negro slaves.[61] Coke's solution of the problem was thus a sounder

---

[59] *East Ohio Gas Company* v. *Tax Commission*, 283 U. S. 465 (1931).

[60] 9 *Works* 305.   [61] *Sommersett's Case* (1771) 20 S. T. 1.

one than Bacon's. Coke found room within the law for both reason and custom. Reason, however, for Coke was no ordinary reason, but "artificial and legal reason" [62] and custom had to be tested by the criteria of the law itself before the law would adopt it.

As a guide in the handling of omitted cases through the analogical technique Bacon laid down a number of general principles. Laws which promote the general welfare should be liberally construed. This amounts to an invitation to judges to appraise the political wisdom of the statutes they are construing. As a rule of construction it is too amorphous to be of real assistance. During the development of democratic theory in the nineteenth century an attempt was made to give the rule more concreteness by holding that laws which promoted the security of individual rights should be liberally construed and that statutes in favor of the power of the state should be strictly construed. Bacon accepted the rule that penal statutes should be strictly construed against the state; however, he thought that if the offense were an old one and taken cognizance of by the laws, but an unprovided case appears, we ought by all means to depart from the decrees of law rather than leave offenses unpunished. In its modern form the rule has been best stated perhaps by Mr. Justice Story. In referring to the rule that penal statutes are to be strictly construed, he said: " I agree to that rule in its true and sober sense; and that is that penal statutes are not to be enlarged by implication, or extended to cases not obviously within their words and purport. But where the words are general, and include various classes of persons, I know of no authority which would justify the court in restricting them to one class, or in giving them the narrowest interpretation, where the mischief to be redressed by the statute is equally applicable to all of them. And where a word is used in a statute, which has various known significations, I know of no rule, that requires the court to adopt one in preference to another, simply because

[62] Co. Litt. 62a.

it is more restrained, if the objects of the statute equally apply to the largest and broadest sense of the word. In short, it appears to me that the proper course in all these cases is to search out and follow the true intent of the legislature, and to adopt that sense of the words which harmonize best with the context, and promotes in the fullest manner, the apparent policy and objects of the legislature." [63] Thus, the Motor Vehicle Theft Act made it an offense to transport in interstate commerce any " self-propelled vehicle not designed for running on rails." In holding that the transportation of a stolen airplane was not under the act, Mr. Justice Holmes observed that " although it is not likely that a criminal will carefully consider the text of the law before he murders or steals, it is reasonable that a fair warning should be given to the world in language that the common world will understand, of what the law intends to do if a certain line is passed. To make the warning fair, so far as possible the line should be clear. When a rule of conduct is laid down in words that evoke in the common mind only the picture of vehicles moving on land, the statutes should not be extended to aircraft simply because it may seem to us that a similar policy applies." [64] Although Bacon's rule may be thus rejected in modern decisions, it has nevertheless been applied from time to time by the common law courts. [65] When a statute repealed the common law (especially in matters of frequent occurrence and long standing), Bacon did not approve proceeding by analogy to omitted cases. When the state has long been without a statute on a matter, even on those matters to which attention has been particularly called, there is little danger in allowing the cases omitted to want for a remedy from a new statute. Statutes framed for an emergency should not be used as an analogy for omitted cases. Consequence does not draw consequence, but the analogical extension should stop within the next case; otherwise there will be a gradual lapse into dissimilar cases, and sharp-

[63] *U. S.* v. *Winn*, 3 Sumn. 209, Fed. Cas. No. 16,740 (1838).
[64] *McBoyle* v. *U. S.*, 283 U. S. 25 (1931).
[65] *U. S.* v. *Wiltberger*, 5 Wheat. 76, 96 (1820).

ness of wit will have greater power than authority of law. When laws and statutes are concise in style, then extend them freely; when they enumerate particular cases, proceed more cautiously; for as exception corroborates the application of law in cases not excepted, so enumeration invalidates it in cases not enumerated. Thus, in a case suggested by Bacon " if the law be that for a certain offense a man shall lose his right hand, and the offender hath before had his right hand cut off in the wars, he shall not lose his left hand, but the crime shall rather pass without the punishment which the law assigned than the letter of the law shall be extended." [66] An explanatory statute stops the streams of the statute which it explains, and neither of them admit of extension afterwards. The judge must not make a superextension, when the law has once begun an extension. Formality of words and acts does not admit of an extension to similar cases; for formality loses its character when it passes from custom to discretion; and the introduction of new things destroys the majesty of the old. Bacon thought that the extension of the law to posthumous cases, which were not in existence at the time of the passing of the law was easy. Where a case could not be expressed, because it had no existence, a case omitted is taken for a case expressed, if there exists the same reason for it.

Bacon's first remedy for the achievement of certainty in the process of judicial decision was thus a resort to the method of analogical reasoning. No method is indeed more fundamental in legal thinking. It is the basis of the theory of precedents and is therefore at the root of the common law system of case law. From the *non est simile* and *n'est pas semblable* of the Year Books to the " not in point," " distinguishable " and " on all fours " of the modern courts the method has been the constant mainstay of the judicial process.

Bacon's little treatise on jurisprudence went into numerous editions on the Continent. We know that Savigny thought highly of Bacon's system, or at least parts of it; and the basic

[66] 14 *Works* 238.

ideas in Savigny's notable discussion of legal analogy in the
law bear a close resemblance to those of Bacon.[67] In Savigny's
view opinions on the methods to be followed in filling gaps in
the law may be reduced to two positions. Either the gap
is filled by a deduction from a principle of natural law, or it is
filled by the process of reasoning from analogy. Savigny
believed the latter procedure to be the only sound one. The
ascertainment of law by analogy may present itself in his
opinion in two forms. There may first appear a new legal
relation previously unknown which cannot be incorporated in
any typical institution of existing positive law. In our day we
are witnessing the appearance of such a relation. It is impossible to fit the labor relationship under any of the typical legal
institutions now existing—master and servant, contract, associations, or other major division. Nevertheless, as Savigny insisted, if friction is to be avoided, the new institution must be
brought into harmony with existing law. In the second form,
and this is the common case, a new question arises in a domain
of law already established. Thus, in the field of labor law, the
question is presented to what extent ought unions be subject
to anti-trust measures. In Savigny's view a question of this
kind must be determined on the basis of the internal kinship
of the principles of law which obtain in its field. In both forms
analogy becomes the instrument of legal progress. It may
operate in the legislative domain where it can be applied with
the greater freedom. It may also operate as a method of
strict interpretation which enables the judge to resolve novel
questions.

Savigny pointed out that analogy assumes an inner consistency in the law; not necessarily, however, a rigid deductive
system, but an organic consistency produced by seeing, as a
whole, the practical nature of the jural relations and the institutions governing them. Our starting point must always be a
particular datum and the solution of the difficulty will result

---

[67] For Savigny's view of Bacon's jurisprudence see *Vom Beruf unserer Zeit für
Gesetzgebung und Rechtswissenschaft* (1892) 12. For his theory of analogy see 1
System des heutigen Römischen Rechts (1840) 290.

from our development of it. Sometimes the datum is a rule of positive law and then the decision is said to be reached *ex argumento legis*; but more frequently we start with a theory of law which itself has been created by abstract reasoning. In both cases the procedure is essentially different from extensive interpretation with which it is often confounded. Extensive interpretation does not aim to fill a gap in the law, but endeavors to rectify the erroneously expressed letter of the law by having recourse to its spirit. When, on the contrary, we use the analogical method we assume a gap in the law which we wish to fill in harmony with the organic unity of the law. Analogical interpretation cannot be applied if the datum which is taken as the point of departure has the character of an exception to the general rule. In such a case the application of analogy must be rejected because a fundamental requisite for the application of analogy, namely, the absence of a rule, is not present. If, for example, a statute is partially repealed by a new statute, what is not repealed is still in effect. If it is decided to extend the repeal to the portion still in force that would not be employing analogy because the rule is present. It would rather be a case of extensive interpretation, but of an arbitrary and groundless character. For the same reason, analogy must not be employed to interpret privileges since the rule in such case is never lacking. Similarly, Savigny insisted we must never extend an anomalous law, a *jus singulare* beyond its immediate limits, because in that case the rule is present and would only be destroyed by being extended. If an anomalous law is used, not to extend the exception which it sanctions, but to decide an open question of the same general type, there is a true analogy which is not subject to rejection. Nevertheless, in such a case the analogy ought not to be sought in the *jus singulare*, but in the usual rules of law, for analogical interpretation depends solely upon the internal consistency of the whole body of the law. Anomalous rules are transplantings to the legal field from other domains and it is impossible to attribute to them the organic creativeness of ordinary law.

Analogical reasoning can be reduced to the formula that when two things resemble each other in one or more respects, and a certain proposition is true of the one, it is therefore true of the other.[68] X has the properties p_1, p_2, p_3 . . . and f; Y has the properties p_1, p_2, p_3. . . . Therefore, Y also has the property f. Thus, Francesco Sizzi, a seventeenth century writer, argued that Galileo's discovery of Jupiter's satellites was impossible because " there are seven windows in the head, two nostrils, two eyes, two ears, and a mouth; so in the heavens there are two favorable stars, two unpropitious, two luminaries, and Mercury alone undecided and indifferent. From which and many other similar phenomena of nature, such as the seven metals, etc., which it were tedious to enumerate, we gather that the number of planets is necessarily seven." In modern Aristotelian logic it is insisted that analogical reasoning, when entirely quantitative, is mathematical in character, and is necessary, like other mathematical reasoning. If, in respect of weight, $a:b::c:d$, and if a weighs twice as much as b, then c must weigh twice as much as d. However, it is also insisted that as soon as we connect with the relation $c:d$, on the ground of its identity with the relation $a:b$, a consequence which is not known to depend entirely on that relation, our reasoning ceases to be demonstrative. Suppose that by rail the distance from Washington to Fredericksburg bears the same relation to the distance from Washington to Baltimore as the distance from Washington to Annapolis bears to the distance from Washington to Gaithersburg; and that it costs half as much again to send a ton of coal to Baltimore from Washington as to Fredericksburg; we cannot infer that the rate from Washington to Gaithersburg will be half as much again as it is to Annapolis; for the rate need not depend entirely on the relative distance, which is all that is alleged to be the same in the two cases. It is therefore argued that analogy should be restricted to arguments turning on similarity of relations alone.[69] However, it has been pointed

---

[68] Mill, *Logic* (1864) 332.
[69] Joseph, *An Introduction to Logic* (2nd ed. 1916) 532.

out that the mathematical statement is not analogical in the sense that it states a *similarity* of relations; the proportion of *a* to *b* is identical with that of *c* to *d*; each is twice the other. In an empirical case, if it could be established that the relations of *a* and *b* are identical with those of *c* and *d*, then the consequences entailed by these relations in the one instance would necessarily be entailed by the same relations in the other instance. But, in fact, it can never be shown that any pairs, triads, tetrads, etc. of actual things are identical in their relations. They are only similar. And this means that an empirical analogy, turning on resemblance in relations, does not differ in principle from one turning on resemblance in properties.[70]

In modern logic analogy is treated as a case of probable inference the force of which is dependent upon the character of the initial resemblance and the relative comprehensiveness of the properties which are asserted to be connected.[71] That is to say, the initial resemblance must be such that a relationship of inference or implication may exist between the property that forms the basis of the analogy and the property to be inferred from it. If it is granted that man's existence is dependent upon the presence of air, then the question whether Mars possesses air would be an important one in determining whether it was inhabited by man. A relationship of inference exists between the property of possessing air and the conclusion that man may inhabit Mars. The strength of the analogy depends upon the existence of a resemblance having this initial character. When we pass from the character of the initial resemblance to the comprehensiveness of the inferred properties we find that the more comprehensive they are the less likely is the conclusion to be true. Keynes gives an example of a poor analogy from Hume: "Nothing so like as eggs; yet no one, on account of this apparent similarity, expects the same taste and relish in

---

[70] Eaton, *General Logic* (1931) 552.
[71] This position was established by Keynes, *A Treatise on Probability* (1921) 222. For a non-mathematical exposition see Stebbing, *A Modern Introduction to Logic* (1930) 249.

all of them." There would be some probability for the conclusion on the basis of the outward resemblance of the eggs.
Keynes points out that " if Hume had expected the same degree
of nourishment as well as the same taste and relish from all of
the eggs, he would have drawn a conclusion of weaker probability." There is therefore a dependence of the probability of
an analogical conclusion upon its scope or comprehensiveness.
Those of a wider scope are less probable than those of narrower
comprehensiveness. " It is important to understand," Keynes
adds, " that the common sense of the race has been impressed
by very weak analogies." [72]

If the gap in the law could not be filled by a parity of reasoning, then, Bacon thought, there should be a resort to examples
which have not yet grown into law.[73] He distinguishes on the
one hand between custom, which is a kind of law, and of
examples which by frequent use have passed into customs as
a tacit law, and on the other, examples which happen seldom
and at distant intervals, and have not yet acquired the force
of law. He is concerned solely with the latter, and his object
is to show when, and with what caution, the rule of justice
may be sought from them where the law is deficient.

Argument by example has always been a frequent practice
of the courts. Sometimes the example is used to mark a limit,
or borderline, which the case before the court either falls short
of or overpasses. Thus, the United States Supreme Court had
before it the question whether an attorney should be disbarred
because he had participated in a lynching. It marked a limit
through the example of lynch law itself. It said: " Whatever
excuse may ever exist for the execution of lynch law in savage
or sparsely settled district, in order to oppose the ruffian
elements which the ordinary administration of law is powerless
to control, it certainly has no excuse in a community where the

---

[72] *Ibid.* 247. Elsewhere he states that "scientific method, indeed, is mainly
devoted to discovering means of so heightening the known analogy that we may
dispense as far as possible with the methods of pure induction." *Ibid.* 241.
[73] 9 *Works* 314, 317.

laws are duly and regularly administered." [74] More frequently, however, the court uses examples for what might be termed the argument from the fearful. In order to meet a contention of counsel the court will suggest an example; but the court then points out that even to suggest that the practice embodied in the example is valid would be unthinkable. Now the matter before the court is similar to the example; ergo, to approve it is also unthinkable. Thus, the United States Supreme Court was called upon to determine whether certain provisions of the Agricultural Adjustment Act of 1933, involving the payment of money to promote a plan of crop control were in conflict with the Federal Constitution. The Court remarked: "It is said that Congress has the undoubted right to appropriate money to executive officers for expenditure under contracts between the government and individuals; that much of the total expenditures is so made. But appropriations and expenditures under contracts for proper governmental purposes cannot justify contracts which are not within federal power. And contracts for the reduction of acreage and the control of production are outside the range of that power. An appropriation to be expended by the United States under contracts calling for a violation of a state law clearly would offend the Constitution. Is a statute less objectionable which authorizes expenditure of federal moneys to induce action in a field in which the United States has no power to intermeddle? The Congress cannot invade state jurisdiction to compel individual action; no more can it purchase such action." [75] The argument from the fearful is a handy weapon for dissenting judges and is widely employed by them, particularly to make the rule established by the majority self-evidently ridiculous. Thus the Supreme Court refused to intervene in a criminal case in which the State Court had held that the requirements of fairness had been met. Due process under the Federal Constitution did not, in the Supreme Court's view, require a separate examination by the Federal Court of the facts. In his dissent Mr. Justice Holmes observed

---

[74] *Ex parte Wall*, 17 Otto 265 (1883).   [75] *U. S.* v. *Butler*, 297 U. S. 1 (1936).

that it was significant that the State did " not go so far as to say that in no case would it be permissible on application for *habeas corpus* to override the findings of fact by the state courts." He seized upon this as the crux of the matter, and proceeded to put some cases of such a character that the majority decision could not be applicable to them. " To put an extreme case and show what we mean, if the trial and the later hearings before the Supreme Court had taken place in the presence of an armed force known to be ready to shoot if the result was not the one desired, we do not suppose that this Court would allow itself to be silenced by the suggestion that the record showed no flaw. To go one step further, suppose that the trial had taken place under such intimidation that the Supreme Court of the State on writ of error had discovered no error in the record, and still imagine that this Court would find a sufficient one outside of the record, and that it would not be disturbed in its conclusion by anything that the Supreme Court of the State might have said. We therefore lay the suggestion that the Supreme Court of the State has disposed of the present question by its judgment on one side." [76] The argument from example is the stock in trade of the rhetorical approach and was so treated by Aristotle who regarded it as the rhetorical form corresponding to induction. He also observed that it was the type of argument best suited for deliberative arguments.[77]

Bacon's rules for the use of examples are merely a formulation of common sense guides. Examples are not to be sought from tyrannical, factious or dissolute times, but from those which are good and moderate. The latest examples are to be accounted the safest. If something has been done recently without inconvenient consequences it may probably be repeated without hazard. However such cases have less authority; and if a reform is needed, modern examples savor more of their own age than of right reason. Ancient examples are to be received

[76] *Frank* v. *Mangum*, 237 U. S. 309, 345 (1915).
[77] *An. Post.* 71ᵃ 9; *Rhet.* 1356ᵇ 2, 1393ᵃ 25; *Rhet.* 1368ᵃ 30. For the method of refuting the argument from example see *Rhet.* 1403ᵃ 5.

cautiously and with proper selection; for lapse of time produces changes so that what in respect of time appears ancient is, by reason of the changes really new. Therefore, the best examples are those of the middle time, or else such a time as is most in conformity with the present age; sometimes this is to be found in a more remote age rather than in that immediately preceding. Bacon also insisted that the courts should keep within, or rather on this side of the limits of the example, and on no account go beyond them. He pointed out that where there is no rule of law everything should be looked on with suspicion; and therefore, as in obscure cases, the courts should proceed with great caution. The courts should beware of fragments, and epitomes of examples, and should look carefully into the whole of examples and all the attendant circumstances. If it is unreasonable to judge of part of a law, without examining the whole, the rule is even clearer in examples, the use of which is doubtful if they do not exactly correspond. It is of great importance to consider the hands through which examples have passed, and to consider also by whom they have been sanctioned. If they stem only from functionaries in the ordinary business of the court, without the manifest knowledge of the higher officers, or from the teacher of all errors, the people, they are to be condemned and held of little account. But if they have passed under the eyes of legislators, judges, or the principal courts in such a manner that they must necessarily have been strengthened by at least tacit approval, they are entitled to more authority. Examples which have been published, although little used, but which have been thoroughly discussed, deserve more authority; but those, which have fallen into oblivion, deserve less. Examples, Bacon remarks, like waters are most wholesome in a running stream. Examples which relate to the law should not be sought from historians, but from public acts and the most careful traditions. It is a misfortune even of the best historians that their legal knowledge is deficient. An example which the same or the succeeding age has upon the recurrence of the case rejected, should not be readily readmitted. The fact that it was once adopted does not tell so much in its favor as the subsequent abandonment tells against it. Examples are to be used for advice, not for rules and orders. Therefore, they should be so employed as to turn the authority of the past to the use of the present.

If, however, neither a parity of reasoning nor the use of examples is available, what then? When the rule of law is deficient in such a case Bacon's solution is the ancient Greek one. He would entrust the matter to the judgment and discretion of a conscientious man. New matters arise both in criminal causes which require punishment, and in civil causes which require relief. The courts which should take cognizance of the former Bacon calls Censorian, and of the latter, Praetorian.[78] Bacon's commentators have usually condemned the institution of these courts; an evidently troubled authority begins his note on them with the remark " Hic vera utopia proponitur." [79] However, it is clear that Bacon was attempting an idealized description of the Court of Star Chamber, and of the equity jurisdiction of the Court of Chancery.[80] Bacon [81] regarded the Star Chamber as " one of the safest and noblest institutions of this kingdom," a view which was shared by Coke [82] who described it as " the most honorable Court (our Parliament excepted) that is in the Christian world." In 1616, when James I decided the dispute between the common law courts and the court of chancery in favor of the latter, Bacon pointed out that the order made the Chancery the court of the King's " absolute power."

Bacon proposed that Censorian Courts should have power and jurisdiction, not only to punish new offenses, but also to increase the punishments appointed by law for old ones, where the cases where heinous and enormous, provided they were not capital. An enormous crime has something of the nature of a new one. Similarly, the Praetorian Courts should have power both to abate the rigor of the law and to supply its defects.

---

[78] 9 *Works* 321.
[79] 3 *Works* 145.
[80] *Ibid.*

[81] 11 *Works* 130.
[82] Fourth Instit. 65.

If relief is due to a person whom the law has neglected, much more is it due to one whom it has wounded. The Praetorian and Censorian Courts should, therefore, entirely confine themselves to monstrous and extraordinary cases, and not encroach upon the ordinary jurisdictions, in order to avoid an inclination to supplant rather than to supply the law. These jurisdictions should reside only in the Supreme Courts, and not be shared by the lower; for the power of supplying, extending and moderating laws differs little from that of making them. The courts should not be entrusted to the charge of one man, but should consist of many. Decrees should not be issued silently, but the judges should give the reasons for their decisions openly and in full court. What is free in point of power would thus be restrained by regard to character and reputation. There should be no authority to shed blood; nor should sentence be pronounced in any court upon capital cases, except in accordance with known and certain law. In the Censorian Courts there should be opportunity for three verdicts so that the judges would not be obliged to acquit or condemn, but would be at liberty to declare the fact " not proven." In addition to the penalty there should be power also to admonish or to inflict a light disgrace; punishing the offender, as it were, with a blush. In the Censorian Courts attempts at great crimes and offenses should be punished even though the end has not been consummated. This might even be the principal function of these courts. It is as well the part of severity to punish attempts, as of mercy to prevent the completion of crimes, by punishing the intermediate acts.

The Praetorian Courts must be careful not to afford relief in such cases that the law has not so much omitted as treated as unimportant, or because of their character, held not worth redress. Under no circumstances should the Praetorian Courts be permitted to hold that everything is a matter of discretion under color of mitigating the rigor of the law; to proceed otherwise would break the strength of the law and relax its sinews. The Praetorian Courts should not have authority under any pretext of equity to decree against an express statute. This would transform the judge into a legislator, and would permit him to hold everything to be discretionary. The law courts must be kept separate from the equity courts. If the jurisdictions are mixed, the distinction of cases will not be retained, and discretion will in the end supersede the law. Judges in the Praetorian Courts ought, as far as possible, to establish rules for their own guidance, and should announce them publicly. It is clear that the best law is the one which leaves the least to the discretion of the judge; similarly, the best judge is the one who leaves the least to himself.

RETROSPECTIVE LAWS

In order to make his theory logically complete Bacon glanced hastily at retrospective laws. He was concerned with the situation when one law follows and amends another, and draws the omitted cases along with it. He was in accord with our present day view that laws of this kind must be used seldom, and with great caution. He did not approve of a Janus in laws. However, he believed that any person who evades and narrows the words or meaning of a law improperly deserved to be himself ensnared by a subsequent law. Thus in cases of fraud and captious evasion it is just that laws should be retrospective, and mutually assistant; that a man who plots to deceive and upset the present laws should at least be apprehensive of future ones.

However, laws which confirm the real intention of statutes against the defects of forms and usages very properly include past actions. The principal inconvenience of a retrospective law is that it creates disturbance; but confirmatory laws of this sort tend rather to promote peace and to settle past transactions. However, there are other types of retrospective laws. There is the type which prohibits and restrains future acts, but which necessarily is connected with the past. Thus, in Bacon's view, which was certainly not widely shared at the time of the passage of the National Prohibition Act, a law which would prohibit certain artisans from henceforth selling their wares seems only to bear upon the future, yet it operates in the past; for that type of artisan is deprived of a skill which he learned in his youth and is now too old to acquire another one. He thought that declaratory laws should not be enacted except in cases where they may be justly retrospective. He argued that every declaratory law, though it does not mention the past, yet by the very force of the declaration must necessarily apply to past transactions. This is true because the interpretation does not date from the time of the declaration, but is made, as it were, contemporary with the law itself.

To sum up, Bacon took the view that in order to achieve justice in the cases not clearly provided for by statute or otherwise the judge has three courses open to him. He may proceed on the analogy of precedents, or by the use of examples, or by his own sound judgment and discretion. This theory was put forward as an attempt to meet the problem of certainty. It can be looked at, however, from another and equally important point of view.

It can be taken as a seventeenth century effort to describe in logical terms the nature of the judicial process. In its wonderful generality it is an extraordinary achievement, and easily holds its own with the notable analyses of modern times. At one pole is the frankly amorphous estimate by Cardozo. " My analysis of the judicial process comes then to this, and little more," he [83] wrote. " Logic, and history, and custom, and utility, and the accepted standards of right conduct, are the forces which singly or in combination shape the progress of the law. Which of these forces shall dominate in any case, must depend largely upon the comparative importance or value of the social interests that will be thereby promoted or impaired. . . . The judge legislates only between gaps. He fills the open spaces in the law. How far he may go without traveling beyond the walls of the interstice cannot be staked for him upon a chart. He must learn it for himself as he gains the sense of fitness and proportion that comes with years of habitude in

[83] *The Nature of the Judicial Process* (1921) 112.

the practice of an art." This is an altogether admirable statement of the elusive qualities of the judicial process. But is the art of judicial decision really so elusive? May we not, as Bacon did, call logic to our aid and endeavor, in spite of the transcendent subtlety of the material, to exhaust the possibilities that confront the judge? At the other pole from Cardozo is the severely analytical analysis of Pound. " Supposing the facts to have been ascertained," he [84] writes, " decision of a controversy according to law involves (1) selection of the legal material on which to ground the decision, or as we commonly say, finding the law; (2) development of the grounds of decision from the material selected, or interpretation in the stricter sense of the term; (3) application of the abstract grounds of decision to the facts of the case." As an abstraction from countless thousands of opinions of the apparent behavior of judges when engaged in the process of deciding cases the statement is as admirable as Cardozo's. Moreover, in his exposition Pound gives full recognition to all the evasive qualities of law and life that were the burden of Cardozo's discourse. Nevertheless, does not Pound's analysis err as much at one extreme as Cardozo's did at the other? Is not Pound's approach too analytical, or more properly, is it an accurate description of the judicial process? It states a theory of the way a judge's mind functions in reaching a decision. Dewey's [85] analysis of that very process seems much closer to the truth. The judge begins with an indeterminate or problematic situation. An important step is for the judge to determine exactly what the problem is. To ask the right question, Bacon long ago observed, is the half of knowledge. The way in which the problem is conceived decides what specific suggestions are entertained and which are dismissed; what data are selected and which rejected; it is the criterion for relevancy and irrelevancy of hypotheses and conceptual structures. Upon the determination of the problem, a possible solution then presents itself as an *idea.* Ideas are the anticipated consequences or forecasts of what will happen when certain operations are carried out. Various activities are involved in executing the operations, and in the process the problem may be further delimited. Eventually, the ideas that represent possible modes of solution are all tested and a final conclusion is reached. It is unnecessary to dwell upon the material difference between this conception of the process of judicial decision and the one put forward by Pound. The vital point is that the judge does not first find the facts, then ascertain and develop the law, and then apply the results to the facts. He does even not know what the operative facts of the case are until the apparently relevant facts have been tested in conjunction with the ideas that forecast the solution. He does not know what the law is until he has settled upon the solution which he believes he will accept. At that point the judge then " finds the law," and it may well be that the provisional solution will have to be abandoned if the " law " as the judge " finds it " will not permit the proposed solution. The judge will then seek a different solution, and again " find the law." This process will continue until a solution is found which will withstand the test of the law, the facts and any other materials the judge deems relevant.

Bacon's analysis falls far short of Dewey's in point of logical completeness; but it is not opposed to it. It suggests that the judge when he develops an idea that anticipates the solution is limited to the three possibilities discussed above, namely, the idea must have an analogical basis, or be grounded on the use of examples, or flow from a conception of justice or reason. Bacon does not suggest that the judge, after his solution has been anticipated, is limited to any particular method of reasoning or the use of any particular material; but he does insist that if there is a gap in the law the judge's possibilities of closing it are confined to three channels.

So far it has been assumed that there are " gaps " in the law; that, in fact, in most litigated cases no statute is clearly applicable and no previous decision is plainly controlling. One branch of modern legal theory denies the validity of this assumption, and asserts that there is no such thing as a genuine gap. The argument turns on the meaning to be given the word "gap." A municipal corporation was authorized by statute to open and widen streets according to the procedure described in the statute; but the statute prescribed no procedure for cases of widening streets, and the court held the statute to that extent inoperative.[86] In one sense there was such a gap in the law in this instance that the court was powerless to close it. Kelsen,[87] however, argues that there is no such thing as a genuine gap in the sense that a legal dispute cannot be decided according to the valid norms, by reason of the omission of a provision directed to the concrete case. That is to say, in the street-widening case the court disposed of the controversy and therefore no "gap" exists. Kelsen would probably apply the same argument to those instances in which the courts hold that the matters submitted to them are not within their province at all, e. g., the determination of political questions. Kelsen points out further that when we speak of a "gap" what we generally mean is not, as the expression might deceive us into thinking, that a decision is logically impossible for lack of a norm, but only that the logically possible decision, confirming or disposing of the claim, is felt, by the agent competent to decide, that is, to apply the law, to be too inexpedient or too unjust, or so inexpedient or so unjust, as to give rise to the impression that the legislator could never have considered this case, and that had he considered it, would and could not have decided in this way. The so-called "gap" is, therefore, nothing else than the difference between the positive law and some other order considered to be better, truer and juster. There is a large element of truth in this analysis; but it is not complete. It does not cover the case handled in Bacon's inquiry. All that Kelsen says can be granted; but there will still remain for analysis the nature of the task which confronts the judge when he has

---

[86] *Chaffee's Appeal*, 56 Mich. 244, 22 N. W. 871 (1885).
[87] *The Pure Theory of Law* (1935) 51 Law Q. Rev. 517.

before him for settlement a matter which is not clearly embraced within the statutes or the controlling decisions.

Obscurity of Laws

We have the second kind of uncertainty in the law, of which Bacon spoke, where the law is ambiguous and obscure. He thought obscurity of law arose from four sources: either from an excessive accumulation of laws, especially if they are mixed with those which are obsolete; or from an ambiguity, or want of clearness and distinctness in drafting them; or from negligent and ill-ordered methods of interpreting law; or lastly, from a contradiction and inconsistency of judgments.[88]

Bacon's remedy for an excessive accumulation of laws was an adaptation of ancient Athenian practice. Every year the Athenians appointed six men to examine the contradictory titles of their laws—the so-called *Antinomies*—and to report to the people those which could not be reconciled so that a definite resolution might be passed with respect to them. However, Bacon insisted that there ought not to be too great an eagerness to reconcile those contradictory titles by fine and far-fetched distinctions. Obsolete laws as well an antinomies should be repealed.

If the laws are too voluminous or too confused to be handled by that method, there should be a new digest. The preparation of the digest should be considered an heroic work, and its authors should be reckoned among legislators and reformers of law. In this regeneration and reconstruction of the laws, the words and text of the old laws and law books should by all means be retained, although it is necessary to extract them by scraps and fragments, and afterwards connect them together in proper order. In laws we ought not so much to look to style as to authority, and its patron, antiquity. Otherwise the work will appear rather a matter of scholarship and method, than a body of commanding laws. This new book of laws ought to be confirmed by the legislative power of the state, since under

[88] 9 *Works* 326.

pretence of digesting old laws, new laws might be secretly imposed.

Bacon approved neither of prolixity or too much conciseness in drawing up laws. He thought it impossible to achieve certainty by attempting to enumerate and express every particular case in apposite words. That procedure, in fact, raises a number of questions about words. The interpretation which proceeds according to the meaning of the law is rendered more difficult because of the conflict of words. Bacon's opposition to brevity, as being the style of majesty and command, was based on the fear that the law should become like Aristotle's Lesbian rule; that is to say, it might fit any situation. We should therefore aim at a mean, and look for a well-defined generality of words. This mean will not attempt to express all the cases comprehended, and it will exclude with sufficient clearness the cases not comprehended. However, in ordinary laws and proclamations of state, in which lawyers are not generally consulted, but every man trusts to his own judgment, everything should be fully explained, and pointed out at a level of meaning possible to the capacity of the people. Although he does not refer to Plato explicitly, it is a fair guess that Bacon was aware of his plea for the use of the preamble. Bacon lived at the end of the great age of the preamble in English statutory law [89] and he thought that preambles were necessarily used in most cases, at least as times were then. They were not needed so much to explain the law, as to persuade Parliament to pass it, and also to satisfy the people. However, he thought it best to avoid preambles as much as possible, and to let the law commence with the enactment. Though the intention and purport of a law is sometimes understood from the prefaces and preambles, yet its latitude or extension should by no means be sought there. For the preamble often selects a few of the more plausible and specious points by way of example, even when the law contains many other things.

The influence of Bacon's experience as a practicing lawyer

---

[89] Plucknett, *A Concise History of the Common Law* (2nd ed. 1936) 288.

on his theory of jurisprudence is nowhere better shown than in his remarks on the methods of legal exposition. He believed there were five methods of expounding law and removing ambiguities: namely, by reports of judgments; by authentic writers; by auxiliary books; by prelections; or by the answers and decrees of learned men. He believed that if all these methods were properly instituted they would be of great service against the obscurity of laws.

Above everything else, he insisted that the judgments delivered in the supreme and principal courts on important cases be reported, especially if the questions were doubtful, difficult or novel. For, as he observed, judgments are the anchors of laws, as laws are of the State. The cases should be recorded precisely, the judgments themselves word for word; the reasons which the judges allege for their judgments should be added; the authority of cases brought forward as examples with the principal case should not be mixed with it; the perorations of counsel should be omitted unless they contain something very remarkable; reporters should be drawn from the ranks of the most learned counsel and receive a liberal salary from the State; judges themselves should not meddle with the reports—they may be too fond of their own authority and thus exceed the province of a reporter.

The body of law itself should be composed only of the laws that constitute the common law, the constitutional laws or statutes, and reported judgments. Besides these, no other should be deemed authentic, or at least they should be sparingly accepted. Bacon thought that nothing contributed so much to the certainty of laws as to keep the authentic writings within moderate bounds and to get rid of the enormous multitude of authors and doctors of law. He believed that because of them the meaning of laws is distracted, the judge is perplexed, the proceedings are made endless, and the advocate himself, as he cannot master so many books, takes refuge in abridgements. Perhaps some one good commentary and a few classic authors, or rather some few selections from some few of them may be received as authentic. The rest should be kept for use in libraries so that the judges or counsel may inspect them if necessary; they should not be allowed to be pleaded in court or to pass into authorities.

There should be many auxiliary books. Students should be educated and trained through the use of Institutes, or comprehensive surveys of the law apparently after the model of Justinian and Coke. The Institute should be arranged in an orderly manner and run through the whole private law, giving a slight sketch of everything; so that when a student comes to study the body of law he will find nothing entirely new or of which he has not had a slight notion beforehand. Public laws should not be treated in the Institutes, but should be drawn from the original sources. It is not clear whether Bacon intended his Institutes to be arranged alphabetically or on the composite plan of Justinian's Code and Digest, and Coke's Institutes. By the Fourteenth Century English lawyers had discovered the great advantages of the alphabetical arrangement as the best scheme to make English law accessible, although the first alphabetical encyclopedia written in English was not published until 1704.[90]

To these remarks Bacon added observations on the proper construction of books dealing with legal terms, rules of law, antiquities of law, summaries, and forms of pleading. He thought it was a sound precept not to take the law from the rules, but to make the rule from the existing law; the proof is not to be sought from the words of the rule, as if it were the text of law. The rule, like the magnetic needle, points at the law, but does not settle it. The law should be taken from sworn judges and not from the answers of learned men. Care should be taken that judgments proceed after mature deliberation; that courts preserve mutual respect for one another; and that the way to a repeal of judgments be narrow, rocky, and as it were, paved with flint stones.

---

[90] 12 Holdsworth, *Hist. Eng. Law* (1938) 174.

Conclusion

Bacon's great merit as a legal philosopher lay in his firm grasp of method, the distinctness with which he formulated the task before him, and the resoluteness with which he adhered to the ideal he had set himself. He possessed a synoptic view of knowledge generally, and the main direction of his thought was towards methodology. He saw that the principles of a scientific methodology were as applicable to law as to other departments of knowledge. In considering those principles in relation to jurisprudence he perceived with the utmost clearness that much previous juristic speculation had fallen into either utopianism on the one hand or provincialism on the other. He therefore aimed at a jurisprudence which would be always practical but which would possess all the necessary characteristics of a genuine scientific theory. Modern logic has dealt harshly with his theory of inductive generalization; that, however, was only one aspect of his conception of scientific method, although it is the part on which he lavished the greatest attention. There is no evidence, or at least none has been suggested, that his ideas of the inductive process have vitiated his theory of jurisprudence. His juristic speculations are in fact the product of no single method. So far as he went in reducing his ideas to writing he realized what he considered to be the ideal of jurisprudence. He developed a general theory of large practicality. He was able to do that because he always kept before him the facts of English legal history. That deprived his system of a measure of generality, but it increased, at least for the Anglo-American lawyer, its utilitarian value. His actual achievement in jurisprudence is of a high order. In his first principles he perhaps takes too much for granted; but his analysis of the nature of the judicial process goes unerringly to the central problem and his proposed solutions merit, in the main, more attention than they receive in modern thought.

CHAPTER VII

HOBBES

> *I say it advisedly, if you would
> think clearly of rights and duties,
> sovereignty and law, you must
> begin with the criticism of
> Hobbes.*
>
> Pogson Smith

HOBBES divided philosophy into three parts, *Corpus, Homo,
Civis*, that is, a system of Matter, Man and the State,
and he aimed to give a complete account of the entire domain.[1]
His starting point was the idea of motion. Hobbes' philosophical views were not presented to the public until he was in
middle age, and it is not clear at what stage of his thought he
became impressed with the fundamental importance of the
ubiquity of motion in nature. On his third trip to the continent,
which lasted from 1634 to 1637, he was haunted during the
whole journey by the idea. He himself traces his realization of
the significance of the conception to the following incident,
which has not been dated.[2] At a gathering of learned men,
where he happened to be, someone mentioned sensation. It
was at once disposed of with the contemptuous question:
"What is sense?" Hobbes thought it singular that men who
regarded themselves as wise should be ignorant of the nature
of their own senses. He pondered long about the matter, and
concluded finally that if all bodies were at rest or all moved
alike, no distinction could be made, and therefore all sensation

---

[1] 1 *Works* 12. References are to *The English Works of Thomas Hobbes*, edited
by Sir William Molesworth, 11 vols., (1839-45). References to *The Elements of
Law* are to Tönnies' edition, *Cambridge English Classics*, (1928). All citations to
the *Leviathan* have been compared with the text of the 1651 edition. For the
Latin works the references are to the *Opera philosophica quae latine scripsit omnia*,
edited by Sir William Molesworth, 5 vols. (1839-45) and are cited "*L. Works.*"
For the most acute interpretation of Hobbes' political philosophy that has appeared
in recent years, see the Introduction by Professor Michael Oakeshott to his edition
of the *Leviathan* (1946).

[2] 1 *L. Works* xx.

would be abolished. Hence the cause of all things must be sought in the difference of movements. On the basis of this principle, Hobbes planned to explain the nature of Matter, Man and the State.

Inasmuch as all things have but " one universal cause, which is motion," [3] Hobbes thought that all inquiry must begin with geometry, which investigates simple motion. All writers, he remarks, " as are ignorant of geometry, do but make their readers and hearers lose their time." [4] From a consideration of the principles of simple motion, the inquiry would pass to the motions of bodies, or physics, and thence to Man, inasmuch as the " motions of the mind . . . have their causes in sense and imagination," [5] which are subjects of physics. Finally, from these inquiries there would be deduced " the causes and necessity of constituting commonwealths." [6] Thus Hobbes thought he would be able to deduce a theory of law and justice from a principle of mechanics. He did not live to complete his system, or even to organize all that he was able to compose.

At bottom Hobbes therefore envisaged an explanatory deductive system necessarily of a postulational character. He was attempting something more than a classification of the fields of inquiry—the ethic, physics and dialectics of Plato, the theoretical, practical and productive of Aristotle, the *trivium*

---

[3] 1 *Works* 69.

[4] 1 *Works* 73.

[5] 1 *Works* 72-3.

[6] 1 *Works* 74. The idea that motion is the starting point of Hobbes' philosophy is to be understood in the sense that it is an explicitly avowed postulate of Hobbes' system. Professor Oakeshott has shown that when Hobbes' system is analyzed from the point of view of political philosophy generally, its assumptions are of a different kind. Professor Oakeshott isolates three great traditions in political thought, that of Reason and Nature, exemplified by Plato's *Republic*; Will and Artifice, typified by the *Leviathan*; and the Rational Will, represented by Hegel's *Philosophie des Rechts* (op. cit. xii). He concludes that " the system of Hobbes' philosophy lies in his conception of the nature of philosophical knowledge, and not in any doctrine about the world. And the inspiration of his philosophy is the intention to be guided by reason and to reject all other guides." Consequently, " the lineage of Hobbes' rationalism lies, not (like that of Spinoza or even Descartes) in the great Platonic-Christian tradition, but in the sceptical, late scholastic tradition " (p. xxvii). Nevertheless, on the issue whether the predicament of mankind arises from the nature of man, or from a defect in the nature of man, he is with Plato and Spinoza (as opposed to St. Augustine) in holding that it is due to the former (p. liv).

and *quadrivium* of the Middle Ages, and the history, poesy and philosophy of his employer, Bacon. His definition of philosophy allowed for such a classification: " Philosophy is such knowledge of effects or appearances, as we acquire by true ratiocination from the knowledge we have first of their causes or generation: And again, of such causes or generations as may be from knowing first their effects." [7] This definition at once marks off history, which is the record of past experience; " whereas sense and memory are but knowledge of fact, which is a thing past and irrevocable; science is the knowledge of consequences and dependence of one fact upon another." [8] It also distinguishes theology, since by definition God had no cause. Although his approach yielded a classification, his aim had a much greater significance. He sought, and believed he had found, a formula that embraced all the phenomena of the universe, insofar as they were capable of expression through matter and motion treated from the point of view of causal processes. Such formulae are not unusual in the history of thought, and may be traced to the Stoics, who were perhaps the most vigorous proponents of the idea of the full causal linkage of all events.[9] In view of the recurrence from time to time of the idea of a " total deduction " Meyerson [10] is inclined to think that it may have a special importance. It implies a belief in the rationality and unity of nature, and therefore the possibility of a deduction of all events. But apart from these considerations, the scheme that Hobbes set himself to carry out placed him at once in the group of great European system-builders who even then were working a transformation of the metaphysical and scientific bases of Western thought. No contemporary rose to such an idea of progressive, scientific explanation, and not until two centuries had elapsed was the idea again so distinctly conceived and seriously carried out.[11]

---

[7] 1 *Works* 3.
[8] 1 *Works* 11; 3 *Works* 35.
[9] 1 Meyerson, *De l'explication dans les sciences* (1921) 111.
[10] *Ibid.* 116.
[11] Robertson, *Hobbes* (1886) 45.

Hobbes thought of scientific method as reasoning from the effect to the cause, or from the cause to the effect.[12] He believed that the whole method of scientific demonstration is of the latter type—the former being hypothetical—and consists in deducing the conclusion syllogistically from first principles.[13] Now such principles are nothing but definitions which, in turn, are nothing but the explication of the meaning of names.[14] A name is defined to be " a word taken at pleasure to serve for a mark, which may raise in our mind a thought like to some thought we had before, and which being pronounced to others, may be to them a sign of what thought the speaker had, or had not before in his mind," and originally was given arbitrarily.[15] From this it followed, in Hobbes' opinion, that the fundamental principles of science are constituted arbitrarily, and are not to be demonstrated. Truth and falsity are therefore solely a function of speech,[16] and the truth of our first principles is something man himself has made.[17] All this led Hobbes to a position of extreme nominalism, and to his emphasis upon the arbitrary character of science.

His mature views on methodology were published after he had put forward his psychological and political works. " What was last in order, is yet come forth first in time," he writes.[18] To give those works validity he had to allow for their methodology, which was not strictly in accord with the ideal system just sketched. Thus, he observes that the causes of the motions of the mind are known, not only by ratiocination, but also by every man who takes the pains to observe those motions for himself.[19] Inasmuch as the principles of politics rest upon a knowledge of psychology, political knowledge itself may be arrived at through man's experience and the examination of his own mind. Self-observation thus becomes a warranted method for psychology and the social sciences, including jurisprudence. His legal theory is therefore not necessarily a deduc-

---

[12] 1 *Works* 312.
[13] 1 *Works* 81.
[14] *Ibid.* and 1 *Works* 70.
[15] 1 *Works* 16.
[16] 1 *Works* 36-7.
[17] 1 *Works* 388.
[18] 2 *Works* 20.
[19] 1 *Works* 73.

tion from the laws of mechanics. In fact, its ultimate basis is an empirical psychology. He was the first to develop that field in modern times, and his contributions to it have been described as epoch-making. This does not mean that he lost sight of the idea of motion in either the *Human Nature* or the *Leviathan*. Thus sensation is held to be a motion inside the body caused by the action of external objects; and delight, pain, love, and hatred " are nothing really but motion about the heart." [20] However, those assertions are more or less taken for granted, and in any event are not deduced in accordance with the principles of his ideal methodology.

NATURAL LAW

From the elaborate psychological analyses prefixed to the various expositions of his political theory, Hobbes drew conclusions of major importance. He believed that he had set forth a complete account of the whole nature of man, which could be reduced to four basic elements, the natural powers of man's body and mind: strength of body, experience, reason, and passion.[21] In the course of the argument that led him to this position he had concluded that good and evil were relative terms. Whatever is the object of any man's appetite or desire, he calls " good "; whatever is the object of his aversion he calls " evil." For these words " are ever used with relation to the person that useth them: there being nothing simply and absolutely so; nor any common rule of good and evil to be taken from the nature of the objects themselves, but from the person or the man (where there is no commonwealth), or (in a commonwealth) from the person that representeth it, or from an arbitrator or judge, whom men disagreeing shall by consent set up, and make his sentence the rule thereof." [22] If there is no general moral law, it follows that the desires and passions of man are not in themselves censurable. Similarly the actions that proceed from those passions cannot be condemned, until

[20] 3 *Works* 42, *Elements* 22.   [21] *Elements* 53.   [22] 3 *Works* 41, *Elements* 22.

there is a law that forbids them.[23] Now the first aim of man, it seemed clear to Hobbes, was the assurance of a contented life. That aim can be realized only if man obtains power which, if we take it in a universal sense, means his present means of obtaining some future apparent good.[24] "So that in the first place, I put for a general inclination of all mankind, a perpetual and restless desire of power after power that ceaseth only in death. And the cause of this, is not always that a man hopes for a more intensive delight, than he has already attained to; or that he cannot be content with a moderate power; but because he cannot assure the power and means to live well, which he hath present, without the acquisition of more."[25]

His next proposition is that nature has made men so equal in body and mind that one man, on the basis of any supposed difference, cannot claim for himself any benefit to which another may not pretend as well as he.[26] The strongest of body may be overcome by the weakest, either by secret machination or through confederacy with others; as for the mind, setting aside special aptitudes, and coming to prudence, which is experience, there is a greater equality among men than that of strength. All men think that they have it in a greater degree than others; but this proves rather that men are in that point equal, "for there is not ordinarily a greater sign of the equal distribution of anything than that every man is contented with his share." From this equality of ability there arises equality of hope in the attainment of our ends. The life of man, he says, may well be compared to a race that has no other goal nor other garland, than to be foremost.[27] Men are moved by three principal passions, a desire

---

[23] 3 *Works* 114.

[24] 3 *Works* 74, 85.

[25] 3 *Works* 85. *Cf.* Nietzsche's definition of psychology: "All psychology hitherto has run aground on moral prejudices and timidities, it has not dared to launch out into the depths. In so far as it is allowable to recognize in that which has hitherto been written, evidence of that which has hitherto been kept silent, it seems as if nobody had yet harbored the notion of psychology as a doctrine of the development of the will to power and of the forms it takes (Morphologie und Entwicklungslehre des Willens zur Macht)." *Beyond Good and Evil*, § 23.

[26] 3 *Works*, c. 13.   [27] *Elements* 36.

for gain, for safety and for reputation. Those passions are thus the three great causes of quarrels. Hence, the natural condition of man, which is his state in the absence of a superior power to keep him in order, is one of war " of every man against every man." If there is any doubt upon this score consider what opinion man has of his fellow citizens when he arms himself for a journey, and locks his doors, and chests. Hobbes thinks that there is as much an accusation of mankind by these actions as there is in Hobbes' words. And man does all this when he knows that there are laws and public officials to revenge all injuries done him. For further evidence Hobbes brings forward as examples the life of savages, and the immoral relations which obtain between independent states. He does not hesitate to draw the necessary conclusions of his view of man in his natural state:

" In such condition, there is no place for Industry; because the fruit thereof is uncertain: and consequently no Culture of the Earth; no Navigation, nor use of the commodities that may be imported by Sea; no commodious Building; no Instruments of moving, and removing such things as require much force; no Knowledge of the face of the Earth; no account of Time; no Arts; no Letters; no Society; and which is worst of all, continuall feare, and danger of violent death; And the life of man, solitary, poore, nasty, brutish, and short. . . . It is consequent also to the same condition, that there be no Propriety, no Dominion, no *Mine* and *Thine* distinct; but onely that to be every mans, that he can get; and for so long, as he can keep it."

Plato had erected his imaginary community on the basis of his psychological analysis of human nature, and Hobbes' own views are similar to those advanced by Glaucon in the *Republic*.[28] But the significance of Hobbes' theory is its opposition to the Aristotelian doctrine that " man is by nature a political animal." Twenty-six years before the appearance of the *Leviathan* Grotius had given a new twist to the Aristo-

[28] *Republic* 358E-359B.

telian view in his principle of sociability (*socialitas*). " Among
the traits characteristic of man," he wrote, " is an impelling
desire for society, that is, for the social life—not of any and
every sort, but peaceful, and organized according to the measure
of his intelligence, with those who are of his own kind; this social
trend the Stoics called ' sociableness.' Stated as a universal
truth, therefore, the assertion that every animal is impelled
by nature to seek only its own good cannot be conceded." [29]
The Horatian view that " just from unjust Nature cannot
know " must not for one moment be admitted. Grotius' theory
was an effort to solve the problem of the existence of natural
law in a state of nature where men were completely independent
in their relations. Could individuals be bound by a common
law unless at the same time they were united in a community? [30]
But a basic postulate of natural law was the assumption that
status naturalis was the antithesis of *status socialis*. Grotius
and his followers held that natural law commanded sociable
behavior, and they therefore believed that the state of nature,
if it were not yet a state of society, was at least a state of
sociability. On this assumption it could be shown that civil
society and positive law were outgrowths of an original sociability and the original natural law. However, in Hobbes' theory
society was a radical departure from the natural order of human
relations; it was an institution founded partly on the passions
and partly on reason.

Thus, those Continental followers of Hobbes who insisted
that the state of nature did not contain even the germ of the
community were advancing a point of view not shared by
Hobbes. How did man ever escape from the melancholy condition in which Hobbes first finds him in nature? There are
certain passions, Hobbes answers, that incline men to peace:
fear of death, desire of such things as are necessary to commodious living, and a hope to obtain them through industry.
Reason therefore suggests convenient articles of peace, upon

[29] *De Jure Belli ac Pacis Libri Tres* (Kelsey trans. 1925) 11.
[30] 1 Gierke, *Natural Law and the Theory of Society* (1934) 96-105.

which men may be drawn to agreement, and dictates to every man for his own good to seek after peace, as far as there is hope to attain it. Those articles of peace are nothing other than the so-called laws of nature.

Legal and speculative philosophy prior to Hobbes had given much thought to distinguishing the various kinds of law. There was not only a *ius naturale*, a *ius gentium* and a *ius civile*, but there was also a *ius naturale prius*, a *ius naturale posterius*, a *ius gentium praevium* and a *ius gentium secundarium*. Hobbes' first step was to eliminate some of the important categories and to revise the general classificatory scheme. He had prepared the way in his discussion of man's condition in a state of nature by maintaining that every man by nature has a right to all things; but, as he at once saw, the right of all men to all things is in effect no better than if no man had a right to anything.[31] His next step was to distinguish law and right, *lex* and *ius*. He held that they were completely opposed to each other. Right is the liberty which the law leaves us; laws are the restraints by which we agree mutually to abridge one another's liberty.[32] " Law is a fetter, right is freedom; and they differ like contraries." [33] This analysis permitted him to make a further advance and to distinguish natural rights (*ius naturale*) from natural law (*lex naturalis*). He defined a natural right as the liberty of each man to use his own power, as he wills, for the preservation of his own life; consequently man may do anything which in his own judgment best accomplishes that end. By " liberty " he means the absence of external impediments. Natural law, however, is inconsistent with this conception. A law of nature he defined as a precept or general rule, found out by reason, by which a man is forbidden to do that which is destructive of his life, or which takes away the means of preserving it, and to omit that by which he thinks it may

---

[31] *Elements* 55, 109. Hobbes' critics customarily urged this point against his theory of rights, as though he himself were not aware of the contradiction in principle.

[32] *Elements* 148.

[33] *2 Works* 186.

best be preserved.[34] At this point he repeats his argument that the theory of rights leads to anarchy, and in effect to no rights at all. The argument has at least two purposes in view. First, the theory of rights accounts for the state of nature as the "*bellum omnium contra omnes.*" By the state of nature Hobbes, of course, does not mean a past condition of mankind. He means the situation that must obtain in the absence of civil power. He regarded men "as if but even now sprung out of the earth, and suddenly, like mushrooms, come to full maturity." [35] Thus, the anarchic condition of the state of nature, which must inevitably be assumed from the hypothesis of natural rights, is transformed into the order of civil society by the logical addition of the natural law element. Second, he stated the natural right concept in the extreme form of the right of all to everything in order to eliminate it from further consideration. He made the individual omnipotent, as Gierke says, with the object of forcing him to destroy himself instantly in virtue of his own omnipotence; then the right would survive only in the form of a *ius ad omnia* left in the hands of a single man, or a single body of men, and would proceed to convert itself into mere naked power. Furthermore, it seems clear that whatever salutary function a theory of natural rights fulfilled, that function could also be deduced from the natural law theory set forth by Hobbes. The concept of natural right was therefore unnecessary once the idea of natural law was admitted.

Hobbes also endeavored to eliminate other ideas which he believed were superfluous. In his discussion of the customary division of law into divine, natural and civil he was able to eliminate the divine law because he held that it was identical with the natural law.[36] Again, he disposed of the idea of the

---

[34] 3 *Works* 116-7.
[35] 2 *Works* 109. *Cf.* 3 *Works* 114. Hobbes is here following the Polybian tradition which maintains that government originates when the ferocity and force of primitive man yield to the supremacy of reason. *Histories*, VI. 6. 12. He is of course denying the truth of the Aristotelian position that man is by nature a political animal. In other words he thought government was an invention and not a development.
[36] *Elements* 149.

ius gentium on the ground that its precepts were exactly those of the natural law.[37]

Hobbes arrived at the formulation of his laws of nature by assuming as an objective a condition for man the opposite of the one which obtains in the anarchic state of nature. If the life of man in the state of nature is solitary, poor, nasty, brutish and short; if there is no security to any man, no property and no dominion; and if all this follows from the fact that in that state there is a war of all against all; then it is plain, at least to Hobbes, that amelioration can be found only in the establishment of an antithetical principle. Consequently, Hobbes proposed as the supreme rule " that every man ought to endeavor peace as far as he has hope of obtaining it; and when he cannot obtain it, that he may seek and use all helps and advantages of war. The first branch of which rule containeth the first and fundamental law of nature, which is *to seek peace and follow it*. The second, the sum of the right of nature, which is by all means we can to defend ourselves." [38] This is the basic " general rule found out by reason " from which Hobbes at once deduces nineteen more. However, the reservation of the right of defense (which includes the natural right of each to all things) in the first law which, if fully exercised, would defeat the end Hobbes has in view, leads him immediately to propose the second law for the purpose of closing that gap. In substance, the law obtains that each man by agreement should lay down the right to all things, and be content with so much liberty against other men as he would allow other men against himself. Then, as the cornerstone, his third law provides " that men perform their covenants made "; for without this law " convenants are in vain, and but empty words, and, the right of all men to all things remaining, we are still in the condition of war." Hobbes devoted many pages to the analysis of the idea of contract and reached finally the novel position that " the definition of injustice is no other than the not performance of covenant. And whatsoever is not unjust is

[37] 3 *Works* 342; 2 *Works* 187; 2 *L. Works* 317.
[38] 3 *Works* 117.

just." Thus in a state of nature there can be no injustice. This follows because in a state of nature it is each man's natural right to disregard his promises if to his advantage. Promises are assured only if a coercive power exists to enforce them, and as there is no such power in a state of nature, covenants in that state are meaningless. Justice, which by definition is the performance of covenants, therefore has existence only in the presence of coercive power.

Hobbes next proceeds to the deduction of his remaining laws which, in the main, are general precepts intended to insure order and peace in society; for example, every man should strive to accomodate himself to the rest, and no man should declare hatred or contempt of another. Here Hobbes realized that his rules may have become too tenuous as guides to action. Men would not take notice of them, either because they were " too busy in getting food " or because they were " too negligent to understand." He therefore reduced them all to one simple formula " intelligible to the meanest capacity ": *Do not that to another which thou wouldest not have done to thyself.* By stating this precept in a negative form, in contrast with its Biblical positive counterpart, Hobbes perhaps emphasized the idea that morality was based on instructed prudence. In Professor Oakeshott's opinion the rule is stated negatively because the felicity of another can be promoted only negatively by forbearance, not positively by activity. The laws of nature are " immutable and eternal "; for injustice, ingratitude, arrogance and the rest can never be made lawful, since it can never happen that war should preserve life and peace destroy it. Nevertheless, the laws of nature are not binding upon men everywhere and at all times. They are obligatory merely in the sense that everyone should desire their observance. For a man that would be modest and tractable, and perform all his promises, while other men were the opposite, would make himself a prey to others, and procure his own certain ruin, which would be contrary to the law of nature which demands self-preservation. It follows as a corollary that the laws of nature are not strictly laws, but " conclusions or theorems concerning what conduceth to the conservation and defense of " men. Law, properly speaking, is the word of him that by right has command over others. However, Hobbes is prepared to admit that if the theorems are to be considered as delivered in the word of God then they are properly called laws.

Now Hobbes has here succeeded in stating the important factors which make group life possible under the conditions of an ordered community. Contemporary social thought has carried the analysis much further, and has added a number of elements for the sake of formal completeness which never occurred to Hobbes. At the same time, since it ignores the teleological, the reduction of group life by modern thought to the elements of contract, physical basis, homogeneity, structure, energy, and plurality of units is not to be counted altogether a gain, notwithstanding its formal clarity. Hobbes had a more significant end in view than the production of a mere descriptive sociology. His book was intended as a guide to action, and he therefore seized upon the essentials, leaving the rest for the systematizers. His critics continue to repeat that his laws of nature are negative, that he can hardly be said to have any real belief in social institutions as the instruments and bearers of progressive civilization. He is held to have accepted the Aristotelian maxim that the state comes into being that man may live, but to have ignored the equally vital truth that it continues in order that he may live well. No doubt part of this charge is true. Hobbes was not a hopeful man and he did not tend to overrate his fellow human beings; he was assuredly no believer in the childish notions of progress which sustain so many men. Nevertheless, he had a clear idea of the state as an instrument of the good life. It was the heart of his whole theory to assert that without the coercive power of the state the life of man was anarchic and brutish, and that the way of the good life was solely through its instrument. His entire problem, as he saw it, was the reconciliation of liberty and authority. He was an apologist for the supremacy of the sovereign on the ground that peace and security were thus best secured; but he was a Spencerian in his insistence that Government should abstain from regulating the lives of its citizens, except in the most urgent matters. " In a way beset," he writes, " with those that contend on one side for too great liberty, and on the other side for too much authority, 'tis hard to pass between the points of both unwounded." [39] The *Pax Hobbesiana* that the *Leviathan* establishes is a compromise one; it lacks the elements of nobility that distinguish many of the great political schemes devised by other philosophers. It was invented for a world that was neither the best nor the worst of all possible worlds; it partook of the necessary limitations of that circumstance.

THE LAW OF THE STATE

In his theory of positive law Hobbes at the outset put his finger unerringly upon a vital distinction. He attempted a separation which, in the Continental languages, is expressed by separate words: *ius, lex; diritto, legge; droit, loi; Recht, Gesetz; derecho, ley;* but which in English is indicated only by the difference between the terms " law " or " the law " and " a law " or " the laws." [40] Thus we speak of corporation law or the law of torts, meaning thereby not any particular law, but the whole body of law prevailing in those fields; we speak also of a law of Congress, or the income tax laws, by which we mean the specific norm or collection of norms. It is the distinction between the general and the particular, and Hobbes saw at once that the primary concern of legal theory was with the former and not the latter. He perceived that law was something more than an aggregate of laws, and that the latter could be subsumed under any sound general theory of the former. There was also an historical reason for his choice. In the legal system of his time the courts and not the legislature or ruler were at

---

[39] 3 *Works* v.

[40] For the relationships of the Greek τὸ δίκαιον and νόμος to Latin *ius* and *lex* see Barker, *Greek Political Theory* (1918) 180.

the center of gravity; their preoccupation was with law and not laws. But in an age such as ours of almost overwhelming legislative activity, or in periods of political absolutism, as during the ancient regime in France or in much of the world today, the common focus of interest may well be laws and not law. In any event, Hobbes declared it was his design not to show what is law here and there; but what is law. He proposed to study the law that men are bound to observe because they are members, not of this or that state in particular, but of a state. He offered many definitions of such law, of which the following perhaps raises the least number of difficulties: " Law, properly, is the word of him that by right hath command over others." [41] This conception was founded on the premise that once the sovereign power had been created through the instrumentality of men agreeing amongst themselves to submit to some man, or assembly of men, voluntarily, that power henceforth was authorized to will in the place of the contracting parties to the end that they might live peaceably amongst themselves and be protected against other men.

For, as Hobbes had already shown, before the institution of sovereign power all men had a right to all things. This necessarily caused discord because no man knew what goods he might enjoy or what conduct he could observe without being molested by his fellow men. Inasmuch as the sovereign power was established to keep the peace, and alone is authorized to do so, it has the whole power to prescribe the rules of property and of conduct which constitute the civil laws, that is to say, the laws of each commonwealth in particular. For the same reasons the sovereign has the right of hearing and determining all controversies that may arise concerning law, either civil or natural, *i. e.*, it has the right of judicature. Without

---

[41] 3 *Works* 147. See also 3 *Works* 250. Elsewhere the *Leviathan* contains a more elaborate definition: " Civil law, is to every subject, those rules which the commonwealth hath commanded him, by word writing or other sufficient sign of the will, to make use of, for the distinction of right and wrong; that is to say, of what is contrary, and what is not contrary to the rule." 3 *Works* 251. *Cf.* " Law is the command of that person, whether man or court, whose precept contains in it the reason of obedience." 2 *Works* 183.

the decision of controversies one man has no protection against the injuries of another; the laws of *meum* and *tuum* are in vain; and to every man remains, from the natural and necessary appetite of his own conservation, the right of protecting himself by his own strength, which is the condition of war, and contrary to the end for which every commonwealth is established.[42] Elsewhere he had expressed the argument almost syllogistically: " The desires and other passions of men are in themselves no sin. No more are the actions that proceed from those passions, till they know a law that forbids them; which till laws be made they cannot know; nor can any law be made, till they have agreed upon the person that shall make it." [43] Once men reduced their wills, by a plurality of voices, into one will they created an obligation of obedience to the commands of the sovereign power. Hobbes admitted a few exceptions to this obligation. Men can refuse to kill, wound, or maim themselves; can refuse to accuse themselves of crimes; and when the sovereign is no longer able to protect them from harm they are at liberty to disobey its commands.[44]

This argument, which formed the basis of political thinking from the sixteenth to the eighteenth century, no longer carries persuasion since the rights of governments are now deduced from the needs of society and not from a purely rational conception of the primitive rights of man. Until that fundamental shift in political thinking occurred Hobbes' argument was attacked with regularity by most of his successors; now it is no longer attacked, it is merely ignored. In its time it was much more than a formal political doctrine; it was one of the most powerful weapons forged from the fierce social struggles of the seventeenth century. As we look at it today it suffers from two principal weaknesses. First, it ignores the great mediaeval conception of law as the custom of the community, the idea that law was not primarily the expression of the will of the ruler, but that it was the expression of the habit of life of the community.[45] In the actual historical development of

---

[42] 3 *Works* 165.   [43] 3 *Works* 114.   [44] 3 *Works* 204, 208.
[45] 6 Carlyle, *History of Mediaeval Political Theory in the West* (1936) 507.

the state there is no sharp break between pre-political and political society. A general theory of law is therefore defective unless it accounts for law both as custom and as legislative command. Second, the idea of a social contract is unnecessary, inasmuch as the observance of the contract must depend on something other than the naked contract itself. We must argue that a social ideal—in Hobbes' case, peace—makes it obligatory to observe the contract. But then, that ideal would also act as the basis for the conduct we are insisting upon, and the idea of contract is thus superfluous. At the same time, the idea of contract has some merit. It insists upon the mutuality of social life; and although Hobbes drew from the conception a justification of absolute monarchy, that is not the necessary deduction as is shown by Rousseau's use of it to establish the absolute authority of the will of the people.

From his conception of the nature of law Hobbes was able to deduce a number of consequences which had the effect of disposing, for him at least, of many troublesome questions. The sovereign is the sole source of law, is not subject to it, and alone has the power to abrogate it. Custom obtains the authority of law through the will of the sovereign signified by his silence. Austin, whose jurisprudence seems to have taken its point of departure from Hobbes', insisted that custom was not law until it was expressly recognized by the sovereign; but his position on this question was ultimately the same as Hobbes', since he insisted that a command could be tacit.[46] Hobbes held further that the law of nature and the civil law are equal in extent; that the law of a conquered country is that of the victor; that the law can never be against reason, *i. e.*, the reason of the sovereign; finally, that law obliges only those who can take notice of it and therefore does not command the insane, children or animals. It was a vital principle of Hobbes that it belonged to the essence of the civil law to be made known to every man to whom it is directed.[47]

---

[46] 1 Austin, *Lectures on Jurisprudence* (Campbell's ed.) § 36.
[47] 3 *Works* 259.

Hobbes at this point saw that his theory of law needed the addition of a further material element if all the gaps were to be closed. There was still the problem of interpretation. His theory in that field, apart from the formal elements which tied it to his doctrine of sovereignty, is in the main the one generally accepted today, although usually on the authority of Austin. He held that it was " not the letter, but the intendment or meaning, that is to say the authentic interpretation of the law (which is the sense of the legislation) " [48] in which the nature of the law consists. From this it followed that the interpretation of all laws depends on the sovereign authority, and its interpreters must be those who owe obedience to the sovereign. " For else, by the craft of an interpreter, the law may be made to bear a sense contrary to that of the sovereign; by which means the interpreter becomes the legislator." [49]

It has sometimes been supposed that a perfection of statement is possible and that in theory there is therefore no need for interpretation. But Hobbes took the flat position, which is now the accepted one, that all laws have need of interpretation. He saw that the meanings of almost all words are either in themselves or in their metaphorical use ambiguous, and that they may be drawn in argument to make many senses. No written law, he pointed out, whether it be expressed in few or many words, can be well understood without a perfect understanding of the end for which the law was made. But the knowledge of that end is in the legislator, and to him therefore there cannot be any insoluble knot in the law. He unravels the knot by discovering the ends, or Alexander-wise he cuts it by making what ends he will through the legislative power.

At the center of Hobbes' theory of interpretation was the judge. In opposition to Bacon and the common law tradition he ruled out the commentator altogether in the interpretation of both the law of nature and the written law. The opinion of a

[48] 3 *Works* 262.
[49] *Cf.* Hoadly, *Sermon Preached Before the King* (1717) 12: " Whoever hath an *absolute authority* to *interpret* any written or spoken laws, it is *he* who is truly the *Law-giver* to all intents and purposes, and not the person who first wrote or spoke them." Quoted, Gray, *Nature and Sources of the Law* (2nd ed. 1924) 102.

writer who speaks without the authority of the commonwealth is not law, no matter how sound it may be. Even what Hobbes himself had written in the *Leviathan*, though it was evident truth, is not therefore presently law. Hobbes states precisely that the interpretation of the law of nature is the sentence of the judge constituted by the sovereign authority to hear and determine controversies, and consists of the application of the law to the case. For in the act of judicature the judge does no more than consider whether the demand of the party is consonant with natural reason and equity; and the sentence he gives is therefore the interpretation of the law of nature. That interpretation is authentic, not because it is his private sentence, but because he gives it by authority of the sovereign; thus it becomes the sovereign's sentence, which is law for that time to the parties pleading. Similarly, the interpreter of the written laws is not the commentator. For commentaries are commonly more subject to cavil than the text and therefore need other commentaries, and thus there will be no end of such interpretation. The interpreter of the written law is no other than the ordinary judge, and his sentence is to be taken by the parties as the law in that particular case. From this analysis to the position of the realist of the present day the step is almost too brief to be measured.

Hobbes accepted the view of the sixteenth century that the courts were not bound to follow precedents, a practice to which we are now returning, whatever may be the present state of of our theory. He argued that judges, and even the sovereign, may err in matters of justice; in a subsequent similar case the judge may find it more consonant with justice to give a contrary sentence, and in such instances he is obliged to do so. " No man's error becomes his own law," Hobbes writes, " nor obliges him to persist in it. Neither, for the same reason, becomes it a law to other judges, though sworn to follow it." The law of nature is the eternal law of God, and cannot change or pass away. No precedent, therefore, can establish a rule of law which is contrary to natural equity; nor can an example of a former judge warrant an unreasonable sentence nor discharge the present judge of the trouble of determining the equitable disposition of the case before him. Hobbes put the case of a man, accused of a capital crime, who fled because of the power and malice of his enemies and the corruption and partiality of the judges. Later he is captured, tried and acquitted, but is nevertheless condemned to forfeit his goods because of his flight. To Hobbes this is a manifest condemnation of the innocent, and would therefore be against the law of nature. He admitted that a written law may forbid innocent men to flee, and they may be punished for fleeing; but that fleeing for fear of injury should be taken for presumption of guilt after the man was judicially absolved of the crime, for which there was authority in English law at the time, seemed to Hobbes preposterous.

On the ancient question of whether the letter of the law or the intent of the lawmaker should prevail Hobbes attempted a reconciliation. He agreed that if by the letter of the law is meant merely what can be gathered from the bare words, then a real problem existed because of the notorious ambiguity of words. But if by the letter is meant the literal sense, then the letter and the intention of the law are one. For the literal sense is that which the legislator intended, and should be clear from the letter of the law. Now the intention of the legislator is always assumed to be just, and a judge therefore ought, if the word of the law does not fully authorize a reasonable conclusion, to fill the omission from the law of nature; or, if the case contains greater difficulties, to withhold judgment until he has received more ample authority. Hobbes put two cases: In the first, the statute provides that he who is put out of his house by force shall be restored by force. A man negligently leaves his house unguarded and, returning, is kept out by force. Hobbes holds that the case is covered by the statute, otherwise there would be no remedy, which would be against the intention of the legislator. Again, the word of the law directs that the judge should decide according to the evidence. A man is falsely accused of an act which the judge himself saw done by another and not by the accused. In this case the letter of the law shall not be followed to condemn the innocent, nor shall the judge give sentence against the evidence of the witnesses because of the rule above stated. The judge should retire in favor of another judge and himself be a witness. In its essentials this theory is identical with a recent carefully formulated proposal to clarify the almost intolerable confusion which obtains in the field of statutory construction.[50] Among its many virtues is the circumstance that it involves a frank recognition in theory of what in large part is the actual practice of the courts. But the practice itself has not always been a happy one, as in the cases where personal predilections of the judges have overridden necessary public requirements.

Hobbes was aware of this weakness in his theory, and attempted to meet it by describing the qualities that make a good judge. He thought that the abilities required in a good interpreter of the laws, that is to say, in a good judge, were not those which had to be possessed by an advocate, namely, a knowledge of the laws. This doctrine has, of course, been accepted in those American states which permit the appointment or election of lay judges. Hobbes himself cited the example of the Law Lords in Parliament who, as he said, were not much versed in the study of the law. But the real basis of his doctrine was his theory of sovereignty. He argued that inasmuch as a judge should not take notice of facts except from witnesses, so also he should not take notice of the law except from statutes and constitutions of the sovereign, either alleged in the pleading or declared to him by those having sovereign power to do so. However, there were certain positive qualities that a judge should possess. He should have a sound sense of justice, should not be swayed by hope of reward or preferment, should be able in judgment to divest himself of fear, anger, hatred, love and compassion, should be diligent and patient in hearing causes, and should have the memory to retain, digest and apply what he has heard.

[50] Radin, *A Short Way with Statutes* (1942) 56 Harv. L. Rev. 388, 422.

In recent times the idea that obscure statutes should be interpreted in accordance with the intention of the legislature has been under attack. It is argued that the legislative intention is actually undiscoverable, and, further, even if it were, that the real difficulty occurs when it clearly had no intention at all with respect to the particular situation before the court. The first contention is met when the legislature in the preamble, in the policy section of the statute, or in the committee reports, agrees formally upon its intention; but the second contention still remains. Two remedies have been suggested to meet the problem raised by the circumstance that the legislature may never have contemplated the relevance of the statute to the particular situation before the court. It has been proposed that the court refer the matter back to the legislature. This procedure was adopted in France in 1790, but was abolished in 1837, since it brought about intolerable delays in the administration of justice and also violated the doctrine of the separation of powers by delegating to the legislature work that was essentially judicial. We are told now that instead of looking for the intention of the legislature we should attempt to find the meaning of the statute. Logic has still not developed the rules which should be applied to propositions in order to determine their meaning; but it recognizes the problem as a legitimate one and an increasing attention is given to it. In jurisprudence, especially on the Continent, the idea that the meaning of a statute is to be found in the social consequences that follow from the possible interpretations has gained wide support. The judge, in other words, has a limited freedom in the decision of marginal cases: he must consider himself an ideal legislator and decide the case in accordance with standards which such a legislator would heed if he were drafting a statute to meet the situation. The logical basis for this theory of the meaning of propositions is found in Peirce's doctrine that the meaning of a proposition consists of its possible deductions or consequences. The classical legal exposition of the doctrine is Gény's *Méthode d'interprétation et sources en droit privé positif* (1899).

Theory of the Common Law

At about the age of seventy-six Hobbes undertook an analysis of the English common law. Aubrey had urged him to embark upon the task, but he had replied that he could not count upon life enough. However, under the stimulus of a gift from Aubrey of Bacon's *Elements of the Common Laws of England* he wrote out the *Dialogue between a Philosopher and a Student of the Common Laws of England*.[51] It belongs to the period when Hobbes was under investigation by a parliamentary committee as a suspected heretic, and feared for his own safety. At that time he wrote an essay on the English law of heresy to prove that he could not be legally burnt, the argument of which he restated in the *Dialogue*. But the primary object of his study of the common law was to refute the theories of the constitutional lawyers, particularly those founded on the great mediaeval conceptions advanced by Coke. He believed that the limitations on the royal prerogative, such as the denial of the sovereign's right of militia, were among the main causes of the catastrophe of the Rebellion, and that a good share of the blame was attributable to the ideas of the constitutional lawyers, which needed correction from the point of view of the new doctrine of sovereignty.

The general theory of the *Dialogue* is merely an application of the doctrine of the *Leviathan* to the specific case of the common law. There is no advance in theory, but the analytical skill with which Hobbes tackled concrete problems contributed in no small measure to his rescue in the nineteenth century from the solitary and opprobrious position to which the critics of the two preceding centuries had assigned him. At the outset he disputed Coke's assertion that reason is the life of the law and that the common law itself is nothing else but reason. It did not help to say that the reason which is the life of the law is artificial and not natural. Hobbes understood that knowledge of the law is gotten by much study, as in other sciences, and

---

[51] 6 *Works* 3 *et seq.*

that such knowledge is an art. He held that it is not wisdom, but authority, that makes a law. He therefore rejects the view of Bracton and Coke that " *lex est sanctio justa, jubens honesta, et prohibens contraria,*" and defines it instead as " the command of him or them that have the sovereign power, given to those that be his or their subjects, declaring publicly and plainly what every of them may do, and what they must forbear to do." [52] Thus it followed that no record of a judgment was a law save only to the party pleading,[53] and that custom by its own nature could never amount to the authority of a law.[54] He interpreted Coke's use of the phrase " legal reason " to mean that the reason of a judge, or of all the judges, together without the king, is that *summa ratio,* and the very law; and he denied that the proposition is true.[55] No judge without the authority of the King can make law; but a judge possessing the authority can give an authentic judgment, which thereby becomes the sovereign's, and " is law for that time to the parties pleading." [56] His conception of case law as binding only on the parties themselves permitted him to argue against the authority of precedents, which he attempted also to meet on the additional ground that, if carried back far enough, would make all the justice in the world depend upon the sentence of a few learned or ignorant men.

Throughout the *Dialogue* Hobbes maintained a running fire of criticism against Coke's views. He observed that Coke everywhere in the *Institutes* endeavored to diminish the king's authority and to insinuate his own opinions among the people for the law of the land; [57] that Coke in maintaining that judicature belonged only to the judges failed to distinguish between a transfer and a commitment of power; [58] that it is impossible to understand Coke's assertion that to cause the death of a man and to declare it is all one thing; [59] that Coke's understanding of unintentional homicide is entirely his own

[52] 6 *Works* 26.
[53] 6 *Works* 54.
[54] 6 *Works* 62.
[55] 6 *Works* 5.
[56] 3 *Works* 263; *Cf.* 6 *Works* 14.
[57] 6 *Works* 62.
[58] 6 *Works* 52.
[59] 6 *Works* 75.

invention; [60] that his definition of theft leads to absurdities; [61] that his discussion of heresy is defective inasmuch as it omits the main point, *i. e.*, what it is; [62] that Coke's constant citation of ancient authorities does not represent his own reading, but are quotations at second-hand; [63] that he misunderstood his common-law authorities; [64] and, finally, that in no other English legal writing had Hobbes encountered weaker reasoning than in the *Institutes*.[65] Putting aside the political and personal elements in Hobbes' criticisms, the principal defects noted in Coke's exposition are defects of the law itself, that Coke had inherited. That Coke failed to perceive numerous instances in which the law stood in need of modernization is undoubtedly a weakness, and that Hobbes, with the tremendous power of the analytical method as a weapon, was on sound ground in exposing it, cannot be doubted. Nevertheless, if Coke was wrong in insisting that the life of the law is reason, Hobbes was equally in error in urging that it is authority. Hale, who took up the cudgels for Coke, put his finger on the flaw in Hobbes' theory when he observed that philosophers generally make " the worst Judges that can be, because they are transported from the Ordinary Measures of right and wrong by their over fine Speculacions, Theoryes and distinctions above the comon Staple of humane Conversations." [66] Hale's criticism could at most be taken as a prophecy of the logical excesses to which the followers of Hobbes, Bentham and Austin carried the refinements of analytical jurisprudence. Hale displayed extraordinary perception in isolating the flaw in Hobbes' theory of law when viewed as a rigid system. Actually, however, it was Hobbes, the authoritarian, who allowed for the tolerance of human affairs, and it was Coke, the rationalist who, on logical grounds, wished to punish the innocent [67] and who maintained that growing corn and grain could not be the subject of larceny [68] because they were annexed to the realty.

---

[60] 6 *Works* 87.   [62] 6 *Works* 96.   [64] 6 *Works* 129.
[61] 6 *Works* 92.   [63] 6 *Works* 144.   [65] 6 *Works* 144.
[66] Hale's tract against Hobbes is printed as appendix III in 5 Holdsworth, *History of English Law* (1924) 499.
[67] 6 *Works* 137; 1 Coke, *Instit.* (5th ed. 1656) 373.
[68] 6 *Works* 92; 3 Coke, *Instit.* (1648) 109.

Conclusion

Hobbes' great contribution to legal philosophy was his justification of the criterion by which analytical jurisprudence since his day has identified law. He held that the legal order derived its authority from politically organized society, and that a law was a rule for which the state had commanded obedience. In thinking of law he thus took his departure from neither the ethical nor the rational, and his ideas in that respect culminated in the Austinian doctrine that no positive law can be legally unjust. He admitted the validity of ethical rules and conceded that they were anterior to the establishment of the state. But he insisted that if they were to be obeyed generally they had to be commanded by a properly established authority possessing adequate force to compel obedience. Thus he made the hallmark of the state the criterion for the identification of law, and in doing so repudiated the theory that law was the habit of life of the community, an idea which in English law found expression in Bracton's theory of law as primarily custom. In the hands of the later analytical jurists Hobbes' idea became one of the most powerful weapons for the analysis of legal phenomena ever devised. Though it has numerous rivals today, it is still employed with fruitful results and seems historically to be at the root of the contemporary realist's conception that law is whatever is done officially about disputes. No doctrine has been so continually criticized and none has showed such tenacity. Every young intellectual, Warburton [69] pointed out in the eighteenth century, "would needs try his arms in thundering upon Hobbes's steel cap," an observation which Holmes [70] was to repeat for our own time but with the addition that he thought "the old pot will serve for a few days longer." That the recent trends towards state absolutism, both in practice and in theory, are in the main current of Hobbes' speculation scarcely needs to be remarked. If those trends continue, his basic legal ideas, in one form or another, will continue to attract a large share of legal speculation.

---

[69] *Divine Legation of Moses* (Hurd's ed. 1811, IV. 31).
[70] 1 *Holmes-Pollock Letters* (1941) 30.

Chapter VIII

SPINOZA

> All our modern philosophers,
> though often perhaps unconsci-
> ously, see through the glasses
> which Baruch Spinoza ground.
>
> Heine

S PINOZA approached law from the point of view of both wisdom and science. He inherited from the Scholastic tradition a sense of order, a way of looking at society that was essentially legal. As a central figure in the great scientific renascence of the seventeenth century he was dominated by the idea of the necessary. At the same time, his experience of life prompted him to allow for the contingent, for those details of conduct which need not, or could not, be subsumed under general principles. He knew that scientific research required the construction of ideally isolated systems in which the necessary relations of things in their essential aspects would be revealed. But no such construction is ever final, particularly in the realm of human affairs; there are omissions and rearrangements which demand a continuous process of correction.

A convenient edition of the Latin works is *Benedicti de Spinoza, Opera quotquot reperta sunt*, recognoverunt J. Van Vloten et J. P. N. Land, 3rd ed. 1913, 4 vols. A translation of the principal works of interest to the legal student was published in the Bohn Library: *The Chief Works of Benedict de Spinoza*, trans. by R. H. M. Elwes, revised ed. 1903, 2 vols. Although it appears that the number of commentaries devoted to Spinoza may some day surpass those on Aristotle, studies of his legal thought are rare. The most important studies in English are *Spinoza's Political and Ethical Philosophy* by Robert A. Duff (1903); Pollock, *Spinoza's Political Doctrine*, 1 *Chronicon Spinozanum* (1921) 45; Green, *Lectures on the Principles of Political Obligation* § 32 *et seq.*, 2 *Works* (1890) 355 *et seq.* Reference to the Latin works are given as "L. Works"; to Elwes' translation as "Elwes." However, I have departed from Elwes' version in many cases. I have also utilized White's translation of the *Ethic* (4th ed. 1937) and the 1862 translation of the *Tractatus Theologico-Politicus*. References to the letters are to Wolf, *The Correspondence of Spinoza* (1928).

Spinoza is surpassed by no other philosopher in the steadiness with which he kept before him both the requirements of his system and the importance of what it had failed to embrace.

As the professed aim of his philosophy Spinoza had a practical end in view. Experience had taught him that all the common aims of social life are vain and futile; that they have no intrinsic value, and are good or bad solely in the effect they have upon the mind. He resolved therefore, so he tells us, to inquire if there were anything so that if he discovered and attained it he would enjoy continuous, supreme and permanent happiness.[1] All the sciences, he maintained, have but one end: the attainment of supreme human perfection.[2] He argued that the foundation of virtue is the endeavor we make to preserve our own being, and that happiness consists exactly in the fact that a man can preserve his own being;[3] to act in conformity with virtue is to preserve our being as reason directs;[4] such an effort of the mind is nothing but the effort to understand, and this effort is the primary and sole foundation of virtue;[5] to understand, therefore, is the absolute virtue of the mind.[6] Thus man reaches ultimate happiness through understanding.

This doctrine Spinoza carried over explicitly into his social and legal views. His views, he held, contributed to the welfare of our social existence since they taught social cooperation and contentment. They contributed also to the advantage of common society to the extent they teach us by what means citizens are to be governed and led, not in order that they may be slaves, but that they may freely do those things which are best.[7]

In all this there is little to alarm the most timid. We have still to reach the views that have been condemned as evil from the time of his own Amsterdam synagogue to that of the present day.[8] These views flow from the naturalistic theory he held of

---

[1] 1 *L. Works* 3; 2 *Elwes* 3.

[2] 1 *L. Works* 6; 2 *Elwes* 7.

[3] *Ethic*, iv, 18.

[4] *Ethic*, iv, 24.

[5] *Ethic*, iv, 26.

[6] *Ethic*, iv, 28.

[7] *Ethic*, ii, 49.

[8] Walsh, *The Mystery of Haushofer*, 21 Life 106 (1946).

the universe. This theory led him to assert that in nature every man has as much right as he has power.[9] Every individual is conditioned by the rules of nature to live and act in a given way. Fishes, for example, are naturally conditioned for swimming and the greater for devouring the rest; therefore fishes enjoy the water, and the greater devour the less by sovereign natural right.[10] Taken abstractly it is certain that nature has the sovereign right to do anything she can. In other words, her right is co-extensive with her power.

As a corollary to this doctrine Spinoza was cautious in holding out any hope for improvement in the social lot of man. The avowed aim of the *Tractatus Theologico-Politicus* was to demonstrate that freedom could be granted without prejudice to the public peace, and that without freedom religion could not flourish nor the public peace be secure.[11] But the *Tractatus Politicus* had a different aim. Spinoza was dissatisfied with the political theories of both philosophers and statemen although he held that the latter, inasmuch as they had had experience for their mistress, wrote far more happily about politics than the former. Philosophic political theory was too moralistic for Spinoza. Since it conceives that men fall into vice by their own fault it generally takes the form of a manual of abuse. It praises what is nowhere to be found in nature and attacks what, in fact, exists; it never conceives of men as they are, but as the philosophers would like them to be. As a result the theories are of no practical interest and are completely Utopian. It is possible that the theories of statesmen suffer from an equally serious but different defect. Statesmen may consult their own interests rather than those of mankind. For himself Spinoza was persuaded that experience had revealed all possible commonwealths which are consistent with men living in unity and also the methods by which people may be guided or kept in fixed bounds. He found it difficult to believe that anything new of service to mankind could be discovered. His whole

[9] *Tract. Polit.*, c. 2.
[10] 2 *L. Works* 258; 1 *Elwes* 200.
[11] 2 *L. Works* 87; 1 *Elwes* 6.

intention therefore is to demonstrate, not what is novel, but only such things as agree best with practice. Of necessity, men are liable to passions. If the well-being of a government depends on any man's good faith, if its affairs cannot properly be administered unless those who conduct them will act honestly, then it will be very unstable indeed. Spinoza turned here to a principle at the basis of the United States Constitution.[12] The public affairs of a government should be so ordered that those who administer them, whether guided by reason or passion, cannot be led to act treacherously or basely.[13]

In nature man is not, Spinoza insisted, a kingdom within a kingdom. Nothing happens in nature which can be attributed to any vice, or flaw, of nature; for nature is always the same and everywhere one, and her virtue and power of acting are everywhere and always the same.[14] Spinoza hoped therefore for little improvement in the lot of man. If man lived a life of reason his lot would be a happy one; but it is very seldom indeed that men live according to the guidance of reason.[15] Spinoza apparently anticipated that his doctrines at the best would have only an indirect effect upon practical affairs. He addressed himself specifically to philosophers and did not commend his thoughts to mankind, for he could not expect that his ideas would please them. He asked the masses not to read his book; they would gain no good themselves and might prove a stumbling block to others.[16]

Spinoza gave much attention to the development of a method that would yield the knowledge necessary for virtue. He wrote a still valuable study of philosophic methodology in which he held that clear and distinct ideas, *i. e.*, ideas formed by pure intellectual activity, were the necessary components of adequate knowledge. He associated methodology with the theory of definition, and held that the definition of a thing must include its proximate cause, and also be such that from it

---

[12] Merriam, *A History of American Political Theories* (1924) 76.
[13] *Tract. Polit.*, c. 1.
[14] *Ethic*, iii, praef.
[15] *Ethic*, iv, 35.
[16] 2 *L. Works* 91; 1 *Elwes* 11.

all the properties of a thing can be inferred.[17] But as a sympathetic critic has pointed out, the rules are too abstract and formal to have any value.[18] Logically they are worthless for they do not embody a positive theory of definition. In practice they are of little use because they do not explain, in any given case, how the mind is to reflect upon and to analyze its true ideas. They have a negative value, however. They are formal canons of criticism, inasmuch as no formula which does not meet them is a genuine definition. In the *Ethic* Spinoza adopted a so-called geometrical method, with an elaborate apparatus of axioms, postulates, corollaries and propositions. However successful the Euclidean method may be in mathematics, it suffers in philosophy from a fatal defect, as a correspondent pointed out to Spinoza.[19] From a mathematical definition we are able to deduce at least one property; if we desire more properties then we must relate the thing defined to other things. Spinoza's deductions from his definitions are not really strict deductions; he is assuming other definitions which he has not explicitly stated. In truth, Spinoza's method, as he himself recognized, is the general method of naturalism. What he did was to examine those aspects of nature which appeared to him important for the purposes of his inquiry, and on the basis of the observations to formulate various propositions from which he made further deductions,[20] correcting them, as his writings show and as he himself claimed, by experience when necessary.[21]

It is difficult to determine the extent of Spinoza's knowledge of positive law. Probably it was not profound. In his library was a copy of *Justinian*—was it the *Institutes?*—but no one has ever claimed that he read it. He knew Hobbes' writings and probably Grotius' *De iure belli ac pacis*, although of this there is some doubt. He made no formal study of law, and so

[17] 1 *L. Works* 29; 2 *Elwes* 35.
[18] Joachim, *Spinoza's Tractatus de Intellectus Emendatione* (1940) 204.
[19] *Ep.* 82. Wolf, *The Correspondence of Spinoza* (1928) 364; Joachim, *A Study of the Ethics of Spinoza* (1901) 115 *et seq.*
[20] 2 *L. Works* 172; 1 *Elwes* 99.
[21] 2 *L. Works* 4; 1 *Elwes* 288.

far as his life is known, had little association with jurists.[22] He had, however, as his writings reveal, a complete command of the traditional law of the Jews, and since for Judaic thought law has always been a central idea, its significance was early impressed upon him. Throughout his writings he kept his theory of law at the initial stages of speculation. He was occupied with the general conceptions and the basic postulates. He did not follow the consequences of his theory to the subsidiary levels to which Hobbes, for example, conducted his own. It is clear that his grasp of Judaic law would have permitted Spinoza to follow this course if he had so chosen. That he did not do so must therefore be attributed to choice and not to lack of knowledge. Perhaps he was guided in this action by the consideration that at the level at which he formulated his theory the doctrine of necessity was fully operative, that excursions into what appeared to be legal minutiae would conduct him into the realm of the arbitrary.

CONCEPT OF LAW

Spinoza's theory of the nature of law is a clear anticipation of an idea which has been an influential one from Kant to the present day. It is the theory which conceives of law as a form of social control, as the device which has as its aim the ordering of human behavior through coercion.

Three proper objects of desire were acknowledged by Spinoza: to know things by their first causes; to control our passions, or acquire virtuous habits; to pass our lives in safety and in health.[23] The means of acquiring the first two were in the nature of man himself, so that their acquisition lies entirely within our own power or depends on the laws of human nature alone. For this reason it may be concluded that these gifts belong to no nation in particular, but are and always were common to the whole of the human race. But the means which insure security of life and good health resides chiefly in external circumstances. They depend for the most part on the current

---

[22] Pollock, *op. cit.* 48. [23] *Tract. Polit.*, c. 3.

of external things, of the causes of which we are ignorant; we are inclined to regard them as gifts of fortune. Nevertheless human forethought and watchfulness are of great avail in attaining security of life. Reason and experience both show no more certain means of reaching this object than the establishment of a society governed by definite laws, occupying a particular territory, with the strength of all the members concentrated in one body. It takes great ability and care to form and preserve a society, and one which is founded and administered by prudent and watchful men will be more secure and lasting than one ruled by men without skill. Nations are therefore particularly distinguished from one another by the institutions and laws under which they live.

Spinoza has accomplished several important objectives in this theory of the structure of the social state. He has carried over into politics the doctrine that the foundation of virtue is self-preservation. At the same time he has carefully excluded morality from his political theory. He admits that the acquisition of virtuous habits is a legitimate end; but their attainment is something for each man to achieve for himself if he can. Morality is not, in Spinoza's theory, the business of the state, which is concerned solely with security. This is, it need scarcely be remarked, a complete repudiation of the Platonic tradition; Spinoza is " not content to rave with the Greeks." [24] He has deliberately associated himself with the doctrines of Machiavelli, Bodin and others that the origin and end of the state is security.[25] In modern days the idea has been put forward with his customary pithiness by Bagehot: " The compact tribes win. . . . Civilization begins because the beginning of civilization is a military advantage." [26] Spinoza's statement of the theory was his own, adapted to his philosophy as a whole, and led specifically to his idea of law.

The root idea of law (*lex*) in Spinoza's system is uniformity.

[24] 2 L. *Works* 89; 1 *Elwes* 7.
[25] Machiavelli, *Discourses* (Modern Library ed. 1940) 105-106; Bodin, *Six Bookes of a Commonwealth* (Knolles trans. 1606) 47.
[26] 4 *Works* (1889) 464.

This allows him to connect the idea with the laws of the universe at one extreme and with the ordinances of the community at the other. In its most abstract or absolute sense the word law means, he says, that in virtue of which things of the same species act in a certain determinate manner. This comes about either because of natural necessity or human decree. A law which depends on natural necessity is one which follows necessarily from the very nature, or definition, of the thing. A law which depends on human decree, and Spinoza thinks it more correctly called an ordinance (*Jus*), is prescribed by men for themselves and others in order to live more safely or conveniently, or for other reasons. He offers as examples of laws which depend on natural necessity a law of mechanics and a psychological law of memory. But when men cede or are forced to cede a right (*jus*) which they have by nature, and bind themselves to a certain manner of living (*ratio vivendi*), this depends on human decree.[27]

However, Spinoza was a determinist. He readily admitted that all things are predetermined by universal natural laws to exist and operate in a given, fixed and definite manner. How then can a certain class of laws depend on human resolution? Spinoza gives two answers. First, because man, in so far as he is a part of nature, constitutes to this extent a part of the power of nature. If something follows necessarily from the necessity of human nature (that is, from nature herself conceived as acting through man) it follows, even though it be necessarily, from human power. Hence, Spinoza argues, laws for the regulation of society depend on man's decree. Second, because we must define and explain things by their proximate causes. To take a wide view and regard events as always determined, can be of little aid to us in arranging and forming our ideas about particular objects. Moreover, we are obviously ignorant about how things are ordained and linked together. Hence for practical purposes it is necessary for us to consider things as contingent. So far as this argument is concerned

[27] 2 *L. Works* 134; 1 *Elwes* 57.

Spinoza holds that the laws of a nation are subject to the operation of the principle of determinism; however, we must act when we devise them as if the principle did not apply.

So far Spinoza has been discussing law in its abstract or absolute sense. In common speech, he observes, it is taken to signify a command (*mandatum*), which men can either obey or neglect, for it restrains human nature within bounds that were exceeded in the state of nature, and therefore lays down no rule beyond human strength. Spinoza advances a theory to account for the command idea of law. He argues that few perceive the true object of legislation, and that most men are almost incapable of grasping it. Legislators therefore, in order to secure obedience to law, have wisely put forward another object, very different from that which necessarily follows from the nature of law. They promise to the masses in return for obedience that which the masses chiefly desire; they threaten violators with that which violators chiefly fear. They endeavor, in other words, to restrain the masses as a horse is checked with a curb. Thus the word law is chiefly applied to the modes of life enjoined on men by the sway of others; those who obey the law are said to live under it and to be under compulsion.

It is clear that Spinoza had before him the conception advanced by Hobbes that " law, properly, is the word of him that by right hath command over others." [28] He held it to be an unsatisfactory concept; in fact, men living under law so conceived were in a kind of slavery. A man who renders to each his due because he fears the gallows, acts under the sway of others and cannot be called just. A man is just only if he gives to each his due because he understands the true reason for laws and their necessity, and acts from a firm purpose and of his own accord. Spinoza took this to be the meaning of St. Paul's statement that those who live under the law cannot be justified by the law.

Through this analysis Spinoza arrived at his own conception

---

[28] 3 *Works* (1839-45) 147.

of law: A plan of living which serves only to render life and the state secure, prescribed by the community under the sanction of a penalty.[29] In its original formulation Spinoza omitted, in accordance with his criticism of the Hobbes' concept, the idea of penalty. Further reflection apparently convinced him that a punitive sanction was necessary to complete the idea, although, he endeavored to save something from his original argument by maintaining that men should be moved to obey the law by hope and not fear; they should be led to do their duty from good-will and not compulsion. When the state has to resort to punishment it is a sign that it has failed in one of its major tasks.

Spinoza's idea of law, although it represents a repudiation of Hobbes' theory that it is a command, is nevertheless not original. Actually, it was one of the aspects from which Aquinas viewed law. " Law," Aquinas wrote, " denotes a kind of plan directing acts toward an end." [30] But the interpretation that Spinoza put upon his conception differed radically from Aquinas'. Here Spinoza was a Hobbesian. The community was free to impose any plan it liked upon itself.[31] It was true that some plans would work better than others, but in any event the choice of the plan was a matter for the community to decide. This could not be admitted by Aquinas. All plans to be valid were to be measured by the common good.

DIVINE LAW

From the tradition of legal speculation Spinoza inherited a variety of types of law which he proceeded to sort out. Hobbes had eliminated divine law and the *ius gentium* by identifying them with natural law. This solution was not satisfactory to Spinoza, it may be assumed, since it failed to account for the idea of necessity. He therefore reinstituted divine law, but gave the idea his own interpretation.

---

[29] 2 *L. Works* 136; 1 *Elwes* 59; 1 *L. Works* 210, 2 *Elwes* 214.

[30] *Summa Theologica*, I-II, 93, Art. 3.

[31] 2 *L. Works* 11-13; 1 *Elwes* 298-300.

The Divine Will had, from the earliest days of Greek thought, been associated with the notion of law. " All human laws are nourished by the one divine law," Heraclitus [32] had written. This conception had been insisted upon by the Stoics, whose views were accepted by Cicero.[33] It also came into Western thought through the Hebrew tradition, as the writings of Philo [34] bear witness. The rise of Christianity gave the idea a special emphasis, and from the time of Lactantius [35] and St. Augustine [36] onwards it was customary to distinguish between eternal law and human law. But the problem of natural law still remained. Behind it was the great authority of Aristotle, Cicero and Justinian, and it would therefore be unthinkable to dismiss it. How was the Church to maintain the authority of the divine law, which enabled her to speak with supremacy on matters of faith and morals? Not until the twelfth century was the answer given with clarity. In anticipation of Hobbes, the Romans had identified their *ius gentium* with the law of nature; and the Church in a similar move identified the law of God with the natural law in the Decretum of Gratian.[37] This step was taken, Pollock writes, " with a thoroughgoing boldness which almost deserves the name of genius." [38] Gratian found the archetype of natural law in the Golden Rule, " Do unto others what thou wouldest wish others to do unto thee "; he held also that natural law was immutable, that it was in agreement with the Scriptures, that it is supreme, just as the Divine Will and the Scriptures are supreme, and that customs and laws contrary to it are void. However, this solution also raised difficulties which Gratian and others attempted to meet. If natural law is contained in the law of the Scriptures, why is

---

[32] *Frag.* 91.

[33] *De Re Publica* III, 22.

[34] *Quod Omn. Prob.* 46.

[35] *Div. Inst.* V, 18.

[36] *De Lib. Arb.* I, 6. 15, 32 Migne, *Patrologiae Latinae* 1229 (1861).

[37] *Decretum,* D. i.

[38] *The History of the Law of Nature* (1901), 1 Col. Law Rev. 11, 17. See also 2 Carlyle, *History of Mediaeval Political Theory in the West* (1909) 98; Salmond, *The Law of Nature* (1895), 11 Law Quarterly Rev. 121, 132.

much of that law no longer obeyed? Again, if natural law is immutable, why are conditions allowed to exist which are contrary to that law? [39] The answers to these questions were worked out with great ingenuity, but the result was that Aquinas found it necessary to classify law into four types—the eternal law, the natural law, the Divine law, and the human law. Divine reason governs the universe and is the eternal law; natural law is the participation of the rational creature in the eternal law; Divine law is the law of God as revealed in the Old and New testaments. Divine law is not in opposition to natural law, but permits men to share in the eternal law in a more perfect manner.[40] By the time of Hooker, Aquinas' theory, with various modifications, had become a commonplace [41] and was followed by Grotius.[42]

Spinoza discarded these classifications, but he was nevertheless influenced by them and by the reasons which had led to their formulation. He defined the Divine law to be that which regards the highest good, the true knowledge of God and love.[43] The love of God is the supreme good, the ultimate end and aim of man; hence he alone lives by the Divine law who loves God, not from fear of punishment, but solely because he has knowledge of God or is convinced that the knowledge and love of God is the highest good. The first precept of the Divine law, indeed its sum and substance, is to love God unconditionally as the supreme good. Spinoza, like Aquinas,[44] recognizes the existence of both a natural Divine law and a positive Divine law. Spinoza gives the laws of Moses, which he holds to have been ratified by prophetic insight, as an example of the latter. But his main concern, at this point, is with natural Divine law.

He holds that it is universal or common to all men, for it can be deduced from universal human nature; it does not

[39] Carlyle, 109 *et seq.*
[40] *Summa Theologica*, I-II, 91, Arts. 1, 2, 4.
[41] *Laws of Ecclesiastical Polity* (1594) Bk. I.
[42] *De Jure Belli ac Pacis Libri Tres* (1625) Bk. 1, c. 1, X.
[43] 2 *L. Works* 136; 1 *Elwes* 59.
[44] *Summa Theologica*, II-II, 57, Art. 2.

depend on the truth of any historical narrative whatsoever; it does not demand the performance of ceremonies; its highest reward is the law itself, namely, to know God and to love Him of our free choice; its penalty is the absence of this knowledge and love and the presence of an inconstant and wavering spirit.

Here Spinoza comes to his central point. He denies that we can conceive of God as a lawgiver or potentate ordaining laws for men. When God is described as a lawgiver or prince, and styled just and merciful, it is merely a concession to popular understanding and the imperfection of popular knowledge. In reality, God acts and directs all things simply by the necessity of his nature and perfection. His decrees and volitions are eternal truths, and always involve necessity. For example, the necessity of a triangle's essence and nature, in so far as they are conceived of as eternal verities, depend solely on the necessity of the Divine nature and intellect; from eternity he has decreed that three angles of a triangle are equal to two right angles. Hence, if God said to Adam that he was not to eat of the forbidden fruit, it would have been a contradiction for Adam to have eaten of it; it would have been impossible that he should have so eaten, for the Divine command would have involved an eternal necessity and truth. Nevertheless, Scripture states that God did give this command to Adam, and that Adam ate of the tree. Spinoza concludes that we must perforce say that God revealed to Adam the evil that would follow upon his act, but did not disclose that the evil would of necessity come to pass. Adam took the revelation to be not an eternal and necessary truth, but a law, an ordinance followed by gain or loss. Through Adam's lack of knowledge God was thought of by him, in his ignorance, as a lawgiver and potentate.

Spinoza's example contains some elements of obscurity. If he means that man can transform the necessity of God's commands into obligations which he is free to follow or ignore, man can also construct three angles of a triangle that are equal to four right angles. It is true that non-Euclidean geometry may perform such feats. but, nonetheless, it still preserves the idea of necessity. Spinoza, in fact, seems here to be attempting to adapt to his own position an idea worked out by Aquinas. Eternal law, Aquinas held, is binding upon the whole of nature in all its actions and movements because God has imprinted upon it the principles of its proper actions, *i. e.*, necessity. However, the eternal law merely obligates man, since he is rational and subject to passions, and his knowledge of what is good, and his inclination towards it, may be imperfect.[45] Man is therefore free to break the eternal law but not with impunity. The substance of his thought seems to be that the evil resulting from the breaking of eternal law is a necessity even in cases where the observance of the law is not a necessity.

However confusing Spinoza's argument and examples may be, his intention is clear enough. He wishes to preserve the idea of necessity, as his example of the triangle shows. He wishes to deny that God is a lawgiver whose edicts can be ignored with impunity, and to deny also that the law of the Scriptures binds necessarily. In part this task had already been performed by Gratian through his doctrine of *mistica*, or regulations which, under certain circumstances, may be altered since they are concerned with ceremonies and sacrifices, and which differ therefore from the moral precepts (*e. g.*, Thou shalt not kill), which are immutable.[46] Spinoza generalizes this idea to include all the injunctions of the Scriptures except that universal law which signifies the true manner of life, and not ceremonial observances. He argues, for example, that Moses does not teach the Jews as a prophet not to kill or steal, but gives these commandments solely as a lawgiver or judge. He does not attempt to justify his doctrine rationally, but affixes for its non-observance a penalty which may and very properly does vary in different nations.

---

[45] *Ibid.*, I-II, 93, Art. 6. In Epist. XIX Spinoza attempts to answer a criticism of his position advanced by Blyenbergh. However, here he does not assume that God in fact instructed Adam not to eat of the forbidden fruit. The Scriptures, he says, should be understood as a parable, and should not be taken literally.

[46] Carlyle, 109.

NATURAL LAW

In Hobbes' theory natural law was part of the science of ethics. Natural laws were precepts which had as their aim the preservation of human life. Law properly is the word of him that by right has command over others. Hence, natural laws are not properly laws, unless we hold them as delivered in the word of God, that by right commands all things. Natural laws are, in fact, apart from the theological reservation, nothing but dictates of reason.[47]

This view of natural law was adopted by Spinoza. When he speaks of " natural right " he uses the phrase *ius naturae*;[48] when he refers to the " laws " or " rules " of nature in accordance with which everything takes place he employs the phrase *leges naturae*.[49] But when his topic is " natural law " in the sense of Hobbes' *lex naturalis* he takes his cue from Hobbes and abandons the word " law " altogether. As a substitute he uses the phrase " dictates of nature " (*dictamina rationis*)[50] or " guidance of reason " (*ductus rationis*).[51] Accordingly the idea is treated in the *Ethic* and not in the political treatises.

Spinoza's justification of the theory of the dictates of reason is carefully worked out, and with him it is completely a moral doctrine; however, it is associated with his theory of law. He held that a man is necessarily always subject to passions, and that he follows and obeys the common order of nature, accommodating himself to it as far as the nature of things requires.[52] Hence men do not necessarily follow the dictates of reason although those dictates are not difficult to discover.[53] Reason does not demand anything that is opposed to nature. It therefore demands that everyone is bound to seek his own profit; *i. e.*, what is truly profitable to him, that really leads him to greater perfection. In its absolute sense it means, as Hobbes

---

[47] *Leviathan* (1651) c. 15 *ad fin.* *Elements of Law* (1928) 58, 74. Hobbes had inherited this theory from Grotius and others. *De Jure Belli ac Pacis Libri Tres* (1625) Bk. I, c. 1, X.

[48] 2 *L. Works* 6.

[49] *Ibid.*

[50] 1 *L. Works* 196.

[51] 1 *L. Works* 199.

[52] *Ethic* 184.

[53] *Ethic* 193-5.

had previously held, that everyone should endeavor, as far as he is able, to preserve his own being. From these premises Spinoza at once deduced some principles: (1) the foundation of virtue is that endeavor itself to preserve our own being, from which it follows that happiness consists of the fact that a man can preserve his own being; (2) virtue is to be desired for its own sake, nor is there anything more excellent or more useful to us than virtue, for the sake of which virtue ought to be desired; (3) all persons who kill themselves are impotent in mind, and have been thoroughly overcome by external causes opposed to their nature; (4) we can never free ourselves from the need of something outside ourselves for the preservation of our being, and we can never live in such a manner as to have no intercourse with objects which are outside us; (5) men who are governed by reason (*i. e.*, seek their own profit) desire nothing for themselves which they do not desire for other men, and thus are just, faithful and honorable. This leads to the doctrine that the end of the State, in accordance with the dictates of reason, is not domination, but liberty.[54]

Law of the State

Although Spinoza was an individualist he insisted that the individual could attain his highest good only in the State. In the state of nature each person judges what is good and evil, consults his own advantage as he thinks best, avenges himself, and endeavors to preserve what he loves and to destroy what he hates. This condition could be tolerated if men lived according to the guidance of reason; for then every one would enjoy the benefits of the state of nature without injuring any one else.[55] But men are subject to passions which are stronger than human power or virtue, and their interests draw them in different directions. Inevitably they discover that by mutual help they can more easily procure the things they need, and

[54] 2 *L. Works* 306; 1 *Elwes* 259.
[55] *Ethic* 210.

that it is only by their united strength they can avoid the dangers which everywhere threaten them.[56]

Men must therefore necessarily come to an agreement to live together in harmony and be a help to one another. Only in this way will they be able to enjoy as a whole the rights which naturally belong to them as individuals. By the agreement they will cede their natural right and instil confidence in each other that they will do nothing to injure each other. However, no one will abide by his promises unless under the fear of a greater evil, or the hope of a greater good. Society must therefore claim for itself the right possessed by man in a state of nature; it must also possess the power to prescribe a common rule of life, to promulgate laws and support them, not by reason, which cannot restrain men, but by penalties. So far this theory appears indistinguishable from Hobbes' doctrine. But the conclusions which Spinoza drew from the theory would not have been recognized by Hobbes. He succeeded in this accomplishment by virtue of the principle—which he held clearly differentiated his doctrine from Hobbes'—that natural right as exercised by the State must be preserved intact so that the supreme power in a State has no more right over a subject than is proportionate to the power by which it is superior to the subject.[57] By this Spinoza meant that in the civil state as well as in the natural state, right would be identified with power.

Here Spinoza anticipates the objection that it is contrary to reason to subject one's self wholly to the judgment of another, and consequently that the civil state is repugnant to reason.[58] To this objection Spinoza gives several answers. So long as men are moved primarily by passions reason cannot hold that they should remain independent. Reason teaches altogether to seek peace, and peace cannot be maintained if the commands of the State are not obeyed. But above all it should be remembered that the ultimate end of the State is not dominion, nor

[56] *Ethic* 206; 2 *L. Works* 260; 1 *Elwes* 202.
[57] *Ep.* 50.
[58] 2 *L. Works* 14-15; 1 *Elwes* 303.

restraint by fear, nor the exaction of obedience; on the contrary, its end is to free every man from fear, so that he may live securely; in other words, to make it possible for him to possess in the best sense his natural right to existence and work without injury to himself or others. It is not the end of the State to change men from rational beings into beasts or automata. Its end is to enable them to develop their minds and bodies in security, and to employ their reason unshackled so that hatred, anger, deceit, and strife should cease. In fact, the true aim of the State is liberty.[59] But this is only part of the answer. Although right may be coextensive with power, power, in fact, in the civil community is limited, or, in modern phraselogy, there are limits to effective legal action. There are some things which men cannot be induced to do, either by rewards or threats. It is impossible to make a man believe against his judgment; no rewards or threats can bring a man to believe that the whole is not greater than its part. A man cannot be compelled to love one whom he hates or to hate one whom he loves. There are some things so abhorrent to human nature that they are regarded as actually worse than any evil; for example, that a man should be a witness against himself, or torture himself, or kill his parents, or not strive to avoid death. We can still say that the State has the right or authority to order these things; but this amounts to no more than that a man has the right to be mad or delirious. Finally, the power of the State is limited absolutely by the fact that if it behaves unwisely men will conspire together to overthrow it. The State, to maintain its independence, is bound to preserve the causes of fear and reverence, otherwise it ceases to be a State.

With this argument Spinoza executes a return in part, at least, to the position of Aquinas, that to be valid all plans for the community must be measured by the common good. Spinoza has attempted to show that there is an inescapable connection between power and its proper exercise. If power is wielded blindly, if it is exercised without regard to what

---

[59] *Ibid. op. cit.* note 54.

men hold to be abhorrent, it will defeat itself. Since the end of the State is peace and security of life, power is exercised for the best where men pass their lives in unity and the laws are kept unbroken. However, this is merely Spinoza's conception of the ideal State. He would not affirm that power exercised contrary to that end was not a legal exercise of power; he would not say, as Aquinas did, that an unjust law was no law. A free multitude, he argued, is guided more by hope than by fear; a multitude subject to a despot is guided more by fear than hope. Nevertheless between the dominion created by a free multitude and that gained by a despot, if we regard generally the right of each from the point of view of the science of politics, we can make, he held, no essential distinction. Their ends and the means to the preservation of each are very different; but so far as power, and hence right, is concerned, they belong to the same species.[60]

On the basis of this political view of society Spinoza came to his theory of positive law. It was a mixture of his own thoughts and those of his predecessors. It was also destined to be one of the most influential theories ever proposed; it contains the root idea of the Kantian system, and thus of all nineteenth century metaphysical and twentieth century sociological jurisprudence.

He concurred in the Hobbesian idea that the supreme authority in the State has the sole right to lay down laws, to interpret them, and to decide whether a given case is in conformity with or in violation of the law.[61] He followed the theory of Aquinas and others that laws must be founded on reason,[62] and that the public welfare is the supreme law to which all laws should be made to conform.[63] He anticipates Bentham in his insistence upon the point that the end of law is the security of the individual and the state.[64] At this point he reaches his own doctrine of the state as one mind. Without law the state

---

[60] 2 *L. Works* 23; 1 *Elwes* 313.

[61] 2 *L. Works* 20; 1 *Elwes* 309.

[62] 2 *L. Works* 12, 263; 1 *Elwes* 206, 299.

[63] 2 *L. Works* 36, 298; 1 *Elwes* 249, 330.

[64] 2 *L. Works* 23, 136; 1 *Elwes* 59, 313. "Security," writes Bentham, "is the pre-eminent object" of law. *Theory of Legislation* (1864) 97.

is impossible. When a state is formed the power of making laws must be vested either in all the citizens, or in some of them, or in one man. Men's free judgments are diverse and each believes that he alone knows everything; it is therefore impossible that all should think alike in any subject and speak with a unanimous voice. Hence it is impossible for men to preserve peace unless individuals abdicate their right of acting entirely on their own judgment. Spinoza is careful to point out here that the individual cedes only his right to act, not the right to reason and judge.[65] When the right to act is ceded to the State it permits it to be guided as by one mind. It is the law which fulfills this function, but the laws must, as he has insisted, be founded upon reason.[66] Spinoza's use of the phrase " one mind " is, of course, a figurative one. Just as the human body is guided by one mind so must the body of the state be guided by one mind. In the realm of the State the one mind is the collective will which must be taken to be the will of all.[67]

Consequently, law in the state is a harmonizing of wills in the interests of freedom. Men are not born fit for citizenship but must be made so. If men's wills are not harmonized, if men are permitted in civil society to pursue their own ends, then it would be difficult to distinguish that society from a state of nature.[68] Although Hobbes held that law was a fetter Spinoza argues that it is the way to freedom. Peace and freedom cannot be attained unless the general laws of the State are respected. Therefore the more a man desires freedom the more constantly will he respect the laws of his country, and obey the commands of the sovereign power to which he is subject.[69] Spinoza had perhaps learned this lesson early in life from the Judaic tradition which teaches as a religious ideal, not freedom from the law, but freedom in the law. The idea

[65] 2 *L. Works* 306; 1 *Elwes* 259.
[66] 2 *L. Works* 12; 1 *Elwes* 298.
[67] 2 *L. Works* 14; 1 *Elwes* 302.
[68] 2 *L. Works* 23; 1 *Elwes* 313-14; *Ethic* 210.
[69] 2 *L. Works* 327; 2 *Elwes* 276.

of law as the instrument through which wills are harmonized
for freedom is customarily attributed to Kant; in any event the
idea is still with us. It is a fundamental element in today's
jurisprudence. "Kant's conception of the legal order," Pound
writes, "as a reconciling or harmonizing of wills in action by
means of universal rules becomes in the hands of the social
utilitarian a compromise or adjustment of advantages, a balance of interests. In the hands of economic realists it becomes a
reconciliation or harmonizing of wants—'the satisfaction of
every one's wants so far as they are not outweighed by others'
wants.' In the hands of the positive sociologists it becomes an
adjustment of social functions. In the hands of psychological
sociologists it becomes a reconciling or harmonizing or adjusting of claims or demands or desires." [70] None of the schools of
jurisprudence, since Kant revived or developed the idea, has
escaped its influence.

Spinoza, like his predecessors, recognized that the affairs of
human beings could not be regulated entirely by laws. He had
been instructed by the Judaic tradition that the subtle matters
of morality were altogether beyond the reach of the law; they
were matters which were left to the heart. He recognized
specifically that the laws give weak assistance if the continuation of public liberty is dependent upon them alone.[71] Things
should be so arranged that the citizens of the state will always
do their duty spontaneously rather than under the pressure of
laws; when we have to resort to laws they should be so framed
that the people will be moved to obey them from hope and not
fear.[72] He held sumptuary laws to be not only vain, but a
stimulation to the desires and lusts of men.[73] "We are ever
eager," Ovid had written long before, "for forbidden fruit, and
desire what is denied." The constitution is the soul of the
dominion, and must be defended by both reason and passion.
If it relies only on the help of reason it is weak and easily

[70] *Immanuel Kant* (1925) edited by E. C. Wilm, 81-82.
[71] 2 *L. Works* 34; 1 *Elwes* 328.
[72] 2 *L. Works* 78; 1 *Elwes* 382.
[73] 2 *L. Works* 78; 1 *Elwes* 381.

overcome.[74] The aim of Spinoza's thought was to devise the principles by which a dominion would be so ordered that of necessity, rulers and governed alike, whether they will or no, should do what makes for the general welfare.[75] To guard against all evils and form a dominion where no room is left for deceit; to frame institutions so that every man, whatever his disposition, will prefer public right to private advantage—that, says Spinoza, is the task and that the toil.[76] It is the dream no less of the closet philosopher than of the men of action as the writings of those who devised the American Constitution show.

From the Reformation Spinoza had inherited an individualistic tradition, which no doubt helped to color his views on liberty. But there were nevertheless definite limits to the liberty which he allowed the citizen. His most important ideas on this subject are to be found in his doctrine of obedience. He insisted that it was the citizen's duty to obey the law even if he believed it to be a bad law. To hold otherwise could lead only to the ruin of the State.[77] What the State decides to be good must be held to be so decided by every individual. Hence, however iniquitous the subject may think the State's decisions, he is nonetheless bound to execute them. But what should the subject do if he is ordered by the State to disobey the word of God? Spinoza answers, obey God when you have a certain and indisputable revelation of His will. But men are very prone to error on religious subjects and on this pretext might assume unbounded license, and thus set at naught the sovereign power. The only remedy is for the State to have supreme authority to make any laws about religion it sees fit.[78] Actually this is not a great concession, for the mind, so far as it makes use of reason, is dependent only on itself and not on supreme authorities. Hence the true knowledge and love of God cannot be subject to the dominion of any one.[79] This doctrine had also

[74] 2 *L. Works* 79; 1 *Elwes* 383.
[75] 2 *L. Works* 25; 1 *Elwes* 316.
[76] 2 *L. Works* 271; 1 *Elwes* 217.
[77] 2 *L. Works* 14, 307; 1 *Elwes* 260, 302.
[78] 2 *L. Works* 268; 1 *Elwes* 211-212.
[79] 2 *L. Works* 17; 1 *Elwes* 305.

been advanced in substance by Calvin. He had held that it was the duty of the citizen to obey bad rulers, for an unjust ruler is a fulfillment of God's purpose to punish people for their sins.

In Calvin's theory the citizen was also to give priority to God's commands over the laws of the State; but here Spinoza parted company with him. The Calvinistic doctrine, not by direct statement, but by clear inference, permitted the citizen to judge of such matters.[80]

Conclusion

Since Spinoza did not live to complete his system he can scarcely be blamed for the gaps which it contains. We have, for example, only a hint of his theory of legislation and how he would have developed it we do not know. It would have been coupled, we can be sure, with his idea that might makes right, just as his doctrine of freedom of thought was coupled with it. A State should, for the reasons he urged, allow freedom of thought; but as a matter of fact it has to allow it, since it lacks the power to control it. In the ethical field he saw his subject as a whole and in all its detail. He worked it out as a logical system with a finish which cannot fail to command admiration. He was not so successful with his jurisprudence. Law was at the basis of his political thought, and he isolated elements of the legal process which are of prime importance. But none of them was analyzed to the degree with which he studied his ethical ideas. He kept to a neutral path so far as the doctrines of the previous philosophers went, and he at no time lost sight of the demands of practical affairs. If he had lived to perfect his thought we would, in all probability, have been given a jurisprudence of the stature of his ethics. We have been given instead a jurisprudence which anticipates the most influential jurisprudence of modern times.

---

[80] *Institutes* Bk. IV, c. xx, § 25. Gooch, *English Democratic Ideas in the Seventeenth Century* (2d ed. 1927) 5.

CHAPTER IX

LEIBNIZ

> *He combined two great qualities which are almost incompatible with one another—the spirit of discovery and that of method.*
>
> Diderot

L EIBNIZ brought to legal philosophy the set of ideas which has explicitly controlled all scientific inquiry since his day— identity, system, consistency, possibility, and causality. "Our reasonings," he insisted,[1] "are grounded upon *two great principles, that of contradiction,* in virtue of which we judge *false* that which involves a contradiction, and *true* that which is opposed or contradictory to the false; and *that of sufficient reason,* in virtue of which we hold that there can be no fact real or existing, no statement true, unless there be a sufficient reason, why it should be so and not otherwise, although these reasons usually cannot be known by us." What Leibniz intended as the full meaning of these two principles is not entirely clear; but from them he developed his doctrine of necessary and contingent truth, the former being demonstrable by the principle of contradiction, the latter by that of sufficient reason.

Leibniz' writings on jurisprudence, so far as they have been collected, are contained in 4 Dutens, *G. G. Leibnitii, opera omnia* (1768), cited here as "Dutens," and Mollat, *Mittheilungen aus Leibnizens ungedruckten Schriften* (1887), cited here as "Mollat." But there are many discussions of juridical matters in his other writings and in his letters. For secondary sources, my greatest indebtedness is to Hartmann's *Leibniz als Jurist und Rechtsphilosoph* (1892); Zimmermann's *Das Rechtsprinzip bei Leibnitz* (1852); and Cassirer's *Leibniz' System in seinen wissenschaftlichen Grundlagen* (1902).

[1] *The Monadology*, Latta's ed., (1898) § 31-32. Elsewhere he rephrased the principle of contradiction: "The principle of contradiction is in general: *A proposition is either true or false;* this comprises two true statements; *one, that the true and the false are not compatible in the same proposition, or that a proposition cannot be true and false at the same time*; the other, that the opposite or the negation of the true and the false are not compatible, or that there is no middle ground between the true and the false, or better, *that it is impossible for a proposition to be neither true nor false.*" Erdmann, *God. Guil. Leibnitii opera philosophica* (1840) 339.

Thus he held that the criterion of truth is thought; this permitted him to substitute, in place of the dominant theological attitude of the time, a rationalistic approach to natural law and the positive law deductions made from it. His method resulted in the construction of one of the great philosophical systems, of which his legal theory forms an integral part; but that system was never expounded in any unified form and must be put together from many papers and letters. As a philosopher his ultimate views were as comprehensive as the outlook of that domain demands; but the naturalistic science of his time led him also to piecemeal investigation, to the detailed study of the part rather than the whole. It is this latter method of approach which predominates in his jurisprudence and which accounts for the many gaps in that aspect of his thought. His basic legal ideas are clearly enough attached to his main philosophical system, but the connections between them and many of his concrete suggestions in the field of positive law often have to be surmised.

Leibniz' immense theoretical powers were always guided in the area of human affairs by an intense awareness of the practical. No other philosopher has participated more intimately in the practical concerns of his time and none has been more perceptive in the isolation of the essential forces. In this achievement Hobbes, one of the architects of the British colonial empire, alone approaches him. Among Leibniz' many achievements in this field are his suggestions to Peter the Great which led to the administrative reforms that placed the Russian system on approximately the same footing as that of the Western powers, and his arguments addressed to Louis XIV on the importance of Egypt in the plans for an Eastern empire, arguments which are thought to have guided Napoleon's Egyptian campaign.

PRELIMINARY WRITINGS

Leibniz' views were not settled until his fortieth year; as he confessed, he had changed them again and again in accordance with the fresh knowledge he had acquired. However, his early writings on jurisprudence, a field with which he began to occupy himself when he was eighteen years old, reveal clearly the mixture of scholasticism, novelty of insight, and scientific analysis that was to characterize his mature studies. Throughout his life he continued to value these preliminary excursions into juridical theory, although he frankly conceded that they stood in need of revision. At his death the most important of them, his *Nova methodus juris*, lay open in his study, marked with marginal alterations.

In his early writings, his method was predominantly that of the formal logic of the preceding centuries; he nevertheless was plainly feeling his way towards the philosophical approach and the substitution of reason for authority, ideas which dominated the thought of the seventeenth and eighteenth centuries. It was always one of his leading ideas, that the usefulness of a science varied directly with the speculative depth it was able to attain. His thesis for the degree of Master of Philosophy, the *Quaestiones philosophicae amoeniores, ex Jure collectae,*[2] was aimed avowedly at saving law students from the dangers of over-specialization and of curing them of any contempt which they might hold for the other departments of knowledge, particularly philosophy. This idea is a remarkable anticipation of the current doctrine, now insisted upon by many jurists, that jurisprudence is not a self-sufficient science, and that it must cooperate with the other disciplines, such as history, economics and sociology, which face similar problems. " I am undertaking a difficult matter," Leibniz wrote in the preface to the paper, " one which is beyond my power, but which is productive and welcome to myself. I was raised on philosophy and thus became a student of jurisprudence; and as often as the opportunity presented itself I went back to philosophy and made a note of what either originated in philosophy or was related to it. The examination which I am about to undertake will also serve to remove the disdain of the expert jurists for philosophy

[2] Dutens, pt. 3, 68.

when they see how many parts of their ' jus ' would be an
inextricable labyrinth without the guidance of philosophy and
how the ancient authorities were as thoroughly familiar with
its profundities as with their own science. It is certainly
understandable that Ulpian called jurisprudence the science of
divine and human things because he was convinced that without this previous philosophic insight the jurist could neither
come to his own nor, in consequence, could the science of right
and wrong be achieved." Leibniz developed the idea in an
unsystematic fashion by propounding seventeen questions
which were intended to show connections between law and such
subjects as metaphysics, logic, mathematics, and physics. Some
of the questions appear to us today to raise matters of no
moment, or to be handled in an overly subtle fashion; but it
would not be difficult to match Leibniz' attenuated reasoning
with present-day court opinions on such topics as the taxation
of foreign corporations. Leibniz asked, for example, if property
is a relation, a question which he, in company with some
modern jurists, answered affirmatively, but which he, unlike
them, pushed on to the further question: Can a relation
subsist upon a relation? More practically, he raises the question
whether bees are wild animals, a matter which modern courts
have had to face in determining the liability of bee-keepers
for injuries committed by their bees. His formal logic is perhaps
put to its best use in his discussion of the maxim *affirmanti
incumbit probatio*; here he shows that an affirmation is not
dependent upon a form of words, and that the same idea can be
expressed in either negative or positive form. At the time of
the writing of this paper, and for a considerable period thereafter, Leibniz was still strongly under the influence of the
scholastic tradition, and his premises and arguments were
both formulated in strict accordance with the technique of
that school.

His succeeding paper, the *Doctrina conditionum*,[3] published
the next year in 1665, dealt with the doctrine of conditions

---

[3] Dutens, pt. 3, 92.

and the rules of interpretation, subjects made to order for his formal methods. The doctrine was pronounced to be a part of juridical logic and its conclusions to be susceptible of mathematical demonstration.[4] It is, he insisted, a prime example of jurisprudence as a science in the true sense of the word, and all the genius and profundity of the classical Roman jurists is to be found in its development. " The ancient jurists," he wrote, " have displayed so much genius and shown such penetrating judgment in the definition of law that to give their explanations the form of a completely positive and almost mathematical argument is a work which requires sifting rather than further ingenuity." The doctrine is to be treated rigorously, beginning with definitions and proceeding syllogistically to the deduction of theories and rules of law. Thus, " when the ship arrives from Asia, Titius shall have a hundred " is taken by Leibniz to assert a condition of fact independent of temporal consideration. The mere arrival of the ship, altogether apart from the time of its arrival, is the condition to be satisfied. From this it followed, in Leibniz' view, that the money would be due at once on a certification from an officially approved Oracle that the ship would arrive; in the absence of such transcendental intervention, it is also clear, on the actual arrival of the ship, that the money was due at the time of the bargain. Notwithstanding results of this kind, which may be taken as illustrative of the dangers of a too-rigid application of formal logic to the circumstances of the legal order, the paper was received favorably by the more advanced professors of the day. Even in modern times it is regarded as containing a grain of truth; that once the premises of a legal system have been validly established, it should be possible, in accordance with the methods of the physical sciences, to make proper deductions from them.[5] However, the infinitude of variables to be ordered in the construction of any such system in the juristic field necessarily reduces the effectiveness of the system to a minimum area.

[4] Dutens, pt. 3, 94.   [5] Hartmann, 16.

At the age of twenty, in his *Dissertatio de Arte Combinatoria,* Leibniz put forward an idea to which he was to return frequently throughout his life. This was the conception of a *Characteristica Universalis* or Universal Mathematics which would solve all problems and end all disputes. Apparently through the symbolic method, in which formal rules would supplant rational analysis, results could be achieved in all sciences comparable to those which had been produced by the same method in mathematics. The procedure, he pointed out, would enable us to reason in morals as we do in geometry. If controversies were to arise, he added, disputation between two philosophers would be as unnecessary as between two accountants. All they would need do would be to take their pencils in their hands, sit down to their slates, and say to each other (with a friend as witness, if they desired it) : Let us calculate.[6] Bertrand Russell [7] points out that Leibniz thought that by establishing the premises in any *a priori* science, the rest could be effected by mere rules of inference; and to establish the right premises, it was only necessary to analyze all the notions employed until simple notions were reached from which all the axioms would follow as identical propositions. Leibniz regarded the syllogism as the most fruitful of human inventions, a kind of universal mathematics, and he evidently held the Universal Characteristic to be akin to the syllogism. Leibniz' idea has been a basic one in an important branch of modern mathematics, but it has failed in philosophy because of the almost insuperable difficulty of formulating premises which are significant.

Nevertheless, Leibniz in the same year at once gave the idea a legal application in his tract *De Casibus Perplexis;* [8] his theory was that the legal system is a complete science in which no problem can arise for which an answer cannot be found. This idea is still widely held by practicing lawyers and also by some jurists. As a descriptive statement of the existing legal order

[6] [7] Gerhardt, *Die philosophischen Schriften von G. W. Leibniz* (1931) 200.

[7] Russell, *Philosophy of Leibniz* (1900) 170.

[8] Dutens, pt. 3, 45.

it is clearly erroneous; it is true only in the sense, as Ehrlich [9] observes, of an expression of the practical endeavor to supply the judge with a store of norms for decision, sufficient for all cases that might arise, and to make them binding upon him as effectively as possible. Leibniz defined the " perplexing case " as the entangled knot of a juridical nature which apparently could not be unraveled because of an inner logical conflict. He promised to decide all such cases *ex mero jure*, and he thus put aside the arguments that they were insoluble, or should be decided by lot or by an arbitrator. Since he defined " ex mero jure " as embracing the positive law of the land, plus natural or general human law, he had the same virtually illimitable latitude for decision as is accorded the modern American judge, allowing only for a difference in phraseology.

Nor did Leibniz hesitate to attack problems of the kind known in the logic books as dilemmas. Logicians had long wrangled over one of the dilemmas he chose for discussion.[10] Eulathus, a pupil, had agreed to pay his rhetoric teacher Protagoras half of his fee when he won his first case in court. Eulathus delayed going into court, however, and Protagoras brought suit against him for the balance due. Protagoras then argued to the jury: If Eulathus loses this case, he ought to pay by the judgment of the court; and if he wins, he ought to pay by his own agreement. But he must either win or lose. Therefore, he ought to pay. This argument was rebutted by Eulathus as follows: If I win this case, I ought not to pay, by the judgment of the court; and if I lose, I ought not to pay by my own agreement. But I must either win or lose. Therefore, I ought not to pay. It is reported that the jurors were so profoundly perplexed by the argument that they put off the decision to a distant day, which in effect gave the verdict to Eulathus.

Leibniz, prompted no doubt by motives of abstract justice, awarded the ultimate decision to Protagoras. He would first

[9] *Fundamental Principles of the Sociology of Law* (1936) 20.
[10] Aulus Gellius, *Noctes Atticae*, v. 10.

have Protagoras' suit dismissed on the ground that it was
filed prior to the time of the condition of the agreement. Protagoras could then at once sue again successfully, inasmuch as
the previous victory of Eulathus had fulfilled the condition of
the agreement. The argument of *res judicata* would not apply
because the previous suit would have been dismissed without
prejudice, since Protagoras' right to sue would accrue only
after the termination of the first action. Perhaps what Leibniz
really meant was that the case should·be treated as an exception, either because it did not occur to the parties at the
time of the agreement or because Protagoras had in mind as a
legally inoperative mental reservation, such an exception in
his favor. This argument is an anticipation of the theory of
types, on the analogous basis of which modern logic holds that
Protagoras did not mean by his pupil's first case any case whatsoever. If he did, his own suit fell under the agreement. Inasmuch as this was plainly not Protagoras' intention, the case
was an exception. Such dilemmas are not altogether the sport
of logicians' fancies, and we sometimes meet them in judicial
proceedings heavy with the weight of tragedy. When Henry
VIII attempted to force the oath of supremacy upon Sir
Thomas More, the question was put to More whether he
thought the statute " giving to the King the title of Supreme
Head of the Church under Christ " had been " lawfully made
or not." He answered that the act was like a two-edged sword,
for " if he said that it were good, he would imperil his soul; and
if he said contrary to the statute, it were death to the body."
Sir Thomas More declined to swear at all and was put to
death.

THE NEW METHOD OF LEARNING AND TEACHING JURISPRUDENCE

It is not surprising that at this point in Leibniz's career he
should undertake a complete reformation of the whole field of
jurisprudence. His previous papers were all marked with the
unmistakable hopes of youth—the conviction that the impasses
of one discipline can be surmounted by recourse to the ideas of

other domains, and a belief in the competency of reason, functioning through a formal methodology, to meet the tasks of
any inquiry. All the intellectual ferment of the seventeenth
century met in Leibniz, and its effects were evident even in his
early writings. Whitehead has remarked that the intellectual
life of Europe during the succeeding centuries up to our own
time has been existing upon the accumulated capital of ideas
provided by the genius of the seventeenth century. When
Leibniz first began to publish the century was two-thirds over,
and he drew heavily on the work of his immediate predecessors.
He aimed frankly and audaciously at an application of the new
ideas to the study of jurisprudence. He pursued this ideal
throughout his entire life, but his first major attempt to
achieve it was the *Nova Methodus Discendae Docendaeque
Jurisprudentiae* of 1667.[11] This paper, which brought Leibniz
great fame, bears many resemblances to the *Novum Organum,*
which Bacon wrote at the age of fifty-nine. If Leibniz' early
age, twenty-one, was any handicap in the production of his
paper, it was balanced by the ideas already formulated in the
century and available for application by someone possessing his
insight. Leibniz' only reservation about the paper was the
fact that it was composed while travelling, without the benefit
of libraries, and without the necessary leisure to polish it.

Leibniz' paper was a protest against the jurisprudential
methods of his period, and an outline of the grounds on which
they could be reformed. These methods were an inheritance of
the techniques devised by Irnerius and his successors during the
twelfth century revival of jurisprudence at Bologna and elsewhere. Irnerius, through his glosses, examined fully the meaning of the passages of the *Corpus Juris*, and by the use of
questions and discussion he clarified for his students whatever
obscurities or apparent contradictions remained. Basically it
was the method which was also applied to the problems of
theology and science—the so-called scholastic method. Through
the instrument of logic it proceeded dialectically to analyze

[11] Dutens, pt. 3, 159.

conceptions and construct syllogisms.[12] Rashdall sums it up
thus: "An almost superstitious reverence for the *littera
scripta*, a disposition to push a principle to its extreme logical
consequences, and an equally strong disposition to harmonize
it at all costs with a seemingly contradictory principle; a
passion for classification, for definition and minute distinction,
a genius for subtlety—these, when associated with good sense
and ordinary knowledge of affairs, are at least some of the
characteristics of a great legal intellect."[13] The results of the
method represented a great achievement in legal history; but
by the middle of the thirteenth century, with the appearance
of the extraordinary *Glossa ordinaria* of Accursius, the high-
water point of the school, the method already stood in need of
revision. There were complaints that the glosses were a plague
of locusts which covered up the text, and the saying was prevalent that only glossed portions would be recognized in court.
When the jurists began to gloss the glosses the end was in
sight.[14] The Glossators were succeeded by the Commentators,
whose method was known as the *mos Italicus*. Instead of confining themselves to an understanding of the Roman law of
Justinian's day, they attempted to know the Roman law of
their own time. Their great achievement was in making over
the old law into an Italian law. Although the way for a new
approach had been opened to them by the Humanists, they still
pursued the dialectical method. They gave a new impetus to
legal studies by their emphasis on logical reasoning; but disadvantages were present from the beginning. "When their
system," Calisse[15] writes, "after a formative period, was finally
developed, it stood forth as the apotheosis of a painstaking
logic. The jurist's ideal now was to divide and subdivide; to
state premises and then to draw the inferences; to test the
conclusion by extreme cases, sometimes insoluble and always
sophistical; to raise objections and then to make a parade of

---

[12] Vinogradoff, *Roman Law in Medieval Europe* (1929) 56.
[13] *The Universities of Europe in the Middle Ages* (1936) 254.
[14] Haskins, *The Renaissance of the Twelfth Century* (1933) 202.
[15] *General Survey of Continental Legal History* (1912) 142.

overthrowing them—in short, to solve all problems by a fine-spun logic." But soon the lectures and treatises became so prolix that only a small topic would be treated in each. The jurists therefore discussed only the easier points, and passed the difficult ones over in silence. Cujas summed up in an aphorism the case of their critics: *Verbosi in re facili, in difficili muti, in angusta diffusi.* Aristotelianism also had its place. To know is to know by means of causes, according to Aristotle; and thus the four causes—the "*causa efficiens*," "*materialis*," "*formalis*," and "*finalis*"—were extensively employed as the basis of a methodological scheme into which the elements of the legal process were fitted. The third revival of jurisprudence came with the work of the Humanists. Dante had complained that the jurists had rejected the new knowledge and were too literal in their interpretations of the texts. Petrarch dismissed them as venal and ignorant in their refusal to look to other sciences for aid, and he accused them of wasting their lives in vain, imaginary quibbles; Boccaccio washed his hands of law altogether, saying it was no science at all. The crowd of pedants and imitators who produced the so-called learning of the Italian Renaissance added little to juristic knowledge; their goal was scholarship as such, improved taste, purer Latin, applied antiquarianism and the moderation of dialectical subtleties.[16] The lack of significance in such puerile objectives was known to the handful of serious students of the period: " I am no Humanist," said Leonardo da Vinci. Among the Humanists, Lorenzo Valla was the great exception. He regarded Greek and Latin scholarship as instruments to greater ends. His dislike of the Commentators, and his enthusiasm for classic Roman law, led him to the development of a bold method of textual criticism. He was followed by his pupil Pomponius Leto, who was a pioneer in the reconstruction of Roman legal history. Leto's younger contemporary, the gifted poet and scholar Politian, formed a great plan, which was cut short by his untimely death, for the compilation of a variorum edition of

[16] *Ibid.*, 396.

the Roman texts. Altogether the labors of these men and others in their textual studies opened a new horizon in jurisprudence. "Not only in textual criticism," Calisse [17] writes, "but also in topics and methods, legal research was broadened and advanced. Public law was now included, not merely private law. To textual interpretation was added synthetic reconstruction and general treatises. Practice ceased to be the sole objective; a legal science in the true sense was the inspired aim; and history and philology were pressed into service."

In the northern lands one of the legacies of the Humanist movement was the work of Peter Ramus; and it was against Ramus and the "Ramistic" that Leibniz' reforms were specially directed. At its inception Ramism had claimed for itself all the liberalizing qualities of its predecessors. [18] Men's minds should not be controlled by pedagogical rules, but should have all the freedom allowed them by the laws of nature. Those laws should be discovered by observing carefully how men's minds actually work in practice. After the laws had been collected they should be set forth in their natural order, and the rules established in model form for those who wish to reason well. Dialectics is thus a system founded upon the practice of those who are best fitted to reason, *i. e.*, the wise. Ramus defines dialectics as the art of discussing well, and it is more concerned with persuasion and exposition than the discovery of truth. [19] It consists of two parts, invention and arrangement. "*Inventio*" is that which is concerned with the "invention of arguments," and "*judicium*" or "*dispositio*" with the "suitable arrangement of things invented, with the combination and classification of these elements into a complete whole." "Invention" and "arrangement" are further subdivided into two groups, and these subdivisions in turn fall into still further groups, and so on, until the domain of dialectic

---

[17] *Ibid.*, 150.

[18] For a summary of the movement see Waddington, *Ramus, sa vie, ses écrits et ses opinions* (1855) 364 *et seq.*

[19] Graves, *Peter Ramus and the Educational Reformation of the Sixteenth Century* (1912) 148.

appears to be accounted for. Ramus held that wise deliberation was always from the general to the particular, and that if "method" were neglected in either science or practical life nothing but chaos could result. His method was widely adopted in Europe, particularly that part of it which insisted upon the utilization of the four causes of Aristotle. It yielded some notable legal textbooks, particularly Lauterbach's *Collegium theoretico-practicum* (1690), a work that held its place as a fundamental manual in German universities until the middle of the eighteenth century. The chief merit of the method lay in the fact that it did not permit the jurist to ignore difficult problems, a freedom accorded him by less restraining methods, but compelled him to take account of all the troublesome points in the subject under investigation. Ramism fell into the same quagmire, however, that had engulfed the methods it was designed to supplant. Instead of a pure naturalism it yielded a new formalism, and eventually perished in the strangling rigidity of its methodology.[20]

One central idea is implicit in Leibniz' theory of legal education: Law should be taught both as a science and as a practical discipline. If instruction is carried on entirely at the scientific level, that is to say, on an academic basis, the student acquires knowledge by means of lectures, recitations, and the memorizing of textbooks. The recitative system, which is the basic method in most universities for instruction in the humanities, has many merits, not the least of which is that, if properly handled, it inculcates in the student a synoptic view of the subject, and a clear understanding of the principles upon which it is constructed. But the method is not adequate for instruction in a professional subject such as law. At the level at which law is sometimes practiced the lawyer and judge may be mere reciters—formalists and merchants of lifeless ideas. Legal instruction, however, aims among other things at an imaginative grasp of the principles of the legal process; and the testimony of lawyers is abundant that it is at this precise point

[20] *Op. cit.* note 15 at 400.

that the recitative method fails. It does not permit the student to perform the same operations that are employed by the creative judge or lawyer when confronted with a legal task.[21] To meet this defect of purely academic instruction, resort has been had to various devices such as the requirement in England that a candidate to practice as a solicitor must serve for a term of years as an articled clerk in a solicitor's office, and the widespread adoption by American law schools of the case system of instruction. All this was clearly perceived in the universities of the Middle Ages, and Leibniz' paper was an attempt to reinstate, against the excessive formalism of his day, this essential idea.

Like North,[22] Leibniz insisted upon the necessity of a liberal education for the skillful lawyer. He must have a firm grasp of history, politics, philosophy, ethics, mathematics, and logic.[23] The grounds for this belief, although not stated by Leibniz, are not difficult to surmise. When we train students in the law we are instructing them in one of the most vital functions of a culture—the maintenance and development of a dominant order of the society. But that order is interrelated with many other orders, and its propositions, if they are to be effective, must be similarly interrelated. Leibniz' new method of legal instruction aimed at a reduction in the time necessary for the course from five to two years. It was to open with what we would call today a course in legal history and bibliography. The authentic sources of the law, including contemporary statutes and decrees, were to be explained to the student. Technical terms, on the pedagogic value of which Leibniz laid great stress, were to be fully explained, and their use illustrated through actual cases. At this point the student was to proceed to the study of the original legal sources, the main course of instruction. With a little help from the teacher, but for the most part left to his own enterprise, the student was to be required to

[21] See, *e. g.*, Ames, *Lectures on Legal History* (1913) 362.
[22] *A Discourse on the Study of the Laws*, published in 1824, but written many years before his death in 1734.
[23] Dutens, pt. 3, 200-201.

master the problems of the texts and to understand them in the context of actual cases. " We have to remember that the valuable intellectual development is self-development," Whitehead has written, and Leibniz made this truth one of the main principles of his system. In the second year, for the so-called *curriculum polemicum*, Leibniz proposed what was essentially a system of moot courts. It was intended to supplant the traditional syllogistic method of treating legal propositions, and the procedure was to be in accordance with actual German court practice. Sessions were to last two hours, with a participation of twelve students, each maintaining or defending two propositions. Inasmuch as a number of *quaestiones* could be combined, as in actual practice, in one *casus*, Leibniz thought that about 3,600 *quaestiones* could be covered in a year. The teacher was to act as judge, and was to decide the case with a full statement of the grounds of his decision. The propositions to be maintained were to be originated by students from half the class, and defended by those from the other half. The arguments were to be direct, brief, and in German—not Latin. But the proceeding was not to be superficial, and the questions to be argued should therefore be disclosed one day in advance to the teacher and the students. Resourcefulness in argument was to be attained through the extemporaneous verbal replies that the students would have to originate to defend their positions.

On the analogy of theology, Leibniz divided the law curriculum into four parts, the didactic, the historical, the exegetic and as we have seen, the polemic. For this classification he called for the composition of a new set of textbooks. The first text should be elementary, consisting entirely of " *definitiones et praecepta*," expounded with the conciseness of a mathematical argument; he wanted also a " *novum corpus juris* " based on Justinian but newly arranged. For the second, he demanded an " *historia mutationum juris*," and an " *historia irenica*." For the third there was to be a " *philologia juris*," a " *grammatica legalis seu lexicon juridicum*," an " *ethica et politica legalis*,"

and a "*logica et metaphysica juris.*" In the actual work of
exegesis, the *mos Italicus* should be followed. For polemics, he
asked for a vast "*syntagma juris universi*" with a natural law
foundation. The conception of these volumes is strikingly
similar to the three texts proposed by Bacon in the *De
Augmentis* for a science of law: a book of Institutes, which
was "to be a key and general preparation to the reading of
the course"; a treatise "*de regulis juris*" which would acquaint
the student with the leading principles of the law; and a dic-
tionary of legal terms, not arranged alphabetically, but rather
on the principle of Roget's *Thesaurus.* Leibniz closed his paper
with a list of thirty-one desiderata demanded by the new
method, beginning with a "*partitiones juris,*" closing with a
"*pandecta juris novi,*" and including such items as an "*arith-
metica juris.*" That the list was inspired by the desiderata at
the end of Bacon's *Novum Organum* seems clear. Leibniz at
once undertook to supply at least one of the desiderata, a
"reconcinnation" of Justinian; the state of legal science, however, made it impracticable to carry it to a conclusion. One
commentator [24] would excuse him on the analogy of Bacon,
who has had a large influence notwithstanding his similar
failure to supply the philosophical desiderata. Another,[25] whose
attitude is distinctly favorable, dismisses the plan to the
extent that it calls for new texts as "just unfermented cider of
a roaring and foaming youth." Lists of desiderata are notori-
ously easy to compile; but perhaps the wisest attitude is merely
one of regret that Leibniz never found the time to execute his
projects.

PHILOSOPHY OF LAW

Leibniz' general theory of law was worked out by the controversial method that distinguishes most of his writings. Like an
organism, he did not act, he reacted. Thus we owe many
of his most significant ideas in jurisprudence to his critical
reformulation of propositions put forward by Hobbes, Grotius,
Pufendorf, Descartes, Locke, and many others now forgotten.

[24] Landsberg, *op. cit.* note 15 at 422.   [25] Hartmann, 25.

Some idea of what jurisprudence has lost by his failure specifically to formulate his legal philosophy systematically can be gained from a reading of the *Monadology*. That paper was an attempt to bring into a coherent order the philosophical principles, with their important implications, that he had scattered through many brochures and letters. That the most careful student of Leibniz could have constructed it is more than doubtful. The composition of the paper generated a burst of creative activity in him, which led to such a bold and imaginative statement of his principles that it amounted to an innovation in his thought. However, his legal principles are not inconsistent even with the doctrines of the *Monadology*, and it is possible to form some idea of the kind of system he might have devised in jurisprudence if he had understaken the task.

He had a distinct idea of the plan on which the ideal treatise on jurisprudence should be constructed, although he was never to write it. Its point of departure would be a set of clear definitions, and the argument would proceed deductively from correct premises to proper conclusions; it would fix the foundations of social behavior in their fit systematic setting and would allow for the exceptions authorized by nature; it would establish a determinate method by which all legal questions could be overcome. He had no doubt that jurisprudence could be made into such an absolute and methodical science, and that its author might have been Grotius if he had not been occupied with other matters, or Hobbes if he had not run after depraved principles. Selden could easily have initiated the science if he had devoted his extraordinary abilities to the undertaking.[26]

Leibniz' first task was to establish natural law on a rational basis, and to divorce it from both theological and political absolutism. His aim was to show that natural law is wholly an ethical law of reason. It is very true, he said, that God is the author of all natural law—not, however, through His will, but rather through its own nature, in the same sense in which He is the author of truth, which also does not depend upon His will.

[26] Dutens, pt. 3, 276.

It is possible for both geometricians and jurists to be atheists, and Grotius correctly remarked that the natural law is intelligible in itself even if one should imagine that there is no God. Just as the mathematical rules of equality and proportion rest upon eternal reason, so do the rules of fairness and decency. It is impossible that God Himself could violate them, and somehow at some time could wish that someone should torture innocent persons just because he has an itch to do so.[27] Leibniz expressly rejected Descartes' belief that there are truths which are dependent upon God's arbitrariness, and he thought it absurd for Descartes to maintain that God was perfectly free to make it untrue that the three angles of a triangle should be equal to two right angles.[28] God could neither bring it about that a triangle have four sides, nor that four be an uneven number. If in this field there is something exempt from God's will, then the case is even stronger in the domain of morals and jurisprudence. Here it is completely beyond His power to turn good into evil, wrong into right, and *vice versa*. The eternal truths, Leibniz insisted, are above God's will, even though they are not above His understanding; for otherwise the latter would not be the most perfect.[29] The reason for these eternal truths, however, is not to be found in His understanding. They are not truths because He understands them, but, rather, He must understand them by virtue of His most perfect knowledge, because they are truths. And *that* they are truths is as little His work as *why* they are truths. Truth, whatever subject it concerns, is immutable, eternal. Truth exists in God's mind, but not as a result of God's mind. God knows all truths, but He does not create them.[30] The conception of God, Leibniz said, signifies the pinnacle of the moral philosophy—not however, the foundation upon which it is constructed.[31] Again,

---

[27] *Monadology*, 267; Dutens, pt. 3, 273, 279.

[28] Dutens, pt. 3, 272; *Monadology*, 242.

[29] See *Monadology*, 242, note 72.

[30] Zimmermann, 13. See *op. cit.* pages 32 *et seq.* and 44 for a reconciliation of statements by Leibniz apparently in conflict with this doctrine.

[31] 3 Gerhardt, 429.

Locke maintained that God had laid down a rule according to which mankind should behave. In opposition to Locke's idea of a positive precept it was generally argued that the ideal basic rules of judgment would be transformed into arbitrary norms subject to cancellation at any time. Leibniz rejected this argument, and held that the true measure of the moral was the unalterable rule of reason which God had obligated Himself to maintain (*la règle invariable de la raison, que Dieu s'est chargé de maintenir*).[32] Thus it is true that the conception of God is considered related to jurisprudence in so far as it forms the explanation and guarantee of the final realization of the ethical demands for the individual, as well as for the totality— it is not, however, the motive and the legitimization of those demands themselves.[33]

Leibniz' argument against Hobbes and other exponents of the absolute State is substantially identical with that advanced by present-day advocates of natural-law doctrines. Power or authority, he said, cannot decide the formal reason of a binding force, cannot answer the deeper question of its *why*. Power is not the formal reason which makes the just *just*. Otherwise, all power would be just, exactly in proportion to its power; but this is against experience. To put right and might on the same plane is the sign of a fundamental misconception of the true relation between the " is " and the " ought." It is one thing to be able, another thing to be commanded. The necessary and demonstrative sciences, such as logic, metaphysics, arithmetic, geometry, mechanics, and the science of right and wrong, are not founded on experience or facts, but serve rather to give an account from the facts themselves and to regulate them in advance (*à rendre raison des faits et à les régler par avance*).[34] The conception of right would therefore remain in force even if there were no laws in the world. The mistake of those who make justice conditional upon might originates in the confusion of right with law, the ideal principle itself with its empirical coinage. The " ought " must not be read off from the existing

[32] Erdmann, 286.   [33] See *op. cit.* 451.   [34] Mollat, 51.

order of things and its patterns, but must be recognized as a regulative factor whose function is to direct the creation of the positive law. Thus Leibniz set the positive law against justice, the " is " against the " ought," and appealed from the former to the latter. In essence, he argues for a hypothetico-deductive system of natural law, in which the claims of rival hypotheses would receive adequate analysis. This is the method of the sciences that have passed beyond the classificatory or descriptive stage, and appears to be the only one on which a rational natural-law doctrine can be founded. Leibniz often pointed out that Thrasymachus' definition of justice as the interest of the stronger was the model for the absolutistic theories of his day. " With this remark," as Cassirer [35] observes, " he himself denoted the historical perspective from which his doctrine is to be viewed and judged. It is the struggle of the Socratic teachings against those of the Sophists, of the eternal ' idea ' of right against its relativeness to convention, which renews itself here in modern philosophy." That there are definite limits to the realization of the ideal in the realm of the empirical Leibniz clearly recognized; this limitation, however, is no contradiction, but in such a system is merely a stimulus toward the greater understanding of the rôle of the ideal. [36]

With natural law grounded on reason, rather than on the will of God or State absolutism, Leibniz proceeded to elaborate his system. The object of the highest reason is to act in such a manner that as much good as possible is done for as many as possible, and that as much happiness flows over all and everything as they are able to contain. This is the supreme command, and the being who acts according to this principle is of a truly divine nature; for if we wanted to take the opposite view, namely, that God rules with such despotic arbitrariness that he is influenced by neither rational creatures' happiness, nor by irrational expediency, then He could be called neither wise, good, nor just in the hitherto accepted sense of the words. [37] Jurisprudence itself Leibniz defines as the science of just and

[35] *Op. cit.* 453.   [36] Hartmann, 89.   [37] Dutens, pt. 3, 273.

unjust actions, the just and the unjust are what is useful or injurious to the public.[38] The " public " is the world and its Ruler, God, the human race, and the State. These elements are so arranged that in case of conflict, the will of God takes precedence over that of the human race; the latter over that of the State, and the State over personal advantage. There is thus a three-fold science of jurisprudence: a divine, a human, and a civil. The doctrine of the promotion of personal advantage is not a part of jurisprudence, Leibniz declared; it belongs to politics.

This general theory, and even the arguments in support of it, have much in common with the ideas advanced by Grotius and Suárez, which in turn have their antecedents in the tradition which extends back to Cicero, the Stoics and Plato. The immutability of the moral law which is beyond even God's power to alter, was a premise of Grotius;[39] that He could make right that which by reason is wrong is as incomprehensible as that He could make two times two something other than four. Reason for Grotius also was the basis of morality, and would be a sure guide even if there were no God. Again, Grotius understood politics to be the wise arrangement of the conditions peculiar to every human being and to every State as entities. Leibniz himself freely acknowledged many of his indebtednesses and thought that he had combined with his own system sound conceptions that had been advanced previously. Thus, he called attention to Grotius, who deduced law from a society of intelligent beings; to Hobbes who traced peace within the State to the war of all against all in the natural state; and to Sforza Pallavicino who found law in the wise origin of the world, motion and rest.[40] Leibniz' eclecticism, however, has often been remarked, and need not be explored here. Nor, in the other direction, need we concern ourselves with the relations between his thought and that of Bentham. That there are affinities between their ideas seems clear enough.

[38] Dutens, pt. 3, 185.
[39] *De Jure Belli ac Pacis Libri Tres* (1625) Bk. I, c. 1, sec. 5.
[40] Dutens, pt. 3, 212.

Leibniz' next step is the development of the idea of right,[41] which he attempted to do systematically. In stating the elements of natural right, he observed,[42] there must be expounded, first, the common principles of justice, the charity of the wise man; secondly, private right or the precepts of commutative justice, concerning what is observed among men in so far as they are regarded as equal; thirdly, public right, concerning the dispensing of common goods and evils among unequal people for the greatest common good in this life; fourthly, inward right, concerning universal virtue and natural obligation toward God, that we may have regard to perpetual happiness. To these must be added the elements of legitimate and divine right: human right both in our own commonwealth and between nations, divine right in the universal church.

Right, he said, is a certain moral power, and duty (*obligatio*) a moral necessity. Moral is that which is equivalent to " natural " in a good man; for as a Roman lawyer admirably says, it is not to be believed that we are capable of doing things which are contrary to good morals. Further, a good man is one who loves all men, so far as reason allows. Justice, therefore, will be most fittingly defined as the charity of the wise man, that is to say, charity in obedience to the dictates of wisdom.[43] Therefore the saying attributed to Carneades that justice is supreme folly, because it bids us attend to the interests of others, neglecting our own, proceeds from the ignorance of the definition of justice. Charity is universal benevolence, and benevolence is the habit of loving or esteem-

---

[41] Preface to the *Codex Juris Gentium Diplomaticus* (1693). It is translated in part by Latta, *op. cit.* 282 *et seq.* For the full text see Dutens, pt. 3, 287.

[42] Mollat, 19. See Latta, *op. cit.*, 282.

[43] The idea of justice is *a priori* according to Leibniz. "Since justice consists in a certain congruity and proportion, the just may have a meaning, although there may neither be any one who practices justice nor any one towards whom it is practiced, just as the ratios of numbers are true, although there may neither be any one who numbers nor anything which is numbered, and it may be predicted of a house that it will be beautiful, of a machine that it will be effective, of a commonwealth that it will be happy, if it comes into existence, although it may never come into existence." *Juris et aequi elementa* (Mollat, 23). The doctrine of Right must therefore be deduced from definitions, in Leibniz' view. For other definitions of justice by Leibniz see those collected in Latta, *op. cit.*, 283 note 7.

ing. But to love or esteem is to take pleasure in the happiness of another, or what comes to the same thing, to adopt another's happiness as our own. In this way is solved the difficult problem, also of great importance in theology, of how there can be a disinterested love, a love apart from hope and fear and every consideration of advantage; the solution being that the happiness of those in whose happiness we take pleasure becomes a part of our own happiness, for things which give us pleasure are desired for their own sakes. And as the very contemplation of beautiful things is pleasant, and a picture by Raphael moves him who understands it, although it brings him no gain, so that it becomes dear and delightful to him, inspiring in him something like love; so when the beautiful thing is also capable of happiness, his feeling for it passes into real love. Divine love excels other loves, for God can be loved with the happiest results, since nothing is happier than God and nothing more worthy of happiness can be conceived. And since He possesses supreme power and wisdom, His happiness not only becomes a part of ours but even constitutes it (if we are wise; that is, if we love Him). But since wisdom ought to direct charity, wisdom also requires to be defined. It is nothing but the very science of happiness, so that we are brought back again to the notion of happiness.

With this statement, as Zimmermann remarks,[44] we have reached the crux of the matter. Justice is perfection in accordance with wisdom,[45] and wisdom is the science of supreme happiness; hence the definition of justice depends upon the definition of supreme happiness, and the latter is the conception which supplements the former upon which everything depends. It is through the idea of supreme happiness that, in Leibniz' opinion, the hitherto empty, formal notion of justice is to receive its specific content. Supreme happiness is defined as " a state of permanent joy." [46] Joy, he said, does not produce happiness if it is not lasting; rather, he who for the sake of brief joy falls into prolonged sadness, is unhappy. Joy, how-

---

[44] *Op. cit.*, 26.   [45] Dutens, pt. 3, 261.   [46] Erdmann, 671; Mollat, 3.

ever, is a desire (*lust*) if the soul itself registers it; desire is the feeling of perfection or superiority, either about ourselves or about something else. Supreme happiness, accordingly, is the permanent feeling of one's own perfection, or of a perfection external to oneself.

Now from this source flows natural Right (*jus naturae*) of which there are three degrees: strict Right (*jus strictum*), equity, and piety, or, civil, human and divine law. The first of these refers to the State, the second to humanity, the last to God and the universe: Strict Right in commutative justice, equity (or charity in the narrower sense of the word) in distributive justice, and piety (or uprightness) in universal justice.[47] Hence come Ulpian's precepts that we should do injury to no one, that we should give each his own, that we should live virtuously (or rather piously). Each degree that follows is more complete than the preceding one, confirms it, and in case of conflict neutralizes it.

Strict Right is basically nothing but the law of war and peace. Between two people the law of peace prevails so long as one does not start war, that is to say, violates the law. Between the person (the intelligent being) and the thing (which has no intelligence) there exists a continual law of war (*jus belli*). The lion may tear a man to pieces and a mountain may crush him; a man on the other hand may subdue the lion and tunnel through the mountain. Victory of the person over things and the reduction of the latter is called possession. Thus, under the law of war, possession gives the person the right to a thing if it is ownerless. If someone injures the person or the thing of another, then that act gives the other person the right to obtain redress through force. Deception also is a violation of right, inasmuch as a disadvantage is coupled with other intentions, and out of this flows the necessity of keeping promises. The single rule of the pure natural law therefore is: Injure no one so that the right to use force does not arise.[48] Otherwise, if the injury occurs within the State,

---

[47] *Cf.* Aristotle, *N. E.* 1130 [b] 30, 1131 [b] 27, 33.   [48] Dutens, pt. 3, 213.

the person injured would have ground for an action at law, or if it be without the State, he would have the right to make war. From this there comes the justice which the philosophers call *commutative*, and the *right* which Grotius called *right proper* (*facultas*).[49]

The next higher degree of natural right is equity (*aequitas*) or, in the narrow sense of the word, charity (*caritas*). This degree extends beyond the rigor of strict Right to those obligations which those to whom we are obliged have no right of action to compel us to perform. These include gratitude, pity, and the things that were said by Grotius to have *imperfect right* (or fitness, *aptitudo*), not *right proper* (*facultas*). Equity requires as a condition for its existence some sort of " society." A society may exist in which the strict law alone is recognized, but it will not be a happy one, for it will be full of " perpetual quarrels."[50] Equity demands that though I make war upon him who has injured me, I do not carry it to the point of annihilation, but only so far as to receive indemnification; that I admit arbitrators; that I do nothing against others that I do not want them to do to me; that I do not particularly aim at the punishment of imprudence, but rather only at wickedness and deception; finally, that the cunningly contrived contract be rectified and the dupe assisted. For the rest, equity commands the observance of strict Right.[51] As the precept of strict Right was to injure no one, so that of equity is to do good to everyone so far as befits each person or so far as each deserves, since we cannot equally befriend all men. Thus we have here *distributive* justice, and that precept of law (*jus*) which bids us give to each his own. And to this our related political laws in the State, laws that have to do with the happiness of persons, and which usually bring it about that those who had only a moral claim (*aptitudo*) acquire a jural claim (*facultas*), that is, they are enabled to demand what it is fair that others should give. But while in the lowest degree of natural Right no regard

[49] Latta, 288. Grotius, *De jure belli et pacis*, bk. i, ch. 1, par. 5, *et seq.*
[50] Mollat, 15. Latta, 289, note 29.
[51] Dutens, pt. 3, 213.

was paid to the differences among men, (except to those which arose from the particular matter in hand), and all men were regarded as equal, now in this higher degree merits are weighed, and hence privileges, rewards and punishments appear. Equity itself leads us in business to act upon strict Right, that is, the equality of men, except when a weighty reason of greater good requires us to depart from it.

The highest degree of Right is that of uprightness, or rather piety. For what has been said so far may be understood in such a way as to be limited to the relations of a mortal life. Strict Right has its source in the need of keeping the peace; equity or charity strives after something more, so that while each to the other does as much good as possible, each may increase his own happiness through that of others; in a word, strict Right avoids misery, whereas Right in the higher sense (*jus superius*) tends to happiness, but of such a kind as falls to our mortal lot. We ought to subordinate life itself and whatever makes life desirable to the great good of others, so that it behooves us to bear patiently the greatest pains for the sake of others. This is beautifully inculcated by the philosophers rather than thoroughly proved by them. Moral dignity and glory and the soul's feeling of joy on account of virtue, to which philosophers [52] appeal under the name of rectitude, are indeed great goods, but not such as to prevail with all men nor to overcome all the sharpness of evil, since all men are not equally moved by imagination; especially those who have not become accustomed to the thought of honor or to the appreciation of the good things of the soul, either through a liberal education, or a noble way of living, or the discipline of life or of method. In order that it may be concluded by a universal demonstration that everything honorable is beneficial and that everything base is hurtful, we must assume the immortality of the soul, and the Ruler of the Universe, God. Thus it is that we think of all men as living in the City of God, that is to say, in the most perfect State that is possible, under the most perfect of Monarchs.[53]

---

[52] *E. g.*, Cicero, Mollat, 30.   [53] *Monadology*, Par. 85.

That Monarch cannot be deceived because of His wisdom, and His power cannot be avoided; He is also so lovable that it is happiness to serve such a master. By His power and providence it comes to pass that every *right* passes into *fact*, that no one is injured except by himself, that nothing done rightly is without a reward and no sin without a punishment. It is on this account that *justice* is called *universal* and comprehends all other virtues; for things which otherwise do not seem to concern any one else, as for instance whether we abuse our own body or our own property, are nevertheless forbidden by the law of nature, that is, by the eternal laws of the Divine Monarchy, since we owe ourselves and all that is ours to God. For as it is of importance to a commonwealth, so much more is it to the universe, that no one should make a bad use of that which is his own. Accordingly from this is derived the force of that highest precept of the natural law which bids us live virtuously.

Thus the highest degree of Right formally completes Leibniz' scheme. It expresses the will of a superior; but the superior is either superior by nature, as God is: and His will natural, hence *piety* or law, hence positive Divine Right; or the superior is superior by agreement *(pactum)*, as a man is; hence civil Right. Piety therefore is the third degree of natural Right, and it gives perfection and effect to the others. For God, since He is omniscient and wise, confirms bare right and equity; and since He is omnipotent, He carries them out. Hence the advantage of the human race, and indeed the beauty and harmony of the world, coincide with the Divine will.[54] Now there must be a higher degree of right than mere equity, for God is supremely just and good, and the justice of God differs not in kind but in degree from the justice of man. " But it is not for His ease nor in order to keep the peace with us, that God shows us so mucn goodness; for we could not make war upon Him. What then will be the principle of His justice and what will be its rule? It will not be that equity or that equality which has its place among men. We cannot regard God as having any other motive than perfection." [55] Thus the highest degree of Right equalizes the antagonisms of the first two; strict Right can come into conflict with equity, and equity can come into conflict with strict Right. In the external world, both cannot prevail side by side without an equalizing physical force. Here God is the mediator and arranges that whatever is of benefit to the public welfare also brings advantages to the individual; and thus that all that is moral is useful, and all that is immoral is destructive. The existence of an omniscient and omnipotent Being is therefore the last foundation of natural Right. [56]

Leibniz' theory is thus both metaphysical and ethical, but it is not theological. God is the foundation of all natural Right, in the sense that without the assumption of God's existence it is impossible to speak of the existence of a legal order in the world, inasmuch as the world itself would be non-existent. Since God is the last cause of being, He is also the cause of its *being so*. [57] It is the assumption of God's existence which serves as a sufficient guarantee of the existence of the highest possible legal and moral condition in the universe. But God is merely the originator of the condition and not of the laws that substantiate Him. These latter are entirely independent of Him, and flow out of the nature of truth itself. They form the object and substance of His cognition, not however of His arbitrariness. God desires what is right; but right would also remain right if He did not desire it. [58]

What is the interest of Leibniz' philosophy of law for us today? His general philosophical system, together with those of Plato and Aristotle, St. Thomas, Descartes, Hobbes, Spinoza, Locke, Kant, Hegel and the rest, has long ceased to be accepted as embodying a final account of the truth. Yet those systems are still studied with the greatest care, a tribute not accorded—apart from purely historical concerns—the various scientific systems advanced in the past, such as the Hippocratic and the Ptolemaic. The answer appears to be that the systems are

[55] Mollat, 65, Latta, 291, note 37.   [57] Zimmermann, 32.
[56] Dutens, pt. 3, 214.   [58] *Ibid.*, 44.

occupied with problems which are still persistent, that they contain certainly not the whole truth but perhaps some part of it, and that the methods of the systems have not been overthrown completely, as has, for example, the practice of divination in the treatment of disease.

Leibniz' philosophy of law is addresssed to the attempted solution of a central enduring problem of jurisprudence—the determination of a just legal order. That determination was the object of Socrates' proposition that law tends to be the discovery of reality, and it is the ultimate concern of the twentieth century revival of natural law. Under the influence of nineteenth century positivism the problem of a just legal order was held to be insoluble, on the ground that human processes are subject to the rule of causality, so that evaluative judgments are without significance. It was urged also that it is impossible to test such judgments scientifically. Notwithstanding a contemporary revival of natural-law doctrines, this is the dominant attitude today. We are told that the only legitimate concern of jurisprudence, that is to say, the only scientifically possible one, is the study of the law that is, and not the law that ought to be. Judgments of value must be eliminated not only from jurisprudence but from all the social sciences; the concern in such fields of inquiry is solely with what happens. That this view has a certain plausibility it is impossible to deny, in view of the large number of distinguished adherents who profess it; but that it has been refuted on numerous occasions it is also certainly possible to affirm.

It is indisputable that values constitute an omnipresent factor in the legal process. In the realm of statute-making we have to determine whether conduct shall be ordered in this way or in that, and what kind and degree of penalty shall be imposed for an infraction of the rule. Here there is clearly a competition among ideals, which demands some sort of resolution. In the realm of judicial decision the competition is no less intense, and extends from Mr. Justice Peckham's [59] denial of

[59] *Lochner* v. *New York*, 198 U. S. 45 (1904).

the validity of particular social legislation as " meddlesome interference " to Mr. Justice Cardozo's [60] allowance of a claim in tort on the ground of " considerations of analogy, of convenience, of policy, and of justice." Early in the history of American law the problem of values assumed an acute form. The States were faced with the task of determining the extent to which English law should operate within their domains. Some States admitted as authoritative only decisions prior to colonization, and regarded those between the reign of James I and the Revolution as merely persuasive. In a letter written in 1788 Jefferson [61] held " it essential, in America, to forbid that any English decision which has happened since the accession of Lord Mansfield to the bench, should ever be cited in a court; because, though there have come many good ones from him, yet there is so much sly poison instilled into a great part of them, that it is better to proscribe the whole." And this of the man now held to be the greatest lawyer of his century, and who succeeded in revitalizing the entire common law! Although human actions may be causally determined, must not the jurist study the ideals of the eighteenth century if he is fully to understand the structure of contemporary American law? And may he not test Jefferson's position by assuming that Jefferson's ideals had triumphed, and that Mansfield's doctrines were thus initially excluded from American law? A little reflection would reveal to him that the common law prior to Mansfield was inadequate to cope with the commercial society of the nineteenth century, and that Mansfield's doctrines, or their equivalent, were essential if the common law was to meet its full responsibility.

But Leibniz' philosophy of law raises an apparently deeper issue. He proposes an evaluation of values, not at the historico-descriptive level, but as a measure for the future. In principle, this proposal is substantiated by the considerations just advanced, but it may be well to make it explicit. Scientific inquiry, in its essence, proceeds by the so-called hypothetico-deductive method. It formulates hypotheses on the firmest ground available, makes logically proper deductions from them, and tests the results dialectically or empirically. No sound arguments appear to have been brought forward against the view that ethical systems can be made scientific through the development of adequate hypotheses as to what is good or bad, or what is necessary to achieve certain ends.[62] At bottom, and this is its great merit, Leibniz' philosophy of law is a specimen of such a scientific system, put forward by one of the greatest minds in Western philosophy, and rigorously thought out by the identical methods which have achieved much success in the exact sciences. He began his system with two hypotheses: " (a) The Monad is nothing but a simple substance which enters into compounds. By ' simple ' is meant ' without parts ';" (b) "There must be simple substances, since there are compounds; for a compound is nothing but a collection or *aggregatum* of simple things." These hypotheses culminated, through steps which seemed to Leibniz inexorable, in the theory of the City of God, the apex of his philosophy generally, as well as of his philosophy of law. The elements of his hypotheses are ideal elements, exactly comparable to the ideal bodies whose masses are concentrated into ideal points for the purposes of physics. For the objectives of this theory, as for that of the physicist, it is irrelevant whether or not they exist in nature. He proceeded by the same method in his philosophy of law: " *jus strictum*," " equity " or " *caritas*," and " *uprightness* " or " *piety* " are all ideal entities that exist nowhere in the social world, but against which actual social events can be measured. That the system is defective on many grounds, principally in that it cannot be applied to the actual world in any meaningful sense, need not be denied. Similar failures in the history of science do not impugn the validity of the method. Nor need it be denied that the difficulties in the way of the construction of a system which will yield applicability are

[62] For a recent discussion, see Cohen, *A Preface to Logic* (1944) 155 *et seq*.

immense. But that does not necessarily mean, as the contemporary positivist asserts, that the construction of such systems is impossible. A theory of natural law that possesses no application is at best an idle game; but a theory of positive law that ignores the normative is fatally incomplete.

LAW AND THE SOCIAL ORDER

Parallel with his theory of natural law, Leibniz developed a theory of law in society. He was, as his numerous papers on specific contemporary legal issues amply reveal, an intensely practical man, and his grasp of the problems of positive law was as firm as his hold on those in the domain of natural law. In the sphere of positive law his thought was basically sociological, that is, it took its departure from the idea of the group, or the human plural, the pivotal concept, as it has been called, of present-day sociological theory. At the same time, his social values were of such an ameliorative nature that his nineteenth century followers felt themselves compelled to deny that his ideas were " socialistic." Among other things, he proposed that the State safeguard the opportunity to work, that it promote an adequate insurance system, a wise colonial policy, a modernized tariff system and a State liquor monopoly.[63] The whole tendency of his temperament, as of his philosophy, Russell[64] remarks, was to exalt enlightenment, education and learning, at the expense of ignorant good intentions. If his thought in this respect is not always as clear as it might be, it is because the Church had explicit views on the topics with which he was concerned. He consistently attempted in all fields to harmonize his views with those of that powerful institution, and where that was not feasible he did not hesitate to defer. But it is impossible to mistake the true direction of his thought, or fail to realize the extent to which it was permeated with social considerations. " Laws," he remarks, " are not made for the purpose of destroying man, they are made to preserve man."[65]

---

[63] Hartmann, 80.
[64] *The Philosophy of Leibniz* (1900) 202.
[65] Dutens, pt. 3, 256.

At the root of his social theory of law was a conception of law
and justice as a totality, a resolute opposition to any attempt
at a bifurcation of the legal order into law on one side and
justice on the other. This does not mean that in the social
world law and justice are not frequently in opposition. Right,
he remarked, for example, can never be unjust, for that would
be a self-contradiction; law, however, can very well be unjust.
For it is force that gives and maintains the law; and if this
force lacks wisdom or good will, it can give and maintain very
bad laws.[66] In such cases the duty of the magistrate is identical
with that of the citizen: there must be absolute obedience to
the rules of the legal order, even when it is unmistakable that
they run counter to the true right.[67] If Leibniz was here
attempting to be practical he was not being practical enough.
Much closer to an accurate description of the social process, in
the sense that it allows for the facts of individual resistance
and social revolution, is the doctrine associated with the name
of Rousseau, that the basis of obedience is consent. Since this
means that the activities of the State are subject to examination it means also that authority under certain conditions will
pass over into anarchy. History is replete with the record of
men who have defied the instructions of the legal order, from
an overwhelming sense of duty. The Anabaptists rejected all
law, since the Holy Spirit, who was unfettered, would be the
complete guide for the good man. A theory such as that of
Leibniz, which condemns them on *a priori* grounds, ignores a
permanent tradition of human society.

In his social theory of law Leibniz conceived of justice as a
communal virtue, that is, a virtue which preserves the community, and which therefore can come into being only with the
existence of a community. A community is defined as " a union
of various human beings for a common aim." [68] Now law
originates in the community not as a result of a natural social
condition, but as a consequence of the desire for happiness.

[66] Mollat, 51.   [67] Mollat, 108.
[68] 1 Guhrauer, *Leibniz' Deutsche Schriften* (1838) 414.

Human beings do not establish the legal order because they, like certain animals, possess originally an inclination to live socially, and because, as Aristotle taught, man is a social animal. On the contrary they live socially because they desire happiness, and because every individual sees his own welfare advanced and less endangered by others if, instead of standing isolated, he unites with others for common protection and advancement, thus forming a community. The most perfect community is one with the objective of common and supreme happiness, from which it follows that any community that desires perfection should have the sole objective of common and supreme happiness. It may be well to add that Leibniz' theory of happiness was based ultimately on a doctrine of unconscious or insensible perceptions. At every moment there are an infinite number of perceptions in us, but not accompanied by apperception and reflection, *i. e.*, changes in the soul itself of which we are not conscious, because the impressions are either too slight and too great in number, or too even, so that they have nothing sufficient to distinguish them from one another; but joined to others they do not fail to produce their effect and to make themselves felt at least confusedly in the mass. They form, Leibniz knows not what, these tastes, these images of the sense-qualities, clear in the mass, but confused in the parts, these impressions which surrounding bodies make upon us, which involve the infinite, this connection which each being has with all the rest of the universe. We may even say that in consequence of these minute perceptions, the present is big with the future and laden with the past, that all things conspire, and that in the least of substances eyes as penetrating as those of God could read the whole course of things in the universe. These unconscious perceptions form the inclinations and propensities, but not the passions. Happiness is, so to speak, a road through pleasures, and pleasure is only a step and an advance towards happiness, the shortest that can be made according to present impressions, but not always the best; one may miss the true road in desiring to follow the shortest. Thus we know that it is the reason and the will that lead us towards happiness, but the feeling and appetite carry us only towards pleasure. At bottom, however, pleasure is a feeling of perfection, and pain a feeling of imperfection, provided it be marked enough to make us capable of perceiving it. Out of the fountainhead of the unconscious perceptions flow ultimately the recognizable impulses and the perceptible inclinations.[69]

Leibniz defined six types of communities, each with its own type of law. There are the three elementary types made up of a few persons: the marital community, the family community of parents and children that results, and the community of master and servant. The fourth is the community of the household, which combines the first three types. Then there is the civil community, comprising the city, province, and state. Finally, the series is crowned by the supreme, all-embracing community, the Church of God, whose destiny it is to be general and catholic, as a moral world within a natural world, with God Himself at the head as invisible Lord and Ruler. These are natural communities because they are the kind " that nature wants." We know nature desires them, because nature has given us a desire for them and an ability to satisfy that desire; for nature does nothing in vain, particularly when the matter is necessary or when it is of permanent advantage, for nature dispenses everywhere for the best. Out of the natural community flows the natural law, the purpose of which is to preserve and further the natural community.

Each community is interpreted in the light of this principle. The community of husband and wife serves " to preserve the human race." Preservation is the fundamental assumption for all happiness and, to that extent, a condition for its satisfaction, The community of parents and children is cultivated and preserved by the parents for the pleasure of enjoying grateful children, and by the children in order that they themselves may reach perfection. Thus the family community serves the pur-

---

[69] *New Essays concerning Human Understanding*, translated by A. G. Langley (1916) 48, 200.

pose of happiness, although, as Zimmermann remarked, it is plain that Leibniz' conception has not exhausted the meaning of the family. The careless and sketchy manner in which the idea is presented probably explains why Leibniz himself never made public the paper in which it appears. The third natural community, that of master and servant, exists in accordance with nature if one person lacks intelligence but not the physical strength to earn a living. Such a person is a servant by nature and must work as instructed by someone else, he thus makes a livelihood, but the surplus belongs to the master. Leibniz apparently did not want this argument used as a justification for slavery or serfdom, however, for he at once added that he doubted whether an example of such bondage, in which the servant exists solely for the master's sake could be found, particularly since souls are immortal and someday can acquire knowledge and participate in the happiness of the master's life. For if there is hope that the servant may acquire knowledge, then the master is obliged to further his servant's freedom through education, to the extent the servant needs it for his happiness. Accordingly, he concluded that this type of community exists only between man and cattle. The household community has as its purpose the meeting of " daily exigencies." The civil community serves the purpose of attaining happiness more quickly and, at the same time, of remaining secure. Its aim is temporal welfare. The aim of the ecclesiastical community is eternal happiness.

Two ideas of importance emerge from Leibniz' theory, the first an attempt to find a ground for law in a principle of society, and the second an endeavor to work out a conception of the end of law within the framework of that principle. As to the first, his principle is merely that society has a structure, and that positive law is grounded upon that structure and its character is determined by it. This idea is now a commonplace of contemporary social thought, which recognizes many types of organization—the community, crowds, classes, the family, and the organized groups such as the state and the various economic organizations. This structure holds together and perpetuates itself through various controls, of which one of the most important is the legal order. The idea of finding the basis of law in the structure of society is familiar enough to sociologists, but it is rarely attempted by jurists, who generally associate law with the state, or with an ideal of morality, or with some principle of power, either in a naked form or as expressed through the sovereign, the legislature, the courts or officials. Perhaps the most successful formulation by a jurist in modern times of the structural principle in its legal aspect is Maine's hypothesis that ancient society was organized on the basis of status and that modern society had its focus in contract. We hear much from jurists today of law as an instrument of social control, but we receive little or no analysis of that aspect of the legal order in the only terms that appear to be valid. Sociologists have developed the foundations of the structural principle in a seemingly unanswerable manner, but so far they have lacked the technical knowledge to make its application to the legal order fruitful. Leibniz' sketch of the principle was hardly more than a beginning, but its power and objectivity when united with the tasks of legal analysis in the hands of its two most eminent juristic exponents, Maine [70] and Jordan,[71] should long ago have awakened a wide conception of its possibilities. At its very outset, it may be noted, the structural principle challenges the foundations of the most influential of contemporary legal philosophies. Since Jhering we have been taught that the State is a harmony of conflicting interests, and that law is the instrument of effecting and maintaining the harmony. In the words of Pound, who has given this theory its classic form, " an interest is a demand or desire which human beings either individually or in groups seek to satisfy, of which, therefore, the ordering of human relations in civilized society must take account." [72] Does this theory fall because of the argument that no organization of subjective

---

[70] *Ancient Law* (1861).
[71] *Forms of Individuality* (1937).
[72] *Outlines of Lectures on Jurisprudence* (5th ed. 1943) 96.

phenomena is possible, that subjective facts do not submit to order, that the order of mind is not the superficial juxtaposition of mental states? We do not know, since nowhere, notwithstanding the advancement of this explicit criticism, is the problem faced by the exponents of the theory of an order of interests.

Leibniz' theory of the end of law emphasizes two tasks that are also at the bottom of most present-day legal thinking about the problem: (1) insistence upon a proper consideration of the human being, and (2) the attainment of the common end as the measure of social values. An economic relationship, such as that of master and servant, has validity in Leibniz' system only in so far as it expresses an intellectual class relationship. This at once eliminates any idea of property, as in slavery, or of individual privilege, and refuses to admit the conception of the individual as a mere expedient. This ethical ideal of self-realization has its metaphysical correlate in the idea of immortality. Intellectual priority, representing the legal title of authority, contains within itself the obligation to produce an effect upon the spiritual community which at once abrogates absolute dependence.[73] The master-servant relationship itself sets the aim and task of education for freedom. These values fix a barrier to the idea of exclusive property, which has no place under an ideal constitution. Although the necessity of individual proprietors is recognized, under present conditions it must be held to be a sympton of ethical bondage and immaturity.[74] Above the idea of property stands society, with its right of control. At the stage of strict Right the aim is to limit and guarantee to the human being a highly circumscribed circle of individual operation. But at the stage of equity, this negative rule is transformed into the positive principle of furtherance of individual purposes, through active social participation and cooperation. This demands of the individual a voluntary renunciation of the advantages that arise from separation and isolation.[75] As Cassirer put it, " the objective goal

---

[73] Mollat, 16.   [74] Mollat, 9.   [75] Mollat, 14.

of the community alone decides the legal and social structure." [76]
The gulf that separates this conception of the end of law from
Plato's idea of its task as the preservation in their distinctness
of the principal functions of society, or from Cicero's and St.
Thomas Aquinas' idea that it was to give to each his due, need
scarcely be remarked. Not until the twentieth century did
Leibniz' idea of the task of the legal order receive full expression
in the writings of jurists. But that contemporary jurists are
now putting forward in this field ideas that he long ago formulated cannot be doubted.[77]

CONCLUSION

Leibniz presented his ideas in what for many must be a
somewhat strange and baffling form. His writings on law
represent an amalgam of conceptions drawn from the three
great divisions of thought of his time, science, philosophy and
theology, with the addition of a fourth that we would call today
the social sciences. He did not see any of these divisions as
self-contained departments of knowledge, and he expected any
proposition which he asserted to be valid, whether tested
scientifically, philosophically or theologically. Consequently,
the system which he constructed in any particular field was apt
to contain elements from other domains and to be related to
them explicitly. Such a method, when used by a man of
Leibniz' powers, makes for great complexity and apparent
obscurity. It also accounts for the fact that although his intellectual abilities were undoubtedly the equal of Plato's his
philosophy even yet has not been fully expounded in its generality, and no complete collection of his writings has ever been
published. In studying any major philosopher, Russell [78] has
remarked, the right attitude is " a kind of hypothetical sympathy, until it is possible to know what it feels like to believe
in his theories, and only then a revival of the critical attitude,

---

[76] *Leibniz*, 456.
[77] For a summary of the present-day leading ideas, see Pound, *Twentieth Century
Ideas as to the End of Law*, Harvard Legal Essays (1934) 357, 365-366.
[78] *A History of Western Philosophy* (1945) 39.

which should resemble, as far as possible, the state of mind of a person abandoning opinions which he has hitherto held." This counsel is peculiarly appropriate to the study of Leibniz, whose complexities of thought may appear without much reflection to embrace too large a share of the fantastic. But it is the part of wisdom to remember always, when confronted with elements of this character, that Leibniz' methods were as rigidly scientific as they could well be. " An abstraction is not an error," he wrote pointedly, " provided we know what it is that we feign therein," and on this ground he justified not only the employment by mathematicians of perfect lines, uniform motions and other ideal entities, but also the comparable use of similar abstractions in other fields.[79] The main task in the study of Leibniz is to grasp the full content of such abstractions.

[79] *New Essays*, 51.

CHAPTER X

LOCKE

Probably the most important contribution ever made to English constitutional law by an author who was not a lawyer by profession.

Sir Frederick Pollock

LOCKE hoped in his political theory, at the core of which was his idea of law, to find, as a basis for the State, some sagacious principle the self-evident virtues of which would be plain to practical men. He was an intelligent man with a large experience in constitutional affairs who wrote on philosophical subjects. But his dominant impulse was not philosophical: he was fearful of the unfamiliar. " Our business here is not to know all things," he wrote, " but those which concern our conduct." [1] His philosophy was thus a philosophy of the middle area; he began with the familiar, and for the most part did not pass beyond it in either of the two directions in which speculative inquiry moves. He did not attempt, in one direction, to justify the primary ideas on which his whole system rested. On this subject he took for granted the thought of his time. Thus, although his connections with the Cambridge Platonists were close, he nevertheless undertook an examination of the nature and extent of knowledge without any prior inquiry into the character of reality, a procedure entirely foreign to their practices and, indeed, to that of philosophy generally. He also failed to move very far in the other direction, towards a consideration of the consequences of the propositions established in his system. This is not a matter of much importance, provided indicia are present in the system which will enable

---

The Two Treatises of Government and *An Essay Concerning Human Understanding* were both first published in 1690. The fourth edition of the latter work, with Locke's final revisions, appeared in 1700. All references to the *Two Treatises* are to the sections of Part II, unless otherwise specified.

[1] *Essay*, I, i, 6.

readers to draw the necessary conclusions themselves. But on
significant issues Locke has too frequently halted his speculation at a point which does not permit readers to draw conclusions. Thus Locke argued that government is established by
society, and may therefore be disestablished by it. But who
is to judge when the government has betrayed its trust to the
extent necessary to justify an act of revolution? Locke answers,
" the people." [2] But by what means is this judgment to be
taken? By a plebiscite? Rioting in the streets? An act of
revolution itself? Locke does not provide the answer to the
question, nor is it possible to deduce it from the propositions
of his system.

By avoiding abstractness at one end and complexity at the
other, Locke kept his philosophical position free of elements
which are held to discourage popular interest. It may be
remarked, however, that the wide acceptance at various times
of certain theological systems which embraced those elements
to a high degree might have indicated that the foundations of
this supposition needed examination. At any rate, not the least
of the interest we have in Locke's philosophy today is due to its
vast influence on practical affairs. That his basic ideas are at the
root of much of the political theory of the eighteenth century
is clear; and that the framers of the Declaration of Independence and the architects of the French Revolution, both directly
and through the interpretations of such men as Rousseau and
Paine, were inspired by his principles is also clear. The power
of Locke's system, in fact, is nowhere else so strikingly illustrated than in the idea of the men of 1776 that it was applicable,
although framed about the structure of English aristocratic
society of 1688, to the entirely different society of the American colonies. Notwithstanding this popularity, his principles
throughout the nineteenth century came increasingly under
attack at the hands of formal political theorists, and it may well
be that World War II will be taken historically as conveniently
marking the close of their practical influence, together with that

[2] *Treatise,* 240. It is arguable that he means a majority. See 168 and 209.

of the even more profound doctrines of 1789.[3] Nevertheless, altogether apart from their problematical future, Locke's ideas deserve study as a typical way of approach to the problems of the legal order. It is not the approach of the philosophical specialist, who can exclude nothing from his purview, but that of the temperate sagacious man, whose efforts are directed to things which seem to him really to matter.

PREPOLITICAL SOCIETY

Locke's first step in the development of his theory of law was to deny, in accordance with his general philosophical position, that the law of nature was innate. He argued that a rule of conduct imposes a duty; but what a duty is cannot be understood without a law, and a law cannot be known, or supposed, without a lawmaker, or without reward and punishment. It is therefore impossible for a rule of conduct to be innate (that is, imprinted on the mind as a duty) without supposing the ideas of God, law, obligation, punishment, and a life after death, also to be innate. But these ideas are so far from being innate, that it is not every studious man, much less every one that is born, in whom they are to be found clear and distinct. However, because Locke denies an innate law, he must not be thought as holding there are nothing but positive laws. He believes there is a great difference between something imprinted on our minds at the outset and something that we, being ignorant of, may attain to the knowledge of by the due application of our natural faculties. Thus, he believes they equally forsake the truth who, running into the contrary extremes, either affirm an innate law, or deny that there is a law knowable by the light of nature, that is, without the help of positive revelation.[4]

Jurisprudence must here wait upon philosophy for a decision

[3] Locke's principles, oddly observes one of the most acute of contemporary English thinkers, " were embalmed in the Constitution of the United States which survives like an ancient family ghost haunting a modern sky-scraper." Broad, *John Locke* (1933) 31 *Hibbert Journal* 249, 256.

[4] *Essay*, I, iii, 12-13.

on the relative claims of empiricism and rationalism. Although
jurisprudence may not be entitled to speak upon such an issue,
the problem of knowledge is nevertheless involved in legal
speculation. In general, jurists either fail to perceive the problem and stop just short of the issue, thus leaving the whole
matter in the air, or they impliedly assume some solution,
or they deliberately avoid raising the issue since it has no
bearing upon their speculation. Thus, Cardozo in a strong
plea for the use of natural law as a part of the method
of sociology takes the position that the judge must appeal
to the "teachings of right reason and conscience." [5] But
it is important to know if these teachings are to have their
basis in experience or if they are to be found in the mind as a
creator of knowledge. Until we know the answer to this
question we are unable to take even the first step in Cardozo's
program, which is to consult the "teachings." Again, theories
of law based on such contemporary conceptions of biology and
psychology as the "subconscious," "inborn tendencies," and
"introspection" seem, insofar as the notions have any meaning
at all, to be bringing in by the back door, and not too well
disguised with false whiskers, what Locke put out the front,
namely, Innate Ideas. [6] Finally, and more soundly, writers such
as Pound consciously construct their proposals so that the
issue is not immediately raised. Thus Pound's so-called "jural
postulates of civilized society in our time and place," which
are in reality natural law doctrines of a highly sophisticated
nature, are intentionally framed as the necessary "presuppositions" of a particular legal system or systems. [7] They are thus
simply logical constructs, and at the point at which Pound
proposes them the issue of empiricism versus rationalism is
irrelevant; that is to say, however that controversy may be
decided in the future the content of the presuppositions would
not be affected unless the decision demanded a change in the
legal system itself. We have so far been spared a nominalist-

[5] *The Nature of the Judicial Process* (1922) 137.
[6] Timasheff, *An Introduction to the Sociology of Law* (1939) 34-36.
[7] Pound, *Social Control Through Law* (1942) 113.

realist controversy, with the nominalists sharply demarcated as the upholders of positive law, and with the realists similarly segregated as the supporters of natural law. However, a nominalist-realist controversy would not arise if the natural law system were solely a logical construct.

Locke's next step [8] is to invoke the conception of a state of nature. This condition he defines for men as "a state of perfect freedom to order their actions, and dispose of their possessions and persons as they think fit, within the bounds of the law of Nature, without asking leave or depending upon the will of any other man." [9] This conception is a strict deduction from the proposition which he lays down with respect to political power, the self-evident validity of which he takes for granted and which he consequently advances no arguments to sustain: "Political power. . . . I take to be a right of making laws, with penalties of death, and consequently all less penalties for the regulating and preserving of property, and of employing the force of the community in the execution of such laws, and in the defence of the commonwealth from foreign injury, and all this only for the public good." [10] Locke's idea of political power is thus a formal one. He finds in the law-making function the single element which distinguishes the power of the state from that of a father over his children, a master over his servant, a husband over his wife, and a lord over his slave. In spite of the large element of truth in Locke's assertion, we must recognize that as a complete factual description of political authority it is inadequate. It enables him to distinguish the State from the family and from economic organizations. But if, as Ratzenhofer and Small have done, we choose to look at the social process as one of a conflict of group interests, we arrive at a conception

---

[8] That is, the "next step" in Locke's own theory. Prior to his attempt to establish this premise, Locke had indulged in a long detour in which he answered the argument of Filmer's *Patriarcha* (1681) that Charles I derived his title and authority from Adam. However, the substance of Filmer's contention is not as silly as it is made to appear by Locke and his modern supporters. Actually it paved the way for the idea of natural rights as developed by Locke and Rousseau. See Figgis, *The Divine Right of Kings* (1914) 148 *et seq.*

[9] *Treatise*, 4.

[10] *Treatise*, 3.

of political power as an arrangement of combinations by which mutually repellant forces are brought into some measure of concurrent action.[11] In the performance of that function law is an important, but not the only, tool. Conciliation, propaganda, war, and many other devices, are instruments to that end. Locke's premise should therefore be understood as valid only for the purposes of his argument, and inasmuch as one of his conscious and valid techniques was the employment of such abstractions, it is fair to assume that he meant it to be taken in that manner.

Thus Locke arrived at a conception of a state of nature on purely rational grounds; he did not appeal to the thought of the Middle Ages, to the Roman lawyers, to the Stoics or to Aristotle as authorities upon which to base it. He argued merely that political power is the right to make law and to punish for the public good. Take away that power and men have perfect freedom to order their actions within the bounds of the law of nature. As a strictly formal argument—apart from the introduction of the idea of natural law, in which Locke is anticipating himself—no exception can be taken to it. However, the argument must not be understood as asserting an actual historical condition. Locke himself was fully aware of the force—and the limitations—of that criticism by his opponents. "It is often asked as a mighty objection," he remarks,[12] thus anticipating his modern critics, "where are, or ever were, there any men in such a state of Nature?" To show that the conception is not entirely fictitious he suggests that the actual state of nature in his sense exists between independent princes and rulers, and between men of different societies who bargain with each other in a place where there is no government, *e. g.* between a Swiss and an Indian who bargain for truck in the wilds of America. "They are perfectly in a state of Nature in reference to one another," he remarks, "for truth and keeping of faith belong to men as men and not as members of society." However, he implies that these two

[11] Small, *General Sociology* (1905) 253.   [12] *Treatise*, 14.

examples are really superfluous, inasmuch as he wishes to affirm that all men are naturally in a state of nature, and remain so until they make themselves members of a political society.[13]

Locke next asserts that all men in a state of Nature are equal by nature, and it is at this precise point that his argument breaks down. He here evokes a studied ambiguity of statement which makes it impossible to ascertain with any confidence his true meaning; but his proposition falls if taken in either of its two possible interpretations. Locke's [14] actual words are: men are naturally in " a state also of equality, wherein all the power and jurisdiction is reciprocal, no one having more than another, there being nothing more evident than that creatures of the same species and rank, promiscuously born to all the same advantages of Nature, and the use of the same faculties, should also be equal one amongst another, without subordination or subjection, unless the lord and master of them all should by any manifest declaration of his will, set one above another, and confer on him, by an evident and clear appointment, an undoubted right to dominion and sovereignty." This statement, if taken formally, in accordance with Locke's argument up to this point, means that no man in a society which is not politically organized has any political authority over any other man. As such, the statement is a truism, and we are at once in the dilemma supposed by Hobbes: [15] Where there is no political authority, the right of all men to things, is in effect no better than if no man had right to anything. But even within the framework of Locke's argument there is a deeper objection. If he intends his assertion to be taken in a formal sense, then he has reached an impasse. His objective is to pass from a state of nature to a state of politically-organized society; but this he cannot accomplish on his hypothesis if the inhabitants of his society remain formally equal. Thus, when he comes to make the transition he does so by making those inhabitants " biased by their interest," " ignorant " in their knowledge of it, refuse to allow the application of the law of nature to them-

---

[13] *Treatise*, 15.   [14] *Treatise*, 4.   [15] 4 Hobbes, *Works* (1840) 84.

selves, "partial," motivated by "passion" and "revenge,"
"negligent," and most important of all, without power to back
their rights.[16] Now in Locke's formal system the equality of
the members should be self-executing; if it is not, there is no
equality. But if the equality is self-executing, in Locke's system
the condition would have been an idyllic one, and Locke's imaginary beings would never have consented to the substitution
for it of a political society.

But Locke's assertion can be understood in a different sense,
one which is equally invalid but which has the virtue of allowing the argument to progress. It also seems to be the sense in
which he meant it, if we judge by the subsequent development
of his thought. It can be taken to mean that in a state of nature
the physical and mental differences among men are so slight
that no man can claim authority over another because of
them. This is Hobbes' argument, and in Locke's case it can be
understood in either an ethical or an empirical sense. We may
dismiss the empirical meaning at once—that men would not in
fact claim that authority could be predicated on their differences—since Locke's subsequent argument seems to show that
he meant it to be taken ethically. Furthermore, Locke could
not safely at this stage base his argument on what men would
or would not do in fact in a state of nature; he would have to
admit on historical grounds that they both would and would
not make such claims. He therefore argues: "The state of
Nature has a law of Nature to govern it, which obliges every
one, and reason, which is that law, teaches all mankind who
will but consult it, that being all equal and independent, no
one ought to harm another in his life, health, liberty or possessions; for men being all the workmanship of one omnipotent and
infinitely wise Maker; all the servants of one sovereign Master,
sent into the world by His order and about His business; they
are His property, whose workmanship they are made to last
during His, not one another's pleasure. And, being furnished
with like faculties, sharing all in one community of Nature,

---

[16] *Treatise,* 124-126.

there cannot be supposed any such subordination among us that may authorize us to destroy one another, as if we were made for one another's uses, as the inferior ranks of creatures are for ours." [17] In its ethical significance, as distinguished from its theological, the doctrine is an anticipation of Kant's maxim that we ought to treat every man as an end, never as a means only. This asserts that every man is the judge of his own good; and no man, and therefore no government, can impose another good upon him. But this would make government impossible unless everyone acquiesced in the good established by the government for the community. The doctrine of Locke and Kant is the modern democratic doctrine of individualism, but it plainly needs restatement in order to fit the facts of that type of government.

We are therefore at the stage in Locke's argument at which he has abandoned his method of conscious abstraction. Henceforth, his discussion is on an ethical or an empirical level, and may thus be tested by criteria, such as the historical, which would be inappropriate had he continued his initial method. In this respect he stands in sharp contrast to a philosopher such as Leibniz, who constructed two theories of law, one formulated on a set of ideal postulates, the other empirical and based on the facts of positive law.

Locke's state of Nature, as we have seen, was governed by a law of Nature, the basis of which was established both theologically and ethically. The law of Nature, which was known through reason, was at bottom the rule of self-preservation, which was generalized by Locke to include the preservation of all members of the society. "Every one as he is bound to preserve himself," he wrote,[18] "so by the like reason, when his own preservation comes not in competition, ought he as much as he can to preserve the rest of mankind." In terms as concrete as Locke thought it advisable to make them, this meant that no one ought to harm another in his life, health, liberty or possessions. From this it followed, in Locke's view, that the

---

[17] *Treatise*, 6. [18] *Ibid.*

execution of the law of Nature was in every man's hands. Not only may a man punish for the injury done him, but others may assist in that process, because an injury is social as well as personal.[19] Nevertheless, the punishment must not be arbitrary, but must be proportionate to the transgression, that is to say, will be such as will serve for reparation and restraint.

Apparently Locke was concerned over his proposal that every man in a state of Nature had a right to punish and to be the executioner of the law of Nature. He referred to it specifically as a " strange doctrine," [20] as indeed it was, and he attempted to bolster it by two arguments. The first argument we have already noticed: that an offence is a trespass against the whole society; and since every man has a right to preserve mankind in general, every man therefore has a right of punishment. His second argument bore upon a principle of English law that had just been established. By what right, Locke asked, except on his argument, can a State punish an alien for a crime committed in its country? [21] It is certain, he says, that the laws of a State, by virtue of any sanction they receive from the promulgated will of the legislature, do not reach a stranger. Therefore, if by the law of Nature every man does not have a power to punish offences against it, Locke does not see how the magistrates of any community can punish an alien of another country, since in reference to him, they can have no more power than what every man naturally may have over another.

It is curious that Locke should have advanced such an argument, since the question of the liability of an alien for violations of the local criminal law had recently been settled on another ground by the English courts. Moreover, the argument contradicts a position Locke was to assume later on in the *Treatise*. Queen Elizabeth's lawyers had been confronted with the problem in the case of Mary Stuart, both as a question of political necessity and as a matter of law. Elizabeth defended her right to retain her prisoner on the ground that " a man offending in another's territory, and there found, is punished in the place of

---

[19] *Treatise*, 10.　　　[20] *Treatise*, 9.　　　[21] *Ibid.*

his offence, without regard of his dignity, honor, or privilege." [22]
But a few years earlier, in 1545, the authorities had turned over
to his captain a Spanish soldier who had committed a murder
in England. [23] Later, Sherley, a Frenchman, committed an act
of treason in England against the king, and the court recognized
that he owed a local and temporary obedience so long as he was
within the king's protection. [24] Again, in 1594, in the case of the
wretched Portuguese Jew, Dr. Lopez, who was Elizabeth's physician and who was accused by Essex of a conspiracy against
her life, the judges followed the principle of the Sherley case.
This principle was recognized by way of obiter in 1609 in
Calvin's Case, the longest and weightiest case in substance,
according to Coke, that was ever argued in any court. [25] Finally,
in 1662, the court expressly decided, in the case of a Quaker
born in France, who was on trial for a violation of the Act to
Suppress Seditious Conventicles, that aliens owed a temporary
allegiance to the government of the country in which they were
resident. [26] Locke was well acquainted with the rule established
by these cases, because he stated it approvingly in section 122
of the *Treatise*. " Thus we see," he writes, " that foreigners, by
living all their lives under another government, and enjoying
the privileges and protection of it . . . are bound, even in
conscience, to submit to its administration as far forth as any
denizen." This rule is binding, in Locke's opinion, upon the
alien in conscience because the alien, through the enjoyment of
the government's protection, has given his tacit consent to
obey the rules of the government. [27]

Locke defined a state of nature as a society of " men living
together according to reason without a common superior on
earth, with authority to judge between them." [28] This grouping
of men is a society, but it is not political, [29] its members possess
natural rights, and the ordering of the group is regulated by

[22] 1 Walker, *History of the Law of Nations* (1899) 172.

[23] 1 Dasent 170.

[24] *Sherley's Case* (1557), Dyer 144a.

[25] 7 Co. Rep. 6a-6b.

[26] Kelying, 38.

[27] *Treatise*, 119.

[28] *Treatise*, 19.

[29] *Treatise*, 77.

natural law. There are also certain institutions in the society which are antecedent to the organization of political society: executive power to punish,[30] property,[31] money,[32] war,[33] slavery,[34] the family,[35] religion,[36] education,[37] inheritance,[38] and other elements. Thus Locke's prepolitical society contains all the institutions, some of which are surplusage, for the necessary functioning of a society. He omits, in fact, only one institution— the state, or sovereign governmental group—which is customarily found in societies. That the society he contemplated, from the point of view of the elements he assigned to it, is a possible one, is now entirely free from doubt, inasmuch as many such societies are known to be in existence at the present time and are also known to have been in existence for many generations past. The Pygmies of the Andaman Islands exhibit the characteristics of Locke's society in an even more rudimentary form than Locke was willing to allow.[39]

Yet, in Locke's view, as we have seen above, the state of nature in reality is such an intolerable one that its inhabitants, however free, are willing to quit it. Every man's life, liberty and property are constantly exposed to invasion by others; the rules of justice and equity are only partially obeyed; and his condition generally is full of fears and continual dangers.[40] Men therefore agree with other men to unite into a community for their comfortable, safe and peaceable living, and when they have so consented to make one community a government, they are thereby presently incorporated, and make one body politic, in which the majority have a right to act and conclude the rest.[41]

Thus, political society is established by the freely given

[30] *Treatise*, 11.
[31] *Treatise*, C. v.
[32] *Treatise*, 46 *et seq.*
[33] *Treatise*, C. iii. By definition Locke distinguishes the state of nature from the state of war; but it is clear from his discussion that he envisages the existence of war in his prepolitical society.
[34] *Treatise*, C. iv.
[35] *Treatise*, 77.
[36] *Treatise*, 56 and *passim.*
[37] *Treatise*, 69.
[38] *Treatise*, 72.
[39] Brown, *The Andaman Islanders* (1922).
[40] *Treatise*, 123.
[41] *Treatise*, 95.

consent of the men who are to be members of that society. Every individual has the natural right to be free from any superior power on earth, and not to be under the will or legislative authority of other men, but to have only the law of nature for his will. He may, however, abrogate that right by consenting to form a political society. When he forms that society he surrenders his power to preserve his property—that is, his life, liberty and estate—against the injuries and attempts of other men, and he surrenders also his power to judge of and punish breaches of the law. At the moment of the formation of political society these natural powers pass to it. In Locke's opinion the possession of these powers by a society constitutes the sole criterion by which to judge whether it is politically organized or not. " There, and there only," he writes, " is political society where every one of the members hath quitted this natural power, resigned it up into the hands of the community in all cases that exclude him not from appealing for protection to the law established by it." [42] The formation of a political society excludes the private judgment of every particular member, and the community comes to be umpire, and to possess the power to punish. The community is authorized to make laws for the public good, but its actions cannot be arbitrary; for the law of nature rules in political society also, and men have surrendered to the community not all their natural rights, but only their right of executive power. Thus Locke holds that an absolute monarchy is inconsistent with civil society, and cannot be a form of civil government at all.[43] Locke further separates the compact which forms the political society from the act which creates the kind of government which will rule the society.[44] Finally, when the government, which is a fiduciary power to act for certain ends, violates its trust, the people have the right to save themselves and to constitute a new government.[45]

Two mistaken assumptions are at the basis of Locke's account of the transition from pre-political to political society,

---

[42] *Treatise*, 87. [43] *Treatise*, 90. [44] *Treatise*, 132. [45] *Treatise*, 149.

one that he could predict how men would actually behave in a pre-political society; and the other, that he could determine how men ought to behave at all times and everywhere. As for the first, it was a matter of necessity for Locke to establish that conditions resulting from human behavior in the state of nature would be so unsatisfactory that men would be instigated or compelled to form a political society; otherwise mankind would never abandon their liberty to the extent required to submit to a government. But how men will behave in the theoretical circumstances established for them by Locke is clearly beyond the limits of present knowledge to predict. In its abstract form the problem is analogous to a much simpler one in mathematics which is still unsolved—the problem of three bodies. Newton was able to account for the motions of a single planet revolving about its primary; but the determination for a particular time of the positions and motions of three mutually gravitating bodies when their positions and motions are known for some other time, is still so complex a matter that its full solution has never been accomplished. The social sciences are not even at the stage at which they can handle the problem of two bodies. Two men, sworn enemies, are turned loose on an uninhabited island; one is stupid and weak, the other strong and intelligent. Who can conjecture which will survive? We know further that many communities have existed in an even more rudimentary state of nature than the imaginary one constructed by Locke and were not under any apparent compulsion to form a government. Among such communities the most rudimentary are the Andaman Islanders, the Paiute Shoshone of Utah and Nevada, and the Yahgan of Tierra del Fuego, none of whom possess coercive agencies in Locke's sense, either in the form of institutions or chiefs. Nor need we confine ourselves to the so-called primitive peoples for illustrations of communities functioning for long periods of time in a state of nature. The numerous utopian colonies such as the Shakers, founded in many parts of the United States for the purpose of achieving a communist commonwealth and a life in accordance with literal Christianity, are examples of the fact that some men at least find the state of nature, as Locke defined it, a desirable one. In this respect in fact, the ideal of theoretical communism is precisely the condition which Locke rejected as intolerable. When organizing production anew on the basis of a free and equal association of the producers, Engels insisted, society will banish the whole State-machine to a place which will then be the most proper one for it—the museum of antiquities, side by side with the spinning-wheel and the bronze axe. Thus, the necessity which in Locke drives men from a state of nature to a political society, becomes in Engel's theory the necessity which compels a reversal of the process.

Locke's belief that he could, through reason, frame a set of moral rules which would be universally applicable was put forward in the most emphatic terms. " I doubt not," he wrote, " but from self-evident propositions, by necessary consequences, as uncontestable as those in mathematics, the measures of right and wrong might be made out, to any one that will apply himself with the same indifferency and attention to the one as he does to the other of these sciences." [46] This, of course, is a reversal of the Aristotelian doctrine that ethics is concerned with things which are for the most part so, things which are capable of being otherwise, and that we must not expect from ethics the perfect demonstrations that are possible for a science which, like mathematics, deals with things that are of necessity. Locke gives two examples of his mathematical morality which he thinks are as certain as any demonstration in Euclid: " Where there is no property, there is no injustice " and " No government allows absolute liberty." These statements appear to be merely descriptive propositions, and it is not clear why Locke regarded them as moral rules. However, in the *Reasonableness of Christianity*, Locke took the position that human reason needed the assistance of religion in order to work out a system of ethics. Human reason, he said, never from unquestionable principles made out an entire body of the law of nature. He does not tell us what science would have produced the ideal he had in mind, and Sidgwick [47] conjectures that he would probably have demonstrated from man's nature the body of laws which he had inherited from Grotius and Pufendorf under the name of the law of nature. But as Alexander [48] observes, there is an unresolved problem here: How can propositions which follow from abstract human nature be applicable to or true of a world of concrete men? Moral judgments are relative, and this was one of Locke's reasons, and a correct one, for denying the innateness of moral principles. Nevertheless he clung fast to his belief in the abstract character of moral laws. Yet it implies either that these varying and conflicting judgments are not moral or else that morality is not abstract. There is the further difficulty, that whether a man has been harmed in his life, health, liberty or possessions must always depend upon the facts of the particular case. It is not enough to promulgate a rule that prohibits such harm. It is exactly the problem of fitting the general rules to this particular case which the courts of the land are attempting to determine every day; and that there is a large element of uncertainty in the solutions, the reversals, new trials and dissenting opinions bear witness. Locke's principles are so general that opposite results are fully in accord with them. In one type of society, that of the Shakers, an absolute equality in the distribution of property assists in the realization of the ideal end for which it was organized. In another, that of U.S.S.R., a different method of distribution has the same result. But in both instances no member of the society has been harmed in his possessions.

Nevertheless, in its essence, Locke's method of approach contains a large element of truth. He began by asking a legitimate question, *i. e.*, one for which there exists some possibility of an answer: What is the origin of government? He endeavored to answer the question conjecturally through abstract reasoning, and, from such material as was available in the seventeenth century, empirically. In all this his methods,

[47] Sidgwick, *Methods of Ethics* (1884) 202.   [48] *Locke* (1908) 72.

abstractly considered, do not differ essentially from those employed in such a work as Lowie's *The Origin of the State*, which exhibits the most refined of modern techniques. Locke's error, however, lay in the fact that he lost sight of his objective. His objective, unlike Lowie's, was not to discover the origin of government, but to prove a political theory. He was therefore compelled to introduce elements, such as ethical norms and the idea of necessity, in a manner which distorted his inquiry and led him to erroneous results if judged historically. But that he was on the right track, apart from his political distortions, the most approved methods of contemporary ethnology are ample evidence.

THE RULE OF LAW

At the heart of Locke's theory of civil society was the idea of law. His argument was constructed entirely in terms of law, and the ideal society which he contemplated was organized on the basis of institutions deduced from legal practices. When he came to summarize his view of the state of nature and to make the vital shift from prepolitical to political society his approach was exclusively through legal institutions. The great and chief end of men uniting into commonwealths, and putting themselves under government, is the preservation of their property, he observed.[49] This could not be accomplished in the state of Nature, he thought, because there are many things wanting. First, there is lacking an established, settled, known law, received and allowed by common consent to be the standard of right and wrong, and the common measure to decide all controversies between them. The law of Nature is, of course, plain and intelligible to all rational creatures, but men are biased by their interest, as well as ignorant for lack of study of it, and are not apt to allow it as a law binding on them in the application of it to their particular cases. Secondly, there is lacking a known and indifferent judge, with authority to determine all differences according to the established law. Inasmuch as every

[49] *Treatise*, 124 *et seq.*

one in the state of Nature is both judge and executioner of the law of Nature, and since men are partial to themselves, passion, revenge, negligence and unconcernedness, are apt to carry them too far, and with too much heat in their own cases, and make them too remiss in other men's. Thirdly, there often is lacking power to back and support the sentence when right, and to give it due execution. Those who are offended by any injustice will seldom fail where they are able by force to correct their injustice; constant resistance to injustice makes punishment of resistance dangerous, and frequently destructive to those who attempt to punish it. Thus mankind, notwithstanding all the privileges of the state of Nature, are actually in an ill condition while they remain in it and are quickly driven into a political society. In such a society, which has no other end but the peace, safety, and public good of the people, the legislative or supreme power of the commonwealth is bound to govern by established standing laws, promulgated and known to the people, and not by extemporary decrees; controversies will be decided by indifferent and upright judges in accordance with those laws; and the supreme power of the commonwealth will employ the force of the community at home only in the execution of such laws, or abroad to prevent or redress foreign injuries and secure the community from inroads and invasion.

In his emphasis upon the desirability of the rule of law Locke was in full accord with one of the great traditions of Western thought. Plato had accepted the rule of law as a " second-best " when contrasted with the administration of a philosopher-king; but from the point of view of the government which society in reality was likely to achieve, he regarded law as a necessity, and accordingly made its observance or non-observance the criterion by which all governments should be judged.[50] To Aristotle, the rule of law seemed preferable to that of any individual.[51] This idea was insisted upon by the mediaeval lawyers and political philosophers [52] and found expression in

[50] *Politicus.*
[51] *Politics* 1287 ª 20.
[52] 3 Carlyle, *Mediaeval Political Theory in the West* (1916) 52 *et seq.*

Bracton's doctrine that the law and not the prince was supreme.[53] " There is no king," Bracton said in a famous phrase, " where will rules and not law." But it was Cicero who clearly formulated three of Locke's basic ideas. Law for Cicero was the bond of civil society,[54] the state was a partnership in law,[55] and was actually a large assemblage of people associated by consent under law.[56] However, he expressly repudiates Locke's view that men are impelled to form political societies because of individual weaknesses; they come together and form a civil society because, in Aristotle's words, man is by nature a social animal.[57]

To lawyers and political theorists schooled in legal thinking the idea of the rule of law, of society held together by its bonds, is apt to be especially appealing. But it is well to remember that the theory has been repudiated as the embodiment of evil by thinkers fully as acute as Locke, and as earnestly concerned with the public good. From Godwin to Proudhon, from Spencer to Kropotkin, it has been insisted that government *per se* is evil, and that the human action of men in society is best regulated by the uncoerced power of reason, which alone will produce a just and harmonious social order. In Locke's estimate the character of human nature requires government and law; in that of the philosophical anarchist and extreme individualist it does not. It is on the truth or falsity of Locke's proposition that the entire argument of the two attitudes turns. Both schools have an unlimited faith in the rational nature of man, but one demands anarchy as the ideal solution, and the other a form of limited government.

Law to Locke was a branch of ethics, and laws in their essence were moral rules.[58] Rules of morality, including rules of law, were distinguished from other rules by the fact that they were enforced, or were associated with rewards and punishments. The rules or laws that men generally refer their actions

---

[53] *De Legibus et Consuetudinibus Angliae,* f. 5b.
[54] *De Re Publica* I, 32.
[55] *Ibid.*
[56] *Ibid.,* I, 25.
[57] *Ibid.*
[58] *Essay* II, 28, 6 *et seq.*

to, to judge of their rectitude or obliquity, seemed to Locke to fall into three classes; the divine law, the civil law, and what he termed the law of opinion or reputation, by which he meant the practice of condemning certain actions as evil or praising them as good. By the divine law he meant the law which God has set to the actions of men, whether promulgated to them by the light of nature, or the voice of revelation. He thought there was nobody so brutish as to deny that God has given a rule whereby men should govern themselves. He has a right to promulgate such rules, we are his creatures. He has goodness and wisdom to direct our actions to that which is best; and he has power to enforce it by rewards and punishments, of infinite weight and duration, in another life; for nobody can take us out of his hands. This is the only true touchstone of moral rectitude; and by comparing them to this law it is that men judge of the most considerable moral good or evil of their actions; that is, whether as duties or sins they are likely to procure men happiness or misery from the hands of the Almighty.

Locke held that it would be utterly vain to suppose a rule set to the free actions of man, without annexing to it some enforcement of good and evil to determine his will. We must, therefore, wherever we suppose a law, suppose also some reward or punishment annexed to that law. It would be vain for one intelligent being to set a rule to the actions of another, if he did not have it in his power to reward the compliance with, and punish deviation from, his rule, by some good and evil that is not the natural product and consequence of the action itself. For that, being a natural convenience or inconvenience, would operate of itself without a law. This for Locke is the true nature of all law which, in a phrase anticipatory of Austin, is " properly so called."

The civil law was defined by Locke as the rule set by the commonwealth to the actions of those who belong to it. This law nobody overlooks; the rewards and punishments that enforce it being ready at hand, and suitable to the power that makes it. This is the force of the commonwealth, engaged to protect the lives, liberties and possessions of those who live according to its laws, and has power to take away life, liberty, or goods from him who disobeys; this is the punishment of offenses committed against this law. Locke is here following the imperative theory. Hobbes had held that the civil law is to every subject those rules which the commonwealth has commanded him to make use of for the distinction of right and wrong; that is to say, of what is contrary and not contrary to the rule.[59] Similarly, Pufendorf had held a law to be an enactment by which a superior obliges one subject to him to direct his actions according to the command of the former.[60] It is true that Locke elsewhere refers to law as a " positive command," [61] but at this point he studiously avoided the use of the term.

He did not in truth think of law as a command, but as that which is set up by authority as a rule for the measure of conduct. Law is the standard to which men refer their actions, and by which they judge of their rectitude or pravity, of their criminality or lack of it. In Locke's phrase " law is the rule set to the actions of men," a conception entirely different from Hobbes' view of law as command. One of the important objects of Hobbes' system was to establish an absolute governmental authority. With Locke, his most significant aim was to prove that government must necessarily be limited. " Absolute arbitrary power, or governing without settled standing laws, can neither of them consist with the ends of society and government," he wrote.[62] Positive laws of a society must be made in conformity with the laws of nature,[63] for " the obligations of the law of Nature cease not in society " but stand " as an eternal rule to all men, legislators as well as others." [64] In civil society the legislative power is supreme, " for what can give laws to another must needs be superior to him." [65] In

[59] *Leviathan* (1651) 137.
[60] *Elementa jurisprudentiae universalis* (1672) def. 13.
[61] *Treatise*, 160.
[62] *Treatise*, 137.
[63] *First Treatise*, 92.
[64] *Treatise*, 135.
[65] *Treatise*, 150.

making a distinction between law as a " command " and law as a rule which is " set," Locke seems to be distinguishing between a command and a norm coupled with an enforcement mechanism. In Hobbes' sense law was a direct command from the sovereign power in the State to the citizen to follow a particular course of action; in Locke's system the capacity of the supreme power is fiduciary, and accordingly it establishes merely a pattern to which behavior should conform, and with which is associated rewards and penalties for conformity or infractions. Locke's rules of civil law thus partake no more of the character of commands than do his laws of nature, which are based upon " reason," and which " teach " mankind the rules it is to observe. Austin's accomplishment was to add Locke's phraseology to Hobbes' idea of sovereignty, and thus to arrive at the idea of a law as " a rule laid down for the guidance of an intelligent being by an intelligent being having power over him." [66] In this sense, he observes, law comprises " law set by God to men, and laws set by men to men." Moreover, the essential criterion of a positive law is that it is set by a sovereign power which is absolute.[67] Austin also went back to Hobbes in his terminology by explicitly introducing the idea of command as the essence of law. It is not clear what Austin gained by his repeated employment of the Lockean phrase to describe law as a rule which is " set to men," since in Locke's system the words had an entirely different meaning. Locke's theory of law in fact appears to be an anticipation of the powerful modern continental view which Pound has termed the " threat theory of law " and which is exemplified in Binding, Jellinek, Lévy-Ullmann, Kelsen and others. That theory holds that law in its essence is the establishment of norms by the proper authoritative political power, and the enforcement of threats that, given a defined act or situation, neither qualified as good nor bad, certain legal coercion will follow.[68]

[66] *Province of Jurisprudence Determined* (1832) sec. 2.

[67] *Ibid.*, Lect. VI. Bentham's theory of law as a volition expressed by a sovereign power in the form of a command was an immediate influence upon Austin's terminology; but Bentham's theory itself also took its origin in Hobbes and Locke.

[68] Pound, *Social Control Through Law* (1942) 28.

Locke introduced two additional elements into his conception of law which must not be overlooked—the idea of reward as well as punishment, and the idea of sanction itself. Austin believed that the extension by Locke (in which he was followed by Bentham) of the idea of sanction to rewards produced only confusion and perplexity. He argued that rewards are, indisputably, motives for our compliance with the wishes of others; but to talk of commands and duties as sanctioned or enforced by rewards, or to talk of rewards as obliging or constraining to obedience, is surely a wide departure from the established meaning of the terms. If you expressed a desire that I should render a service, and if you proffered a reward as the motive or inducement to render it, you would scarcely be said to command the service, nor should I, in ordinary language, be obliged to render it. In short, Austin held that I am inclined to comply with the wish of another by the fear of disadvantage or evil. I am also inclined to comply with the wish of another, by the hope of advantage or good, but it is only by the chance of incurring evil that duties are sanctioned or enforced. This argument has not been accepted by Austin's followers in the form in which it is stated. There is the authority of Ulpian that legal obedience is secured " not only by the fear of punishment, but also by the hope of reward." [69] As Jhering pointed out, public recompense had a legal expression at Rome. The general of the army had a right to the triumph, a soldier a right to one or other of the Roman military orders, and in either case the right was one of which the tribunals would take cognizance. In addition, Austin's supporters admit it would be possible to go further than Locke, and claim that a command may be sanctioned by the reverence for an authority as well as the fear of punishment or the hope of recompense. " He alone lives by the Divine Law," said Spinoza, " who loves God not from fear of punishment, or from love of any other object, such as sensual pleasure, fame, or the like; but solely because he has knowledge

[69] Digest I, i, 1. I am here summarizing Brown, *The Austinian Theory of Law* (1920) 8-9n, 342.

of God or is convinced that the knowledge and love of God is the highest good." Divine law as thus defined is a command, not through fear of punishment, but for love and reverence of the Divine Being. Locke's modern followers as represented by Kelsen regard punishment and reward as the two typical sanctions, although in social reality they hold the first to play a far more important role than the second.[70]

Taken strictly, Locke's idea of sanction breaks down when applied to criminal statutes for the violation of which no penalty is provided. Thus a Federal statute makes it a misdemeanor to harbor or conceal any alien not duly admitted by an immigration inspector or not lawfully entitled to enter or to reside within the United States, but imposes no penalty for the offense.[71] So far as the offense of harboring is concerned, a citizen of the United States may commit it without fear of a direct visitation of the State's coercive power. It is possible that power might be exercised indirectly should the occasion arise; but that would be a different case and would fall within the sanction known as nullity. Thus a landlord who harbored an alien might not be permitted to enforce the terms of his lease. In *Cowan* v. *Milbourn* it was held that a contract to let a lecture room for an anti-Christian lecture was void for illegality.[72] Baron Bramwell observed in his judgment: " It is strange there should be so much difficulty in making it understood that a thing might be unlawful, in the sense that the law will not aid it, and yet that the law will not immediately punish it. If that only were unlawful to which a penalty is attached the consequence would be that, inasmuch as no penalty is provided by the law for prostitution, a contract having prostitution for its object would be valid in a court of law." This type of negative punishment is regarded by Austinians as included within his conception of sanction.[73] " I agree with critics of Austin,"

[70] *General Theory of Law and State* (1945) 17.
[71] 8 U. S. C. 144; *U. S.* v. *Niroku Komai,* 286 Fed. 450, 451 (1923); *U. S.* v. *Evans,* 333 U. S. 483 (1948).
[72] (1867) L. R. 2 Ex. 230.
[73] Brown, 9.

Sidgwick writes, " in thinking that the conception of ' command '—implying announcement of wish, together with power and purpose of punishing its violation—can only be applied in an indirect way, and by a process of inference sometimes rather complicated, to many of the rules that make up the aggregate of civil law. Still I think that Austin's conception is always applicable, if it is interpreted as meaning only that the expectation of some penalty, to result from the action or inaction of government or its subordinates, constitutes one motive for conforming to the rules that we call ' laws,' and supplies a broadly distinctive characteristic of such rules: though the penalty (1) may consist only in the enforced payment of damages to a private individual injured by the violation of the rule, or (2) may be merely negative, and consist in the withdrawal from the law-breaker of some governmental protection of his interests to which he would otherwise have been entitled." [74] Whatever may be the case with Austin, it is impossible from Locke's language to determine whether he would have regarded the sanction of nullity as a punishment of sufficient coerciveness to comply with his theory. On one interpretation, however, he would have accepted the sanction of nullity as an additional punishment to be applied in the proper case, and which might or might not arise; but if the prohibition itself provided for no punishment in its particular case then, on his theory, it would not be a law.

By introducing the idea that laws must be enacted solely for the good of society,[75] Locke avoided a difficulty that later was to plague the Austinian dialectic. Austin's idea that the essence of law is command, and that its object therefore is to impose duties, leads to a police conception of the function of law under the restrictions of which the individual moves at his peril. But law is plainly more than a set of police regulations. It is one of the forms of social ordering which allows society to function to maximum effectiveness. This was clearly seen by Locke. " Law, in its true notion, is not so much the

[74] *Elements of Politics* (1891) 22n. [75] *Treatise*, 135, 142.

limitation as the direction of a free and intelligent agent to his proper interest, and prescribes no farther than is for the general good of those under that law. . . . So that however it may be mistaken, the end of law is not to abolish or restrain, but to preserve and enlarge freedom." [76] Where there is no law there is no freedom, he argues with Spinoza. For liberty is to be free from restraint and violence from others, which cannot be where there is no law. A person who is at liberty to dispose and order as he wishes his person, actions, possessions, and his whole property within the allowance of those laws under which he lives, is not subject to the arbitrary will of another, but is freely following his own.

Locke's theory for the remainder of its development passes over into politics. Long ago Joubert pointed out that Locke's theories in general are incomplete. They do not fully embody their subject matter, because Locke did not have that subject matter all in his mind beforehand. As a matter of political theory Locke held that the legislative is the supreme power, " for what can give laws to another must needs be superior to him." [77] However, the legislature in pursuance of its functions must not be arbitrary over the lives and fortunes of the people; it cannot assume to itself a power to rule by extemporary arbitrary decrees, but is bound to dispense justice and decide the rights of the subject by promulgated standing laws, and known authorized judges; it cannot take from any man any part of his property without his own consent; it cannot transfer the power of making laws to any other hands, for it being but a delegated power from the people, they who have it cannot pass it over to others; there are also other limitations.[78] These rules, and much else from Locke beside, were substantially adopted by Blackstone, and thus through him and other sources have had a profound influence on the legal and political thinking of the United States. Today they are all in process of modification, but what will supplant them is not yet clearly discernible.

---

[76] *Treatise*, 57.   [77] *Treatise*, 150.   [78] *Treatise*, C. xi.

Conclusion

Philosophical theories live long after their brains have been knocked out, Leslie Stephen once observed. Locke's theories have displayed this customary vitality. In spite of the attacks made directly upon them and indirectly through criticism of the Austinian position, they survive today in the fundamental thought of one of the most vigorous of the modern schools of jurisprudence. Locke is in fact the propounder of an original and profound theory of law. It has been said that had Locke's mind been more profound, it might have been less influential. Whatever may be the truth in other respects, the depths of his legal analysis have rarely been surpassed by any other philosopher or jurist. His theory of law was incidental to his main argument, and he did not develop it in all, or even in many, of its possible ramifications. But he paused long enough to state its essence, and only today are we aware of the power of the idea he formulated.

CHAPTER XI

HUME

> *Upon the whole, I have always
> considered him, both in his life-
> time, and since his death, as
> approaching as nearly to the idea
> of a perfectly wise and virtuous
> man, as perhaps the nature of
> human frailty will admit.*
>
> Adam Smith

H<small>UME</small>'s theory of law, which he worked out as a part of his general philosophical system, was based in his own eyes on the employment of a new approach to the problem of knowledge. It is easy, he says, for one of judgment and learning to perceive the weak foundation even of those systems of philosophy which have obtained the greatest credit. Principles taken upon trust, consequences lamely deduced from them, want of coherence in the parts, and of evidence in the whole, these are everywhere to be met with in the systems of the most eminent philosophers, and seem to have drawn disgrace upon philosophy itself. This was a view which he had entertained since the age of eighteen. At that time he could find in the books which he read " little more than endless disputes "; he therefore sought for himself, " some new medium by which truth might be established." In philosophy, the thoughts of youth are centered generally upon questions of method, and Hume was no exception. In the spring of 1729 he found the medium which he sought. " There seemed to be opened up to me a new scene of thought," he wrote, " which transported me beyond measure, and made me, with an ardor natural to

---

The editions of Hume's work cited in the following notes are *A Treatise of Human Nature*, edited by L. A. Selby-Bigge, Oxford, 1896 (hereafter referred to as *Treatise*); *An Enquiry concerning the Human Understanding*, and *Enquiry concerning the Principles of Morals*, edited by L. A. Selby-Bigge, Oxford, 1894 (hereafter referred to as *Enquiry*); and *Essays, Moral, Political, and Literary*, Longmans, Green and Co., London, 1875, 2 vols., edited by T. H. Green and T. H. Grose (hereafter referred to as *Essays*). For a contemporary criticism of Hume's legal views see Reid, *Essays on the Active Powers of Man* (1788) 387 *et seq.*

young men, throw up every other pleasure or business to apply entirely to it." Hume proceeded to distinguish himself from most other young men who believed they had found a new way to truth by actually applying his method to the problems which occupied the men of his time. By the age of twenty-six his book was almost complete, and he had written the greatest single work in the whole range of English philosophy.

Hume's " new medium " through which he proposed to redeem philosophy was the experimental method; it was to be focussed upon a new subject matter—human nature—which would result in the establishment of a Science of Man.[1] Hume maintained that all the sciences bear some sort of a relation to human nature; even mathematics and physics are in some measure dependent on the science of man, since they lie under the cognizance of men, and are judged of by their powers and faculties. Other sciences, such as logic, morals, and politics, have a connection with human nature which is more close and intimate.[2] In any event human nature is the only science of man, and up to Hume's time had hitherto been the most neglected.[3] He believed that human nature was not modifiable,[4] and that there was a general course of nature in human actions, as well as in the operations of the sun and the climate. There are also characters peculiar to different nations and particular persons, as well as common to mankind. The knowledge of these characters is founded on the observation of a uniformity in the actions that flow from them; and this uniformity forms the very essence of necessity.[5] Nevertheless, a distinction exists among the various sciences with respect to the certainty of their knowledge. Algebra and arithmetic are the only sciences in which we can carry on a chain of reasoning to any degree of intricacy and yet preserve a perfect exactness and certainty.[6] Knowledge derived from the other sciences is only probable. In the field of the science of man there is a further difficulty which is not present in the natural sciences. We are unable, in

---

[1] *Treatise*, xx.
[2] *Treatise*, xix.
[3] *Treatise*, 273.
[4] *Treatise*, 537.
[5] *Treatise*, 402.
[6] *Treatise*, 71.

estimating human affairs to perform controlled experiments. We must therefore in the science of man " glean up our experiments " from a cautious observation of human life, and take them as they appear in the common course of the world, by men's behavior in company, in affairs, and in their pleasures. Hume thought that when experiments of this kind are judiciously collected and compared, we may hope to establish on them a science, which would not be inferior in certainty, and will be much superior in utility to any other human comprehension.[7]

There are many obscurities in Hume's application of his " new medium," but in substance he appears to be advocating an application of the comparative method to the study of sentiments and institutions. His avowed aim is to deduce general principles from a comparison of particular instances.[8] Those instances are not to be derived one by one from an *experimentum crucis*, but are to be found, as his practice shows, in history. Since Hume cited Bacon as among those who had " begun to put the science of man on a new footing," [9] we may take it that he shared the still popular belief that modern science is inductive, in contrast with the science of past times which was supposed to be deductive. Nevertheless, he drew a valid distinction between knowledge which is certain and that which is probable; or in other words, between inferences which are necessary and those which are probable. It is true as contemporary logic has shown, that the evidence for universal propositions which are concerned with matters of fact can never be more than probable. But the crucial question which arises when we apply Hume's method to social phenomena is: How probable is the universal proposition which is constructed by this method? From the vast range of social data which history offers us it is a poor philosopher who cannot construct a reasonable number of propositions to exemplify the theory to which he is wedded. In Hume's hands the comparative method suffered from this rudimentary weakness. But his insight trans-

---

[7] *Treatise*, xxiii.   [8] *Enquiry*, 174.   [9] *Treatise*, xxi.

cended his method, and he was able to arrive at a view of both society and law which contains many elements that are at the foundation of much of today's social and legal speculation.

JUSTICE

Hume's posthumous fame is founded to a considerable degree on his analysis of the idea of causation. But in the scheme of the *Treatise* the idea of justice occupies as important a place as that of causation and is no less extensively treated. Since his day philosophy, for the most part, has abandoned any interest in the subject matter to which the idea of justice is usually attached, and his examination of the idea has not received a consideration which at all approaches the attention paid to his analysis of causation. His conclusions with respect to the idea of causation are held to be of great significance in philosophical thought; his final determination of the meaning of justice is no less significant, though scarcely recognized, for the understanding of social and legal phenomena. It is of special concern to the student of jurisprudence since, unlike the theory of justice propounded in Plato's *Republic*, it is a theory of legal justice as distinguished from an ethical one.

It was Hume's central contention that " reason is, and ought only to be the slave of the passions, and can never pretend to any other office than to serve and obey them." [10] From this doctrine he proceeded to prove that moral distinctions are not derived from reason. He argued that reason is concerned with the discovery of truth or falsehood, which he held to consist in an agreement or disagreement either with respect to the real relations of ideas, or with respect to real existence and matter of fact. Whatever, therefore, is not susceptible to this agreement or disagreement is incapable of being true or false, and can never be an object of our reason. Now it is plain that our passions, volitions and actions cannot fulfill this condition, since they are original data, complete in themselves and imply

[10] *Treatise*, 415.

no reference to other passions, volitions and actions. It is impossible therefore to pronounce them either true or false and to be either contrary or conformable to reason. From this argument Hume concluded that actions do not derive their merit from their conformity to reason; and that as reason can never immediately prevent or produce any action by contradicting or approving of it, it cannot be the source of moral good and evil, inasmuch as the application of value terms to action possesses such an influence.[11] Hume's attempted syllogism here may be defective, but his point at least is clear.

Moral distinctions, therefore, are derived in Hume's view, from a moral sense. This is the sense which causes us to feel satisfaction in the contemplation of virtue, and uneasiness in the presence of vice.[12] But is it possible to carry the analysis further and determine what acts upon the moral sense to cause it to manifest emotions of approval? Hume answers that approval is bestowed upon whatever is *useful* to its possessor or to others, or upon whatever is *immediately agreeable* to its possessor or to others.[13] This was the part of the *Treatise* which caused Bentham [14] when he read it to exclaim, " I felt as if scales had fallen from my eyes. . . . That the foundations of all *virtue* are laid in utility, is there demonstrated, after a few exceptions made, with the strongest evidence: but I see not, any more than Helvétius saw, what need there was for the exceptions." At this point Hume found it necessary to assume the existence of another principle. The emotion of approval is a general one, and is not confined to the person involved; it is extended to the presence of happiness wherever located. We frequently bestow praise on virtuous actions, Hume observes, performed in very distant ages and remote countries, where the utmost subtlety of imagination would not discover any appearance of self-interest, or find any connection of our present happiness and security with events so widely separated from us.[15] Hume accounts for the universality of moral approbation

---

[11] *Treatise*, 458.
[12] *Treatise*, 471.
[13] *Enquiry*, 268.

[14] *Fragment on Government* (Footnote).
[15] *Enquiry*, 215-216.

on the basis of what he terms the principle of benevolence. The notion of morals implies some sentiment common to all mankind, he writes, which recommends the same object to general approbation, and makes every man, or most men, agree in the same opinion or decision concerning it. It also implies some sentiment, so universal and comprehensive as to extend to all mankind, and render the actions and conduct, even of remote persons, an object of applause or censure, according as they agree or disagree with that rule of right which is established. Hume insisted that these two requisite circumstances belong alone to the sentiment of humanity or benevolence.[16] Thus Hume arrives at the existence of this sentiment in accordance with his empirical method. Men in fact do bestow their approval upon conduct which is agreeable to others, and, hence, men are benevolent.

With this argument as a background Hume takes up the discussion of the idea of justice, which in his system serves both an ethical and a sociological function. In ethics, since he has asserted that what is approved is pleasant or promotes human happiness, he must account for the fact that in adhering to certain standards we not infrequently follow a course which seems unpleasant to ourselves or to others. Sociologically, he had to determine whether the principle of benevolence was sufficient to account for the functioning of society, or whether fully to explain its operations some additional elements were necessary.

Hume began by observing that the social virtues of humanity and benevolence operate chiefly in particular cases, not as part of any system, and with no view to the consequences resulting from the concurrence, imitation or example of others. A parent flies to the assistance of his child, transported by the sympathy which actuates him and without reflection on the sentiments or the rest of mankind in like circumstances. In such cases the motivating actions contemplate a single individual object, and pursue the safety or happiness alone of the person, loved and

[16] *Enquiry,* 272.

esteemed. This is sufficient to satisfy the activating impulses. And as the good, resulting from their benign influence, is in itself complete and entire, it also excites the moral sentiment of approbation, without any consideration of further consequences. On the contrary the action of the individual who stands alone in the practice of beneficence is enhanced in value in our eyes, and joins the praise of rarity and novelty to its other merits.[17]

But this is not the case with justice. As a social virtue it is highly useful, or indeed absolutely necessary to the well-being of mankind; but the benefit resulting from it is not the consequence of every individual single act. It arises from the whole scheme or system concurred in by the whole or greater part of society. General peace and order are the attendants of justice; but a particular regard to the particular right of one individual citizen may frequently, considered in itself, be productive of pernicious consequences. Riches, inherited by a bad man from his parents may be an instrument of mischief, and the right of inheritance in that case would be hurtful.[18] Thus a single act of justice is frequently contrary to public interest; and were it to stand alone, without being followed by other acts, may, in itself be very prejudicial to society.[19] But however single acts of justice may be contrary to public or private interest, it is certain that the whole plan or scheme of which justice is a part, is highly conducive, or indeed absolutely requisite, both to the support of society, and the well-being of every individual. It is necessary that society be regulated by general inflexible rules,[20] and exceptions should not be made in hard cases, otherwise the utility of the whole system will disappear. Such rules as are adopted are intended as best may be to serve the public interest; but it is impossible for them to prevent all particular hardships, or make beneficial consequences result from every individual case. It is sufficient, if the whole plan or scheme be necessary to the support of civil society, and if the balance of good, in the main, thereby preponderates much above that of evil.

---

[17] *Enquiry*, 303.　　[18] *Enquiry*, 304.　　[19] *Treatise*, 497.　　[20] *Enquiry*, 305.

Thus Hume takes the position that a legal system to be socially useful must adhere strictly to its rules even at the expense of injustice in individual cases. Aristotle's view, of course, was different. He thought that equity should rectify law where law was defective because of its generality,[21] and his discussion makes it clear that he had in mind both the unprovided case (where the matter for decision is not covered by the law) and the hard case (where the matter is covered but the application of the law would result in an injustice).[22] Hume's argument is addressed to the hard case alone, and his conclusion is the one that has prevailed in the Anglo-American legal system. As early as the fourteenth century the maxim developed that a " mischief " (an injustice in a particular case) would be permitted rather than an " inconvenience " (a departure from the law). Hume's own argument is expressly stated in the sixteenth century by St. Germain, the earliest of the founders of the English equity system: " It is much more provided for in the law of England that hurt nor damage should not come to many than only to one." [23] No other attitude seems consistent with the development of a mature system of law. " A community," Maine observed, " which never hesitated to relax rules of written law whenever they stood in the way of an ideally perfect decision on the facts of particular cases, would only, if it bequeathed any body of judicial principles to posterity, bequeath one consisting of the ideas of right and wrong which happened to be prevalent at the time. Such a jurisprudence would contain no framework to which the more advanced conceptions of subsequent ages could be fitted. It would amount at best to a philosophy marked with the imperfections of the civilization under which it grew up." [24] Nevertheless the problem still remains. A system of law must consist of a body of invariable rules or it will neither grow nor persist; at the same time it must do substantial justice. Perhaps the only feasible solution is the one proposed by Aristotle and

---

[21] *Eth. Nic.* 1557b.
[22] *Rhet.* 1374a-1374b.

[23] *Doctor and Student* I, c. 18.
[24] *Ancient Law (World Classics ed.)* 62.

restated for contempory thought by the Swiss Civil Code of
1907 and various modern jurists: The judge must not sacrifice
the law to do justice in the hard case, but within the " inter-
stitial limits " of precedent, custom, and the judicial process he
possesses an area of discretion which is ample for the requirements of abstract justice.[25]

Hume advances several arguments to support his contention
that public utility is the sole origin of legal justice and the sole
foundation of its merit.[26] He begins by imagining four situations in which justice would be totally useless, and he then
attempts to show that its essence is thereby totally destroyed
and its obligation upon mankind suspended. (a) Let us suppose that nature has bestowed on the human race a complete
abundance of external conveniences so that every individual
finds himself fully provided with all that his most voracious
appetite can want. For what purpose make a partition of
goods, Hume asks, where every one has already more than
enough? Why give rise to property, where there cannot possibly
be any injury? Why call this object *mine*, when upon the
seizing of it by another, I need but stretch out my hand to
possess myself to what is equally valuable? Justice, in that
case, being totally useless, would be an idle ceremonial, and
could never possibly have a place in the catalogue of virtues.
However, little reflection is needed to show us that this particular argument is without merit. Property is valued because
it satisfies some need; but what is desired by a particular individual is not determined alone by its scarcity. Sentiment,
religious ideas, aesthetic appreciation, and other factors all
enter into the valuing process. The possessor of a family
heirloom will not exchange it for a similar article in better
condition and of greater monetary worth. A Melanesian who
is within the *Kula* exchange places a high value upon his shell
necklace and armshell, although similar shells are available

---

[25] Aristotle, *Rhet.* 1375b, would limit the application of equity to well defined
classes of cases, *e. g.* mistakes and accidents. For the present day view see Cardozo
The Nature of the Judicial Process (1922) Lecture III. The provision of the Swiss
Civil Code of 1907 is quoted by Cardozo, *op. cit.* 140.

[26] *Enquiry*, 183 *et seq.*

everywhere and for the mere appropriation. He values them because, like many of our collections of crown jewels which are ugly and even tawdry, they are enmeshed in a web of historic sentimentalism.[27]   (b) Hume reverses his supposition and imagines a society where there is such a want of all common necessaries that the utmost frugality and industry cannot preserve the greater number from perishing, and the whole from extreme misery. He believed that in such a case the strict laws of justice would be suspended, and give place to the stronger motives of necessity and self-preservation. Is it any crime after a shipwreck, he asks, to seize whatever means or instruments of safety one can lay hold of, without regard to former limitations of property? This same case was put by Cicero and answered by him the other way;[28] it was also determined adversely to Hume by an American court.[29] Here again other considerations than mere utility are determinative of the question. In the American case a sailor in charge of a foundering long boat caused a certain number of men to be put overboard to keep the vessel afloat. He was convicted on the theory that selection by lot was the only proper method. In this case utility did not enter, and abstract justice alone was insisted upon, a rule which it does not appear ethically possible to have otherwise.   (c) Hume assumes a supply of goods as at present, yet all men moved by perfect benevolence. Every man, upon this supposition, being a second self to another, would trust all his interests to the discretion of every man, without jealousy, partition or distinction. The whole human race would form only one family, where all would be in common, and be used freely, without regard to property; but cautiously too, with an entire regard to the necessities of each individual, as if our own interests were most intimately concerned. This example, however, does not prove that there would be no system of legal justice established, but only that the legal justice which is implied would be self-executing.   (d) Finally, Hume assumes

[27] Malinowski, *Argonauts of the Western Pacific* (1922) 89, 502.
[28] *de Officiis* III, 90.
[29] *U. S.* v. *Holmes*, 1 Wall Jr. 1 (1842).

a state of complete anarchy, the *bellum omnium contra omnes* of Hobbes. In such case, a virtuous man's particular regard to justice being no longer of use to his own safety or that of others, he must consult the dictates of self-preservation alone, without concern for those who no longer merit his care and attention. Of course an individual present in a community in which no system of legal justice obtains cannot conform to what is nonexistent. But in the ethical sphere, where Hume seems to place his argument in this instance, the possibility of the operation of justice is not eliminated by the example. It seems to be implied in the case Hume puts that conduct which exceeds the " dictates of self-preservation " would be unjust, as in the wanton killing of innocent children. This same principle is recognized in the Anglo-American legal system. A criminal has fewer rights than an innocent man, but he nevertheless is accorded some measure of protection by the law. A man in danger of his life at the hands of a criminal may use no greater violence in defense of his person than is necessary to protect himself.

Hume argued that the common situation of society is a medium amidst all these extremes.[30] Hence the ideas of property become necessary in all civil society; hence justice derives its usefulness to the public; hence alone arises its merit and moral obligation. Once the laws of justice have been fixed by the views of general utility the harm which results to any individual from a violation of them is a source of the blame which attends every wrong. A violation of the laws of justice is a wrong to the individual because it disappoints expectations which the rules allow; it is also a public wrong because it is a violation of the general rules of equity.[31]

If, Hume asserts, we do not accept the theory that justice arises from its tendency to promote public utility and to support civil society, we must then take the position that justice arises from a simple original instinct.[32] That being so, it follows that property, which is the object of justice, is also

---

[30] *Enquiry*, 188.   [31] *Enquiry*, 310.   [32] *Enquiry*, 201.

distinguished by a simple original instinct. But the rules of property are so infinitely complex we must assume ten thousand different instincts to account for them. A hundred volumes of law and a thousand volumes of commentators have not been found sufficient to account for the ideas involved in the concept of property. Does nature, Hume asks, whose instincts in men are all simple, embrace such complicated ideas, and create a rational creature, without trusting anything to the operation of his reason? Furthermore, where will we draw the line? Have we original innate ideas of praetors and chancellors and juries? Is it not clear that these ideas arise merely from the necessities of human society? In fact, however various may be the particular rules of law, in their chief outlines there is a fair regularity, because the purposes to which they tend are everywhere exactly similar. In like manner, all houses have a roof and walls though diversified in their shape, figure and materials. Thus Hume argues, utility is the only principle that accounts for both identity and diversity. At the present day the ideas of a property instinct, and even of a legal instinct are once again to the fore; but we may accept Hume's arguments as still unanswered, at least until the idea of instinct itself is assigned some intelligible meaning. Thus McDougall,[33] who conceives of an instinct as an inherited or innate psycho-physical disposition which determines its possessor to perform a specific action in a specific way, accepts the existence of an acquisitive instinct which is accompanied by a feeling of ownership and possession. However, even assuming there is an innate tendency, apparently observable in children, to grasp and to handle objects, it may represent a form of behavior not primary in itself, but merely a type at the service of a more fundamental need such as hunger. If the idea of instinct is understood in the more watered down sense of response of function to environment we are at the beginning again, and the legitimacy of the idea will turn upon the meaning attributed to the terms. Hume himself recognized that perhaps there were further alternatives to

---

[33] *An Introduction to Social Psychology* (15th ed. 1923) 30.

his theory of utility, other than the idea of instinct, although he insisted that his own proposal was the only truly sound one. He suggested that justice may be nothing more than a habit; however, he argued that even in day to day life we have every moment recourse to the principle of utility and ask: What must become of the world, if such practices prevail? How could society subsist under such disorders? [34]

But the real difficulty with Hume's position lies not in his arguments but in his presuppositions. He was impressed with Newton's achievements, and he believed that, like Newton, he had found a principle which had great force in one instance, and that he was therefore entitled to ascribe to it a like force in all similar instances.[35] His analysis took its departure from the basic assumption that society was best analyzed in terms of what promoted its " peace and interest," what was necessary for the " good of mankind." [36] On this assumption it is not difficult to argue that the existence of property rules promotes the happiness of mankind; where it is useless to have such rules none would obtain; therefore legal justice is grounded solely in utility. But if we assume that social analysis should proceed on the basis of a different set of concepts we will arrive at a different answer. If we believe, as is the present day tendency, that the fundamental concept in social science is Power, in the same sense in which Energy is the fundamental concept in physics, we will see property as one of the forms of power, and we will conclude that it is responsible for evil as well as for good, and that like other forms of power it should be tamed.[37] But social science is still far short of the knowledge and certainty achieved by physics; and while it is legitimate to argue for the existence of certain fundamental concepts in its domain none so far have been proposed which in practice have exhibited the systematic force of the basic ideas of the exact sciences. Until we have achieved that level of scientific analysis

[34] *Enquiry*, 203.
[35] *Enquiry*, 204.
[36] *Enquiry*, 192.
[37] Russell, *Power* (1938) 12-13 and *passim;* Cohen, *Law and the Social Order* (1933) 41 *et seq.*

Hume's theory, together with all similar ones, are at the best shots in the dark which later investigation may or may not show to have hit the target.

THE CONVENTIONALITY OF THE RULES OF LAW

In the *Treatise* Hume was at great pains to prove that justice was not a natural but only an artificial virtue, and his editor is of the opinion " it is pretty plain that he meant to be offensive in doing so." [38] It is difficult to perceive on what basis this extraordinary appraisal rests. By the time Hume had come to write the *Enquiry* he was so perplexed by the multitudinous senses of the word " natural " that he was inclined to dismiss the question as " vain " and " verbal "; [39] nevertheless, he did not depart from his position. [40] It is obvious, of course, that Hume was raising one of the oldest problems in the history of jurisprudence, and one upon which he had decided views—whether right was right by nature or only by convention and enactment. From the Sophists to his beloved Cicero and to Hooker the question had been endlessly discussed and it would be fruitless to speculate upon the source which suggested it to his mind. But that he handled the matter with what he felt was the deference due the theological and moral atmosphere of his time is clear from the reservations which he attached to his ultimate conclusion.

Justice according to Hume, is approved because of its utility, and this recognition of its necessity is discovered by reason; [41] but inasmuch in Hume's theory " reason is and ought to be the slave of the passions " the approval we bestow upon justice must be due to something other than reason. Hume therefore raises the question: Why does utility please? [42] We are able through reason to understand the utility of justice in promoting human happiness. What is that to me? [43] Perhaps the

---

[38] *Enquiry*, xxviii. Hobbes previously had argued that the " pacts and covenants " by which the State was held together were " Artificial." *Leviathan* 1.

[39] *Enquiry*, 307.

[40] *Enquiry*, 307 n. 2.

[41] *Enquiry*, 183.

[42] *Enquiry*, 212 *et seq.*

[43] *Enquiry*, 217.

application of justice will result in an increase of general human happiness, but bring only misery to the individual. Hume answers this problem by observing that the ultimate ends of human actions can never, in any case, be accounted for by reason, but recommend themselves entirely to the sentiments and affections of mankind, without any dependence on the intellectual faculties.[44] Reason is not alone sufficient to produce any moral blame or approbation. Utility is only a tendency to a certain end; and were the end totally indifferent to us, we should feel the same indifference towards the means. It is requisite that a sentiment should here display itself, in order to give a preference to the useful above the pernicious tendencies. This sentiment can be no other than a feeling for the happiness of mankind, and a resentment of their misery; since these are the different ends which virtue and vice have a tendency to promote. Here therefore reason instructs us in the several tendencies of actions, and humanity makes a distinction in favor of those which are useful and beneficial.[45] Thus sympathy with the public interest is the source of the moral approbation which attends justice.[46] We begin therefore with the proposition that justice, although an artificial virtue, owes its moral approval to a feeling.

Hume initiated his argument in the usual manner of the period. He began with a quest for the First Origin, and inasmuch as the discovery of that elusive condition defies, in the nature of things, the customary historical analysis, he fell back upon invention. He assumed that man in a solitary condition was ill equipped by nature to secure food, clothes and shelter.[47] It is through society alone that he is able to supply his needs. But in order to form society, it is necessary not only that it be advantageous, but also that men be sensible of its advantages. However, it is impossible, in their wild uncultivated state, that by study and reflection alone, they should ever be able to attain this knowledge. Fortunately another necessity exists which may justly be regarded as the first and original

[44] *Enquiry*, 293.
[45] *Enquiry*, 286.
[46] *Treatise*, 500.
[47] *Treatise*, 485.

principle of human society. This necessity is the sexual drive which unites man and woman and preserves their union until a new tie takes place in their concern for their common offspring. This new concern becomes also a principle of union between the parents and offspring, and forms a more numerous society. In time, custom and habit operate on the impressionable minds of the children, make them sensible of the advantages which they may reap from society, and fashion them by degrees for it.[48]

This view of the origin of society is deceptively plausible and has had many adherents. However, it may be answered on several grounds. If taken in a strict historical sense, it is completely speculative and may therefore be dismissed. If taken as a logical reconstruction, it is inconsistent with many of the facts of ethnology, on the basis of which alternative theories of greater plausibility can be constructed. Thus, as Briffault[49] maintains, the primitive social instincts of humanity, which constitute the bond that knits that primitive social group and actuates its collective mentality, thus affording the conditions of all human mental and social development may not be the sexual instincts; they may be the maternal instincts and the ties of kinship that derive directly from their operation. This hypothesis would account for the fact that in many societies the family group, in the patriarchal sense, does not exist. Finally, if Hume's theory is taken as a sociological concept, the comparable but more complex theory of Aristotle, recently revived by Mead, promises greater usefulness. Man is by nature a social animal, said Aristotle; but he alone of all animals possesses the power of speech[50] which means that nature has fitted him for a social life. He is the best of all animals when perfected, but he can realize perfection only in society; therefore society is philosophically prior to the individual in the sense that the whole is prior to the part; it is also prior in time in the sense that the individual is not

---

[48] *Treatise*, 486.
[49] *The Mothers* (1927) 518.
[50] *Politics* 1253a. Mead, *Mind, Self and Society* (1934) 277 *et seq.*

complete until he becomes a part of it. Without society and the elements it adds to man's personality, he would be either a " beast or a God." As Rousseau was later to remark, one becomes a man by being a citizen.

Hume argued that there are three different species of good of which we are possessed: the internal satisfaction of our minds, the external advantages of our body, and the enjoyment of such possessions as we have acquired by our industry and good fortune.[51] We are perfectly secure in the enjoyment of the first; someone may tear the second from us, but it can be of no advantage to him. The last only is both exposed to the violence of others, and may be transferred without suffering any loss or alteration; at the same time, there is not a sufficient quantity of them to supply every one's desires and necessities. The fact that a society has come into being is not sufficient to protect these goods, the proper care of which is the chief advantage of society. Our natural uncultivated ideas of morality would, in fact, increase the hazards which attend ownership. The remedy, then, is not derived from nature, but from artifice; or more properly speaking, nature provides a remedy through reason for what is irregular in sentiment. For when men, from their early education in society, have become sensible of the infinite advantages that result from it; and when they have observed that the principal disturbance arises from those goods, which Hume calls external, and from their looseness and easy transition from one person to another; they must seek for a remedy, by putting those goods, as far as possible, on the same footing with the fixed and constant advantages of the mind and body. This can be done after no other manner, than by a convention entered into by all the members of the society to bestow stability on the possession of those external goods, and leave everyone in the peaceable enjoyment of what he may acquire. This convention is not of the nature of a promise; for promises themselves arise from human conventions. It is only a general sense of common interest; and this sense all the

[51] *Treatise*, 487.

members of the society express to one another, and it induces them to regulate their conduct by certain rules. Two men who pull the oars of a boat do it by an agreement or convention, although they have never given promises to each other. After the convention is entered into there immediately arise the ideas of justice and injustice; and then those of property, right and obligation.

To avoid giving offense, Hume [52] remarks he must observe, when he denies justice to be a natural virtue, he makes use of the word *natural*, only as opposed to *artificial*. In another sense of the word, as no principle of the human mind is more natural than a sense of virtue, so no virtue is more natural than justice. Mankind is an inventive species; and where an invention is obvious and absolutely necessary, it may as properly be said to be natural as any thing that proceeds immediately from original principles, without the intervention of thought or reflection. However, Hume observes, although the rules of justice are artificial, they are not arbitrary.

Here Hume has set forth what in its elements is the accepted sociological theory of today. He has described the process through which societary control is formed, and he has correctly emphasized the fact that culture traits, such as the rules of law, are all ultimately the product of invention.[53] Translated into contemporary terms, we have first an *emotion* of approval or disapproval in a *particular* case; second, a *judgment* of approval or disapproval constituting a generalization as to the desirability of cases of this type; third, *folkways*, *mores*, and *usages*, informal non-institutionalized embodiments of previously formed judgments of approval or disapproval, but generally understood and commonly accepted as applying to all cases of this *general class*; finally, accepted *institutions*, culminating in *law*, the formal crystallization of the previously formed judgments of approval or disapproval, into *express*

---

[52] *Treatise*, 484.
[53] For a more complete account of these two factors in their relationship to law, see my *Theory of Legal Science* (1941) 26-27 and c. 3.

statutes, with definite penalties for violation.[54] Hume's account
of the formation of the rules of laws is plainly enough the
forerunner of the present day hypothesis. Moreover, he
centered his whole account upon the crucial element—that
rules of law come into existence through the process of invention. They are inherited from one generation to another, and
they are also borrowed from other cultures. But at some
stage they had to be originated, and it was this fact which,
in his insistence upon invention, Hume always kept in view.

The Nature of Law

Nowhere did Hume attempt a formal analysis of the nature
of law, but it is clear from his text that he thought of it as
embracing at least three elements. There was first the general
system of morality, which he termed " equity," that guided the
judges in the decision of cases.[55] Again, he thought of law in
the sense in which jurists now speak of the " legal order "—the
regime which adjusts relations and orders conduct by the
systematic and orderly application of the force of a politically
organized society.[56] Thus he writes, " We are, therefore, to
look upon all the vast apparatus of our government, as having
ultimately no other object or purpose but the distribution of
justice, or in other words, the support of the twelve judges." [57]
Hume's vocabulary is not clear and at times he seems to define
justice as meaning " property." However, for the most part
he treated the two ideas as distinct concepts,[58] and in any event
he was perhaps using the term " property " in the broad sense
employed by Locke and which embraced the individual's rights

---

[54] This is Eubank's summary of the results of investigations by Westermarck,
Hobhouse, Sumner and others. *The Concepts of Sociology* (1932) 249.

[55] *Treatise*, 483, 537-38; *Enquiry*, 188.

[56] Pound, *Social Control through Law* (1942) 40.

[57] 1 *Essays*, (1875) 113; see also *Treatise*, 544. Presumably the reference to the
" twelve judges " is to the twelve common law judges who constituted the common
law judicial system at the time.

[58] *Treatise*, 484 *et seq.*; *Enquiry*, 200-201. Property he defines as anything which
it is lawful for a man, and for him alone, to use, *Enquiry*, 197. See also his denun-
ciation of what he termed the vulgar definition of justice—the constant and
perpetual wish to give each man his due. *Treatise*, 526.

to life, liberty and health. Finally, he thought of law in its customary sense as a body of precepts.[59] Thus Hume distinguished many of the separate ideas which jurists now find in the concept " law."

Political obligation, or submission to authority, was founded by Hume on the interest which all men have in the security and protection afforded by political society.[60] He believed that on the strict observance of what he termed the three fundamental laws of nature—that of the stability of possession, of its transference by consent, and of the performance of promises— depended entirely the peace and security of human society.[61] These laws are antecedent to government and are supposed to impose an obligation before the duty of allegiance to civil magistrates has been thought of.[62] Upon the first establishment of government Hume is willing to admit that it derives its obligation from the three laws of nature, and in particular from the one concerning the performance of promises. Men would naturally promise their first magistrates obedience, and a promise is therefore the original sanction of government, and the source of the first obligation to obedience. Although the rules of justice are sufficient to maintain any society, men soon discover in advanced societies that a further element must be added if the rules are to be observed. They therefore establish government as a new invention to attain their ends; by a more strict execution of justice they preserve the old or procure new advantages. Our civil duties are therefore connected with our natural duties, and the former are chiefly invented for the sake of the latter. Thus the principal object of government is to constrain men to observe the laws of nature. However, the law of nature with respect to the performance of promises is only comprised along with the rest; and its exact observance is to be considered as an effect of the institution of government, and not the obedience to government as an effect of the obliga-

---

[59] *Treatise,* 501 *et seq.; Enquiry,* 192 *et seq.*

[60] *Treatise,* 550; *Enquiry,* 197 n. 1.

[61] *Treatise,* 526.

[62] *Treatise,* 541.

tion of a promise. Although the object of our civil duties is the enforcement of our natural duties, yet the first (in time, not in dignity or force) motive of the invention is nothing but self-interest. But the interest in obeying government is separate from that in the performance of promises, and we must therefore allow a separate obligation. To obey the civil magistrate is requisite to preserve order and concord in society. To perform promises is requisite to beget mutual trust and confidence in the common offices of life. The ends, as well as the means, are perfectly distinct; nor is the one subordinate to the other.[63]

Hume's solution of the problem of why men obey the law is essentially a sociological and not an ethical one. It is also the basis of most later thinking on the subject, which has not contributed an analysis which has taken the question much further. Hume's theory, simply stated, is that society is an advantageous condition, and for society to function properly it is to everyone's advantage to obey the rules that permit the attainment of that end. Contemporary thought would add to this statement, as the program of a sound political theory, the conditions that the rules which the government establishes command obedience by virtue of their quality, and that the formation of the rules be accomplished on the basis of the widest possible participation. The first condition presupposes the establishment of some standard of values which political theory has yet to propose; the second begs the question since participation rarely results in unanimity, and with a situation short of that the fact of the government of the dissenters by the majority must still be accounted for. Other elements than self-interest have been suggested as the basis of obedience—utility, which is merely a generalization of Hume's idea; and habit, which Hume himself allowed for.[64] Hume also admitted the right of revolution on the argument that if interest first produces obedience to government, the obligation to obedience must cease, whenever the interest ceases in any great degree and in a considerable number of instances. That is to say, whenever the civil magistrate carries his oppression so far as to render his authority perfectly intolerable, we are no longer bound to submit to it. The cause ceases; the effect must also cease.[65] However, he rejected as an absurdity the mediaeval doctrine of passive obedience, which had its origin in the right of the Christian minority to resist, at least passively, the actions of an unchristian or heretical authority.[66] We must, he insisted, make allowances for resistance in the more flagrant instances of tyranny and oppression.

In Montesquieu's theory of law Hume found an account which appeared sound to him, and he adopted it in its essential aspects. In general he thought that the authority of civil laws extends, restrains, modifies, and alters the rules of natural justice according to the particular convenience of each community.[67] The laws have, or ought to have, a constant reference to the constitution of government, the manners, the climate, the religion, the commerce, the situation of each society. However, Hume observed that Montesquieu's premises for this conclusion differed from his own. Montesquieu supposed that all right was founded upon certain relations, which was a system, in Hume's opinion, which would never be reconciled with true philosophy. It excluded all sentiment and pretended to found everything on reason; it has therefore, Hume observed, not wanted followers in this philosophic age. He argued that the inference against Montesquieu's basic theory was short and conclusive. Hume admitted that property was dependent on civil laws; civil laws are allowed to have no other object but the interest of society: This therefore must be allowed to be the sole foundation of property and justice, not to mention that our obligation itself to obey the magistrate and his laws is founded on nothing but the interests of society. If our ideas of justice are not in accord with those of the civil law, this is a confirmation, he insists, of his theory. A civil law which is

---

[65] *Treatise,* 551-553.

[66] For the doctrine, see Kern, *Kingship and Law in the Middle Ages* (1939) 97 *et seq.*

[67] *Enquiry,* 196.

against the interest of society, loses all its authority, and men judge by the ideas of natural justice which are conformable to those interests. Civil laws also sometimes, for useful purposes, require a ceremony or form to a deed; and where the formality is not observed, the legal consequences may be contrary to justice; but one who takes advantage of such chicanery is not commonly regarded as an honest man. Thus, the interests of society require that contracts be fulfilled; and there is not, Hume thought, a surer material article either of natural or civil justice; but the omission of a trifling circumstance will often, by law, invalidate a contract, *in foro humano,* but not *in foro conscientiae.* In these cases the magistrate is supposed only to withdraw his power of enforcing the right, not to have altered the right. Where his intention extends to the right, and is conformable to the interests of society, it never fails to alter the right—a clear proof, Hume believed, of the origin of justice and property as he had expounded it.

Possession and Property

Hume recognized that the general rule that possession must be stable, although not only useful but even absolutely necessary as he thought to human society, was a formula of too great generality to serve any practical purpose.[68] He therefore proposed to find a method by which we may distinguish what particular goods are to be assigned to each person, while the rest of mankind are excluded from their possession and enjoyment.

It is obvious, he thought, that the reasons which modify the general rule of stability are not derived from any utility or advantage which either the particular person or the public may reap from his enjoyment of any particular goods, beyond what would result from the possession of them by any other person. As a general rule, no doubt it is better that everyone is possessed of what is most suitable to him and proper for his use; but this relation of fitness may be common to several at once,

[68] *Treatise,* 501.

and men are so partial and passionate in disputes involving property that such a rule would be incompatible with the peace of human society. The general rule of stability is not applied therefore by particular judgments, but by other inflexible general rules. When society is first established Hume assumes that property would be assigned to its present possessor. But his real search is for the rules which control the disposition of property after society is once established. The most important of these he found in the ideas of occupation, prescription, accession, and succession. Here he was influenced by his reading of Roman law.[69] Property he defined as such a relation between a person and an object as permits him, but forbids any other, the free use and possession of it, without the laws of justice and moral equity.[70]

Men are unwilling, Hume observed, to leave property in suspense, even for the shortest time, inasmuch as it would open the door to violence and disorder. Thus we have the rule that property belongs to him who first possesses or occupies it; further, if this rule were not recognized there would be no color of reason to assign property to any succeeding possession. Locke's labor theory had held that everyone has a property in his own labor, and when he joins that labor to anything, it gives him the property of the whole. Hume pointed out that there are several kinds of occupation where we cannot be said to join our labor to the object we acquire, as when we possess a meadow by grazing our cattle upon it. Further, the labor theory accounts for the problem by means of accession, which is taking a needless circuit. Finally, we cannot be said to join our labor in anything but in a figurative sense. Properly speaking, we only make an alteration on it by our labor. This joins a relation between us and the object; and then arises the property, in accordance with Hume's principles.[71]

If property belongs to him who first possesses it, what do

---

[69] For the little that is known of Hume's legal studies as a youth see Greig, *David Hume* (1931) 64 *et seq.*

[70] *Treatise,* 310. *Cf. Enquiry,* 197.

[71] *Treatise,* 505.

we mean by possession? Few, if any, questions have been more discussed by writers on jurisprudence, and neither the Roman nor the English law ever worked out an adequate theory.[72] In modern times the point of departure for speculation on the subject is Kant's theory of acquisition,[73] which in Savigny's hands became the doctrine that possession means physical control, with the intention to hold as one's own—detention with *animus habendi* or *domini*. Jhering, who rejected the idea of *animus domini* defined possession as the externals of ownership. As Buckland says, " a man possesses who is in relation to the thing in the position in which an owner of such things ordinarily is, the *animus* needed being merely an intelligent consciousness of the fact, so that a *furiosus* cannot acquire possession." [74] Savigny thought, as did Hume, that possession was protected in the interest of a public peace, a view which Ihering rejected in favor of the idea that it was an outwork of ownership. There is much in Hume that anticipates this great nineteenth century debate, but the extent to which his influence was a direct one is indeterminable. At all events, his ultimate view is very much the present day one, namely, that the problem is insoluble, a position which, unlike that of contemporary theorists, he attempted to demonstrate.

We are said to be in possession of anything, Hume maintained, not only when we immediately touch it, but also when we are so situated with respect to it, as to have it in our power to use it; and may move, alter, or destroy it, according to our present pleasure or advantage. It follows that this relation is a species of cause and effect; and as property is nothing but a stable possession, derived from the rules of justice or the conventions of men, it is to be considered as the same species of relation. However, as the power of using any object becomes more or less certain according as the interruptions we may meet with are more or less probable; and as this probability may in-

---

[72] Buckland and McNair, *Roman Law and Common Law* (1936) 65.

[73] Holmes, *The Common Law* (1881) 206.

[74] *Textbook of Roman Law* (1921) 200. For the references to Savigny and Ihering see Buckland, *ibid.*

crease by insensible degrees, it is impossible to determine when possession begins or ends. Nor is there any certain standard by which we can decide such controversies. A wild boar that falls into our snares is deemed to be in our possession, if it is impossible for him to escape. But what do we mean by impossible? How is the impossibility separated from the improbability? And how would that be distinguished exactly from a probability? Hume concluded that we would never find a solution for these difficulties in reason, public interest or the imagination.[75] As for the latter, the qualities which operate upon it run so insensibly and gradually into each other that it is impossible to give them any precise bounds. The same power and proximity will be deemed possession in one case but not in another. A person who has hunted a hare until it falls from exhaustion would look upon it as an injustice for another to rush in before him and seize his prey.[76] But the same person, advancing to pluck an apple that hangs within his reach, has no reason to complain if another, more alert, passes him, and takes possession. Not only may disputes arise concerning the real existence of property and possession, but also concerning their extent. These disputes, Hume thought, are often susceptible of no decision, or can be decided by no other faculty than the imagination. A person who lands on the shore of a small island that is deserted and uncultivated is deemed its possessor from the very first moment, and acquires the property of the whole; because, Hume thought, the object is there bounded and circumscribed in the fancy, and at the same time is proportioned to the new possessor. The same person landing on a deserted island as large as Great Britain extends his property no farther than his immediate possession; but a numerous colony is regarded as the proprietors of the whole from the instant of the debarkment.

When the title of first possession becomes obscure through the passage of time, long possession or prescription will give a

---

[75] *Treatise,* 506.
[76] *Cf. Pierson* v. *Post,* 3 Caines (N.Y.) 175 (1805).

person property in anything he enjoys. Nevertheless it is certain that however everything be produced in time, there is nothing real that is produced by time; it follows, that property being produced by time, is not anything real in the objects, but is the offspring of the sentiments, on which alone time is found to have any influence. We acquire the property of objects by accession, when they are connected in an intimate manner with objects that are our property, and at the same time are inferior to them. Thus the fruits of our garden, the offspring of our cattle, are all held to be our property, even before possession. This source of property, Hume thought, could never be explained except through the imagination. The right of succession he justified on the ground of the presumed consent of the parent or near relation, and from the general interest of mankind which requires that men's possessions should pass to those who are dearest to them, in order to render them more industrious and frugal. Plain utility and interest also require a mutual exchange and commerce; for this reason the transference of property by consent is founded on a law of nature. But the civil laws, and perhaps also the law of nature, commonly require delivery or a sensible transference of the object as a necessary circumstance in the transference of property. This is so because it aids the imagination in conceiving the transference of property; we take the sensible object and actually transfer its possession to the person on whom we would bestow the property. The supposed resemblance of the actions, and the presence of this sensible delivery, deceive the mind and make it fancy that it conceives the mysterious transition of the property. Men have even invented a symbolical delivery to satisfy the fancy, where the real one is impracticable. Thus the presentation of the keys of a granary is understood to be the delivery of the corn contained in it.[77]

In all this Hume has attempted no more than the sketch of a general theory of property justified by a psychological analysis. His basic ideas and his examples, with unimportant

[77] *Treatise*, 515.

exceptions, are drawn from Roman law, but in its detail his account lacks the richness of the Roman theory with its endless putting of cases to test the general rule. In some of his insights, as in his theory of possession and in his conception of property as being in essence a relation, he nevertheless anticipated the thought of a much later day.

CONCLUSION

Hume was a pioneer in the attempt to explain law in psychological terms. He began with the fundamental assumption that all our ideas are derived from impressions, and he attempted to show that morality was founded on feeling and not reason. All ethical ideas, including that of justice, are based on a feeling, he thought, of advantage to the person or to others. Justice in particular can be understood only on the basis of sympathy for the welfare of human life generally. Hume's psychology of an endless series of disparate experiences was a force until the passing of the association psychology in the middle of the nineteenth century; but his idea that law should be explained in psychological terms is once again to the fore. Its value is apparent in Tarde's studies, and in Ward's exploration of the psychic factors of civilization. We are told today that every important legal problem is at bottom a psychological problem, and that the rapid rise of psychology in recent years supplies a background for a natural science of society which has hitherto been lacking.[78] No doubt Hume would have found these observations gratifying. But it is well to remember that he was careful to point out there were limits to the method of psychology so far as truth or falsity were concerned. Jurisprudence differed from all the other sciences, he thought, in that in many of its nicer questions there cannot properly be said to be truth or falsehood on either side.[79] The choice afforded the judge turns more often on taste and imagination than on argument.

[78] Robinson, *Law and the Lawyers* (1935) 49, 51.
[79] *Enquiry*, 308.

Chapter XII

KANT

> *There is always something about*
> *Kant, as about Luther, which*
> *reminds one of a monk, who has*
> *indeed quitted his cloister, but*
> *who can never quite rid himself*
> *of its traces.*
>
> Schiller

IN THE realm of legal speculation Kant's thought was no less influential than it was in philosophy generally. Through Austin, who studied his works in Germany, and also directly, he affected the current of nineteenth century English legal theory; on the Continent during the same period the power he exerted gave him a position of unique eminence. In the history of legal philosophy only one or two other thinkers can be placed beside him in the ascendency which he has exercised over the study of jurisprudence. If the aim which he held before himself had been fully realized the explanation of his influence could be accounted for on that ground alone. In the Preface to the *Critique of Pure Reason* he asserted the extraordinary claim " I have made completeness my chief aim, and I venture to assert that there is not a single metaphysical problem which has not been solved, or for the solution of which the key at least has not been supplied "; a similar claim, though more guardedly put, is made for his work in jurisprudence in the Preface to his *Philosophy of Law*. He there states, by

Kant's principal work in the philosophy of law is his *Metaphysische Anfangsgründe der Rechtslehre* (2nd ed. 1798), translated by Hastie as *The Philosophy of Law* (1887) and cited here as *P. L.* Kant's other legal works—*Idee zu einer allgemeinen Geschichte in weltbürglicher Absicht* (1784), *Über den Gemeinspruch: Das mag in der Theorie richtig sein, taugt aber nicht für die Praxis* (1793), and *Zum ewigen Frieden, ein philosophischer Entwurf* (1795)—were also translated by Hastie as *Kant's Principles of Politics* (1891), and are cited here as *P.P.* The best exposition of Kant's legal philosophy in English is 2 Caird, *The Critical Philosophy of Immanuel Kant* (1889) 315 *et seq.*; the best critical analysis is Cohen, *A Critique of Kant's Philosophy of Law* in *The Heritage of Kant* (1939) ed. Whitney and Bowers.

means of indirect assertions, that he has put forward a rational system of jurisprudence which is complete and comprehensive. That it to say, the system is complete from the point of view of principle; Kant expressly disclaims any suggestion that he made a practical application of the system to all cases. In its structure the *Philosophy of Law* follows the scheme of the Roman jurists, and no doubt Kant thought that this method afforded him an external measure of the persistent problems of law. It did not bring him to completeness, since even the vast experience that was classified in the Roman system failed by much to exhaust the legal possibilities of human conduct. However, it provided him with a view of many problems of universal currency and he was able to perceive the obstacles which must be overcome in the construction of a general theory of law. But his influence was due even more to the fact that he seized the principal threads of eighteenth century thought, particularly those which culminated in the French Revolution, and wove them into a pattern to which the mind of the nineteenth century was peculiarly sympathetic. He accepted the view of Aristotle that man was social by nature; he also believed with Hobbes that man was antisocial. Kant endeavored to find a place for these and related ideas, as they found expression in Rousseau and others, in a rational theory of society. In the view of the present day world his efforts led to some curious conclusions; but they also directed him to conclusions which are still unshaken.

Kant's theory of law is an application to the domain of jurisprudence of his general system of ethics. His declared aim was to establish a metaphysic of morality entirely divorced from empirical psychology, theology, physics and the hyperphysical. If such a system were constructed it would dispose of the eighteenth century dispute whether man as a natural being was guided by benevolent or selfish impulses, or whether as a rational being he was governed by the idea of perfection. His solution is as follows. " Nothing," he wrote, " can possibly be conceived in the world, or even out of it, which can

be called good without qualification, except a Good Will." [1]
Through the will we reach reality, a goal which the senses
and the intellect cannot achieve; they are confined to the world
of experience and thus we can never know " things-in-them-
selves," but only the appearance of things under *a priori* forms
of reason. However, when we will we are not contemplating
phenomena under the inescapable limitations of experience.
The rational will has freedom to legislate to itself; it is, in
Kant's phrase, autonomous. Thus the will takes us beyond
experience into the realm of value. Man, as a part of the
phenomenal world, is subject to the laws of cause and effect,
and in that world things merely are; it is impossible at that
level to talk of moral values and rational freedom. In the
inner world of the moral Self, however, we are in the presence
of the idea of " ought," and this idea has no meaning in the
empirical realm. "Ought," Kant says, " expresses a kind of
necessity which is found nowhere else in the whole of nature.
We cannot say that anything in nature *ought to be* other than
what it actually is. When we have the course of nature alone
in view, ' ought ' has no meaning whatever. It is just as absurd
to ask what ought to happen in the natural world as to ask
what properties a circle ought to have." [2] But when we act
we must determine if our choice is one that we ought to make,
and in making that choice we ought not to act in accordance
with our feelings, but upon a principle which we would admit
as universally valid. Objective principles of this kind, which
are obligatory for the will, Kant called commands, and the
formula of the command he called an imperative. All imperatives are either hypothetical or categorical. A hypothetical imperative is a principle of conduct on which we act, not because
of its intrinsic merits, but because of something else, such as an
end which we wish to achieve. A categorical imperative we
accept for its own merits and not as a means to something else.
Thus he arrived at his famous conception that there is only

---

[1] *Critique of Practical Reason* (1898, trans. Abbott) 9.
[2] *Critique of Pure Reason* (1933, trans. Smith) 472-473.

one categorical imperative, namely: Act only on that maxim which will enable you at the same time to will that it be a universal law. Kant followed this with a second formula to determine the end of the moral law: Act so that in your own person as well as in the person of every other you are treating mankind also as an end, never merely as a means.

Kant's theory of law is also closely connected with his view of history. He held that whatever may be the metaphysical status of the freedom of the will, the manifestations of the will in human actions are determined like all other external events by universal natural laws.[3] It may be hoped, therefore, that when these manifestations are examined on the great scale of universal history, a pattern will be discovered in their movements; in this way, what appears to be tangled and un-regulated in the case of individuals, will be recognized in the history of the whole species as a continually advancing, though slow, development of the species' original capacities and endowments. Individual men, and even nations, in pursuing their own purposes are advancing unconsciously under the guidance of a purpose of Nature which is unknown to them; furthermore, if the purpose were known to them it might be held to be of no significance. Philosophy recognizes that no rational conscious purpose can be supposed to determine the actions of mankind as a whole; but philosophy can attempt to discover if there is a universal purpose of Nature in the paradoxical movements of humanity—that is to say, whether a history of creatures who proceed without a plan of their own may nevertheless be possible according to a determinate plan of Nature. Kant stated that if he found such a clue to history, he was prepared to leave the development of the idea to some future Kepler or Newton. Kant's argument is apt to appear obscured by the eighteenth century optimism and the Greek teleology which dominate it; but he is actually posing a problem which, as the labors of Spengler, Toynbee and others bear witness, still appears to be a legitimate one, *i. e.*, is capable of a solution. In its simplest

[3] *P. P. 3 et seq.*

terms the task is to ascertain whether the historical process is random or whether it falls into some kind of a pattern, and if the latter, to isolate the determinative elements.

Teleology and the idea that Nature does nothing superfluous are the concepts which dominate Kant's attempt to solve the problem. He holds that all the capacities implanted in a creature by Nature are destined to unfold themselves completely and conformably to their end, in the course of time. In man, as the only rational creature on earth, those natural capacities which are directed towards the use of his reason, can be completely developed only in the species and not in the individual. This is so because reason experiments in a multitude of ways, and the life of an individual is too short for him to learn by himself how to make a complete use of all his natural endowments. Since nature has provided man with reason, he must produce everything out of himself and is not to be guided by instinct, nor instructed by innate knowledge. All his material inventions, all the sources of delight which make life agreeable, including the goodness of his will, must be entirely his own work. The means which nature employs to bring about the development of all the capacities implanted in men, is their mutual antagonism in society, but nature employs this antagonism only so far as it becomes the course of an order among men that is regulated by law. The antisocial side of man's nature is exhibited in his disposition to direct everything merely according to his own desires. Thus arises the wish for honor, power, wealth and rank. Because of this impulse the first real steps are taken from barbarism to civilization. Without those qualities of an antisocial kind, men might have led an Arcadian shepherd life in complete harmony, contentment and mutual love, Kant observes with Rousseau's argument plainly before him; but in that case all their talents would have forever remained hidden. We owe thanks then to Nature for this unsociableness, for this envious jealousy and vanity, for this insatiable desire for possessions and power; without them all the excellent capacities implanted in mankind by Nature would slumber forever undeveloped.

Therefore the greatest practical problem for the human race, to the solution of which it is compelled by nature, is the establishment of a civil society, universally administering right according to law. Kant insisted that in only one type of society could the highest purpose of Nature, which is the development of all her capacities, be attained in the case of mankind. It is the society which possesses the greatest liberty, and which consequently involves a thorough antagonism of its members—with, however, an exact determination and guarantee of the limits of this liberty in order that there may be mutual freedom for all the members. Now Nature also wills, Kant says, that the human race shall attain through itself to this, as to all the other ends for which it was destined. Hence a society in which liberty under external laws may be found combined in the greatest possible degree with irresistible power, or a perfectly just civil constitution, is the highest natural problem, according to Kant, prescribed to the human species. This is so, because Nature can only by means of the solution and fulfillment of this problem, realize her other purposes with our race. Kant believed that this problem is also the most difficult of its kind and that it is the latest to be solved by the human race. Kant insisted that it was not easy to perceive how man could provide for a supreme authority over public justice that would be essentially just, whether such an authority was in a single person or in a group of persons. The highest authority has to be just in itself, and yet administered by a man. Kant indeed thinks that the perfect solution of this problem is impossible. He is certain, however, that any solution is dependent on the problem of the regulation of the external relations between States conformably to law. The same antagonisms which lead to the establishment of a single government are also present, he argued, in the international field and until a great International Federation regulated by law is established the ideal civil society is unrealizable.

Thus social conflict is the clue, in Kant's eyes, to the historical process, and its goal the universal administration of right according to law. Right in the Kantian system comprehends the whole of the conditions under which the voluntary actions of any one person can be harmonized in reality with the voluntary actions of every other person, according to a universal law of freedom.[4] That the historical process can be explained in terms of conflict is an idea that has often been proposed but never proved. Society is in a constant flux, and as Simmel was one of the first to point out, societary phenomena in that aspect are perhaps best interpreted through the concept of reciprocal action. In the hands of contemporary sociologists the idea is seen to consist of four elements—conflict, competition, combination, assimilation—which extend all the way from direct personal antagonism to the degree of cooperation manifested in the formation of a corporation, which involves the creation of a single entity to act for numerous separate personalities. All these elements are important in the social process, and it is conceivably possible that their relative importance may some day be measured; but today we have not the tools for that task. Kant's ideal of right under law has a great appeal, but here again no theory of values yet proposed will enable us to estimate its worth with any reasonable degree of confidence. Aristotle's own teleological method led him to assert that the object of the State was to promote the good life. The Kantian system permits the pursuit of pleasure as the sole goal of the members of society, an end which Aristotle thought fit only for slaves and beasts; Aristotle's system, however, allowed slavery, a condition which Kant condemned as immoral. However defective the ideals of Kant and Aristotle may be as ultimate standards it is significant that both philosophers built their conceptions upon the idea of law. The aim of legislation, Aristotle believed, was to make men good; in Kant's opinion right could not be sustained without the force of law. Such an estimate of the importance of law should be a source of gratification to jurists; but it is well to remember that ethical systems other than legalistic ones are possible in theory.

[4] *P. L.* 45.

On the basis of these general ideas Kant developed his philosophy of law. His purpose was to treat the subject as a system of principles that originate in Reason.[5] He termed his main excursion into jurisprudence *The Metaphysical Principles of the Science of Right*, and he held that although the conception of right was purely rational in origin, it was also applicable to cases presented in experience. Nevertheless he held it was impossible to survey experience in all its details, and the empirical conceptions which embraced those details could not form integral elements of the system itself, but could only be introduced in subordinate observations, and mainly as furnishing examples to illustrate the general principles.

THE GENERAL THEORY

At the basis of Kant's thinking was the belief that we could attain to a knowledge of the principles of human conduct, and that from this science the principles of all positive law could be deduced by judges and legislators.[6] This idea in its essence is not peculiar to Kant, but is the necessary presupposition of all efforts to discover in legal phenomena a system of ordered relationships. Stated simply, it is the attempt to ascertain the first principles of law. We may say that law has no first principles, that as it exhibits itself in society it is haphazard and fundamentally meaningless. In the long run we may be driven to this view. But over against it is the persistent hope that some form of order can be isolated in the multitudinous varieties of the legal process. It is customary to attack the problem in any one of three different ways. A special field of the law, the analysis of which would appear to yield a set of logically coherent principles, is studied by itself with little or no reference to other special fields. Products of this way of attacking the problem are the volumes on such subjects as tort, contract, and

---

[5] *P. L.* 4. Earlier he had expressed the hope that instead of the endless multiplicity of civil laws we should someday be able to fall back on their general principles. He insisted it was only in those principles that we could find the secret which would enable us to simplify legislation. *Critique of Pure Reason* 302.

[6] *P. L.* 43-44.

criminal law. Their point of departure is the root idea of their special field: What is a tort? What is a contract? What is crime? A second way of attacking the problem is found in works on jurisprudence, which attempt to develop the principles underlying all the particular domains of positive law and to unite them in a systematic and non-contradictory manner. Their starting point is the idea of law itself, conceived as broad enough to embrace all its manifestations and at the same time framed with a definiteness that will permit it to be carried out in practical applications. The third way of attacking the problem is found in the investigations which originate in an area beyond the domain of law, but which are nevertheless regarded as containing the principles in accordance with which law is or must be fashioned. Theology, ethics, economics, anthropology, sociology, biology and numerous other areas have all been suggested as such points of departure. It is in this way that Kant, and all the systematic philosophers who have devoted themselves to law, approach the problem.

For the purposes of his jurisprudence Kant began with the idea of right, although the roots of his theory extend back to the heart of his metaphysical system. He saw at once that a solution in terms of the laws of some one country at a particular time would not be a solution of the general problem. He thought it was easy to say that what is right in particular cases is what the laws of a certain place and time may determine; but it is much more difficult to ascertain whether what they have enacted is right in itself, and to lay down a universal criterion by which right and wrong and justice and injustice in general may be recognized. The search for such a criterion must, in the Kantian theory, be conducted in the realm of pure reason and not in the empirical world. Kant agreed that empirical laws may indeed furnish excellent guidance; but a merely empirical system that is void of rational principles is, like the wooden head in the fable of Phaedrus, fine enough in appearance but unfortunately it wants brain.

Kant arrived at his basic conception through the process

of exclusion. As he defined it, the idea of right refers only to the external and practical relations between individuals in so far as their actions as *facts* can have a direct or indirect influence on one another; right does not indicate the relation of the action of an individual to the *wish* or mere desire of another, as in acts of benevolence or of unkindness. It indicates only the relation of his free action to the freedom of action of another; in this reciprocal relation of voluntary actions, the idea of right does not take in account the *matter* willed, in so far as the end which any one may have in view in willing it is concerned. In other words, when the problem of right is involved the question, for example, would not be asked whether a person who purchased goods for his business realized a profit by the transaction or not. Only the *form* of the transaction is taken into account in considering the relation of the mutual acts of will. Furthermore, acts of will are thus regarded only in so far as they are free, and so far as the action of one person harmonizes with the freedom of others, according to a universal law. By these steps Kant thus reached his famous definition of legal right, which was held to consist of the totality of conditions under which the will of one can be harmonized with the will of others according to a universal law of freedom.

There are two objections to Kant's theory that should be noticed. His idea that there is a " law-giving faculty," [7] and his idea that in pure reason alone, altogether apart from experience, we can find the basis of all law, are not proved. In the actual formulation of his theory of right he constantly appeals to experience; and the final statement of his theory signifies little until empiricism discloses its meaning. Furthermore, the theory ignores, or rather fails to meet, the problem of ends. In Kant's theory the social ideal is security of freedom of will to each person limited only by the like freedom of will of all other persons. This formula represents perhaps the ultimate possible statement of the idea of freedom in society. However, notwithstanding Hegel's famous statement that

[7] *P. L.* 13.

history is the history of liberty, different ages and different societies insist upon striving for other ends and even for varying ideals of liberty. From the year 1000 to the year 1500, from the Emperor Henry II to the Emperor Maximilian, the ideal was one of right embodied in law; from 1500 to the French Revolution it was one of force, power and the supremacy of dynasties; from the French Revolution to the present day the ideal has been one of ideas—liberty, nationalism, self-government, among others.[8] Kant's formula would have been unworkable in the achievement of such ends or, if applied, its results we would hold undesirable today. In the medieval period the idea of right was exemplified on a wide scale in private warfare, a practice consistent with Kant's rule, but which we would hold intolerable. In the same period the different classes of society were ruled by different laws and, as Holdsworth[9] observes, "even at the present day, when the equality of all men and women is an accepted political fiction, we find that the law must draw distinctions between different classes and between different professions and trades." The Statutes of Labourers, enacted after the Black Death had eliminated nearly half the population, even in their beneficial provisions were violations of the Kantian rule, *e. g.*, they permitted only the impotent poor to solicit alms. Today we have the application of Kant's standard to the same circumstances. "The law," as Anatole France observed, "in its majestic equality forbids the rich as well as the poor to sleep under bridges, to beg in the streets, and to steal bread." The twentieth century ideal of a welfare state requires the recognition of classes needing special treatment from the legal point of view, as certainly as the medieval ideal demanded it. Further, the rise of vast cities makes the application of Kant's formula impossible. State regulated mono-

---

[8] Stubbs, *Lectures on Medieval and Modern History* (1887) 239 *et seq.*

[9] 2 *Hist. Eng. Law* (1923) 464. Patterson has pointed out that Kant's principle, that a human being should treat both himself and others as an end and not a means, has found expression in the abolition of slavery, and in the hostility of American courts to any legal arrangement which makes possible coerced labor or peonage. See *Pollock* v. *Williams* (1944), 322 U. S. 4; Patterson, *An Introduction to Jurisprudence* (2nd ed. 1946) 182.

polies, such as electric light and telephone companies, which possess exclusive franchises, but whose rates are fixed in the public interest, are impossible in the Kantian system since everyone would have the same right to conduct those businesses. Kant's ideal of freedom is a noble one, but we possess no yardstick to measure it against other ideals equally noble. There is no international state or court, Hegel observed, which passes judgment upon the peoples, and none is possible; the judgment of the nations is found in the fate which awaits them in the process of world-history.[10]

Nevertheless, Kant's formula has proved useful and has exerted an immense influence on nineteenth century legal thinking. At the outset, it eliminated the idea, which was dominant in the eighteenth century, of immutable, eternal natural rights. Next, as Pound has shown, " the metaphysical element was decisive in the doctrine of the historical school. For the idea which it found was the idea of right held by and as formulated by the metaphysical jurists. In fact the historical method in jurisprudence was a historical verification of that idea." [11] Savigny translated the Kantian formula of right into a theory of law which was to prevail for several generations: " Man stands in the midst of the external world, and the most important element in his environment is contact with those who are like him in their nature and destiny. If free beings are to co-exist in such a condition of contact, furthering rather than hindering each other in their development, invisible boundaries must be recognized within which the existence and activity of each individual gains a secure free opportunity. The rules whereby such boundaries are determined and through them this free opportunity is secured are the law." [12] In the view of the thinkers who succeeded Kant the end of the law was visualized as the effort to secure the maximum amount of liberty to each individual. In Herbert Spencer's [13] hands the Kantian rule

[10] Stace, *The Philosophy of Hegel* (1924) 438.
[11] *Interpretations of Legal History* (1923) 23.
[12] 1 *System des heutigen römischen Rechts* (1840) § 52. Quoted, Pound, *op. cit.* 29n.
[13] *Justice* (1891) § 27.

became the celebrated injunction: "Every man is free to do that which he wills provided he infringes not the equal liberty of any other man." As a force the idea in the United States reached what was perhaps its apogee in *Lochner* v. *New York* in which the Supreme Court invalidated a statute establishing hours of labor for bakers. Mr. Justice Holmes, dissenting, quoted Spencer's injunction, remarked that the citizen's liberty was interfered with by school laws, by the Post Office, by every State or municipal institution which takes his money for purposes thought desirable, whether he likes it or not, and denounced the rule as a "shibboleth." To secure the point he then added what has since become one of his most famous aphorisms: "*The Fourteenth Amendment does not enact Mr. Herbert Spencer's Social Statics.*" [14] Holmes' opinion has been termed "the most famous dissent in all legal history." [15] Whether Kant's theory is dead or only stunned it is too early to say; but at least its capacities for concrete application have been fairly tested.

From his conception of right Kant next developed what he termed the Universal Law of Right: "Act externally in such a manner that the free exercise of thy Will may be able to co-exist with the Freedom of all others, according to a universal Law." [16] His argument in support of this law is as follows: Every action is right which in itself, or in the maxim on which it proceeds, is such that it can co-exist along with the Freedom of the Will of each and all in action, according to a universal Law. Kant called this the universal Principle of Right. Hence, I am wronged when any one interferes with actions of mine conducted in accordance with this definition; for such an interference cannot co-exist with Freedom according to a uni-

---

[14] 198 U. S. (1905) 45, 74. Earlier, in *The Path of the Law*, 10 Harv. Law Rev. (1897) 457, Holmes had remarked that Spencer's rule was not "self-evident." Patterson interprets Holmes' "bad man" theory of law as a rejection of the Kantian view that morality depends upon motives. However, he thinks that Kant is not at variance with Holmes in his position that law imposes duties of external conduct motivated by the fear of consequences. *Op. Cit.* note 9 at 186.

[15] Walton Hamilton in *The Constitution Reconsidered* (ed. Read, 1938) 186.

[16] *P. L.* 46.

versal law. However, it cannot be demanded that I make this
universal Principle of Right the maxim of my actions. The freedom of other persons is indifferent to me, even to the extent of
wishing in my heart to infringe it, so long as I do not actually
violate that freedom by my external action. It is here that Kant
makes a sharp distinction between ethics and law. Ethics, as distinguished from law, does impose upon me the obligation to
make the fulfillment of Right a maxim of my conduct. By these
steps Kant thus arrives at his universal law of Right as a rule of
external action. There is no question in Kant's mind that this
law imposes obligation upon me; but it does not at all imply
and still less command that I *ought*, merely on account of this
obligation, to limit my freedom to these very conditions.
Reason here says only that it *is* restricted thus far by its Idea,
and may be likewise thus limited in fact by others; and it lays
this down as a Postulate which is not capable of further proof.
Furthermore, Kant's argument to the present point has not
been to teach virtue, but to explain the nature of Right. The
Law of Right as thus laid down is therefore not to be understood as a motive principle of action.

Kant's attempt to confine the sphere of law to actions
manifested in the external world touched off a debate which
has continued to the present day. At the end of the Middle
Ages we find Brian, C. J., remarking " The thought of man
shall not be tried, for the devil himself knoweth not the thought
of man." [17] Similarly, Hale, in speaking of witchcraft, asserted
" it cannot come under the judgment of felony, because no
external act of violence was offered whereof the common law
can take notice, and secret things belong to God." [18] Nevertheless, in the fourteenth century we find the lawyers appealing to the maxim, *Voluntas reputabitur pro facto*.[19] A test case
in English legal history is the statute of Edward III which

---

[17] Y. B. 7 Edw. IV. f. 2. Quoted 2 Pollock and Maitland, *Hist. Eng. Law.* (2nd
ed. 1899) 474.

[18] 1 P. C. 429. Quoted *ibid.* 475.

[19] Maitland regards the maxim as but a " momentary aberration " (*ibid.* 477
n5.) but Holdsworth disputes this (3 *Hist. Eng. Law* 373 n4.).

made treason not the killing of the king, but the compassing or imagining his death, *i. e.*, the intention to kill him. However, it was obvious that an intention to kill the king had to be proved from overt acts, which showed that the person doing them had such an intention.[20] This was Coke's view: " This compassing, intent, or imagination," he said, " though secret, is . . . to be discovered by circumstances precedent, concomitant, and subsequent." [21] But the facts of the legal process are much more complicated than these few examples indicate. The statement that " a mere mental condition unaccompanied by any external act is, legally speaking, *nullius momenti*, and produces no legal result whatever," [22] is contrary to certain medieval English precedents which seem to show that mere words displaying such an intention were treasonable.[23] In modern juristic thought it is argued that when it is said that an act of thought is not punishable it means only a known act of thought, for otherwise the statement is senseless. In truth, the law does take notice of psychic acts, as in the punishment of certain religious beliefs which may be proved by confession. Kant's doctrine is really a political one, and had its origin in the effort to prevent the State's exercise of coercion over intimate individual beliefs. The proposition that law *cannot* invade psychic life and is *by its nature* indifferent to developments within the consciousness is an untenable one. If the law does not attempt to encompass that area it is because that is its choice and it is not due to an inherent limitation.[24] Moreover, assuming Kant's distinction to be a valid one we still must ask: What is an external act? The life of the law is complex, and has been confronted with numerous situations which Kant apparently did not contemplate, *e. g.*, a landowner neglects to warn an invitee of a hidden danger not created by the landowner; a man perceives the mistake of another who is about to

[20] 8 Holds. 311.
[21] 3 Instit. 6.
[22] Markby, *Elements of Law* (6th ed. 1905) 123.
[23] 3 Holds. 393.
[24] Del Vecchio, *The Formal Bases of Law* (1914) 139 *et seq.*

build on the former's land, but stands by in silence. Instances such as these, as well as estoppel from silence, admissions from silence, tacit ratification, negligence by omission and so on have resulted in formidable schemes of classification in an effort to rationalize a juristic theory of acts. Thus we have positive and negative acts, the latter divided into omissive and commissive acts, and the latter again divided into direct and indirect acts, plus even further divisions.[25] In this department, Kant started a hare which neither he nor his successors have run to earth. It may well be that the whole concept of action is an unnecessary one for jurisprudence in the sense that its validity has not been established empirically; nor does it seem to be formally necessary.

Right is not self-executing, even in the rarified atmosphere of the Kantian system, and it was therefore necessary for Kant to associate it with compulsion. In accordance with his approach his argument for the necessity of authority is a purely logical one, and it was therefore unnecessary for him to turn either to sociology or to ethics for support, as is the present-day practice. The resistance which is opposed to any hindrance of an effect, he said, is in reality a furtherance of this effect, and is in accordance with its accomplishment.[26] He had already shown that everything that is wrong is a hindrance of freedom, according to universal laws. Therefore, compulsion of any kind is a hindrance to freedom. Consequently, when the exercise of freedom is itself a hindrance of the freedom that is in accordance with universal laws, it is a wrong; and the compulsion which is opposed to it is right, as being a hindering of a hindrance of freedom, and as being in accord with the freedom which exists in conformity with universal laws. Hence, according to the logical principle of contradiction, all right is accompanied with an implied title or warrant to bring compulsion to bear on any one who may violate it in fact. This is a neat solution, for the task Kant had in hand, of the problem of

---

[25] Kocourek, *Jural Relations* (1927) 259 *et seq.* These pages represent about the best that has been done with the matter.
[26] *P. L.* 47.

authority; but it is valid only within the formal juristic system Kant was in process of constructing. If we do not accept his theory of right—he never shows logically or empirically how it is possible for a society of completely free-willing individuals to exist—his theory of compulsion is without force. In the absence of the acceptance of his premises we are free to view authority from the position of individualists like Max Stirner: " Away: you deprive me of sunshine."

Rights in the strict legal sense, Kant further insisted, may also be represented as the possibility of a universal reciprocal compulsion in harmony with the freedom of all according to universal laws. The external is the sole measure of a right in the strict legal sense, as it is of right in general. Strict legal rights are no doubt founded upon the consciousness of the obligation of every individual according to law; but to be taken in its pure form it must not refer to this consciousness as a motive to determine the free act of will. It must be grounded upon the principle of an external compulsion, such as may co-exist with the freedom of every one according to universal laws. As an illustration Kant pointed out that where it said that a creditor has a right to demand from a debtor the payment of his debt, this does not mean merely that he can bring him to feel in his mind that reason obliges him to do this; but it means that he can apply an external compulsion to force any debtor to discharge his debt, and that this compulsion is quite consistent with the freedom of all, including the parties in question, according to a universal law. Right and the title to compel thus indicate the same thing. The law of right thus amounts to a reciprocal compulsion necessarily in accordance with the freedom of every one, under the principles of a universal freedom. This formulation of the rule is regarded by Kant as an ideal, and not an empirical, statement, and is to be understood as a pure intuitive perception *a priori* analogous to Newton's physical law of the equality of action and reaction. This law asserts that reaction is always equal and opposite to action; that is to say, a body that pulls or presses another body is pressed or pulled in exactly the same degree by that other body. Hence, ideally we are to conceive of individuals as reacting upon each other under a reciprocal compulsion within the framework of the principle of freedom. Kant's mechanistic interpretation of the idea of right was probably suggested by the great social physics movement of the seventeenth century, among whose chief exponents were Descartes, Hobbes, Spinoza, Leibniz, Grotius, Pufendorf, Malebranche and Berkeley. This movement, which gave social expression to the Newtonian ideas of inertia, gravitation, equilibrium and dynamics, attempted to create a social mechanics founded on a mathematical method, and purported to perceive in societary phenomena the type of mechanistic analogy put forward by Kant.[27] Further, in the ideal constructions of mathematics only one solution is possible for certain types of problems, and on this analogy Kant held that the science of right aims at determining what every one shall have as his own with mathematical exactness. This aim is not possible in ethics, Kant recognizes, because there must be a certain latitude for exceptions. However, are not the so-called equitable rights and the right of necessity comparable to the exceptions demanded by ethics? Kant disposes of this point by excluding both cases from the realm of law.

He argues, in the case of equitable rights, that the necessary conditions are not present to enable a judge to determine the proper satisfaction to be accorded such claims. He cites two examples. In the first, one of the partners of a mercantile company formed on the basis of equal profits, has, however, done more than the other members, and in consequence has also lost more. Kant thinks that it is in accordance with equity that he should demand from the company more than merely an equal share of advantage with the rest. But from the point of view of strict legal right he can furnish no definite data to establish how much more belongs to him by the contract. In the second case, a servant is paid his wages at the end of a

[27] For a summary of the movement see Sorokin, *Contemporary Sociological Theories* (1928) 5 *et seq.*

year of service in a coinage that became depreciated within that period. Kant holds that since there was nothing bearing on this point in the contract a court could not give a decree on the basis of vague or indefinite conditions. His holding in both cases represents the result which English and American courts would reach, though not necessarily on the ground which he proposed. To reach a different result would require a departure from the terms of the contract; but assuming such a departure, and the presence of other factors, a court would not be powerless to determine the proper satisfaction. With respect to the first case, the customary action for work and labor is, of course, in *quantum meruit*, a procedure which the courts have not found difficult to apply. Where currency depreciation is involved the courts have not been inclined to substitute a commodity or other measure for the monetary measure expressed in the contract, which they must necessarily do if they recognize a currency depreciation. But this is a matter of policy, and does not rest on an inability of the court to ascertain a satisfactory measure. "An obligation in terms of the currency of a country takes the risk of currency fluctuations," Holmes observed, "and whether creditor or debtor profits by the change the law takes no account of it." [28] Moreover, the so-called "escalator contracts" now in use today, which make express provision for currency depreciation, are presumably regarded by their draftsmen as presenting enforcement problems not beyond the competence of the judiciary. Kant's cases actually involve difficulties of much less moment than the attempt to value the feelings or honor of an injured person. As Pound has pointed out, in words quoted from Kipling, the common law's solution of this task passeth the understanding of the Oriental: "Is a man sad? Give him money, say the Sahibs. Is he dishonored? Give him money, say the Sahibs. Hath he a wrong upon his head? Give him money, say the Sahibs." [29] Kant's main points are nevertheless well taken.

---

[28] *Die Deutsche Bank Filiale Nurnberg* v. *Humphrey*, 272 U. S. 517, 519 (1926).
[29] *Social Control Through Law* (1942) 60.

Courts are constantly confronted by well-founded moral claims for which the law can provide no remedy; further, in numerous situations the legal mechanism necessarily offers only rough tools with which to grasp the delicate insubstantialities of human association, so that social and ethical ideals frequently fail of realization. Kant thinks that the doctrine of equitable rights may be summarized as "the more law, the less justice" (*summum jus, summa injuria*). Parallel with this is the rule of the right of necessity: "Necessity has no law" (*necessitas non habet legem*). In its general aspect the right of necessity raises the question whether I may use violence against one who has used none against me. Concretely, may a man who is shipwrecked, and struggling in extreme danger for his life, in order to save it thrust another from a plank on which he had saved himself.[30] This is not the case of a wrongful aggressor making an unjust assault upon my life, and which I anticipate by depriving him of his own. Kant holds that the case put is beyond the reach of the criminal law, inasmuch as the punishment threatened by the law could not possibly have greater power than the fear of the loss of life in the case in question. Such a penal law would fail altogether to exercise its intended effect; for the threat of an evil which is still uncertain—such as death by judicial sentence—could not overcome the fear of an evil which is certain, as drowning is in such circumstances. An act of violent self-preservation of this kind is not beyond condemnation; it is only exempt from punishment. Moreover, there cannot be a necessity that could make what is wrong lawful. Thus, the law is confronted with rights which cannot be enforced and with enforcement which is without right.

Kant's final step in laying down his general theory was the establishment of the classifications of his subject. In his eyes the philosophy of law consisted in the determination of its fundamental principles, which in turn were regarded as an expression of the science of right. Kant divided the science of

---

[30] See *People* v. *Martin*, 13 Cal. A. 96, 108 Pac. 1034 (1910); *Reg.* v. *Dudley*, 14 Q.B.D. 273 (1884); *U. S.* v. *Holmes*, 26 Fed. Cas. No. 15, 383, 1 Wall. Jr. 1 (1842), where a view contrary to Kant's is maintained.

right into a " General Division of the Duties of Right " and a
" Universal Division of Rights." [31]   In the first category he put
the three formulae of Ulpian—*honeste vive, neminem laede,
suum cuique tribue*—as the basis of a division of the system of
juridical duties. Kant regarded Ulpian's formulae as merely
devices of convenience to be taken in a general sense, perhaps
not fully realized by Ulpian, but a sense which the formulae
could receive. He translated the formulae into the following
propositions: " Do not make thyself a mere means for the use
of others, but be to them likewise an end; do no wrong to
anyone, even if thou shouldst be under the necessity, in observing this duty, to cease from all connection with others and to
avoid all society; enter, if wrong cannot be avoided, into a
society with others in which every one may have secured to
him what is his own." At the same time the formulae suggest
to Kant a division of the system of juridical duties into
Internal Duties, External Duties and Connecting Duties.

As a scientific system of doctrines, the system of rights is
divided into natural right and positive right. Natural right
rests upon pure rational principles *a priori*; positive or statutory
right is what proceeds from the will of the legislator. However,
the system of rights can be regarded from another point of view.
Society is composed of individuals who possess implied powers
of dealing morally with each other on the basis of obligations;
that is, each person possesses a legal foundation for his actions
in relation to the other members of the society. In this aspect,
the system is divided into innate right and acquired right. Kant
defines innate right as that right which belongs to everyone by
nature, independent of all juridical acts of experience. Acquired
right is that right which is founded upon such juridical acts.
Innate right may also be called the " Internal Mine and
Thine "; for external right must always be acquired.

However, Kant maintained that there was only one original
inborn right that belonged to every man in virtue of his
humanity. This is the right of freedom, which Kant defined as

independence of the compulsory will of another. It is an inborn right in so far as it can co-exist with the freedom of all according to a universal law. This conception enabled Kant to dispose of a series of rights or qualities regarded as innate by seventeenth and eighteenth century thought—equality, justice, common action—on the grounds that they are included in the principle of innate freedom and are not easily distinguishable from it even as divisions under a higher species of right. Kant claimed that his classification of rights served a practical purpose. He thought that it would assist in the ready determination of controversies over acquired rights; for the party repudiating an obligation, and on whom the burden of proof might rest, would be able to point to his innate right of freedom as specified in a particular right, which would be the warrant for his action.

Up to this point Kant has classified rights from two points of view—the general division of the duties of right, and the universal division of rights. He now added a final classification —the methodical division of the science of right. He rejected the not uncommon division into natural and social right, and put in its place the classification natural right and civil right. By the first, he meant private right, and by the second, public right, and it is under these two headings that his treatise is divided. He argued that it is the " civil state," and not the " social state," that is opposed to the " state of nature "; for a society of some sort may exist in a state of nature, but there is no civil society as an institution securing property by public laws. Right when considered with respect to the state of nature thus involves the conception of private right, that is, the system of those laws which require no external promulgation. Under the conception of public right is to be considered the system of those laws which require public promulgation.

Kant's principle of right thus turns out to be the rule in terms of which legal principles are to be measured. He has not attempted to determine the basic principles of jurisprudence applicable to all conscious law-making in its various applica-

tions. That task he will take up immediately. His present
principles are anterior to such an inquiry. He has attempted to
establish the formal principle by which the first principles of
jurisprudence may be tested. To dismiss the principle of right
as merely formal is, therefore, to misunderstand Kant's argument. Kant expressly pointed out that in pure mathematics
we cannot deduce the properties of its objects from a mere
abstract conception, but can only discover them by figurative
construction. Thus it is, he says, with the principle of right.
It is not so much the mere formal conception of right, but
rather that of a universal and equal reciprocal compulsion as
harmonizing with it, and reduced under general laws, that
makes representation of that conception possible.[32] Thus, the
relation of the principle of right to particular rights, such as
the right of parents to the management and training of the
child, is not regarded by Kant as similar to the relation that
obtains between the law of gravitation and Kepler's laws of
planetary motion.[33] The relationship is rather more like that
which exists between the principle: " all arguments of the form
' all M is P and all S is M entail all S is P ' are valid " to the
specific case of " all men are mortal and all Greeks are men,
therefore all Greeks are mortal." As Broad observes, it is
impossible to deduce any particular argument from the general
principle of the syllogism; but, if any particular argument in
syllogistic form claims to be valid, its claim can be tested by
seeing whether it does or does not have the formal structure
required by the general principle. However, as Aristotle saw,
logical principles express the general nature of things; that is
to say, while logic, through its investigation of being as being,
achieves the utmost generality in its principles, it nevertheless
has an empirical reference.[34] If the principle of identity were
not applicable to statesmen, and to telegraph operators, to ships
and to chemical elements, to concepts and to emotional states it
would be defective in a necessary requirement. But Kant's

[32] *P. L.* 49.
[33] Broad, *Five Types of Ethical Theory* (1930) 122.
[34] See *P. L.* 72.

principle of right fails at just this point. He has abstracted the individuals that compose society to identical points in motion in space, and in that sense his principle no doubt possesses validity. But it appears to be of the essence of a sound social and legal theory to take account of the individual differences of the classes that constitute society. All the classes are not equally weighted in strength, and the law has always found it desirable to adjust those differences through the mechanism of special protection and privilege, as in the labor laws and the rules for the protection of minors. Kant's principle, as we have seen above, ignores those differences and to that extent at least does not have an empirical reference. As a rule of thumb, however, in the framing of general legislation it possesses some merit. It warns us against the promulgation of rules that benefit powerful classes in society which do not stand in need of special protection.

The Principles of the External Mine and Thine

Although Kant occasionally employed the term " property " and, in fact, gave the idea specific consideration,[35] his theory of the " mine and thine " embraced a much wider area than the customary judicial conception of property as rights or interests attaching to whatever may be the subject of ownership. Anything is " mine " by right, Kant says, when I am so connected with it, that if any other person should make use of it without my consent, he would do me an injury.[36] He defines possession as the subjective condition of the use of anything. However, for an external thing to be mine I must assume it to be possible that I can be wronged by the use which another might make of it when it is not actually in my possession. Consequently Kant assigns to the term possession two meanings: sensible or physical possession, which is perceived by the senses, and rational or juridical possession, which is perceivable only by the intellect. To describe an object as external to me may mean either that it is different and distinct from me as a

[35] *P. L.* 98. [36] *P. L.* 62.

subject, or that it is a thing placed outside of me, and to be found elsewhere in space or time. In the first sense the term possession means rational possession, and in the second sense, empirical possession. Rational possession, if it is possible, is possession viewed apart from physical holding or detention. Kant holds that it is an assumption *a priori* of the practical reason to regard and treat every object within the range of my free exercise of will as objectively a possible mine or thine. He terms this postulate a " permissive law " of the practical reason, since it gives us a special title which cannot be deduced from the mere conception of right generally. This title permits us to impose upon all others an obligation, to which they are not otherwise subject, to refrain from the use of certain objects of our choice, because we have already taken them into our possession. Finally, any one who would assert the right to a thing as his, must be in possession of it as an object; otherwise he would not be wronged. On the basis of this theory Kant held that there can only be three external objects of my will in the activity of choice: a corporeal thing external to me; the free-will of another in the performance of a particular act; and the state of another in relation to myself.

Little reflection is needed to perceive the acuteness of this analysis. It represents the most finished proprietary theory advanced by any philosopher of the first rank up to the time of its promulgation. Its central idea—the exclusion of other persons from the thing appropriated—has become a common-place of juridical thought, and has established itself as a work-able idea for both text writers and judges. Thus Wigmore writes, " The Property-Right is essentially a guarantee of the exclusion of other persons from the use or handling of the thing. Its most absolute form amounts to no other than that. The common mode of definition, therefore, as a right of use by the owner himself, is fallacious." [37] Holmes' theory of property is just as close to Kant's conception, and possesses the same reservations Kant entertained in his view of the labor theory.

[37] 2 *Select Cases on the Law of Torts* (1912) 858.

" Property, a creation of law," Holmes held, " does not arise
from value, although exchangeable,—a matter of fact. . . .
Property depends upon exclusion by law from interference, and
a person is not excluded from using [it] . . . merely because . . .
it took labor and genius to make it." [38] But Kant, notwithstanding his enthusiasm for the principles of the French Revolution, did not hesitate to extend his theory to situations to
which it appeared applicable, although in the process he ran
counter to many of the ideals of his time and our own. His
first extension presented no difficulty from this point of view,
and represents in fact a position to which the courts are beginning to give increased adherence. Kant held that one of the
external objects of the will covered by the conception of the
external mine and thine was the free-will of another in the
performance of a particular act. To enforce this right the holder
of it must be able to assert, " I am in possession of the will of
the other, so as to determine him to the performance of a particular act, although the time for it has not yet come." [39] This
principle plainly covers all types of property which depend for
their being upon the existence of a promise or grant, such as
the property evidenced by certificates of stock, bonds, pro-
missory notes and franchises. But it goes further, and embraces
such matters as the property interest of the plaintiff in *Lumley
v.Gye*,[40] where it was held that the defendant, in enticing an
opera singer not to carry out her contract with the plaintiff
to sing at his theatre, had interfered with a property interest
in a manner that was actionable. However, Kant's extension of
the proprietary idea to domestic and other relational interests
presents an obvious difficulty which has troubled his commentators. Is it possible to say in modern times that the head
of the household has a " property " interest in the wife, child,
or domestic? The action of the parent in the instance of sexual
intercourse with his child developed as trespass or case for loss

[38] *International News Service* v. *Associated Press*, 248 U. S. 215, 246 (1918)
(Concurring opinion).
[39] *P. L.* 65.
[40] 2 *El. & Bl.* 216 (1853).

of services—a proprietary interest—which apparently was the
most convenient device available.[41] This idea has now almost
vanished, so that any trivial service, such as making a cup of
tea for the parent, or even the mere right to service, is sufficient.
Some courts have recognized that loss of services is an obsolete
fiction and is no longer necessary to maintain the action. What,
then, is the basis for an action for interference with family
relations? It is asserted that the harm is not done to person or
to property but rather to rights incident to them.[42] However,
as has been pointed out, this is not true historically.[43] Criminal
conversation and alienation of affections, the two best-known
marital causes of action, are both based upon the proprietary
interest of the husband in the body and services of his wife.
Moreover the adoption of the theory of incidental rights by the
courts has led to unfortunate results. When there is a change
in the marital relationship, as through judicial separation, the
guilty party may lose the right to the custody of the child. But
the same party does not lose the right to sue for criminal conversation. In the first case the right is an incidental one which
is lost when the relationship changes; in the second case the
proprietary right to exclusive sexual intercourse persists. This
distinction had important consequences in the interpretation of
women's enabling acts. The first view led to the extension of
the action to the wife; the second would have resulted in its
extinction. As the result of the absence of a sound theory
"consortium has been thrown into hopeless confusion."[44]
Whatever may be the drawbacks of Kant's theory, it has at
least the merit of avoiding logical dilemmas of this kind.

In order to make his theory formally complete Kant had
some further difficulties to explain, some raised by the theory
itself and some by his own philosophy. His theory assumed
that every object within the range of the free exercise of his
will was objectively a possible mine or thine. Consequently,

---

[41] Prosser, *Law of Torts* (1941) 933.
[42] Street, *Foundations of Legal Liability* (1906) 264.
[43] Lippman, *The Breakdown of Consortium* (1930) 30 Col. L. Rev. 651, 658-59.
[44] *Ibid.* 672.

since this assumption applied to things which I may not be physically holding, things located outside of me in space or time, I must be in some kind of possession of an external thing, if the thing is to be regarded as mine. A rational possession must therefore be assumed as possible if there is to be an external mine and thine.[45] But this at once raises the question: How is a merely juridical or rational possession possible? Here, however, Kant encountered a difficulty created by his own philosophy. He had defined an analytic proposition as one in which the predicate was contained in the subject, and on the basis of which, through an application of the principle of contradiction, we could make further statements independently of additional knowledge. " A black book is black " is such a proposition. But the predicate of a synthetic proposition is not contained in the subject, and must be derived from other sources, as in the proposition, " The book is on the table." Kant held that all propositions of right, as juridical propositions, are propositions *a priori*.[46] A proposition *a priori* with respect to empirical possession is analytic, since it implies nothing beyond the right of a person in reference to himself. But a proposition with respect to rational possession, since it asserts a possession even without physical holding and therefore looks beyond the subject to experience, is synthetic. How is this possible *a priori*?

Kant's attempt to answer this question led him to his important conception of an *original* community of the soil, as distinguished from the idea of a *primitive* community which he regarded as a fiction. He argued that the first possessor of a portion of the earth's surface based his claim to it upon an innate right of common possession of the earth's surface, and also upon the universal will that corresponded *a priori* to it, and which allows a private possession of the soil. If this were not so, freedom would deprive itself of the use of its voluntary activity in thus putting useable objects out of all possibility of use. It would annihilate the objects by making them *res nullius,* notwithstanding the fact that acts of will in relation to such things would formally harmonize, in the actual use of them, with the external freedom of all according to universal laws.[47] Thus a first appropriator acquires originally by primary possession a particular portion of the ground; and by right he resists every other person who would hinder him in the private use of it. However, his resistance during the continuance of the " state of nature " would be extra-juridical, because public law does not yet exist. Kant therefore laid down the postulate that every external object of the free activity of my will, so far as I have it in my power, although not in the possession of it, may be reckoned as juridically mine. This postulate, in turn, was founded upon the postulate: It is a juridical duty so to act towards others that what is external and useable may come into the possession or become the property of someone. The conception of possession as embracing the non-physical is to be understood in conjunction with this latter postulate. But the conception of non-physical possession cannot be proved or comprehended in itself, because it is a rational conception for which no empirical perception can be furnished. However, if we follow the dictate of the postulate, the rational condition of a purely juridical possession must also be possible.

At this point Kant introduced his important idea of " having." [48] This was a necessary conception in order to account for the application of the principle of the possibility of an external mine and thine to objects of experience. A purely juridical possession is not an empirical conception dependent on conditions of space and time. Since the conception of right is contained merely in the reason, it cannot be immediately applied to objects of experience, so as to give the conception of an empirical possession, but must be applied directly to the mediating conception in the understanding of possession in general. Therefore the mind, in place of physical holding as an empirical representation of possession, substitutes the formal conception of " having " abstracted from all conditions of space and time, and only as implying that an object is in my power and at my disposal. This conception has certain significant consequences. The term " external " carries no significance of existence in another place than where I am; my acceptance refers to no other time than the moment in which I have the offer of a thing; " external " signifies only an object different from or other than myself. When I say that I possess " White-acre " although I am in a different place, I do not mean that there is an intellectual relationship between myself and " White-acre," but that I have " Whiteacre," as a practical matter, in my power and at my disposal, a meaning which is independent of space; it is also mine, because my use of it in accordance with the determination of my will is not in conflict with the law of external freedom. The mode then, of having something external to myself as mine, consists in a specially juridical connection of the will of the subject with that object, independently of the empirical relations to it in space and time, and in accordance with the conception of a rational possession.

Civil society alone furnishes a common, collective, and authoritative will, that can furnish a guarantee of security to all. Kant therefore held that to have anything external as one's own is only possible in a civil state of society under the regulation of a public legislative power.[49] In the state of nature, if anything external is held as one's own, it is mere physical possession, with a presumption of right that eventually it will be made juridical. It amounts, in other words, to a kind of potential juridical possession.[50]

Since Kant is sometimes criticized for failing to offer a justification of private property it seems advisable to consider the specific theory he advanced on this question. His defence of property was a highly refined version of the occupation theory, which held that the act of taking occupancy of things without an owner, with the intention of making them one's own property, was the principal method by which title was originally acquired. From the Roman jurists to Kant the theory had been

[49] *P. L.* 76.   [50] *P. L.* 79.

an influential one. Kant's justification, which has been discussed from another point of view above, is that if the will is
not exercised with respect to external objects in accordance
with a universal law the objects are thereby annihilated by
making them *res nullius*.[51] But this negation of the will is not
possible. The pure practical reason lays down only formal laws
as principles to regulate the exercise of the will. In this process
all qualities of the object are ignored except the single one of
being an object of the activity of the will. Hence the practical
reason cannot contain, in reference to such an object, an
absolute prohibition of its use, because this would involve a
contradiction of external freedom with itself. Kant's attempt
to establish a formal proof of the proposition that everything
ought to have an owner is an important illustration of the
power of philosophical analysis in legal theory. In the efforts of
the historical jurists to work out a justification for the same
proposition the only arguments apparently available were that
it was supported by an historical " presumption " and a " feeling " that it was " naturally " right.[52]

REAL RIGHT

How are things acquired? Kant answers that I acquire a
thing when I act so that it becomes mine. The idea was
expressed by him in the Principle of External Acquisition as
follows: Whatever I bring under my power according to the
law of external freedom, of which as an object of my free
activity of will I have the capability of making use according
to the postulate of the practical reason, and which I will to
become mine in conformity with the idea of a possible united
common will, *is* mine.[53] Three practical elements are involved
in original acquisition: seizure of an object which belongs to no
one; a formal declaration of possession of the object; appropriation, as the act, in idea, of an externally legislative common

[51] *P. L.* 62-63.
[52] Maine, *Ancient Law* (World's Classics ed. 1931) 213.
[53] *P. L.* 82.

will, by which all are obliged to respect my act of will. The original primary acquisition of an external object of the action of the will Kant calls " occupancy," and it can occur only with respect to corporeal things. However, we are faced here with the task of accounting for title to accessory things, such as alluvial deposits. Strictly, under Kant's theory, an original occupier could claim land formed in this manner. In order to meet the question Kant invoked the scholastic (or Aristotelian) doctrine of accident, *i. e.*, that which has no independent being, but adheres in some other substance. Accidents inhering in the substance of the soil, he held, are mine *jure rei meae*. He extended the category to include everything which is so connected with anything of mine, that it cannot be separated from what is mine without altering it substantially, *e. g.*, gilding on an object, mixture of a material belonging to me with other things, and alteration of the adjoining bed of a river in my favor so as to produce an increase of my land.[54] But the last case seems to beg the question. The Roman lawyers held that if a river altered its bed, the old bed belonged to the owners on each side, and the new bed became public.[55] One of the great virtues of Kant's exposition of his theory of law is his constant putting of difficult cases, mostly drawn from Roman law sources, to illustrate his theory. A further virtue is his uniform endeavor to set forth the reasons for his position. In later jurisprudence, unencumbered by the will theory, it is held that original acquisition can take place either with or without an act of possession, the latter class embracing *accessio, confusio* and *commixtio*.[56] But the categories, for all that appears, are purely empirical, and no effort is made to relate them to a general theory. Jurisprudence, by definition, if it is not theory is nothing.

When A holds an external object that belongs to B, B can compel A to return it to him. Kant's theory of real right is an effort to explain why this is possible. He denies that the exter-

[54] *P. L.* 97-98.
[55] Buckland, *Textbook of Roman Law from Augustus to Justinian* (1921) 212.
[56] Holland, *Elements of Jurisprudence* (10th ed. 1906) 207-209.

nal juridical relation of the will is a kind of immediate relation
to an external thing. A right on one side has always a duty
corresponding to it on the other; but to affirm an obligation of
persons towards things, and conversely, Kant thinks is absurd.[57]
He holds that there is only one condition under which it is
possible to exclude every other possessor from the private use
of a thing; that is the condition of common collective possession.
The collective will of all united in a relation of common possession gives rise to an obligation on the part of another person to
abstain from the use of the thing. Therefore the definition of
right in a thing is a right to the private use of a thing, of
which I am in possession—original or derivative—in common
with all others. Further, the term " real right " means not only
the " right in a thing " but also the constitutive principle of
all the laws which relate to the real mine and thine. It is
evident, however, that a man entirely alone upon the earth
could properly neither have nor acquire any external things as
his own, because between him as a person and all external
things as material objects there could be no relations of obligation. There is therefore, literally, no direct right in a thing,
but only that right is to be called " real " which belongs to any
one as constituted against a person who is in common possession of things with all others in the civil state of society.

Moveable property is defined by Kant as everything that
can be destroyed; and it is to be regarded as an inherence
in the soil which is a substance.[58] Since accidents cannot exist
apart from their substances, so in the practical relation, move-
ables on the soil cannot be regarded as belonging to any one
unless he is supposed to have been previously in juridical possession of the soil so that it is thus considered to be his. Kant
therefore holds that the first acquisition of a thing can only be
that of the soil. An assumption *a priori* of the practical reason
was that every object within the range of my free exercise of
will was objectively a possible mine or thine. From this it
follows that every part of the soil may be originally acquired.[59]

[57] *P. L.* 85.   [58] *P. L.* 87.   [59] *P. L.* 88.

Chance or nature has placed men upon the earth at particular places, and they are therefore originally and before any juridical act of will in rightful possession of the soil. That possession is common because of the interconnectedness of the places of the earth, which is a globe. If the earth had been an infinite plain, social community would not have been a necessary consequence of existence on the earth. Possession prior to juridical acts is an original possession in common, and Kant holds that it is not derived from experience, nor is it dependent on conditions of time, as is the case with what he regards as the imaginary and indemonstrable fiction of a primeval community of possession in actual history. Occupancy is the acquisition of an external object by an individual act of will. The original acquisition of a limited portion of the soil is an act of occupation, and its essential condition is its priority in respect of time. In the state of nature acquisition can only be provisory, and only within a civil constitution can anything be acquired peremptorily. Kant limits the right of taking possession of the soil to the extent of the capacity to defend it. Thus, within the range of a cannon shot no one has a right to intrude on the coast of a country that already belongs to a particular State. What the fishing rights are in the English Channel, now that guns can shoot across it, would be impossible to determine on this principle. How people settle themselves upon the earth, provided they keep within their own boundaries, is a matter, Kant holds, of mere pleasure and choice on their part. Thus he repudiates, as a " flimsy veil of injustice," all attempts to rule by force the so-called backward peoples of the earth, or to establish colonies by deceptive purchase.[60]

Kant's important contribution in his conception of real right is his idea that right in a thing presupposes a collective will of all united in a relation of common possession. His insistence upon this point emphasizes the significance of system in legal analysis. Through system we pass beyond knowledge which may be incomplete to knowledge in which all the necessary

[60] *P. L.* 93.

propositions are explicitly set forth. If knowledge is not organized in this manner the foundations of our analysis may rest upon unapprehended assumptions of the utmost dubiety. We may also be led to the useless exploration of propositions which possess no meaning in the domain of inquiry. System also promotes economy in the statement of the necessary propositions of the subject. In a modern treatment of the subject of possession no less than seven factors are described in connection with the explanation of only one element of the idea, and admittedly the enumeration is incomplete or, in some aspects, erroneous.[61] Kant's isolation of a collective will united in a relation of common possession furnishes not only a basis for the explanation of a right in a thing, but it separates law as a study of man in his social aspects as distinguished from such subjects as anatomy and zoology, which study him as an individual. In present-day sociology the counterpart of Kant's theory is the idea of psychic interaction, or intermindedness, the reciprocal play of mind upon mind which results in mutual influences. It is held to be not only the distinguishing mark of the group, but the very factor by which the group's character as a group is determined.[62]

PERSONAL RIGHT

One of the most influential of Kant's ideas in jurisprudence was his theory of contract which he based on his conception of the external mine and thine. It is a philosophical justification of the so-called subjective theory of contract which was authoritatively stated by Savigny [63] and further developed by the later historical jurists. Kant's problem was to provide a justification for the enforcement of contracts. In the natural law theory which preceded him promises were self-justifying on the basis of their own inherent moral force.[64] Kant asserted emphatically that is was impossible to give any proof of the proposition

---

[61] Salmond, *Jurisprudence* (8th ed. 1930) 302 *et seq.*
[62] Eubank, *Concepts of Sociology* (1932) 163-64.
[63] 3 *System des heutigen römischen Rechts* (1840) § 140.
[64] Grotius, *De Jure Belli ac Pacis Libri Tres* (1625) Bk. II, c. 13.

" promises ought to be kept," a task on which previous writers on jurisprudence had expended much labor.[65]

Kant's whole justification of enforcement turned on his idea of a common collective possession.[66] One of the forms of right, according to Kant, is the possession of the active free-will of another person which includes the power to determine it by my will to a certain action according to the laws of freedom. It is possible to have several such rights in reference to the same person or to different persons. The principle in the Kantian system which justifies such possession is that of personal right, and there is only one such principle. The acquisition of a personal right can never be primary or arbitrary, nor is it permissible, Kant insisted, to employ an unjust means in such acquisition. Acquisition by means of the action of another is always derived from what that other has as his own. As a juridical act the derivation can never be a mere negative reliquishment or renunciation of what is his, because such a negative act would only amount to a cessation of his right, and not to the acquirement of a right on the part of another. There must therefore be a positive transference or conveyance. But this is only possible on Kant's theory, by means of a common will, through which objects come into the power of another, so that as one renounces a particular thing which he holds under the common right, the same object when accepted by another, in consequence of a positive act of will, becomes the property of that other. Kant calls the transference of the property of one to another its " alienation "; and the act of the united wills of two persons, by which what belonged to one passes to another, he terms " contract."

Four juridical acts of will are involved in every contract, Kant held; two of them are preparatory acts, and two of them constitutive acts. There is first an offer, which in turn is followed by an indication that the offer will be received; these two acts are followed by a promise and an acceptance. For an offer cannot constitute a promise before it can be judged that the

thing offered is something that is agreeable to the party to
whom it is offered, and this much is shown by the first two
declarations; but by them alone there is nothing as yet acquired.
In the civil law theory Kant's separation of offer and promise
still prevails, but the corrections in the theory that are made
from time to time are worked out on an empirical and not an
abstract basis. A merchant who exposes an article for sale may
be regarded as offering it at that price to any one; but he may
also be permitted to substitute an identical article; and when he
offers it in the window he may, under certain circumstances, not
be required to sell it at all. An offer of reward to the finder of
lost property is not invalid because the offeree is indeterminate;
but a " To Let " notice on a house is not an offer, but merely an
offer to negotiate.[67]

In contemporary common law theory it is argued that an
offer is a promise, but the question is not free from doubt.[68]
Unless an offer is a promise it is difficult to imagine on what
basis general offers, such as an offer of reward for the apprehension of criminals, could be sustained. The common law
theory of contract recognizes a manifestation of a general
intention or willingness to contract, but which nevertheless does
not amount to an offer, *i. e.*, a promise. Thus A may say to B:
" Would you be interested in buying my horse? " This category
of the common law theory, the logical justification of which
goes back to Plato's argument in the *Sophist*, that false knowledge is knowledge, does not differ from Kant's idea of " offer."
In the Kantian theory an " offer " is a necessary step, from the
point of view of the will-idea, in the formation of a contract;
but it is not a juridically necessary one.

But a further difficulty remains. Kant points out that it is
not by the particular wills of the promisor and promisee that
the property of the former passes over to the latter; [69] this is
effected only by the combined or united wills of both, and

[67] Amos and Walton, *Introduction to French Law* (1935) 151.
[68] 1 Williston, *Treatise on the Law of Contracts* (1936), 49 *et seq.*; Goble, *Is an
Offer a Promise?* (1928) 22 Ill. L. Rev. 567; Green, *Is an Offer Always a Promise?*
(1928) 23 Ill. L. Rev. 95, 301.
[69] *P. L.* 102.

consequently so far only as the will of both is declared at the same time or simultaneously. This idea is at the basis of the common law rule, settled by *Cooke* v. *Oxley*,[70] that an offer must be accepted instantaneously, or it ceased to exist. But as Kant pointed out, simultaneity is impossible by empirical acts of declaration, which can only follow each other in time, and are never actually simultaneous. For if I have promised, and another person is now merely willing to accept, during the interval before actual acceptance, however short it may be, I may retract my offer, because I am thus far still free; and on the other side, the acceptor, for the same reason, may likewise hold himself not to be bound, up till the moment of acceptance, by his counter-declaration following upon the promise. After Kant the civil law lawyers found no reason in theory why an offer was not revocable; but the offeree would frequently act upon the offer as soon as it was received. Furthermore an offer clearly was terminated by death or insanity. Jhering first solved the problem by holding the offeror liable for losses actually sustained by the offeree in reliance on the offer, but not for the profits which would accrue under the contract. Eventually, the German Civil Code, and the codes of other countries, provided that an offer cannot be revoked for a reasonable time or for the time provided in the offer, unless the offer provides against the irrevocability.[71] Kant argued further that the external formalities on the conclusion of a contract—such as shaking hands or breaking a straw held by two persons— prove in fact the embarrassment of the contracting parties as to how and in what way they may represent declarations, which are always successive, as existing simultaneously; and the forms fail to do this. They are, by their very nature, acts necessarily following each other in time, so that when the one act is, the other either is not yet or is no longer. The same problem is present in the common law which holds that offer and acceptance must exist simultaneously. British and Ameri-

---

[70] (1790) 3 T. R. 653; 1 Williston, *op. cit.* note 68 at 142-43; 12 Holds. 532.
[71] 1 Williston, *op. cit.* note 68 at 186.

can courts have sometimes attempted to meet the problem with the fiction of a relation back of the acceptance of the offer. Thus Lord Ellenborough, in a case involving a contract by mail, said, " the acceptance must be taken as simultaneous with the offer." [72] But this is objected to by Williston on the ground that the offer is not merely evidence of a state of mind. It is an element in the formation of a contract irrespective of the offeror's mental attitude, and may continue effective in spite of a change in that attitude. He therefore believes that the resort to a fiction is unnecessary, and that the only accurate way to express the matter is to say that the offeree's power of acceptance continues till the acceptance. This solution is in accord with the rule that a revocation requires communication; but this seems inconsistent with the requirement that the formation of a simple contract demands a manifested mutual assent, inasmuch as there can be a manifested mutual dissent, but if the revocation has not been communicated, the contract is nevertheless formed upon the acceptance of the offer. There is the further difficulty of applying the rule to general offers. Must every member of the public who sees the general offer receive notice of its revocation? In an additional departure from the rule the Supreme Court has held that a reasonable effort to give notice of revocation, *i. e.*, full publication so far as possible in the same way as the original offer, is sufficient.[73] All this points merely to the great difficulty of framing a general theory into which can be fitted the unforeseeable complexities of legal phenomena.

Kant accepted all the conditions of his contract theory and met the simultaneity problem squarely. His solution turned on his concept of " having " discussed above. The two juridical acts of promise and acceptance must necessarily be regarded as following one another in time. But the juridical external relation which is established when I take possession of the free-will of another is purely rational in itself. The will as a law-

---

[72] *Kennedy* v. *Lee* (1817) 3 Mer. 441, 454. Quoted 1 Williston, *op. cit.* note 68 at 143 n4.

[73] *Shuey* v. *U. S.*, 92 U. S. 73 (1876).

giving faculty of reason represents this possession as intelligible in accordance with the conceptions of freedom and under abstraction of the empirical conditions. But then the two acts of promise and acceptance are not regarded as following one another in time, but as proceeding from a common will (Kant's presupposition of a collective will of all united in a relation of common possession), and the object promised is represented, under elimination of empirical conditions, as acquired according to the law of the pure practical reason; *i. e.*, the *a priori* assumption to treat every object within the range of the free exercise of the will as objectively a possible mine or thine. Thus the modern common law theory, and Kant's theory both come to the same thing: an offer and an acceptance must exist at the same time; but simultaneity in the common law is preserved through the fiction of a continuing power in the offeree, and in Kant's theory through the elimination of the condition of time.

Kant's idea of a union of wills as the necessary element in the formation of contracts has been supplanted in the modern common law by the so-called objective theory. This theory, in the words of one of its most vigorous proponents, insists that the legal meaning of such acts on the part of one man as induce another to enter into a contract with him, is not what the former really intended, ncr what the latter really supposed the former to intend, but wnat a " reasonable man," *i. e.*, a judge or jury, would put upon such acts.[74] In an extreme case this means that when adverse parties who speak different languages and cannot understand each other voluntarily agree upon an interpreter to translate for them, his representations are chargeable to each although his statements may be erroneous.[75] However, it is interesting to note that there is a retreat from the rule, founded on the objective theory, that the offeror is bound by an inaccurately transmitted telegraphic offer. It is now proposed not to bind him but to put him under a duty

[74] Holland, *op. cit.* note 56 at 256.
[75] *Bonelli* v. *Burton*, 61 Or. 429, 123, Pac. 37 (1912).

to use due care to mitigate damages,[76] a solution which would meet Jhering's analysis of a hundred years ago. Kant does not discuss the question of mistake in offer and acceptance, but there is no question that his theory would not permit the formation of a contract where there was not a union of wills. But there is some ground in his language for thinking that he may be closer to the objective theory than is generally supposed. How are we to determine when there is a union of wills? Again, Kant does not expressly take up the point, but he nowhere suggests or implies that the hearts of the offeror and offeree shall be searched. On the contrary, he refers to the " various modes of confirming the declarations " and cites two instances of an objective nature; further, he expressly states that the contract relation " is conceived at first empirically by means of the declaration and counter-declaration of the free-will of " the parties,[77] which seems to indicate an objective measure.

By the contract, Kant held, I acquire the promise of another, as distinguished from the thing promised. I have become the richer in possession by the acquisition of an active obligation that I can bring to bear upon the freedom of another. Nevertheless it is only a personal right, valid only to the effect of acting upon a particular physical person and specially upon the causality of his will, so that he shall perform something for me. It is therefore not a real right through which alone I can acquire a right valid against every possessor of the thing; for it is in this that all right in a thing consists. On the basis of the current American theory that a contract is a promise for breach of which the law gives a remedy,[78] the answer to the question what is acquired by a contract would be the same as Kant's. It was held further by Kant that a thing is not acquired by the acceptance of the promise, but only by the delivery of the object promised. Kant is here following the rule of the

[76] *Holtz* v. *Western Union Telegraph Co.*, 294 Mass. 543, 3 N. E. (2nd) 180 (1936).

[77] *P. L.* 102-103.

[78] *Restatement of Contracts* § 1.

Roman law which insisted upon delivery before a transfer of the property was effected; [79] but this rule was already on its way towards abandonment by the common law by the time of Henry VI.[80]

REAL PERSONAL RIGHT

Personal right of a real kind, the last of the categories of the mine and thine, is the right to the possession of an external object as a thing and to the use of it as a person.[81] This right refers specially to the family and household; and the relations involved are those of free beings in reciprocal real interaction with each other. The household forms a society composed as a whole of members standing in community with each other as persons. Kant held that individuals acquire this social status neither by arbitrary individual action nor by contract, but by a natural permissive law, based on the right of humanity in our own person. This law is not only a right, but constitutes possession in reference to a person; it is therefore a right which rises above all mere real and personal right. In the household a man acquires a wife; the husband and wife acquire children, thus constituting the family; and the family acquire domestics. These objects can be acquired, but they are inalienable; and the right of possession in the objects is the most strictly personal of all rights.

To the great pain of subsequent moralists Kant defined marriage as a mutual lease of the sexual organs.[82] He held that the domestic relations were founded on marriage, which in turn was founded on the natural reciprocity or intercommunity of the sexes. This natural union of the sexes could proceed according to the mere animal nature (*fornicatio*) or according to law, *i. e.*, marriage. In spite of the formality of his approach to the problem Kant, probably under the influence of Protestant theology, here adopted what has since become a widely

[79] Jolowicz, *Historical Introduction to the Study of Roman Law* (1932) 302.
[80] Ames, *Lectures on Legal History* (1913) 77; 3 Holds. 354-57.
[81] *P. L.* 108.
[82] *P. L.* 110.

shared ethical point of view. He admitted two factors as the
end of marriage—the erotic and procreative elements. Mon-
taigne, whose analysis of such matters was anything but formalistic, refused, following the classical tradition, to admit the
legitimacy of the erotic element and, in fact, condemned its
presence as a kind of incest.[83] On the basis of his conception
Kant proceeded to lay down a series of highly edifying rules.
In the relationship of natural reciprocity—in the strict Kantian
sense of *usus membrorum sexualium alterius*—there is an enjoyment for which the one person is given up to the other. But in
this relationship the human indivídual makes himself a *res*,
which is contrary to the right of humanity in his own person.
However, this is possible under the one condition that as the
one person is acquired by the other as a *res*, that same person
also equally acquires the other reciprocally, and thus regains
and re-establishes the rational personality. The acquisition
of a part of the human organism being, on account of its unity,
at the same time the acquisition of the whole person, it follows
that the surrender and acceptation of, or by, one sex in relation
to the other, is not only permissible under the condition of
marriage, but is further only really possible under that condition. Moreover, the personal right of this relationship is real
in kind. Therefore if one of the married persons runs away or
enters into the possession of another, the aggrieved spouse is
entitled to bring the erring one back to the former relation as
if that person were a thing. Since marriage is a relationship of
equality it is only truly realized in monogamy; on the same
principle Kant condemns both concubinage and morganatic
marriages. But how is the case of the legal supremacy of the
husband to be justified? This is not contrary to natural
equality, Kant said, if it is based only upon the natural superiority of the faculties of the husband compared with the wife,
in the realization of the common interest of the household, and
if the right to command is based merely upon this fact. For
this right may thus be deduced from the very duty and

equality in relation to the end involved. Finally, he held that the contract of marriage is completed only by conjugal cohabitation. If there is a secret agreement before marriage not to cohabit the marriage may be dissolved at will by either party; if the incapacity arises after marriage no such right exists. Kant wrote, of course, before the great revolution in the social status of women had occurred. But the doctrines of Condorcet, and Mary Wollstonecraft's little book, which had been translated into German, were an indication that a new wind was beginning to blow. This gentle zephyr left Kant, however, unmoved.

Kant's treatment of the relationship of parent and child, and of master and servant, was also a faithful reflection of eighteenth-century thought. From the fact of procreation there follows the duty of rearing children as the products of the union. Children accordingly as persons have a congenital right to be reared by their parents until they are capable of maintaining themselves.[84] Parents have no right to destroy their child as if it were their own property, or even to leave it to chance. Kant is here speaking of legitimate children; his opinion of the treatment of illegitimate children was, as we shall see, different. From these duties of the parents there arises the right of the parents to the management and training of the child, which continues until the period of practicable self-support. The domestic relationship of the household is not founded on social equality, but is of the kind that one commands as master and another obeys as servant.[85] Domestics belong to the master as if by a real right; for if any of them run away, he is entitled to bring them again under his power by a unilateral act of will. But in the master's use of domestics he is not entitled to conduct himself towards them as if he were their owner. His power rests only on contract, and particularly on a restricted contract. For a contract by which the one party renounced his whole freedom for the advantage of the other, ceasing thereby to be a person and consequently having

[84] *P. L.* 114.   [85] *P. L.* 119.

no duty even to observe a contract, is self-contradictory, and is therefore of itself null and void. In the American law of slavery the self-contradictory feature of contractual relations with slaves was recognized, but from an entirely different point of view. Unless granted by statute, a slave possessed no legal capacities at all, and attempts to extend positive rights to him were regarded as an effort to reconcile inherent contradictions.[86] " It was an inflexible rule of the law of African slavery, wherever it existed," the Supreme Court observed, " that the slave was incapable of entering into any contract, not excepting the contract of marriage." [87] The court added that this rule was harsher than the one applied to the Roman bondman, the Saxon villein, the Russian serf and the German and Polish slave. The domestic relationship contract in the Kantian system never permits an abuse of the domestic, and in what constitutes an abuse the servant is as competent to judge as the master. Servants should therefore never be held in bondage as slaves or serfs. On the same principle a domestic contract cannot be concluded for life, but in all cases only for a definite period. Children, including even the children of one who has become enslaved owing to a crime, are always free; for every man is born free, because he has at birth as yet broken no law.[88]

Kant concludes his survey of the principles of private right with an account of what he terms ideal modes of acquisition, that is to say, acquisition which involves no causality in time and which is founded upon a mere idea of pure reason. He holds there are three such modes of acquisition—usucapion, inheritance, and the continuing right of a good name after death, the latter mode representing an attitude to which the law of defamation generally has not given its approbation. Kant also considers certain forms of acquisition—gifts, loans, lost property, and the security which is gained through the taking of an oath—from the point of view of their association

[86] *Ex parte Boylston*, 2 Strob. 41 (S. C. 1846).
[87] *Hall* v. *United States*, 2 Otto 37 (1876).
[88] *P. L.* 132-40.

with the judicial process.[89] But he introduces no new principles
at this point in his argument, and it is therefore unnecessary to
examine it in any detail.

Thus in the Kantian system, the principle of the external
mine and thine carries the whole burden of the private rights
of persons. At the opening of the Institutes of Justinian we
are told that the study of law is divided into two branches:
public law was that part which has to do with the government
of the Roman Empire; private law was that part which concerned the interests of individuals.[90] Kant's public law, as will
be seen, is also a system of constitutional law. However, Kant
has transformed the Roman classification into a formal system
of law based upon a set of postulates which purportedly, in
themselves and in the conclusions deducible from them, express
the regulatory principles applicable to private and public rights.
Kant's principle of the external mine and thine has the merit of
great generality. By its terms it covers such basic categories as
property and contract in their root aspects. But it goes further
than that: Its generality is such that the modern theory of
interests, which classifies interests as (a) interests of personality; (b) domestic interests; and (c) interests of substance,
admittedly builds directly upon Kant's three-fold classification
of rights as personal, real-personal and real.[91] On its face,
therefore, the Kantian analysis, at least in its abstract phase,
is sufficiently general to embrace the entire contemporary field
of private rights, *i. e.*, the individual interests which are secured
by law. But the most cursory inspection reveals that in
actuality it falls far short of this. That is to say, there are large
areas of the law occupied by doctrines relating to individual
interests—trusts, for example—which in principle may be
covered by Kant's theory but which he does not discuss at all.
It is easy to perceive that the theory of trusts falls within the
principle of the external mine and thine; but it is also apparent
that adjustments would have to be made in the principle if it is

[89] *P. L.* 141-54.
[90] I. 1. 4.
[91] Pound, *Interests of Personality*, 28 Harv. L. Rev. 343, 349-50 (1915).

fully to account for the law of trusts, since it is clear that many
trust doctrines cannot be deduced from the premises established
by Kant. In the modern theory of interests this difficulty is
avoided through the use of the method of enumeration. In
the Kantian system the classes of rights are deduced from
the principles; in the modern theory they are established
inductively.

Stated generally, the task of formalistic theories of law is
to achieve the universality which will comprehend the possible
legal systems, and at the same time allow for the differences
which the separate systems necessarily will exhibit. But to
accomplish this end the formalistic theory must establish indicia
which will show when the determination is juridically indifferent
and when it is significant. The requirement in Anglo-American
law of a sufficent consideration in the formation of informal
contracts is not paralleled by the Roman or modern Continental
law. Is this a matter to which a formal theory of law should
be indifferent or not? Formalism's great weakness is that it is
nondiscriminating in an area where discrimination is necessary.
This is clearly shown by Kant's insistence on the proposition
that a lie is never justified; but moralists have never accepted
the idea that a lie told to an intended assassin in order to save
an innocent life is not justified. In the Kantian theory a
discrimination of this kind is condemned on the ground that it
destroys the universality of the system. However, it is precisely
this kind of discrimination which formalistic systems must
make if they are to be effective. Formalistic theories must also
provide for the growth of the system and supply indicia from
which rules can be deduced to cover new situations. Kant put
illicit sex relations on the level with cannibalism; [92] he also, as
we saw above, placed such a value upon the worth of a good
name that he would permit satisfaction for the calumny of a
dead person.[93] To date the rule of the American courts is that
no damages will be allowed for the mental distress and humiliation caused a woman who receives a proposal of illicit inter-

[92] *P. L.* 239.   [93] *P. L.* 139.

course, "the view being, apparently, that there is no harm in asking." [94] It is arguable that Kant would hold otherwise; but there is nothing in his system from which that conclusion can be strictly deduced.

THE JURIDICAL STATE

Kant has now isolated the rights which individuals may claim as their own, and he has worked out the principles on which those rights are founded. But he has not yet told us how the rights are to be secured. His solution of this problem contained little that was new, and is clearly derived from Hobbes [95] and others. He argued that the juridical state alone contains the conditions under which it is possible for every one to obtain the right that is his due. [96] The formal principle of actually participating in such right is public justice, which has three aspects: protective justice, commutative justice and distributive justice. In protective justice the law declares merely what relation is internally right in respect of form; in commutative justice it declares what is likewise externally in accord with a law in respect of the object, and what possession is rightful; in distributive justice it declares what is right, and what is just, and to what extent, by the judgment of a court in any particular case coming under the given law.

Now the non-juridical state is that condition of society in which there is no distributive justice, and is commonly called the state of nature. Its opposite is the civil state, which possesses distributive justice. Juridical forms of society, such as marriage and parental authority, may exist in a state of nature; but there is no incumbent obligation *a priori* to enter into any of those forms. However, in the juridical state, persons ought to enter into them. Private right therefore finds its domain in the non-juridical state, and public right finds its domain in the civil state. But the latter state contains no more and no other

---

[94] Magruder, *Mental and Emotional Disturbance in the Law of Torts* (1936) 49 Harv. Law Rev. 1033, 1055.

[95] *Leviathan* (1651), 98 *et seq.*

[96] *P. L.* 155.

duties of men towards each other than what may be conceived in connection with the former state. Thus the matter of private right is exactly the same in both. The laws of the civil state, therefore, only turn upon the juridical form of the co-existence of men under a common constitution; and in this respect these laws must necessarily be regarded as public laws.

In contemporary social theory Kant's main point is now a commonplace. It is important, for certain purposes, to distinguish the state from other groupings of individuals, such as society, associations and communities. Kant locates in the legal order the precise criterion which marks the difference between the state and other groupings. This conception does not necessarily involve any commitment with respect to either a liberal or an authoritarian view of the state. In the hands of a liberal sociologist such as R. M. MacIver, whose attitude on this question is identical with Kant's,[97] it can lead to a completely liberal theory of state power. But Kant's constitutional theory was autocratic in important doctrines, and he therefore at this point prepared the way for it. He denied that the civil union in a strict sense was a society, on the ground that there was no sociality in common between the ruler and the subject under a civil constitution. They are not co-ordinated as associates in a society with each other; the subject is subordinated to the ruler. Those who may be co-ordinated with one another must consider themselves as mutually equal, in so far as they stand under common law. Kant therefore held that the civil union is to be regarded not so much as being, but rather as making a society. Whether or not the ruler was *legibus solutus* was, of course, a much debated question prior to Kant. The early Christian Fathers, St. Augustine, St. Ambrose and St. Isidore of Seville, apparently favored the idea that the prince ought to obey his laws; but later civilians such as Baldus held that the prince was not under his laws, that he rules others and is ruled by no one.[98] However, in the mediaeval Germanic practice, which may have influenced Kant, it was customary for the princes frequently to acknowledge that they were bound by the law; [99] and it was this rule, notwithstanding the autocratic element in his thinking, that Kant urged. Although at first glance it would appear that the prince ought to be subject to the law, the proposition is not self-evident. Is the state subject to the same morality that is applicable to its citizens? " It is ridiculous," Montesquieu said, " to pretend to decide the rights of kingdoms, of nations, and of the whole globe, by the same maxims on which (to make use of an expression of Cicero) we should determine the right of a gutter between individuals." [100] The same thought was also expressed by Holmes: " A State is superior to the forms that it may require of its citizens." [101] However, this doctrine appears to have its roots in expediency; at least we still await its theoretical justification.

On the basis of the conditions of private right in the natural state Kant formulated the postulate of public right: In the relation of unavoidable co-existence with others, thou shalt pass from the state of nature into a juridical union constituted under the condition of a distributive justice.[102] Kant accepted Hobbes' view that the state of nature was a war of all against all; but it cannot be said, Kant maintained, that even in cases of actual hostility that the individuals involved do wrong or injustice to one another. However, in general they must be considered as being in the highest state of wrong, as being and willing to be in a condition which is not juridical.

Kant therefore defines public right as the whole of the laws that require to be universally promulgated in order to produce a juridical state of society.[103] It is the necessary system of laws to order the conduct of the people who constitute a nation,

6 *ibid.* (1936) 82. Under the common law the king's powers were limited. 4 Holds. 201-202.

[99] Kern, *Kingship and Law in the Middle Ages* (1939) 75.

[100] *Esprit des Lois* (1748, Nugent's trans.) XXVI, c. 16.

[101] *Virginia* v. *West Virginia*, 220 U. S. 28 (1911).

[102] *P. L.* 157.

[103] *P. L.* 161.

and to regulate the relations of nations themselves. Since men and nations have a mutual influence on one another, they require a juridical constitution uniting them under one will, in order that they may participate in what is right. In the relationship of the individuals of a nation to one another we have the civil union in the social state; taken as a whole in relation to its constitutent members, it forms the political state.

What Kant hoped to gain by a separation of public right from private right is not clear. Since he identified private right in the non-juridical state with natural law, and since he further maintained that private right in both the juridical and non-juridical state were identical, he could for all that appears have made his point with a brief excursus on natural law. In truth, he appears to be the victim of the distinction taken in Roman law between public and private law. It is not a necessary distinction in legal systems, and while it is held to have been a useful factor in the development of Roman legal science, it is also recognized that it had certain disadvantages.[104] In the actual ordering of the life of a state the two sets of rules are intimately associated; but the distinction keeps them vividly apart. Thus Roman jurists gave little or no attention to constitutional and administrative law, to the law relating to public property, to the public law relating to real property, public acquisition of real property, and the public law limitations on land ownership. This method of treatment has resulted, for example, in a distorted view of the Roman law of real property, which takes on an appearance of liberality which it did not possess if the public law limitations are taken into consideration. However, as an advantage, Roman private law attained the form of a highly developed system, " tinged," Savigny wrote, " with an assurance not found elsewhere except in mathematics, and it is no exaggeration to say that they made calculations with their conceptions."[105] This resulted, as in the Kantian system, in Roman private law taking on a natural

---

[104] Schulz, *Principles of Roman Law* (1936) 27 *et seq.*
[105] *Vom Beruf unser Zeit f. Gesetzegebung u. Rechtswissenschaft* (1840) 29. Quoted *op. cit.* note 104 at 36.

law aspect, so that with its revival in the Middle Ages it was regarded as a kind of law of nature, a *ratio scripta*. [106] Perhaps the truth of the matter lies in Jhering's observation that at bottom private law and public law were indistinguishable in their " subject "; one but had to do solely with the private rights of individuals, and the other was available to all citizens generally.[107]

CONSTITUTIONAL LAW

Political theory and law are hopelessly intertwined in Kant's treatment of public rights. No doubt a sound constitutional system must have its foundation in valid political conceptions; but Kant's political theory is a hash of the principles of Hobbes, Montesquieu, Rousseau and others, and the legal conceptions which he puts forward are not, for all their apparent mixture, necessarily related to the political principles.

He defines a state as the union of a number of men under juridical laws, and he holds that the laws as such are to be regarded as necessary *a priori*, and not as merely established by statute. The form of the state is thus involved in the idea of the state; and this ideal form furnishes the normal criterion of every real union that constitutes a commonwealth. Every state contains three powers—legislative, executive and judicial.[108]

The legislative power can only belong to the united will of the people. All rights proceed from this power, and it is therefore necessary that its laws should be unable to do wrong to anyone. Kant attempts to explain this point through the idea of a united and consenting will. If any one individual determines anything in the state in contradistinction to another, it is always possible that he may perpetuate a wrong on that other; but this is never possible when all determine and decree what is to be law to themselves. Hence it is only the united and consenting will of all the people—in so far as each of them

---

[106] *Op. cit.* note 104 at 37.
[107] 1 *Geist des Römischen Rechts* (1852) 195.
[108] *P. L.* 165.

determines the same thing about all, and all determine the same thing about each—that ought to have the power of enacting law in the state. Kant is here insisting upon a doctrine which Madison [109] had urged in other terms, the doctrine that the greatest enemy of popular government is the growth of faction or, in modern phraseology, pressure groups. But the mere vesting of ultimate power in the legislature is not, as contemporary democratic practices make clear, the final solution of the problem, however much it may be a necessary step towards that solution. Further, if the legislature decrees a course of action to which I am opposed and have duly voted against, does it express the united and consenting will of all? Rousseau, through the idea of the General Will, answers that it does, on the ground that the conflict is only apparent; the legislature gives expression to what I really desire although I am not aware of it, and may in fact by my action oppose it. Kant does not reveal whether his idea of a united will embodies this conception.

The citizen of the state possesses three juridical attributes that inseparably belong to him by right: The right to have to obey no other law than that to which he has given his consent or approval; the right to recognize no one as a superior among the people in relation to himself, except in so far as such a one is as subject to his moral power to impose obligations, as that other has power to impose obligations upon him; the right to owe his existence and continuance in society not to the arbitrary will of another, but to his own rights and powers as a member of the commonwealth; and consequently, the possession of a civil personality which cannot be represented by any other than himself. These noble-sounding principles disclose with what ease Bills of Rights may be devised, and with what difficulty their draftsmanship is attended if they are to possess any significant meaning. For in the next breath Kant excludes apprentices, servants, women, and all who are compelled to maintain themselves under the control of others, *e. g.*, wood-

---

[109] *The Federalist*, No. 10.

cutters, resident tutors, and ploughmen, from civil personality. However, they are entitled to be treated according to laws of natural freedom and equality, as passive parts of the state.

Kant makes a distinction between the universal sovereign as head of the state, which he defines as the people itself united into a nation,[110] and the individual person who possesses the executive power.[111] This is an essential distinction in constitutional theory occupied with any state short of an absolute autocracy, and arises immediately upon the denial of the truth of Louis XIV's purported assertion " l'état c'est moi." So far as can be determined from his writings Kant has only one object in view: the ascertainment of the form of the state which he considers ideal, and the justification of the principles which should prevail in that state. Unlike Aristotle he therefore ignores all other possible forms of the state, from absolute autocracy at one limit to anarchy at the other. At the same time, his theory of the state contains elements which liberal opinion would repudiate as characteristic of the authoritarian approach.

The universal sovereign is the ruling power and its function is to govern; the individuals of the nation are the subjects, the ruled constitutents, and their function is to obey. The people constituted itself a state by an original contract; by this act they gave up their external freedom in order to receive it immediately again as members of a commonwealth. The individual, therefore, has not sacrificed a part of his inborn external freedom for a particular purpose; he has abandoned his wild lawless freedom wholly, in order to find all his proper freedom again entire and undiminished, but in the form of a regulated order of dependence, that is, in a civil state regulated by laws of right. It is thus on the basis of the individual's own regulative law-giving will that Kant accounts for the relation of dependence. Furthermore, he carefully limits the idea of the original contract to merely an outward mode of representing the conception by which the rightfulness of the process of organizing the constitution may be made conceivable. But it needs little reflection to perceive that consent is not a sufficient justification ethically upon which to base authority. Many slaves in the Southern states at the close of the Civil War would willingly have consented to a continuation of their slave status. Kant himself held that it was morally impossible for an individual voluntarily to give up his whole freedom to another.[112] Consent may be a desirable element in the recognition of authority; but it cannot transform the morally unjustifiable into the morally proper.

From these general premises Kant drew the logically necessary conclusions; but no actual state has ever exhibited them, and it is unlikely that ethics could sustain them. He held that the three powers of the state in their relations with each other are (a) co-ordinate with one another as so many moral persons, and the one is thus the complement of the other for the completion of the constitution of the state; (b) they are also subordinate to one another, so that their separate function cannot be usurped; and (c) through the union of both relations they assign distributively to every subject his own rights. In its dignity, the will of the sovereign legislator, in respect of what constitutes the external mine and thine, is to be regarded as blameless; the executive function of the supreme ruler is to be regarded as irresistible; and the judicial sentence of the supreme judge is to be regarded as irreversible, being beyond appeal.[113] Kant's view of the blamelessness of the legislative power involves a direct denial of the ancient conception of natural law as a form of higher law. The enactment in the United States, on the authority of a duly adopted constitutional amendment, of repressive minority laws, would in his theory be fully valid. But a natural law theory would deny this. It would hold, as Cooley argued, that amendments to the Constitution " cannot be revolutionary; they must be harmonious with the body of the instrument." [114] For such a theory to be effective, it would

---

[112] *P.L.* 119.
[113] *P.L.* 170.
[114] *The Power to Amend the Federal Constitution,* 2 Mich. L. Jr. 109 (1893).

have to be widely held as an article of faith by the electorate; but in that event no such amendment would be adopted. A society which believes in the desirability of legislation of this type is closer in its thinking to Kant than to Antigone, and if the modern doctrine is sound that courts should follow the will of the people, it is unlikely that natural law would be much of a refuge.

The executive authority in Kant's theory is the supreme agent of the state. It appoints the magistrates and promulgates the laws enacted by the legislature; as a moral person it constitutes the government.[115] Kant insists that the orders issued by the government to the people, the magistrates and the administrators are not laws but rescripts or decrees; for they terminate in the decision of particular cases, and are given forth as unchangeable. Furthermore, if they were law the government would be a despotic one. It is true that rescripts are not law under the Kantian conception that law is the whole of the circumstances according to which the free will of individuals may be reconciled according to a universal rule of freedom.[116] But in the Roman law rescripts sometimes had the force of law,[117] and in the United States today it would be difficult, from the point of view of their effect, to distinguish many executive orders from legislation. Nevertheless the point Kant makes is an important one. Is there an essential difference between law and administration? Kelsen, the leader of the neo-Kantians, tells us, contrary to the teachings of Kant, that there is not.[118] Pound, the chief of the sociological school, assures us with Kant that the distinction is a vital one.[119] It is argued, on the one hand, that functionally it is impossible to perceive any difference, on the other, that unless one is made absolutism is inevitable.

Kant held that the legislative power should be clearly sepa-

[115] *P. L.* 171.
[116] *P. L.* 45.
[117] *Op. cit.* note 55 at 20.
[118] *General Theory of Law and State* (1945) 274 *et seq.*
[119] *Administrative Law* (1942) *passim.*

rated from the executive, inasmuch as the ruler should stand under the authority of the law, and is bound by it under the supreme control of the legislator. The legislative authority may therefore deprive the governor of his power, depose him, or reform his administration, but not punish him. He makes the curious assertion that this is the proper and only meaning of the English maxim "The King can do no wrong." But it was specifically provided that Henry VI, who was nevertheless King although under age, should be physically chastised whenever he "trespasseth or doth amys." Kant argued that an application of punishment would necessarily be an act of that very executive power to which the supreme right to compel according to law pertains, and which would itself be thus subjected to coercion; and this would be self-contradictory. This argument was also advanced in the debates on the Federal Constitution at the Philadelphia Convention in 1787, except that it extended to impeachment itself. In spite of the apparent force of the proposition that officials who violate their public trust should be removable from office, to say nothing of being subjected to punishment, the final vote on the issue in the Convention was eight to two, with Massachusetts and South Carolina in the negative.[120] To date the American constitutional solution which allows both impeachment and punishment, but refers the latter to the regular processes of law seems a wise course. But it has not been tested in a crucial case; and Hamilton's fears may some day be realized that if the issue ever arises it will be impossible to divorce the political from the juridical aspects of the matter, so that the question will not be resolved on its proper grounds.

Finally, Kant insists upon separating the judicial function from both the legislative and executive powers, although he argues that it is by means of the executive authority that the judge holds power to assign to every one his own.[121] It is only

[120] 5 Elliot, *Debates* (1845) 343. Kant's argument is also stated by Hamilton but refuted by him on the ground that the doctrine of the separation of powers permits a "partial intermixture." *The Federalist*, No. 66.

[121] *P. L.* 173.

the people, Kant holds, that can properly judge in a cause; either the executive or the legislative authority might do an individual wrong in their determinations in cases of dispute with respect to the property of individuals, inasmuch as individuals are merely passive in their relationship to the supreme power which assigns to any one what is his. It is even beneath the dignity of the Sovereign to act as judge; for by so doing he would put himself in a position in which it would be possible to do wrong, and thus to subject himself to the demand for an appeal to a still higher power. Kant recognizes that the people can judge in a cause only indirectly, *e. g.*, by representatives elected and deputed by themselves, as in a jury. Judges should be appointed, Kant holds, by the executive power. On the basis of the British experience, which follows this method, Kant's proposition has much to support it. The American state practice of electing judges has little or nothing to recommend it, and in some states an attempt has been made to meet its obvious defects, through the cooperation of the principal parties in the re-election of able judges irrespective of their political allegiance. However, the Swiss system of legislative appointment of judges has apparently worked well in that country. If we put aside appointment by election as impossible, on the ground that the electorate does not possess the technical information to estimate properly the judicial qualities of candidates, we are faced with only two other methods—legislative or executive appointment. Either system will work satisfactorily if coupled with an adequate sense of responsibility; both will break down if that factor is absent. It is argued that in the nature of things the executive would have a greater awareness of the obligation involved than would the legislative power, where political pressures and the necessity for compromise are more immediate. But the historical evidence adduced for this position is far from conclusive.

When there is cooperation of the three divisions of government the state realizes its autonomy. This autonomy consists in its organizing, forming and maintaining itself in accordance

with the laws of freedom. In the union of the three divisions
the welfare of the state is achieved. This does not mean merely
the individual well-being and happiness of the citizens. Kant
expressly follows Rousseau in arguing that the welfare of the
group is more important than the welfare of the citizens. If
we look merely for individual well-being it can perhaps be
attained, Rousseau asserted, more desirably in a state of nature.
But the welfare of the state as its own highest good is reached
when the greatest harmony is attained between its constitution
and the principles of right. To individualist theory this argument, of course, makes no appeal. That the welfare of the
state is something different from the welfare of its citizens
is an abstraction that is either meaningless or else is an attempted justification of state power that cannot be admitted;
the welfare of the state means the welfare of the citizens, and it
is the citizens and not the state who are the ultimate judge of
that condition. If the Rousseau-Kant argument is taken sociologically, in the sense of the group versus the individual, the
anarchist position has still to be met. In the last resort the
individual must determine for himself whether he will follow
collective action or oppose it. If he opposes it, he must accept
whatever penalties that position entails, from execution at one
end, as in the case of Socrates, to relatively harmless social
displeasure at the other.

Kant attempted to solve several constitutional questions
which had vexed his predecessors. Today they possess for the
most part little beyond an historical interest; but the twentieth
century tendency towards autocracy may again give them an
immediacy. Is the sovereign, viewed as embodying the legislative power, to be regarded as the supreme proprietor of the
soil, or only as the highest ruler of the people by the law?
Martinus in the twelfth century had argued that the Emperor
had a true ownership of all things; at the same time Baldus had
" taught that above private ownership there stood only a
Superiority on the part of the State, which was sometimes
expressly called a mere *iurisdictio et protectio*, and which even

when it was supposed to be a sort of dominium, a sort of over-ownership, was still treated in a purely ' publicistic ' manner." [122] Kant maintained that the sovereign was the supreme proprietor of the land, but only in the sense of an idea of the civil constitution, objectified to represent, in accordance with juridical conceptions, the necessary union of the private property of all the people under a public universal possessor. [123] The representation of the relation in this manner forms a basis for the determination of particular rights in property. It also denies any private property in the soil to the supreme universal proprietor; for otherwise he would make himself a private person. Private property in the soil belongs only to the people, taken distributively and not collectively. The supreme proprietor accordingly ought not to hold private estates, either for private use or for the support of the court. If the opposite rule were permitted the extent of the sovereign's domains would depend upon his pleasure, and all land would be taken by the government and all citizens treated as bondsmen of the soil. To meet this same point, and others, various American states have placed limitations on the quantity of land which may be owned by corporations. Kant therefore concludes that the supreme proprietor of the land possesses nothing of his own except himself; otherwise disputes with others would be possible and there would be no independent judge to settle the cause. However, this problem, as earlier and later history shows, can be solved in a different manner. If the state possesses property, then there must be, as Kant saw, an independent judiciary to adjudicate claims. This is one of the principal meanings of the growth of remedies against the crown in England from the thirteenth century to the present day. In an autocratic state an independent judiciary no doubt is not to be looked for; but in other forms of government it can be taken as a matter of course. The mediaeval idea of a *judex medius* was fully expressed in the Aragon constitution, [124] and has its counterpart today in such in-

---

[122] Gierke, *Political Theories of the Middle Age* (1938) 79.
[123] *P. L.* 183.
[124] *Op. cit.* note 99 at 125.

stitutions as the United States Court of Claims and in the practices of the Supreme Court in suits in which the government is a party in interest. Although the sovereign possesses nothing, it may also be said, Kant argued, that he possesses everything; for he has the supreme right of sovereignty over the whole people to whom all external things severally belong; and as such he assigns to every one what is to be his. Kant is here merely stating one of the dogmas of the doctrine of sovereignty which, however much it may be exemplified in today's practices, has still not been satisfactorily stated. Should the state be allowed to take or destroy private property without compensation? That it does so does not mean that the practice is sound constitutionally; for an ideal of health, the vast liquor industry in the United States was wiped out without compensation; for an ideal of race, the private property of the Jews was expropriated in Germany; for an ideal of economics, private property of certain classes is appropriated by the European and other governments which adopt the communist system. A sound theory of ideals, which would permit a discrimination, might provide the bases for a solution of the problem; but there is little room in history for any expectation that a people in the grip of a reform movement will heed the dictates of a rational ethics which runs counter to their frenzy.

On the basis of the sovereign right to assign property distributively Kant would permit the state to reclaim corporate and church property, and that of the nobility, whenever the usefulness of the particular institution has ceased to exist. But in all cases survivors must be indemnified for their interests.[125] Kant also insisted upon a correlative doctrine. The government is justified in compelling those who are able to furnish the means necessary to preserve those who are not themselves capable of providing for the most necessary wants of nature to furnish them. In particular, he urges relief for the poor, the establishment of foundling asylums, and aid to charitable and

---

[125] *P. L.* 184. cf. *Ruppert* v. *Caffey*, 251 U. S. 264 (1920), where the government was permitted, under the prohibition laws, to close the breweries without compensation.

pious foundations. However, the actual cost of maintaining the church should fall, he thinks, only upon the people who profess the particular faith of the church. He does not express any opinion on the legitimacy of indirect state subsidies to churches, such as exemption from taxes. To the supreme authority in the state Kant assigned the right of distributing offices and conferring dignities. He asked whether the sovereign has the right, after bestowing an office on an individual, to take it away again at his mere pleasure, without any crime having been committed by the holder. He answered emphatically, *No.* As Mr. Justice Brandeis observed, in his dissent against the view that the President could remove officials without the consent of the Senate, an essential of free government was held in 1787 to be the protection of officials against " the arbitrary or capricious exercise of power." [126]

Kant's absolutistic attitude is best illustrated in his arguments against a right of revolution.[127] He argues that the supreme power in the State has only rights and no duties towards the subject. If the head of the state violates the law the subject may oppose a complaint to the injustice, but not active resistance. In no case is resistance on the part of the people to the supreme legislative power legitimate. It is the duty of the people to bear any abuse of the supreme power, even though it should be considered to be unbearable. Kant's reason is that any resistance of the highest legislative authority must always be contrary to law, and must even be regarded as tending to destroy the whole legal constitution. There cannot, he says, even be an article contained in the political constitution that would make it possible for a power in the state, in case of the transgression of the constitutional laws by the supreme authority, to resist or even to restrict it in so doing. The argument is that it would be self-contradictory for the constitution so to provide. But this point is easily met through Locke's theory that the legislative is only a fiduciary power;

[126] *Myers* v. *United States,* 272 U. S. 52, 294 (1926).
[127] *P. L.* 174 *et seq.*

therefore " the community perpetually retains a supreme power of saving themselves from the attempts and designs of anybody, even of their legislators, whenever they shall be so foolish or so wicked as to lay and carry on designs against the liberties and properties of the subject." [128] In the constitutions of New Hampshire, Pennsylvania and Delaware, in the Declaration of Independence and in the Declaration of the Rights of Man of 1789, the right of revolution was expressly recognized. Kant's argument that it is impossible for a constitution to provide for its own forcible change is thus met by actual historical cases to the contrary. Of course, constitutions can be self-contradictory, and perhaps ought not to be. But apart from Locke's theory, there seems to be no reason why the community may not substitute one legal order for another, and by revolutionary means if it so desires. Even if the legal order which it is preparing to overthrow embodies absolute perfection, which is the only possible argument for a denial of the right, it is certainly within the competence of the community to desire an order which might perhaps subject them to a different mode of living. In a twentieth-century version of the myth of the Creation, when God saw " that Man had become perfect in renunciation and worship, he sent another sun through the sky, which crashed into Man's sun; and all returned again to nebula." [129] Revolutions, as historical examples show, may come about simply out of a desire for change.[130] For legal theory to attempt to declare such a process inherently criminal or impossible would be to subject itself to the likelihood that it will be overruled by future events.

CRIMINAL LAW

Kant's anti-utilitarianism is nowhere better exhibited than in his theory of punishment. His whole conception of the criminal law turns on the idea of retributive justice, to which he commits

---

[128] *Two Treatises of Government,* II, sec. 149.
[129] Russell, *Mysticism and Logic* (1925) 47.
[130] Ortega y Gasset, *Concord and Liberty* (1946) 36-37.

himself without reservation. He holds that punishment can never be administered merely as a means for promoting another good either with regard to the criminal himself or to civil society, but must in all cases be imposed only because the individual on whom it is inflicted has committed a crime.[131] A man ought never to be dealt with merely as a means subservient to the purpose of another, nor be mixed up with the idea of rights in things. Against such treatment his inborn personality has a right to protect him, although he may be condemned to lose his civil personality. He must first be found guilty and punishable, before there can be any thought of drawing from his punishment any benefit for himself or his fellow-citizens. To this point Kant's argument seems beyond attack. He has not ruled out reformation or deterrence as possible objects of punishment; he has insisted that these purposes ought not to be brought into view until it has first been determined that a crime has been committed by the person on trial. In the present state of our knowledge, the proposition that the criminal law could operate upon an individual before there had been a transgression of the law would be untenable. In the future, psychiatry or some other branch of knowledge may be able to predict with disturbing certainty that particular individuals will commit certain specified crimes. Remarkable instances of this kind have occurred in the past; but they have not been numerous enough to warrant a reconsideration of the basic principle which Kant has set forth.

However, Kant goes further and argues that retribution is the only rationally just principle of punishment. The penal law, he maintains, is a categorical imperative; and woe to him who creeps through the serpent-windings of utilitarianism to discover some advantage that may discharge him from the justice of punishment, or even from the due measure of it, according to the Pharisaic maxim: "It is better that one man should die than that the whole people should perish." Kant puts the case of a criminal condemned to death, but who agrees to

[131] *P. L.* 195.

permit a dangerous medical experiment to be performed upon him on the understanding that his life will be spared if he survive. Kant would execute the criminal on the ground that justice would cease to be justice if it were bartered away for any consideration whatever. Retaliation is the only principle which can definitely assign both the quality and the quantity of a just penalty; all other standards are wavering and uncertain. Thus, whoever has committed murder must die. In this case there is no judicial substitute or surrogate that can be given or taken for the satisfaction of justice. There is no likeness or proportion between life, however painful, and death; and therefore there is no equality between the crime of murder and the retaliation of it but what is judicially accomplished by the execution of the criminal. Kant then states his famous case of a civil society ready to dissolve itself with the consent of all its members—as might be supposed in the case of a people inhabiting an island resolving to separate and scatter themselves throughout the world. Under those circumstances the last murderer lying in prison ought to be executed before the resolution is carried out. The murderer will then realize the desert of his deeds, and there will be no bloodguilt upon the people; otherwise they might all be regarded as participators in the murder as a public violation of justice.

From Plato [132] to the latest volume on criminology the retributive view of punishment has met with vigorous condemnation. However, it has not been without enlightened support since Kant's day.[133] The opposing theories of reformation and deterrence are attacked on the ground that their supporters will not face the logical consequences involved. If punishment is a deterrent, then the family of the offender should also be punished, since this would increase the deterrent element. Further, the heaviest punishment should be inflicted in cases of the maximum provocation, since they need a greater deterrent. Thus crimes of passion would be punished severely, but a crime

---

[132] *Protagoras* 324 B.
[133] Kohler, *Philosophy of Law* (1914) 283; 1 Westermarck, *Origin and Development of the Moral Ideas* (2nd ed. 1912) 79 *et seq*.

of parricide would be viewed leniently since filial affection is already present as a restraining influence. If reformation is the guiding principle, the petty offender, such as drunkards and vagrants might receive life sentences, since they are the most incorrigible of all offenders, while perpetrators of serious crimes might be treated lightly, since statistics seem to show that they are the most easily reformed. However, arguments by way of horrible examples are not conclusive; there is no compulsion on society to adopt all the consequences of any view to which it adheres. England, as Disraeli observed, is not governed by logic; she is governed by Parliament. The fatal error in the Kantian theory is its conception of justice as an end in itself. If the sole end of society is justice then Kant's argument is unassailable; but if some other good is sought, such as Aristotelian happiness, then the retributive theory may not be the agency to accomplish that end. To analyze the problem properly it appears that we need ask only two questions: What is the end of the criminal law? Does punishment assist in the realization of that end? If the end of the criminal law is the promotion of the common interest, as most jurists from Aristotle to the present have insisted, that common interest must still be determined for the particular society before the first question can be answered properly. It may be happiness, economic security, religious freedom, military superiority or other objectives or mixtures of them. But not until the end is precisely envisaged and a correlation established between that end and retribution, deterrence, reformation or some other objective is a concrete solution of the problem possible. It may well be that the whole idea of punishment may be found to have no foundation and ought to be abandoned. In that event criminals might be segregated, as are the mentally disordered, until they could safely be restored to society.

In spite of the logical rigor of his position Kant found himself forced to make three exceptions to the categorical imperative that the murderer must die. Suppose there are so many accomplices to the murder that the State, in resolving to be without such criminals, would be in danger of soon also being deprived of subjects. In that case the sovereign as a matter of necessity may assign some other punishment and thereby preserve the people.[134] It is difficult to perceive why the principle of this exception would not also justify sparing the life of a criminal who survived a dangerous medical experiment the results of which preserved the population from the ravages of a calamitous plague. Kant would also not apply the death penalty to the survivor of a duel. He does not think that killing under those circumstances is murder, inasmuch as it takes place publicly, with the consent of both parties, and is intended to satisfy an idea of honor. In this position Kant joined hands with Utilitarianism. Bentham thought that duelling served a social purpose by filling a gap which the law ignored. If the law gave the same protection to honor that it gave to the person then duelling could be safely abolished.[135] Finally Kant would not inflict the death penalty in cases of maternal infanticide with respect to an illegitimate child. He argues that the child is beyond the protection of the law, that it is analogous to smuggled goods, and as it has no legal right to existence its destruction may be ignored.

In the maintenance of his position Kant took account of the arguments of Beccaria against the justice of the death penalty. Beccaria argued that capital punishment is wrong because the penalty of death could not be contained in the original social contract; for in that case every one would have had to consent to lose his life if he committed murder. But such a consent is impossible, because no one can thus dispose of his own life. Kant denounces this as mere sophistry. No one undergoes punishment because he has willed to be punished, but because he has willed a punishable action. The individual who, as a co-legislator, enacts penal law, cannot possibly be the same person who, as a subject, is punished according to the law; for, *quâ* criminal, he cannot possibly be regarded as a legislator, who is rationally viewed as just and holy. If any one then enact a

[134] *P. L.* 200.   [135] 1 *Works* (1843) 380, 542.

penal law against himself as a criminal, it must be the pure juridically law-giving reason (*homo noumenon*) which subjects him as one capable of crime, and consequently as another person (*homo phenomenon*), along with all the others in the civil union, to this penal law. Beccaria's chief error, in Kant's view, consists in regarding the judgment of the criminal himself, necessarily determined by his reason, that he is under obligation to undergo the loss of his life, as a judgment that must be grounded on a resolution of his will to take it away himself. Thus the execution of the right in question is represented as united in one and the same person with the adjudication of the right.

Kant allowed the right of pardoning, but only in the case of treason or some form of it. He would not permit the right to be exercised in application to crimes of the subjects against each other; for exemption from punishment would be the greatest wrong that could be done them.[136] He defined a crime as any transgression of the public law which makes him who commits it incapable of being a citizen.[137] This definition would limit crimes to felonies; but it contains the germ of the present-day conception of crime as an act forbidden by the criminal law.

INTERNATIONAL LAW

Kant's speculations on international law were a development of his view of human history. Does the human race, viewed as a whole, he asks,[138] appear worthy of being loved; or is it an object which we must look upon with repugnance, so that, while in order to avoid misanthropy, we continue to wish for it all that is good, we yet can never expect good from it, and would rather turn our eyes away from its ongoings? Kant assumes a continuous progress towards the better. He does not attempt to prove this assumption, but takes his stand on the proposition that every member in the series of generations is prompted by his sense so to act in reference to posterity that they may always become better; the possibility of this must be assumed.[139]

---

[136] *P. L.* 204.   [137] *P. L.* 194.   [138] *P. P.* 65.   [139] *P. P.* 68.

Nevertheless, there was no easy hopefulness behind this attitude; in fact, so strongly marked is Kant's pessimism that Schopenhauer's conclusion that of all conceivable worlds this is the worst, is one of the speculations for which Kant may be held ultimately responsible.[140] But for the Kants of this world pessimism seems inevitable. "Neither paganism nor Christianity," Acton [141] wrote, "ever produced a profound political historian whose mind was not turned to gloom by the contemplation of the affairs of men. It is almost a test to distinguish the great narrators from the great thinkers,—Herodotus, Livy, Froissart, Schiller, Macaulay, Thiers from Thucydides, Polybius, Tacitus, Machiavelli, Raleigh, Gibbon, Guizot, Niebuhr."

But if human nature is worthy to be loved it must establish a civil society, universally administering right according to law; [142] for it is only in such a society that the highest purpose of nature, which is the development of all her capacities, can be attained in the case of mankind. Thus the natural state of nations as well of individual men is a state which it is a duty to pass out of, in order to enter into a legal state.[143] National rights which exist before this transition are merely provisory; they can only become peremptory in a universal union of states analogous to that by which a nation becomes a state. It is only through this means that a real state of peace can be established. However, perpetual peace, which is the ultimate goal, is in fact an impracticable idea. The too great extension of a union of states over vast regions makes government, *i. e.*, the protection of individual members, impossible; and the existence of a multitude of separate states would again bring round a state of war. The political principles, however, which aim at such an end and which enjoin the formation of such unions among the states as may promote a continous approximation to a perpetual peace, are not impracticable; they are as practicable as this approximation itself, which is a practical

---

[140] Bury, *The Idea of Progress* (1920) 250.
[141] Quoted, Mathew, *Acton: The Formative Years* (1946) 98.
[142] *P. P.* 12, 76.
[143] *P. L.* 224.

problem involving a duty and founded upon the rights of men and states. This view is similar to the one advanced by Plato with respect not only to the ideal form of the State, but to all ideal forms; he said that the ideal form could only be approximated and never realized, although the urge toward perfect form is inherent in all things.

No state, Kant recognizes, is for a moment secure against another in its independence or its possessions.[144] The will to subdue one another or to reduce each other's power, is always rampant; and the equipment for defence, which often makes peace even more oppressive and more destructive of internal prosperity than war, can never be relaxed. Against such evils there is no possible remedy but a system of international right founded upon public laws enjoined with power to which every state must submit—according to the analogy of the civil right of individuals in any one state. A lasting peace on the basis of the so-called balance of power in Europe is a mere chimera. It is like the house described by Swift, which was built by an architect so perfectly in accordance with all the laws of equilibrium, that when a sparrow lighted upon it, it immediately fell. But, he asks, will the State submit to such compulsory laws. Is not his proposal a pretty theory, but of no value for practical purposes? As such has it not always been laughed at by great statesmen as a childish and pedantic idea fit only for the schools from which it takes its rise?

For his part, Kant replies, he trusts to a theory which is based upon the principle of right as determining what the relations between men and States ought to be; and which lays down to these earthly gods the maxim that they ought so to proceed in their disputes that such a universal international state may be introduced thereby, and to assume it therefore as not only possible in practice but such as may yet be presented in reality. This theory is further to be regarded as founded upon the nature of things, which compels movement in a direction even against the will of man. Under the nature of

[144] *P. P.* 75.

things, human nature is also to be taken into account; and as in human nature there is always a living respect for right and duty, Kant neither can nor will regard it as so sunk in evil that the practical moral reason could ultimately fail to triumph over this evil, even after many of its attempts have failed.

Every neighboring state is free to join the Congress of Nations which Kant envisages.[145] But he means by a Congress only a voluntary combination of different states that would be dissoluble at any time and not such a union as is embodied in the United States, founded upon a political constitution, and therefore indissoluble.

Kant couples with his idea of international law his conception of so-called cosmopolitical law. This is the right of man as a citizen of the world to attempt to enter into a communion with all others, and for this purpose to visit all the regions of the earth.[146] It does not embrace a right of settlement upon the territory of another people, for which a special contract is required. The relations between the various peoples of the world have now advanced everywhere so far that a violation of right in one place of the earth, is felt all over it.[147] Hence the idea of a cosmopolitical right of the whole human race is no fantastic mode of representing right, but is a necessary completion of the unwritten code which carries national and international right to a consummation in the public right of mankind. Thus the whole system leads to the conclusion of a perpetual peace among the nations.

Historically Kant's solution of the problem of international anarchy may be traced to mediaeval thought which conceived of a world state based on a universal ethic under divine guidance. Perpetual peace may be possible only through the establishment of the system of states contemplated by Kant; but on the empirical level it remains true that the mind of man has been able to devise only two systems which have given mankind peace for any appreciable periods of time—the balance of power and world domination by one state. It was on the latter method that mediaeval thought seized. At no time, says Dante, since the fall of our first parents, has the world been quiet on every side except under the perfect monarchy of the divine Augustus.[148] Kant's proposal is of course, a modification of this idea. For the world sovereignty of a single state, he would substitute the world sovereignty of a union of states. However, since Kant wrote there has developed no further evidence that the progress of nature is toward the realization of his idea.

Conclusion

Kant's philosophy of law was put forward in the year 1797,[149] when he was seventy-three years of age, and has often been dismissed by unsympathetic students as the product of an enfeebled old age. But this estimate in no way accounts for the fact that Kant's system has been the fountainhead of one of the most acute schools of legal philosophy which the nineteenth and twentieth centuries have known. With Stammler, Del Vecchio, and Kelsen the Kantian point of view has been carried forward to the present day in the form of an aggressive, acute philosophy of law possessed of at least as much power as any other system to capture the allegiance of contemporary thinkers. Perhaps one of the secrets of Kant's strength is that his followers can repudiate so much of what he would have regarded as vital in his thought, and still regard themselves as inspired by his teaching. Stammler [150] held the basic Kantian formula of an act as right when it is consistent with every one else's freedom, according to a universal law, to be erroneous because it undertakes at the same time to define the concept of law as well as to determine when its content is just. We are told by Kelsen [151] that the Kantian ethic can be regarded as the most perfect expression of the classical doctrine of natural law as it evolved in the seventeenth and eighteenth centuries on the

---

[148] *De Monarchia,* I, xvi.
[149] Or perhaps 1796. See 2 Erdmann, *History of Philosophy* (1909) 368.
[150] *Theory of Justice* (1925) 162.
[151] *General Theory of Law and State* (1945) 445.

basis of Protestant Christianity. For Del Vecchio Kant was not a great innovator; he merely corrected and clarified, by a rigorous method, the ancient teachings of natural law. However, he believes the natural law school had stated a sound principle: that the basis of law is in man himself; but it had given an historical meaning to what was only a rational principle; it had represented as an empirical growth what was only an ideological development. Kant's great merit lay in his suppression of the confusion between the historic and the rational, in his affirmance of the purely rational value of the principles of natural law.[152]

These criticisms suggest that Kant's continuous appeal can be accounted for by two considerations. Notwithstanding the autocratic elements to be found in his system, in its main principles it follows the liberal philosophy of Rousseau and the eighteenth century. It is a significant coincidence that the year which saw the publication of Kant's *Philosophy of Law* witnessed also the great *Defense* of Babeuf, similarly Rousseauistic in its origins, and from which the whole movement of European socialism stems. In his *Philosophy of Law* Kant set forth for the world of legal theory the possibilities of a doctrine of freedom as the basis of a legal philosophy which could not fail to appeal to subsequent liberal thought however purged of romanticism it might be.

More important was Kant's doctrine that knowledge should be based on principle, which means the power to see the particular in the universal by means of concepts. Perhaps some day, he insisted, we may find out the principles of the civil law, instead of being confronted with their infinite multiplicity. That remains not only the essential task of the Neo-Kantians, but of all jurisprudence; as an ideal it has for the jurist almost overpowering attractiveness. Stated this way the Kantian approach does not appear to raise any crucial problems. But the basic idea of Kant's system is the conception of right which is held to be purely rational in origin. In legal terms this means

[152] *Lezioni di filosofia del diritto* (1936) 90.

that the actual content of laws can be determined from purely formal principles. But Kant never demonstrates how it is possible to pass from a purely logical form, apart from material premises, to the actual content of a law.[153] There is a further difficulty. Kant's formal test of the rightness of acts is so general that it leaves room for numerous possibilities, but his system as actually presented does not contemplate those possibilities. He defines marriage as the union of two persons of different sexes for lifelong reciprocal possession of their sexual faculties. But this is an arbitrary definition. That is to say, so far as the universal law of freedom is concerned it could just as well have been otherwise. It would have been completely in accord with his universal law of freedom if he had provided that marriages should be for a term of years, as they were in old Japan. Similarly, he could have held that marriage had for one of its chief ends the production and care of children. He could then have asserted in accordance with a frequent practice that the contract of marriage is completed only by the birth of a child or by signs of pregnancy, instead of providing that it was completed only by conjugal cohabitation. But this difficulty is necessarily present in all formalistic theories of law. It was not solved by Kant or by any of his successors. It does not mean that we must abandon the valuable elements in formalism, particularly the search for principle. It teaches us specifically that a pure formalism can never cope with the facts of the legal order. It is here that the great merits of Kant are apparent. No one else has surpassed him in revealing the force of principles, if due account is taken of empirical circumstances, in the attempt to order the infinite diversity of legal phenomena.

---

[153] Cohen, *Law and the Social Order* (1933) 295.

Chapter XIII

FICHTE

*The true self, thinks Fichte, is
something infinite. It needs a
whole endless world of life to
express itself in. Its moral law
couldn't be expressed in full on
any one planet.*

Josiah Royce

FICHTE's theory of law is an attempted deduction from the
nature of self-consciousness. He held that the task of
philosophy is to explain experience, and since the whole matter
of man's thinking is contained in experience, experience must
be the starting point of philosophical analysis.[1] When we
analyze experience we find that it consists of ideas of things;
that is to say, there is an objective aspect and a subjective
aspect. There are thus, according to Fichte, two possible
systems of philosophy, idealism and dogmatism. Idealism
endeavors to explain the thing in terms of the idea; dogmatism
endeavors to explain the idea in terms of the thing. The explanatory ground of idealism is an intelligence in itself; that
of dogmatism, a thing in itself. For Fichte, idealism was the
only possible philosophy, since he held that it was beyond the
capacities of dogmatism to overcome the gulf between things
and ideas.[2]

Fichte's principal legal work is the *Grundlage des Naturrechts nach den Prin-
cipien der Wissenschaftslehre* (1796) translated by A. E. Kroeger as *The Science
of Rights* (1869). Unless otherwise specified the references are to the translation
which is cited as " S. R." In 1812 Fichte put forward a new presentation of his
legal doctrines in his *Das System der Rechtslehre.* This work is printed in vol.
II of the *Nachgelassene Werke,* 3 vols., edited by I. H. Fichte (1834-35) and is
cited here as " N. W." The most thorough account of Fichte's life and work is the
great study by Xavier Léon, *Fichte et son temps,* 3 vols. (1922-27), cited here as
" Léon." References cited as " S. W." are to Fichte's *Sämmtliche Werke,* 8 vols.
(1845-46). There is a convenient edition of the *Naturrechts* edited by Medicus
(1908), and keyed to the pages of the " S. W."

[1] *S. W.* 425.
[2] *S. W.* 438.

This point of view was inspired by Kant's failure to suggest a satisfactory theory of the thing in itself. Fichte was Kant's ablest follower, and so thoroughly had he absorbed Kant's teaching that his first work, which through an error appeared anonymously, was widely attributed to Kant himself. His theory of law, which is a remarkable approximation of Kant's own system of law, is an astonishing production; it was worked out before the appearance of Kant's system, and even before the publication of Kant's *Essay on Perpetual Peace*.[3] Fichte's excursion into jurisprudence was directly inspired, however, by a series of articles in German periodicals on natural law by several now forgotten jurists.[4] Fichte's dissatisfaction with jurisprudence as it then existed stemmed principally from the fact that little or no attempt was made to separate law from ethics. In his subsequent work he claimed that he was the first to accomplish this task, and that its realization made all other volumes on jurisprudence antiquated, with the exception of Kant's *Philosophy of Law*.[5]

For Fichte, the initial step of philosophy is the discovery of the first principle of knowledge. It is the nature of consciousness to know, and it is thus the business of philosophy to explain how that is possible and what it means. When I think about this problem I observe my self-consciousness, just as I observe any other object. Philosophy is therefore defined by Fichte as the artificial consciousness, as the consciousness of consciousness.[6] As the starting point in an effort to reach the basic principle of knowledge Fichte analyzes a simple act of judgment. He states that any universally accepted affirmative judgment could be utilized for this purpose, and the one he chooses is A =

[3] *S. R.* 22. But the basic idea of the Kantian system, which was adopted by Fichte, had been stated in the *Kritik der reinen Vernunft* (1787). The necessary idea of all law, Kant there remarked, is that of " allowing the greatest possible human freedom in accordance with laws by which the freedom of each is made to be consistent with that of all others." (Smith's trans. 1933) 312.
[4] For a summary of the leading ideas of the articles, see 1 Léon 472 *et seq.*
[5] *N. W.* 498. Schneider, *J. G. Fichte als Sozialpolitiker* (1894) 9, supports Fichte's claim.
[6] 1 *S. W.* 219; 3 Hegel, *Lectures on the History of Philosophy* (1896) 484.

A.[7] That is to say, whatever else A may be when viewed empirically, it is itself. By an intricate process of reasoning Fichte then arrives at the first principle of consciousness: The ego posits itself. Fichte's reasoning is open to many objections, of which the first is that the law of identity, $A = A$, states, if anything, only a partial truth if it refers to objects. To affirm that a thing is itself is to ignore its connection with the remainder of the universe, both from the point of view of what it contains of the universe within itself by implication, and also from the point of view of the relationship of the universe to it. If $A = A$ is regarded as expressing a judgment with respect to the object A, then it is denied in logic that the judgment is thinkable at all, since it is impossible for us to think pure identity; all actual thought is held to imply difference of some kind.[8] There is more in the consciousness than the ego, and Fichte is therefore forced to formulate a second principle which he connects with the logical assertion A is not not-A. This principle states that the " ego posits a non-ego to which it is absolutely opposed." [9] Through these two principles the affirmative and the negative aspects of judgment are accounted for. But precisely because the two principles express only aspects of judgment they cannot be in real contradiction, their opposition cannot be final. He therefore formulates a third principle which asserts that the " ego posits a divisible ego in opposition to a divisible non-ego." [10] This third principle returns the opposition of the first two principles to consciousness, and means that within the consciousness, not as a result of something forced upon it by the outside world, the ego and the non-ego mutually limit each other.

From these three principles Fichte then proceeded to deduce

---

[7] 1 *S. W.* 92.

[8] Keynes, *Formal Logic* (4th ed. 1906) 453; 1 Sigwart, *Logic* (1895) 84 *et seq.* Fichte recognized that $A = A$ was to be viewed only from the point of view of form and not from that of content; but from $A = A$ he at once deduced that Ego = the Ego $(I = I)$ which he held was valid not only in form but also in content.

[9] 1 *S. W.* 104.

[10] 1 *S. W.* 125.

certain of the categories. It was an heroic undertaking, and
the first of its kind in the history of philosophy. It extended
even to the deduction of space and time, light and air.[11] However, in its theoretical presentation Fichte's system was a purely
formal one, and was dismissed by Kant as simply an abstract
logic. It may well be, as Goethe remarked, that Fichte too often
forgets that experience is not in the least what he has imagined
it to be. At the same time no one was ever more completely
aware than Fichte that it is a logical impossibility to deduce
the material propositions of a legal order from the principles of
a purely formal system of the type he constructed.[12] A system
of philosophy, he said, which pretends to resolve human life
entirely into logical principles defeats its own purpose, and in
attempting to explain the whole of life, misses it altogether. A
philosophical system, even when perfected in its theoretical
aspects, always remains inapplicable to human affairs until
adjusted to the facts of experience, where the true inner
principles of life are to be found.[13] What, then, in his legal
philosophy, purportedly deduced from the proposition $I = I$,
was Fichte's aim? He was the declared enemy of what he
termed mere formal thinking,[14] and he held that it had
been indescribably injurious in philosophy, mathematics,[15] the
natural sciences, and indeed in all the pure sciences. A formalism which overstresses the dialectical element and permits it

[11] Fichte later remarked on the merriment in philosophical circles which greeted
this effort: "Light and air deduced *a priori* by Fichte! Think of it! ha! ha! ha!
— ha! ha! ha! — ha! ha! ha! Come! Enjoy it with us! ha! ha! ha! — ha! ha! ha! —
ha! ha! ha! Air and light *a priori!* *tarte à la crême* ha! ha! ha! Light and air *a
priori! tarte à la crême* ha! ha! ha! . . . . . . and so on endlessly." 2 *S. W.* 472-473.
And these men, Fichte added contemptuously, call themselves Kantians.

[12] 6 *S. W.* 365.

[13] 5 *S. W.* 343.

[14] *S. R.* 15.

[15] German philosophy from Kant to Schopenhauer entertained curious views of
the nature of mathematics. Whitehead's reaction to those views, however, may be
taken as a warning: "I have never been able to read Hegel," he writes. "I
initiated my attempt by studying some remarks of his on mathematics which
struck me as complete nonsense. It was foolish of me, but I am not writing to
explain my good sense." *Autobiographical Notes* in *The Philosophy of Alfred
North Whitehead* (ed. Schilpp, 1941) 7.

to contradict the existential aspects of nature can, of course, result only in absurdities. But to dismiss formal thinking as such, as Fichte appears to do, would result, since it is the root of scientific method, in greater absurdities. Fichte's condemnation of purely formal thinking was based on the belief that it yields a system of conceptions without objects, and is, hence, empty thinking. This argument, if heeded, would have prevented the construction of the tensor calculus, which appeared to possess only formal interest until it was disclosed as one of the tools which made possible the formulation of the theory of relativity.

Thus, according to Fichte, a genuine philosophy posits conception and object together, and never treats one without the other. The conception of rights, as will be seen later, is assumed to be an original conception of reason. This conception, as Fichte attempts to demonstrate, is the conception of the necessary relation of free beings to each other. The object of the conception is therefore the possibility of a community of free beings. But the idea of such a community is, as Fichte recognizes, altogether arbitrary. It is necessary, he says, that every free being should assume other free beings as existing; but it is not necessary that all these free beings, as free beings, should form a group. However, a community of free beings appears possible on the assumption that each member will limit his freedom in such a manner that others can also be free. There is no requirement in the conception of rights that such a community be erected; there is only the requirement that, if it be erected, it shall be established on the basis of the conception of rights.

Fichte's theory of rights is thus purely an *a priori* one. He has set himself the abstract problem of determining the necessary legal structure of a community of free beings, assuming such a community is desired. If philosophy, in accordance with Leibniz' definition, is understood as the science of the possible, Fichte's inquiry is then, to this extent, a strictly philosophical one. Empiricism insists that we must study only what is; but scientific thought owes much of its fruitfulness to the study of the non-existent, as the analysis of frictionless engines, free bodies, and the ether makes clear. There is thus ample warrant for Fichte's method of approach; but the value of his system will depend in the last resort on the knowledge it brings us of the external world in general, and of substantive legal systems in particular. Nevertheless, Fichte's method raises a number of problems not usually so sharply encountered in the philosophies of law. Fichte's preliminary assumptions, from which the rest of his system is deduced, seem to be at the ultimate limit of abstractness; all other systems of law rest to some extent at least upon empirical elements. Even Hobbes' system took its departure from the idea of motion, an empirical concept. But abstractness creates a special problem, *e. g.*, how is it possible for abstract rules to have an empirical application? It is one of Fichte's merits that he attempts to meet issues of this sort, and if his solutions are not always satisfactory it is not because he was not aware of the issues or endeavored to minimize them. His explicit object was to establish his propositions on the basis of reasoning of the utmost rigor, and from that aim he never deviated.

LEGAL RELATIONS

For Fichte the basis of law is the idea of the legal relation. It is the one firm foundation of jurisprudence, and in it everything is contained.[16] The conception of law is the conception of a relation between human beings.[17] It can come into existence only when such beings are thought of as in relation to each other. Fichte defines this relationship as the compulsion upon each individual to restrict his freedom in recognition of the possibility of the freedom of others.[18] He terms this formula

[16] *N. W.* 495. Spencer and others have gone further, and have purported to see in relations the universal form of thought. "We think in relations. This is truly the form of all thought; and if there are any other forms they must be derived from this." *First Principles* (1880) 135.

[17] *S. R.* 81.

[18] *S. R.* 78.

" the fundamental principle of the science of rights," and he calls the relationship itself the " relation of legality."

It would be difficult to overemphasize the importance for jurisprudence of the conception Fichte has here isolated. Nevertheless the idea was not subjected to anything approaching a thorough analysis until the latter part of the nineteenth century, and even today the leading American exposition of the concept attributes " the first theoretical discussion " of it to Savigny.[19] Although much of jurisprudence is concerned with the idea, it has never received the attention it apparently deserves. This neglect is perhaps due in large part to the circumstance that jurisprudence has never been worked out in detail as a logical system. Many of its leading ideas have received extensive critical treatment, but their logical foundations and the connections between the ideas have escaped rigorous analysis. Thus Hohfeld,[20] in one of the most influential studies in the field, set forth the eight basic ideas in terms of which he held all legal analysis could be stated. All these ideas were, as he held, " strictly fundamental legal relations "; [21] but no critical scrutiny of the idea of " legal relation " itself is undertaken at all. This condition was paralleled until recently in the history of mathematics, where natural, real, complex and other numbers, were studied with great care, but before any satisfactory conception of " number " itself was developed. The idea of " legal relation " seems to be as fundamental in jurisprudence as the idea of " number " in mathematics. As Kocourek emphasizes, " no legal phenomenon can exist without dealing with one or more jural relations. The purpose of every legal rule is to create the formal conditions for the existence of jural relations. No technical analysis of a legal question can be made without the manipulation, whether consciously or not, of jural relations. No legal solution is scientifically understand-

---

[19] Kocourek, *Jural Relations* (1927) vi. Savigny's discussion seems clearly to have been inspired directly by Fichte. 2 *System des heutigen römischen Rechts* (1839) 52 *et seq.*
[20] *Fundamental Legal Conceptions* (ed. Cook, 1923) 5.
[21] *Ibid.* 36.

able without the interplay of jural facts and jural relations." [22]
All this Fichte saw with one of his flashes of deep insight which
enabled him to crystalize the essence of the matter.

Fichte's philosophical scruples would not permit him to take
the conception of the legal relation for granted, and he therefore
attempted to justify it by elaborate proof. He began with his
favorite proposition $I = I$.[23] He asserts that a finite, rational
being cannot posit itself without ascribing to itself a free
causality. But since a rational being by definition has the power
of free causality,[24] the purported proof which follows is unnecessary. Fichte argues that the activity of the rational being in
contemplating the world is determined in its content in the
sense that the objects of that world must be represented as they
are. An activity opposed to this activity would therefore, in
order to be its opposite, have to be free in regard to its content.
Since the activity of the rational being in reflecting upon itself
is the opposite of the determined activity which contemplates
the world, it must also be opposite in its nature, *i. e.*, free. But
Fichte has already argued, as we have seen above, that the
principles of the affirmative and negative aspects of judgment
are not in real contradiction; he is able to return both principles
to consciousness. Further, a mere matter of direction of contemplation cannot in itself assure the free causality of the individual. If I glance to the left and am bound, and if I glance to
the right and am free, it must be because of something I
perceive in those two directions. In Fichte's case, the rational
being, turning his thoughts inward, found a being who by
definition possessed the power of a self-determining activity.

But something lies beyond the sphere of the absolutely self-
active. It is the sensuous world, which the rational being must
posit as not produced nor producible through the activity of
free causality. In that sensuous world the rational being must
assume that the other rational beings which inhabit it are also

---

[22] *Op. cit.* note 18 at v. Kocourek draws a distinction, not important here,
between " jural relations " and " legal relations."

[23] *S. R.* 126.

[24] *S. R.* 31.

free. But no free being can recognize the other as such unless both mutually thus recognize each other; and no one can treat the other as a free being, unless both mutually thus treat each other. Hence the relationship between rational beings is a determined one, and is the legal relation. In essence, this is Fichte's deduction of the idea of the legal relation.

Fichte's formula of the legal relation differs from Kant's principle of right in an important respect. Kant's formula is a standard against which the first principles of the system of jurisprudence are to be measured. Fichte's formula is itself the first principle of jurisprudence, and from it the rules of positive law are to be deduced. The difference is vital. Kant is under no compulsion, in framing his system of jurisprudence, to secure an absolute conformity between the first principles which he chooses to establish and his yardstick. He measures the principles by the yardstick, but empirical considerations may dictate adjustments. He is at liberty to make these adjustments inasmuch as the principles are not deduced from the formula. With Fichte the case is otherwise. The rules of the system he proposes are allegedly deductions from the formula, and may or may not exhibit a congruity with the empirical conditions of the sensuous world. Fichte's system of jurisprudence is therefore in essence a hypothetical one, its incorruptibleness being a direct function of the rigorousness of Fichte's logic. On the contrary, Kant's system is of a logico-empirical nature, directly related to the circumstances of the sensuous world.

Certain consequences follow at once from Fichte's argument in the construction of the legal relation formula. Since the idea of law is deduced from the conception of man as a rational being, it follows that the idea of law is not something we are taught, nor does it come from experience, nor does it arise from arbitrary arrangements among men.[25] At the same time, Fichte insists that the conception is not an empty, *a priori* form waiting for the impress of experience. When the conception is

[25] *S. R.* 79.

manifested in the empirical consciousness it is conditioned by the fact that it is to be applicable to men. Man cannot be man isolated; he only becomes man amongst men. The case of application must therefore occur since, as Fichte has been at pains to show, a rational being cannot posit itself without positing a rational being outside of itself.

In no sense, Fichte insisted, was his formula to be connected with morality. Jurisprudence, he remarked in his *System der Rechtslehre*,[26] had been mistaken for a branch of ethics until he came along. He held that all attempts to deduce law from morality had utterly failed. His argument, however, is valid only for his own system and not for law generally. The starting point of Fichte's argument is a logical form, which contains no elements of the " ought "; his deductions therefore, if an " ought " is not smuggled in, will be distinct from morality. His assertion that his system has no connection with morality is therefore a valid one to the extent that his declared intentions have been rigorously carried out. Moreover, the distinction is inherent in the arbitrary character of his system, as he is careful to emphasize. Morality may demand that every rational being is bound to desire the freedom of all other rational beings; but Fichte's system of rights merely shows each rational being the consequences of his acts if he chooses to accept or to reject the principle of right. But Fichte argues further that there is a generic difference, apart from his system, between law and morality. Law merely permits, he insists, but morality commands categorically.[27] He is here opposing the idea of " duty," a moral conception, to the idea of " right," a legal conception, and he observes that the law does not command an individual to make use of his rights. It is true that individuals are not under a legal compulsion to exercise their rights. This is clearly revealed in the case of the establishment of new rights which have been made compulsory duties by political action. Thus the State may command its citizens to

---

[26] *N. W.* 497.　　　　　　[27] *S. R.* 81.

exercise their right to vote,[28] to attend school in order to obtain their right to an education,[29] and to be vaccinated in order to secure their right to be free from certain diseases;[30] but in all such cases the courts hold that the individual is under a duty to perform the required act, not that he is under a legal compulsion to exercise a right. In the Hohfeldian system the confusion between "right" and "duty" is eliminated by making them strict correlatives; but it can scarcely be denied that in a large area of legal activity the law commands the performance of duties, *i. e.*, the duty to file an income tax return, to drive on the right hand side of the road, etc. Fichte was on sounder ground when he argued that morality often forbids the exercise of a legal right. Thus, if law were derived from morality, morality would contradict itself, since it would first grant a right and then prohibit its exercise.

Since law results only when there is a relationship between human beings, there are no rights between man and the objects of nature, such as land or animals. This view now is the accepted one,[31] but the idea that legal relations extend to animals has also been advanced on the ground that when animals are willed property they become the proprietors of the goods and possess certain rights.[32] When two persons are related to the same object the question of the "right to a thing" arises; or more properly, the right which one person has against another to exclude him from the use of such things. Rational beings are placed in a relationship of mutual causality with each other only through acts, through manifestations of their freedom, in the sensuous world. Hence, Fichte's conception of rights applies only to what manifests itself in the external world. What occurs subjectively has no causality in the sensuous world, and therefore belongs to morality and not to law.[33] On this

---

[28] *Judd* v. *McKen*, 38 C. L. R. 380 (1926); 32 A. L. R. 389.

[29] *State* v. *Bailey*, 157 Ind. 324, 61 N. E. 730 (1901).

[30] *Jacobson* v. *Mass*, 197 U. S. 174 (1904); *Zucht* v. *King*, 260 U. S. 174 (1922).

[31] Salmond, *Jurisprudence* (8th ed. 1930) 239.

[32] Korkunov, *General Theory of Law* (2nd ed. 1922) 201.

[33] This is also the view of Amos, *The Science of Law* (1874) 32.

basis Fichte denies a right, in the legal sense, to freedom of thought and to freedom of conscience. The individual has the power to perform these internal acts, and he may have duties concerning them, but it is improper in the Fichtean system to refer to them as rights. Kant's theory permitted an action to lie for the calumny of a dead person. This would not be possible under Fichte's conception since the system is applicable, by definition, only to the living.[34]

THE APPLICABILITY OF FICHTE'S SYSTEM

The arbitrary character of Fichte's system was developed in the course of his attempt to answer the question: How is a community of free beings, as such, possible? His argument had led him to the assertion of two apparently contradictory propositions: Persons, as such, are to be absolutely free, and dependent only upon their will. But as persons they are to be reciprocally influenced by each other, and hence not to be dependent solely upon their will. His task was to reconcile these two statements.[35]

Every person thinks of every other person as a free being, and not as a thing. If this conception were actually dominant, no person could ascribe to himself the power to influence another as a thing, and hence could not have that power. But this is not the case. Every person has posited the body of every other person as modifiable matter. Hence every person, since his will can be limited only through his thinking, can will to modify the bodies of other persons. But because the individual is free, he can also establish the rule that he will never treat the body of any other person as a mere thing. However, the validity of the rule will depend upon whether or not the individual is consistent. But consistency in this case depends upon freedom of the will; and there is no more reason why an individual should be consistent, unless he is compelled to be so, than there is why he should not be consistent. This is the boundary line between necessity and freedom in Fichte's

[34] S. R. 83.   [35] S. R. 125.

system, the line which separates the science of rights from that of morality. Precisely stated the line is: The rational being is not absolutely bound by its character of rationality to desire the freedom of all other rational beings. Morality shows this desire; but the science of rights merely shows that the individual has the freedom to desire it or not to desire it, and then shows the consequences of either act.

The fundamental principle of the science of rights, " limit thy freedom in such a manner that others can also be free," rests therefore on no absolute ground. However, *if* an absolute community is to be established between persons as such, every member of the community must assume the law; for only by treating each other as free beings can they remain free beings. The law therefore has only hypothetical validity; namely, if a community of free beings is to be possible, then the law must be observed. Fichte's law is thus not a mechanical law of nature, but, as he terms it, a law for freedom. Individuals are free to accept or reject it; and it possesses relevancy only on the condition that a community of free beings is to be established.

It is apparent that Fichte is adhering more closely to the method of science than to that of philosophy in the construction of his system. Traditionally science abstracts from the circumstances of the world, and concerns itself only with those distilled realities which yield to its manipulation. Its view of the world is necessarily incomplete, but it nevertheless achieves an insight into the nature of things which for its purposes it accepts as satisfactory. Philosophy's business is to account for the whole of things, and this is particularly so when it attempts to understand the varieties of human conduct. In the legal sphere it must see the phenomena as examples of the principles of the system. This means that the principles must be framed with the totality of the legal world in view. A system as admittedly partial as Fichte's may be in accord with the usual practices of science, but that is no assurance it will yield the complete knowledge that a jurisprudence seeks.

THE DEDUCTION OF POSITIVE LAW

Positive law, according to Fichte, arises in the following manner. The end of law is a community of free beings. This end can only be achieved if all persons subject themselves to the principle of right; but the principle is not applicable to a person who has not subjected himself to it, since the end no longer exists for which I adopted the principle. I have adopted the principle for myself, but not for the person who has not adopted it. Thus I acquire a right of compulsion against that person, and may apply force whenever he violates any of my original rights. I also at the same time acquire a right of judgment with respect to that person. There is no limit to the right of compulsion unless the violator subjects himself to the principle of right. But it is impossible to determine with any certainty whether the violator's submission is complete and permanent, since the reality of his submission is a matter of inner sincerity. If I possessed foreknowledge of the violator's whole future life, I could then tell whether the acceptance of the principle was real. Both parties must be externally convinced that each will be free from attack by the other thereafter. This is possible only by means of a guarantee, and the guarantee is only possible if both parties unconditionally transfer their physical power and their power of judgment to a third party. In that transfer I must be guaranteed perfect security of all my rights, not only as against all other individuals, but as against the third party himself. I must be convinced that all possible decisions of a legal nature with respect to affairs of mine will always be precisely what I should be compelled to pronounce, under the principle of right. The rules which will determine those future decisions must, therefore, be submitted to my examination, and those rules must apply the principle of right to all possible future cases which may occur. Those rules are what Fichte calls positive law.[36]

All positive laws are, Fichte held, deduced more or less from

---

[36] *S. R.* 151.

the principle of right. They cannot be arbitrary, and they must be such as every rational being would make them. Fichte here draws a distinction between the decision of the court and positive law. At one end is the principle of right; at the other, the decision of the court. Positive law floats in the middle between them. In positive law, the principle of right is applied to the specific objects which the rule comprises; in the decisions of the court, the positive law is applied to particular persons. Fichte's view of the judicial process was a wholly unsophisticated one. He held that the judge has only to ascertain what has occurred, and then to state the law which applies to that event. If the law is clear and complete, Fichte asserts, the decision or sentence should already be contained in it.

But the bare transference of my rights to the law is plainly, as Fichte recognized, not a sufficient guarantee that my rights will be protected in the future. The law is a mere conception, and how can a mere conception be realized in the external world? Even if the law announces that my rights will not be violated who will guarantee that the will of the law will be realized? Fichte solves this problem by asserting that the law must be a power, and that it only becomes an obligatory power from the consent of individuals who unite themselves into a commonwealth. His argument is that superior power over a free being can only be realized by the union of many free beings, since the sensuous world holds nothing so powerful as a free being—for the reason that it is free and can direct its forces with matured consideration—and holds nothing more powerful than a single free being, except many. For present purposes then, power depends upon whether they will the will of the law. Thus the strictest and only sufficient guarantee which each individual can demand is that the existence of the commonwealth itself be made to depend upon the effectiveness of the law.

ORIGINAL RIGHTS

Original rights in Fichte's system were concededly a fiction, but one necessary for the purposes of his jurisprudence. Since man only becomes man in association with men it is impossible to think of him as one individual. It is therefore, Fichte held, a fiction to ascribe original rights to him. The rights of free persons cannot coexist at all unless they reciprocally limit each other, that is, unless the original rights are changed into rights which exist in a commonwealth. There is a further limitation: the conditions of personality can be thought of as rights only in so far as they appear in the sensuous world, and can be obstructed by other free beings. There is thus a right of sensuous self-preservation, that is, a right of preserving my body as such; but there is no right freely to think or to will. I have a right of compulsion against the man who attacks my body, but not against the man who disturbs me in my peaceful convictions, or who annoys me by his immoral behavior.[37] Thus in principle Fichte's system would not allow the protection of interests which are now slowly coming under the guardianship of the legal order.

Fichte asserts two original rights: The right to the continuance of the absolute freedom and inviolability of the body, and the right to the continuance of the individual's free influence upon the whole sensuous world.[38] These rights are a deduction from the principle that the individual demands as his original rights a continued reciprocal causality between his body and the sensuous world, determined and determinable solely through his freely formed conception of that world. It is claimed by Fichteans that the rights to life, liberty and the pursuit of happiness asserted by the Declaration of Independence are expressions in other terms of the two rights deduced by Fichte.[39] But without further definition the two principles can scarcely

---

[37] For the difficulties inherent in according legal protection to the "peace and comfort of one's thoughts and emotions" see Pound, *Social Control Through Law* (1942) 58.

[38] *S. R.* 169.   [39] *S. R.* 169 n.

serve as guides to conduct. The first principle would appear to
outlaw war, and Fichte in fact held, at least in one stage of
his thought, that all wars were unlawful; but it would appear
also to outlaw capital punishment. Although Fichte permits
the imposition of the death penalty, he seems to recognize this
consequence for he will not allow the state to execute the
criminal. The only public act of the state is the exclusion of
the criminal from the state; he is then civilly dead and killed in
the memory of the citizens. They do not care what is done
with the physical man after the sentence of expulsion. If the
criminal is then executed it is through the function not of the
judicial power, but of the police power, and is carried out by
sheer necessity, and not in the exercise of a positive right.[40]
In its more popular form Fichte's second principle is the right
to happiness, the right of the individual to be left alone in his
conduct.[41] But is the state to secure the happiness of its citizens
by allowing them freedom to follow their own inclinations, or
shall it force them to be vaccinated, to remain sober, to save
their money, and to attend school? Fichte, as one of the
founders of modern European socialism, was committed to the
belief that men could be made happy by law, or at least
materially helped to that condition by legal means. He was
also, as he recognized, committed to a belief in the freedom of
the will. I have the right to will the exercise of my rights
because I have the right to will them, a proposition which
Fichte regarded as closing the circle of his investigations. If
freedom of the will is denied, then the reality of absolute rights
is also denied. This, in fact, is what Spinoza [42] held, who conceived of a natural right as what a man did in accordance with
the dictates of his own nature, so far as his power extended.

The Equilibrium of Rights

Original rights in Fichte's system are infinite. How then is
it possible for a free being in the exercise of those rights to

[40] *S. R.* 367.
[41] Ritchie, *Natural Rights* (1895) 272.   [42] *Tractatus Politicus* II, § iii.

violate the rights of another? If A says to B: "Don't do that, because it limits my freedom," B can reply "But you are limiting my freedom by taking that position." Fichte proposes to solve this problem by the idea of the equilibrium of rights.

It is possible that the idea of an equilibrium of rights was suggested to Fichte by the theory of the balance of power. In that doctrine equilibrium is conceived of as a mutual or inhibiting limitation of two or more forces, which is the sense in which Fichte employs the term. In any event, the conception, which possesses a legitimate scientific use, is too vague, notwithstanding its extensive employment today, to be applicable to the relations of the social order.[43]

Fichte's theory of equilibrium asserts that free beings must mutually recognize and determine the sphere of their rights, since those acts are evidence that they have subjected themselves to the principle of right.[44] There is an actual self-limitation of a free being by his mere cognition of other free-beings; this mere cognition also determines the limit which the free being must put upon his own freedom. There must be a similar self-limitation on the part of the other free beings, otherwise a state of lawlessness prevails. All legal relations between persons are therefore conditioned by their mutual cognition of each other, and are, at the same time, completely determined thereby.[45]

Fichte's original right of freedom and inviolability of the body excludes my causality as a free being from operating in the space occupied by the body of another free being at any time. Since this self-limitation is dependant upon a similar self-limitation in the other free being, my self-limitation is therefore problematical. Free beings are posited as free causes in the sensuous world, and it must be assumed that they desire to have some effect in that world in order to correspond to the conception. The objects subjected by the free beings to their particular purposes must be mutually inviolable if they are known.

---

[43] I have discussed the idea more in detail elsewhere. See Cairns, *The Theory of Legal Science* (1941) 124.

[44] *S. R.* 189.   [45] *S. R.* 174.

But this subjection remains within the consciousness of the free beings, and does not manifest itself in the sensuous world. Thus the objects of the right remain also problematical. I am bound to respect the objects which the other person has subordinated to his ends only in so far as that other person respects mine. But this is not possible unless the objects are known. But there is complete ignorance on this point, and no legal relation is possible. Everything is and remains problematical.

From this impasse the only possible solution is for every person by reciprocal declaration to state what each desires exclusively to possess. This is the condition, Fichte believed, of all lawful relations between persons. The declarations may agree, or they may conflict. If they agree there is no further problem; if they conflict the question can be settled by compromise, or a quarrel or war can ensue. But all wars are unlawful, and the parties are therefore bound to transfer the decision of the dispute to a third party, or in other words, they must join a commonwealth. Each has the right to compel the other to join a commonwealth with him, since only thus the maintenance of law and a legal relation between men is made possible.

The right of property, that is, the right of exclusive possession, is therefore completed and conditioned by mutual recognition, and does not exist without it. All property is based upon the union of many wills into one will. Through mutual recognition possession changes into property. Future appropriations must be governed by a generally valid rule to be agreed upon. In order to avoid endless disputes Fichte thought that there should be a possession of the object followed immediately by a declaration of ownership, otherwise some one else might declare his possession of the same object. If possession and declaration are not thus united, the occupied object must contain a sign that it has been occupied. Since the signs are signs only in so far as they have been agreed upon, they may be of any nature, *e. g.*, fences or ditches around land.

In this application of the principle of right to property Fichte believes that he had answered the most important question raised by his system of jurisprudence: How can a purely formal rule of law be applied to determined objects? [46]

THE RATIONALE OF COMPULSION

Fichte's principle of an equilibrium of rights is, as he recognizes, only a partial solution of the problem of mutual security. That principle is based ultimately upon the fidelity with which the persons who agree to respect one another's spheres of freedom observe their promises. Fichte argues that mutual fidelity and confidence are not dependent upon the conception of right and cannot be compelled by law, nor is there a right to compel confidence and fidelity, since they cannot be externally manifested and, hence, do not appertain to the sphere of the conception of right. It is true that persons may have made the agreement without the intention of keeping it, or they may have made it sincerely and have changed their minds later. Fichte says that the moment one party can suppose this possible of the other he has no security any longer, and the agreement is annulled because mutual confidence is annulled. This argument, although it opens the way for the introduction of a novel justification of compulsion, seems to contradict the theory of Fichte's system. Time and again Fichte asserts that his system has no concern with subjective states. It should therefore make no difference if a subjective condition of distrust should arise, so long as the terms of the agreement are kept in practice. At this stage in his argument Fichte cannot rely upon the fact of an actual breaking of the agreement to make his point, since his task is to justify a law of compulsion prior to the externally manifested event which requires its application. He has therefore been driven to the espousal of a subjectivism which it is one of the objects of his system to avoid.

In order to meet the problem which arises through the loss

[46] *S. R.* 189.

of fidelity and confidence, Fichte proposes an arrangement which will relate to the will itself, so as to induce and compel the will to determine itself never to will anything inconsistent with lawful freedom.[47] He rejects compulsion through the mechanical power of nature, because man is free and could overcome such a power, and because he would be changed into a mere machine in his legal state and would not be supposed to have any freedom of will to secure which the whole legal relation is established. Therefore, if it could be arranged that the willing of an unlawful end would necessarily—in virtue of an always effective law—result in the very reverse of that end, then the unlawful will would always annihilate itself. A person could not will that end for the very reason because he did will it. His unlawful will would become the ground of its own annihilation.

As a free being I propose to myself an end, and the opposite of that end I must detest as the greatest evil possible to me. The end proposed is the end established by the agreement. Hence, if I can foresee that an act, which I undertake to realize the proposed end must necessarily result in the opposite of that end, I cannot then wish to realize the original end for the very reason that I do desire it and do not desire its opposite. I cannot will the end because I will it. The problem is therefore solved. The lawless will annihilates itself and confines itself within its own limits.

Fichte has here described, in a highly abstract form, a situation which is encountered only too frequently in the legislative process. Legislation intended to eliminate or control what are regarded as abuses sometime stimulates those abuses to greater activity, or encourages the growth of other and even larger evils. Thus, the so-called " Raines Law " of 1896 was devised to suppress so far as possible the drinking of alcoholic liquors on Sunday in the State of New York. Hotels, but not saloons, were permitted to sell drinks on Sunday; a hotel was defined in the legislation as a hostelry with at least ten properly

[47] S. R. 193.

furnished bedrooms. At once the saloon keepers transformed their establishments into hotels with the required number of bedrooms. By 1905 Manhattan and the Bronx alone possessed 1407 certified hotels, of which it was estimated that 1150 were created by the Raines Law.[48] But the saloon keepers could not afford to maintain in idleness ten thousand bedrooms for which there was no real demand; they were therefore converted into places of assignation and houses of prostitution. Legislation intended to discourage Sunday drinking not only did not achieve its end, but it had the worse effect, in the eyes of its draughtsmen, of encouraging prostitution.

Fichte believed that if a contrivance could be secured which would operate with mechanical necessity so as to cause each lawless act to result in the very opposite it was intended to produce, then such a contrivance would compel the will to desire only what is lawful; and would restore the security which must be restored after fidelity and confidence have been lost. The good will would be rendered superfluous for the external realization of right, since the bad will would be forced by its very badness to effect the same end. In the case of a trespass through carelessness the trespasser, in Fichte's view, may be said to have no will at all; hence the law of compulsion produces of itself the will which is lacking. It does this by making the violation of the rights of others a violation of my own rights; I will therefore certainly take as much care to protect the other person's rights as to protect my own.

Thus the law of compulsion is to work in such a manner that every violation of the rights of another is to result for the violator in the same violation of his own rights. But is this a solution of the problem in the terms in which Fichte stated it? I may have entered into the agreement without the intention of keeping it. I may desire an end different from the one proposed by the agreement; and the fact that my rights are to be violated to the extent I violate the rights of others under the agreement may be a matter of indifference to me.

[48] Ellis, *The Task of Social Hygiene* (1916) 29.

An agreement to establish a law of compulsion must contain a provision that both parties agree to treat, with united strength, the one of them who shall violate the rights of the other, in accordance with the provisions of the law of compulsion.[49] But this is an impossible condition, because it means that one person would lend his own strength to repel his own attack. A contradiction remains even if we assume that the violator voluntarily submits to punishment. If the aggrieved party inflicts the punishment who is to guarantee to the aggressor that the aggrieved party will not purposely step beyond the provisions of the law of compulsion, or that he has not made a mistake in applying it? Thus the aggressor must have an impossible confidence in the justice and wisdom of the other, a confidence which Fichte assumes that he cannot possess. A revengeful mind, Sir Thomas Browne remarked, " holds no rule in retaliations, requiring too often a head for a tooth." The agreement could be realized only if the aggrieved party had always superior power, extending only to the limit provided by the law of compulsion, and if he lost all that power as soon as he had reached that limit.

Hence the necessary condition of such an agreement is that each party possess precisely as much power as right.[50] But this condition can be realized only in a commonwealth, and thus the law of compulsion is not possible except in a commonwealth. Outside a commonwealth compulsion is only problematically lawful, and for that reason is always unlawful if really applied. With this argument Fichte reaches the conclusion that natural law, or a legal relation between men, is not possible at all except in a commonwealth and under positive laws. This conclusion is also dictated, as Gierke [51] observes, by Fichte's initial conception of the ego as omnipotent. Right, prior to the state, is the absolute freedom of the individual to be a free cause in the sensuous world.[52] Natural law, therefore,

---

[49] S. R. 200.
[50] S. R. 201.
[51] 1 *Natural Law and the Theory of Society* (1934) 102 and notes.
[52] S. R. 176.

has no other sanction, in the free state period, than fidelity and confidence, which are not sufficient, in Fichte's system at any rate, as we have seen above, to constitute a legal sanction. However, law which is supported by the state must be based upon reason. This argument enabled Fichte to assert two propositions: " All law is purely the law of reason," and " all law is the law of the state." [53] The great merit of his analysis, Fichte asserted, was to have raised the latter proposition beyond all doubt.[54]

In essence, Fichte's rationale of compulsion, as he recognized,[55] amounted to a justification of the principle of the *lex talionis*. This principle asserts that there must be an equivalence between the wrong and the punishment which is imposed for the commission of the wrong. As a justification of punishment the principle is now almost universally held to be a product of savagery. However, it has not been without its enlightened defenders. Kant himself adopted it, but with limitations. Cohen,[56] while recognizing its practical limitations, such as our inability to measure the severity of punishment, believes that the principle contains elements of value. There is a natural desire for vengeance which must be met and satisfied by the orderly procedure of the criminal law or we will revert to the more bloody vengeance of the feud and the vendetta. Further, the principle suggests that a just system of punishment must eliminate all traces of favoritism.

CONSTITUTIONAL LAW

In Fichte's system the object of the state is the enforcement of the conception of rights, or that which all persons necessarily will, among persons who live together in a community. Those persons seek through their common will a common security. They are motivated by self-love and not by morality, and thus each subordinates the common end to his private end. Through the law of compulsion the two ends are supposed to

---

[53] *N. W.* 599. [54] *Ibid.* [55] *S. R.* 346.
[56] *Moral Aspects of the Criminal Law* (1940) 49 Yale Law Jr. 987, 1011.

be united in the sense that the welfare of each is combined
with the security and welfare of all. Fichte's problem is therefore to discover a will in which the private and the common
will are synthetically united.[57]

He accomplishes this by means of the organization of the
state, which rests upon three compacts. There is, first, a
property compact by which each pledges all his property as
security that he will not violate the property of all others.
Fichte contemplates an agreement of all with all, inasmuch
as every free being has the right to traverse the whole sphere
of the commonwealth, and thus can come in conflict with all
other persons. This means that the conception of rights can be
realized only in a universal commonwealth of all mankind. The
right of the individual to claim the world as a sphere of
causality is defined in the separate commonwealths, but a
universal determination of the right is not possible until a
universal confederacy has been realized.

The rights guaranteed by the property compact have to be
protected by compulsion, if necessary. A second compact would
therefore provide that each individual will protect the specified
property of other individuals to the extent of his physical
powers, provided they will protect his property in the same
manner. In the first compact the parties agreed not to do
certain things; in the second, they agree to do certain things.
But the protection compact is effective only on condition that
if A protects B's rights B will protect A's rights. I therefore
obtain the right to claim the protection of others only by
actually protecting the rights of others. But if this is so, no
one will ever obtain a strictly legal claim to the protection of the
other. It will always remain problematical whether the obligation required by the protection compact has been met or not, and
hence, whether the other party has obligations or not. However, this uncertainty can be removed if mere membership in
the state organization carries with it the fulfillment of the
obligation demanded by the protection compact; in other words,

[57] *S. R.* 206.

if promise and fulfillment are united, if word and deed are one and the same.

This problem is solved by a third compact which provides for a protective power to which each member of the organization must furnish his contribution. This contribution would be the fulfillment of his promise to protect the rights of all other members. There could thus be no further uncertainty as to his affording that protection to the others upon which his own claim to protection is grounded. This protective power is established with a totality consisting of all the members of the community. The totality is the second party to the contract. Fichte insists that the totality is not an abstract conception, as a *compositum*, but is, in fact, a *totum*. Thus in the state nature unites what she has separated in the production of many individuals. Fichte compares this conception to an organized production of nature such as a tree. If each part of the tree has consciousness and a will, then each part, as it desires its own preservation must also desire the preservation of the whole tree, because its own preservation is possible only on that condition.[58] The individual makes a contribution to the protecting body in the form of votes, services, money and other things. That which is to be protected embraces all that each one possesses. What the individual does not contribute to the totality is his own, and in respect to it he remains individual, a free independent person. This is the freedom which the state has secured to him, and to secure which he became a member of the state. Man separates himself from his citizenship in order to elevate himself with absolute freedom to morality; but in order to do so he becomes a citizen.[59]

---

[58] Fichte's remarks at this point have been much admired. Thus Vaughan observes that " in the image of the natural organism is found the germ of all that has been most fruitful in subsequent political speculation. It forecasts the idea that dominates the work of Hegel and of Comte; and Fichte himself, in his later work, did much, more perhaps than is generally acknowledged to unfold its true significance. It is this that makes the *Grundlage* so memorable a landmark in the history of political thought." 2 *Studies in the History of Political Philosophy* (1925) 118.

[59] *S. R.* 229.

The three compacts establish a state organization in which
the common will is manifested and has become the law of all.
But the common will has been realized as mere will, not as a
power to maintain itself, not as a government. Fichte's next
task is to solve that problem. He excludes both the trans-
gressor and the offended party from the execution of the
common will, and concludes that a third party has to be the
judge since it would not be to his private advantage to decide
in favor of either side. Nevertheless, there is the possibility
that the third party may combine with one side or the other
and work an injustice. To avoid this every one must be convinced that the unlawful treatment of any member of the state
will infallibly result in his own unlawful treatment. This conviction could be produced if the unjust violence against an
individual were legalized by its having occurred once. Because
something has been allowed to occur once, each citizen must
thereafter have a perfect right to do the same. But this would
mean that justice was annulled for all time and would contradict the conception of rights. The conception of rights
means that no single case of a violation of law must ever be
allowed to occur. The protective power can never, therefore,
remain inactive in any single case. This problem is met through
a provision that a law shall have no validity for future cases
until all previous cases have been decided according to it. No
one shall be punished under any law until all previous violations
of this law have been discovered and punished.

How is this power of compulsion to be secured? It cannot
be secured through the people as a whole, since they would be
both judge and a party in the administration of the law. Fichte
rules out both a democracy, in the sense of the direct rule of
the people without a government, and a despotism, as unlawful
forms of government. A representative government is therefore
absolutely required by the conception of rights.[60] It is impossible for the members of the state to be convinced that rights
will never be violated so long as the administrators of the

---

[60] *S. R.* 244.

supreme power are not held accountable. The people of a commonwealth must therefore relinquish the administration of the supreme power to one or more persons who remain responsible for the proper application of that power. Hence, it is a fundamental law of every rational and legal form of government that the executive power, which, in Fichte's system, embraces the executive and judicial, should be separated from the power which controls and checks the administration of that executive and judicial power. Fichte calls the checking power the Ephorate. It must remain with the entire people, while the executive power must not remain with them.

Fichte gives elaborate consideration to the Ephorate as a power to check the government. The Ephors must be completely independent, must have a certain and sufficient income, and must have as few friendships, personal connections, and attachments as possible. If a law is violated the Ephors utterly suspend the government, and a convention of the people is called. The issue is there decided, and either the government or the Ephors are declared guilty of high treason. The idea of the Ephorate had, of course, its root in the Spartan system of Ephors; in modern times the theory is held to be derived from Calvin's *Institutes*, and its principal proponents have been Althusius and Fichte. The Pennsylvania constitution of 1776 and the Vermont constitution of 1777 provided for a Council of Censors who were charged with the duty of inquiring whether the constitution had been preserved inviolate. Pennsylvania abolished the Censors in 1790, but the institution persisted in Vermont until 1870; they met thirteen times and ten times proposed constitutional changes.[61]

However, in the *Rechtslehre* Fichte withdrew his idea of an Ephorate on the ground that there was no one to watch the Ephors. They might start a revolution, although the government had not violated the law. Further, the government with all its power might suppress the Ephorate at the very start, just as the Roman patricians killed the tribunes of the people.

[61] Gettell, *History of Political Thought* (1924) 318 n.

Once the Ephors were killed the government would find arguments and false charges enough to justify its conduct. Notwithstanding his inability to find a satisfactory solution, Fichte has raised a vital problem of government: How shall the government be made to obey the law? Under the American Constitution, congressional committees of inquiry and the threat of impeachment are the principal devices to this end. They would fail, of course, at the very time when they should be effective, if a situation comparable to that which existed during the Augustan period ever arose.

CIVIL LAW

Since the property compact is the basis of the legal relation in Fichte's theory, it is equally the basis of the civil law. Fichte therefore attempted an exhaustive analysis of that compact in order to complete his inquiry.

He held that the need of nourishment was the original incentive of man's activity, and its satisfaction was the final end of the state, and of all man's life and activity.[62] The highest and universal end of all free activity is therefore that men may live. The spirit of the property compact is the guarantee of this end. It is the fundamental principle of every rational form of government that each person shall be able to live from the results of his labor. If a man cannot live from the results of his labors, the others must provide him with sufficient property to support him. They have also the right to compel others to work when they are able to do so. There must be no poor man in a rational state, and there must also be no idler.

Fichte then proceeded to deduce a set of rules with respect to the various classes of property. Those rules were to be further amplified in his work on the *Closed Commercial State* which he published in 1800. This latter work attracted little attention at the time of its publication, and for the most part it is ignored by the histories of socialism; but thirty years after its appearance its ideas came into the main stream of

[62] *S. R.* 291.

European socialism through Lassalle's *Theory of the State,* which was constructed on Fichte's foundation.[63] All shades of opinion at the present day, from extreme nationalism to revolutionary bolshevism,[64] have been sustained by Fichte's thoughts in this field.

The right to land is limited in Fichte's system to the use of it, *e. g.,* the farmer cannot prevent some one else from using the land provided it does not conflict with his own use. After the harvest others may use the land for pasturage unless the farmer also possesses the right of cattle-raising. Thus only the products of the land are the property of the farmer. He owns them, substance and all, but of the land he owns only the accidence.[65] This idea has reappeared in modern times in the distinction taken between " property for use " and " property for power." " Those things are rightly privately owned," A. D. Lindsay [66] thus summarizes the principle of communism, " which are necessarily privately used, and in so far as they are so used." But the distinction taken by Fichte is an arbitrary one in his system. An economic arrangement which would permit all men to live is not necessarily incompatible with fee simple title. Mines and the products of mines (precious stones, marble, sand, etc.) are to be owned by the state which, however, may transfer them by franchise to individuals if it desires to do so. Fichte permitted private property in tame animals, but not in wild animals until they were caught or killed. The government should regulate the professions, which include workers' unions, and limit their membership to the number that can support themselves. The members of the profession are to have the exclusive right to produce the objects assigned to it; raw materials are obtained from merchants, who also comprise

[63] Engelbrecht, *Johann Gottlieb Fichte* (1933) 82.
[64] *Ibid.* 190.
[65] *S. R.* 299. Hegel thought that Fichte's distinction was an empty subtlety. If I take possession of a field and plough it, the furrow and all the rest are my property. That is to say, I will to take the whole thing into my possession, and the form which I have imposed is precisely a sign that I claim the thing as mine. Hence there is nothing left to be taken into possession by someone else. *Philosophy of Right* (Knox trans. 1942) 238.
[66] *Property: Its Duties and Rights* (1922) 77.

a limited profession, in exchange for finished products. The producer must always dispose of his property; but if he does not want wares he is entitled to receive money. Artists are subject to the same requirement. The money thus received is absolutely pure property over which the state has no control; for the state to attempt to tax it, Fichte thought, would be the height of absurdity. Similarly a man's house is his absolute property, and what is in the house is beyond the supervision of the state.

Penal Law

Fichte's theory of penal law rested upon what he termed a a compact of expiation. He who violates the law has not accepted the fundamental principle of the community as his constant rule of action. But his rights are conditioned upon his observance of that principle; and when he does not observe the principle he loses his rights and becomes an outlaw. But the object of the state is to secure to each the full enjoyment of his rights, and if this can be accomplished without the imposition of outlawry, the punishment need not necessarily be affixed. By compact all citizens promise to all citizens that they shall not be outlawed, provided that this is compatible with the public security. Fichte's argument thus led him to announce the extremely advanced principle that every citizen has the right to expiate offences.[67] However fundamental the idea of expiation may be in the penitential discipline of the Christian and other churches, its adoption in the regulation of criminal behavior is unlikely so long as punishment continues to be based in large part upon motives of revenge. " Blood it is said will have blood," Bentham[68] writes, " and the imagination is flattered with the notion of the similarity of the suffering, produced by the punishment, with that inflicted by the criminal." However, Fichte would not permit the right of expiation to extend further than is compatible with public security; to do otherwise would be irrational.

[67] *S. R.* 344.
[68] *Rationale of Punishment* (1830) 191.

Punishment is not an end in itself, Fichte argued, and contrary to Kant, he insisted that the maxim " he who has killed must die " is positively meaningless. The end of the state is the maintenance of public security, and punishment is merely a means to that end. The only purpose in providing punishment is to prevent by threats transgressions of the law. The end of all penal laws is therefore, Fichte saw with great acuteness, that they may *not* be applied.[69] But the continuance of the argument led Fichte to support the idea of the *poena talionis.* The original intention of punishment was solely to deter the criminal from crime. When he commits a crime his punishment has another end: to deter other citizens from committing the same offense. The punishment must therefore be equal to the crime.

Fichte outlined the rules which determine the sufficiency of the counterpoise, or equality of the punishment and the crime. Thus in the case of a wrong committed through carelessness a fine equal to the amount of damage done is equal to the injury committed; but in the case of a deliberate crime, the criminal must not only restore what is taken but must, moreover, pay an equal amount from his own property; only by that additional payment is the punishment made equal to the offense. Somewhat oddly Fichte held that murder did not allow of an attempt to reform the criminal, and the punishment, as we have seen above, must be absolute exclusion from the community. He would, however, permit the establishment of private institutions for the purpose of attempting the reform of such criminals; but such societies would have to guarantee to the state the safe keeping of the murderer.

It cannot be said that Fichte's theory of the criminal law represents more than a generous effort, under the impetus of the liberal movement initiated by Beccaria, to rationalize the archaic penology of the eighteenth century. Fichte was not able to free himself altogether from the crude ideas of his contemporaries, as in his infliction of the pillory for slander; [70]

[69] S. R. 245. [70] S. R. 371.

but his theories on the whole, notwithstanding the absolute
indeterminacy as a standard of the idea of the *lex talionis*, were
in the current of the reforms which the nineteenth century was
later to recognize as necessary.

POLICE LAW

Fichte drew a distinction between the civil laws and what he
termed the police laws (*Polizeigesetzen*). In his system the
civil laws prohibit merely the actual violation of the fundamental compact, but the police laws are intended to prevent the
possibility of such violation.[71] Accordingly, the police laws may
prohibit acts which appear to be indifferent, and which in themselves are harmless, but which are calculated to facilitate the
promotion of wrong, and to render difficult the protection of
citizens' rights. Thus the state may forbid a citizen to carry
arms although on the surface it is a matter of indifference to
other citizens what I choose to carry about my person. Unfortunately, Fichte proposes no standard by which a proper
exercise of the police power is to be judged. His enthusiasm for
the power led him to propose that all citizens shall carry passports, and, further, when they venture on the streets at night
they must be equipped with lights so as to be instantly
recognizable.

INTERNATIONAL LAW

No task occupied more of Fichte's attention than the one
of working out the system of law which should control the
relations of states, and his legal philosophy nowhere else led to
results of greater value. His first reflections upon the subject
were initiated perhaps by Kant's *Essay on Perpetual Peace*
(1795) which he enthusiastically reviewed in 1796.[72] In the

---

[71] *S. R.* 377. In his *Philosophy of Right*, Hegel was later to develop further the
idea of " police law." Professor Knox, however, points out that *Polizei* has a wider
sense in Hegel's system than that conveyed by " police " in English. In his own
very careful translation Professor Knox therefore generally translates it " public
authority." *Hegel's Philosophy of Right* (1942) 360.

[72] 8 *S. W.* 427.

Grundlage he returned to the subject again in the same year, and with a greater dialectical skill than Kant exhibited;[73] he reconsidered the question again, apart from his less formal discussions, in 1800,[74] in 1812,[75] and finally in 1813.[76] His thought during this period was by no means consistent; but at all times it was in advance of the dominant conceptions of his day. He wrote during a period of great political turmoil, and all his political treatises reflect the turning points of that struggle. The *Beiträge* corresponds, Vaughan[77] writes, " to the Jacobin domination and the Reign of Terror; the *Grundlage* to the first decisive triumph of Napoleon, ' the child and champion of Jacobinism,' in Italy; the *Geschlossene Handelstaat*, a strange forecast of the continental Blockade, to the First Consulate, the Constitution of the year VIII, and the battle of Marengo; the *Reden* to the Treaty of Tilsit and the uprising of the Spanish nation against the insolent usurpations of Napoleon; the *Staatslehre* to the humiliation of the universal tyrant at Moscow, and the birth of the German nation amid the throes of the war of liberation." Fichte's juristic thought is the bridge from Kant, which is to say from Rousseau and the Revolution, to Hegel; its beginning is a theory of the individual and his natural rights, its close a doctrine of state socialism and the national state, which would he thought culminate in the future in a Christian world community.

Fichte's theory of international law is a strict logical extension of his general theory of law. The relations of states are based upon the legal relation of their citizens.[78] In itself the state is nothing but an abstract conception; only the citizens, as such, are actual persons. Further, the relation is based

---

[73] It should be remembered, as pointed out above, that Fichte claimed to have developed his jurisprudence before the appearance of Kant's *Essay on Perpetual Peace*. However, in the *Grundlage* international law is treated not in the body of the work, but in the Appendix.

[74] *Der geschlossene Handelstaat*, 3 *S. W.* 389.

[75] *Das System der Rechtslehre*, 2 *N. W.* 495.

[76] *Die Staatslehre*, 4 *S. W.* 369.

[77] *Op. cit. supra* note 57 at 95. Cf. Frank, *Fate and Freedom* (1945) 6-10, 231-43, 342-43.

[78] *S. R.* 475.

expressly upon the law, or necessity, that citizens who meet each other in the sensuous world must guarantee security to each other. Thus the relation of the states lies in their mutually securing to each other the security of their citizens. The formula of that agreement is: I agree to hold myself responsible for all the damage which my citizens may do to your citizens, provided you will make yourself responsible for all the damage which your citizens may do to mine. Such a compact necessarily implies a mutual recognition of the legal organization and interdependence of states, as well as their equality. The treaty fixes boundaries and defines the rights of fishing, hunting, navigation and so on; it also permits states to send ministers to each other to make certain that the provisions of the treaty are being observed. Violation of the treaty gives a right to declare war, for the state which is made war upon has shown that a legal relation with it is impossible, and hence that it has no rights at all.

Nothing is more characteristic of eighteenth century thought than Fichte's attitude toward the conduct of warfare. From Gibbon [79] to Toynbee [80] historians have commented upon the moderateness of the warfare of that period, which extended from the punctiliousness of the soldiers towards each other to the care which the armies observed in preserving the permanent capital equipment of social life in the war-zone. With the introduction of the *levée en masse* in Revolutionary France, war, which had been kept to a minimum of destructiveness through the conception of it as the " sport of kings," passed into its nineteenth and twentieth century phase as *la guerre totale*. Fichte observes that since only the armed powers of the states carry on war it is not made upon unarmed citizens.

---

[79] 2 *History of the Decline and Fall of the Roman Empire* (Bury ed. 1946) 1221, 1223. " In war the European forces are exercised by temperate and undecisive conflicts," Gibbon wrote. " The balance of power will continue to fluctuate, and the prosperity of our own or the neighboring kingdoms may be alternately exalted or depressed; but these partial events cannot essentially injure our general state of happiness, the system of arts, and laws, and manners, which so advantageously distinguish, above the rest of mankind, the Europeans and their colonies." Quoted Toynbee *op. cit. infra* note 79 at 148.

[80] 4 *A Study of History* (1939) 141.

The object of war is not to kill, but merely to drive away and disarm the armed force which protects the country and its citizens; reason therefore seems to require that we should always advise the enemy when we intend to open fire upon his posts, just as we demand the surrender of fortresses before opening fire upon them. Nevertheless Fichte thought that the usual manner of carrying on war was certainly irrational and barbarous. He thought the practice of sharpshooting was illegal. The sharpshooter from a hidden place, where he is safe himself, cold-bloodedly takes aim upon a man as upon a target; with him, Fichte thinks murder is the end. He observes that the first use of sharpshooters, by Austria against Prussia, created universal indignation throughout Europe. He writes that we are now accustomed to it, and imitate it; but it is not to our honor.

Fichte saw that the right of war, like all rights of compulsion, is unlimited. The opponent has no rights because he refuses to recognize the rights of the war-making power. He may of course sue for peace and promise to recognize those rights. But how shall the other party be convinced that he is in earnest and is not merely seeking a better opportunity to subjugate? Hence the natural end of war is always the annihilation of the opponent.

But since every state does not possess the same amount of strength as of right, war may as often promote the cause of injustice as the cause of justice. Hence Fichte once again sought for a contrivance which would arrange matters in such a way that the just cause will always be victorious in war. Strength arises from the mass; hence a number of states must form a confederacy for the maintenance of law and for the punishment of all unjust states. It is clear that the combination will result in a power that will be always victorious. But how can it be arranged that this combination of states always will decree justly?

The states would guarantee each to the other their independence and the inviolability of the compact. The formula of the confederation would be: We all promise to exterminate with united force any state, whether it belong to this confederation or not, which shall refuse to recognize the independence of any one of us, or which shall violate a treaty concluded between it and us. The compact, Fichte insists, creates a *confederacy* (*Völkerbund*) and not a *state* (*Völkerstaat*); the distinction is that an individual can be compelled to become a member of a state, since otherwise it is impossible to establish a legal relation with him; but a state can not be compelled to enter the confederacy because a legal relation with it can be established otherwise. Whether one state has recognized the independence of another state, appears from the fact whether or not it has concluded a treaty with it. Hence the confederation has a sure means of deciding this question; and it is not to be presumed that the confederation will knowingly and intentionally pronounce a wrong judgment, since all the world would see immediately the injustice of such judgment. If a state does not appear before the confederation to justify itself it thereby virtually admits its guilt. Since all treaties are concluded under the guarantee of the confederation, it can tolerate no indefiniteness in their terms. The states of the confederation cannot well have a common interest to act unjustly, for the principles which they apply to others will be applied to them. The confederation must have the power to execute the decisions, and hence must be armed; Fichte is against the establishment of a standing army, because it will be idle most of the time, and in favor of an army called out only in times of war by contributions from the separate states.

Fichte readily admits that he has not established the impossibility of an unjust decision by the confederation. Until reason herself appears in person upon earth and assumes judicial power, he writes, we shall always have a supreme court, which, being finite, is liable to error or to evil motives. The practical problem therefore is simply to discover a tribunal from which there is the least likelihood to expect this. His final thought is an optimistic one. As the confederation extends to embrace the whole earth, eternal peace will be established. It is the only lawful relation of states, since war is as likely to give victory to the just as to the unjust; at the very best, under the direction of a confederation of states, war is only a means for the ultimate end, the maintenance of peace.[81]

Grotius had based the relations of states on a natural law doctrine which applied to states the same moral standards applicable to individuals. With the rise of the corporate state and the passing of the sovereign as the embodiment of state activity, the international lawyers substituted the idea of the compact as the ground for the regulation of state behavior.[82] Fichte's theory is squarely in this tradition and is a remarkable anticipation of nineteenth and twentieth century thought. As our current wars indicate the idea of the compact has proved as inadequate to control international relations as Grotius' natural law theory. But in the years which have elapsed since Fichte wrote the wit of man has not been able to improve upon Fichte's thoughts, as the theory of the League of Nations and United Nations shows.

Conclusion

In its abstractness Fichte's theory of law is almost without parallel and it thus raises, as precisely as may be, the question of the value of such systems. It may be said at once that as aids to the understanding of any known legal system, or of any that is likely to be known, their value is slight. The subject matter of jurisprudence exists in the same sense that the subject matter of the various natural sciences may be said to exist. The histories of those subjects show us that advances are seldom made unless the ideas which control the investigation are constantly brought into a relationship with the available

---

[81] *S. R.* 489. In the later studies Fichte's thought oscillated from a pessimism inspired by contemplating the selfish motives of men and states (*Rechtslehre,* 2 *N. W.* 645) to the idea of a league of Christian states which would eventually embrace even the non-Christian peoples (*Staatslehre,* 4 *S. W.* 600).

[82] Cairns, *Foreword, A Symposium in Juristic Bases for International Law* (1946) 31 Iowa Law Rev. 493.

factual data. There must be a constant reciprocal checking of data by ideas and of ideas by data. It is explicitly not the aim of the Fichtean type of legal system to explain an existential subject matter. Its aim is avowedly to establish the necessary principles of a particular kind of legal system which, in Fichte's case at any rate, is not, and in all probability will never be, existential. Such a procedure is entirely legitimate and, at the worst, is a harmless intellectual exercise which runs, however, the risk of being dismissed as utopian.

However, since philosophical inquiry of the type exemplified by Fichte has not attained the abstractness of pure mathematics, empirical elements are always present. It is therefore always possible that the results of such an inquiry may be applicable to some extent to existential legal systems. In Fichte's case there are a number of such instances, two of which at least possess interest. His conception of the legal relation, although jurists have subjected it to nothing like the analysis it deserves, is plainly an important one. Again his conception of the necessary requirements of an international order has not been improved upon in its general outlines since he proposed it. It is in such directions that the Fichtean type of analysis may possess great value. They may either uncover fundamental legal conceptions which jurists take for granted and thus pass over in their studies; or they may indicate new lines of development in new areas, but based on presently existing legal ideas, as in Fichte's generalization of the conception of contract to control the relations of states. Fichte's system is an advance over the one put forward by Kant in the fact that it takes much less for granted, and analyzes with great care propositions which Kant felt he could safely assume; but the case is otherwise with respect to the empirical elements of the two systems. However much we may deplore the absence of anything approaching a satisfactory treatment of them by Kant, in comparison with Fichte he could appropriately be regarded as a gross empiricist.

CHAPTER XIV

HEGEL

*Even if Hegel's construction has
failed, Hegel's criticism is on our
hands. And whatever proceeds
by ignoring this is likely, I will
suggest, to be mere waste of time.*

F. H. Bradley

W^{E ARE} told by Hegel that philosophy was accessible to the
ordinary knowledge of the cultured public until Kant.
Beginning with Kant's intricate idealism it passed beyond their
understanding, and its subtleties are now open only to the
grasp of the professional.[1] If Hegel's remark is an accurate
description of a difficulty of modern philosophical thought,
his own system, notwithstanding his insistence that it is the
duty of all individuals to occupy themselves with philosophy,[2]
did nothing to overcome it. The intricacy of his thought is
the theme of the commentator and the experience of the
student. But Hegel also brings a special burden to the student
who wishes to understand him. We are assured that Hegel

References cited as *PR* are to *Hegel's Philosophy of Right* (1942) translated
by T. M. Knox. There is an earlier translation by S. W. Dyde (*Hegel's Philosophy
of Right*, 1896) which, however, has now been superseded by Professor Knox's
excellent version. For the German text there is a convenient edition, with an
elaborate introduction by the editor, in the *Philosophische Bibliothek: Grundlinien
der Philosophie des Rechts*, edited by Georg Lasson (3rd edition, 1930). References
cited as *JE* are to the Jubilee edition of Hegel's *Werke*, edited by Hermann
Glockner, 20 vols. (1927). The best single volume account in English of Hegel's
philosophy in its entirety is W. T. Stace's *The Philosophy of Hegel*. Hugh A.
Reyburn's *The Ethical Theory of Hegel* (1921) is an admirable introduction to the
Philosophy of Right itself. Other studies of the *Philosophy of Right* are: *Hegel's
Philosophy of Right*, by T. C. Sandars, *Oxford Essays* (1855), the first exposition in
English and still unsupplanted; *Lectures on the Philosophy of Law*, by J. H.
Stirling (1873) the author of the *Secret of Hegel* (new ed. 1898), of which latter
work the joke is still repeated, although unjustifiably, that if he had discovered the
secret he had successfully kept it to himself; Bosanquet, *The Philosophical Theory
of the State* (1920) c. X; *The Political Philosophies of Plato and Hegel* (1935) by
M. B. Foster; *Reason and Revolution*, by Herbert Marcuse (1941) c. VI, an
analysis of the social background.

[1] 3 *Lectures on the History of Philosophy* (1896) 505.
[2] *Op. cit.* 218.

during the course of the exposition of a particular point not only had his entire system present to his mind, but that he kept equally before him all the philosophy of the past.

An introduction to Hegel's thought is thus likely to begin with a preliminary sketch of philosophical ideas to the first years of the nineteenth century. An exposition of a particular aspect of Hegel's system is usually preceded by an account of the major ideas upon which it rests. In all this there is much merit. When we are concerned with a thinker of Hegel's stature we cannot know too much about the interconnections of his thought. What he has to say on other topics, and especially the process by which he arrives at the specific conclusion he is expounding, are valuable in our efforts to reach the essence of his thought. This would seem to be the case with Hegel's theory of jurisprudence. It was first put forward as an integral part of the volume which he regarded as the methodical summary of his system.[3] It was later reconsidered and expanded as a separate volume.[4] Further, the latter part of the jurisprudence was itself additionally developed in the form of the lectures, published after his death, on the philosophy of history.[5] Finally, Hegel himself apparently presupposed on the part of the reader some knowledge of his general system, particularly the exposition of his philosophic method in the *Science of Logic*.[6]

Nevertheless, it appears possible to comprehend Hegel's philosophy of law without a preliminary excursus on his general system or on the systems of his predecessors.[7] Indeed the first English expositor of the system thought that " we may take down the volume of Hegel's works containing the *Philosophy*

---

[3] *Encyklopädie der philosophischen Wissenschaften im Grundrisse* (1817). The work is divided into three parts, Logic, Nature, and Mind. The third section, which contains the philosophy of law, was translated by Wallace as *Hegel's Philosophy of Mind* (1894).

[4] *Grundlinien der Philosophie des Rechts* (1821).

[5] *Vorlesungen über die Philosophie der Geschichte* (1837).

[6] *PR* 2.

[7] This is now particularly so in view of the publication of Professor Knox's edition of the *Philosophy of Right* with its skillful apparatus of explanatory and critical notes.

of Right, and although we have never opened any of the other volumes, we shall not find what we read unintelligible. . . . We need not travel beyond the limits of this particular sphere in order to apprehend its true character." [8] Hegel himself took pains in the Introduction to the *Philosophy of Right* to sketch the elements of his general theory; but it may be doubted that his full meaning will be understood in the absence of a knowledge of his more elaborate statements. Nevertheless his legal theory, and the ethical theory of which it forms a part, can be stated without difficulty. There is no likelihood that legal thought will adopt either the philosophical basis or the technical apparatus of Hegel's jurisprudence. We have a vital interest in understanding as fully as may be the meaning and the grounds of the conclusions he has reached in jurisprudence. But it is the conclusions themselves which are our primary concern, since it is possible to deduce them from premises other than those which Hegel employed. Many of those conclusions have passed over into jurisprudence, and are part of the stock of ideas of legal theory today. Our task is to ascertain the meaning of those conclusions as they were expounded by Hegel, and to understand, so far as necessary for the purposes of the inquiry, the presuppositions which led him to reach them. That is an undertaking which appears possible although accompanied by a minimum of explanatory exegesis.

Hegel's purpose in publishing a treatment of the philosophy of right in a separate volume is made abundantly clear from his preface. He felt that the audience which attended his lectures on the subject needed the guidance of a manual in order fully to understand the import of his remarks; he felt also that the lectures stood in need of clarification and amplification, and that writing them out in the form of a manual provided the opportunity to accomplish those ends. His manual was thus to be a compendium, with its subject-matter circumscribed by the limits of the science. But it was to be a compendium with a difference. Hegel believed that philosophy possessed a logic or

[8] Sandars 216.

method of its own, one that was peculiar to itself, and which constituted philosophy's own kind of scientific proof. This was the dialectical method, which proceeds through the development of the concept. It is the process by which from the first member of a triad, say Being, a second element, Nothing, is deduced. This is possible because Being in its completely abstract form, devoid of all qualities, is Nothing. But we are able at this point to perceive the presence of the member of the triad, Becoming. In fact, we are forced to take this step according to Hegel because, unless we do so, we are asserting the paradoxical proposition that Being and Nothing are the same—that a thing both is and is not. We must therefore search for what Hegel calls the unity of opposites. In the present case it is found in Becoming; a thing both is and is not when it becomes.[9] It is on this basis, says Hegel, that " the system of concepts has broadly to be constructed, and go on to completion in a resistless course." [10] Hegel explicitly rejects two other methods of procedure, that which he terms *raisonnement* and the mathematical method of Spinoza. *Raisonnement* [11] in Hegel's view was the method of the Sophists. It consists of the finding of reasons which justify the conclusions the individual wishes to uphold. These reasons, or grounds, have therefore no objective or essential principles of their own, and it is as easy to discover grounds for what is wrong as for what is right. It is the method especially adapted by the Sophists to the consideration of questions of law; it is still

[9] *The Logic of Hegel* (trans. Wallace 2nd ed. 1892), 163. Hegel does not offer a precise quotable description of the dialectic. However, it is described by Mc-Taggart in the following general terms: " Hegel's primary object in his dialectic is to establish the existence of a logical connection between the various categories which are involved in the constitution of experience. He teaches that this connection is of such a kind that any category, if scrutinized with sufficient care and attention, is found to lead on to another, and to involve it, in such a manner that an attempt to use the first of any subject while we refuse to use the second of the same subject results in a contradiction. The category thus reached leads on in a similar way to a third, and the process continues until at last we reach the goal of the dialectic in a category which betrays no instability." *Studies in the Hegelian Dialectic* (2nd ed. 1922) 1.

[10] 1 *Hegel's Science of Logic* (trans. Johnston and Struthers 1929) 65.

[11] *Op. cit.* supra note 9 at 228; see also *op. cit.* supra note 10 at 67.

followed in the legal profession and its products are known as "lawyer's arguments." To the mathematical method he objects that it necessarily involves presuppositions and that it is the method of the understanding.[12] By presuppositions he means that Spinoza's method of beginning with definitions and axioms, notwithstanding the fact that they are a great storehouse of speculative truth, is basically the method of dogmatic assertion. Hegel held that his own method made no assumptions of this character. By the method of the understanding Hegel means the type of reasoning which is based upon the law of identity $A = A$. In jurisprudence, he pointed out, since we argue from a specific law or precedent to another, advances are primarily regulated by identity.[13] But when we pass to the speculative method we are at the level of the concept and have passed beyond identity to the unity of opposites. In the Hegelian system methodology occupied a preeminent place, and it was from the point of view of the application of his own philosophical method to the problems of law that Hegel wished his jurisprudence primarily to be judged. He took the view that jurisprudence at bottom was a philosophical science (*Wissenschaft*) and in such a subject, he held, form and content are inseparable.

At this point we come to one of Hegel's most controversial ideas and, at the same time, one of the most important in his philosophy. This is his assertion that the rational is actual and the actual is rational. Perhaps the best course, in order to grasp the meaning of this proposition, is to follow the steps which led to its assertion.

We can assume that the task of the philosopher is to state the truth about the subjects with which he is concerned. Philosophers in their books keep serving up hashes which purport to set forth these truths, but they are merely rewarmed dishes which are supplanted by each new serving. Through the philosophical method we can really arrive at the truth. So far as jurisprudence is concerned the truth is nothing new. It was embodied long ago in the various systems of law which the

---

[12] *Op. cit.* supra note 9 at 369.   [13] *Op. cit.* supra note 9 at 144.

world has known. Philosophy's problem is to isolate those truths and to exhibit their logical necessity. This does not mean, as Hegel's critics have asserted, that legal institutions or rules are immune from criticism, or, in other words, that whatever is, is right. Hegel makes this perfectly clear in the distinction he draws between the laws of nature and positive law.[14] The laws of nature are given and their measure is outside man. No matter how well we know them we can add nothing to them nor can we assist in their operation. Our ideas about them, however, can be false. Positive law, on the contrary, is posited, it originates with man. For the posited, however, man insists that the measure is within him. When we are confronted with nature we do not go beyond the truth that there is a law; but we cannot accept positive law simply because it exists. There is thus the possibility of a conflict between the ought and the is.[15] It is the assignment of the philosophy of law to establish the rationality of law or right, and in this respect it stands in contrast with the study of positive law which is mainly occupied with the revelation of contradictions. Thought is now seen to be the essential form of things, and philosophy must therefore attempt to grasp law or right as thought. Again, this does not mean that right must yield to a supposed supremacy of thought, or that random opinions are entitled to weight. Thought which is valid must take the form, not of a mere opinion, but of a concept about the thing. We arrive at this position only through the employment of the philosophic methodology. Above all we cannot know the truth through the method of either intuitionalism or subjectivism.[16]

[14] *PR* 224-225.

[15] Kelsen, who is a declared neo-Kantian, asserts that the State is a normative order and therefore is not a fact. If it were a fact it could not be in "conflict" with an individual, "since facts of nature never are in 'conflict' with each other." *General Theory of Law and State* (1945) 189. To this Professor Cahn replies: "It does not seem to have occurred to Dr. Kelsen that individuals (graciously conceded to be facts of nature) can be in conflict with each other." *1945 Annual Survey of American Law* (1946) 1233.

[16] *PR* 6-7.

Philosophy's concern is with the rational. This means that it is an effort to apprehend the actual. For the world that the philosopher contemplates is a world of appearance and essence, the outward and the inward, the unity of which constitutes actuality. Now the mere existent is not the actual, since if it were it would include caprices of fancy and evil, which are not rational. Caprices of fancy and evil represent the fortuitous, something of no greater value than the possible, something which may as well be as not be. It is the actual alone which is rational, which can be grasped in thought.[17] But when rationality is actualized it assumes a multitude of forms, and it is not the business of philosophy to concern itself with such an infinite variety of affairs. Thus Plato [18] should not have urged that nurses with children in their arms should continually rock them; nor should Fichte have insisted that passports should be signed and have the portraits of their owners painted upon them. Attempts to pass judgment upon matters of this sort are a form of supererudition in which philosophy loses its way. At bottom Hegel's book has as its aim the effort to understand the state as an inherently rational institution. It is not an endeavor to construct the state as it ought to be, but only to reveal how the state, which is the world of the ethical, is to be understood.

We can approach Hegel's position from another point of view. His system, like Kant's, is based upon a principle of knowledge, reason, which acts universally. But reason in Kant's hands is a formal principle. The ethical rules which are to guide individuals must be given a universal form, otherwise the individual could, in his behavior, indulge in self-contradictions. Kant

---

[17] *Op. cit.* supra note 9 at 9-12, *PR* 10.

[18] *Laws* 789 E. Professor Knox observes that Hegel " seems to have forgotten that Plato is saying that to make such a regulation is unnecessary and would be ridiculous." *PR* 303 n29. Plato thought the rule a necessary one but that the legislator would be subject to ridicule if he enacted it as law; further that nurses with their womanish and servile minds would refuse to obey it. The individual citizen, Plato thought, should therefore adopt the rule as law for himself. So far as Hegel's point is concerned it is a matter of indifference whether the philosopher recommends the adoption of the rule or not. In either event the philosopher should not concern himself with such trivia.

puts the case of the person who adopts the maxim: "I may increase my fortune by every safe means." That person has in his hands a deposit the owner of which is dead; but there is no proof of the deposit. Is it possible, in accordance with the maxim, to permit the law: Everyone may deny a deposit of which no one can produce a proof? Kant answers "No," because such a law would annihilate itself since there would be no deposits.[19] But as Hegel observes, suppose there are no deposits, where is the contradiction? [20] Kant's system can tell us whether the action is self-consistent or not, but we want to know whether the practice of making deposits is morally valid. An evil man can be perfectly consistent and can thus meet the test of universality. Hegel's theory of the concrete universal, the concept, attempts to meet exactly this point. It gives a material content to the universal. Hegel shows also that the Kantian morality itself is self-contradictory. We can take as a universal maxim the rule: "Help the poor." But the best way to help the poor is to abolish poverty. But this would mean the abolition of a moral duty, since our duty to help the poor would vanish with the poor themselves. We must therefore keep poverty so that we can perform our duty. But in that case we are not really doing our duty, which is to give the most effective assistance possible to the poor.[21]

Hegel was careful to warn his readers not to expect too much from philosophy. It always comes too late to teach the world what it ought to be. Philosophy, as the thought of the world, appears only when the formative process of actuality has been completed. Only when actuality is mature can the ideal be contrasted with the real; it is only then that the ideal apprehends the substance of the real world and shapes it into an intellectual realm. "The owl of Minerva," Hegel observes in his greatest Delphic utterance, "takes its flight only with the falling of the dusk." [22] If this is an impractical philosophy, as critics of Hegel allege,[23] it is nevertheless not without its

---

[19] Kant, *Critique of Practical Reason* (Abott trans. 1909) 115.

[20] 1 *JE* 466.

[21] 1 *JE* 470.

[22] *PR* 13.

[23] Hook, *From Hegel to Marx* (1936) 23.

justification. The impulse to understand the world is justified by the fact that it gratifies legitimate curiosity. It needs no further support in the hope or desire that practical results will issue from it. In fact, that some philosophies may have no practical consequences is at present perceived to be a virtue, now that the wave of utilitarianism is receding. "This subject," Hardy wrote of pure mathematics, "has no practical use; that is to say, it cannot be used for promoting directly the destruction of human life or for accentuating the present inequalities, in the distribution of wealth." That Hegel himself was not always a consistent Hegelian in the non-utilitarian view he took of his philosophy need not concern us here.

THE FOUNDATIONS OF THE PHILOSOPHY OF LAW

Hegel's philosophy of law takes as its subject-matter the Idea of right, that is, the concept of right and the actualization of that concept.[24] Law itself, we are thus told at the outset, is to be explored from the point of view from which Hegel customarily regarded the world. Hegel held that mathematics, formal logic, and related subjects operated at the level of the understanding; they are concerned with "thoughts" or "universals" (the form) and with "particulars" (the content). But at the level of reason we encounter the "concept," the principle of which is the identity of opposites. When opposites such as form and content, universal and particular, are synthesized at the level of reason, they become concrete thought, the concept. By concreteness Hegel means that the concept has a content which it has given to itself through the process of synthesis. But this process can also be applied to the concept itself and, in turn, it yields the Idea. When we see the concept in its development, that is, when the concept itself has become concrete through its own self-determination, it is the Idea. The concept and its existence are two sides of the same thing; they are distinct, yet, like body and soul, to use Hegel's own example, they are united.[25] Body and soul are one life, yet both can be

[24] *PR* 14. [25] *PR* 225.

regarded as lying outside one another. A soul without a body would not be a living thing, and vice versa. Thus the determinate existence of the concept is its body, while its body obeys the soul which produced it. Hence the unity of determinate existence and concept, is the Idea. It is not a mere harmony of the two, but their complete interpenetration. However, it is important to emphasize that the process which transforms the universal into the concept, the concept into the Idea, is not to· be viewed as a series of stages possessed of a temporal or historical nature. They are philosophical stages; they represent an order of logic and not of time. Thus we cannot say that property existed prior to the family; but in the logical development of right it must be treated first.[26]

For the purposes of the exposition of his philosophy of law Hegel emphasized two ideas—will and personality. Philosophy he regarded as a circle; but it is necessary to make a beginning somewhere, and these two ideas are the most appropriate through which to breach the circle. For the most part the justification of his assertions with respect to these two ideas are presupposed; in fact, what comes after is also presupposed for his philosophy of law is not the climax of his general system; the final phase is reached in the apprehension of the Absolute through art, religion and philosophy. But will and personality take us directly to the heart of his philosophy of law; for present purposes we need only grasp the meaning he assigns to them.

Right in general has its foundation in mind, or, as precisely as may be, in the will. The will is free, and thus freedom is both the substance and goal of the will; the system of right is therefore the province of actualized freedom. Freedom is, in Hegel's view, as characteristic of the will as weight is of matter.[27] Matter, in fact, is weight; the two cannot be separated. It is the same with freedom and the will, since the free entity is the will. Without freedom will is an empty word; freedom becomes actual only as will, as subject. But a will which resolves on nothing is not an actual will.[28] The absolute goal or impulse of free mind is to make freedom its object.[29] When it resolves, the will posits itself as the will of a specific individual, as a will which is separated from the will of another individual. In its activity the will overcomes the contradiction between subjectivity and objectivity, and its aims assume an objective instead of a subjective character. Hence right is an existent of any kind which embodies the free will. Right therefore is by definition freedom as Idea.

But we must pass beyond the single will of a subject, the stage of the abstract absolutely free will. Personality arises when the subject is conscious of himself as a completely abstract ego in which all concrete limits and values are negated and without validity. Thus the abstract will consciously self-contained, is personality. But personality implies a capacity to possess rights, and constitutes the concept and abstract basis of abstract, and therefore formal, right. Hence the mandate of right is: " Be a person and respect others as persons." At the stage of formal right the person possesses rights simply because he is a person. There is no question here of particular interests, advantages or welfare. Further, abstract right is only a possibility; such a right is therefore only a permission or a warrant.[30] Hence its only command, unconditionally its own, is: " Do not infringe personality and what personality entails." In accordance with these views Hegel divides his subject into three stages to correspond with the development of the Idea of the absolutely free will: (a) the sphere of abstract or formal right, where the will is abstract, that is to say, personality, embodied in an external form; (b) the sphere of morality, where the will has turned inward; it is the subjective will in relation, from the point of view of the good, to the right of the world and the right of the Idea; (c) the sphere of ethical life, where the good is not only apprehended in thought but is realized in the subjective will and the external world. This latter

---

[29] *PR* 32.
[30] This idea was probably suggested by Kant's doctrine of a *lex permissiva*. See Kant, *Philosophy of Law* (1887) 95.

category can be viewed as the realm of the family, civil society and the State.

From the ideas of will and personality Hegel develops the categories of the sphere of abstract right. There is first possession or property. This is freedom of the abstract will in general, or the freedom of a single person related only to himself. There is secondly contract. This category recognizes the existence of more than one person, and it is only as owners that two persons exist for one another. Their implicit identity is realized through a transference of property in conformity with a common will, and without detriment to the rights of either. Thirdly, there is wrongdoing and crime. This occurs when the individual will is at variance with and opposed to itself as an absolute will. With these categories Hegel believed that he had exhausted the classification of the field of abstract right.[31]

Hegel's analysis is the culminating product of several centuries of study by philosophers and mathematicians. For the modern age the analysis begins with the explicit formulation of the systems of Descartes, Hobbes, Spinoza, and Leibniz. To use once again the phrase coined by the mathematician Pieri, the systems are basically of a hypothetico-deductive nature. Since Hegel is the last of the classical philosophers to put forward a system of law it may be well to state from the point of view of a scientific theory, the characteristics of that system. He aimed at a consistent set of premises as the foundation of his system; in other words, any deductions that were made from the premises should not lead to contradictions. The premises should also be complete in the sense that they would permit the possible deduction of propositions adequate to embrace the entire existential subject-matter of the field. If Hegel had been successful in the accomplishment of those two aims his system of law would have taken the form of a set of related propositions. If his method, as applied to jurisprudence, had not been interrupted by the rise of the ethnographical and sociological methods of the nineteenth century, it would have

[31] *PR* 38.

tended on its formal side towards the ideal of the most successful of modern forms of analysis, that of logistics. The program
of logistics was formulated in a statement by Russell as the
attempt to prove " that all pure mathematics deals exclusively
with concepts definable in terms of a very small number of
fundamental logical concepts, and that all its propositions are
deducible from a very small number of fundamental logical
principles " and to explain " the fundamental concepts which
mathematics accepts as indefinable." [32] In jurisprudence this
would mean the deliberate adoption of the logistic method of
analysis, already implicit in Leibniz. It would mean, in the
initial construction of the system, the explicit formulation of
both the primitive or undefined concept, and the primitive or
undemonstrated proposition. Its great virtue would be that
the student of jurisprudence would know what he was doing,
his undisclosed assumptions would be revealed, and his results
would possess the utmost generality. It is true that a method
of analysis which in mathematics requires a whole volume of
the *Principia Mathematica* to demonstrate that $m \times n = n \times m$
would probably break down of its own weight in a subject so
complex as jurisprudence, although the amount of space devoted to the attempt to define the word " law " in jurisprudence far exceeds the space occupied by the whole of the
Principia. Hegel's method in its elements was nevertheless
approaching this type of analysis, and jurisprudence together
with economics, which has since developed a mathematical
phase, possessed a subject-matter which would lend itself to
such an approach. Jurisprudence was diverted from this path
by nineteenth and twentieth century methods of " fact grub-
bing " so that it stands today badly in need of theory of a
kind that gives proper allowance to both the existential and
the abstract.

Before we pass to the further aspects of Hegel's system it
is important to notice what he has accepted and rejected in the
traditional jurisprudence. He rejects the usual approach to

[32] *Principles of Mathematics* (1903) xv.

jurisprudence which begins with definitions. To possess validity definitions, he held, should be stated in universal terms; but this is impossible because of the contradictions inherent in material legal systems and also because of the wrongs they contain. Thus in Roman law there could be no definition of " man " since the definition could not cover " slave," *i. e.*, if a " slave " were a " man " then slavery is a denial of rights. He believed that the only proper approach was through the concept, or what we would term today " hypothesis." [33] He held that natural law, or law from the philosophical point of view, is distinct from positive law; but they are not in opposition or contradiction, their relation being something like that which exists between the *Institutes* (conceived as a statement of general principles) and the *Pandects* or body of case law in which the principles are worked out.[34] He believed that the historical element in positive law was correctly understood by Montesquieu, namely that legislation, both in general and in its particular provisions, should be treated not in isolation and abstractly, but rather as a dependent element of one totality, interconnected with all the other elements which make up the character of a nation and an epoch.[35] He believed that the historicism of Savigny had its place, but that its function was limited and that it did not fall within the province of a philosophy of law. A particular law may be wholly grounded in and consistent with the circumstances and with existing legally-established institutions, and yet it may be wrong and irrational in its essential character.[36] He rejects Kant's universal principle of right [37] on the ground that it opened the

---

[33] *PR* 15, 305 n4. However, as Whitehead observes, once we abandon the strictly logical point of view, definitions are at once seen to be of vital importance, since they determine the concepts which will be employed in the system. *The Axioms of Projective Geometry* (1906) 3.

[34] *PR* 16.

[35] *Ibid.*

[36] *PR* 17, 121, 135.

[37] " Every action is right which in itself, or in the maxim on which it proceeds, is such that it can co-exist along with the freedom of the will of each and all in action, according to a universal law." *Op. cit.* supra note 30 at 45.

way to caprice by exalting the private self-will of the single person over the absolute or rational will. As popularized by Rousseau [38] the idea made the individual more important than the group. It has produced an attitude in the minds of men, and situations in the world such as the Reign of Terror, which are paralleled in frightfulness only by the shallowness of the thoughts upon which they are founded.[39] He rejects as perverse and lacking in speculative thought both the *Institute's* classification of the system of right into *jus ad personam, jus ad rem,* and *jus ad actiones,* and Kant's classification of *jus reale, jus personale,* and *jus realiter personale.*[40] Finally he repudiates altogether caprice and the sentiments of the heart when they are set in opposition to law and positive right. That force and tyranny, he remarks, may be an element in law is an accident and has nothing to do with its nature. Above all, there is no possibility that the outcome of the philosophy of law shall be a code of positive law for use by an actual state.[41]

PROPERTY

Hegel's theory of property, which is based on the idea of personality, originated in a rudimentary form with Kant. Everyone, Kant said, is invested with the faculty of having as his own any external object upon which he has exerted his will. Anything is rightfully mine when I am so connected with it that anyone who uses it without my consent does me an injury. These principles demand that everything external and useable have an owner; for if any useable thing were to remain without an owner freedom to that extent would deprive itself of the use of its voluntary activity in thus putting useable objects out of all possibility of use.[42] Fichte transformed this

---

[38] "The problem is to find a form of association which will defend and protect with the whole common force the person and goods of each associate, and in which each while uniting himself with all, may still obey himself alone, and remain as free as before." *Contrat Social* (1762) Bk. I, c. vi.

[39] *PR* 33.

[40] *PR* 39.

[41] *PR* 16. *cf.* Kant, *op. cit.* note 30 at 4.

[42] *Op. cit.* supra note 20 at pp. 79, 61-2. "It is a juridical duty so to act towards

theory into the doctrine that beings are absolutely free in their self-determination to have causality; that since they are free causes in the sensuous world they necessarily desire to have an effect in the sensuous world to correspond to the conception; hence, they have subsumed certain objects of the sensuous world, which must be mutually inviolable, to their ends.[43]

With Hegel the philosophical theory of property reached its ultimate level of sophistication. In order to exist as Idea the freedom of a person must be actualized in an external sphere. We must therefore oppose to free mind the idea of " thing " which is the external pure and simple, something not free, impersonal, and without rights. Since things have no end in themselves, and obtain their destiny and soul from the will, persons have as their substantive end the right to put their will into things thereby making the objects their own.[44] Possession is to have extrinsic power over a thing. When I make something my own because of my natural want, impulse, or caprice possession satisfies that particular interest. However, the true aspect of the matter is not the satisfaction of wants, but that property is the first embodiment of freedom and is therefore in itself a substantive end. Thus Hegel does not repudiate the social basis of the theory of interests, which is the ground upon which all jurists, from Jhering to Pound, have placed it. If we start with the wants of the individual human being, as the theory of interests does, then the possession of property, even in the Hegelian system, appears as a means to their satisfaction; but since I am an actual will for the first time in what I possess, the requirements of the Hegelian system demand that this latter ground be taken as the true one.

Perhaps the greatest weakness in Hegel's theory of property is the point to which he next turns—the justification of private property. Since my individual will becomes objective in property, he argues, property acquires the character of private

others that what is external and useable may come into the possession or become the property of some one." *Ibid.* 71.

[43] Fichte, *The Science of Rights* (1869) 176.

[44] *PR* 41.

property.[45] Where property is owned in common by separate persons it has the character of an inherently dissoluble partnership in which the individual's retention of his share is a matter of arbitrary choice. From these principles Hegel argues that such things as water and air are incapable of private ownership; that when there is a clash between public and private ownership of land, the former must give way to the latter; that the state has the right in exceptional cases to abolish private ownership, but it is only the state that can do this; that the state can re-establish private property as in the case of the dissolution of the monasteries, for the rights of a community to property are inferior to those of a person.[46]

There are three immediate objections to this theory. In the first place, it violates the law of parsimony, or Ockham's razor. In the realm of law we are concerned with an existential subject-matter. Unless compelled to do so—and this Hegel has not shown—we ought not to pass to the transcendental realm of metaphysical free will to account for what is existential; if property is to be justified in the context of an existential subject-matter, namely law, it should be done at that existential level. Second, in the terms of Hegel's own system the theory is erroneous. As we pass to the higher realms of his ethical order a person ceases to be an exclusive unit, but partakes of the nature and ends of other persons. *Pari passu*, property keeps its private character, but a common character is also added to it. Thus, as society becomes more organized the nature of property changes so that what is true of it at one period is not necessarily true of it at another.[47] Finally, we are unable to deduce from the principle the proper distribution of property in present-day societies. Green thought that the value of property lay in the fact that it allowed the individual to carry out a plan of life. Present-day distribution, however,

---

[45] *Ibid.* Green, Ahrens, Lorimer, Ely and many others who have insisted that property is the realization of freedom have attempted, although without success, to meet the difficulties inherent in the proposition. For a discussion of their views see my *Law and the Social Sciences* (1935) 69 *et seq.*

[46] *PR* 44, 236.

[47] Reyburn, 130.

is far from meeting this need, and Green's only solution was to propose that society bestow on every individual at least enough property to develop a sense of responsibility.[48]

Hegel accepts the principle of *occupatio*, but with the reservation that the first person to occupy a thing is the rightful owner not because he is first but because he is a free will; he can only become first if another succeeds him. He also agrees with Kant and Fichte that the mere exercise of the will toward a thing is not enough to make it mine; the thing must be occupied. Occupancy makes the matter of the thing my property, since matter in itself does not belong to itself. In the relationship of the will to the thing there are three types of connection. We may take possession of the thing directly, or, in other words, occupy it; we may use it; or we may alienate it. Occupation itself has three modes: we take possession of a thing by seizing it physically, by forming it, and by marking it as ours.[49]

These modes of taking possession exhibit a process in which we pass from the particular to the universal. When we directly grasp an object we take into possession no more than what we can touch with our body. Further, the mode is subjective and temporary. It is true that the intellect not only draws the inference that what I grasp is mine, but also what is connected with it. But at this juncture the concept is exhausted and nothing further can be deduced from it; positive law must handle the question through its statutes. When I give form to a thing the character it acquires as mine is independent of my presence. This mode applies also to the formation of the organic, such as tilling the soil, cultivating plants, and taming animals. If we consider this mode in relation to man himself we see that it is only through the formation of himself, through the cultivation of his body and mind that he takes possession of himself and becomes solely his own property. If we believe

---

[48] Green, *Principles of Political Obligation* (1895) § 221. However, Hegel observes that a solution of this sort is only a moral wish, but like anything that is only well meant it lacks objectivity. *PR* 44.

[49] *PR* 46.

that man is absolutely free, then slavery is condemned. However, the slave's own will is responsible for his slavery, just as the will of a people is responsible for its subjugation. Hence the wrong of slavery lies not with the masters and conquerors, but with the slaves and conquered. Slavery occurs in the passage from the state of nature to true moral and ethical conditions. It is found in a world where a wrong is right. In those circumstances the wrong has its value and finds a necessary place.[50] Taking possession by marking is of all the modes the most indefinite, but at the same time it is also the most complete, since the prior modes have also more or less the effect of a mark. A mark may be arbitrary, and need not signify a connection between the mark and the thing. A cockade may mean citizenship in a state, though the color has no connection with the nation, and represents not itself but the nation. Man shows his lordship over things through his ability to acquire them by the use of marks.

After we have taken possession of property and it is ours, the next step in the relation of the will to it is the use that is made of it. At this point Hegel accepts the present-day theory which places interests on a social basis. He argues that things exist only for my need and are to serve it; my need is the particular aspect of a single will which finds satisfaction in the use of things. Use is the external realization of my want through the change, destruction and consumption of the thing. In this way the thing is revealed as selfless and so fulfills its destiny.[51] Here we encounter a problem raised by Locke. Assuming that a right of private property has been established, how far does that right extend? May a person acquire as much as he will? Locke denied that the principle of private property gave any such right. " As much as any one can make use of to

---

[50] *PR* 239. Hegel's argument appears to be a philosophical expression of the theological position maintained in Carlovingian times, that slaves were slaves not by nature but because of sin. However, from this it was deduced that they should be set free. 5 d'Achery, *Spicilegium* (1661) 53. Dante also argued that the submissive victim of violence abets the violence and hence is morally accountable. *Paradiso*, IV, 76-80.

[51] *PR* 49, 239.

any advantage of life before it spoils, so much he may by his labor fix a property in," was the limit set by Locke.[52] Hegel approached the question from the doctrine of the equality of men, from which it was sometimes deduced that property holdings should be equal. He admitted the equality of men, but only as persons. As men their capacities are different and an equality of the sort proposed would be wrong. Hence what and how much I possess is a matter of indifference from the standpoint of right.[53]

But Locke's argument has also been given the further development that things which are not used may cease to be the private property of the owner if social considerations so dictate. Hegel attempted to answer this contention by arguing that use is a secondary and subordinate modification of property; the owner's will, by virtue of which a thing is his own, is the fundamental principle. This question is by no means a settled one as we can observe from the series of United States Supreme Court cases which involve the right to suppress patents. It has there been argued that a patentee is in the position of a quasi trustee for the public, and is under a moral obligation to permit the use of the invention. So far, however, the Court has followed Hegel rather than the implications of Locke's argument. "If the patent is valid," Mr. Justice Brandeis observed, " the owner can, of course, prohibit entirely the manfacture, sale or use " of a patented article.[54]

If I have the full use of a thing I am the owner of it, is Hegel's argument. When we pass beyond completeness of use there is nothing left over to be the property of another. The relation of use to property is that of accident to substance, outer to inner, force to its manifestation. Hegel insisted that

[52] *Second Treatise on Civil Government* (1690) § 30.
[53] *PR* 44. 237.
[54] *Carbide Corporation of America* v. *American Patents Development Corporation*, 283 U. S. 27, 31 (1931). But see the dissenting opinion in *Special Equipment Co.* v. *Coe*, 324 U. S. 370 (1945) where three justices take the position that the rule should be abandoned. To suppress individually is not the same as to restrict in combination with others, and action of the latter type may violate the federal anti-trust laws. *Hartford-Empire Co.* v. *U. S.*, 323 U. S. 386, 324 U. S. 570 (1945).

the total use of a thing cannot be mine, while the abstract property is vested in another person. To make such a distinction is, he held, the work of the empty Understanding. However, he recognized that use may be separated from proprietorship, but only for a temporary period. He thus allowed for usufruct and all the gradations recognized by legal systems between that interest and full ownership, the instances of which he regarded as mere titbits culled from the history of the right of property. But when I withdraw my will from a thing it ceases to be mine. Property may thus be lost by prescription. Hence prescription is not a mere arbitrary introduction into systems of positive law; it is a deduction from the principles of right. It is necessary for a thing to remain mine that my will continue in it. This principle can be extended to national monuments. So long as they enshrine the spirit of remembrance and honor they are national property. When they lose that quality they become *res nullius* and the private possession of the first comer, *e. g.*, the ancient monuments of Greece and Egypt when in the possession of Turkey.

Since a thing is mine only in so far as I put my will into it, I may abandon as a *res nullius* anything that I have or may yield it to the will of another and thus into his possession.[55] This is the final mode by which property is modified through the relation of the will to it. Alienation raises the subsidiary question whether a product of my mind, such as a book or an invention, which is given an external form, may be reproduced when it comes into the possession of other people. Hegel upholds copyright and patent laws on the ground that the author and inventor remain the owner of the right of reproducing their products. Reproduction rights are capital assets and a special type of property; they are a distinct source of wealth and may be separately possessed. Copyright and patent laws are therefore comparable to laws against theft.

[55] *PR 52.*

CONTRACT

Contract is thought of by Hegel in terms of property; a promise is conceived as a subjective volition which, because it is subjective, can be altered. Property as an external thing exists for other external things, *i. e.*, the will of another person. Property can thus be a relation between a thing and my subjective will; but to this relationship can be added the will of another person, so that the thing is held because of my participation in a common will. This latter is the sphere of contract. Hegel here again rejects the idea that contracts are formed because of needs or wants; reason, or the Idea of the real existence of free personality, is the driving force.[56]

Contract is the process which expresses and mediates the contradiction that I am and remain an independent, exclusive owner of something only by identifying my will with that of another and ceasing to be an owner. There is a unity of different wills, a unity in which there is a surrender of differences and peculiarities; yet each will retains from its own point of view a special character of its own, so that independent property ownership can exist. In a real contract both parties surrender and both acquire property, *i. e.*, an exchange; a contract is formal where only one of the parties acquires property or surrenders it, *i. e.*, a gift. From these principles Hegel argues that to subsume marriage under contract, as Kant did, is shameful; but in fairness to Kant it is necessary to add that marriage can be subsumed under contract in the Hegelian system provided the Kantian view of its existential aspect is accepted. Hegel also rejects the idea that the state is a " social contract "; an individual does not have the option to enter or leave the state, since we are already citizens of the state by birth. False also is Fichte's theory, which he maintained at one time, that the obligation to keep a contract begins only when the other party begins fulfilling his side of it. Fichte said that up to that point I am uncertain whether the other party is really in earnest. But the real question is not whether

[56] *PR* 57.

the other party can fail to carry out his undertaking, but whether he has the right not to do so. In other words, Fichte has raised a moral point and not one lying in the field of the philosophy of right. Hegel is careful to add that he is speaking of the " real contracts " of the civil law, which are looked upon as fully valid only when there has been an actual performance of the undertaking. This is a matter which does not concern the nature of the relation of the stipulation to performance, but only the manner of performance.

The classification of contracts should, in Hegel's opinion, be derived from the distinctions inherent in the nature of contract, and not from external circumstances. The distinctions are those between formal and real contracts, between ownership, possession and use, and between value and specific thing. In the main, as Hegel recognizes, this classification is that proposed by Kant. The classification is as follows: A. Gift; comprising (1) gift of a thing—gift properly so called, (2) loan of a thing without interest, (3) the gift of a service, *e. g.*, the mere storage of a property (excluding a gift to take effect on the death of the donor, since testamentary disposition presupposes civil society and positive law). B. Exchange; comprising (1) exchange as such either as (a) barter or (b) purchase or sale, (2) rent either (a) of a specific thing or (b) of a universal thing, *e. g.*, money at interest, (3) wages for service. C. Completion of a contract through pledges. When the owner is not in actual possession of the thing itself, the pledge puts him in possession of its value.

Hegel's statement of the will theory of contract, if looked at closely, disposes of the usual objections to that theory. It is denied that the law can concern itself with the question whether there is an actual agreement of wills. " The law has nothing to do with the actual state of the parties' minds," Holmes observed. " In contract, as elsewhere, it must go by externals, and judge parties by their conduct." [57] In his disposition of Fichte's theory of contract Hegel, as we have seen

---

[57] *The Common Law* (1881) 309.

above, seems to adopt this same argument. Suppose two parties
enter into a contract, but one of them the whole time is determined not to perform his share of the agreement. There is
certainly here no agreement of the will, but courts will nevertheless enforce the contract. And so apparently would Hegel.
" The question therefore is not whether the other party *could*
have had different private intentions when the contract was
made or afterwards," he writes " but whether he had any right
to have them." [58] Thus, Hegel as well as Kant looks to the
physical acts of the parties to ascertain whether or not there
has been an agreement of wills. In other words, they both are
in accord with the so-called present-day objective theory of
contracts. If this is the real meaning of the theory it disposes
of the objection that the abstract will is too tenuous an entity
to be grasped by an empirical legal system. It also allows for
the doctrine that an offeror is bound by an offer which is erro-
ously transmitted by the telegraph company and accepted as
transmitted in good faith. It allows finally for the doctrine that
parties to a contract will be bound, within certain limits, by
the consequences of the agreement although unforeseeable. It
cannot be said that in these two latter cases there has been an
agreement of wills; but neither can it be said of the case put
by Hegel. What then becomes of the will theory? Perhaps the
answer is that the law should give effect, so far as possible, to
what the parties voluntarily intended; that in contract the wills
should be at one; but that if there is a conflict between the inner
will and the physical act, it is the latter that will prevail in the
interpretation of the intent of the inner will and its consequences. In the three cases just put the will was an active
element. In the first the will through physical acts expressed a
particular intent, but was secretly resolved upon something
else; in the second, there was a will to create a contract, but the
actual intent of that will was wrongly transmitted; in the third,
there was an agreement of wills at the beginning, but the parties
were unable to foresee all the consequences of that agreement. If

---

[58] *PR* 61 (Translator's italics).

we attempt to eliminate the will altogether we run at once into an excessive contractualism, which sees a contract in such cases as the dropping by a passenger of a coin in the conductor's box, or which argues that marriage is a contract although the relations of the parties are entirely established by law. This type of contractualism is condemned even by the critics of the will theory.[59] If we preserve the will as an element to which weight will be given, we avoid at least this defect. That is to say, there must be an intent to create a contract, possessed of a certain meaning and the nature of that intent will be determined by both subjective and objective factors; but in the case of an absolute conflict the objective factors will control. The courts distinguish between the weight to be given objective acts, and they also consider the force of subjective factors. Thus, when the meaning of the contract is plain, the acts of the parties will not be allowed to prove a construction contrary to the plain meaning; further, the declarations of the parties to the contract with respect to what they intended it to mean will be received by the court.[60] It is difficult to perceive on the basis of the strict objective theory how the latter declarations could be received.

In contract two wills are related as a common will. But the private will and the common will may not agree; the particular will may act in opposition to the general abstract right. This leads Hegel to the third stage of abstract right, that which is occupied with wrong.

WRONG

In contract there is an appearance of right, a correspondence between right, or the universal will, and the particular will. In wrong this appearance of right becomes a mere show, a seeming reality; wrong arises when the particular will and the universal will are not in accord. Wrong occurs in three cases: nonmalicious or unpremeditated wrong, fraud, and crime. In

---

[59] Cohen, *Law and the Social Order* (1933) 85, 92.
[60] Williston, *Treatise on the Law of Contracts* (1936) § 623.

the first class both parties recognize rightness and desire to see it realized, but their private interests obscure their view of it. This is the realm of civil suits at law. When A asserts that a rose is not red he still admits that it has color. It is the same with this type of right. Both parties will the right and desire the action to reach that result. The wrong lies in each holding that what he wants is right. In the second category, fraud, the wrongdoer alleges that he respects the right, but deliberately attempts to see that it is not realized. The person who is defrauded is made to think that right has been recognized. In the final category, crime, the wrongdoer is aware that his actions are wrong and makes no effort to assert the contrary. In fraud the particular will is apparently respected, since the defrauded person believes that what has been done is in accord with right. In crime both the particular will and the universal will are openly negated.[61] Now if right is negated, it must annul what infringes it; for it thereby proves itself to be a necessary reality. This leads us to recompense and punishment. In non-malicious wrong there is no need of punishment, for right as a universal has not been infringed. Hence the compensation which is given in a civil suit is sufficient to justify right. But fraud and crime can be vindicated only by punishment, since in these cases right has been set aside as such, and mere recompense or restitution are not adequate to restore what has been altered. The particular will of the criminal must be penalized in order to annul the crime.

Hegel's purpose is to justify punishment as an expression of the criminal's own inherent will, as a visible proof of his freedom and his right; by being punished the criminal is honored as a rational being. Hence the concept and measure of his punishment are deduced from his own act.[62] In substance Hegel's argument is that force is directly self-destructive because it is a manifestation of a will which cancels the expression

---

[61] *PR* 64 *et seq.*

[62] *PR* 70-71. Children, imbeciles and lunatics were excepted from Hegel's general theory on the ground that the individual had the right to know his act as good or evil, legal or illegal. *PR* 88.

of a will; taken abstractly force is therefore wrong.[63] Since in its very conception force destroys itself its principle is that it must be cancelled by force. Under certain conditions it is not only right but necessary that a second exercise of force should annul the first. A crime is something negative so that its punishment is a negation of the negation. The injury resulting from the crime exists only as the particular will of the criminal; hence to injure this particular will is to annul the crime and to restore the right. Crime is the will which is implicitly a nullity and it contains its negation within itself. This negation is manifested as punishment. This punishment is only the manifestation of crime, the second half which necessarily presupposes the first. The elimination of crime is retribution, which means only that crime has turned back upon itself; hence it is the very act of crime itself which vindicates itself. Punishment is thus not only implicitly just; it is an embodiment of the criminal's own freedom, a right established within the criminal himself.

This justification of punishment implied at least two limitations which Hegel was careful to insist upon. Crime is annulled through retribution which has the appearance of something immoral, such as revenge, which has a personal element in it. " Vengeance is mine, saith the Lord." Actually, however, the personal element must never be permitted to exist. The idea of retribution is used by Hegel only in a formal sense; he means only that the crime is turned round against itself. If the subjective will interferes in punishment retribution passes over into revenge and becomes a new transgression. This is a defect of the Jewish, Roman and English law, which permit some crimes to be punished not as *crimina publica* but as *crimina privata*. A wronged person is apt to go too far in redressing the injury done him. Among the Arabs, for example, revenge is deathless and continues from generation to generation.[64] Hegel also recognized that requital, except in one case, simply cannot be made specifically equal to the crime. The Eumenides sleep, but crime

---

[63] *PR* 67 *et seq.*　　　　[64] *PR* 247.

awakens them, he remarks. It is true that their principle is
" an eye for an eye, and a tooth for a tooth." But mere thinking
cannot determine how any given crime is to be punished;
positive laws are necessary. With the advance of education,
opinions about crime become less harsh, and criminals are not so
severely punished. If the punishment to be meted out to crime
is determined without due regard to empirical circumstances we
may be led to adopt the Stoic view that there is only one virtue
and one vice, or the view embodied in the laws of Draco which
prescribed death as a punishment for every offence. Murder,
however, is of necessity liable to the death penalty; life is the
full compass of a man's existence and punishment can consist
only in taking away a second life.[65]

Hegel's theory of punishment involved a rejection of other
theories prominent in his day. Klein [66] had argued that crime
and punishment are both evils, and that it is unreasonable to
will an evil merely because another evil exists already. This
argument follows from the view that crime is a wrong done to
a particular person, and punishment is an equivalent wrong
done to the wrongdoer. But if crime is viewed as a violation
of right, rather than as an injury to a person, Klein's argument
is without force. Feuerbach [67] had argued that punishment is
a threat, and if a crime is nevertheless committed, punishment
is justified because the criminal was aware of the threat. But,
Hegel asks, is the threat justified? A threat assumes that a man
is not free, and its aim is to coerce him by the idea of an evil.
It is equivalent to the act of a man who threatens a dog with a
stick. Threats treat a man not in accordance with his honor
and dignity, but as a dog; they may arouse him to demonstrate
his freedom. Beccaria had denied to the state the right of in-
flicting capital punishment, since in entering into the social
contract the individual could not be presumed to have consented to his own death. Hegel denied that the state was a

[65] *PR* 68, 246.
[66] *Grundsätze des peinlichen Rechts* (1796) § 9 *et seq.*
[67] *Lehrbuch des gemeinen peinlichen Rechts* (1801).

contract at all.[68] He agreed that Beccaria was right in his insistence that men should give their consent to being punished. But he held that the criminal gives his consent through his very act. He agreed also that Beccaria's efforts to have capital punishment abolished had had beneficial effects. The theories of punishment which regard it as preventive, deterrent, or reformative are, in Hegel's opinion, equally superficial. Fundamentally such theories hold punishment itself to be an evil; equally superficially they regard the results of punishment as a good. But the question at issue is not a good that, or evil this; it is wrong and the righting of it. If you brush aside the objective attitude, you fall into the moral attitude, *i. e.*, the subjective aspect of crime, intermingled with trivial psychological factors.

Since Hegel wrote the theory of punishment has undergone a radical transformation. Emphasis is no longer placed upon the crime or the victim, but upon the criminal. It is denied that the criminal act is one of pure intention; it is asserted on the contrary that it is a product of many causal relations. This theory does not justify punishment itself; on the contrary it suggests that punishment should not be applied at all. Under the influence of the doctrine of natural selection sociologists such as Stanley Hall and Giddings have attempted to justify punishment on the ground that it is a mechanism of social selection. It eliminates or adjusts those who are not adapted to social life. This is an empirical argument, and at that level it may be answered that the history of punishment does not reveal that punishment is effective as an instrument of social selection. Further, who is to judge whether a particular individual is adjusted satisfactorily to social life? The natural selection theory justifies the condemnation of Socrates, as well as that of the American Revolutionary leaders, had they fallen into the hands of the British and been convicted of treason.

---

[68] *Dei delitti e dei pene* (1764). English trans. *Crimes and Punishments* (1880).

CIVIL SOCIETY AND THE THEORY OF POSITIVE LAW

Civil society in the Hegelian system is the logical, not the historical, stage between the family and the state. It is the battlefield of private interests where each member is his own end; but a member cannot attain his end unless he enters into relations with other persons. Civil society is an association of members in a relationship of complete interdependence, where however their actions as individuals are still allowed maximum play. To reach this position Hegel had passed from a consideration of abstract right, in which the will is universal, to an analysis of morality, where the will is subjective. But abstract right and the subjective will need to be united in an objective whole. The true conscience of the individual is subject to fixed principles which it knows as objective determinants and duties. The conception is transformed into the Idea when we pass beyond the individualism of morality to the sociality of the ethical order. Three phases mark the realm of social ethics: the family, civil society, and the state. Civil society emerges when the family is disrupted. This occurs when the children grow to maturity and form new families of their own.

Civil society as Hegel develops it contains three momen s: the system of needs; the administration of justice; and the police and the corporation.[69] He is not here asserting that law and the courts, which he treats under the classification the administration of justice, are prior to the state. Civil society as a logical category can be isolated from the state and considered separately; but civil society itself requires the state in order to exist.

" My notion is," says Socrates, " that a state comes into existence because no individual is self-sufficing; we all have many needs." [70] The idea that the satisfaction of human wants is the organizational principle of society was also the basis of Hegel's theory. He thought that the full explanation of the

---

[69] *PR* 126.
[70] *Republic* 369 B (Trans. Cornford). *Cf.* Herodotus, 1.32.14. " No human being is self-sufficing. He has some things, but requires others."

system of needs was the task of economics, which he held as a science to be a credit to thought. Economics also begins with the idea of needs and thereby accounts for mass relationships and movements in their complexity and their qualitative and quantitative character. The astonishing thing in this mutual interlocking of economic particulars, in Hegel's opinion, is the evidence of ordered phenomena, paralleled by the regularity which the astronomer has perceived in the apparent irregularity of the solar system. What the English call comfort is something inexhaustible and illimitable; for any comfort can be shown to be a discomfort, and so the need for discoveries is endless. Further, we desire to imitate our neighbors and at the same time to preserve our own individuality; these two feelings are powerful factors in the creation of wants. As social conditions tend to multiply and divide wants and their satisfactions indefinitely, we soon find ourselves in the presence of luxury. Wherever luxury is extreme, distress and depravity also prevail; and in such case the Cynicism of Diogenes is the outcome. Should man therefore not confine himself to the simple necessities of nature? In that case, it is argued, he would have the freedom of the so-called "state of nature." Hegel replies that this is a false view. If the individual is confined to the satisfaction of physical needs the mental is submerged in the natural, which is the condition of savagery and unfreedom. Freedom is to be found only in mind's differentiation from nature.

Since Hegel wrote the idea of the system of wants has been extensively analyzed by sociologists. Small and Vincent held that all social interpretation must begin with desires and the wants expressed by these desires.[71] However, Ward later took the position that "in the beginning were interests."[72] They are prior to desires, and account for them. Interests are "something in men that make them have wants, and something outside of men that promise to gratify the wants." This idea is

---

[71] *Introduction to the Study of Society* (1894) 173.
[72] *General Sociology* (1905) 196.

now an influential aspect of contemporary legal thought, since it is one of the tenets of sociological jurisprudence. However, as a philosophical doctrine the theory of wants, in spite of its plausibility, is not a self-evident one. It was opposed, for example, by Zeno who asserted that man should be self-sufficient. The Stoic Wise Man towards outside things has intentions but no desires.[73]

At this point Hegel effects a transition from the sphere of abstract right to that of positive law. He accomplishes this task through the medium of the important idea of relationship. Relationships arise from the system of reciprocity which obtains among persons in civil society because of the interdependence of needs and labor for their satisfaction. At the level of abstract right this relatedness is turned into itself as infinite personality. But this very sphere of relatedness gives abstract right a determinate existence in the form of positive law. When abstract right is objectified into something universally recognized, known, and willed, and at the same time possesses a validity and an actuality, it becomes positive law. Thus the realm of positive law is the objective sphere of relationships which obtains in civil society.[74]

Kant [75] had worked out the category of relation as a logical concept and we have already seen the application of the idea to law in the hands of Fichte. In Hegel it is a strictly deduced idea, and a pivotal point in his philosophical analysis of law. Since Hegel the idea of relation as a fundamental element in the structure of society has been extensively developed by European sociologists, particularly Durkheim,[76] Vierkandt,[77] and von Weise.[78] As in Hegel's theory relations are held by

[73] Bevan, *Stoics and Sceptics* (1913) 59.

[74] *PR* 134. Elsewhere I have discussed the idea of the system of legal relations from the sociological point of view. *The Theory of Legal Science* (1941) 106 *et seq.* Cf. Vaihinger, *The Philosophy of "As If"* (1924) 147: "Law is not really a science of objective reality but a science of arbitrary human regulations."

[75] *Critique of Pure Reason* (1933, Smith trans.) 113 *et seq.*

[76] *Les règles de la méthode sociologique* (8th ed. 1927).

[77] *Gesellschaftslehre* (1923).

[78] *Allgemeine Soziologie* (2nd ed. 1933). For an English version see the

sociologists to be objective realities which possess an independent existence.

We have already seen that Hegel held jurisprudence to be a philosophical science. As a science, therefore, its form and content are inseparable. Thus he holds that right is positive in general (a) when it has the form of being valid in a particular state, and (b) this criterion is accepted as the basis for the recognition of right in its positive form.[79] In other words, it is from the State that law derives its legality. Hegel is not asserting here, it must again be insisted, that a law is right because it exists; he is asserting that a law exists if the State says it does. In his system a bad law would be one that had mere existence, but no genuine reality.[80] As Aristotle pointed out a severed hand looked like a hand; it existed, but had no actuality.[81] Thus Hegel thought that a number of provisions in Roman private law which followed logically from the Roman matrimonial institution and from the *patria potestas* were wrong and irrational in their essential character.[82] Right as positive acquires the positive element in its content in three ways. First, through the particular character of a nation, the stage of its historical development, and the interconnection of all the relations which are necessitated by nature. Hegel is here according explicit recognition to the doctrines of Montesquieu; he is also laying the foundation for the subsequent efforts to explain legal phenomena in terms of geographical, ethnological, and biological factors, which came to the forefront in later nineteenth century legal thought.[83] Second, right receives a positive element in its content through the circum-

---

"augmented adaptation" entitled *Systematic Sociology* (1932) by von Weise and Howard Becker.

[79] *PR* 15.

[80] *PR* 283.

[81] *Politics* 1253a 20.

[82] *PR* 17, 120-121, 266.

[83] For an exposition and criticism of these views see Pound, *Interpretations of Legal History* (1923) 69 *et seq.* For an acute criticism of the idea of a "spirit" of legal institutions see Seagle, *The Quest for Law* (1941) 151 *et seq.* Cf. *PR* 217-218. For Hegel's views on the geographical basis of history see *The Philosophy of History* (1900) 79 *et seq.*

stance that the universal concept must be applied to particular objects and matters which are existential. Thus, the concept of theft eventually will come to be applied to a case of literary plagiarism, a matter not even originally envisaged when the law against theft was promulgated.[84] Finally, right becomes positive through the operation of the judicial process.

These principles are further justified and explained by Hegel as follows. To possess an objective actuality right must be known in some way or other to consciousness; it must possess the power which the actual has through the characteristic of validity. Thus right in its objective actuality becomes universally known.[85] From the point of view of the legal process how is this accomplished? Hegel answers, when it is posited. That is to say, when thinking makes it determinate for consiousness and reveals it as right and valid. In thus acquiring this determinate character, the right becomes positive law in general. Thus for Hegel the distinguishing mark of law is its universality; and it can only acquire this characteristic when it possesses a determinate existence. Hence there is much more to the establishment of law than the mere promulgation of a rule of behavior valid for everyone, though that is one moment in the legislative process. The true essence of the matter is knowledge of the content of the law in its determinate universality, *i. e.,* comprehension of the objectification of right through the process of positing. Custom differs from law only in that it is known in a subjective and accidental way; customs are therefore less determinate than law and their universality is obscure. The valid laws of a nation do not cease to be its customs even when collected and given the form of a legal code. The collection is a legal code, but one that is formless, indeterminate and fragmentary. Such a collection differs from a code properly so-called in that in the latter the principles have been apprehended and expressed in their universality. In Hegel's opinion the monstrous confusion of the English common law was due to the fact that English judges were essentially legislators.

[84] *PR* 306. Trans. note 10.   [85] *PR* 134.

As a result, England possessed no code of laws which met the test of rationality, determinateness, universality and form. To argue, as Savigny did, that customary law was " living " and therefore had a special vitality, is only part of the matter. No greater insult, Hegel said, could be offered to a civilized people or to its lawyers than to deny them ability to codify their law. Law (or right, *Recht*) must be known by thought, it must be a system in itself, and only as such can it exist in a civilized nation.[86]

Thus, in answering the question why law has a binding force Hegel's theory comes to this. There is an identity between the implicit and posited character of positive law which gives it a specific rightness and therefore an obligatory force. But when right is posited in positive law contingent elements, because of self-will and other factors, may creep in. Hence there may be a discrepancy between the law as formulated and rightness. It follows therefore that in positive law we must turn to that which is lawfully established as the source of our knowledge of our legal rights. To that extent the science of positive law is an historical science based upon authority. It is the task of positive law to study the given laws, their historical growth, their applications and subdivisions. For the philosophy of law is reserved such problems as their rationality and their ultimate nature.[87]

If the science of positive law, in Hegel's opinion, has its limitations, he is equally frank in admitting those of philosophical jurisprudence. It cannot concern itself with questions of morality which are of a private and subjective nature; it must take as its subject matter only those relationships which in principle can be externalized. In practice the laws of the nations differ widely in their recognition of this rule. In China, for instance, a husband is required by law to love his first wife more than the others, otherwise he is flogged. However, apart from nations, in the case of the oath, where the conscience is involved, integrity and honor must be taken into account as matters of substance. Further, philosophical jurisprudence in the application of positive law to the particular case can lay down only a general limit. It can not decide whether forty lashes or thirty-nine shall be inflicted. It may therefore properly allow for the contingent and the arbitrary by permitting a judge to impose a sentence of not more than forty lashes nor less than some other number. The judge by the necessities of the case is still confronted with the making of a finite, positive, decision. All codes to this extent are therefore incomplete. But it is in precisely this aspect of the law that completeness in this definite sense cannot be achieved, and codes must therefore be taken as they stand.[88]

In agreement with some of his philosophical predecessors, Hegel insisted that law must be made universally known. This rule is not, however, put forward as a self-evident ethical maxim, but is a deduction from principles previously constructed. Right concerns freedom, the worthiest and holiest thing in man, the thing which he must know if it is to have binding force upon him. [89] Caligula posted the laws so high that no citizen could read them. The modern practices of burying them in cumbrous legal tomes, and in collections of judicial decisions, of writing them in foreign languages, are equally wrongs. Law is not the monopoly of a special class, although jurists customarily take that position. But we do not need to be a shoemaker to find out if the shoe fits; law is a matter of universal interest and our knowledge of it does not depend upon our status as professionals.

Nevertheless Hegel recognized that we were here in the presence of an antinomy. Law should be a comprehensive whole, closed and complete; yet it is impossible to escape new determinations. The conflict between the need for stability and the need for change is, Pound [90] has argued, the central problem of the science of law; in one way or another, Pound maintains, all the vexed questions of jurisprudence prove to be

[88] *PR* 137-138, 272.
[89] *PR* 273, 88.
[90] *Interpretations of Legal History* (1923) 1.

phases of this same problem. Hegel is not here attempting to
solve the problem from the point of view of the construction
of a sound legal system; he is concerned only with showing that
the antinomy is a genuine one, that is, that it does not involve
a logical fallacy. Hegel envisages, on one side, a set of simple
general principles, universal in themselves and inherently and
actually rational; on the other side, is the finite material to
which the principles are applied. The very nature of the finite
material entails an infinite process in the application of the
principles to it. The subject-matter of a field like private law
can never be "complete." Its "completeness" is merely a
perennial approximation to completeness. No branch of knowledge can ever be complete in the sense that it can make an
exhaustive collection of all that pertains to its field. To argue
therefore that we ought not to have a code of laws because
no code can be complete is to misunderstand the problem.
Every code of course can be better. An old tree sends out
new branches without becoming a new tree in the process; it
would be folly not to plant a new tree because it might produce
new branches. The best answer to empty abstractions of the
sort Hegel is here combatting is, he thinks, the commonsense
proverb, *Le plus grand ennemi du Bien, c'est le Meilleur.*

Jurists as well as the public frequently reveal an antipathy
to the formalities which the law requires. Hegel takes a middle
of the road course with respect to them. Form can not be
repudiated by feeling which never rises above the subjective,
or by reflection, which holds to its abstract essences; nor can
the understanding insist upon clinging to formalities in opposition to the thing itself and infinitely increasing their number.
Legal events must be recognized as having taken place. Formality gives objectivity to my will. It is essential because what
is inherently right must also be posited as right. My will is a
rational will; it has validity; and this validity should be recognized by others. It is through form that this end is accomplished. Similarly, boundary stones are placed as symbols for
others to recognize. Vinogradoff, from the sociological point of

view, traces the formalism of early law to its intimate connection with religion, the reverence for traditional custom and the federal organization of society where the psychological desires of individuals are subordinated to those of the group; he recognizes however, that formality may have a practical importance. In Bavaria and Alamannia land transfers take place in the presence of a number of small boys, who are then boxed on the ears so they will keep a vivid remembrance of what happened.[91]

THE THEORY OF COURTS

Hegel's philosophy of law does not take for granted any legal institution which he regards as essential for the operation of his system. He therefore takes pains to establish that the judicial process is rational in principle and therefore necessary. In the Hegelian theory the administration of justice must be looked upon as both the duty and the right of the public authority. Whatever may have been the historical origin of the judge and his court does not therefore concern Hegel. His theory also involves both the repudiation of the idea that the establishment of a system of judicial administration is a matter of optional grace or favor on the part of the ruler, and the idea that the judicial system is an improper exercise of force, a suppression of freedom, and a despotism.

When right takes the form of law it becomes existential. It then has its own career, it is self-subsistent and has to vindicate itself as something universal. This is achieved through the recognition and realization of right in the particular case without the subjective feeling of private interest. It is the business of the court of justice to carry out that task.

Hegel had argued previously that the individual may maintain right against crime, that is, may take revenge. But revenge is only right implicit, not right in the form of right; revenge therefore becomes a new transgression. In the court of law it is the injured universal that appears, not the injured party. It

[91] 1 *Outlines of Historical Jurisprudence* (1920) 364.

is the function of the court of justice to pursue and avenge crime. This pursuit is not a mere subjective revenge, but is a pursuit transformed into a true reconciliation of right with itself, that is, into punishment. Both the objective and subjective aspects of Hegel's theory are here brought into agreement. In the former, law is reconciled with itself; by the annulment of the crime the law is restored and its inherent validity is realized. In the latter, the criminal is reconciled with himself, that is, with the law which he must know as his own, as valid, for him and his protection; when the law is applied to him he recognizes it as the satisfaction of justice and his own completed act.

From these principles certain requirements, in Hegel's opinion, necessarily followed. Every member of the community has the right to bring his case before the court, and is also under the duty to acknowledge the court's jurisdiction and to accept its decision whether he is plaintiff or defendant; rights which are to be vindicated must be proved; judicial proceedings must be public, since the aim of the court is justice, which is a universal belonging to all, and it is through publicity that the citizens become convinced that a just result has been reached.

After the facts have been ascertained, judicial decision is today said to involve three steps, as was seen in the discussion of Bacon's theory: (1) choice of the legal material on which the decision will be based, or the process of finding the law; (2) interpreting by logical methods the legal material thus selected with the intent of ascertaining its meaning; (3) application of the results to the facts of the case.[92] Hegel's analysis of the judicial process places the emphasis differently, but his results are the same. He divides the work of judgment into two separate parts. There is first the necessity of ascertaining the facts. The result of this inquiry is to fix the case as a unique, single, occurrence and to fix its general character. It tells the judge whether he is concerned with contract, tort, crime, some other matter, or combination of matters. Hegel advances the

[92] Pound, *The Theory of Judicial Decision* (1923) 36 Harv. Law Rev. 641, 945 *et seq.*

naive view that the ascertainment of fact involves in itself no pronouncement on points of law. The determination of the facts, he holds, is knowledge ascertainable by any educated man.[93] But facts are not naked events; they are events seen from a special point of view and the way they are seen determines their character, and hence the judgment. Herman Duker, during the course of a hold-up, committed murder. He and an accomplice pleaded guilty and threw themselves on the mercy of the court. The accomplice was sentenced to life imprisonment and, at the same time by the same judge, Duker was sentenced to be hanged. The judge held Duker to be legally sane but a psychopathic personality. The judge also thought that it was "a confession of social and legal failure" and a "tragedy" to hang Duker, but no other course was open to him inasmuch as Duker, who was legally sane, could not be committed to a mental institution, and to commit him to the penitentiary would endanger the lives of the guards. The Governor, in commuting Duker's sentence to life imprisonment, held the judge's findings with respect to mental institutions and Duker's future behavior to be irrelevant and observed that "the plain fact is that psychopaths when found guilty of crime are in this country sent to the penal institutions."[94] As Garlan remarks, "to formulate the ' facts ' in one way and not in the other is to get one kind of a decision and not another."[95] However, Hegel admits that the determination of the facts is ultimately a subjective matter; it depends upon single details and circumstances which are objects of sensuous intuition and subjective certainty. The determination does not contain in itself any absolute, objective, probative factor. Hence, finding the facts turns in the last resort on subjective conviction and conscience (*animi sententia*), while the proof, which rests on the statements and affi-

---

[93] *PR* 143.

[94] Ulman, *A Judge Takes the Stand* (1933) 211 *et seq.* 273 *et seq.*

[95] *Legal Realism and Justice* (1941) 38. See also Cook, "*Facts*" and the "*Statement of Facts*" (1937) 4 University of Chicago Law Review 233. Isaacs, *The Law and the Facts* (1922) 22 Col. Law Rev. 1.

davits of others, receives its final though purely subjective verification from the oath.[96]

In the second aspect of the judicial process Hegel holds that the task is that of subsuming the case under the law that right must be restored. Hegel argues that the judge is the organ of the law and the case must be prepared for him in such a way as to make possible its subsumption under some principle. That is to say, Hegel says, it must be stripped of its apparent, empirical, character and exalted into a recognized fact of a general type.[97] Hegel recognizes the three elements into which later jurists have analyzed the process of judicial decision, though he does not do so with formal explicitness. In his argument that the case must be subsumed under some principle, he admits that the judge must ascertain the legal rule to be applied; he admits that the law must be interpreted, but he rejects spurious or legislative interpretation, which he holds to be arbitrary, and favors genuine interpretation, where the scope of the judge's activities is confined to the logical ascertainment of the meaning of the law;[98] he recognizes expressly that the law as determined must be applied to the cause in hand.[99] To analyze the judicial process in these explicit terms, however, either did not occur to him, or seemed of small moment. He stresses other elements, particularly the importance of making the final result a general one. On this latter point, he is not opposed, as is clear from his recognition of the function of equity,[100] to what is known as the individualization of application of legal rules and precepts; he is insisting that judicial decisions should not turn upon factors which lead to the abuses of favoritism and arbitrariness.

[96] Hegel makes a distinction between the establishment by proof of a rational category, such as the concept of right itself, and the establishment of a fact. In the first, the process is that of apprehension of rational necessity and demands a different method from that required in the proof of a geometrical theorem; in the second, the process is that of putting two and two together from the testimony and affidavits. *PR* 144.

[97] *PR* 143.

[98] *PR* 135, 271. On genuine and spurious interpretation see Pound, *Spurious Interpretation* (1907) 7 Col. Law Rev. 607; *Courts and Legislation* (1915) 7 Amer. Polit. Sc. Rev. 361.

[99] *PR* 142-143.   [100] *PR* 142.

But the rights of individuals cannot be protected by the courts alone. There must be an undisturbed safety of person and property so far as that can be attained; there must also be an attempt to secure the conditions which make for the well-being of the individual. To the police Hegel assigns the first task, and to trade guilds or corporations the second. Hegel's theory of the corporation, by which he means a community of citizens possessing a common interest, has its present day counterpart in the doctrine of political pluralism. His argument for the existence of such communities is placed on a high plane. In modern times, he points out, the citizens participate only slightly in the public business. Nevertheless it is essential to provide men—ethical entities—with work of a public character over and above their private concerns. This work can be found in the corporation or association. The individual, while maintaining himself in the civic community, acts also for others. But this unconscious necessity is not enough; it is in the corporation that a conscious and reflective ethical reality is first reached. Corporations of course must fall under the direction of the state, otherwise they would ossify and degenerate into castes. In itself, however, a corporation is not a closed caste. Its purpose is to bring isolated groups into the social order and elevate them to a sphere where they gain strength and respect.

Although it is the essence of his political theory we need not follow Hegel into his discussion of the State. What he has to say is almost entirely of a political nature and has little bearing upon his legal doctrines. In Hegel's scheme the State as a political entity has three divisions: the legislative, which has the power to determine and establish the universal; the Executive, which has the power to subsume single cases and the spheres of particularity under the universal; and the Crown, which has the power of ultimate decision. The legislature is concerned with the laws as such in so far as they require fresh and extended determination. Laws are not originated by the legislature, they are merely adapted and extended to new situations.

International Law

At the heart of international law Hegel discerned an antinomy which he was unable to resolve. International law arises from the relations of autonomous states. Its realization therefore is dependent upon a number of different wills each of which is sovereign. For this reason Hegel holds that international law in its essence must always remain in the realm of " ought."[101]

Machiavelli [102] was the first of the modern theorists to put forward the principle, which Spinoza and others subsequently adopted, that the moral and legal rules which are held to bind citizens in their private actions are not binding upon States in their relations with one another. Hegel justified the principle by the following argument, which strengthened further his view of the " oughtness " of international law. A state, unlike a private person, is a completely autonomous totality; hence a relationship between States differs from relationships of morality and private right. Private persons are subject to the judicial process, which realizes what is intrinsically right. It is clear that State relationships ought also to be intrinsically right, but in mundane affairs a principle ought also to be coupled with power. As matters now stand there is no power to decide against the State what is intrinsically right and to actualize the decision. Hegel therefore concludes that in international relations we cannot get beyond the " ought." This leads to the circumstance that international relations are relations between autonomous entities which enter into mutual stipulations but which at the same time are superior to those stipulations.[103]

This is a position which moralists have always found offensive since the time when it was first outlined by Plato. No one has surpassed Plato in regard for the virtue of good faith and truth,[104] but he held that under special circumstances the virtue was not an absolute one. To make his point he used his

---

[101] *PR* 212.
[102] *The Prince*, c. 18 and *passim*.

[103] *PR* 297.
[104] *Laws* 730 BC; *Gorgias* 224 et seq.

favorite analogy of the physician. He held that falsehoods are useful to mankind only as medicines; but medicines should be handled only by physicians. Hence the rulers of the State may lie for the public good; but for the citizens to have the privilege of lying would be subversive and destructive.[105] Cicero explicitly decided that promises were not always to be kept, and attempted a classification of the circumstances which permitted their violation.[106] St. Augustine would not allow a lie even to save a life,[107] but the Church did not accept the doctrine and held that a promise, although under oath, was not binding if contrary to the good of the Church.[108] This doctrine played an important political rôle when associated with the theory of the consequences of excommunication and the claim of the Church to absolve a man from the obligation of an oath to a king.[109] In modern times it has been argued by followers of Kant that unless promises are kept rational society would be impossible.[110] As an absolute proposition, however, as Cohen [111] observes, this is untenable. In the actual world, which is certainly among the possible ones, not all promises are kept; moreover, as Cicero pointed out, the actual world is so full of surprises that we must always allow for contingency, and a system so rigid that promises could never be broken would promote evil as well as good, *i. e.*, we should not keep a promise when it would do only harm to the person to whom it was made. Hegel's view that the actions of States are superior to the promises of States, however morally opprobrious that view may be, is thus not without some historical and rational justification.

Hegel therefore, while accepting Fichte's contractual basis of international law, holds, on the basis of the principle of sover-

[105] *Republic* 389 BC.

[106] *De officiis* iii. 24 *et seq.*

[107] *De mendacio* 6; 40 Migne, *Patrologia Latina* (1861) 494.

[108] Gregory IX, *Decretales*, ii. 24, 27. Burchard of Worms follows Cicero in classifying the oaths which need not be kept. *Decretum* XIX. 5; 140 Migne, *Patrologia Latina* (1853) 951.

[109] 2 Carlyle, *History of Mediaeval Political Theory in the West* (1909) 203 *et seq.*; 3 *ibid.* (1916) 163 *et seq.*

[110] Reinach, *Die apriorischen Grundlagen des bürgerlichen Rechts* (1922) §§ 2-4.

[111] Cohen, *Law and the Social Order* (1933) 90.

eignty, that states are, to the extent the principle is given effect, in a state of nature in relation to one another. Their rights are realized, not in a general will duly constituted as a superior power, but only in their particular wills. He is forced to reject Kant's idea of a perpetual peace through the device of a League of Nations. But the success of Kant's plan turned ultimately on a particular sovereign will and the plan for that reason was infected with contingency. Hegel is unable or unwilling to attempt any modification of the principle of sovereignty, and on that basis his argument is a sound one. Inasmuch as he held that the relations of States ought to be inherently right, it is difficult to understand why he did not depart from the merely actual and outline the requirements of a system that would permit the realization of that rightness. Instead he held that disputes between States could be settled in the last resort only by war.

CONCLUSION

With Hegel legal philosophy leaves by the same door it entered with Plato. Law for Plato was the way to the discovery of reality, the rule of right reason,[112] the ascertainment of the ordering of human affairs which is in accord with the immortal element within us.[113] For Hegel law is a deduction from Being —the first of the categories—and its proper sphere is the Philosophy of Spirit or Mind. It is the realization of freedom as Idea, the grasping of right as thought, the apprehension of the essential form of things.[114] Translated into the same terminology Plato and Hegel both hold that law may be found by reason, and that it is to be found through the analysis of an ultimate category. They both employ a logical process to arrive at their views of the nature of law, but Hegel's is immeasurably more formalized. Plato associates law with the good society, a society in which every member performs the social services for which his nature is best adapted;[115] Hegel makes the same association[116] except that in his hands the good society is one

---

[112] *Minos* 314E; *Laws* 659CD.
[113] *Laws* 714A.
[114] *PR* 33, 225.
[115] *Republic* 433A.
[116] *PR* 79, 86 *et seq.*

in which the concept of freedom is actualized.[117] Their views of the nature of law seem therefore to differ in no significant particular;[118] their views of the end of law are radically apart. In its answer to the primary question of every jurisprudence— What is law?—legal philosophy has thus with Hegel come full circle.

In contrast with the views of Plato and Hegel are those of Hobbes. He held that man makes and constitutes the truth of the first principles on which our reasoning depends.[119] Natural law is therefore nothing but the precepts which are deduced from whatever first principles man chooses to reason from;[120] positive law is whatever the sovereign commands.[121] In sum, law is an invention, a contruction of our mind, and not something revealed through an analysis of reality or Being. These opposed theories have important consequences. In the case of Plato and Hegel the theory leads to a search for the ultimate nature of law. It leads also, since law has a final essence, to a definition of law from a point of view which cannot be varied. What is not embraced by the definition is not law since it does not partake of the essential character which the definition discovers. It follows also that the effort of jurisprudence should be directed at an understanding of law in the condition in which it stands closest to reality. It should not be occupied with the particular laws of States which, in the scholastic sense, are

---

[117] *PR* 105.

[118] In an acute study it has been argued that Hegel's theory of law differs from Plato's in two main respects: (1) Hegel "regards law as the product of an activity of 'positing,' which yet imports into its nature no element impenetrable by the speculative reason; (2) he so limits the consequence of speculative reason in the determination of law, as to make it stop short of the particular detail of its actualization." Foster, *The Political Philosophies of Plato and Hegel* (1935) 120. These differences do not appear to me to be real ones. (1) By positing Hegel means that process of thought by which the principle of rightness is made determinate for consciousness and made known as what is right and valid. *PR* 134. Plato had no term for this process but there is no question that this process is illustrated in the Dialogues. (2) Hegel and Plato differed in their formulations of the rules of law but both agreed that there were limits to the process. *Republic* 425B; *Laws* 842 CD, 788B.

[119] 1 *Works* (1839) 388.

[120] 3 *Ibid.* cc. 5, 14.

[121] 3 *Ibid.* 147.

merely accidents, and reveal only the inessential aspects of reality. It is genuine reality, law in its true essence, that jurisprudence should study, and not just appearance. In the Hobbes tradition, which includes Locke, Hume, Bentham, Austin and the present-day so-called " realists," all this in large part is denied by the implications of the theory, notwithstanding the fact that there may be a lack of courage to face all its consequences. If law is an invention, it has no final reality and we are free to define its rules as we choose; particular laws are important, and on them it is legitimate to base assertions with respect to the general nature of law.

In brief, jurisprudence in its philosophical aspect was realist at its inception, reacted during one phase to an extreme nominalism, and closed in the Hegelian speculation with a reassertion of realism. In the main, philosophical jurisprudence has been realistic, and it is difficult to perceive how it could be otherwise. Even Hobbes and the present-day so-called legal " realists " (whose ideas are nominalistic) assume that a jurisprudence of general principles is possible; but if particular laws are unique events distinct from all other particular laws, if universals have no objectivity, a system of general principles cannot be constructed.[122] In the courts the realist tradition of classical philosophy is as plainly marked. Their constant appeals to some form of a natural law doctrine, to ideals, to the nature of justice, to the good of society, and to right, are possible only in a realist view of the legal order. But realism as well as nominalism has its excesses, and Hegel as well as Plato is chargeable with them.

Realist jurisprudence has a tendency to remain at such an abstract level that its conclusions are of little or no help in the solution of the controversies which the study of actual systems of law engenders. That is the substance of Bryce's famous criticism of metaphysical jurisprudence.[123] In part at least,

---

[122] " I believe," Hardy writes, " that mathematical reality lies outside us, that our function is to discover and *observe* it, and that the theorems which we prove, and which we describe grandiloquently as our ' creations ' are simply our notes of our observations." *A Mathematician's Apology* (1940) 63.

[123] *Studies in History and Jurisprudence* (1901) 609-612.

Hegel is open to this charge, but certainly not with respect to all his analyses and conclusions. It may be leveled at him when he forces the legal order into the Procrustean bed of the dialectic; but not when he insists upon the force of custom in the making of law, or points out the irreconcilability of the idea of sovereignty and the theory of perpetual peace. Bryce admits that in the books of the metaphysical school " one finds legal conceptions analysed with an acuteness which cannot but sharpen the reader's wits," and that there is " much ingenious and subtle thinking." With this concession the case for the metaphysical type of analysis could rest. Have any of the other schools—analytic, historical, sociological—done more? The difficulty with the metaphysical school is not, as Bryce maintained, that it was abstract, but that it is not abstract enough. It aimed at an analysis of law at a level sufficiently abstract to encompass the possible legal systems. It succeeded only in devising systems that are inescapably of their time and place. Therefore it has been insisted that a legal system such as Hegel's cannot be studied as if it were a world constitution presented for adoption or rejection. It must be taken as the thoughts of a wise and learned man who in his logical grasp of the subtleties of some problems of jurisprudence has been surpassed by no one. His " reflections may often be valuable because they are suggestive," Sandars wrote at the beginning of Hegelianism in England, " suggestive in many different ways, and of many kinds of truth; but yet may not bear to be sifted and analysed and ranged as true or false." [124] Hegelianism was a product of the intellectual currents of its time; it has become itself one of the currents which has formed modern thought. Throughout the nineteenth and twentieth centuries in jurisprudence it was at the basis of many of the separate schools—historical, ethnographic, economic. Today's legal speculation is too predominantly nominalistic for Hegel's views to be taken with the seriousness with which they were once studied. His influence remains nevertheless inescapable.

[124] *Op. cit.* 249.

CHAPTER XV

CONCLUSION

JURISPRUDENCE AS PHILOSOPHY

Everything has been said already; but as no one listens, we must always begin again.

André Gide

FROM Plato to Hegel legal philosophy was an effort to see law in its rational relation to some general scheme of things. It was also an attempt to see law imaginatively, to state the principles of its elements in their ideal forms rather than in the casual guise through which they are known in existing legal systems. It strove to depict the pattern to which the law of the community should aspire but would never attain. Plato was content to regard his own legal theory as scarcely more than a fairy tale about justice, and no doubt the description may be applied with propriety to all the philosophies of law formulated by succeeding philosophers. The problems which the philosophy of law has raised continue to attract a large share of juridical attention and the solutions which it has proposed are still everywhere relied upon in the judicial process. Moreover, the philosophical ferment which the twentieth century has witnessed has given a new impetus to legal theory.

Recent philosophy has been marked by two general movements both of which are significant for their bearing upon jurisprudence. There has been an explicit return to the philosophies of the past where it has been found that theories formerly held to have the status of museum pieces were still fruitful guides in current speculations; there has been also a radical effort at reconstruction in philosophy, the full impact of which has only begun to be felt in legal thinking. For the most part the leaders in these movements have not extended their activities to the philosophy of law, although to some of them,

as with Whitehead, the idea of legality is a fundamental constituent of their thought. It therefore does not appear premature to attempt to indicate the nature of the task which
confronts jurisprudence if it would adjust itself to contemporary philosophical thought.

A characteristic of contemporary philosophical thought is its
highly self-critical state. This self-criticism asserts that the condition of our philosophical knowledge is very much what it
was in the days of the ancient Greeks. Philosophical issues
turn today on the same unresolved problems the Greeks left
behind them, and philosophy has given us no store of knowledge comparable at all to that accumulated in the intervening
centuries by science. " All new theories do but add to the babel
and confusion," Hoernlé writes. "There is no cumulative
coöperative advance from generation to generation, no funded
stock of philosophical truths which can be taught as its established rudiments to beginners, and which are taken for granted
by all experts as the basis of further inquiry. The same problems are ever examined afresh." [1] But the criticism extends
further. It maintains that the constructive speculation of
classical philosophy is an unjustifiable pursuit. It argues that
the traditional philosophical proposition, *e. g.*, law is right by
nature and not by convention, is a mere pseudo-proposition
because there is no known way of verifying its truth or falsity; [2]
finally, that all philosophical systems, since they are framed by
individuals, are necessarily partial and assume peripheral facts
to be central and typical facts. "How," Santayana asks,
" should a complete chart of the universe descend into the
twilight of an animal mind, served by quite special senses,
swayed by profound passions, subject to the epidemic delusions
of the race, and lost in the perhaps infinite world that bred
it? " [3] The classical philosophy of law stands in no more secure
position in relation to this attack than philosophy generally. If

---

[1] *Studies in Contemporary Metaphysics* (1920) 48.
[2] Ayer, *Language, Truth and Logic* (1936) 19-20.
[3] *Obiter Scripta* (1936) 102.

it is a valid criticism of philosophy, it is a valid criticism of the classical philosophy of law.

It is true that notwithstanding the serious nature of the attack upon all efforts to devise a constructive metaphysics the present age has seen no abatement in the practice of formulating comprehensive systems, as the work of Whitehead, Alexander, Bergson, Croce and others bear witness. However we have no basis to believe that the future will view our current systems in a light different from that in which we regard those of the past. The constructive philosophies of the present ignore, but do not answer, the criticism that has been advanced. The task of answering the criticism has fallen to the critics themselves who, naturally, concede its validity but meet it by offering new conceptions of the nature of philosophy and its proper aims and method. They would abandon what has been traditionally regarded as the domain of metaphysics, and would substitute as legitimate philosophical pursuits, the systematic study of meaning, the analysis of logic, the investigation of syntactical sentences, the exploration of social problems, or the historical ascertainment, *i. e.*, without regard to their truth or falsity, of the views philosophers have held at different times. The student of jurisprudence who is not a professional philosopher cannot pass with any competence upon the merits of this attempt of philosophy to reconstitute itself. But he should not close his eyes to the warning, that many of the problems with which he is concerned may be pseudo-problems, that many of the propositions upon which he and the courts rely for the solution of the difficulties which confront them may be pseudo-propositions, and that he may be bemusing himself in large part with vain techniques in the pursuit of a knowledge that is unattainable. His task is therefore to examine the philosophy of law in the light of the attacks now made upon its foundations. He must do this, not from the point of view of philosophy generally, but from that of its bearing on the undertakings of his own domain of jurisprudence. When that task is accomplished he should know what hopes he may legitimately entertain for his subject and what he must forsake.

Our own age has very much the attitude of mind of the later Academy. The Ionian thinkers, whose studies lay principally in the physical sciences, had attempted to answer the question " What is the world made of? " Their speculations were of a high order, but they were contradictory and dogmatic; they were undermined by Zeno who showed that empirical evidence was far from demonstrative. With Protagoras, who doubted the existence of objective truth, and Socrates, who doubted the possibility of the discovery of physical truth, Greek philosophy began the analysis of a new problem: " What is the nature of our values? " Socrates believed that values could be determined with certainty if his method for the discovery of error and the establishment of truth were followed. Ethics was studied with such success that, as Gilbert Murray has observed, it may almost be said that no important idea in that field has occurred to mankind since the fourth century B. C. But the effort to understand values ended in the same scepticism that befell the attempt to solve the problem of the physical world. It was argued by the later Academy that the wisest and most honest philosophers were in hopeless disagreement; that knowledge is relative inasmuch as it is a function of the physical and mental condition of the observer; that it is impossible to demonstrate the first principles of our arguments; and that the syllogism involves a *petitio principii.* The physical problem that Socrates had abandoned as beyond the reach of knowledge continued to be studied by European and Arabian philosophers, and in the seventeenth century the results of their labors began to bear astonishing fruit. The success of seventeenth century thought was so fortunate in devising a system of concepts for the pursuit of scientific research that, as Whitehead points out, every university in the world organizes itself in accordance with it; no alternative system has been suggested, it not only reigns, but is without a rival. The favorable outcome of physical speculation had a pronounced effect upon social thought. It was believed that if values were divorced from the analysis of human affairs, the social studies could be organized as auspiciously as the physical sciences. Under this impulse the study of social behavior has been extensively systematized, but the results have not been attended with the successes that distinguish physical theory. Both fields lack a generally accepted metaphysical foundation on which their primary assertions can rest with security. Social thought, however, is under additional handicaps: its speculations cannot pass over into the practical —which is the principal justification today of physical theory— unless the issue of value is in some way met, and, further, unless a method is devised for the isolation of significant variables. Our elaborate social constructions in large part fail in application because we are unable to perceive the meaningful factors in the social process when we are brought face to face with critical situations; we do not know what is evidentiary and what is not. As in the third century B. C., we find for these reasons our ablest social scientists unable to agree on any major issue—the alleviation of unemployment, the control of prices, the regulation of family life, the minimization of crime or the adjustment of international relations. The arguments of the later Academy are repeated today in strikingly similar form against the possibility of effective social knowledge. We have, however, for whatever comfort may be drawn from it, the witness of physical science which shows, in that field, the successes which can follow upon a reconstitution of the concepts which control inquiry.

Legal Philosophy as the Realm of the Jural Hypothesis

For the worker in the field of jurisprudence the most satisfactory course appears to be the adoption of the view that the function of legal philosophy is the formulation and valuation of jural hypotheses. This attitude enables jurisprudence to stand clear of philosophical quarrels, on the merits of which it cannot hope to pronounce a competent judgment; it permits jurisprudence to salvage all that is important from the extensive accumulations of the past; finally, it assigns to one branch of jurisprudence a necessary and continuing task which must be carried out if we are to have a comprehensive legal science. This view of the rôle of legal philosophy is itself an hypothesis; it is subject to the tests which have been developed to measure valid hypotheses. However, before that is possible the meaning of this approach must be stated with some completeness.

We may begin conveniently with a brief summary of a few of the results that legal philosophy has reached in the past. We have been told by Plato that law is a form of social control, an instrument of the good life, the way to the discovery of reality, the true reality of the social structure; by Aristotle that it is a rule of conduct, a contract, an ideal of reason, a rule of decision, a form of order; by Cicero that it is the agreement of reason and nature, the distinction between the just and the unjust, a command or prohibition; by Aquinas that it is an ordinance of reason for the common good, made by him who has care of the community, and promulgated; by Bacon that certainty is the prime necessity of law; by Hobbes that law is the command of the sovereign; by Spinoza that it is a plan of life; by Leibniz that its character is determined by the structure of society; by Locke that it is a norm established by the commonwealth; by Hume that it is a body of precepts; by Kant that it is a harmonizing of wills by means of universal rules in the interests of freedom; by Fichte that it is a relation between human beings; by Hegel that it is an unfolding or realizing of the idea of right. These are some of the conclusions which philosophers, occupied with the problems of jurisprudence, have attempted to establish. By and large they, or deductions from them, form the main staple of juristic inquiry today. They have entered indelibly into the thinking of students of jurisprudence and, in one aspect or another, are the presuppositions on the basis of which the decisions of our courts are constructed. The labors of philosophers in the vineyard of jurisprudence have presented us with a harvest of extraordinary richness and variety, one that in its conceptual aspect surpasses that gathered in by jurists themselves. How should we regard it?

We may put aside immediately the attractive thought that the fundamental truths of the various philosophies of law should be sifted out and then combined in one harmonious whole. We cannot perform that task because we do not know, and have no way of ascertaining at present, what are the fundamental truths in jurisprudence. The philosophers appear to have stated certain truths with respect to law, but they have not shown us whether they are superficial or basic. If they are superficial, then the truth which they reveal is too accidental to be reduced to the permanent insight that we seek; if they are basic, then neither philosophy nor any other branch of inquiry has discovered how to reconcile them. To the extent that they possess a common denominator it is—as we see the world through our present inescapable spectacles—some form of realism or nominalism. Philosophy today exhibits a certain impatience with this problem; this impatience takes the form of arguing that it should be abandoned as altogether insoluble. Russell, whose position usually possesses elements of novelty, holds that the issue between realists and their opponents is not a fundamental one, and that he could alter his views on the controversy without changing his mind as to any of the doctrines which he wishes to stress.[4] All this means in practice is that Russell for one reason or another refuses to raise the nominalist-realist issue. It does not mean that the question is non-existent for philosophy, or that its solution is not determinative of many philosophical problems, including those with which Russell is concerned. In the present state of our knowledge courts and jurists act in fact as if realism and nominalism were both true, a position which philosophy itself has maintained in some degree when it admits that both the particular and the universal are real. A comparable situation in optics was described in 1921 by Sir William Bragg. Physicists had to

---

[4] *Logical Atomism* in Muirhead (Ed.), *Contemporary British Philosophy* (First Series, 1924) 359. For a critical account of what happens in fact to Russell's views on mathematics when he alters his views about realism see Feibleman, *A Reply to Bertrand Russell's Introduction to the Second Edition of the Principles of Mathematics* in Schilpp (Ed.), *The Philosophy of Bertrand Russell* (1944) 155.

assume the truth of both the wave and corpuscular theories. "On Mondays, Wednesdays, and Fridays we use the wave theory; on Tuesdays, Thursdays, and Saturdays we think in streams of flying energy quanta or corpuscles. That is after all a very proper attitude to take. We cannot state the whole truth since we have only partial statements, each covering a portion of the field. When we want to work in any one portion of the field or other, we must take out the right map. Some day we shall piece all the maps together." [5] In the light of its history philosophy has less ground than physics to hope that the ultimate propositions which it has had under continual analysis since the days of the ancient Greeks will be pieced together to form an intelligible map. Nevertheless legal philosophy must have a view of them, since they lie at the root of juristic speculation.

A few illustrations will be sufficient to show the importance of philosophical presuppositions in the judicial process and the legal order. In *Swift* v. *Tyson* [6] Mr. Justice Story held that the provisions of the 34th section of the Judiciary Act of 1789 did not require the Supreme Court of the United States to follow the decisions of the State tribunals in all cases to which they apply. That section provided " that the laws of the several States, except where the Constitution, treaties, or statutes of the United States shall otherwise require or provide, shall be regarded as rules of decision in trials at common law in the courts of the United States, in cases where they apply." Story's problem was to determine whether the word " laws " as used in the section was broad enough to embrace court decisions. His solution was to adopt an unjustifiably strict version of the nominalism of Hobbes and Austin and to define law as " the rules and enactments promulgated by the legislative authority . . . or long-established local customs having the force of laws." He thought that it would " hardly be contended that the decisions of courts constitute laws. They are, at most, only evidence of what the laws are, and are not of themselves laws."

[5] *Electrons and Ether Waves* (1921) 11.
[6] 16 Pet. 1 (1842).

But this was a view of the nature of law which clearly could not endure. Neither the analytical jurists nor the courts could deny, in the face of the overwhelming empirical evidence to the contrary, that courts as well as legislatures established law. Holmes made precisely this point in his dissent in *Black and White Taxicab Co.* v. *Brown and Yellow Taxicab Co.*[7] which paved the way for the overruling of *Swift* v. *Tyson* in *Erie Railroad Co.* v. *Tompkins.*[8] But he was careful to limit himself to this rigidly circumscribed area. The Supreme Court of a State, Holmes wrote, " says with an authority that no one denies . . . that thus the law is and shall be." He needed to assert no more in order to dispose of Story's doctrine. He was aware that a deeper issue was involved if he went further, namely, whether judges in deciding controversies " legislate," in the sense that they " invent " rules to dispose of the cases. He saw that this issue in turn was associated with the realist-nominalist controversy. Although he himself was a pronounced nominalist his native scepticism cautioned him that in this instance at least a declaration of his views on that question was unnecessary. Whether the Supreme Court of a State, he wrote, " be said to make or to declare the law, it deals with the law of the State with equal authority however its function may be described." That is to say, it was immaterial to Holmes for the purposes of the case whether the common law existed as something prior to and apart from decisions, and a judge in deciding a case merely declared it, or whether a court in giving judgment manufactured the law then and there. Mr. Justice Butler, speaking for the majority, had adopted the view that the common law embodied a Platonic type of reality. " For the discovery of common law principles applicable in any case," he said, " investigation is not limited to the decisions of the courts of the state in which the controversy arises. State and Federal courts go to the same sources for evidence of the existing applicable rule. The effort of both is to ascertain that rule.

[7] 276 U. S. 518, 532 (1928). See also Holmes' reflections on the case in his letters to Pollock. 2 *Holmes-Pollock Letters* (1941) 214 *et seq.*
[8] 304 U. S. 64 (1938).

Kentucky has adopted the common law and her courts recognize that its principles are not local but are included in the body of law constituting the general jurisprudence prevailing wherever the common law is recognized." Holmes' technique was to show the majority how the issue could be avoided. Judges do not traditionally exhibit this self-restraint. " I do not hesitate to declare," said Justice Johnson in *Fletcher* v. *Peck*, " that a state does not possess the power of revoking its own grants. But I do it on a general principle, on the reason and nature of things; a principle which will impose laws even on the Deity." [9] In the Platonic scheme the point was urged with more caution. Platonists insist that the necessities to which God is subject are inferences which follow from God's own nature; they are therefore expressions of His power and not real limitations. Again the New York Court of Appeals had the case of an employee who was struck by the propeller of a " hydroaeroplane " while it was moving on navigable waters. Cardozo held that since the plane was a vessel " while afloat upon waters capable of navigation " and so " subject to the admiralty " jurisdiction, the State Workmen's Compensation Act did not apply.[10] Cardozo, who in this case at least was an Aristotelian, assumed that it was possible to state what a " vessel " was. His holding in this respect was harshly criticized by Cook, whose metaphysics were derived ultimately from Peirce. Cook held that the meaning of a proposition consists of its possible consequences. He therefore thought that in a collision case a hydroaeroplane on the water would be a " vessel " within the meaning of a marine insurance policy; it would not be a " vessel " in the sense that a member of the " crew " who " navigated " it while temporarily on the water could maintain a libel *in rem*. These few examples are sufficient to illustrate the point. They could be extended indefinitely to include such topics as corporate personality, due process of law, contract, property, intent, malice, and the other counters of judicial thought.

---

[9] 6 Cranch 87, 143 (1810).
[10] *Reinhardt* v. *Newport Flying Service* 232 N. Y. 115, 133 N. E. 371 (1921); *The Logical and Legal Bases of the Conflict of Laws* (1942) 160.

That the basic principles of the law often turn on metaphysical presuppositions has often been shown and need not be elaborated upon. In the law of tort when damages are allowed, excluding those of a punitive nature, it is on the theory that the injured party should receive indemnification for the injury wrongfully done him. This is the realist view that a monetary award compensatory for the injury is an objective measure of the wrong. In the Roman action on delict the action is penal and not compensatory. It is founded on vengeance, and although the injured party may be indemnified the suffering of the injuror is also an objective. " The desire for vengeance," Holmes remarks, " imports an opinion that its object is actually and personally to blame. It takes an internal standard, not an objective or external one, and condemns its victim by that." [11] In its complete nominalistic form it leads to Kant's doctrine of the *ius talionis* as the principle of punishment. When the idea of compensation and the idea of penalty are set in opposition they lead to different results in practice. In the Roman law, subject to limitations not here important, if several persons were engaged in a delict, each was liable for the full penalty. This is, of course, also the rule in tort. But in the Roman law, since it is a penalty, the fact that one of them has paid does not release the others. Vengeance cannot be subdivided.[12] In modern realism the infliction of penalties is regarded as not in the least conducive to public or private welfare, and Peirce, in fact, argued that punishment should be abolished altogether. Criminals were to be isolated in relative luxury, but prevented from reproducing themselves.[13]

It is with material of this kind, derived from both the juristic order and the formal studies of professional philosophy, that legal philosophy is concerned. In the prosecution of its inquiry with respect to this material legal philosophy has three general aims in view. It seeks to ascertain the philosophic suppositions,

---

[11] *The Common Law* (1881) 40.

[12] Buckland and McNair, *Roman Law and Common Law* (1936) 269-70. See also Jolowicz, *Historical Introduction to Roman Law* (1932) 176.

[13] 2 *Collected Papers of Charles Sanders Peirce* (1932) 95.

from whatever source derived, of the jural order and the grounds of their justification. It endeavors to determine the nature of the objects of the jural order, *e.g.*, what is law? What is a right? What is property? Finally, it attempts to evaluate the suppositions and objects of the jural order. If we consider each of these tasks separately the rôle of the jural hypothesis and its relation to legal philosophy should be clarified.

Legal philosophy's first desideratum is a systematic collection of the philosophic suppositions applicable to the legal order. In the first instance they should be the suppositions in terms of which the problems of the legal order are approached or are purported to be solved. That is to say, we need to know the suppositions which are generated directly by the effort to solve the tasks of the law. Those suppositions are formulated as responses to questions immediately at issue in the legal process, and thus as propositions make lineal assertions about the subject-matter of jurisprudential inquiry. Suppositions collected on this basis would be related to law in its aspect as a product of social phenomena; they would also be connected with law in the aspects it presents when approached from the point of view of other conceptual schemes. Although law is unmistakably a social product, and its problems take their form from the social environment, we cannot ignore the possibility that the way to a full understanding of the legal order may lie in some other domain. It still remains to be determined whether law or any other subject can be understood in terms only of itself. The history of thought is against such a likelihood; but the advantages of seeking the solution of problems within the domain in which they arise are too obvious to be set forth. That is the great strength of the empirical method, Fechner's [14] working from below, which is opposed to the metaphysical method of working from above in terms of general concepts. The empirical method is not the only road to knowledge, and the proposition that we should keep open all avenues to that goal needs no

[14] *Vorschule der Ästhetik* (1876) 1 *et seq.*

argument. Nevertheless the area from which the suppositions are to be collected is not unlimited. It is confined to those suppositions which are immediately connected with the effort to explain the legal order. In the long run the validity of more remote suppositions, *e. g.*, that a piecemeal analysis of the legal system will lead to knowledge, must be faced; but the investigation of their standing perhaps lies elsewhere.

Legal philosophy is not concerned with these suppositions as true or false, but as hypotheses which are to be tested by their capacity to promote the solution of the problems of the legal order.[15] The supposition logically is expressed in an *if-then* form. " If legal instruction is conducted by the case method, then it is believed that certain consequences will follow." " If law is the rules laid down by the legislature, then the rules established by the courts are not law." " If the rules established by the courts are law, then the Supreme Court of the United States in certain cases has been directed by Congress to apply them." In the first hypothesis the consequences of a particular course of action are predicted. In the two other hypotheses definitions are established. They define " law " so that anything, *e. g.*, the decisions of officials, which does not meet the test of the definitions, is excluded from their scope. When two *if-then* propositions, both of universal application, conflict, a choice must be made between them on the basis of the consequences which flow from them. Story's hypothesis of the character of law led eventually to consequences which the Supreme Court thought undesirable, but which Holmes' hypothesis avoided. There is no question here of the truth or falsity of the hypotheses. Either the consequences which follow assist in the solution of the difficulties of the legal order, or they do

---

[15] The logical justification of this method of approach is fully set forth in Dewey, *Logic, the Theory of Inquiry* (1938). For the philosophical attitude see Collingwood, *An Essay on Metaphysics* (1940). For their rôle in science see Meyerson, *Identity and Reality* (1930) 391 *et seq.* Meyerson thinks that " they have their own value; they correspond certainly to something very profound and very essential in nature itself." A different view was taken by Mill who held that it was a condition of a genuinely scientific hypothesis that it must be certain to be either proved or disproved through comparison with observed facts. *Logic* (1864) 293.

not. Unless they satisfy that criterion their status is merely one of potential usefulness. Suppositions regarded as hypotheses disclose the possible ways in which the perplexities of the legal order may be attacked, not the ways that are necessary. This permits a plurality of hypotheses, a condition which the history of science shows to be desirable in the exploration of any complicated subject-matter.

Scientific method gives us little help in appraising hypotheses before they are tested by their consequences. Jevons in 1874 first worked out the requisites of a good hypothesis, and his rules are at the basis of discussions of the subject in contemporary logical theory.[16] An hypothesis should be subject to testability by consequences. Would the operations of the legal process be different in any respect if either the realist or nominalist view of law were adopted? If the adoption of either hypothesis would make no difference, as Russell argues is the case for at least his own principles, then neither hypothesis has consequences which test it. Further, an hypothesis should have at least the appearance of plausibility, *e. g.*, it should not appeal to the intervention of an angel to explain how courts are able to do justice. Again, it should offer an answer to the problem which it purports to solve. Jevons' formulation of this condition was that the consequences inferred should agree with the facts of observation. But this proposition would have required Bragg to reject both the wave and corpuscular theories of light, whereas both are useful. Finally, hypotheses should possess the type of simplicity which yields system. Story's conception of law required, in its application by the courts, too many exceptions; Holmes' view allowed for Story's idea, but took in a wider field without any loss of precision. It is plain that the present state of scientific method offers us little beyond the obvious as aids to evaluate hypotheses in the stage between formulation and application. For an existential subject matter such as law the *experimentum crucis* lies in the consequences that flow from the application.

[16] *The Principles of Science* (2nd ed. 1892) 510-11.

Legal philosophy also endeavors to determine the nature of the objects of the jural order. It attempts to answer such questions as What is law? What is property? It is far from clear what is involved when we ask such questions. However, in general, it appears that the attempt to answer them, at any rate for jurisprudence, involves two tasks.[17] We want to know first: What are the entities of the legal order? Legal theory, like other sciences, deals with certain entities, and ideas about those entities can be expressed in propositional form. As the approach to law becomes increasingly scientific its deductive character will become more apparent and its logical structure of greater significance. Legal theory may eventually be reduced to something approaching the status of geometry so that we will have sets of entities from which we can account for all the important propositions of the legal order. But our present task is to ascertain the entities in terms of which legal orders operate. Our interest in those entities is not, as Fichte thought, one primarily of logical necessity; that attitude has its own values, not the least of which is the aesthetic satisfaction it gives us. Positive law is a social phenomenon; the entities of importance to legal philosophy are those which relate it to that world. Our second inquiry involves the application of law to the empirical conditions of human conduct. Are the entities with which law operates adequate for its purpose? Are there enough or too many of them, and have they been defined in such a way that law rests upon a firm empirical foundation? This involves the attempt to ascertain whether or not there are any contradictions between the operations of the legal order and the conceptual foundation which endeavors to account for those operations. It is possible that legal philosophy may some day take up the problem of the ultimate entities of the legal order, those from which even the primary entities of juridical thought are constructed. But the advance which jurisprudence and social thought generally must take before that task can be

---

[17] See Russell, *The Analysis of Matter* (1927) 1 *et seq.* On the logical requirements of a valid question see Felix S. Cohen, *What is a Question?* (1929) 39 *Monist* 350.

contemplated belongs to a distant day. In its occupation with
the nature of legal objects, legal philosophy passes into the
realm of ontology. There are no risks in that enterprise provided the empirical nature of its subject matter is kept always
steadily in view.

Finally, legal philosophy must undertake the evaluation
of the suppositions and objects of the legal order. No more
important assignment faces jurisprudence as a whole. Zeller
long ago pointed out that the great weakness of all ancient
thought, including the Socratic, was that it made no appeal to
objective experiment, but that it appealed instead to some subjective sense of fitness. We are told today that values lie
beyond the reach of knowledge, particularly of an empirical
kind; that what we like or dislike is wholly a matter of our
emotions. We are told also that this opinion is false. If the
first view is correct then the idea that law is a form of social
control that can direct human conduct to desirable ends is sheer
fantasy. It means that societal processes, in the great turns and
reversals that they exhibit, are at the mercy of blind impulses
and unseeing imponderables. Against that view is the circumstance that it has not been demonstrated that the methods of
science are not applicable to the evaluation of moral judgments.
There is still reason to believe, therefore, that the ethical aspect
of jurisprudence will some day yield to rational manipulation.
Beyond this point, notwithstanding the elaborate analysis to
which the topic is everywhere subjected, it seems impossible
today to go with caution.

CONCLUSION

From the study of the legal theories of the important
philosophers one central fact emerges: the great theories of
law current today are the extension of philosophical systems.
Duhem [18] in his classical study of the dominant scientific
theories found that they were developments of metaphysical

---

[18] *La théorie physique* (1906) 10 *et seq.*

principles, and it is no less true of jurisprudence than of science. However, jurisprudence, which was at one time the daughter of philosophy, is now not even a stepchild. Philosophy, which nourished jurisprudence from the time of the ancient Greeks to the first part of the nineteenth century, has cast it adrift. It is perhaps possible that jurisprudence is sturdy enough to stand alone. Her workers are in an immediate relationship with the material world at the point where law and society meet. It may be thought that that position is a more advantageous one for the guidance of the vast adjustments which confront the legal order than the more remote perspective which was available to the philosophers of the past. Nevertheless, if it should turn out in the end that philosophy has taught us nothing about law, it would be difficult to deny that it has taught us other things. It has insisted that practice cannot be reformed in any significant sense if fundamental ideas are not clarified and harmonized into a systematic theory of that minute aspect of the world that any science studies; it demands, if practice is to achieve its goal of an ideal society, that the view taken be wide enough for that purpose. " The synoptical man," Plato said, " the man who has a conspectus of knowledge is the philosopher; and the man who is not synoptical, who cannot see two subjects in their relation, is no philosopher." No legal problem is ever solved in isolation; it must be related to the whole structure of phenomena.

INDEX OF PROPER NAMES

INDEX OF SUBJECTS